Scaling Up Affordable Health Insurance

D1717170

Scaling Up Affordable Health Insurance

Staying the Course

Editors

**Alexander S. Preker, Marianne E. Lindner,
Dov Chernichovsky, and Onno P. Schellekens**

THE WORLD BANK
Washington, D.C.

Library of Congress Cataloging-in-Publication Data
Scaling up affordable health insurance : staying the course / editors, Alexander S. Preker, Marianne E.
Lindner, Dov Chernichovsky, and Onno P. Schellekens.
       p. ; cm.
    Includes bibliographical references and index.
    ISBN 978-0-8213-8250-9 (pbk. : alk. paper) — ISBN 978-0-8213-8579-1 (electronic)
    I. Preker, Alexander S., 1951– editor of compilation. II. Lindner, Marianne E., editor of compilation.
III. Chernichovsky, Dov, editor of compilation. IV. Schellekens, Onno P., 1964– editor of compilation.
V. World Bank, issuing body.
    [DNLM: 1. Insurance, Health. 2. Developing Countries. 3. Health Services Accessibility—economics.
W 100]
    RA412.3
    368.38'2—dc23
                                                                                               2013009642

Contents

BOXES

FIGURES

TABLES

Foreword

This book takes the reader on a fascinating historical and global voyage of the pivotal role that health insurance played in expanding access to health care and protecting households from the impoverishing effects of illness from the late 19th to early 21st centuries.

During the early evolution of health insurance at the end of the 19th and beginning of the 20th centuries, the nascent health insurance programs were initiated by professional guilds and communities that helped their members and households weather the loss of income from a breadwinner or critical member of the family rather than pay for health care itself.

When medical interventions became more effective in preventing and treating diseases, the European friendly societies and sickness funds also started to pay for health care itself in addition to the income support they provided to households with sick family members. The state initially played only a marginal role in partially subsidizing premiums for the poor or paying for almshouses and poorhouses.

As time progressed, the role of the state in providing health insurance became more prominent, to the point where in some countries, like the United Kingdom and the great experiment in the former Soviet Union, health insurance was—for a period of time—eliminated altogether. In recent years, even such "noninsurance" countries have reintroduced health insurance for complimentary, supplementary, and even primary coverage.

Although some developing countries tried to leapfrog this process and introduce national health systems or national health insurance programs without first building the social and physical infrastructure that is needed for such systems to work, most low- and middle-income countries are retracing the historical experiences of Europe, North America, and Australia.

The contributing authors conclude this book with a proposal for a new paradigm for health insurance—a pluralistic multipillar system in which both the private sector and the state play a crucial role and in which expansion of health insurance coverage is accompanied by a parallel investment in service delivery to ensure that lofty ideals about equity are matched by access to quality services on the ground.

I congratulate the contributing authors for the overarching research that went into this volume and the invaluable lessons for developing countries trying to improve health care for their populations.

Willem van Duin
Chairman of the Executive Board of Directors, Achmea
Member of the Board, International Federation of Health Plans

Preface

As the world recently turned its attention to the struggle of expanding health insurance coverage for 40 million people in the United States, it is important not to forget the 4 billion people in low- and middle-income countries that face the same hardship.

Millions of the poor have already fallen back into poverty as a result of the ongoing global financial crisis. Millions more are at risk before full recovery. It is the poor and most vulnerable that are at greatest risk due to lack of protection against the impoverishing effects of illness.

Europeans, Canadians, Australians, and many others who live in countries where universal coverage was achieved many years ago, watched with bewilderment the debates in the U.S. Congress and Senate. How could anyone be opposed, they ask, to reforms aimed at securing access to affordable health insurance for the currently unprotected in the world's richest country? What argument, they ask, could anyone possibly give to oppose a reform that would extend protection to those vulnerable segments of the population?

Yet, it is precisely the same type of debate—often fueled by ideologically oriented stakeholders and donors—heard in India, Kenya, Pakistan, Senegal, Uganda, and many other countries struggling themselves to introduce health insurance reforms.

The research for this volume shows that, when properly designed and coupled with public subsidies, health insurance can contribute to the well-being of poor and middle-class households, not just the rich. And it can contribute to development goals such as improved access to health care, better financial protection against the cost of illness, and reduced social exclusion.

The protagonists are divided into several camps. Supporters of expanded health insurance coverage claim that it provides access to care when needed without the long waiting lists, low-quality care, and rudeness often suffered by households using public services provided by Ministries of Health. They highlight that many of the problems observed with health insurance are germane to third-party payment systems and therefore equally true in the case of subsidized or free access to government-provided health services.

Opponents vilify health insurance as an evil to be avoided at all cost. To them, health insurance leads to overconsumption of care, escalating costs—especially administrative costs—fraud and abuse, shunting of scarce resources away from the poor, cream skimming, adverse selection, moral hazard, and an inequitable health care system.

Skeptics of both of these approaches claim that neither health insurance nor government-funded health systems have worked in addressing the biggest health challenges in developing countries. Instead they believe that both government and donor funding would be better spent if channeled into disease-specific areas for which there are well-known and cost-effective interventions. This approach, they claim, is easier to implement and allows more direct monitoring of results.

Critics of this latter approach claim that, although the billions of dollars spent during recent years have had a notable impact on outcomes related to HIV/AIDS, malaria, and TB, these gains have come at a heavy price in terms of parallel deteriorations in the sustainability and capacity of the underlying health system in addressing other health challenges such as maternal and child care.

There is no shortage of anecdotal personal experience to substantiate the arguments on all sides of this debate. Many have been refused care or had to pay informal charges even though they were members in good standing with a health insurance scheme. Others have seen a sick relative wait for hours in a busy emergency room of a public hospital or die because of shortages in essential drugs and skilled staff in public facilities. Doctors earning little over US$500 a month in a public clinic can often walk across the street to an international donor organization willing to pay them over US$5,000 a month.

Today many low- and middle-income countries are no longer listening to this dichotomized debate between vertical and horizontal approaches to health care. Instead, they are experimenting with new and innovative approaches to health care financing. Health insurance is becoming a new paradigm for reaching the Millennium Development Goals (MDGs). In Nigeria, subsidized health maintenance organizations (HMOs) are used to provide health insurance coverage for the population. The National Health Insurance Scheme in Ghana has reached almost 70 percent population coverage through nongovernmental district mutual health organizations. In Rwanda, community-level health insurance has reached coverage rates higher than 80 percent in some areas. These are a few of the many examples provided in this book that challenge common myths about the limited potential role of health insurance in developing countries.

Building on Past Reviews

Scaling Up Affordable Health Insurance: Staying the Course, edited by Alexander S. Preker, Marianne E. Lindner, Dov Chernichovsky, and Onno P. Schellekens is the fifth volume in a series of in-depth reviews of the role of health care financing in improving access to needed care for low-income populations, protecting them from the impoverishing effects of illness and addressing the important issues of social exclusion in government-financed programs. Success in improving access and financial protection through community and private voluntary health insurance has led many countries to attempt to make membership compulsory and to offer subsidized insurance through the public sector. Arguments in favor of this approach include the potential for achieving higher population coverage, broadening the risk pool by collecting at source from formally employed workers, and collective action in securing value for money in purchasing health care from providers.

In an earlier volume, *Health Financing for Poor People: Resource Mobilization and Risk Sharing*, the coeditors Alexander S. Preker and Guy Carrin presented work from a World Bank review of the role of community financing schemes in reaching the poor in outlying rural areas or inner city slums. Most community financing schemes have evolved under severe economic constraints, political instability, and lack of good governance. Government taxation capacity is usually weak in poor countries, formal mechanisms of social protection for vulnerable populations absent, and government oversight of the informal health sector lacking.

In this context of extreme public sector failure, community involvement in the financing of health care provides a critical, though insufficient, first step in the long march toward improved access to health care by the poor and social protection against the cost of illness. Though not a panacea, community financing can complement weak government involvement in health care financing and risk management related to the cost of illness. Based on an extensive survey of the literature, the main strengths of community financing schemes are the degree of outreach penetration achieved through community participation, their contribution to financial protection against illness, and their increase in access to health care for low-income rural and informal sector workers. Some of their main weaknesses are the low level of revenues that can be mobilized from poor communities, the frequent exclusion of the very poorest from participation in such schemes without some form of subsidy, the small size of the risk pool, the limited management capacity in rural and low-income contexts, and their isolation from the more comprehensive benefits that are often available through more formal health financing mechanisms and provider networks. Many of these observations are also true for private voluntary health insurance.

In another related work, *Social Reinsurance: A New Approach to Sustainable Community Health Financing*, the coeditors David M. Dror and Alexander S. Preker detail the use of community, rather than individual, risk-rated reinsurance as a way of addressing some of the known weaknesses of community financing schemes. The authors of this volume show how standard techniques of reinsurance, used for a long time in other branches of insurance, can be applied to microinsurance in health care. This is especially relevant in situations in which the underlying risk pool is too small to protect the schemes against the expected expenditure variance. In this context, the reinsurance provides a "virtual" expansion of the risk pool without undermining the social capital underpinning participation by rural and urban informal sector workers in such small community-based schemes.

In a third volume, *Private Health Insurance in Development: Friend or Foe?*, the coeditors Alexander S. Preker, Richard M. Scheffler, and Mark C. Bassett present work on the economic and institutional underpinnings of private voluntary health insurance in low- and middle-income countries. In the fourth volume, *Global Marketplace for Private Health Insurance: Strength in Numbers*, the coeditors Alexander S. Preker, Peter Zweifel, and Onno P. Schellekens present 12 case studies that illustrate the experience of countries that use private voluntary health insurance around the globe. The research for these volumes was designed specifically to explore health care financing challenges faced at low-income levels such as in the Africa and South Asia Regions, but the reviews also draw upon important lessons learned elsewhere in the world and should therefore also be of interest to a broader readership.

They emphasize the need to combine several instruments to achieve three major development objectives in health care financing: (1) sustainable access to needed health care; (2) greater financial protection against the impoverishing cost of illness; and (3) reduction in social exclusion from organized health financing instruments. These instruments include subsidies, insurance, savings, and user charges (figure 1). Few organizational and institutional arrangements include all four of these instruments under a single system. The authors argue in favor of a *multipillar approach* to health care financing in low- and middle-income countries, which would include an important private voluntary health insurance component (community- and private enterprise–based programs). All volumes in this series strongly recommend prepayment over direct out-of-pocket payment for health services. The use of insurance was recommended to pay for less frequent, higher-cost risks and subsidies to cover affordability for poorer patients to higher-frequency, lower-cost health problems.

There are close parallels between community financing and private health insurance. Both are nongovernmental but often have important interfaces with government programs through subsidies and shared provider networks. Both rely on voluntary membership. Membership is small unless the effective risk pool is enlarged through reinsurance or federation with other schemes. Both depend on trust. Their members must have confidence that their contribution paid today will lead to benefits when needed tomorrow. Both are vulnerable to insurance market failure such as adverse selection, cream skimming, moral hazard, and the free-rider phenomenon.

There are also some important differences. Community financing schemes emerged largely due to governments' inability to reach rural poor and urban

FIGURE 1   Objectives of Different Financing Instruments

Objective	Equity		Risk management			Income smoothing
Financing mechanism	Donor aid	General revenues	Public health insurance	Private health insurance	Community financing	Household savings
Voluntary						
Mandatory						

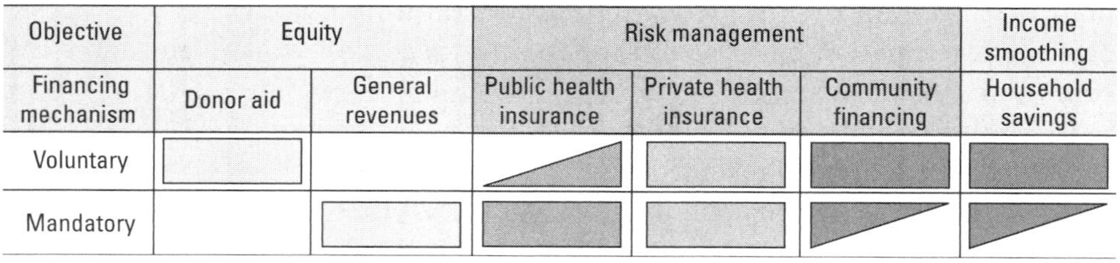

Source: Authors.

informal sector workers. In this context—for lack of better solutions—small communities such as rice growers, fishers, carpenters, and other tradespeople started their own programs, often linked with rural loans, savings, and micro-insurance programs. Many have benefited from donor involvement during the early start-up phase. The populations served are usually poor. The benefits package they can offer is constrained by their limited resources unless they receive a government or donor subsidy.

Private voluntary health insurance schemes were often set up by large enterprises. Such programs were seen as fostering a "self-help" attitude by encouraging employees to pay in advance for the health care benefits that they would receive later. It was hoped that access to health care would cut illness-related absenteeism and improve labor productivity. The populations served are usually formal sector workers. The benefits provided are often generous compared with those provided by community financing schemes and publicly financed government programs. Whereas community financing schemes tend to be not for profit, many private voluntary health insurance schemes are for profit.

Scaling Up Affordable Health Insurance: Staying the Course describes how some countries have tried to "leapfrog" both private and public insurance by introducing legislation to give the population at large access to a free government-subsidized national health service as a basic human right. For several reasons, however, few low- and middle-income countries have succeeded in securing universal access through this approach. First, at low income levels, weak taxation capacity limits the fiscal space available for health and other segments of the public sector. Second, there is a lack of trust in government-run programs into which the population is asked to pay today for benefits that may or may not be available tomorrow due to shifting priorities and volatile resource flows. Finally, public supply-side subsidies often do not reach the poor when programs are designed to provide care for everyone. The resulting underfinanced and low-quality publicly financed and owned health services leave the poor and other households without adequate care and exposed to severe financial risk at the time of illness. "Rights"—without action or accountability and responsibility—have not served the poor well in low- and middle-income countries.

How scarce money is spent in the public sector probably has as much or greater impact on the services available to the poor as does the presence or absence of private and government-run mandatory health insurance. This is the topic of five other past reviews: *Spending Wisely: Buying Health Services for the Poor*, edited by Alexander S. Preker and John C. Langenbrunner; *Public Ends, Private Means*, edited by Alexander S. Preker, Xingzhu Liu, Edit V. Velenyi, and Enis Baris; *Designing and Implementing Health Care Provider Payment Systems: How-To Manuals*, edited by John C. Langenbrunner, Cheryl Cashin, and Sheila O'Dougherty; *Innovations in Health Service Delivery: The Corporatization of Public Hospitals*, edited by Alexander S. Preker and April Harding; and *Private Participation in Health Services*, edited by April Harding and Alexander S. Preker. These five reviews emphasize the important role that markets and nongovernmental providers play in improving value for money spent not only by the public sector but also the range of services available through mandates under health insurance programs. In all cases, strong public policies and government involvement are needed to secure an efficient and equitable system of health care financing. But state involvement by itself is not sufficient.

The 1997 *Strategy on Health, Population, and Nutrition* and the 2007 *Healthy Development: The World Bank Strategy for Health, Nutrition, and Population Results* both emphasized a need for the international development community to support health services and financing with the private sector and civil society, in addition to the public sector. Other bilateral donors working with the Bank, such as the Dutch, German, and French governments and other partner agencies such as the World Health Organization and the International Labour Organization share this vision for development.

The editors and authors contributing to *Scaling Up Affordable Health Insurance: Staying the Course* make a strong case for giving health insurance greater attention than it has received in the past. It is an important instrument—together with other financing mechanisms—for purchasing value for money from both public and private providers, achieving fiscally sustainable access to needed health services, financial protection against the impoverishing cost of illness, and health insurance coverage for social groups that are often excluded from access to publicly provided health care.

Road Map

In "Public Options, Private Choices," the introductory chapter 1 to this book, Alexander S. Preker, Marianne E. Lindner, Dov Chernichovsky, and Onno P. Schellekens describe how low-income countries often rely heavily on government funding and out-of-pocket payments for health care financing.

At an early stage of economic development, a country's ratio of prepaid to out-of-pocket sources of financing is often as low as 20:80. At higher income levels, this ratio is reversed: prepaid sources make up 80 percent of financing sources. Countries on an optimal development path will progress from the 20:80 to 80:20 ratio. But many of the fragile low-income countries are on a slower and suboptimal development path toward a 40:60 ratio. Without a significant shift in policy direction and implementation, out-of-pocket spending will continue to represent a large share of total health care expenditure, leaving many households exposed to financial hardship or impoverishment despite significant government spending on health care. In many countries on a suboptimal development path, a large share of government funding comes from donors rather than from domestic sources of financing. These countries are vulnerable to donor dependence, volatility in financial flows, and fungibility. Furthermore, in many of these poorly performing countries, a large share of out-of-pocket expenditure is on informal payments in the public sector and on private sector spending, exposing households to whatever cost the local market can bear.

The authors highlight that treatments for HIV/AIDS, malarial, and other priority public health programs are often too costly to include in the expanded insurance benefits without additional subsidies. The current approach for dealing with this problem is to leave it to governments and the international donor community to cover the costs of these programs through direct supply-side subsidies for the poor or expensive vertical parallel programs. An alternative approach recommended by the authors would be for donors and government to channel these additional earmarked resources through health insurance programs. Under this approach, these programs could benefit from risk-mitigation mechanisms and be better integrated into the system (figure 2).

The authors stress the important trade-offs that countries face in terms of the depth and breadth of the benefits package, especially in severely resource-constrained environments. In an attempt to rapidly reach universal coverage, low-income countries may end up compromising the adequacy of the benefits package in terms of the range and effectiveness of services provided. This can undermine the policy objectives of both access and financial protection for the poor if patients end up having to pay for care out of pocket for a significant range of services not covered under the publicly mandated benefits. Under a universal entitlement scheme, every dollar of subsidy spent on care for the nonpoor

FIGURE 2   Shift Traditional Subsidies to Cover Premiums for the Poor, 2005–15

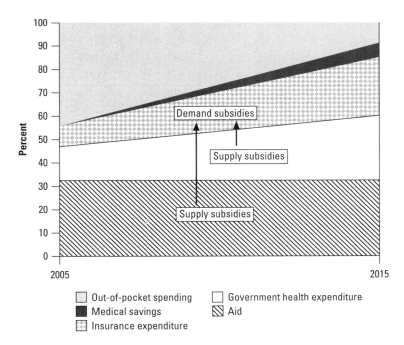

Source: Authors.

is a dollar not spent on the poor. And every dollar spent subsidizing untargeted public hospitals and clinics is a dollar not spent on services focused on providing access for the poor.

The authors of chapter 1 also emphasize the importance of a parallel strengthening and expansion of other parts of the health system such as government stewardship, provider networks, supply chains, and disease prevention programs. Whereas scaling up access to health services for the whole population remains a key policy objective in many countries, rapid introduction of universal entitlement without a balanced expansion in the supply of services, staff, and pharmaceuticals can lead to deterioration in the quality of existing services in clinics left short of staff and drugs.

Part 1 Major Policy Challenges: Preconditions for Scaling Up

Major policy challenges and preconditions for scaling up health insurance coverage in low- and middle-income countries are explored in the first part of this book.

In chapter 2, "Health Protection: More Than Financial Protection," Xenia Scheil-Adlung describes how "scaling up" is more than just insurance coverage. She uses a broader definition of social health protection as part of a cluster of concepts that include human rights to health and social security, equity in access, solidarity in financing based on capacity to pay, and efficiency and effectiveness in the use of funds.

Social health protection is seen by many as an overarching goal. It is understood as a series of public or publicly organized and mandated private measures against social distress and economic loss caused by reduced productivity, reduced or lost earnings, or astronomical treatment expenses that can result from ill health. Social health insurance is a key element of social health protection, and an integral way of achieving universal and affordable coverage through coordinating pluralistic health financing mechanisms. Social health insurance is seen as a necessary element in achieving both social health protection and social security. The author stresses that the ultimate objective of scaling up is to achieve universal coverage and effective access to affordable and quality health care, and financial protection in case of sickness.

To be effective, universal coverage needs to ensure access to care for all residents of a country. This does not preclude national health policies from focusing at least temporarily on priority groups such as women or the poor when setting up or extending social health protection. Coverage should relate to effective and affordable access to quality health services that medically match the morbidity structure and needs of the covered population. Effective access includes both access to health services and financial protection. Financial protection is crucial to avoid health-related impoverishment. Financial protection includes the avoidance of out-of-pocket payments that reduce the affordability of services and—ideally—some compensation for productivity loss due to illness. Compared with legal coverage that describes rights and formal entitlements, effective access refers to the physical, financial, and geographical availability of services.

The author concludes that worldwide experience and evidence show that there is no single right model for providing social health protection or one single pathway toward achieving universal coverage. Countries that use social health insurance have a range of policy options in terms of governance structures, institutional arrangements, financing mechanisms (resource generation, risk pooling, and allocation of resources), and benefits packages. Experience has also revealed that social protection evolves over years or even decades and is contingent upon historical and economic developments, social and cultural values, institutional settings, political commitment, and leadership within countries. In addition, most national health financing systems are based on multiple options that cover disjointed or overlapping subgroups of the population, while others remain uncovered.

In chapter 3, "Making Health Insurance Affordable: Role of Risk Equalization," Wynand P.M.M. van de Ven describes how mandatory health insurance can be used as a *tool* to achieve the *goal* of making health insurance affordable, even for high-risk and low-middle-income populations, irrespective of whether this is in the context of a voluntary or mandatory health insurance. The rationale for doing so is that, if health insurance is not affordable for certain groups of individuals, it makes no sense to mandate it. Conversely, if subsidies can make health insurance affordable, is a mandate to buy such health insurance really necessary?

Free competitive health insurance markets tend to gravitate toward risk-adjusted premiums, leading, over time, to risk selection. To counter this effect, sooner or later governments introduce regulations to make such health insurance accessible to high-risk groups and low-income populations by forcing private health insurance companies or government-run plans to open enrolment and restrict the rate of their premiums. In this context, insurers are often forced to select good risks to avoid insolvency. To overcome this pattern of behavior, which undermines the effectiveness of health insurance in providing financial protection against the risk of illness, an increasing number of countries are looking to various forms of risk equalization as an essential precondition for using health insurance in financing health care.

The author concludes that, although many Western countries are increasingly looking to risk equalization as a way to address traditional insurance market failure, in low-income countries that have restricted capacity for raising taxes, the introduction of risk equalization will be institutionally challenging. This is likely to happen, considering their large informal sector, public distrust of insurance companies, inexperience with the regulatory framework to manage a competitive insurance market, and often insufficient data.

In chapter 4, "Reaching the Poor: Transfers from Rich to Poor and from Healthy to Sick," Sherry Glied and Mark Stabile stress that a core function of insurance is to pool resources and risks across individuals. Without a distribution of risks, insurance pools, regardless of whether they are public or private, cannot successfully cover the costs of care for sick individuals, especially poor people.

The authors emphasize that the goals of most public insurance programs include risk redistribution, not just management of risk. One common way of achieving this goal is to subsidize the premiums of individuals who cannot afford to cover the full cost of insurance themselves. Public insurance programs with mandatory participation cross-subsidize costs from rich to poor. When public programs are not mandatory, and superior private alternatives exist, individuals with strong preferences for medical care and with the resources to exercise those preferences may exit the public program for the private tier. Many jurisdictions with both public and private insurance programs require tax contributions to the public program regardless of the level of participation in order to maintain cross-subsidization across incomes.

The authors conclude that most public financing mechanisms cross-subsidize from young to old, from individuals to families, and (often) from wealthy regions to poorer ones. However, depending on the financing mechanism used and the extent of tax-based redistribution, programs can have varying degrees of cross-subsidization. Payroll taxes are levied only on those who work, thereby cross-subsidizing those who do not work, and those with multiple dependents. Premiums generally vary by dependent status (though not generally by age or region), but in general the difference in premiums does not account for the difference in utilization. Thus, public premium-based programs generate redistribution from the currently healthy to the currently sick.

In chapter 5, "Binding Constraints on Public Funding: Prospects for Creating 'Fiscal Space,' " Peter S. Heller highlights the dramatic recent increase in health expenditure, partially due to the enormous need for health care among the poor and significant increase in spending on such priority programs as those for treatment and prevention of HIV/AIDS and malaria.

The threat of pandemics of flu or other diseases could add to the list of urgent issues that may need to be addressed in the future. In this environment, concern has emerged about how to find the fiscal resources ("fiscal space") to finance the required spending on health, including subsidies for government-funded health insurance. In the broadest sense, fiscal space can be defined as the capacity of government to provide additional budgetary resources for a desired purpose without any prejudice to the sustainability of its financial position. The desire is to make additional resources available for some form of meritorious government spending (or tax reduction).

The author concludes that government can create fiscal space in different ways. Additional revenues can be raised through taxation or by strengthening tax administration. Resources can be borrowed from domestic or external sources. Governments can use their ability to print money to finance public programs. And fiscal space may also be obtained if a government receives grants from outside sources. Low-priority expenditures can be cut to make room for more desirable ones. But global concern about helping countries reach the Millennium Development Goals creates competition for such essential fiscal space from other sectors such as education, water, sanitation, housing, and the physical infrastructure needed to foster rapid economic growth. In this context, the author concludes that, in most low-income countries, much of the fiscal space needed for additional health spending, particularly in the short to medium term, is likely to require external financing, with a strong preference for grants. This underscores the importance of greater predictability and longer-term financing by donors if countries are to be enabled to expand employment comfortably in the health sector.

In chapter 6, "Universal Coverage: A Global Consensus," Guy Carrin, Inke Mathauer, Ke Xu, and David B. Evans revisit the long-standing commitment of the World Health Organization (WHO) to helping countries move toward universal coverage as an important development goal in health care financing.

Public aspirations to cover the whole population for health care go back several millennia to Egyptian times when the pharaohs introduced a system of health care for the slaves they used to build their pyramids. More recent landmarks of note include Chancellor Bismarck's introduction of the Sickness Funds in 1884, expansion of health insurance coverage under the Soviet Union from 1919 onward, the introduction of a National Health Insurance program in New Zealand in 1938, the start of the British National Health Service in 1948, the ILO Convention of 1952 on Social Health Protection, and the WHO Declaration of Health for All of 1978. In 2005, the WHO member states reaffirmed their commitment to the principle of universal coverage by adopting a resolution encouraging countries to develop health financing systems capable of achieving and maintaining universal coverage of health services—in which all people have access to needed health services without the risk of severe financial consequences.

The authors emphasize that a major challenge for many countries will be to move away from out-of-pocket payments, which are often used as an important source of fund collection. Prepayment methods will need to be developed or expanded but, in addition to questions of revenue collection, specific attention will have to be paid to pooling funds to spread risks and to enable the efficient and equitable use of resources. Developing prepayment mechanisms may take time, depending on countries' economic, social, and political contexts. Specific rules for health financing policy will need to be developed, and implementing organizations will need to be tailored to the level that countries can support and sustain.

The authors conclude by presenting a comprehensive framework focusing on health financing rules and organizations that can be used to support countries in developing their health financing systems in the search for universal coverage. They stress long-term solutions, coupled with flexible short-term action plans. They do not recommend that countries follow a blueprint or single formula. Indeed, for many countries, they maintain it will take some years to achieve universal coverage and that the path will be complex. Each country's response will be determined partly by its own history and the way its health financing system has developed to date, as well as by social preferences relating to concepts of solidarity.

Part 2 From Theory to Practice: Evidence from the Ground

In chapter 7, "The French Connection in Francophone Africa," Yohana Dukhan, Alexander S. Preker, and François Diop describe how Francophone Africa has a much longer tradition of health insurance than Anglophone Africa.

Health system financing in Francophone Africa and other low-income countries has been characterized by three major trends over the last 30 years. In the first phase until the 1980s, health care was free and publicly funded and delivered. Public social security systems developed in most countries between the 1950s and 1970s, but few of them specifically covered sickness because health care was already free. Sometimes special provisions were made for family and work injury care. Beginning in the 1980s, budgetary and macroeconomic difficulties confronted governments with growing problems of financing, declining quality of care, mounting inequality in coverage, and proliferating informal payments. There were no arrangements to make health care available to the poorest people.

The second trend, cost recovery (resulting from the Bamako Initiative of 1987) led to user participation in the cost of care. Direct payments by users were to provide health care facilities with additional resources (to cover all or part of operating costs), complementing budgetary allocations. These resources were to be managed at local level and by the community, in concert with health care personnel. It was expected that health care centers would operate more efficiently and that the quality of care would improve. However, the problem of access to care for the poorest persisted. Finally, the third trend, which surfaced in the 1990s, emphasized the development of insurance instruments to protect individuals against health risks by pooling resources, mobilizing additional resources for the health sector, and improving the efficiency and quality of care through formal contractual arrangements.

Thus, insurance-type mechanisms have emerged fairly recently in Francophone Africa. Two major groups of mechanisms are notable: community-based insurance (mutual health organizations and similar systems) and mandatory health insurance (MHI) systems. Despite the movements to extend the mutualist trend (Mali, Rwanda, Senegal) and MHI reforms (Côte d'Ivoire, Mali, Rwanda), health insurance coverage remains sparse, and its contribution to financing is weak, in the subregion. Even if experience in developed countries shows that the development of health insurance is a long process, the literature highlights major economic, social, political, institutional, and cultural constraints that account for the low level of implantation and the relatively slow development of health insurance systems in developing countries. The authors conclude that broad coverage in health care financing is unlikely to be achieved through a continuation of past trends. New and more innovative mechanisms such as those that are being tried in the Anglophone countries may also be applicable in some of the Francophone countries.

In chapter 8, "'Big-Bang' Reforms in Anglophone Africa," Caroline Ly, Yohana Dukhan, Frank G. Feeley, Alexander S. Preker, and Chris Atim combine political science and economics to provide insight into the various stages of, and potential solutions to, scaling up health insurance in Africa's English-speaking countries.

This group of countries inherited a publicly run health care system from their colonial days, in addition to a disconnected group of mission-based and other modern and traditional health care providers. Often modeled after the British National Health Service, the public systems were set up with a belief that government-provided health care was a universal right. General revenues from taxes or exports were used to finance public networks of health care providers. In the decades after their independence, economic and political conditions deteriorated in many of these West and East African countries, and their health systems typically bore the brunt. Publicly funded systems could not provide quality health care to all in their diminishing resource environments. Patients increasingly sought health care outside the public system; and the public health care system turned to user fees to make up for funding shortfalls. As a way to solve the dilemmas of limited public resources, high financial barriers to access, costly disease burdens, and inefficient public systems, some countries started to experiment with alternative forms of health care financing.

The authors of this chapter provide a fascinating account of how suddenly, during the past 10 years, a handful of these countries have begun an aggressive program to scale up government-mandated health insurance for their population. The best-known "big-bang" reforms are in Ghana, where coverage has reached 65 percent of the population in less than five years, and in the Dutch Health Insurance Fund–supported pilot experience in Kwara State, Nigeria. Examples with a longer history such as Kenya have recently been joined by Nigeria and Tanzania, while newcomers such as Ethiopia and Uganda are currently debating their legislative reforms. Many other countries in the region are considering following a similar path, with the objective of finding a more sustainable way of financing health care for their population. A notable feature of their search is the mix of public and private arrangements in financing as well as in service delivery. In parallel with their publicly funded national systems, these countries have introduced district mutual health organizations (Ghana), private health maintenance organizations (Nigeria), community-based health insurance (Uganda, Tanzania, and many other countries), and private for-profit insurance industries (Namibia, South Africa, and Zimbabwe). The authors conclude that the African countries are redefining the rules of the game in health care financing. Old divisions between public and private, formal and informal, purchaser and provider are all being reexamined as new and innovative mechanisms are being tried across the continent with notable examples of both success and spectacular failure.

In chapter 9, "Moving from Intent to Action in the Middle East and North Africa," Bjorn O. Ekman and Heba A. Elgazzar describe the scaling-up experience in this region by looking at a set of key health financing indicators over the period 1995 to 2008. The indicators include such key dimensions as resource mobilization and risk pooling, approaches to purchasing services, and the role of the private sector for health. The countries of the region are divided into three separate income groups: low-income (the Republic of Yemen), a large group of middle-income non-oil-producing countries of the Maghreb and Mashreq, and the high-income oil-producing countries of the Arabian Gulf.

The authors highlight that, although health spending levels vary considerably across the MENA Region, most countries spend less as a share of GDP on health than do other similar countries and income groups. Furthermore, while public spending in some countries seems to have stabilized over the past five years, households and individuals pay increasing amounts of money out-of-pocket to see a health provider and to purchase medicines. This trend is causing many people in the MENA Region to face catastrophic health expenditures, and it is also pushing some households into poverty because they are having to pay for health care directly without sufficient financial protection. It is unlikely, however, that continuing this trend of keeping aggregate public spending down is an effective and sustainable approach for the coming decade. More innovative ways of mobilizing funds, pooling resources, and purchasing services will be called for.

The analysis then highlights three issues of general importance. First, there is an almost complete absence of timely and high-quality data on key health system dimensions in the MENA Region. Second, the vast majority of countries in the region continue to rely on input-based methods to allocate financial resources to providers. Finally, the countries of the MENA Region are still at an early stage in developing strategies for getting the private sectors to contribute to providing financial protection and high-quality services in ways that are conducive to equity and cost control. In line with the situation in most parts of the world, the private sector is a real presence in both health financing and in service provision. In many countries of the region, the private health care sector operates all but independently from the public sector. Identifying the most appropriate mechanisms through which the private sector can be an equal and responsible part of the overall health sector will be a critical policy issue in the MENA Region over the coming years.

The authors conclude that, in parallel to making data more readily available and engaging the private sector more effectively, there is an urgent need to introduce low-cost management information systems as essential tools for both scaling up health insurance coverage and managing existing financial resources more effectively.

In chapter 10, "One-Step, Two-Step Tango in Latin America and the Caribbean," Ricardo Bitrán describes how, with the exception of Brazil, most countries in the region have chosen social health insurance as the dominant model for financing health care and providing financial protection against the cost of illness.

Reforms in Latin America typically began with the formal sector workers through wage-based contributions and subsequent expansion in coverage to informal sector workers and low-income populations through public subsidies.

Most countries in Latin America have segmented health systems under which different organizational and financial arrangements have been put in place to serve the health needs of different population groups. In particular contributory social security has been available for public and private formal sector workers, while a publicly financed ministry of health, operating a broad network of own providers, often offers subsidized health services for low-income people. Private health insurance coexists, but often covers only the small, high-income segment of the population. An integral part of the reform process in scaling up health insurance in Latin America was decentralization in financing and delivery of health services.

Despite these common threads, countries in Latin America have come to rely on a mixed array of health insurance arrangements and service delivery systems. For example, Chile's system mandates health insurance enrolment, but leaves it up to the individuals to select their insurer—either the single public insurer known as the National Health Fund or one of the many competing private insurers known as ISAPREs. Mexico relies on health social security to cover about half of its population. Financing comes from workers, employers, and the federal government; tax-based financing subsidizes part of the premium for the other half of the population through Popular Health Insurance.

Efforts to reform health insurance systems in Latin America have been plagued by a strong ideological debate, one that has often been driven by interest groups defending the status quo. For example, initiatives to improve efficiency among public health care providers, or to promote private participation in provision and insurance, have been characterized or discarded by some as neoliberal or privatizing in nature. Government health workers' unions have often been behind these claims. Likewise, efforts to strengthen the regulation of private health insurers have been attacked by the insurers themselves as "central planning." Initiatives to improve the quality of health care through the implementation of diagnostic and treatment protocols have been rejected by medical professionals on the basis that they threaten their professional independence. Deadlocks in this debate have often hampered progress and prevented most countries in the region from achieving the same degree of scaling-up witnessed in Asia. The authors propose a taxonomy for understanding this large array of health insurance systems and their main characteristics (public versus private; mandatory versus voluntary).

In chapter 11, "Orient Express in South, East, and Pacific Asia," William C. Hsiao, Alexis Medina, Caroline Ly, and Yohana Dukhan describe how East Asia is the one region outside the OECD where several countries have managed to rapidly reach universal coverage during the past few years.

Despite the diversity across the Asian continent, two paths have predominated in the quest for universal coverage through health insurance. The industrial economies such as Japan, the Republic of Korea, China, as well as Taiwan, China, have followed a traditional path like Western Europe and Latin America—starting with formal sector workers then expanding to informal sector workers and the poor. The high-income per capita and formal employment sector in these countries have allowed a significant expansion of government-mandated social health insurance. The middle-income countries such as China, the Philippines, and Thailand have followed a new path, shaped by their own circumstances, targeting and subsidizing from the outset hard-to-reach informal sector workers and the poor. A particular feature has been the establishment of community-based insurance in several of these countries, covering rural populations first and then serving as a base for universal coverage later.

The Asian experience shows that several key drivers enabled the scaling-up process. Economic development is a key driver that reduced the portion of population in the informal sector requiring subsidies and increased government tax revenues. Once the government has the fiscal capacity to subsidize enrolment for low-income households and informal sector workers, expansion in coverage can happen quickly.

Political demand for access to known and affordable interventions by the population can be a key driver of reform. Grassroots demand and organization generate political pressure for governments to take action. In China, Japan, and Thailand when people found health care unaffordable, governments took action to scale up coverage. Demand for equitable treatment was a motivating factor in Thailand, the Philippines, and Taiwan, China, where the uncovered population demanded health insurance coverage similar to that of the formal sector workers. Political will and government capacity are also major reform drivers in the scaling-up process. A clear case of comparison is China and India. Both countries decided to allocate significant new funds to cover the rural population. China, with a strong central government, was able to expand coverage for its rural population rapidly. India has had a slower start although recently it has made significant progress as well in expanding coverage for its rural and poorer populations. Indonesia and the Philippines have similar programs to expand coverage but have been handicapped by weak implementation capacity in executing planned reforms.

Finally, the authors of this chapter discuss the important role of incentives both in expanding enrolment and as drivers for efficiency in the delivery of care. They emphasize that it is not only a question of scaling up, but also how to scale up while using resources efficiently.

In chapter 12, "Bismarck's Unfinished Business in Western Europe," Hans Maarse, Alexander S. Preker, Marianne E. Lindner, and Onno P. Schellekens stress that it took many continental European countries more than a hundred years of gradual, incremental reforms in economic, political, and social policy to reach universal coverage for their population. The resulting health systems are diverse and funding mechanisms, varied.

Notwithstanding this diversity, the authors of this chapter stress several common features among the European health insurance countries. First, the countries that followed this path have complex, multiparty, consensual political systems. The health policy that emerged under this type of political system was by necessity a policy of compromise and appeasement of diverse views. But it also resulted in a social contract that has a very broad base of popular support. Political leaders who have tried during recent years to reform the Bismarckian "social health insurance" systems have been surprised by the resistance of the opposition to any policy perceived as eroding the solidarity-based principles that evolved over time, even though membership was based on a contributory membership.

Second, the chapter highlights that good governance was a central feature in scaling up health insurance in Europe. Governments' capacity to formulate and implement policies effectively was important. But the real litmus test was at election time when citizens were able to hold politicians and parties accountable for their economic and social policy choices. Access to health care and financial protection against the cost of illness become viewed as central parts of the post-war social contract between the state and its citizens. With the exception of Switzerland and the Netherlands, the European vision of national health insurance systems was a vision of a "public insurance" that crowded out private health insurance arrangements that may originally have coexisted.

Third, despite strong principles of solidarity and the role of the state in the social insurance countries, entitlement, redistribution, and equity are viewed as earned entitlements and not as acquired rights. Health care is not viewed as free. The working population expects to contribute, but subsidies for people who cannot pay are closely scrutinized. There are no blank checks. Anything seen as "free-riding" is viewed negatively by the main constituent of the electorate, the working population that has to pay.

Fourth, the expansion of health insurance posed a dilemma for the medical profession. It created an opportunity to earn additional money (payment for care for the poor) but threatened physicians' autonomy (growing state intrusion into the doctor-patient relationship and unfavorable financial conditions). Doctors fought in Europe over three basic principles: free choice of doctors, no predominance of the sickness funds, and economic independence. The policy lesson here is that doctors are likely to fight over many issues in national health insurance. This requires a prudent strategy on the part of the policy makers.

Other issues highlighted by the authors in this chapter include social capital, tolerance for pluralist institutional structures, tension between social classes, categories of insurable risks, optimal number of insurance funds, and contextual factors such as economy development, culture, politics, and institutional structures. The authors also emphasize that health insurance arrangements cannot properly function without adequate supportive legislation on health care planning, workforce planning, cost control, and health care quality.

In chapter 13, "From Cradle to Grave in the United Kingdom, Canada, Australia, and Elsewhere," Alexander S. Preker and Mark C. Bassett review the development paths for introducing universal access to health care in the OECD during the 20th century and their relevance to developing countries that are trying to introduce similar financing reforms.

The authors remind the reader that, at the end of the previous century, most Western countries relied mainly on direct out-of-pocket payment and unregulated markets to finance and provide health care similar to what is observed today in many low- and middle-income countries. In 1938, New Zealand became the first country with a market economy to introduce compulsory participation in and universal entitlement to a comprehensive range of health services, financed largely through the public sector (the United Kingdom followed a similar path when—10 years later in 1948—it established the National Health Service [NHS]). Universal access to health care in many East European countries—Albania, Bulgaria, the Czech Republic, the Slovak Republic, Hungary, Poland, Romania, and the former USSR—was achieved through similar legislative reforms. A number of other middle- and low-income countries have followed a similar path.

Today, the populations in most OECD countries (with the exception of Mexico, Turkey, and the United States) enjoy universal access to a comprehensive range of health services financed through a combination of general revenues, social insurance, private insurance, and user charges. In 13 of the OECD countries, universal access was achieved through "big-bang" landmark legislative reforms that guaranteed their population such benefits, often under a state-funded national health service (United Kingdom–styled NHS). Most other OECD countries achieved similar coverage through a combination of voluntary, mandatory, and regulatory mechanisms under a social health insurance–type of system (Bismarckian). This chapter focuses mainly on the former—those countries that achieved universal access through specific landmark legislative reforms and a single-payer financing mechanism. Chapter 12 focused on the latter—those countries that introduced reforms more incrementally, by expanding coverage through voluntary, mandatory, and regulatory health insurance.

Though often incorrectly credited for having been the first, the British NHS was established as a result of the 1944 White Paper, *A National Health Service*, 10 years after the New Zealand NHS of 1938. The British NHS was certainly the most famous, and it was widely emulated by countries throughout the world in the decades that followed. It set out the two guiding principles. First, that such a service should be comprehensive, with all citizens receiving all the advice, treatment, and care they needed, delivered in the best medical and other facilities available. Second, that the service should be free to the public at point of use.

The authors divide the process of introducing a national health service into two phases: a policy formulation phase; and an implementation phase. During the policy formulation phase, the design of the reform needs to consider both the financing and service delivery aspects. Without access to health services, legislation that mandates universal financing is little more than a paper law. A major stumbling block during the design phase has been the political economy of policy formulation and dealing with various stakeholders with vested interests that may resist such reforms for a variety of reasons discussed in the chapter. During the policy implementation phase, management capacity (staff, resources, and administrative tools such as information systems) and sustain-ability factors (financial resources, political commitment, and institutional infrastructure) play a critical role in securing the success of the reforms.

The authors conclude by challenging the doomsday prediction of many crit-ics that such reforms are financially unsustainable and lead to major cost escala-tion. Data presented indicate that most of the OECD countries that passed major legislative reforms to introduce universal access to health care experienced a decade-long period of stability in health care expenditure following the reform compared with the projected expenditure trajectory had the same countries con-tinued pre-reform spending trends.

In chapter 14, "Great Post-Communist Experiment in Eastern Europe and Central Asia," Adam Wagstaff and Rodrigo Moreno-Serra describe how the post-Communist transition to social health insurance in many of the Central and East European and Central Asian countries provides a unique opportunity to try to answer some of the unresolved issues in the debate over the relative merits of social health insurance and tax-financed health systems. Through a detailed empirical analysis, they conclude that, when controlling for differ-ences in provider-payment reforms and other variables, switching from general revenue to payroll tax–based funding increased national health spending and hospital activity rates, but did not lead to any significant changes in health outcomes.

Under Communism, health care in almost all the ECA countries (except for the former Yugoslavia) was financed from general revenues and out-of-pocket payments. Health care was delivered through a centrally planned "Semashko" model consisting of a tiered system of health providers, each allocated budgets according to population-based norms, with health workers paid by salary. In the early 1990s, as most countries shifted away from Communism, several looked to health insurance as a possible alternative in the hope of addressing a drop in funding following the economic transition and problems in the performance and efficiency of health care providers in addressing the poor health of the pop-ulation and emerging problems in access to health services (including financial barriers created through user fees).

Of the 28 ECA countries, 14 introduced payroll taxes earmarked for health care at some stage between 1990 and 2004, and 4 others had already done so before 1990 (Bosnia and Herzegovina, Croatia, Serbia and Montenegro, and Tur-key). Countries that switched to health insurance early in the 1990s included Estonia, Hungary, Lithuania, the former Yugoslav Republic of Macedonia, and Slovenia (1990–92). Some countries such as Bulgaria introduced health insur-ance later (1999). Often, both the employee and employer are liable, although there were differences between who was legally liable for what and who ended up bearing the incidence of the payroll tax, the latter depending on conditions in the labor and product markets.

Contributions were made mandatory, and in exchange for them the contribut-ing employee was entitled to receive health services under the terms of the health insurance scheme. Groups other than formal sector workers were usually also given some coverage. Contributions were always required from the self-employed and in some countries also from pensioners. Other groups were covered through funds allocated from the state budget although such subsidies were not actuarially calculated to cover the cost of health care for these population groups.

Based on their analysis, the authors question the value of countries' having switched from general revenue to payroll tax–funded health care in the post-Communist period in the ECA Region, in light of the apparent lack of significant funding increases, weak evidence on efficiency improvements, and lack of good evidence on changes in overall health status.

Part 3 Implementation Challenges: Staying the Course

In chapter 15, "Political Economy of Reform," Ashley M. Fox and Michael R. Reich stress that, although a growing number of low- and middle-income countries have sought to introduce universal coverage by scaling up national health insurance during the past 20 years, successful reform has been the exception rather than the rule.

If scaling up health insurance coverage is popular, can greatly improve access to care, and potentially reduces costs through risk pooling, then why is it so hard to adopt and implement? The authors argue that reforms are difficult because political challenges are almost always embedded in each step of the policy reform process. Politics affects whether reform makes its way onto the national agenda, how the reform proposal is designed, compromises needed to produce an acceptable agreement, and ultimately the implementation of reform. Health financing reform is often treated as a technical matter—designing the right policy to produce the intended effect. However, the "technically optimal" rarely equates with the politically feasible.

Health policy analysts and international development organizations are putting increasing emphasis on political economy analysis to provide the missing link between reform processes and policy outcomes. This approach involves deepening understanding of the political, institutional, social, and economic issues at play, the power relations among actors, and the incentives that affect change. Why have some countries been successful at adopting national health insurance while others have failed? Why have leaders preferred particular policy designs over others? Why has the same reform produced the intended effect in certain settings, but not in others? What are the prospects for scaling up health insurance coverage in developing countries?

In analyzing the political economy of health financing reform, the authors stress that there is no consensus about what constitutes a "good" reform because of disagreement about underlying social values. Different ethical assumptions result in different reform policies. They argue that simply exhorting leaders to commit to national health insurance is insufficient to move countries to scale up coverage and that lack of political commitment to reform is inadequate to explain why some countries have been more successful than others.

In addition, they find problems with several other commonly asserted reasons to explain the failure or success of health insurance scale-up (such as economic growth, democratization, and political culture). Instead, the authors conclude that four variables particularly affect the probability of successful reform: institutions, ideas, interests, and ideology. These ideas are explored in greater depth in this chapter.

In chapter 16, "Institutions Matter," Alexander S. Preker, April Harding, Edit V. Velenyi, Melitta Jakab, Caroline Ly, and Yohana Dukhan stress that the ultimate objective of scaling up health insurance should be to improve health system performance in addressing national policy objectives, such as improved access to quality health care, financial protection against the cost of illness, and consumer choice or satisfaction. Although such goals could theoretically be achieved under most forms of collective financing of health care, in reality they often require a major and fundamental realignment in the incentives structure within the health sector, such as the shift to health insurance from core budget financing of health services.

In this chapter, the authors explore the contribution to this agenda by the way insurers are organized and their underlying incentive regime through the lens of industrial organizations. The central question is "How does the organizational structure of insurers make a difference in systemic efficiency and equity?" By controlling the "purse strings," financing organizations are in a powerful position to create the needed incentives for providers to behave in ways that would secure not only the highest quality of care but also be responsive to the needs of the patients they serve. Yet in reality often this does not happen.

In an ideal world, a patient (principal) contracts with a health insurance carrier (agent) to perform certain duties, such as pay for health care efficiently and equitably and protect populations against financial risk. For such a contract to work, it must be attractive to both principal and agent. From the agent's point of view, the contract must be at least as attractive as available alternative contracts (participation constraint). From the principal's point of view, the contract and its incentives must be structured in such a way as to ensure that the agent will act in the principal's best interest (incentive compatibility constraint). The principal (patient or government) cannot exploit the agent because the contract is voluntary. And the agent (health insurer) cannot shirk or cheat if his pay is related to effort and outcomes. A well-designed contract maximizes the utility of this relationship for both the principal and the agent. In practice, because of uncertainty in outcomes, information asymmetry, moral hazard, and adverse selection, health insurers often do not act in this way. Most outcomes depend on factors other than a single agent's actions. The effectiveness of any agent is often codependent on the action of others. Success in terms of outcomes cannot be fully attributed to any single agent. Outcomes often depend on the aggregate effort of a team, making it equally difficult to blame any one agent for failure.

Furthermore, health insurance agencies usually serve as multiplicitous agents for several powerful principals other than individual patients. Three important agency relationships are predominant. They encompass the relationship between financing arrangements and individual health care providers (doctors, nurses, allied health care workers), the relationship between financing agencies and various institutional actors (policy makers, regulators, insurers, and other funding agencies), and the relationship between financing agencies and health care organizations (hospitals, clinics, ambulatory services). In reality, there are more than three agency relationships because the stakeholders under each of these three major categories all exert some influence over the financing agents. Policy makers, regulators, and funding agencies often have very different interests. Hospitals, clinics, and ambulatory services expect different services from financing agencies. While private (self-employed) doctors often have direct contact with financing agencies, nurses and other health care professionals do not. Their expectations will be different.

The authors conclude with a detailed examination of how a number of organizational structures and functions affect the principal-agent relationship in terms of organizational forms (ownership, contractual relationships, and scale and scope of insurers); structure configuration (extent of horizontal and vertical linkages or fragmentation among insurers); and incentive regime (extent of decision rights, market exposure, financial responsibility, accountability, and coverage of social functions).

In chapter 17, "Accountability and Choice," Dov Chernichovsky, Michal Chernichovsky, Jürgen Hohmann, and Bernd Schramm provide an overview of some of the key economic and institutional issues confronted during the implementation of health insurance reforms.

The authors present the rather ill-defined and fuzzy concept of scaling up social health insurance (SHI) as a dynamic process leading from a fragmented and failed health care market, based on individuals' ability and willingness to pay, to an integrated universal system, based on social solidarity, means-tested contributions, and government subsidies to ensure no one is left out. The path from fragmentation to integration is punctuated by milestones set by each country's political, economic, social, and institutional realities.

In the first part of the chapter, the authors propose a typology for different health insurance systems. Population coverage and depth of the benefits package are critical elements in the proposed classification. Other critical elements in the classification include the institutional structures of organizations involved and governance arrangements. The spectrum ranges from informal, fragmented market structures to formal, unified, or universal institutions. Often progress toward universal coverage is associated with an increase in the role of the state, but through demand rather than supply-side involvement. Governance arrangements are usually more participatory than under state-run national health services. Eligibility is determined by a social contract rather than being an automatic entitlement.

In the second part of the chapter, the authors describe some of the major obstacles that countries need to overcome on the path to universal coverage.

As coverage and risk pools expand, erosion occurs in the social capital so central to membership with small community financing schemes. With the loss of small group homogeneity, willingness to contribute to collective programs and responsible use of services by patient behavior often erode. As benefits become more standardized, individual needs may be sacrificed in an attempt to provide everyone with a standard minimum benefits package. Efficiency gains through economies of scale that should go along with larger systems may be lost through the administrative inefficiency of larger bureaucracies. And a large block of vested interest may translate into a "tyranny of the majority" with a disregard for individual variations in needs and expectations. Such vested interests include professional groups, employers, patient groups, retirees, and other large constituencies that may exercise their power through a collective voice.

The authors conclude that, in the end, the true nature of large government-mandated health insurance systems is often defined by the accountability and choice over the use of mandatory contributions and supply of services. Accountability and related legitimacy are served by transparency and good governance. The two are assisted in turn by earmarking contributions and by articulating the benefits they fund. These are key elements of the social insurance contract between individuals and the state, substituting contracts between individuals and groups or corporations, and between the latter and the state. Choice is potentially best served by competition in internal markets where citizens can enroll freely with competing plans, where feasible, and with providers. These plans, replacing groups and corporations, can be self-governing and accountable—also through competition—both to their membership and to the public at large, even when privately owned. Both must be supported by stewardship and leadership.

In chapter 18, "Regulatory and Supervisory Challenges," Hernán L. Fuenzalida-Puelma, Pablo Gottret, Somil Nagpal, and Nicole Tapay stress that health care regulation and supervision have been changing. Deciding which activities to regulate involves economic and social considerations. Deciding who should regulate and how involves legal and institutional concerns. The authors stress that the regulatory domain is one where economics *and* law converge. Regulating health care is complex. Political, social, economic, and legal/institutional considerations deal with a matter critical for individuals and society where vested and conflicting interests abound. From an economic point of view, controlling market failures such as asymmetric information, adverse selection, and moral hazard justifies regulatory interventions. From a political and legal/institutional perspective, health care regulation is also justified on social and equity grounds and on the constitutional role of the state in protecting the common good or public interest.

Regulating requires an institutional/legal framework to translate policies into norms and procedures and clear objectives on which activities are subject to regulation, the type of entity or authority entrusted with regulation, and the regulatory instruments necessary for implementation. Regulatory instruments are varied: laws or legislative acts; decrees and other instruments issued by the executive branch; municipal ordinances; judgments by the judiciary; instructions, standards, circulars, public information by health insurance supervisors/regulators; and professional and ethical standards, licensing, and other matters delegated by private self-regulatory organizations.

Private health insurance supervision and regulation should target critical issues, such as: solvency; competition to avoid cartel-type practices; transparency in coverage and prices; market stability for expansion and better complementarities with social health insurance; price controls and prohibition of age-rating; open enrolments into minimum products and, up to a certain age, guaranteed renewal and portability; integration with social health insurance without allowing opt-outs for supplemental and even comprehensive coverage; quality of care by allowing selective contracting of competent providers and respecting their clinical judgment; and advertising and marketing. Regarding health insurance contracts, typical regulations refer, for example, to standards of full and fair disclosure related to health policies and health plans, terms of renewal, initial and subsequent conditions of eligibility, coverage of dependents, preexisting conditions, termination of insurance, probationary periods, limitations, exceptions, marketing of entitlements, and prices.

As the boundaries between public and private financing and service delivery become increasingly blurred, the authors emphasize, there is a need for health care regulation, supervision, and control in the public sector that involves all aspects related to "what to finance," "sources of funding," "whom to finance," "the financiers," and "how to finance" mandatory government-run health insurance and voluntary private health insurance. Many public and private entities are involved but often not coordinated. New, innovative, and comprehensive approaches to health care financing regulation and supervision are needed to identify, redefine, and restructure the regulatory environment, making it more efficient, less cumbersome, and less costly.

The authors conclude that regulation of health insurance is only as effective as its enforcement. In many countries, the regulation of health care financing and health care provision, public and private, is being integrated into complex health authorities. Few have separated the regulation and supervision of suppliers of health care goods, clinical and nonclinical. The authors feel that this arrangement leads to vulnerability to bureaucratic capture and undermines the authority and enforcement of health insurance regulation. Instead, the authors recommend that government-mandated health insurance should be subjected to the same strict regulatory and supervisory oversight expected for private entities and parastatal corporations. In many countries, this will require reforms that separate the regulatory function from line ministries and that set up separate autonomous regulatory/supervisory authorities.

In chapter 19, "Implementing Change," Hong Wang, Kimberly Switlick-Prose, Christine Ortiz, Catherine Connor, Beatriz Zurita, Chris Atim, and François Diop lead policy makers and health insurance designers through a series of management steps to be taken when introducing and scaling up health insurance. These steps are intended to deepen planners' understanding of health insurance concepts, identify challenges, help them design and implement solutions, and define realistic steps for the development and scale-up of equitable, efficient, and sustainable health insurance schemes.

Despite the many benefits that health insurance offers, the journey to implement insurance and achieve those benefits is challenging, long, and risky. When it comes to successful implementation of health insurance, the "devil is often in the details."

In the Africa Region, several countries have spent scarce time, money, and effort on introducing health insurance to scale up coverage and access to health services. The success of some of these reforms is now threatened, not because of design flaws or the complex political process but rather because of a lack of implementing capacity of the health insurance administration involved and the administrative side of the providers that interact with the insurers. For example, in Ghana the National Health Insurance Scheme has signed up around 70 percent of the population. But many members have not received their health insurance cards, the local insurance offices are buried under truckloads of claims forms coming in for payment every day, hospitals are struggling to keep up with billing, and payment transfers are months behind. Such implementation challenges quickly translate into loss of confidence and aggravate problems they were supposed to solve instead of alleviating them.

The authors conclude that policy makers and technicians that support development and scale-up of health insurance must figure out how to increase their country's financing capacity, extend health insurance coverage to the hard-to-reach populations, expand benefits packages, and improve the performance of existing schemes. Based on the recommendations in a companion manual on implementing health insurance reforms, the chapter provides policy makers and health insurance designers with practical, action-oriented supports that improve their understanding of health insurance concepts, challenges, and realistic steps for the development and scaling up of equitable, efficient, and sustainable health insurance schemes.

Finally, in chapter 20, "New Development Paradigm," Onno P. Schellekens, Jacques van der Gaag, Marianne E. Lindner, and Judith de Groot look into the crystal ball to explore ways that future health insurance systems could build on the successes of the past, address some past shortcomings, and look at some important dimensions of future health insurance systems.

Many governments have failed to finance and deliver health care efficiently through the public sector. As a result, paying for between 60 and 80 percent of their own health care out of pocket, many patients fall into poverty. Private equity investments in the health care supply chain often do not take place because the risk is considered too high. Most donor funding is channeled to the public system through supply-side input financing. At the heart of past crisis is a vicious cycle of low supply of good-quality care and low demand for such care.

Without good-quality delivery (supply), the willingness to pay and prepay for care (demand) is low. If there are no prepaid risk-pooling schemes, revenues for health care providers remain uncertain, and because the investment risk remains high, the health delivery sector cannot attract financing to improve delivery capacity. This keeps quality of care (supply side) low, perpetuating the vicious cycle of failed health systems.

Because of these and other factors, the authors of this last chapter of the book call for a rethinking of the way health care is financed and delivered, moving toward a system in which there is greater complementarity between public and private financing and between sustainable financing and service delivery modalities. Both greater access to affordable health insurance and access capital play an instrumental role in breaking the vicious cycle of underfinancing, low-quality care, low demand, and poor health outcomes.

In appendix A, "Theory of Social Health Insurance," Peter Zweifel develops a theory of social health insurance (commonly known as public health insurance in the United States). While a good deal is known about the demand and supply of private insurance, the theoretical basis for government-run mandatory health insurance (social or public health insurance) is much less well known.

The author starts by posing several fundamental questions. On the demand side, why do governments get into the health insurance arena? Is the objective to provide a public option to private insurance programs by addressing shortcomings in private health insurance related to market imperfections or equity concerns? Or is it to change the rules of the game in terms of financing health care and provide financial protection against the hardships of illness? On the supply side, what are the motives and constraints of public insurance systems? With regard to supply, what do we know about the objectives and constraints of managers who run public insurance systems? Economists can predict properties of the market equilibrium characterizing private health insurance. However, what is the likely outcome ("performance") of government-run programs? At the normative level, one may ask, should there be a shift from private to government-run insurance or vice versa?

Section 2 of appendix A reviews the conventional theory of demand for insurance in general and health insurance in particular. However, it also seeks to offer explanations of the demand for government-run health insurance programs, citing efficiency, public choice, and equity reasons. That may explain the existence (but not necessarily the prominence) of the "public option." Section 3 is devoted to the supply of health insurance in general and public insurance in particular, which comprises more dimensions than just price and quantity. Section 4 reviews the properties of the optimal health insurance contract for providing a benchmark, especially with regard to combating moral hazard. In Section 5, the question is asked whether there are factors limiting the apparently inexorable growth of the government options as countries become richer and spending on health care increases relative to GDP.

The author observes that, on balance, scanty available evidence points to a preponderance of public choice reasons for the public option in health insurance. Social (health) insurance can be seen as an efficient instrument for gaining votes in the hands of politicians seeking (re)election. Ironically, recent political pressure to constrain social health insurance (and social security more generally) may reflect marginal willingness to pay on the part of citizens below marginal cost. Conversely, compensation asked for accepting restrictions in the domain of social health insurance (in the guise of reduced contributions) could be financed by health insurers through cost savings achieved. Recent evidence from Switzerland relates to this second approach. It suggests that if health insurers were permitted to fully pass on savings accruing, for example, in their managed care options, they could compensate the average consumer sufficiently to make this option attractive. In all, there are clear signs of social health insurance encountering several limits.

The author concludes that there are important limits on public health insurance that become more apparent over time and occur increasingly toward the end of human life, when costs increase and can no longer be recovered from increased contributions. Moreover, social health insurance, by modifying the incentives of the great majority of a country's health care providers, induces the very change in medical technology that causes the cost of health care to increase more rapidly than other segments of the economy. The challenge will be to devise contracts that create incentives for consumers to choose lower-technology options when close to death. The other maintains that competitive private, rather than regulated, social health insurance is more likely to meet this type of challenge.

In appendix B, "Empirical Evidence on Trends in Health Insurance," Yohana Dukhan extends the analysis of the factors limiting the development of health insurance presented in the chapters on Francophone and Anglophone Africa. The author tests the existence of relationships between the development of health insurance—public and private—and a set of general factors such as political context, institutional environment, economic development, and social settings as well as more specific health sector factors such as insurance supply and demand, and conditions in the health care system. The relationships between these factors and the level of health insurance development are tested in a sample of 99 developing countries between 1995 and 2010. The results show that variables measuring the political and institutional environment appear among the most significant determinants of health insurance development in low- and middle-income countries.

In appendix C, "Compendium of Health Insurance Terms," Alexander S. Preker and Mark V. Pauly provide a glossary of terms frequently used in the field of health insurance.

Acknowledgments

This project would not have been possible without the support of the Dutch Government and the Health Insurance Fund for Africa. From its inception, the project was impelled by collaboration between the World Bank Group, the International Labour Organization (ILO), the World Health Organization (WHO), and Deutsche Gesellschaft für Technische Zusammenarbeit (GTZ) Germany. Peter Zweifel (University of Zurich) and Mark V. Pauly (Wharton School, University of Pennsylvania) were driving forces behind the exploration of the economic underpinnings of private and public health insurance in low-income countries in earlier volumes. The present volume was edited by Alexander S. Preker, Marianne E. Lindner, Dov Chenichovsky, and Onno P. Schellekens.

Important support was also provided by management from across the World Bank Group. Notable encouragement was provided by several managers: Guy Ellena, Cecile Fruman, and Pierre A. Guislain. Shanta Devarajan, chief economist, Africa Region, chaired the internal review meetings and provided invaluable insights on linking this review of government-run mandatory health insurance to the Bank's broader development agenda.

Financial and in-kind sponsorship was provided over the course of the research by the World Bank, IFC, ILO, WHO, GTZ, International Federation of Health Plans (iFHP), the Dutch Health Insurance Fund for Development, The Bill & Melinda Gates Foundation, the Canadian International Development Agency (CIDA), the Swedish International Development Cooperation Association (SIDA), and the U.S. Agency for International Development (USAID).

The editors are grateful to the authors whose collective contribution made this volume possible. These contributors are: Chris Atim, Mark C. Bassett, Ricardo Bitrán, Guy Carrin, Michal Chernichovsky, Catherine Connor, Judith de Groot, François Diop, Yohana Dukhan, Bjorn O. Ekman, Heba A. Elgazzar, David B. Evans, Frank G. Feeley, Ashley M. Fox, Hernán L. Fuenzalida-Puelma, Sherry Glied, Pablo Gottret, April Harding, Peter S. Heller, Jürgen Hohmann, William C. Hsiao, Melitta Jakab, Caroline Ly, Hans Maarse, Inke Mathauer, Alexis Medina, Rodrigo Moreno-Serra, Somil Nagpal, Christine Ortiz, Mark V. Pauly, Michael R. Reich, Xenia Scheil-Adlung, Bernd Schramm, Mark Stabile, Kimberly Switlick-Prose, Nicole Tapay, Jacques van der Gaag, Wynand P.M.M. van de Ven, Edit V. Velenyi, Adam Wagstaff, Hong Wang, Ke Xu, Beatriz Zurita, and Peter Zweifel.

Two steering groups provided technical guidance. Members of the Economic Steering Group provided valuable insights into the underlying economics of scaling up health insurance. Members of this group included: Alexander S. Preker (World Bank Group), David B. Evans (ILO), the late Guy Carrin (WHO), Michael

Cichon, Xenia Scheil-Adlung (ILO), Wynand P.M.M. van de Ven (Erasmus University, Rotterdam), and Dov Chenichosky (Ben Gurion University).

The following additional organizations were consulted and provided valuable inputs: Agence Française de Développement, AFD (Marie-Odile Waty), America's Health Insurance Plans (Diana Dennett), The Bill & Melinda Gates Foundation (Daniel Kress and Sheryl Scott), Dutch Health Insurance Fund (Christopher van der Vorm and Emma Coles), Dutch Ministry of Foreign Affairs (Aaltje-de Roos), GTZ (Rolf Korte), PharmAccess (Onno P. Schellekens, Marianne E. Lindner, Dorien Mulder, and Judith de Groote), Results for Development (David de Ferranti, Gina Lagomarsino, and Marty Makinen), and the Rockefeller Foundation (Ariel Pablos-Mendez and Stefan Nachuk).

Other current and former World Bank Group staff members who contributed insights during various stages of the review include Cristian Baeza, Enis Baris, Paolo Belli, Peter A. Berman, Mukesh Chawla, Jorge A. Coarasa, Rafael Cortez, Daniel Cotlear, Agnes Couffinhal, Maria Louisa Escobar, Scott D. Featherston, Pablo Gottret, Charles C. Griffin, Dominic Haazen, April Harding, Loraine Hawkins, Richard Hinz, Vijayasekar Kalavakonda, John C. Langenbrunner, Rodney Lester, Gerard Martin la Forgia, Emmett Moriarty, the late Philip Musgrove, Somil Nagpal, Mead Over, Ok Pannenborg, Oscar Picazo, Khama Rogo, Eric de Roodenbeke, Sameh El-Saharty, George Schieber, Nicole Tapay, Robert Taylo, and Marie-Odile Waty.

Kathleen A. Lynch provided invaluable help with editing, and Osongo Lenga helped with text processing.

Abbreviations and Acronyms

AA	Anglophone Africa
ADB	Asian Development Bank
AfDB	African Development Bank
AIDS	acquired immune deficiency syndrome
ALOS	average length of stay
ANS	Agencia Nacional de Saude Suplementar, National Agency for Private Health ("Supplementary") Insurance, Brazil
BUPA	British United Provident Association
CBHI	community-based health insurance
CCSS	Caja Costarricense de Seguro Social, Costa Rica
CGHS	Central Government Health Scheme, India
CIDA	Canadian International Development Agency
CIRC	China Insurance Regulation Commission
CIS	Clinical Information System
CMS	Council of Medical Schemes, South Africa
CVM	contingent valuation method
DALY	disability-adjusted life year
DANIDA	Danish International Development Agency
DFID	Department for International Development, United Kingdom
DHS	Demographic and Health Survey
DOH	Department of Health, South Africa
DOTS	directly observed treatment, short course (for tuberculosis)
DRG	diagnosis-related group
EAP	East Asia and Pacific Region, World Bank
ECA	Europe and Central Asia Region, World Bank
ECOWAS	Economic Community of West African States
EHHUES	Egypt Household Health Utilization and Expenditures Survey
EIMIC	Egyptian International Medical Insurance Company
EISA	Egyptian Insurance Supervisory Agency
EP	Emerging Paradigm
ESIS	Employee State Insurance Scheme, India
EU	European Union
FFF	fee-for-service
FMIS	Fund Management Information System
FNM	Formal, Nonuniversal, Market Model
FNN	Formal, Nonuniversal, Nonmarket Model
FONASA	Fondo Nacional de Salud, National Health Fund, Chile
GCC	Gulf Cooperation Council

GDP	gross domestic product
GIS	Government Insurance Scheme, China
GNI	gross national income
GNP	gross national product
GTZ	Deutsche Gesellschaft für Technische Zusammenarbeit [German Agency for Technical Cooperation], one of three German government development organizations merged as "Deutsche Gesellschaft für Internationale Zusammenarbeit GmbH (GIZ)" on January 1, 2011
HCE	health care expenditure
HDI	Human Development Index
HIC	high-income country
HIF	Health Insurance Fund for Africa
HIPC	heavily indebted poor countries
HMO	health maintenance organization
HSRI	Health Systems Research Institute, Thailand
IFC	International Finance Corporation, World Bank
ILO	International Labour Organization
IMF	International Monetary Fund
INN	Informal, Nonuniversal, Nonmarket Model
IRDA	Insurance Regulatory and Development Authority, India
ISAPRES	Instituciones de Salud Previsional, Private Health Insurance Scheme, Chile
LAC	Latin America and the Caribbean Region, World Bank
LIC	low-income country
LIS	Labor Insurance Scheme, China
LSMS	Living Standard Measurement Survey
MC	managed care
MDGs	Millennium Development Goals
MENA	Middle East and North Africa Region, World Bank
MHI	mandatory health insurance
MHO	mutual health organization
MIC	middle-income country
MOFE	Ministry of Finance and Economy, the Republic of Korea
MOH	Ministry of Health
MOHP	Ministry of Health and Population, the Arab Republic of Egypt
MOHW	Ministry of Health and Welfare, the Republic of Korea
MOPH	Ministry of Public Health, the Arab Republic of Egypt
MSA	medical savings account
NCAER	National Council for Applied Economic Research, India
NCMS	New Cooperative Medical Scheme, China
NGO	nongovernmental organization
NHA	national health account
NHI	national health insurance

NHS	National Health Service
NMC	nonmedical consumption
NSSO	National Sample Survey Organisation, India
OECD	Organisation for Economic Co-operation and Development
OOP	out of pocket
OOPS	out-of-pocket spending
ORT	Organisation for Educational Resources and Technological Training
PHC	primary health care
PHI	private health insurance
PMB	prescribed minimum benefit
PPO	preferred provider organization
PPP	public-private partnership; purchasing power parity
PVHI	private voluntary health insurance
PVO	private voluntary organization
REF	Risk Equalization Fund, South Africa
SAR	South Asia Region, World Bank; special administrative region, Hong Kong and Macao
SARS	severe acute respiratory syndrome
SEA	Southeast Asia
SES	socioeconomic status
SHI	social health insurance
SPH	Social Protection in Health, Mexico
SRP	Social Risk Pool, China
SSA	Sub-Saharan Africa Region, World Bank
SSI	social security insurance
SUS	Sistema Unificado de Saude, Unified Health System, Brazil
THE	total health expenditure
UG	Universal Group Model
UP	Universal Pool Model
VAT	value added tax
VHI	voluntary health insurance
WHO	World Health Organization
WTO	World Trade Organization
WTP	willingness to pay

CHAPTER 1

Introduction: Public Options, Private Choices

Alexander S. Preker, Marianne E. Lindner,
Dov Chernichovsky, and Onno P. Schellekens

Achieving the health-related Millennium Development Goals (MDGs) will require mobilization of significant additional financial resources for the health sector, improved management of financial risk, and better spending of existing scarce resources, in addition to addressing the intersectoral determinants of illness. The cost to individual households is unpredictable and often impoverishes even middle-income families who are not insured. And many interventions are ineffective. Additional resources could be mobilized by increasing the share of government funding allocated to the health sector. This chapter presents a framework for scaling up health insurance. Specific issues will be explored in greater depth in the other chapters in the book. Past reviews suggest that no one mechanism is likely to succeed by itself in securing all the objectives of health financing systems: mobilizing resources to pay for needed services, protecting populations against financial risk, and spending wisely on providers (Carrin and James 2004; Chernichovsky 2002; Hsiao 1995; Londono and Frenk 1997; Preker 1998; Savedoff 2005). Rather, a multipillar approach that combines various instruments—including subsidies, insurance mechanisms, contractual savings, and user fees—is more likely to succeed in meeting these objectives in resource-constrained environments with weak institutions, organizational arrangements, and management capacity. Such a system includes a public option but one in which private choice has an essential role in ensuring the system remain responsive to patients and consumers of care. And it emphasizes a systems approach to scaling up, going beyond health insurance itself to include strengthening of the governance and overall health system in parallel to expanded insurance coverage.

INTRODUCTION

The 20th century saw greater gains in health outcomes than at any other time in history (figure 1.1), yet the world's poor, especially in Africa and South Asia, did not benefit as much as other populations from these gains. Some countries even had setbacks. Many African and some low-income countries in other regions still fall far short of many of the MDG target indicators. Average life expectancy in the poorest countries today has not changed since the 1950s.

FIGURE 1.1   A Century of Unparalleled Improvement, but Some Still Have Far to Go

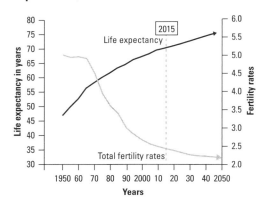

Source: Authors.

FIGURE 1.2   More Public Spending Alone Is Not Enough

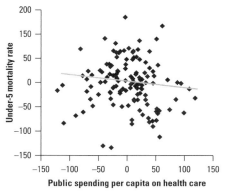

Source: World Bank 2004.

Addressing these problems requires more money and greater protection against financial risk. The correlation between higher income, more spending on health, and better health outcomes is well known. Yet the wide variation in the scatter plot on the correlation between under-5 mortality rates (U5MR) and public spending per capita on health care (figure 1.2) indicates that additional spending on health care—though much needed—is insufficient in itself to achieve good health outcomes (World Bank 2004). It is also necessary to ensure that scarce resources are spent on effective health care directed toward the most critical health challenges to households. Parallel action addressing other important cross-sectoral determinants of poor health is also needed.

Current State of Scaling Up Health Insurance in Low-Income Countries

Direct out-of-pocket spending by households still comprises as much as 80 percent of total health expenditure in many low-income countries (figure 1.3), with still rudimentary formal insurance mechanisms (figure 1.4). Donor aid—with associated volatility and fungibility—often constitutes a significant share of total public resources, as much as 50 percent or more of all resources available to some low-income countries. It is in this context that some countries have begun to experiment with private voluntary health insurance (PVHI)—community and enterprise-based—and government-run mandatory health insurance (Dror and Preker 2002; Preker and Carrin 2004; Preker, Scheffler, and Bassett 2007; Preker, Zweifel, and Schellekens 2010). PVHI complements other forms of health

FIGURE 1.3   Low-Income Countries Have Less Insurance

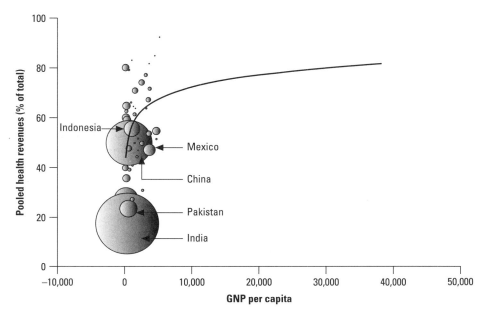

Source: Authors.
Note: The share of the world's 1.3 billion people living on less than US$1 a day is indicated by the size of the bubble.

FIGURE 1.4   Low-Income Countries Spend Less on Social Health Insurance

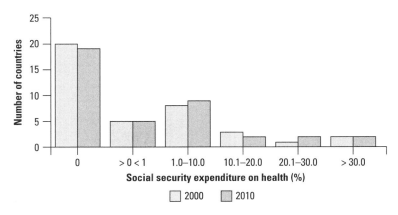

Source: Authors.

financing such as direct charges, donor aid, core budget funding, and voluntary health insurance.

KEY ISSUES

Low-income countries often rely heavily on government funding and out-of-pocket payments for health care financing. Early in a country's economic development, the balance between prepaid to out-of-pocket sources of financing is often as low as 20:80. As wealth grows, these ratios are reversed, with prepaid sources dominating at 80:20. Countries on an optimal development path progress from the 20:80 to 80:20 ratio (figure 1.5). Unfortunately, many of the fragile low-income countries are on a slower, suboptimal development path toward a 40:60 rather than an 80:20 balance. Without a significant shift in policy directions and implementation, out-of-pocket spending will thus continue to pay for a large share of total health care expenditure (figure 1.6), leaving many households exposed to impoverishment and financial hardship despite significant spending by their governments on health care.

In many countries on a suboptimal development path, a large share of government funding comes from donors rather than from domestic sources of financing, leaving them vulnerable to donor dependence and volatility in financial flows and fungibility with no net additionality in financial resources. Furthermore, in many of these poorly performing countries, a large share of out-of-pocket expenditure is on informal payments in the public sector and private sector spending, exposing households to whatever cost the local market can bear.

For several reasons, policy makers all over the world, trying to improve health financing through the introduction of voluntary or government-run mandatory

FIGURE 1.5   Rule of 80 Optimal Development Path

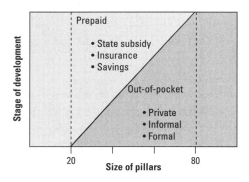

Source: Preker, Zweifel, and Schellekens 2010.

FIGURE 1.6   Fragile States' Suboptimal Development Path

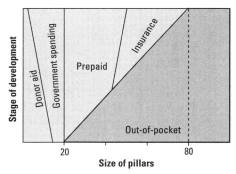

Source: Preker, Zweifel, and Schellekens 2010.

health insurance, are struggling to make progress on the optimal development path from 20:80 to 80:20 ratios.

First Set of Issues: Behavior of Core Financing Functions

A first set of issues relates to the behavior at low-income levels of the three core health care financing functions: revenue collection, financial risk management, and purchasing services from providers. For effective revenue collection, countries trying to introduce health insurance arrangements face the following challenges in mobilizing adequate financial resources through household contributions:

- *Enrolment.* Incomplete population registry (limiting the ability to identify potential members)

- *Choice.* Large informal sector (limiting the pool of employees that can be forced to join a mandatory scheme; other population segments have to be induced to join)

- *Prepayment.* Low formal sector labor participation rates (limiting the employee contributions that can be collected at source under a mandatory scheme); lack of familiarity with insurance and risk-averse behavior (limiting willingness to pay); large share of population with low-income jobs or below-poverty-level earnings with competing demands for scarce household income (limiting ability to pay)

- *Progressivity in contributions.* Lack of accurate income data (limiting information that can be used to construct progressive payment schedules).

In the case of effective financial risk management, countries trying to introduce health insurance arrangements face the following challenges in redistributing resources efficiently and equitably:

- *Size and number of risk pools.* Spontaneous growth of many small funds (limiting size and increasing the number of voluntary pools); social diversity in terms of employment, domicile, and other local social factors (limiting size and increasing the number of voluntary pools); lack of trust in government or national programs (limiting size and number of mandatory pools); weak management and institutional capacity (limiting the size and number of mandatory pools)

- *Risk equalization.* Small share of available fiscal space allocated to health sector (limiting public resources available for subsidizing inactive population groups); lack of national social solidarity (limiting willingness to cross-subsidize from rich to poor, from healthy to sick, and from gainfully employed to inactive)

- *Coverage.* Presence of national health scheme for general public (limiting the need for universal population coverage or comprehensive benefit coverage through insurance).

In the case of effective resource allocation and service purchasing, countries trying to introduce health insurance arrangements face the following challenges in spending scarce resources wisely:

- *For whom to buy.* Lack of good membership data (limiting ability to identify vulnerable groups)

- *What to buy.* Lack of good data on cost-effectiveness (limiting ability to get value for money spent)

- *From whom to buy.* Ambulatory sector dominated by private providers, and inpatient sector dominated by public hospitals (limiting provider choice)

- *How to pay.* Weak management and institutional capacity (limiting sophistication of performance-based payment systems that can be used)

- *At what price.* Lack of good cost data (limiting transparency of prices charged by both public and private providers).

Second Set of Issues: Institutional Environment

The second set of issues relates to the institutional environment of health insurance funds at low-income levels. Often institutional capacity is weak, the underlying legal framework is incomplete, regulatory instruments are ineffective or not enforced, administrative procedures are rigid, and informal customs and practices are difficult to change.

Third Set of Issues: Organizational Structure

A third set of issues relates to the organizational structure of health insurance funds at low-income levels. In countries with many small, community-based funds, both the scale and the scope of insurance coverage and benefits that can be provided are problematic.

Although in theory many government-run health insurance programs have the status of semi-autonomous agencies, they often suffer from the same rigid hierarchical incentive structures as state-owned and -run national health services. This is especially true in countries where the insurance schemes have over time acquired extensive networks of their own providers, thereby undermining the benefits of a purchaser-provider split. In other countries, multiple employment-based funds often do not benefit from competitive pressures but suffer from all the shortcomings of fragmented risk pools and purchasing arrangements (insurance market failure, high administration costs, information asymmetry, and so on).

Fourth Set of Issues: Management Style

A fourth set of issues relates to the management characteristics of health insurance funds at low-income levels. Management capacity is often weak in terms of stewardship, governance, line management, and client services. Management skills are sparse in mandatory insurance. Health insurers as multiplicitous agents for the government, health services, and providers have to serve many masters at the same time. This leads to conflicting incentives and reward structures. Finally, the management tools needed to deliver a health insurance program are often lacking in terms of effective information technology (IT), communications, and other systems needed for effective financial management, human resources management, health information tracking, and utilization reviews.

Box 1.1 summarizes some of the underlying issues and motives for health finance reform at low-income levels.

As highlighted in "New Development Paradigm," the last chapter in this book, reforming and scaling up health insurance in low-income settings has had a checkered history. The authors emphasize three "laws" of economics that hinder this achievement. Underfunding plays an important role: health systems are severely

---

BOX 1.1   UNDERLYING ISSUES AND MOTIVES FOR REFORM

Through the introduction of mandatory government-run health insurance, countries hope to address the following financial mechanism problems (Dror and Preker 2002; Preker, Scheffler, and Bassett 2007; Preker, Zweifel, and Schellekens 2010):

- *Inadequacy of current revenue generation to mobilize sufficient resources to finance the health sector through a combination of government subsidies, user charges, and donor aid.* First, governments' ability to mobilize tax dollars is severely constrained at low-income levels for a variety of reasons that will be reviewed in later chapters. In some countries, as little as 5 percent of GDP passes through the treasury. Second, the fiscal space allocated to the health sector is often small—typically less than 5 percent of total government revenues in many of the poorest countries. Finally, Ministries of Health often receive only a small part of the government's targeted budget appropriation for the health sector—in some cases less than 50 percent. Most out-of-pocket expenditures are collected directly by private providers or as under-the-table informal payments to staff working in public hospitals and clinics. Ability and willingness to pay does not translate into additional resources that can be used to finance public services. When patients run out of money during an episode of illness, the public hospital and clinic have to absorb the cost.

  Despite efforts to secure more medium-term commitment from donors, aid flows remain extremely volatile and unpredictable. Since money is fungible, aid flows often substitute for, rather than supplement, domestic sources of funding. Net additionality is therefore often small. Even when

(continued)

BOX 1.1   UNDERLYING ISSUES AND MOTIVES FOR REFORM (*continued*)

donor money leads to marginal additional financial resources, the shifting priorities of the international donor community have largely prevented most programs from receiving medium-term sustainable financing from external sources. Finally, funding from external donors is often associated with complicated procurement procedures and stringent conditions that have to be met before disbursements are authorized. This leads to volatile revenue flows even after the financing has been fully secured.

- *Inadequacy of current financing arrangements in providing financial protection against the cost of illness.* In principle, universal and free access to general revenue–funded public services should be able to protect individuals against the cost of illness. Since the 1978 Alma-Ata Declaration of "Free for All Health Services by the Year 2000," many countries have tried to secure access to basic health care and financial protection against the impoverishing effects of illness by encouraging countries to build publicly financed health services, run by their Ministries of Health or, in decentralized delivery systems, by local authorities. Under this policy, resource constraints soon forced most countries to restrict the basic package to so few services that most of the population, including the poor, had to seek care out of pocket even for basic conditions for which they were supposedly entitled to free care. Furthermore, even if services are available, resource constraints often lead to such severe deterioration in the quality of public care that patients choose to go to private providers and pay.

  Expansion of coverage through voluntary financing mechanisms (both community- and enterprise-based) has so far been disappointing although populations joining such schemes seem to benefit. In most cases, user fees do not protect individuals against the impoverishing effects of catastrophic or chronic ongoing care. And often the resulting health insurance programs do not have a strong policy framework to take advantage of the financial incentives they could provide through strategic purchasing or performance-based contracting with providers (Preker and Langenbrunner 2005; Preker, Liu, Velenyi, and Baris 2007; Langenbrunner, Cashin, and O'Dougherty 2009).

- *Inadequacy of resource allocation methods within core Ministries of Health service delivery systems.* Despite recent attempts to introduce performance-based payment mechanisms, strategic purchasing of priority services, and other forms of new public sector management techniques under integrated finance and public service delivery systems, the outcomes of these reforms have been disappointing. Ultimately, bureaucratic capture leads to backslipping.

- *Institutional, organizational, and management rigidity.* Under integrated financing and service delivery health care systems, policy makers hope the institutional, organizational, and management rigidities described above will be addressed.

underfunded in countries in which GDP per capita is low. GDP per capita is tightly related to health care expenditures (the first law of health economics), which means that an influx of donor money into the public health sector in a low-income country does not raise the total amount of money in the sector. Instead, it crowds out private funds or substitutes for existing local public expenditures (the third law of health economics). In such countries, out-of-pocket payments are high (the second law of health economics), easily pushing people into poverty.

Scaling up health insurance through the public sector often fails in many developing countries due to weak public sector capabilities and ends up benefiting mainly the interests of groups that have access to state power, which they use for their own benefits. As a result, the public sector often fails to deliver public goods and redistribute income and risk. The institutional framework (legal, financial) is weak or absent, which leads to high levels of uncertainty and risk. This profoundly influences the behavior of patients, providers, and communities. Health care gets stuck in a vicious circle of inadequate funding arrangements, weak governance, and dysfunctional health systems.

A different approach is needed to lower the overall level of risk—by working through local communities and nongovernmental organizations to provide affordable loans and affordable insurance while at the same time raising the quality of services. By reducing market risk, the willingness to invest and to prepay will grow, generating a virtuous effect and turning the vicious circle into a virtuous one. This is the "fourth law" of health economics.

REFERENCES

Carrin, G., and C. James. 2004. "Reaching Universal Coverage via Social Health Insurance: Key Design Features in the Transition Period." Geneva: World Health Organization.

Chernichovsky, D. 2002. "Pluralism, Public Choice, and the State in the Emerging Paradigm in Health Systems." *Milbank Quarterly* 80 (1): 5–39.

Dror, D.M., and A.S. Preker, eds. 2002. *Social Reinsurance: A New Approach to Sustainable Community Health Financing.* Washington, DC: World Bank.

Hsiao, W. 1995. "A Framework for Assessing Health Financing Strategies and the Role of Health Insurance." In *An International Assessment of Health Care Financing: Lessons for Developing Countries,* ed. D.W. Dunlop and J.M. Martins. EDI Seminar Series. Washington, DC: World Bank.

Langenbrunner, J.C., C. Cashin, and S. O'Dougherty, eds. 2009. *Designing and Implementing Health Care Provider Payment Systems: How-To Manuals.* Washington, DC: World Bank.

Londono, J.L., and J. Frenk. 1997. "Structured Pluralism: Towards an Innovative Model for Health System Reform in Latin America." *Health Policy and Planning* 47: 1–36.

Preker, A.S. 1998. "The Introduction of Universal Access to Health Care in the OECD: Lessons for Developing Countries." In *Achieving Universal Coverage of Health Care,* ed. S. Nitayarumphong and A. Mills, 103–24. Bangkok: Ministry of Public Health.

Preker, A.S., and G. Carrin, eds. 2004. *Health Financing for Poor People: Resource Mobilization and Risk Sharing*. Washington, DC: World Bank.

Preker, A.S., and J.C. Langenbrunner, eds. 2005. *Spending Wisely: Buying Health Services for the Poor*. Washington, DC: World Bank.

Preker, A.S., X. Liu, E.V. Velenyi, and E. Baris, eds. 2007. *Public Ends, Private Means*. Washington, DC: World Bank.

Preker, A.S., R.M. Scheffler, and M.C. Bassett, eds. 2007. *Private Voluntary Health Insurance in Development: Friend or Foe?* Washington, DC: World Bank.

Preker, A.S., P. Zweifel, and O.P. Schellekens, eds. 2010. *Global Marketplace for Private Voluntary Health Insurance: Strength in Numbers*. Washington, DC: World Bank.

Savedoff, W. 2005. "Mandatory Health Insurance in Developing Countries: Overview, Framework, and Research Program." Discussion Paper, World Bank, Washington, DC.

World Bank. 2004. *World Development Report 2004: Making Services Work for the Poor*. Washington, DC: World Bank; New York: Oxford University Press.

PART 1

Major Policy Challenges:
Preconditions for Scaling Up

CHAPTER 2

Health Protection: More Than Financial Protection

Xenia Scheil-Adlung

Many developing countries are confronted with low-performing health finance systems, poor health status, and health-related impoverishment of the population. Frequently, the situation is aggravated by limited public funds, inefficient use of available resources, and gaps in mobilizing domestic funds.

For people in the grip of extreme poverty, health is a crucially important economic asset. Loss of health and productivity pose major problems for socially vulnerable persons and their families. When a poor individual or any member of the family falls ill, the entire household may be forced to address the health needs of the sick by skipping school, missing opportunities to gain income, and selling prized livelihood assets. These health and health-related events can be catastrophic, further plunging people into poverty due to income loss and high health care costs. If left unattended, this situation can unleash vicious cycles of poverty and ill health, continuing from generation to generation.

INTRODUCTION

Scaling up social health insurance is one of the mechanisms that address these issues and is integral to achieving universal access to health services. When implementing insurance schemes, their pros and cons must be balanced and specific features adjusted to each country's socioeconomic, political, cultural, and historical context. Schemes are thus often a mix of various forms of health-financing mechanisms and combine both contribution/premium-based financing and use of taxes.

Against this background, and based on long-lasting experience in the field of social health protection, the International Labour Organization (ILO) has developed a pragmatic strategy toward universal access to health care. It is part of the overall Decent Work Strategy and based on ILO Convention 102 on Social Security where health ranks first among the contingencies covered. The strategy responds to the needs of the uncovered population in many developing countries, particularly the informal economy workers and their families, the poor, and the unemployed. The pragmatic approach explicitly recognizes the contribution of all existing forms of social health protection, from tax-funded schemes to various forms of health insurance, and optimizes their outcomes.

This chapter sets forth some basic notions about the strategy with a view to scaling up social health insurance. The first part outlines concepts and definitions of social health insurance. An analysis of trends and developments in the global health-financing situation follows. The chapter concludes with a discussion of the best ways of addressing access deficits.

SOCIAL HEALTH INSURANCE: CONCEPTS, DEFINITIONS, AND OBSERVATIONS

The concept of social health protection and social health insurance is anchored in the human rights to health and social security, equity in access, solidarity in financing based on the capacity to pay, and efficiency and effectiveness in the use of funds. *Social health protection*, an overarching goal, is understood as "a series of public or publicly organized and mandated private measures against social distress and economic loss caused by the reduction of productivity, stoppage or reduction of earnings, or the cost of necessary treatment that can result from ill health" (ILO 2008: 3). *Social health insurance* is a key element of social health protection and an integral means of achieving universal and affordable coverage by coordinating pluralistic health-financing mechanisms. Social health insurance is thus seen as a necessary element in achieving both social health protection and social security. The ultimate objective in the field of social health protection and social health insurance is to achieve *universal social health protection coverage,* defined as effective access to affordable health care of adequate quality and financial protection in case of sickness.[1] In this context, the definition of *coverage* refers to the health protection extended to individuals so that they can obtain health services that are financed through a social risk-pooling mechanism in a way that prevents extremely high out-of-pocket (OOP) costs from posing a barrier to access or restrict poor patients to services of limited quality.

To be effective, *universal coverage* needs to ensure access to care for every resident in a country. This does not preclude national health policies from focusing, at least temporarily, on priority groups such as women or the poor when setting up or extending social health protection. Coverage should relate to effective access to health services that medically match the morbidity structure and needs of the covered population. Compared with *legal coverage,* which describes rights and formal entitlements, *effective access* refers to the physical, financial, and geographical availability of services.

Benefits packages (bundles of health services that are made available to the covered population) should be defined with a view to maintaining, restoring, or improving health; guaranteeing the ability to work; and meeting personal health care needs. Key criteria for establishing benefits packages include the structure and volume of the burden of disease, the effectiveness of interventions, the demand, and the capacity to pay.

Effective access includes both access to health services and financial protection. Financial protection is crucial to avoid health-related impoverishment. Financial protection includes the avoidance of out-of-pocket payments that reduce the affordability of services and—ideally—some compensation for productivity loss due to illness.

Affordability of services is defined as the absence of financial barriers to health service access for individuals, groups of individuals, and societies as a whole. Affordability aims first of all at avoiding health-related poverty. It refers to the maximum share of cost for necessary health care at total household income net of the cost of subsistence. For example, health care costs could be considered affordable if they amount to less than 40 percent of the household income remaining after subsistence needs have been met. Household health care costs below that share are considered noncatastrophic. Universal coverage is thus associated with equity in financing, implying that households should be asked to contribute only in relation to their ability to pay. Out-of-pocket payments in particular have been marked out as especially inequitable and inefficient in that the poor may be unable to pay them at the time and point of delivery, and thus may be excluded from treatment. Premiums or other types of prepayment are recommended by the ILO because they are based on risk pooling between population groups and are thus more equitable.

Fiscal affordability relates to the fiscal space that can be made available to finance a level of expenditure that ensures universal access to services of adequate quality without jeopardizing economic performance or crowding out other essential national services (such as social cash transfers or education, internal security, and so forth). Necessary expenditure levels depend on a population's health status, the availability of infrastructure, the price of services, the efficiency of service delivery, and the ability of a country to mobilize resources. The ILO therefore does not advocate global benchmarks on public spending on health. Quality of care has various dimensions. These include quality of medical interventions, such as compliance with medical guidelines or protocols as developed by the World Health Organization (WHO) or other institutions. The quality of services also includes ethical dimensions such as dignity, confidentiality, respect of gender and culture, and issues such as choice of provider and waiting times.

There are various mechanisms to finance health services with a view to achieving universal coverage. They include different types of tax and contribution/premium-based financing. These mechanisms normally involve the pooling of risks between covered persons—and many of them explicitly include cross-subsidizations between the rich and the poor. Some form of cross-subsidization between the rich and the poor exists in all social health protection systems, otherwise the goal of universal access could not be pursued or attained. The key features are briefly reviewed in figure 2.1.

Funding social health protection from general government revenue might include direct or indirect taxes from various levels, such as national and local

FIGURE 2.1   Overview of Key Forms of Health Financing

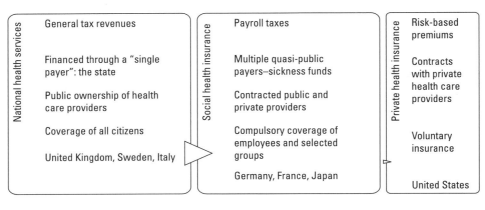

Source: Author.

tax in addition to general or earmarked tax. *Direct taxes,* levied on individuals, households, and enterprises, comprise property taxes, personal income tax, and corporate profit taxes. *Indirect taxes,* conversely, are obtained from goods and services (for instance, excise and/or "sin tax" on consumption of tobacco products). Payments related to indirect tax are based on consumption, not on overall income. *General taxes* can be drawn from different sources and therefore have a broad revenue base; nonetheless, allocation for health care is subject to annual public spending negotiations. *Hypothecated taxes* are earmarked for health and may be less susceptible to political influence. Taxes are often used for various forms of social health protection funding. Besides financing national health services, vouchers, or conditional cash benefits, taxes are used as subsidies for mixed health protection schemes such as national health insurances, whereby government revenues are used to subsidize the poor.

Payroll taxes or contributions are collected to fund social health insurance schemes. Employers and employees share contributions. This usually involves formal labor markets, which translates to coverage extended to formal economy workers and their families. International experience shows (ILO 2008) employee contributions might be as low as 1 percent of covered monthly earnings, as in the Arab Republic of Egypt, and 2.5 percent in Jamaica. In the case of employers' contributions, Egypt provides for 4 percent of covered monthly payroll and Jamaica for 8.5 percent of their employees' gross income. In many countries, contributions are based on the ability to pay, and access to health services depends on needs. Contributions may be collected by a single national health insurance fund—or by one or more social health insurance funds which are often independent from the government but subject to regulations.

Premiums are collected by private insurance schemes, including community-based health insurance schemes and private commercial funds. Community-based schemes are usually voluntary and managed by organizations of informal economy workers, community-based and nongovernment entities, cooperatives, trade unions, and faith-based groups. Premiums are often flat rate and services frequently limited. Premiums for private commercial health insurance funds are usually voluntary and risk based. People in high-risk groups pay more, and those with lower risks pay less. Benefits and services vary depending on the insurance company and insured persons. Very few countries use private health insurance as a main form for organizing and financing health services for the whole population. Rather than using payroll contributions they usually apply risk-related premiums and provide for voluntary coverage.

Unfortunately, *out-of-pocket payments* are also used in many countries as a source of funding health services. They are not considered a means of financing social health protection. They involve payments directly to the health care providers at the point of delivery, based on the services utilized, and may be paid partially or in full. They may take the form of direct payments, formal cost sharing, or informal payments. Reference is made to *direct payments* when the consumer pays the full amount of health services not covered by any form of protection. *Formal cost sharing* (user fees) involves expenditures on health services that are included, but not fully covered, in the benefits package, for example in order to set incentives. An overview of the flow of funds is provided in figure 2.2.

Social health insurance refers to various forms of insurance approaches, ranging from *classical social health insurance,* defined by mandatory coverage and income-related contributions of both employers and employees, and *national social*

Figure 2.2   Flow of Funds

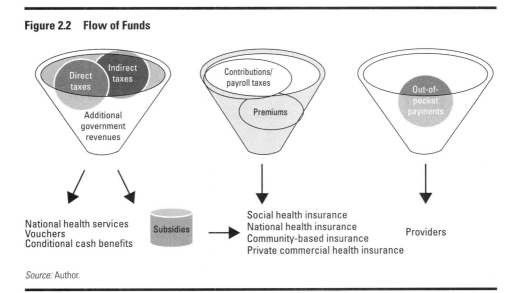

Source: Author.

health insurance, where the poor are fully subsidized. There are manifold forms of *community-based health insurance,* which often complement other schemes and are usually voluntary and financed through flat-rate premiums.

All forms of insurance usually receive some degree of tax subsidy if they are part of the overall health protection system. Also mandated or regulated private nonprofit health insurance schemes and private for-profit health insurance range among these approaches. An overview of the various health insurance approaches is provided in table 2.1.

While private health insurance emphasizes choice, personal responsibility, and market reliance, both social health insurance and national health services are based on solidarity involving high degrees of redistribution. Redistribution is used to support the poorer parts of the population. Besides different sources of funding, health-financing schemes vary with regard to administration. Whereas in national health services (NHS) the state often is a single payer usually providing services through public providers to the whole population, in health insurance schemes multiple quasi-public funds often insure the population and provide services through contracting public or private providers. The social insurance approach is usually based on regulations for sickness funds. These regulations define clearly the scope of the benefits, the compulsory nature of membership, and contracting arrangements with both public and private providers.

All health-financing systems have significant scope to provide for health financing. Figure 2.3 highlights the scope of each health-financing mechanism. It is vital for countries to take account of this aspect when developing policies to improve health-financing mechanisms, design adequate benefits packages, include financial protection, and create institutional and administrative efficiency.

Government revenues usually obtain sizable coverage and outreach, which might imply good performance regarding equity. They also have the potential

TABLE 2.1   Overview of Health Insurance Approaches

	Classical social health insurance	National health insurance	Community-based health insurance	Private for-profit health insurance
Financing: subsidies and contributions	Employers' and employees' contributions (income-related)	Government revenues and contributions of those who can afford it	Flat-rate premiums	Risk-related premiums
Funds collected by	Employers, employees, social security institutions	Government, employers, employees, social security institutions	Insurance fund	Insurance fund
Legal form	Mandatory	Mandatory	Voluntary	Voluntary
Coverage	Formal economy workers and their families	All citizens	Members and their families	Insured persons

Source: Author.

FIGURE 2.3   Scope of Health Care Financing Mechanisms

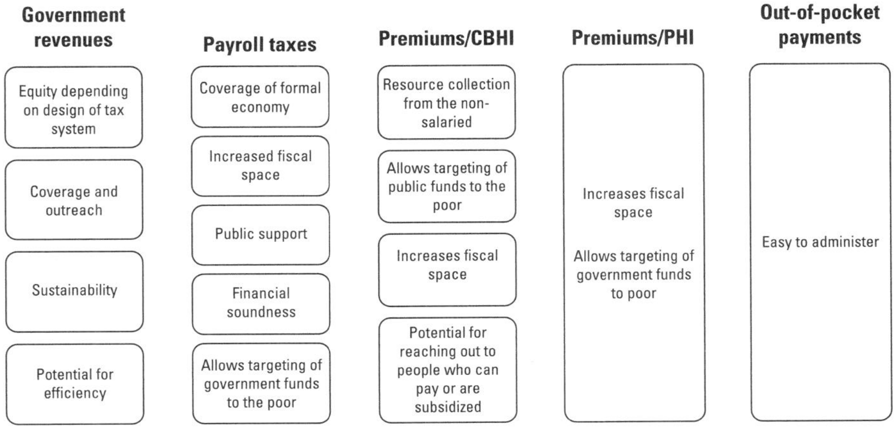

Source: Author.
Note: CBHI = community-based health insurance; PHI = private health insurance.

to achieve efficiency and sustainability. The scope of payroll taxes can bring about increased fiscal space, financial soundness compared with tax funding, and public support—as well as create the possibility of having public funds to target the poor. Regarding the premiums for community-based schemes, the scope may increase fiscal space and reach the poor, those who are unable to contribute—for example, the nonsalaried—and those who are subsidized. Premiums for commercial health insurance demonstrate the capacity for financial soundness.

Criteria for choosing the different mechanisms for particular subgroups of the population usually include the number, structure, and performance of existing schemes; political and cultural context; size of the tax base; size of the informal economy; disease burden; availability of infrastructure; capacity to collect taxes/contributions/premiums; managerial capacity; possibilities for enforcing legislation; and regulation and related impacts on equity.

When deciding on health-financing mechanisms at the country level, both pros *and* cons of each option need to be carefully discussed. The applicability and performance of the different mechanisms need to be judged on the basis of the country's capacity to mobilize funds, efficiency in targeting public funds to the poor, ability to shift funds and power from supply- to demand-side to improve efficiency and quality, accountability stringency and budgeting quality, and capacity to effectively purchase and monitor the delivery of quality health services. A summary of the pros and cons of various financing mechanisms is presented in table 2.2.

TABLE 2.2   Pros and Cons of Key Financing Mechanisms for Social Health Protection

Mechanisms	Pros	Cons
Tax-based health protection	Pools risks for whole population; offers potential for administrative efficiency and cost control; redistributes between high- and low-risk and high- and low-income groups in covered population	Risk of unstable and often inadequate funding due to competing public expenditures; inefficient due to lack of incentives and effective public supervision
Social health insurance	Generates stable revenues; often enjoys strong popular support; provides access to a broad package of services; involves social partners; redistributes between high and low risk and high- and low-income groups in the covered population	Poor are excluded unless subsidized; payroll contributions can reduce competitiveness and lead to higher unemployment; managing governance is complex, and accountability can be problematic; can lead to cost escalation unless effective contracting mechanisms are in place
Microinsurance and community-based schemes	Can reach out to workers in informal economy; can reach the close-to-poor population segments; strong social control limits abuse and fraud and contributes to confidence in the scheme	Poor may be excluded unless subsidized; may be financially vulnerable if not supported by national subsidies; coverage usually extended to only small percentage of population; gives strong incentive to adverse selection; may be associated with lack of professionalism in governance and administration
Private for-profit health insurance	Is preferable to out-of-pocket expenditure; increases financial protection and access to health services for those able to pay; encourages better health care quality and cost-efficiency	Can result in high administrative costs; does not reduce cost pressures on public health-financing systems; is inequitable without subsidized premiums or regulated insurance content and price; requires administrative and financial infrastructure and capacity

Source: Author.

Generally, *taxes* are considered an efficient and equitable source of revenue for the health sector. They may lead to national risk pooling for the whole population and redistribute between high and low risks, and high- and low-income groups. However, the contribution that taxes make to health care financing is largely contingent upon national macroeconomic performance and competing demands from other sectors; the quality of governance; the size of the tax base; and the government's human and institutional capacity to collect taxes and supervise the system. In practice, government schemes are often underfunded due to competing public expenditures, which might lead to a shortage of goods and services, under-the-table payments, and inefficient governance.

The success of *social health insurance schemes* depends on the generation of stable resources as revenues, strong support of the population, provision of a broad package of services, involvement of social partners, and redistribution between risk and income groups. However, schemes are administratively complex, and governance and accountability can be problematic. Also, from a macroeconomic point of view, payroll contributions can reduce competitiveness and lead to higher unemployment.

Furthermore, in countries with sizable informal economies, social health insurance might have an impact on equity if coverage is not universal. Health care for the workforce is not free, and enterprises and the economy have to bear a respective share of the financial burden. In the case of social health insurance schemes, funding should consist of shared financial resources from both employers and employees. For specific benefits such as maternity benefits, particular rules might apply; for instance, full coverage might be provided through public funds to avoid disadvantages for particular groups.

Schemes such as *private or community health insurance schemes* can be an efficient mechanism to cover nonsalaried workers and reduce costs for the poorest at the point of delivery. But they often experience problems of coverage and therefore fail to achieve sufficient pooling; they also frequently find it difficult to organize membership across different ethnic groups and struggle with inadequate management capacity and resources. If these schemes are embedded in a broader framework of social health protection, they often have the potential to include the poor.

Private for-profit health insurance schemes are also found in many countries, ranging from OECD countries to developing countries such as Peru and the Philippines. If the poor are not subsidized, these schemes cover the wealthier part of the population and are based on risk-related premiums. Their exclusive character and high administrative costs are often criticized. Challenges with private health insurance relate particularly to equity and efficiency concerns as outlined in figure 2.4.

FIGURE 2.4   Challenges with Private Health Insurance

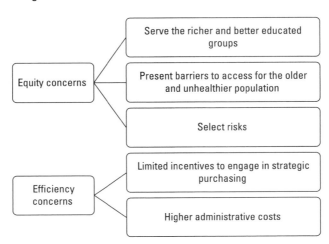

Source: Author.

CURRENT TRENDS AND DEVELOPMENTS IN SOCIAL HEALTH INSURANCE

Social, national, and community-based health insurance and tax-funded schemes coexist in countries and throughout the world. At the global level, the financing of health care costs is shared between government revenues, which contribute 35 percent to global health expenditure; social insurance (26 percent); private insurance (20 percent); and out-of-pocket expenditure and other private spending, which account for 19 percent of worldwide expenditure on health (ILO 2008).

Figure 2.5 shows the range of OOP spending within and among low-, upper-middle-, and high-income countries. The figure reveals a large amount of OOP expenditure paid at the point of service delivery. A high OOP share indicates inequities and lack of coverage of social health protection. OOP spending is the most inefficient way of financing health care spending. It weighs most heavily on the poor and is associated with a high risk of household impoverishment through catastrophic costs.

People in low-income countries such as Cambodia, India, and Pakistan shoulder more than 50 percent of their health expenditures compared with upper-middle- and high-income countries. Such a situation can lead to further inequities, increased poverty, catastrophic health expenditures, and impaired income generation due to sale of assets and borrowing. It also reflects that public expenditure seems to increase in tandem with an increase in country income

FIGURE 2.5   Out-of-Pocket Expenditure, Selected Countries, 2006

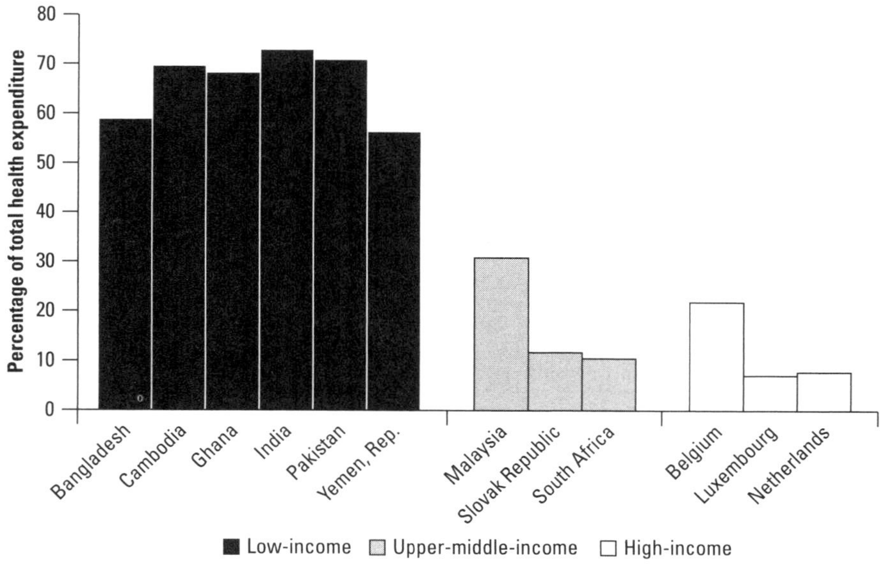

Source: ILO 2008: 9.

levels. Notably, the structure of services purchased in high- and low-income countries varies substantially.

The level of per capita health expenditure also varies significantly among low-, middle-, and high-income countries, ranging between US$1,527, US$176, and US$25 in high-, middle-, and low-income countries, respectively (World Bank 2006). This includes funds from various public, private, and other sources. The share of total health expenditure as a percentage of GDP amounts to 7.7 percent in high-income countries, 5.8 percent in middle-income countries, and 4.7 percent in low-income countries. Public expenditure on health as a percentage of total health expenditure amounts to 70.1 percent in high-income countries, 61.7 percent in middle-income countries, and 51.7 percent in low-income countries (figure 2.6).

As shown in table 2.3, trends in the use of tax revenues for social health protection range from 14.5 percent of GDP in low-income countries to 26.5 percent in high-income countries. Contributions to mandatory social

FIGURE 2.6   Health Expenditure, National Wealth, and Government's Share of Health Spending, 2004

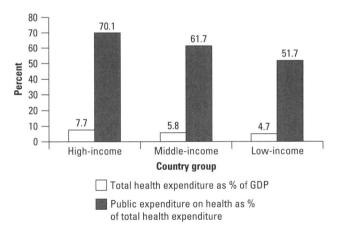

Source: World Bank 2006.

TABLE 2.3   Sources of Social Health Protection Financing, by Country Income, 2002

Country group	Tax revenues for social health protection (% of GDP)	Social security contributions in health (% of GDP)
Low-income	14.5	0.7
Low-/middle-income	16.3	1.4
Upper-middle-income	21.9	4.3
High-income	26.5	7.2

Source: World Bank 2004.

health insurance are significantly lower and range from 0.7 percent in low-income countries to 7.2 percent in high-income countries. Globally, the share of tax revenues is higher than the share of contributions—and both are positively correlated to income.

At the regional level, the share of different forms of social health protection in overall health spending varies significantly (figure 2.7). In 2001, tax spending—at 40 percent—was relatively high in countries of Africa and Europe. Social health insurance ranked particularly high in OECD and transition countries in the European region, in Western Pacific and in Eastern Mediterranean countries. In the Americas, private health insurance played a key role.

Current concerns in low-income countries often relate to the fact that key health policy targets, such as those formulated in the Millennium Development Goals (MDGs), cannot be achieved with the limited funds available. Against this background, mobilizing additional domestic resources through various insurance approaches is an important strategy. Some low-income countries spend as little as 2 percent of GDP on health (figure 2.8).

The impact of this inadequate or low funding in poor countries is enormous. These people lack access to health services and are more likely to die from diseases that are curable in richer countries. For instance, respiratory infections account for 2.9 percent of all deaths in low-income countries but relatively few in high-income countries (Deaton 2006).

FIGURE 2.7   Sources of Health Protection, by Region, 2001

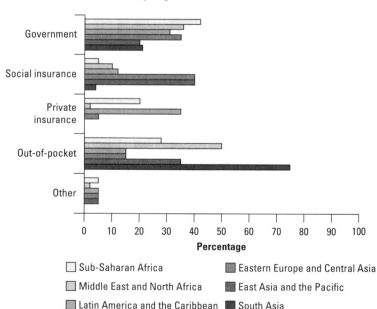

Source: WHO, National Health Accounts Data 2003.

FIGURE 2.8   Total Health Expenditure, Selected Low-Income Countries, 2006

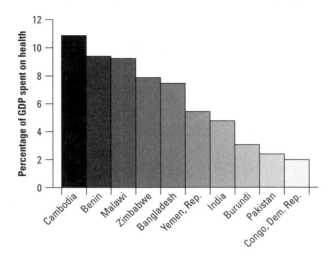

Source: ILO 2008: 11.

The relation between ill health, health insurance, and poverty has been clearly shown in quantitative studies (Scheil-Adlung et al. 2006). In countries such as Kenya, Senegal, and South Africa, the impoverishment level due to health payments amounts to between 1.5 and 5.4 percent of households. This implies that in 2005 alone more than 100,000 households in Kenya and Senegal and about 290,000 households in South Africa fell below the poverty line as a direct result of paying for health services. Table 2.4 shows how catastrophic expenses burden the uninsured and relieve members of health insurance schemes. In addition, out-of-pocket health payments deepen the poverty of already poor people (up to 10 percent of households in Senegal, for example) in all three countries (Scheil-Adlung et al. 2006).

In summary, the global profile of financing social health protection for many low- and middle-income countries is as follows:

- The share of public financing of total health expenditure is low.

- Tax funding is significantly higher than contribution funding, and both are positively correlated to income.

- Solidarity in financing, expressed by risk pooling, is limited.

- A large private share of health financing shifts the burden of health expenditure to households.

- There is a close relation between countries' income levels, access to health services, and mortality.

TABLE 2.4   HOUSEHOLD USE OF FINANCIAL MECHANISMS FOR COPING WITH HEALTH CARE EXPENSES, SELECTED COUNTRIES, 2005

Financial	South Africa		Kenya		Senegal	
mechanism	Uninsured (%)	Insured (%)	Uninsured (%)	Insured (%)	Uninsured (%)	Insured (%)
Sales of assets	5.9	10.6	1.0	0.2	15.4	4.4
Borrowing from family or friends	10.5	7.0	4.1	4.3	27.9	12.3
Borrowing from outside	11.5	3.0	—	—	3.2	6.1

Source: Scheil-Adlung et al. 2006.
Note: — = not available.

- Limited financial protection leads to high levels of OOP spending and ensuing health-related poverty.

- The GDP shares of both social health protection expenditure and total health expenditure are low.

EXPERIENCES IN SCALING UP SOCIAL HEALTH INSURANCE

What experiences have countries had scaling up social health insurance? Most countries simultaneously apply every type of health financing, including tax-based systems, national, social health insurance, community-based insurance, and private health insurance. However, the financing mechanisms are often uncoordinated, resulting in equity and quality issues.

Countries successful in achieving universal coverage, for example, in Asia, mostly applied two approaches:

- Tax-funded schemes with integrated private services and voluntary private provision (Sri Lanka; Hong Kong SAR, China)

- Social insurance with tax subsidies usually requiring sustained government commitment and administrative capacity (Japan; the Republic of Korea; Taiwan, China; Mongolia).

Although increasing national income and the use of risk-pooling mechanisms may be connected, in a number of countries this correlation is not apparent. ILO (2008) data suggest that the extension of social health protection is not necessarily directly linked to a country's income level. For example, Burundi and Tanzania, countries with GDP per capita of US$100 and US$290, respectively, formally cover about 13 percent and 14.5 percent of their population. Conversely, the Democratic Republic of Congo, with a similar GDP per capita, provides coverage at a rate of only 0.2 percent. In Ghana, with a per capita GDP of US$320, 18.7 percent of the population is formally covered by a health protection scheme, while corresponding rates are significantly lower in Togo with 0.4 percent coverage (GDP per capita US$310) and Burkina Faso with 0.2 percent coverage (GDP per capita US$300). A country with a slightly higher GDP per capita like Kenya (US$390) offers formal social health protection to a quarter of its population, and Haiti with no more than US$380 per capita to as much as 60 percent. Countries with a higher level of GDP like Bolivia (US$890, coverage rate 66 percent) and Guinea-Bissau (US$920, coverage rate 1.6 percent) also show very different rates of formal coverage.

A country's specific situation, including a strong political will to set priorities, can therefore have an impact on the extent of social health protection it provides to its constituents. Social health protection is an option for low-income countries, and the extent of population coverage is, to some degree, independent of income levels. The composition and design of the benefits packages are different, however, when comparing countries based on their income level, for instance in the case of Germany and the Republic of Korea.

Experiences with Legal Coverage in the Formal and Informal Economy

The historical developments of national coverage rates also corroborate this trend. Some countries have taken many decades to achieve high levels of coverage; whereas others, starting from similarly low levels of GDP per capita, achieved full coverage in only a few decades or years (figure 2.9).

FIGURE 2.9   Achieving Universal Coverage in Social Health Insurance

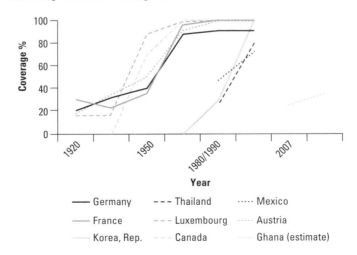

Sources: ILO 2008:19. Compulsory sickness insurance, Geneva, 1927 (for years 1920 to 1925); OECD Health Data 2005 (for years 1970 to 2000).

Coverage, in table 2.5, is measured in terms of the population formally covered by social health protection, for example, under legislation, without reference to effective access to health services, service quality, or other dimensions of coverage discussed later in the section. Formal social health insurance coverage, including community-based schemes in low-income African and Asian countries, ranges from the exceptional rate of 78 percent of the total population in Mongolia to 5 percent in the Lao People's Democratic Republic, and 7 percent in Kenya (WHO 2005; Scheil-Adlung et al. 2006).

In low- and middle-income countries, formal social health protection coverage often remains a challenge. In Latin America, for example, many countries are far from attaining universal coverage, even decades after they introduced their first public insurance scheme. Formal coverage of public and private schemes together is afforded to an average of only 60 percent of the population in Bolivia, El Salvador, and Honduras.

Out-of-pocket payment serves as the key financing mechanism for health care in many low-income countries—up to 80 percent of total health expenditure in countries such as the Republic of the Union of Myanmar, the Democratic Republic of Congo, Guinea, and Tajikistan. These values are above the average OOP expenditure (49.2 percent) of 45 low-income countries. Remaining expenditures are usually financed by taxes and, to a limited extent, by social and community-based health insurance schemes (figure 2.10).

In middle-income countries such as Lebanon and Guatemala, private for-profit insurance reduces the share of OOP spending. However, OOP spending often remains the principal financing mechanism, followed by government budgets and social health insurance. In at least 22 countries (China and India among them), 50 percent and more of the total health expenditure is defrayed out of pocket.

TABLE 2.5   Formal Health Protection Coverage, Selected Latin American Countries and Selected Years, 1995–2004 (percent of population)

Country	Public scheme	Social insurance	Private insurance	Other	Total (%)
Argentina	37.4	57.6	4.6	1.4	100.0
Bolivia	30.0	25.8	10.5	0.0	66.3
Colombia	46.7	53.3	n.a.	n.a.	100.0
Ecuador	28.0	18.0	20.0	7.0	73.0
El Salvador	40.0	15.8	1.5	n.a.	57.3
Haiti	21.0	n.a.	38.0	n.a.	60.0
Honduras	52.0	11.7	1.5	n.a.	65.2
Nicaragua	60.0	7.9	n.a.	0.5	68.4

Source: ILO 2008.
Note: n.a. = not applicable.

FIGURE 2.10   Out-of-Pocket Expenditure, Selected Low-Income Countries, 2006

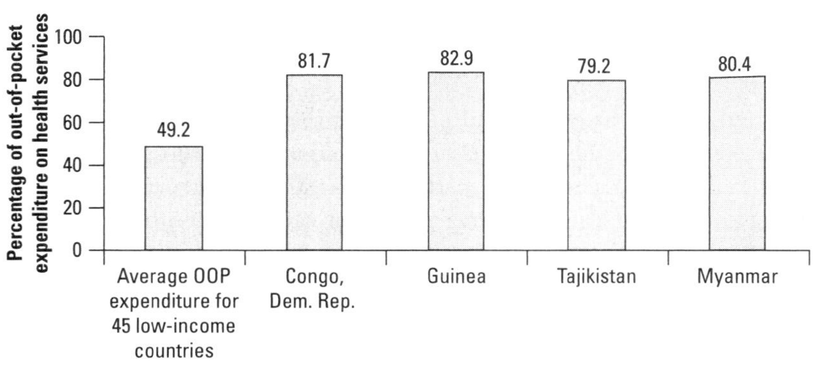

Source: ILO 2008.
Note: OOP = out of pocket.

Health care is imperative for all workers and their families, regardless of their employment status in the formal or informal economy. However, in low- and middle-income countries, many workers and their families do not have suitable health coverage. This is especially true for people in the informal economy. *Informal economy* refers to economic activities not covered by government regulations and laws, including those pertaining to labor protection and social security (ILO 2004c).

Determining the size, composition, and development of the informal economy is exceedingly difficult (ILO 2002d). It may be composed of *informal employment within and outside informal and formal enterprises*. Those *within* informal (for instance small unregistered or unincorporated) enterprises include employers, employees, own account operators, and unpaid family workers. In addition, various types of informal wageworkers work for formal enterprises, households, or have no fixed employer. These include casual day laborers, domestic workers, industrial outworkers (notably home workers), and undeclared workers (ILO 2002c). Informal enterprises are likely to function with low levels of capital, skills, and technology, and limited access to markets; they provide low and unstable incomes and poor working conditions (ILO 2004c). These workers do not have job security or benefits, are frequently exposed to dangerous and unhealthy working conditions, and are insufficiently informed to change their circumstances (ILO 2002c).

In developing countries, informal employment is often characterized by extensive manual/physical labor, long working hours, poor/unhygienic living conditions, deprived benefits, weak bargaining power and voice, and deficient capital and assets. Some migrants, especially illegal migrants, are also part of the informal economy and share the same challenges—particularly with respect to limited access to health care and services. Information about their health is usually scanty on account of their socioeconomic conditions and lack of legal status.

Most workers in the informal economy are vulnerable. High health care costs and serious illnesses often force them to sell their assets and/or borrow money, leaving them heavily indebted and predisposing them to a vicious cycle of poverty and ill health. Social health protection is a vital option to shield members of the informal economy from health and financial risks. Although covering informal economy workers and their families constitutes a major challenge, a number of initiatives have been launched to capture these workers by pursuing universal coverage and/or extending social health insurance.

An example of an organization covering the informal economy is the community-based scheme in India, the Yeshasvini Co-Operative Farmers Health Scheme (Karnataka). A member's annual premium amounts to US$3 per person, which is supplemented by a government subsidy of US$2.50 per person. About 2 million people are covered by the scheme. The benefits package includes surgical procedures and outpatient diagnosis. Maximum benefit per insured individual per procedure is between US$2,300 and US$4,600 per year. Recently, medical emergencies (such as dog bites, accidental poisoning, and road traffic accidents), normal deliveries, and pediatric care within the first five days after birth have been included in the package (ILO 2007: 2).

Access to Health Services

Worldwide, about 1.3 billion people do not have access to effective and affordable health care when they need it. Of those who do, 170 million people are forced to spend more than 40 percent of their household income on medical treatment (ILO 2008). The 1997 *Human Development Report* of the United Nations Development Programme (UNDP 1997) estimates that the majority of the poor without access to health services live in developing countries: 34 percent in South Asia, 27 percent in Sub-Saharan Africa, and 19 percent in Oriental Asia (figure 2.11).

Internationally comparable data on *access to health services* are scarce and incomplete. Often only very specific and incompatible data are available at national and international levels that do not allow assessments of effective coverage and access. Nevertheless, given the close link between access to health services and lack of coverage in social health protection, the availability of such data is vital when developing and advocating strategies for universal coverage. Due to these limitations, numerous conceptual and methodological issues come into play in the provision of data on coverage and access. Ideally, the most useful approach to measuring social health protection coverage would be a combination of key indicators reflecting the situation in a country, including: costs borne by legally covered individuals to obtain the care they need, such as out-of-pocket payments, cost of public and

FIGURE 2.11   Where Poor People without Health Care Live

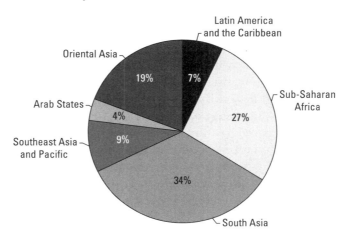

Source: UNDP 1997.

private health expenditure not financed by private households' out-of-pocket payments, total public expenditure on health benefits as a percentage of GDP, and physical access to health services.

National data are fragmented, and more research is required to combine the pieces in a meaningful way. Among the indicators mentioned, physical access to health services is relatively difficult to measure; yet, it is the factual basis for all concepts of coverage. Legal coverage, for example, is meaningless if the necessary physical health care infrastructure and health care staff are not available. Access to health services not only varies among countries and regions, but also within countries. Attempts to describe and quantify access to health care often refer to access to hospital beds. However, this indicator gives too much weight to hospital care if used as a coindicator for social health protection coverage. Indicators on the outcomes of maternal and child health care services might provide a first approach to measure effective access to health services. Until more reliable data become available, births attended by skilled health personnel[2] and density of health professionals[3] can be used as indicators to estimate access to health care, even if they exhibit some inconsistencies.

The birth-attendance access (BAA) deficit was obtained using the difference between 100 and the percentage of live births attended by skilled personnel at a given time—thus revealing the percentage of live births not cared for by a qualified health professional. The health professional density-based access deficit indicator (the staff-related access [SRA] deficit) was measured using the relative difference of the national density levels of health professionals and the Thailand benchmark.[4] Thailand was used as a normative benchmark because it achieves good health outcomes with a staffing ratio of one health professional per 313 individuals (ILO 2008). However, this is a conservative minimum estimate.

If, for example, health professionals are very unevenly spread in a country, the actual deficit may be much greater than the estimate based on national averages. If, however, this "optimistic" indicator signals a national or regional problem, it might be safely assumed that the real problem is bigger than the one indicated by national averages.

Figure 2.12 shows the density of health professionals in selected countries. High-income countries (for instance the United Kingdom with 66 individuals per health professional) have a much higher health-professional-to-population ratio than low- and middle-income countries (e.g., Chad with 3,113 individuals per health professional). Such ratios reflect huge global inequalities in access to health care. The situation is compounded by the migration of health professionals from low- and middle-income to high-income countries.

The ILO calculated the SRA deficit indicator for a significant number of countries, permitting a global estimate of the access deficit. The results yielded an estimated global SRA deficit of between 30 and 36 percent with Thailand as a benchmark. This means that more than one-third of the global population is not receiving the quality of health care that could be provided to them by an adequately staffed network of health professionals. If higher-income countries such as Ireland are used as a reference, the global SRA deficit increases to more than two-thirds of the global population.

Even the Thailand-anchored SRA deficits reveal high national access gaps. In China, the estimated staff-related access deficit indicates that 34 percent of the population lacks access to adequate health services—and this figure rises to 40 percent in Colombia. This is comparable to the staff-related access deficit of 42 percent in Peru. Table 2.6 lists both the SRA deficit and BAA deficit, showing that birth-attendance access deficits are in most cases structurally lower than the staff-related access deficits.

The Human Development Index (HDI) is a composite index and measure of human development based on life expectancy, adult literacy, education, GDP per

FIGURE 2.12   Density of Health Professionals, Selected Countries, 2004

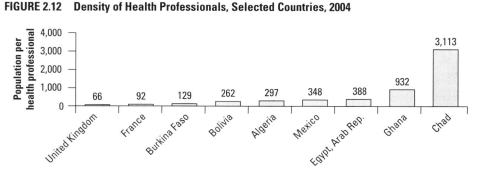

Source: ILO 2008: 25.

TABLE 2.6   Estimated Access Deficits, Selected Countries, 2004

	Estimated access deficit	
Country	Staff-related (% of population)	Births attended (% of live births)
Burkina Faso	85	43
China	34	17
Colombia	40	9
Ghana	66	53
Peru	42	29
Philippines	29	40
Uganda	78	61

Source: ILO 2008.

capita, and the Gini coefficient (as indictors of the economic standard of living) of countries worldwide. HDI provides a large view of human progress in the light of income and well-being. The regression of the HDI and SRA deficit shows that high HDI levels are strongly correlated with low health care deficits (figure 2.13). The obvious interpretation is that countries improve their health infrastructure as they grow economically. However, countries with low overall access deficits are not necessarily countries with a fairly equal income distribution.

The limitations of the SRA index include the fact that, although it indicates overall national staff shortages, it does not specify whether all people face similar access deficits in case of a staff shortage. It is far more likely that people in lower income brackets face much graver deficits than do people with higher incomes. The distributional effects of access deficits can be analyzed only on the basis of individual country studies.

Despite evident gaps in data availability and reliability, as well as the methodological limitations, the analysis of formal social protection coverage and standardized access deficit estimates has given insights into some interesting and challenging developments in a number of countries. These observations are:

• Public health services, though narrowing and deteriorating due to structural adjustment policies, public expenditure cuts, and privatization, continue to play an important role in providing health services through social protection mechanisms.

• Legal coverage of both social health insurance and national health systems has had a heterogeneous effect on out-of-pocket payments.

• Community-based schemes are growing in importance in many countries and can broaden coverage of informal workers.

• Employer-facilitated insurance systems are common in Arab states but not in most developing countries.

FIGURE 2.13   Regression between Access Deficit and Human Development Index

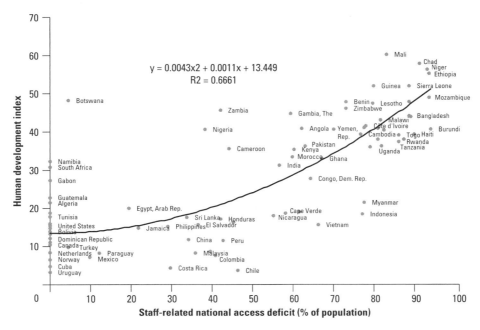

Source: ILO 2008: 28.

Pluralistic Use of Social Health Insurance and Tax-Funded Schemes

Public health services continue to play an important role in providing health services through social protection mechanisms, despite some narrowing and deterioration due to structural adjustment policies, public expenditure cuts, and privatization. For example, formal coverage still amounts to 47.6 percent in the Arab Republic of Egypt and 25 percent in Kenya. Almost all countries use a combination of health-financing mechanisms such as social and national health insurance in combination with national health services, for example, in Egypt and Tunisia. Also in the Republic of Yemen, a number of public, private, and mixed companies offer various types of health benefits schemes ranging from relatively low flat-rate reimbursement to comprehensive coverage packages.

Out-of-Pocket Payments and Legal Coverage

Legal coverage of health expenses does not automatically slash out-of-pocket expenditures. There is a relatively small difference in the share of OOP expenditure as a percentage of private expenditure on health between Tunisia (83 percent), which has almost universal legal coverage, Nicaragua (95.7 percent), where almost 70 percent of the population has formal health protection, and

Niger (89.2 percent), where less than 1 percent of the population is formally covered. At the same time, OOP as a percentage of total expenditure on health accounts for only around 10 percent in Slovenia and South Africa, while it rises to 26.8 percent in Ukraine and to 45.1 percent in Tunisia, although all these countries have achieved universal legal coverage. The burden of OOP spending on uncovered households in Uganda (36.7 percent) is only slightly higher than in Turkmenistan (32.6 percent), where more than 80 percent of the population is covered. The findings indicate that the scope of benefits packages, including financial protection and service quality, has a stronger effect on private health expenditure than does the number of persons or households legally covered by any kind of prepayment system for health.

The Role of Community-Based Schemes

A current trend in low-income countries is to increase the role of mutual health organizations and social health insurance when mainstreaming pro-poor policies in social health protection and addressing issues of high user fees. Voluntary and community-based schemes are also gaining support in many of these countries. Their success and sustainability depend to a great extent on the attractiveness of benefits packages, related financial protection, and service quality. The coverage of workers and their families in the informal economy may also contribute to their success. Key issues concerning sustainability—for example, capacity to pay and adverse selection—are addressed by creating financial and administrative linkages among schemes at various levels based on different ownerships.

Current country examples, among them the Yeshasvini scheme in India, show that schemes can work successfully. Community-based schemes can thus play a role in accelerating progress toward coverage of informal economy workers.

Employer-Facilitated Insurance

Enterprise-based health plans usually provide care directly through employer-owned or on-site health facilities or through contracts with outside providers and facilities. Employer-driven insurance schemes are exclusive, covering only stable workers and in some cases their families. The concept is often closely related to labor legislation on work accidents and occupationally acquired diseases.

Examples from Africa include employer-provided medical care in Zambia and Nigeria. Company health benefits schemes often reflect a paternalistic relationship between employer and employees, relying partly on individual, case-by-case decisions rather than on vested rights. More important is the fact that many schemes are too small to provide effective coverage for catastrophic diseases. Trade union–related health insurance systems may be found in countries like Argentina, Burkina Faso, Guatemala, Mauritius, South Africa, and Zimbabwe. Some foster dual membership and automatically insure all union members through the insurance plan, while others develop mutual insurance systems that are relatively autonomous of the union and open to members and nonmembers alike. Existing approaches are often driven by the need to extend coverage to workers and families in the formal and informal economy by various means to increase fiscal space for health care.

When accepting the coexistence of different subsystems, these subsystems need to be coordinated at the national level to create synergies and avoid gaps in coverage. National, regional, and community-based approaches will have to be incorporated, instead of building new systems or developing a new approach based on only one of the available financing options.

ACHIEVING UNIVERSAL COVERAGE BY SCALING UP SOCIAL HEALTH INSURANCE

Worldwide experience and evidence show that there is no single right model for providing social health protection or single pathway to achieve universal coverage. Countries that use social health insurance also use other means of resource generation, risk pooling, health care delivery, and financing. Experience also reveals that social protection evolves over years or decades and is contingent upon historical and economic developments, social and cultural values, institutional settings, political commitment, and leadership within countries. In addition, most national health-financing systems are based on multiple options that cover disjointed or overlapping population subgroups, while others remain uncovered. Against this background, striving for the following objectives seems to be necessary:

- To rationalize the use of pluralistic financing mechanisms and coordinate with existing social health insurance schemes in order to achieve universal access to essential and affordable care

- To increase fiscal and financial space to fund universal coverage, for example, by improving domestic resource mobilization based on insurance approaches. Coordinating all existing financing mechanisms within a country is suggested to increase the volume of resources and risk pools available for universal health care.

The government should play a pivotal, active role as facilitator and promoter and define the operational space for each subsystem. This entails developing an inclusive legal framework for the country and ensuring adequate funding and comprehensive benefits for the whole population. The framework should also regulate voluntary private health insurance, including community-based schemes, and consider regulations to ascertain good governance and effective protection. This framework establishes a rights-based approach to social health protection, which takes into account needs and capacity to pay, thereby realizing the objective of including the population not covered by social health protection.

When developing the coverage plan, all financing mechanism options—including all forms of compulsory and voluntary schemes, for-profit and nonprofit schemes, public and private schemes ranging from national health services to community-based schemes—should be considered if they contribute, in the given national context, toward achieving universal coverage and equal access to essential services for the population.

The coverage plan should be accompanied by, or include, an overall *national health budget,* making it possible to establish and project—on the basis of a National Health Account—the total resources (such as taxes, contributions, and premiums) available to finance health care. The plan should also estimate each subsystem's expenditures so as to accelerate the process of achieving affordable, sustainable universal coverage and access by building in line with a realistic plan.

A pragmatic strategy to rationalize the use of various health-financing mechanisms with a view to achieving universal coverage and equal access should be developed in two stages:

1. An inventory should be made of a country's existing financing mechanisms, and the gaps in coverage and access should then be assessed.

2. A plan should be made to fill the gaps.

Finding and Assessing the Gaps

Access deficits should be measured by utilizing detailed national health surveys, as well as regionally disaggregated analyses of formal legal coverage by each health-financing subsystem. This involves taking stock of every social health protection mechanism within the country and ascertaining the population segments they cover. The approximation of the coverage gap and access deficit thus obtained would provide guidance to the national coverage plan.

Developing a National Coverage Plan

The national coverage plan should provide a coherent design of pluralistic national health-financing coverage and delivery systems consisting of subsystems, such as national tax-based services, social health insurance schemes, and private insurance schemes. Working toward universal coverage, these would operate within a clearly defined scope of competence and cover defined subsections of the population. The elements of the coverage plan thus consist of: determining subsystems covering all population subgroups; developing adequate benefits packages and related financial protection in each subsystem; determining the rules governing the financing mechanisms for each subsystem, the financial linkages between them, and any needed financial risk equalization between different subsystems; maximizing institutional and administrative efficiency in each subsystem and the system as a whole; and determining the time frame for reaching universal coverage.

Among the activities involved in the development of a national coverage plan are drawing a coverage map, writing a national health budget, improving health-financing mechanisms, building rational linkages between subsystems, designing adequate benefits packages, and creating institutional and administrative efficiency.

Developing a Coverage Map

The coverage plan is directed at closing the coverage gap and access deficit by rational use of a country's health-financing mechanisms. The national coverage plan should establish coverage and access. This map could be used to project intended annual and multiannual progress toward targets set in the coverage plan.

Developing a National Health Budget

Before establishing the coverage plan, the government should document the funds available for social health protection. This requires developing a national health budget that assesses the financial status and development of national health care schemes. A health budget initially compiles the current status of all health sector expenditures and revenues in the form of a national health account.

Improving Health-Financing Mechanisms

Based on the results of the national health budget, issues related to improving health-financing mechanisms and conceiving linkages need to be addressed. There are essentially five ways of improving health-financing mechanisms to broaden social security coverage: implementing and expanding existing social insurance schemes; introducing universal benefits or services financed from general state revenues; establishing or extending means-tested benefits or services (social assistance) financed from state revenues; encouraging microinsurance schemes; and mandating private health insurance. A related health-financing policy checklist is provided in box 2.1.

Improving health-financing mechanisms and extending health protection require increasing funds. In many middle- and high-income countries, revenue collection based on public funds and payroll taxes often encounters obstacles since spending on health is perceived as an unproductive cost that hampers economic development. In many low-income countries, fiscal space and domestic revenues are considered too limited to ensure access to health services for most of the population. Ensuring financial sustainability involves identifying other sources of funds and their collection. Mobilizing additional government resources usually requires a functioning formal economy, yet many low-income countries have large informal economies. Over the past few years, the share of total labor supply in the informal economy has been growing, particularly in Asia. This applies even in countries with high rates of economic growth in the formal sector.

Increasing fiscal space is essential for the improved sustainability of social health protection. It often presupposes changes in government policies—and, for countries relying on international aid—more sustainable support from

---

BOX 2.1   KEY POLICIES ON HEALTH CARE FINANCING

Key policies for financing health care should cover the following:

- Mobilizing and collecting sufficient resources to achieve policy objectives

- Ensuring strong political commitment based on social and national dialogue

- Improving equity and solidarity in financing through income-based burden sharing

- Setting up risk-equalization and solidarity funds where appropriate

- Maximizing risk pooling and reducing fragmentation

- Introducing, in insurance schemes, government subsidies for the poor and for informal economy workers and their families (either direct or for contributions/premiums)

- Minimizing out-of-pocket payments

- Setting user charges according to capacity to pay

- Increasing financial sustainability

- Ensuring efficient and effective use of resources

- Using a mix of health-financing mechanisms to accelerate achievement of universal coverage and to balance equity, efficiency, and quality of care.

Source: Author.

---

donors. Successful methods for increasing fiscal space through government policies include more efficient use of public resources, strengthened efficiency in public institutions and service delivery, budgetary reallocation, greater efforts to collect taxes and contributions, effective governance of funds, and new sources of funding for the national health budget.

These approaches require strong political commitment, priority setting with a view to broadening social health protection, and determination to address transparency and accountability issues. It is crucial that democratic management be established and based on tripartite governance. There should be a participatory approach in scheme management, as well as governance based on social and national dialogue among the stakeholders.

Building Rational Linkages between Subsystems

Another approach to improving health-financing mechanisms consists of creating financial linkages between various schemes. Linkages can achieve redistributive effects, for example, by means of subsidies and financial consolidation (through reinsurance and guarantee funds). To achieve sustainable solutions when conceiving new linkages between different health-financing mechanisms, testing, evaluating, and monitoring integrated approaches linking the schemes are vital. A checklist on administrative and government linkages and related policies is provided in box 2.2.

Designing Adequate Benefits Packages

In addition to improving health-financing mechanisms, the coverage plan should develop *policies on adequate benefits packages, including protection against catastrophic spending* (box 2.3). The health challenges to be addressed in social health protection benefits packages vary in low-, middle-, and high-income countries and should take into account the following aspects:

- Low-income countries are confronted mainly with health challenges relating to primary health care, maternal and child care, and infectious diseases such as HIV/AIDS, TB, and malaria.

BOX 2.2   POLICIES ON BUILDING RATIONAL LINKAGES BETWEEN DIFFERENT HEALTH-FINANCING MECHANISMS

Policies for building linkages between different health-financing mechanisms should include the following:

- Introducing subsidies

- Developing efficient fee schedules

- Setting up risk-equalization and solidarity funds where appropriate

- Maximizing risk pooling by increasing membership

- Introducing, in insurance schemes, government subsidies for the poor and informal sector workers and their families (either direct or for contributions/premiums)

- Mandating private insurers, hospitals, and facilities to cover (e.g., in part) health care services for the poor

- Facilitating reinsurance and guarantee funds

- Establishing joint management functions

- Introducing mutual support in registration and collection of contributions/premiums

- Cocontracting health service delivery networks

- Establishing mutual audit and control.

Source: Author.

BOX 2.3   KEY POLICIES ON ADEQUATE BENEFITS PACKAGES AND PROTECTION FROM CATASTROPHIC SPENDING

Key policies on adequate benefits packages and protection from catastrophic spending should include the following:

- Introducing comprehensive and complementary benefits packages of various schemes providing for an adequate level of services and income protection

- Ensuring acceptability of the protected, professionals, and politicians

- Balancing the trade-off between equity and quality in broad consultations with all actors

- Addressing health-related poverty by covering catastrophic health expenditure (> 40 percent of a household's income net of subsistence)

- Covering out-of-pocket payments/user fees, and so on in order to ensure equal access

- Ensuring adequacy through focus on patients' needs regarding quantity, adequacy, and quality of services

- Minimizing out-of-pocket payments

- Providing access to primary, secondary, and tertiary care (through referral systems), including maternity care, preventive care, and care in relation to HIV/AIDS

- Providing for transportation costs, for instance for groups living in remote areas

- Addressing loss of income through adequate cash benefits.

Source: Author.

- Middle-income countries are saddled by the double burden of infectious diseases found in low-income countries and noncommunicable diseases such as cardiovascular diseases, drug abuse, and tobacco use found in high-income countries.

- High-income countries are faced with the long-term care of the elderly, the treatment of noncommunicable diseases, and stress-related syndromes.

Services covered in the benefits package and financial protection should be based on a consensus derived from broad consultations with all stakeholders involved in social health protection. In the process, the diverging views of the medical profession, various groups in the population (e.g., the poor, the elderly, minorities) should be taken into account.

The size of the benefits package involves a balance between cost and risk protection. It is recommended that benefits packages, including financial protection, be defined, with a view to providing equitable access to a comprehensive range of services as outlined in ILO conventions and recommendations. This may consist of defining primary health care, inpatient care, prevention, and maternity care rather than a "minimum benefits package."

Applying ILO conventions and recommendations avoids inequities in access to health services between formal and informal economy workers, and between the rich and the poor. However, when implementing and extending social health protection systems, deficiencies in infrastructure or, in some cases, the nonavailability of certain services must be taken into account. Against this background, access at an initial stage could be limited, for example, to services available but would include full access at a later stage.

The ILO Social Security (Minimum Standards) Convention, 1952 (No. 102), outlines benefits for sickness and for pregnancy:

- For sickness, benefits should include care by a general practitioner, including house calls; inpatient and outpatient specialist care at hospitals; essential pharmaceutical supplies as prescribed by medical or other qualified practitioners; and any necessary hospitalization.

- For pregnancy, confinement, and their consequences, benefits should include prenatal, confinement, and postnatal care either by medical practitioners or by qualified midwives and any necessary hospitalization.

Because private health expenditures are among the primary causes of impoverishment, benefits packages should be designed with a view to minimizing out-of-pocket payments. This also applies to high-income countries, where long-term care expenditure accounts for a significant proportion of out-of-pocket payments. Here the objective should be to achieve equity in access to health services by designing a benefits package that provides adequate, comprehensive health services and financial protection against impoverishment, particularly from catastrophic health expenditure.[5]

When choosing appropriate mechanisms to promote equity and access to health services, alleviate poverty, and improve health, countries should take into account the following:

- The actual level of spending on benefits matters more than the choice of funding mechanisms (e.g., taxes, contributions, or premiums) for achieving equity, poverty reduction, and health improvements.

- Universal benefits and targeted benefits have a different impact on equity. Universal benefits contribute more to achieving equity than to reducing poverty. Targeted benefits do more to reduce poverty than to improve equity.

Creating Institutional and Administrative Efficiency

The coverage plan for expanding social health protection also requires creating institutional and administrative efficiency. Institutional and administrative efficiency should be sought through leadership, transparency, and economic responsibility. These elements point to good governance and form an integral part of the overall strategy design and implementation. The strategy defines good governance in social health protection as referring to decision making based on existing legal frameworks, accountability, transparency, effectiveness and efficiency, equity and inclusiveness, and participation and consensus.

To fulfill the good governance criteria, the *financial and administrative separation* of health insurance funds from Ministries of Health and Labor is essential. Revenues earmarked for social health protection should be separated from government budgets. Contributions should be used only for health care benefits and plan administration, and not in support of Ministry of Health functions. Ensuring that health care contributions are not used for other contingencies is particularly important.

A recent trend in organizing social health protection with an eye on *efficiency* includes various forms of *decentralization* of responsibilities from the national to local governments or other subnational institutions. However, the related shift of financial burden to the local level is often problematic, since insufficient funds may be transferred from the national level, resulting, for example, in increasing inequities in access for the poor. Another form of decentralization of social health protection concerns community-based schemes. They mobilize additional funds at the local level and provide informal sector workers and their families with some financial protection against out-of-pocket payments (ILO 2006).

Creating efficiency also relates to *purchasing services*. Generally, service delivery can be organized through public or private providers. The most efficient mechanisms for purchasing services are as follows:

- Budgeting such as setting caps on annual expenditure

- Contracting and accreditation of providers based on performance

- Provider payment methods such as salary, capitation, case-based payments, and fee-for-service.

Further, funds—for example social health insurance—may act as purchasers. By doing so, insurance funds shift (financial) power from the supply to the demand side. This might result in important changes in the availability and affordability of services, particularly for poor segments of the population. When implementing social health insurance, capacity building is key to success. Capacity building consists primarily of training; upgrading capacities in designing, implementing, and monitoring; and knowledge development (e.g., through research and exchange of experiences). Building administrative capabilities through training and the establishment of efficient structures and procedures is one of the key preparatory activities for sustainable social health protection. The successful implementation of a reform, along with effective monitoring, good governance, and reliable service delivery, is dependent on well-trained, effective, and committed staff. Moreover, strengthening institutional technical and administrative capacity is essential for ensuring that the necessary conditions are in place to guarantee the viability of national security schemes and their responsiveness to their members' needs. The capacities gained will further contribute to the design, implementation, and testing of national health protection to ensure its viability. Currently, however, many developing countries do not have enough trained staff to ensure successful extension in social health protection. Training the administrators who are expected to implement related reforms is particularly important.

Enhancing the technical capacities of public authorities, social partners, and other stakeholders is crucial for overall governance and supervision. Evidence from many countries proves that successfully extending social health protection to the poor requires the consensus of various levels and entities of government, social partners, civil society, and others. Considering the diverse interests of stakeholders, obtaining the necessary support is a complex and difficult task. Problems often arise when stakeholders and social partners feel that they have been ignored in the process involved in the design and provision of social health protection, that their concerns have been misunderstood, or that the quality and depth of participatory decision making was limited.[6] This might result in a lack of support for new laws and regulations affecting implementation, enforcement, funding, and compliance, leading to a complete failure of important reform activities—even when parliamentary hurdles have been cleared.

Against this background, it is important to enhance the technical capacities of public authorities, social partners, and other stakeholders and improve their participation in social and national dialogue. This can be achieved through appropriate training at a tripartite or broader level.

CONCLUSION

Many low- and middle-income countries suffer from low public health expenditure, poor population coverage and access to health services, as well as from high out-of-pocket expenditures and entrapment in vicious cycles of ill health and poverty. According to ILO data, one-third of the global population does not have access to health care.

Overall, experience shows that there is no single approach and no "pure" insurance or tax-funded approach to providing protection against financial and health risks. Both developed and developing countries are simultaneously employing various health-financing mechanisms such as social health insurance and tax-funded schemes to work toward providing universal coverage to the whole population through adequate benefits packages.

In this context, scaling up social health insurance and its various forms plays an important role, particularly with a view to providing access to affordable health services, mobilizing domestic resources, and ensuring sustainable financing based on ability to pay. Success in scaling up social health insurance depends on a country's socioeconomic context and its institutional and legal environment. A favorable environment is characterized by adequate institutional capacity, efficiency and effectiveness, institutional accountability and popular confidence in institutions, and sufficiently developed and enforced legislation.

The strategy on rationalizing the use of pluralistic financing mechanisms for achieving universal coverage in social health protection is aimed at accelerating the achievement of universal coverage, promoting equity, and supporting global international efforts to alleviate poverty and improve health. The strategy is built on the central credo of incorporating into one pragmatic pluralistic national system all the existing coverage and financing subsystems in a country that meet a number of outcome and process criteria. The system should provide for the following:

- Achievement of universal coverage of the population within a realistic time frame

- Effective and efficient provision of adequate, but not necessarily uniform, benefits packages, including financial protection for all

- Existence of a governance system that confirms the government's overall responsibility for the functioning of the system as a whole, but which also involves covered persons, financiers (contributors and taxpayers, including employers, employees, and workers in the informal economy) and providers of care

- Fiscal and economic affordability.

NOTES

1. This was first formulated in the Medical Care Recommendation, 1944 (No. 69), which provides in its paragraph 8 that "[t]he medical care service should cover all members of the community, whether or not they are gainfully occupied." The universality of the right to health care is also formulated in the Declaration concerning the aims and purposes of the International Labour Organization (Declaration of Philadelphia), 1944, which states: "The Conference recognizes the solemn obligation of the International Labour Organization to further among the nations of the world programmes which will achieve: …(f) the extension of social security measures to provide a basic income to all in need of such protection and comprehensive medical care;…" In addition, the 1948 Universal Declaration of Human Rights provides in its Article 25 (1) that "[e]veryone has the right to a standard of living adequate for the health and well-being of himself and of his family, including food, clothing, housing and medical care and necessary social services, and the right to security in the event of unemployment, sickness, disability, widowhood, old age or other lack of livelihood in circumstances beyond his control."

2. Based on the WHO definition: percentage of live births attended by skilled health personnel in a given period of time.

3. The number of population per health professional (physicians, nurses, and midwives).

4. The actual formula for the SRA for a country X with a population POPx and a number of professionals PROFx is: SRAx = (POPx/PROFx * DENSt)/POPx whereby DENSt denotes the professional density in the benchmark country t (here Thailand).

5. Defined as health care costs that exceed a household's capacity to pay.

6. An example might be seen in recent experience with social health insurance in Kenya: "Ngilu's Fit of Fury," *The Standard* (Kenya), November 16, 2004.

REFERENCES

Asfaw, A. 2006. "What Is the Impact of Social Health Protection on Access to Health Care, Health Expenditure and Impoverishment? A Comparative Analysis of Three African Countries." Country study prepared for X. Scheil-Adlung, F. Booysen, K. Lamiraud, J. Juetting, A. Asfaw, K. Xu, and G. Carrin. ESS Paper No. 24, International Labour Office (ILO), Geneva.

Bailey, C. 2004. "Extending Social Security Coverage in Africa." ESS Paper No. 20, ILO, Geneva. http://www3.ilo.org/public/english/protection/secsoc/downloads/707sp1.pdf.

Deaton, A. 2006. "WIDER Annual Lecture." World Institute for Development Economics Research (WIDER), United Nations University, Helsinki.

ILO (International Labour Office). 1927. *Compulsory Sickness Insurance*. Geneva: ILO.

———. 1999. "More Than 140 Million Denied Access to Health Care in Latin America and the Caribbean. ILO/PAHO Meeting Aims to Reduce Social Exclusion in the Health Sector." Press Release, Geneva. http://www.ilo.org/public/english/bureau/inf/pr/1999/41.htm.

———. 2002a. "Extending Social Protection in Health through Community-Based Health Organizations: Evidence and Challenges." Discussion Paper, Universitas Programme, ILO, Geneva. http://unpan1.un.org/intradoc/groups/public/documents/APCITY/UNPAN018656.pdf.

———. 2002b. *Social Dialogue in the Health Services: Institutions, Capacity and Effectiveness.* Geneva: ILO. http://www.ilo.org/public/english/dialogue/sector/techmeet/jmhs02/jmhs-r.pdf.

———. 2002c. *Women and Men in the Informal Economy: A Statistical Picture.* Geneva: ILO.

———. 2002d. *Decent Work and the Informal Economy.* International Labour Conference, 90th Session, Geneva.

———. 2003a. "Extending Maternity Protection to Women in the Informal Economy: An Overview of Community-Based Health-Financing Schemes." Working Paper, Geneva. http://www3.ilo.org/public/english/protection/socsec/step/download/67p1.pdf.

———. 2003b. "An Inventory of Micro-Insurance Schemes in Nepal." ILO, Kathmandu/Geneva. http://www.ilo.org/amin/download/publ/714p1.pdf.

———. 2004a. *A Fair Globalization: Creating Opportunities for All.* Geneva: World Commission on Social Dimension of Globalization. http://www.ilo.org/public/english/wcsdg/docs/report.pdf.

———. 2004b. "Enabling Women to Address Their Priority Health Concerns: The Role of Community-Based Systems of Social Protection." Working Paper, Geneva. http://www3.ilo.org/public/english/protection/socsec/step/download/666p1.pdf.

———. 2004c. "Financing Universal Health Care in Thailand: A Technical Note to the Government," Geneva.

————. 2005a. "India: An Inventory of Microinsurance Schemes. Community-Based Schemes." Working Paper No. 2, Geneva. http://www.ilo.org/amin/download /publ/831p1.pdf.

————. 2005b. "Improving Social Protection for the Poor: Health Insurance in Ghana." Ghana Social Trust Pre-Pilot Project, Final Report, Geneva. http://www3.ilo.org /public/english/protection/secsoc/downloads/999sp1.pdf.

————. 2005c. *Economía informal en las Américas: Situación actual, prioridades de políticas y buenas prácticas. Resumen.* Lima: ILO, Regional Office for Latin America and the Caribbean. http://www.oit.org.pe/cimt/nn/documentos/economia_informal__resumen.pdf.

————. 2005d. *Social Dialogue in the Health Services: A Tool for Practical Guidance. The Handbook for Practitioners.* ILO: Geneva.

————. 2006. *The Social Protection Perspective of Micro-Insurances.* Geneva: ILO.

————. 2007. *Extension of Social Protection in India: Yeshasvini Co-operative Farmers Health Scheme.* Geneva: ILO.

————. 2008. *Social Health Protection: An ILO Strategy towards Universal Access to Health Care.* Geneva: ILO.

Kwon, S. 2002. "Achieving Health Insurance for All: Lessons from the Republic of Korea." ESS Paper No. 1, ILO, Geneva. http://www3.ilo.org/public/english/protection/secsoc /downloads/509sp1.pdf.

Lamiraud, K., F. Booysen, and X. Scheil-Adlung. 2005. "The Impact of Social Health Protection on Access to Health Care, Health Expenditure and Impoverishment: A Case Study of South Africa." ESS Paper No. 23, ILO, Geneva. http://www.ilo.org/public /english/protection/secsoc/downloads/publ/1007sp1.pdf.

Mesa-Lago, C. 2005. *Las reformas de salud en América Latina y el Caribe: Su impacto en los principios de la seguridad social.* CEPAL/GTZ. Santiago: United Nations. http://www .eclac.cl/publicaciones/xml/8/24058/LCW63_ReformasSalud_ALC_Indice.pdf.

————. 2007. "The Extension of Healthcare Coverage and Protection in Relation to the Labour Market: Problems and Policies in Latin America." *International Social Security Review* 60 (1): 3–31. http://www.blackwell-synergy.com/doi /abs/10.1111/j.1468-246X.2007.00258.x.

————. 2008. "Social Health Insurance: A Development Guidebook." Draft for consultation, ILO, Geneva.

OECD (Organisation for Economic Co-operation and Development). 2005. OECD Health Data 2005. Paris: OECD.

Ron, A., and X. Scheil-Adlung, eds. 2001. *Recent Health Policy Innovations in Social Security.* Edison, NJ: Transaction Publishers for International Social Security Association.

Scheil-Adlung, X. 2001. "Healthy Markets—Sick Patients? Effects of Recent Trends on the Health Care Market." In *Building Social Security: The Challenge of Privatization,* ed. X. Scheil-Adlung, 113–24. Edison, NJ: Transaction Publishers for International Social Security Association.

————. 2004. *Indonesia: Advancing Social Health Protection for the Poor.* Jakarta: United Nations Support Facility for Indonesian Recovery/ILO.

Scheil-Adlung, X., F. Booysen, K. Lamiraud, J. Jütting, A. Asfaw, K. Xu, and G. Carrin. 2006. "What Is the Impact of Social Health Insurance on Access to Health Care, Health

Expenditure and Impoverishment? A Comparative Analysis of Three African Countries." ESS Paper No. 24, ILO, Geneva.

Scheil-Adlung, X., K. Xu, G. Carrin, and J. Jütting. 2007. "Social Health Protection, Poverty Reduction and Access to Care: A Comparative Study on Kenya, Senegal and South Africa." In *Extending Social Health Protection—Developing Countries' Experiences,* ed. J. Holst and A. Brandrup-Lukanow, 132–45. Eschborn, Germany: GTZ.

UNDP (United Nations Development Programme). 1997. *Human Development Report 1997: Human Development to Eradicate Poverty.* New York: UNDP.

———. 2006. *Human Development Report 2006: Beyond Scarcity: Power, Poverty and the Global Water Crisis.* New York: UNDP.

Unni, J., and U. Rani. 2002. *Social Protection for Informal Workers: Insecurities, Instruments and Institutional Mechanisms.* Geneva: ILO.

WHO (World Health Organization). 2003. *National Health Accounts Data.* Geneva.

———, ed. 2004. *Regional Overview of Social Health Insurance in South-East Asia.* SEA-HSD-274. New Delhi: WHO Regional Office for South-East Asia. http://www.searo.who .int/LinkFiles/Social_Health_Insurance_HSD-274.pdf.

———. 2005. *Social Health Insurance: Selected Case Studies.* Manila/New Delhi: WHO.

World Bank. 2004. *World Development Report 2005: A Better Investment Climate for Everyone.* Washington, DC/New York: World Bank/Oxford University Press. http://siteresources .worldbank.org/INTWDR2005/Resources/complete_report.pdf.

———. 2006. *Disease Control Priorities in Developing Countries.* 2nd ed. New York: Oxford University Press.

Xu, K., D. Evans, K. Kawabata, R. Zeramdini, J. Klavus, and C. Murray. 2003. "Household Catastrophic Health Expenditure: A Multicountry Analysis." *Lancet* 362: 111–17. http:// www.who.int/health_financing/Lancet%20paper-catastrophic%20expenditure.pdf.

CHAPTER 3

Making Health Insurance Affordable: Role of Risk Equalization

Wynand P.M.M. van de Ven

Billions of people around the world pay most of their health expenses out of pocket. Scaling up health insurance is seen as a way of reducing catastrophic out-of-pocket health expenses. Two aspects of scaling up health insurance are the focus of this chapter: why and how? Because the advantages of health insurance (risk pooling) seem straightforward, one question immediately comes to mind: Why do people, instead of buying health insurance, pay out of pocket, and why is there a need to scale up health insurance? Next, three tools for scaling up health insurance are examined: different forms of *subsidies* to make health insurance affordable for low-income and/or high-risk individuals, *mandatory community rating,* and *mandatory health insurance.*

INTRODUCTION

Why do people pay most of their health expenses out of pocket, bypassing financial intermediaries that could provide some form of risk management (Hsiao, Medina, and Ly 2008; Leive and Xu 2008; Pauly et al. 2006; Xu et al. 2007)? Unpredictable household health costs can impoverish even middle-income families who are not insured. A survey in 15 African countries showed that between 23 percent and 68 percent of uninsured households financed their out-of-pocket health expenses by borrowing and selling assets (Leive and Xu 2008). Surveys covering 89 percent of the world's population suggest that every year 150 million people suffer financial catastrophe because they pay for health care out of pocket (Xu et al. 2007). In addition, millions of people do not get needed care because they cannot pay for it (Xu et al. 2007). The resulting health problems may lead to impoverishment because sick people cannot work. For households in most low-income countries, health risks are the most important source of impoverishment.

Scaling up health insurance is seen as a way of curtailing catastrophic out-of-pocket health expenses. Many countries are scaling up health insurance by introducing either government-run mandatory health insurance or other insurance-based initiatives such as community health schemes and private voluntary health insurance (Leive and Xu 2008; Carrin et al. 2007). In this way, some of the resources flowing directly from households to providers are to be channeled through some form of prepayment mechanism.

Two aspects of scaling up health insurance—why and how—are the focus of this chapter. Because the welfare advantages of risk pooling through health insurance seem so straightforward, a first question arises: Why are high out-of-pocket health expenses so common, and why is a scaling-up of health insurance needed? Next, three tools for scaling up health insurance are examined: different forms of *subsidies* to make health insurance affordable for low-income and/or high-risk individuals and their different effects on equity and efficiency; *mandatory community rating*; and *mandatory health insurance*. In the final section, some conclusions are discussed.

WHY ARE OUT-OF-POCKET HEALTH EXPENSES SO COMMON?

If health insurance is so welfare improving, why do out-of-pocket payments make up such a large share of total health spending in low-income countries relative to health insurance coverage? Some explanations lie in people's misunderstanding of the insurance concept, the advantages and disadvantages of (scaling up) insurance, and the premium structure in an unregulated, competitive insurance market.

What Is Insurance?

The essence of insurance is risk pooling. Individuals who have an equal probability (p) of a loss (L) in the next contract period pay an insurance premium equal to pL plus a loading fee. Persons who actually incur the loss receive a reimbursement (R) from the insurer; no one else receives a reimbursement. For consumers, insurance implies a *transfer* of their financial risk to the insurer. Statisticians associate insurance with a *reduction of risk* because for a given probability of illness, the distribution of the average rate of illness in a group will collapse around the probability of illness as the size of the group grows (the law of large numbers). Insurance, in contrast with out-of-pocket payments and individual savings, implies income transfers from individuals who incur no loss toward individuals in the same actuarial risk group who do incur a loss. This type of *income transfer by chance* after a loss is the cornerstone of insurance. *A first reason for the reluctance of many people in low-income countries to buy health insurance is that they do not understand the concept of insurance.*

An essential condition for the widespread prevalence of health insurance is that consumers have sufficient trust in insurance companies. In other words, consumers paying their premiums must be sufficiently certain that the insurer will reimburse their future claims, even if the amount claimed exceeds the total amount paid for their premiums. For this reason, insurers in high-income countries must comply with governmental solvency requirements. Few low-income countries have such regulations, however, and they may not mean much in countries that do because of fraud and corruption. In the early days of health insurance in high-income countries, many insurers went bankrupt. For example, Schut (1995: 133) found that the failure rate of health insurers in the Netherlands was 40 percent in 1901–40: 40 out of 100 new insurers stopped writing health insurance or went bankrupt during this period. Failure of health insurance companies may be due, for example, to a lack of government regulation (on solvency requirements), adverse selection, and moral hazard. Thus, *a second reason for the low prevalence of health insurance in low-income countries may be a lack of trust in insurance companies.*

Another precondition for the purchase of health insurance is the willingness and ability to pay the premium. Pauly et al. (2006) conclude that, if people can afford to pay X euros out of pocket for health care, they could afford to pay X euros on health insurance, which would result in a substantial welfare gain. Although this statement seems obvious, it deserves a second thought. The classical expected utility theory, which explains the welfare gain from insurance for a risk-averse individual, is based on the assumption that the individual can fully pay the high expenses out of pocket. However, this assumption is often not fulfilled in low-income countries. In case of a dramatic health problem, most low-income people pay for medical treatment by borrowing or selling assets (shop, car, house), or others in the community pay for their treatment. However, a person's willingness to borrow or to sell assets may be higher in the case of an *identifiable current* health problem than in the case of a *statistical future* health problem. For the same reason, others in the community who have altruistic preferences may be more willing to contribute to the costs of necessary *care* for a specific, serious health problem than to contribute to health *insurance* for a healthy individual. Thus, *a third reason for the low prevalence of health insurance in low-income countries may be a low willingness to pay for health insurance despite a high willingness to pay for catastrophic health expenses in case of a major health problem.*

In summary, three potential reasons for a high percentage of out-of-pocket payments in low-income countries and a low prevalence of health insurance are:

- People do not understand the concept of insurance.

- People do not (sufficiently) trust insurance companies.

- People are reluctant to pay for health insurance against possible illness in the future despite their high willingness to pay for immediate, catastrophic health expenses.

Advantages and Disadvantages of Health Insurance

A necessary condition for the purchase of voluntary health insurance is that the (perceived) advantages outweigh the disadvantages of buying it.

The *advantages* of health insurance are as follows. First, insurance may offer risk-averse individuals a welfare gain. Insurance can be considered a transfer of financial risk from the consumer to the insurer, which reduces the risk (because of the law of large numbers). An individual is risk-averse if he prefers certainty ("paying pL") to uncertainty ("having a probability p of a loss L") and is willing to pay for certainty. Health care expenditures are characterized by large *random* variation across individuals. Because most of this variation is *unpredictable*, risk pooling via insurance may create substantial welfare gains for risk-averse individuals. Second, during the contract period, health insurance provides access to expensive care that would otherwise be unaffordable or would impoverish the family.

These advantages have to be weighed against the *disadvantages* of health insurance: higher health expenses due to moral hazard and the loading fee. *Moral hazard* can be defined as "the use or provision of more, or more expensive, care because the insurer reimburses (a part of) the costs." Moral hazard reduces welfare if the consumer prefers cash reimbursement to care. Health insurance may increase moral hazard because both patient and provider have an interest in the use or provision of more, or more expensive, care than without insurance *and* they have the ability to influence actual expenses, while the insurer, as a "remote payer" does not. The opportunities for providers to generate demand for their services (*supply-induced demand*) are substantially enlarged by the presence of health insurance. Supply-induced moral hazard may be a serious problem, particularly when regulation concerning licensing of health care providers and pricing their services is weak or nonexistent.

A second disadvantage of insurance is the loading fee contained in the premium, in addition to the actuarially predicted health expenses. The loading fee covers the costs of running an insurance company (personnel, administration, computer systems, claims processing, premium collection, fraud prevention, advertising, and other marketing and sales costs); the costs of building up financial reserves to prevent bankruptcy; commissions for insurance brokers; and shareholder profits. Altogether, the loading fee can take a big bite out of the premium.

The desired level of health insurance coverage depends on the trade-off between the welfare gain due to risk reduction and access to otherwise unaffordable care and the welfare reduction due to moral hazard and loading fee costs. Consumers have to weigh these advantages and disadvantages of health insurance, a complicated exercise, because the advantages and disadvantages may interact. For example, Wagstaff and Lindelow (2008) found the curious case that health insurance in China increased rather than decreased the risk of high and catastrophic spending. Their analysis suggests that this is because insurance encourages people to seek care when sick and to seek care from higher-level providers (moral hazard) than they would if uninsured.

In summary, there are five additional potential reasons for a high percentage of out-of-pocket payments in low-income countries and low prevalence of health insurance:

- The willingness to buy health insurance may be low because (both consumer- and supply-induced) moral hazard substantially increases the premium.

- Moral hazard may be more easily controlled by social pressure in small, informal community health schemes than by insurers operating large, impersonal pools.

- The willingness to buy health insurance may be low because people are not (very) risk-averse.

- The willingness to buy health insurance may be low because the loading fee is too high (either absolutely or as a fraction of the total premium).

- Low-income people are not attracted to any of the insurance products offered. A reason for the limited supply of products may be that insurers do not expect any market for their products.

Equivalence of Premiums and Risks

Another necessary condition for the purchase of voluntary health insurance is that individuals who are willing to buy health insurance can afford it. A competitive insurance market tends toward *equivalence* between the premium and the expected costs of each contract (claims plus loading costs). In other words, insurers must set the premium for each contract high enough to cover all the projected costs. They cannot offset predictable losses on the high-risk contracts by making predictable profits on the low risks because competition minimizes predictable profits. An insurer can use three different strategies to achieve equivalence of premiums and projected costs per contract:

- *Risk rating:* adjusting the premium for each product to the individual's risk

- *Risk segmentation:* adjusting the product (for example, coverage, benefits design) to attract different risk groups per product and pricing the premiums accordingly

- *Risk selection:* adjusting the accepted risk to the premium charged for each product.

If insurers pursue only the first strategy (risk rating), they would have to charge widely varying premiums to different individuals because the individual variation in expected health care costs is tremendous. Adjusting for age only, for example, the highest premium would already be more than 10 times higher than the lowest one. In addition to age, insurers can easily identify other risk factors, such as whether the individual suffers from a severe chronic disease. If health insurers in a competitive insurance market fully adjusted premiums to the individual's risk, health insurance would be unaffordable for many high-risk individuals.

In addition to risk rating, health insurers typically pursue the other two strategies (risk segmentation and risk selection). First, by offering different insurance products, insurers can encourage self-selection (for example, by offering a high-deductible plan to attract low-risk individuals (see, for example, Tollen, Ross, and Poor 2004). Under certain conditions, self-selection may result in a separating equilibrium in which the market is segmented by risk type (Rothschild and Stiglitz 1976; Wilson 1977). In the extreme, each risk type buys a separate coverage at an actuarially fair premium. This outcome differs from risk rating in the sense that low-risk groups are forced to signal their risk by purchasing less than full coverage. Second, by refusing high-risk applicants or by excluding treatments for pre-existing conditions from coverage, health insurers can select risks directly (Schut 1995).

A consequence of risk-adjusted premiums is that there is no market for insurance against the financial risk of becoming a future high-risk (Newhouse 1984). In an unregulated competitive market, the premium for an insured consumer who develops AIDS, cancer, or heart disease has to be raised in the next contract period to the expected cost level. Alternatively, the insurer may decide to exclude from coverage the costs related to medical conditions which pre-exist before the new contract period, or not to renew the contract at all. Thus, voluntary health insurance in a competitive insurance market can provide protection against *unpredictable* variation of costs *only during the contract period* (usually a year).

In sum, two additional potential reasons for so high a percentage of out-of-pocket payments in low-income countries and so low a prevalence of health insurance are:

- High-risk people cannot afford to buy health insurance because of risk-rated premiums.

- "Insurance" against becoming a future high risk can be better handled within small informal community health schemes than in a competitive insurance market.

Conclusion

Box 3.1 summarizes 10 potential reasons for the high share of out-of-pocket payments in low-income countries and the low prevalence of health insurance. Further research is needed into the (relative) relevance of each of these potential reasons.

The appropriate tools for scaling up health insurance depend on the different reasons for its low prevalence. These tools may consist, for example, of providing information about "what insurance is," regulation of the insurance market (for example, concerning solvency requirements), tools to reduce (supply-induced) moral hazard, providing subsidies, mandatory community rating, or mandatory health insurance. In this chapter, the last three tools are discussed.

SUBSIDIES FOR HEALTH INSURANCE

Many high-income countries that now have affordable health insurance for high-risk and low- and middle-income people have gone through a long evolutionary process from out-of-pocket payments, voluntary community health

BOX 3.1   WHY OUT-OF-POCKET PAYMENTS ARE SO HIGH AND HEALTH INSURANCE COVERAGE SO THIN IN LOW-INCOME COUNTRIES

1. People do not understand the concept of insurance.

2. People do not (sufficiently) trust insurance companies.

3. People display a low willingness to pay for health insurance but a high willingness to pay for catastrophic health expenses.

4. Willingness to buy health insurance may be low because moral hazard—both consumer- and supply-induced—substantially increases the premium.

5. Moral hazard may be more easily limited in small, informal community health schemes with social controls than in large, impersonal pooling mechanisms like insurers.

6. The willingness to buy health insurance may be low because people are not (very) risk averse.

7. The willingness to buy health insurance may be low because the loading fee is too high, either absolutely or as a fraction of the total premium.

8. There is no supply of insurance products that are attractive to low-income people. One reason for this shortage may be that insurers think there is no market for their products among the poor.

9. High-risk individuals and groups cannot afford to buy health insurance because of risk-rated premiums.

10. "Insurance" against becoming a high future risk can be better handled within small, informal community health schemes than in a competitive insurance market.

Source: Author.

schemes, voluntary health insurance, unregulated competitive insurance market, systems of (mandatory) cross-subsidies, and eventually mandatory health insurance. Unregulated voluntary private health insurance for selected groups has often been a transitional form to develop experience with insurance mechanisms and to build up the institutions and capacities that subsequently enable the gradual expansion of financial protection and affordable health insurance to a larger part of the population. In this chapter, the focus is first on "making health insurance affordable," irrespective of whether the context is voluntary or mandatory health insurance. The rationale for this approach is that if certain groups or individuals lack the wherewithal to buy insurance, requiring them to purchase it makes no sense. However, *if* subsidies make health insurance affordable, the question is whether a mandate to buy health insurance is necessary (discussed below).

In a regulated, noncompetitive insurance market, it is more or less straight-forward to organize subsidies and make health insurance affordable for high-risk and/or low-income individuals. In an unregulated competitive insurance market, where insurers are free to set their premiums and define their products, the organization of (cross-)subsidies is more complicated than in a noncompetitive market. Because the start-up of health insurance in most countries takes place in an unregulated competitive market, this chapter deals primarily with the issue of making health insurance affordable in a *competitive* insurance market.

The subsidies that make health insurance affordable for high-risk and/or low-income individuals may come from an external donor or from low-risk and/or high-income individuals in the same market. In this section, focus is on the different forms of subsidies to the consumer and their different effects on equity and efficiency, not on how the subsidy fund is filled. Individual insurance is discussed, not group insurance. Two main categories of subsidies can make individual health insurance affordable for the high risks: *explicit* premium subsidies and *implicit* cross-subsidies. These two categories of subsidies can be used on their own or in combination.

Explicit Subsidies

Examples of *explicit* subsidies are vouchers, tax deductions, tax credits, and employers' contributions to an employee's individual health insurance. The subsidy system can be organized by a *sponsor* (government, a large employer, a coalition of employers) such that high-risk and/or low-income persons who are confronted with unaffordable premiums receive a premium subsidy from a subsidy fund filled by contributions. The subsidies may be earmarked for the purchase of specified insurance coverage.

Premium-Based versus Risk-Adjusted Subsidies

Two types of explicit premium subsidies can be distinguished: (1) *premium-based subsidies*, which depend on the level of the premium paid (Zweifel and Breuer 2006; Van de Ven 2006), and (2) *risk-adjusted subsidies*, which depend on the risk factors such as age and health status that insurers use in a free market.

Premium-based subsidies are not optimal for three reasons. First, they reduce consumers' incentive to shop around for the lowest premium, and thereby reduce insurers' incentive for efficiency. They reduce the competitive advantage of the most efficient insurers and reduce overall price competition. Second, they stimulate consumers to buy more (complete) insurance than they would have bought without a subsidy, resulting in a welfare loss due to additional moral hazard caused by overinsurance. Third, premium-based subsidies create a misallocation of subsidies. The magnitude of the premiums is determined by many factors, not all of which the sponsor may want to use in determining the subsidies.

Assume that the total set of factors that determine insurers' premiums can be divided into two subsets: factors for which the sponsor desires subsidies, the S(ubsidy)-type factors; and those for which subsidies are not desired, the N(on-subsidy)-type factors (Van de Ven and Ellis, 2000: 768–69). In most countries age, gender, and health status will probably be considered S-type risk factors. But the sponsor could decide that the differences in premiums that are caused by other factors should not be reflected in the subsidies. Potential N-type factors that may result in premium variation are, for example, differences in efficiency among health insurers, regional differences in supply and prices, variations in practice style of contracted health care providers, and differences in individual consumer characteristics such as lifestyle, health behavior, preventive behavior, and taste. If subsidies for health insurance premiums are given *irrespective of the cause of the premium differences*, as is the case with premium-based subsidies, they most likely result in a misallocation of subsidies. The relevance of the distinction between S-type and N-type factors can be illustrated by the decision of the Belgian government that regional variation in supply (for example, the per capita number of providers and hospital beds) is explicitly considered an N-type risk factor, for which the subsidies should not be adjusted. Schokkaert and Van de Voorde (2003: table 2) illustrate the nontrivial impact of this political decision on the subsidies.

Risk-adjusted subsidies do not suffer from the above-mentioned problems. First, risk-adjusted subsidies can be based specifically on S-type risk factors that insurers use in their premium setting. To the extent that a risk factor (region) reflects S-type (health) as well as N-type (oversupply, high prices, inefficiency) factors, the sponsor must decide to what extent premium increases due to this risk factor will (not) be subsidized. Second, in the case of risk-adjusted subsidies, consumers are fully price sensitive at the margin. This avoids the other two problems of premium-based subsidies. The sponsor has to decide what the services should cost, including acceptable treatment quality and intensity, to qualify for subsidy.

Risk-adjusted subsidies can make health insurance affordable at *every new contract period*. If a person's health status deteriorates over time and consequently the insurer has to increase the person's premium to cover the higher expected costs, the future subsidy value will be adjusted to the change in the individual's risk characteristics. In this sense, risk-adjusted subsidies provide protection against the financial risk of becoming a future high-risk.

If consumers received a risk-adjusted subsidy based on the same risk factors that insurers use, the differences in out-of-pocket-premiums (premium *minus* subsidy) would be minimal and would primarily reflect differences in quality, taste, loading fee, or efficiency.

The effectiveness of risk-adjusted subsidies to reduce the differences in out-of-pocket-premiums depends on the risk factors the sponsor uses to calculate the risk-adjusted subsidies and on the risk factors the insurers use to calculate the risk-adjusted premiums and the other tools they have to segment the market.

The transaction costs of giving risk-adjusted subsidies directly to consumers are high. Each consumer must inform the sponsor about his or her risk factors, such as age, gender, prior health care utilization, and health status. These transaction costs can be substantially reduced by giving the subsidies to the insurers who, in a transparent competitive market, are forced to reduce each consumer's premium by the per capita subsidy they receive for this consumer. By giving risk-adjusted subsidies to the insurers, the different risks consumers represent for the insurers are equalized. This way of organizing the risk-adjusted subsidies is called *risk equalization* in this chapter. In practice, all countries that apply risk-adjusted subsidies (including Colombia, Germany, the Netherlands, and Switzerland) do this in the form of risk equalization.

Risk-adjusted subsidies might be insufficient for several reasons, at least in the short run (Van de Ven and Ellis 2000). Therefore, although premium-based subsidies are not optimal, they may provide a (temporary) complement to risk-adjusted subsidies for certain (income) groups.

Excess-Loss Compensations

For several reasons insurers may not be able to accurately adjust the premium to a consumer's risk. For example, collecting sufficient information may be too costly or the group of applicants is too small, so that the law of large numbers is not applicable. This may be particularly relevant in the case of high-risk applicants with a rare disease. Insurers can reduce this problem by exchanging information about an individual's risk factors, if a consumer decides to switch to another insurer. In addition, insurers can develop a nationwide standard rating model based on statistical information from all insurers. This will increase the accuracy of risk rating. (Although a standard rating model provides the nationwide predicted per capita health expenses per risk category, in a competitive market it is essential that *each individual insurer set its own premium rates*.) If, nevertheless, risk-rating an applicant is impossible or too costly, the insurer may set an extremely high premium or reject the applicant.

If insurers cannot calculate a risk-adjusted premium for certain groups of high-risk applicants, most likely the sponsor cannot calculate risk-adjusted subsidies either. To solve this problem, the sponsor can provide the insurers with a subsidy for high-risk subscribers in the form of *excess-loss compensations* (or *outlier payments*). For example, the insurers can be fully or partly compensated by the subsidy fund for an individual's expenses in excess of a certain annual threshold. (Excess-loss compensations can be considered a form of mandatory reinsurance without a reinsurance premium.) These subsidies will substantially reduce the insurers' expenditures for consumers with (extremely) high expected health expenses. This will help the insurers calculate a risk-adjusted premium for the high-risk applicants. In case of full compensation above the threshold, the threshold amount effectively functions as the maximum premium (excluding loading fees) for all insurers. The high risks clearly benefit more from this type of subsidy than do the low risks. Excess-loss compensations are applied in several countries, for instance in Australia and the Netherlands (Colombo and Tapay 2003). The advantages of excess-loss compensations have to be weighed against the disadvantage of reducing the insurers' efficiency incentive.

Implicit Subsidies

A complementary or alternative strategy to make individual health insurance affordable for the high-risk people in a competitive insurance market is to enforce regulations that *implicitly* result in cross-subsidies from low-risk to high-risk individuals. Two types of regulation to enforce implicit cross-subsidies can be discerned: (1) a *guaranteed renewability* requirement; and (2) *open enrolment and universal premium-rate restrictions*.

Guaranteed Renewability

A *guaranteed renewability* requirement generally obliges the insurers to renew the contract with their enrollees at the end of each contract period at the "standard premium and standard conditions" (Pauly, Kunreuther, and Hirth 1995; Herring and Pauly 2006). However, guaranteed renewability has some major limitations. For example, guaranteed-renewability cannot be combined with a free choice of health insurer *for the high-risks* because the "high risks are married to their insurer," because all other insurers offer them insurance at less attractive conditions than their current insurer. This lock-in is a serious problem if the chronically ill are dissatisfied with the quality of care or the benefits package offered by their insurer. They cannot switch at an affordable premium to another insurer because the other insurers will charge them a much higher premium than the standard premium. Another problem is that it is highly questionable whether a guaranteed-renewability clause can really guarantee a "standard coverage" and a "standard premium" 50 years later. These problems can be countered by implementing open enrolment and universal premium-rate restrictions.

Open Enrolment and Universal Premium-Rate Restrictions

Open enrolment and universal premium-rate restrictions hold with respect to *all* applicants, not only those who want to renew a contract with the same insurer, but also those who were previously insured with another insurer. Universal premium-rate restrictions can take several forms: community rating, a ban on certain rating factors (for example, health status, genetic information, duration of coverage, or claims experience) or rate-banding (that is, a minimum and maximum premium). Community rating usually takes the form of a requirement that insurers must charge each enrollee the same premium (in case of risk-equalization: the same out-of-pocket-premium) for the same product, irrespective of the enrollee's risk. The goal of such regulation is to create implicit cross-subsidies from low to high risks in the same pool, in the *current* contract period. However, pooling of people with different risks creates predictable profits and losses for certain subgroups, and thereby provides insurers with incentives for risk selection, which can have several unfavorable effects (box 3.2).

An effective way to reduce incentives for risk selection is to implement a good risk-equalization scheme. In such a scheme, insurers with a relatively large share of predictably high risks receive more compensation than insurers with a relatively large share of low risks. If risk equalization were perfect, it would eliminate all predictable profits and losses for all subgroups that insurers can distinguish. In that case, the initially imposed premium-rate restrictions would be superfluous.

BOX 3.2   UNFAVORABLE EFFECTS OF RISK SELECTION

1. Health plans have a disincentive to respond to the preferences of high-risk consumers. Health plans with a good reputation for chronic care would attract many unprofitable patients and would be victims of their own success. Therefore, health plans may structure their coverage such that the plan is unattractive for the high risks, or they may choose not to contract with providers who have the best reputation for treating chronic illnesses. This in turn discourages physicians and hospitals from acquiring a reputation for excellence, an unfavorable outcome of a competitive market.

2. Efficient health plans, which do not engage in risk selection, may lose market share to inefficient risk-selecting plans, resulting in a welfare loss to society.

3. In case of large, predictable profits resulting from selection, selection will be more profitable than improving efficiency in health care production. In the short run, an insurer that has limited resources to invest in cost-reducing activities may prefer to invest in selection rather than in improving efficiency.

4. To the extent that some health plans succeed in attracting low-risk persons, these selection activities result in risk segmentation, whereby the high risks pay a higher premium than the low risks pay. Alternatively, insurers could specialize in excellent integrated care for chronic diseases and offer contracts at high community-rated premiums if sufficient numbers of chronically ill people can and will buy such a contract. Market segmentation of this type conflicts with the goal of community rating.

5. Selection may induce instability in the insurance market, because low-risk people have a permanent incentive to break the pooling of heterogeneous risks by switching to lower-priced (new) health plans.

6. Finally, resources are wasted, because investments aimed purely at attracting low risks by risk segmentation or selection produce no net benefits to society (zero-sum game among health plans).

Source: Author.

Conclusion

In practice, none of the mentioned forms of subsidies now in use is both fully effective *and* without any market distortion. In principle, the preferred strategy for guaranteeing universal access to affordable coverage in the individual health insurance market is use of risk-adjusted subsidies or (equivalently) risk equalization. In the case of *premium-based subsidies* or *excess-loss compensations,* policy makers are confronted with a trade-off between affordability and efficiency. In the case of implicit cross-subsidies by *open enrolment and universal premium-rate restrictions,* policy makers are confronted with a trade-off between affordability and (the unfavorable effects of) selection. The insurers' incentives for selection can be reduced by implementing a system of risk equalization among the insurers, or by making the premium-rate restrictions less restrictive (which makes health insurance less affordable for the high risks) or by providing the insurers with retrospective compensations (which reduce the insurers' efficiency incentives). Again, policy makers are confronted with a trade-off between affordability, efficiency, and selection.

To the extent that *risk-adjusted subsidies* or *equalization payments* insufficiently subsidize some high-risk consumers, they can be complemented by one or more of the other forms of subsidies. This choice also confronts policy makers with a trade-off between affordability, efficiency, and selection. The better the equalization payments are adjusted for relevant risk factors, the less severe is this trade-off. In the (theoretical) case of perfect risk equalization, there is no need for any of the other forms of subsidies, and the trade-off no longer exists. Each of the other forms of subsidies alone inevitably confronts policy makers with a trade-off. Therefore, good risk equalization offers the only effective means of addressing the trade-off between affordability, efficiency, and selection.

MANDATORY COMMUNITY RATING: DOES ONE PREMIUM FIT ALL?

In contrast with this conclusion, many (if not all) countries with a competitive health insurance market use premium-rate restrictions and an open-enrolment requirement as the major tools to make health insurance affordable for the high-risk people. Mostly the premium-rate restrictions have the (extreme) form of community rating per insurer per product. Community rating usually is in the form of a requirement that insurers must charge each enrollee the same premium for the same product, irrespective of the enrollee's risk. (For a review of community-rated private health insurance in several countries, see Gale [2007].) Despite its social objective, this type of regulation has several adverse effects.

Drawbacks of Community Rating

A first drawback of community rating is that it induces strong incentives for selection, which may threaten good-quality care for the chronically ill, result in failure of efficient health insurers, induce wasteful investments in selection efforts, and reduce insurance market stability (box 3.2). These adverse effects are most pronounced in competitive health insurance markets where community rating is implemented without risk equalization (for example, in Australia, South Africa, and some U.S. states). Since the early 1990s many U.S. states have implemented regulations such as open-enrolment and premium-rate restrictions (often in the form of community rating) for health insurance offered to individuals (US-GAO 1997) and small employers (US-GAO 1995). In the 1990s, there was a gradual trend toward tighter rating reforms in the U.S. small-group market (Curtis et al. 1999). In none of these cases was the regulation combined with risk equalization. The effects of these regulations have been a shift in the composition of insured people from lower to higher risks, a rise in the cost of coverage, an increase in the number of uninsured people, a reduction in the choice of plans available in some instances, and a reduction of the supply of insurers willing to grant coverage (Astorino et al. 1996; Lo Sasso and Lurie 2003; Pauly and Herring 2007).

Next, in contrast to risk-adjusted premiums, community rating does not provide incentives for risk-reducing behavior and cannot discriminate between risk factors (such as differences in health status) for which a sponsor would want to give subsidies and those for which he would not (for example, variations in supply). Moreover, in contrast to explicit subsidies, community rating cannot limit cross-subsidization to low-income people only.

Finally, if direct premium differentiation is forbidden, product differentiation may result in indirect premium differentiation. Insurers may offer special products for various risk groups, for example, depending on life stage, lifestyle, or health status. Such risk segmentation across the product spectrum can be observed in Australia, Ireland, and South Africa, for example, where premiums must be community rated (Gale 2005; Colombo and Tapay 2003; Armstrong 2008; McLeod and Grobler 2008). In this way "community rating per product" results in low premiums for low risks and (unsubsidized) high premiums for high risks, which conflicts with the goal of community rating.

Why Is Community Rating So Popular?

Thus, the question arises: Why is community rating so popular among policy makers? In many countries, community rating seems to be an indisputable axiom, without any debate about whether there are better tools to make health insurance affordable.

Besides the above-mentioned disadvantages, community rating also has some advantages. First, it increases transparency. If insurers risk-rate premiums, it is more difficult for consumers to make an informed choice of insurer than in the case of community-rated premiums. However, if community rating results in extensive product differentiation, the advantage of a transparent premium structure may be largely forgone. A second advantage of community rating is the low transaction costs. Explicit premium subsidies as well as the premium setting and underwriting activities by insurers require administration and transaction costs. Of course, this advantage holds only when community rating is *not* complemented with risk equalization to counteract incentives for risk selection. Another advantage is that community rating requires no public finance, whereas explicit subsidies require a system of mandatory contributions (to the subsidy fund), which may be considered part of public finance. Since most governments are under pressure to restrain public finance, community rating may be politically advantageous in particular in settings (such as low-income countries) where fiscal space is severely limited. Finally, many people believe that community rating offers a better guarantee of making health insurance affordable than a risk-equalization system, which needs to be complemented with additional subsidies. However, as discussed above, if selection is successful and results in a market segmentation where the low-risk and high-risk consumers are no longer in the same pool, and therefore do not pay the same premium (as is the case, for example, in Australia, Ireland, South Africa, and Switzerland), this argument may hold only in the short run.

The popularity of community rating as observed in practice indicates that policy makers attach a higher value to the (perceived) benefits than to the (potential) disadvantages of community rating. This may be partly due to the fact that the direct effect of community rating on affordability is immediately visible, while potential indirect effects such as poor-quality care or high premiums for chronically ill patients may only show up after some years. Thus, in the short run community rating provides a more effective strategy to guarantee affordability than risk equalization. This may at least explain the preference for starting with community rating in combination with poor-risk equalization. The preference for community rating may also be partly due to a general unawareness that community rating implies cross-subsidies also for types of nonhealth-related risk factors, for which most people may not want cross-subsidies. Finally, policy makers may hold the view that risk selection is not a serious problem in practice. One reason for this may be that they ignore or underestimate the forgone opportunities of good-quality, well-coordinated care that would occur if chronically ill people were the preferred clients, rather than nonpreferred "predictable losses." All in all, the justification for mandatory community rating—the most extreme form of premium-rate restrictions—is less straightforward than its popularity in practice suggests.

ECONOMIC MOTIVES FOR MANDATORY HEALTH INSURANCE

Many countries use mandatory health insurance as a tool for scaling up health insurance. In this section, government's economic motives for making health insurance mandatory are explored. Particular attention is given to these arguments under the assumption that health insurance is affordable. As indicated earlier, the rationale for doing so is that, if health insurance is not affordable for certain groups of individuals, it does not make sense to mandate them to buy it. However, *if* subsidies make health insurance affordable, is a mandate to buy health insurance necessary? If so, for *which groups of individuals* should the coverage of *which benefits* be made mandatory?

Mandatory coverage here means governmental imposition of a legal obligation on consumers to obtain coverage. Four economic motives generally prompt government to enforce mandatory coverage: to prevent free-riding, to compensate for a lack of foresight, to cover transaction costs of organizing cross-subsidies, and to prevent adverse selection (Van de Ven 1995; Paolucci, Schut, and van de Ven 2006).

Prevention of Free-Riding

If society is willing to subsidize some health services, some individuals may abuse this willingness by not buying insurance coverage for these services in the expectation that someone else will pay for their health care if they really need it. This free-rider behavior is more likely for low-income people than for high-income people because the willingness to subsidize another's care is lower the greater is that uninsured person's ability to pay. The desire to prevent free-rider behavior can motivate government to make (subsidized) insurance coverage for some health services mandatory for low-income people. For high-income people, this argument is less relevant because they can (and therefore will have to) pay for most health services themselves. Mandatory coverage for high-income individuals may be relevant for catastrophic risks with very high expected costs.

Lack of Foresight

Another motive for government to enforce mandatory coverage may be myopic behavior on the part of the young and healthy who may not always know what is in their best interest. They may underestimate future risks or even think that one or another disease will not affect them. However, the immediate advantage of not paying a premium could mean that they will not be able to afford expensive health care if needed in the future. Such short-sightedness could lead people to make wrong judgments about the relative importance of a certain, direct benefit (no premium) compared with future costs, which are quite uncertain. This argument holds, for example, for long-term psychiatric care, obstetric care, long-term nursing home care, psychogeriatric care, and care for persons addicted to alcohol and drugs (Van de Ven 1995). Based on paternalistic motives, government could make insurance coverage for some services mandatory for some groups of citizens. For high-income people, better educated and better able to afford high health expenditures than low-income people, this motive is less relevant. Nevertheless, this motive is also relevant for high-income people in case of catastrophic health care expenditures.

Transaction Costs of Organizing Cross-Subsidies

Mandatory coverage, also for high-income people, can be justified if otherwise the transaction cost is disproportionally high for organizing cross-subsidies to make health insurance affordable for high-risk people.

Prevention of Adverse Selection

Mandatory coverage can prevent adverse selection. This motive is particularly relevant if the contributions to the subsidy fund have the form of a levy on the insurance premium. In that case mandatory health insurance can prevent an upward premium spiral.

Conclusion

A major argument for mandatory health insurance that is often mentioned by policy makers is to "make health insurance affordable." This is not an appropriate argument. If health insurance is not affordable for certain groups of individuals, it does not make sense to mandate them to buy it. However, *if* subsidies make health insurance affordable, is a mandate to buy health insurance necessary? Four economic motives prompt government to make health insurance for certain *services* mandatory for certain *groups of individuals*: to prevent free-riding, to compensate for a lack of foresight, to cover high transaction costs of otherwise organizing cross-subsidies, and to prevent adverse selection. The relevance of mandatory coverage increases the lower an individual's income and the more catastrophic the health risks are. A pragmatic outcome could be mandatory health insurance for basic services for everyone combined with an income-related voluntary deductible. In case of mandatory health insurance, policy makers should anticipate the question of how to enforce the mandate and what the penalty should be for people who, for whatever reason, do *not* buy the mandatory coverage. It is hard to think of any motive to make duplicate coverage mandatory.

CONCLUSIONS AND DISCUSSION

Billions of people around the world pay most of their health care expenses out of pocket, bypassing financial intermediaries that could provide some form of risk management. Scaling up health insurance is a way of reducing catastrophic out-of-pocket health expenses and a tool for producing net welfare gains in terms of equity and efficiency.

Although scaling up health insurance may improve welfare, the financial protection that insurance offers and its welfare effects should not be overestimated. First, as long as it is not known exactly *why* the share of out-of-pocket payments in low-income countries is so high and the prevalence of health insurance so low (box 3.1), it is hard to come to conclusions about the welfare effects of scaling up health insurance. In addition, to be successful any scaling-up should be done carefully. For example, it is important to pay sufficient attention to control (supply-induced) moral hazard, to keep the loading fee low, and to offer insurance products that are attractive to low-income people.

Second, because many low-income and/or high-risk individuals may not be able to afford health insurance, a substantial part of the perceived protection offered by health insurance comes from subsidies to these groups. In general, these subsidies come from external donors and/or from high-income and/or low-risk individuals. The welfare effects of subsidies allocated to scale up health insurance have to be balanced against the welfare effects of the traditional supply-side subsidies often used by governments or donors.

The reasons for so low a prevalence of health insurance are relevant for the choice of tools for scaling up health insurance. These tools may consist, for example, of providing information about "what insurance is," regulation of the insurance market (for example, concerning solvency requirements), and tools to reduce (supply-induced) moral hazard. The following three tools were discussed for scaling up health insurance: subsidies, mandatory community rating, and mandatory health insurance.

In a regulated, noncompetitive insurance market it is more or less straightforward to organize subsidies and make health insurance affordable for the high-risk and/or low-income individuals. In an unregulated competitive insurance market, where insurers are free to set their premiums and define their products, (cross-)subsidies are more complicated than in a noncompetitive market. Because the start-up of health insurance in most countries takes place in an unregulated competitive market, the focus has been on subsidizing health insurance in a *competitive* insurance market.

In conclusion, a system of *risk-adjusted subsidies* is the preferred form of subsidy in a competitive insurance market with free consumer choice of insurer. Under this approach, insurers are free to sell risk-rated premiums. In practice, all countries that apply risk-adjusted subsidies give the subsidy to the insurer who reduces the consumer's premium with the per capita subsidy they receive for this consumer. This way of organizing the risk-adjusted subsidies is called *risk equalization*. To the extent that some high-risk consumers are insufficiently subsidized, the risk-adjusted subsidies or equalization payments can be complemented by one or more of the following forms of subsidy: premium-based subsidies, excess-loss compensations, and implicit cross-subsidies enforced by premium-rate restrictions for a specified insurance coverage. The choice among these complementary forms of subsidy confronts policy makers with a complicated trade-off between affordability, efficiency, and the negative effects of selection, notably low-quality care for the chronically ill. The better the premium subsidies are adjusted for relevant risk factors, the less are these complementary forms of subsidy needed, and the less severe is the trade-off.

In practice, policy makers appear to have a strong preference for mandatory community rating. Although community rating has some important short-term advantages, it also may have serious negative effects in the long run, particularly as a result of the disincentives to provide good quality care to the chronically ill. Thus, the justification for mandatory community rating, the most extreme form of premium-rate restrictions, is less straightforward than its popularity in practice suggests.

Finally, *mandatory* health insurance was discussed as a tool for scaling up health insurance. A major argument for mandatory health insurance, often mentioned by policy makers, is to "make health insurance affordable." This is not an appropriate argument. If certain groups cannot afford to buy health insurance, it makes no sense to mandate them to buy it. However, *if* subsidies make health insurance affordable, is a mandate to buy health insurance necessary? Government's economic motives for making health insurance for certain *services* mandatory for *certain groups of individuals* are: to prevent free riding, to make up for a lack of foresight by the young and healthy, to prevent the high transaction costs of otherwise organizing cross-subsidies, and to prevent adverse selection. The relevance of mandatory coverage increases for lower-income groups and for more catastrophic health risks. A pragmatic outcome could be a mandatory health insurance for basic services for everyone, combined with an income-related voluntary deductible. In case of mandatory health insurance, policy makers should anticipate the question of how to enforce the mandate and what the penalty is for people who, for whatever reason, do *not* buy the mandatory coverage.

REFERENCES

Armstrong, J. 2008. "Risk Equalization in Ireland." Paper presented at the Risk Adjustment Network (RAN) Meeting, Dublin, March 6.

Astorino, A., V.C. Bunce, P. Hundee, J.J. Jakelis, D. Lack, M. Litow, R. Turner, and J. Whelan. 1996. *State Health Insurance Reform: Experience with Community Rating and Guaranteed Issue in the Small Group and Individual Markets*. Report, Council for Affordable Health Insurance, Alexandria, VA, April.

Carrin, G., C. James, M. Adelhardt et al. 2007. "Health Financing Reform in Kenya: Assessing the Social Health Insurance Proposal." *South African Medical Journal* 97 (2): 130–35.

Colombo, F., and N. Tapay. 2003. *Private Health Insurance in Australia: A Case Study*. OECD Health Working Papers, No. 8, October 30.

Curtis, R., S. Lewis, K. Haugh, and R. Forland. 1999. "Health Insurance Reform in the Small-Group Market." *Health Affairs* 18 (3): 151–60.

Gale, A.P. 2005. "What Price Health? Private Health Insurance Cost Pressures and Product Pricing." Paper presented to the Institute of Actuaries of Australia, Biennial Convention, Cairns, Queensland, May 8–11.

————. 2007. "One Price Fits All." Paper presented to the Institute of Actuaries of Australia, Biennial Convention, Christchurch, New Zealand, September 23–27.

Herring, B., and M.V. Pauly. 2006. "Incentive-Compatible Guaranteed Renewability Health Insurance Premium." *Journal of Health Economics* 25: 395–417.

Hsiao, W.C., A. Medina, and C. Ly. 2008. "Scaling Up Health Insurance in South, East, and Pacific Asia." Draft paper, August 10; chapter 11, this volume.

Leive, A., and K. Xu. 2008. "Coping with Out-of-Pocket Health Payments: Empirical Evidence from 15 African Countries." *Bulletin of the World Health Organization* 86 (11): 849–56.

Lo Sasso, A., and I.Z. Lurie. 2003. "The Effect of State Policies on the Market for Private Non-Group Health Insurance." Institute for Policy Research, Northwestern University Working Paper Series 04-09, October 20.

McLeod, H., and P. Grobler. 2008. "Risk Equalization in South Africa." Paper presented at the Risk Adjustment Network (RAN) Meeting, Dublin, March 6.

Newhouse, J.P. 1984. "Cream Skimming, Asymmetric Information, and a Competitive Insurance Market." *Journal of Health Economics* 3 (1): 97–100.

Paolucci, F., F.T. Schut, and W.P.M.M. van de Ven. 2006. "Categorizing Health Care Financing Schemes: An Economic Approach." Working Paper, Erasmus University, Rotterdam, Netherlands.

Pauly, M.V., and B. Herring. 2007. "Risk Pooling and Regulation: Policy and Reality in Today's Individual Health Insurance Market." *Health Affairs* 26 (3): 770–79.

Pauly, M.V., H. Kunreuther, and R. Hirth. 1995. "Guaranteed Renewability in Insurance." *Journal of Risk and Insurance* 10: 143–56.

Pauly, M.V., P. Zweifel, R.M. Scheffler, A.S. Preker, and M. Bassett. 2006. "Private Health Insurance in Developing Countries." *Health Affairs* 25 (2): 369–79.

Rothschild, M., and J. Stiglitz. 1976. "Equilibrium in Competitive Insurance Markets: An Essay on the Economics of Imperfect Information." *Quarterly Journal of Economics* 90: 629–49.

Schokkaert, E., and C. Van de Voorde. 2003. "Belgium: Risk Adjustment and Financial Responsibility in a Centralized System." *Health Policy* 65: 5–19.

Schut, F.T. 1995. "Competition in the Dutch Health Care Sector." Dissertation, Erasmus University, Rotterdam, Netherlands.

Tollen, L.A., M.N. Ross, and S. Poor. 2004. "Risk Segmentation Related to the Offering of a Consumer-Directed Health Plan: A Case Study of Humana, Inc." *Health Services Research* 39 (S1): 1167–88.

US-GAO (U.S. General Accounting Office). 1995. "Health Insurance Regulation: Variation in Recent State Small Employer Health Insurance Reforms." GAO/HEHS-95-161FS, Washington, DC.

————. 1997. "Private Health Insurance: Millions Relying on Individual Market Face Cost and Coverage Trade-Offs." GAO/HEHS-97-8, Washington, DC.

Van de Ven, W.P.M.M. 1995. "Choices in Health Care: A Contribution from the Netherlands." *British Medical Bulletin* 51 (4): 781–90.

———. 2006. "The Case for Risk-Based Subsidies in Public Health Insurance." *Health Economics, Policy and Law* 1: 171–88.

Van de Ven, W.P.M.M., and R.P. Ellis. 2000. "Risk Adjustment in Competitive Health Insurance Markets." In *Handbook of Health Economics,* ed. A.J. Culyer and J.P. Newhouse, 755–845. Amsterdam, Netherlands: Elsevier.

Wagstaff, A., and M. Lindelow. 2008. "Can Insurance Increase Financial Risk? The Curious Case of Health Insurance in China." *Journal of Health Insurance* 27: 990–1005.

Wilson, C. 1977. "A Model of Insurance Markets with Incomplete Information." *Journal of Economic Theory* 16: 167–207.

Xu, K., D.B. Evans, G. Carrin, A.M. Aguilar-Rivera, P. Musgrave, and T. Evans. 2007. "Protecting Households from Catastrophic Health Spending." *Health Affairs* 26 (4): 972–83.

Zweifel, P., and M. Breuer. 2006. "The Case for Risk-Based Premiums in Public Health Insurance." *Health Economics, Policy and Law* 1: 171–88.

CHAPTER 4

Reaching the Poor: Transfers from Rich to Poor and from Healthy to Sick

Sherry Glied and Mark Stabile

Low-income developing countries spend less than the estimated optimal amounts on health care services. One reason for these low levels of health care spending is that the system for financing health care services is inadequate. Public budgets cannot support the necessary expenditures, and private pooling mechanisms are either nonexistent or quite small. Social health insurance (SHI) offers an opportunity to enhance and expand public financing in these countries.

WHAT IS SOCIAL HEALTH INSURANCE?

Any health insurance system distributes money from healthy to sick people, pooling the financial risks associated with illness and injury. This pooling can occur in a private, voluntary system (Pauly et al. 2006) or in systems with public fiscal or regulatory intervention. Universal national health insurance or national health service systems pool risk by paying for coverage and care through income taxes or other broad-based taxes. SHI models pool risk by requiring that certain groups participate in arrangements that cross-subsidize the costs of health insurance among groups with varying income or health status. In general, social insurance models accomplish this cross-subsidization through mandatory payroll taxes or workplace-based premium payments.

The first large-scale health insurance system, which was developed by German chancellor Otto von Bismarck beginning in 1883, used a social insurance model. Workers and their employers in certain industries were required to contribute to health insurance pools, which at first paid claims only for earnings lost due to illness. Eventually, medical care was also provided. In Germany, this system has evolved into a nearly universal program that includes workers, retirees, dependents, and nonworkers. Many other developed-country health insurance programs also incorporate social insurance principles.[1]

Several developing countries have social insurance programs, usually covering public employees and sometimes selected other formal sector employees (Hsiao and Shaw 2007). In Africa, social health insurance programs have been established in Ghana and Kenya (Hsiao and Shaw 2007). The main financing for these programs comes from payroll taxes or workplace-based premiums, but most also rely on substantial infusions of general revenues. General revenue financing is a necessary element of these systems if they are intended to cross-subsidize people based on their income as well as on their health status, as discussed below.

Economics of Social Insurance

Publicly financed or mandated health insurance has significant economic benefits. These benefits begin with the value of health insurance itself, whether private or public.

Health Insurance

Buying insurance to cover medical care costs instead of paying for them out of pocket serves two important purposes. First, it pools risks across people. Because the direct costs of medical care when ill are extremely high, but few people get very ill, individuals may buy insurance as a way of pooling resources. From this pool, the high cost of care can be covered for the unfortunate few who get extremely ill. Health insurance, transferring income from the healthy to the unexpectedly sick, is valuable because in most circumstances, the marginal utility of income when sick is greater than the marginal utility of income when healthy.

The second important role that insurance can play is allowing individuals to smooth their expected consumption by purchasing insurance. Thus, instead of facing low health care costs when healthy, high costs when sick, and constant uncertainty about whether their health costs will be high or low, individuals can buy insurance such that the costs of medical care can be constant regardless of their actual health status. An important assumption behind this rationale for insurance (beyond that individuals can afford to pay for health care if they fall sick) is that individuals are risk averse and therefore prefer to pay a set amount with certainty against the risk of having to pay a large amount for health care when needed.

Benefits of Public Health Insurance: Adverse Selection

These general benefits of insurance arise in both private and public insurance arrangements. Public insurance may generate additional benefits by overcoming the problem of adverse selection, which can lead to the failure of private insurance markets.

Adverse selection occurs when people incorporate knowledge of their own poor health status into their decisions about insurance coverage. People who expect to use health services that cost more than the price of insurance in the coming year usually buy coverage. People who are healthy and have a low probability of using health care services place a lesser value on health insurance, even if they are risk averse, and this group may not be better off purchasing insurance. Therefore, whatever the health insurance costs, individuals who expect to spend more than its price on health care services will buy, and individuals who expect to spend less may not buy. Even when everyone buys coverage, adverse selection leads healthier people to choose less-comprehensive health plans than they might otherwise buy in order to signal their healthy status.

This process of self-selection can ultimately cause the insurance market to collapse (as occurred in voluntary fraternal health insurance in the United States in the 1920s). In the developing-country context, selection effects (and the fear of such effects) may also confound efforts to establish new private insurance plans. By mandating that both healthy and sick people buy the same health plans, publicly financed or regulated insurance can eliminate the efficiency losses due to adverse selection. Requiring participation in the same health plans also generates long-term risk pooling. In that way, people are assured of obtaining health insurance at reasonable prices in the future, even if they subsequently develop chronic health conditions.[2]

Other Benefits of Public Health Insurance

Public health insurance markets may have other advantages over private insurance. In many situations, these markets operate at lower administrative cost than do private insurers because they can use existing revenue-collection arrangements and do not need to take steps to address adverse selection. When providers exert some monopoly power, large public insurers can serve as an effective countervailing force. When insurance markets do not yet exist, public insurers may be better able to overcome the legitimacy and credibility problems that make it difficult to establish a new private insurer. In some developing countries, however, governments have less legitimacy and credibility than private actors, suggesting that arrangements that rely on private insurance markets (with mandatory side payments) may be more desirable.

Most important, public health insurance arrangements can be a vehicle for redistributing income within the population, from higher-income (or healthier) people to lower-income (or sicker) people. In this role, public insurance systems combine an insurance function with a redistributive function.

Inefficiencies of Public Health Insurance

Publicly financed or mandated health insurance can generate inefficiencies, however, for several reasons. First, mandates and taxes on labor alter the marginal gains from employment. This change in incentives usually leads to changes in the supply of or demand for labor and consequent deadweight losses. Second, the provision of free or subsidized health insurance effectively increases people's income even if they do not work. This income effect weakens the incentive to participate in the labor market. Third, the governance of public insurance is subject to the usual political economy problems of government.

The first two of these inefficiencies of public financing and mandates occur because people's contributions to the system are typically disconnected from the benefits they receive from the system. This disconnect occurs whenever redistribution is an important element of the public insurance arrangement.

It is avoidable, however, in the case of nonuniversal, nonredistributive mandatory health insurance when the beneficiaries fully value the benefits they receive (Summers 1989).

Nonuniversal Social Insurance

Consider a situation in which employees in one sector of the economy value health insurance at its full cost. Private insurance plans do not arise, however, because of the above-mentioned problems of selection, legitimacy, and so forth.

Now suppose that all employees in this sector are mandated to contribute to and participate in a single health insurance plan, but those outside this sector do not participate in the plan. In this case, employees do not perceive the mandatory premium as a tax. They are willing to accept a decrement in wages equal to the full cost of the health insurance plan, since they desire health insurance and can obtain it only by working in this sector. The mandatory payment buys equally valuable services and therefore does not alter the marginal gains from employment. It may even increase the gains from employment—workers may be willing to give up more than the cost of insurance in wages—if desirable health insurance is efficiently provided through the mandatory workplace program. This implies that there are no deadweight losses from the mandate and that revenues associated with the mandatory program do not detract from fiscal space. In this scenario, mandatory health insurance generates a Pareto improvement (figure 4.1).

FIGURE 4.1   Labor Market Effects of Mandated Health Insurance

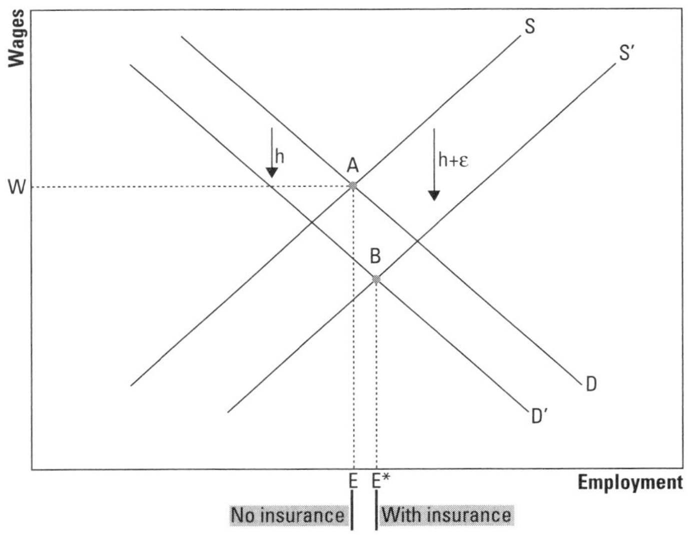

Source: Authors.
Note: Point A = no health insurance; point B = nonuniversal social health insurance; h = the cost of benefits; ε = the amount that workers value benefit in excess of cost.

This favorable situation exists only as long as workers value the health insurance package at (at least) its full cost. If health insurance is available to nonworkers at a lower cost (for example, through a publicly financed program), workers will not be willing to trade wages for mandatory health insurance benefits 1:1 and there will be deadweight losses. If worker premium payments are used to finance benefits for nonworkers (such as the unemployed), these additional payments will be perceived as taxes. The payments will alter the marginal benefit of working, generating deadweight losses and reducing fiscal space.

Labor Market Effects

While nonuniversal social insurance programs limit deadweight losses, they may generate distortions within the labor market. First, if the provision of insurance is less costly under the mandatory program than otherwise, the existence of the mandate will reduce the total cost of labor in the covered sectors. Some workers will be willing to accept reductions in wages greater than the cost of coverage in order to obtain access to health insurance. The mandate may artificially induce growth of the formal sector.

Second, the opportunity to obtain insurance through the mandatory program may make jobs in the covered sectors particularly attractive to workers who value health insurance more than average. Workers who value coverage highly may make job choices based on coverage and not productivity. As a result, worker mobility may decrease, leading to labor market inefficiencies.

Summary

As the above discussion suggests, there is an inherent tension in the design of a social insurance program. Mandatory insurance programs that are narrow in scope and cover only one economic sector can, at least in principle, generate Pareto improvements for the limited population they serve. Narrowing the program can, however, generate distortions in favor of the covered sector and reduce worker mobility. Moreover, narrow programs do not address the widespread need for health care financing and do not generate redistribution. Efforts to expand the comprehensiveness of services and populations covered in these programs can, however, generate deadweight losses and consume fiscal space. A "social insurance" program that covers the entire population and the full scope of services is simply a national health insurance (or national health service) program financed through a payroll tax.

DESIGN CONSIDERATIONS

As the above discussion suggests, social health insurance can take a wide variety of forms, from very narrow programs to near-universal initiatives. Social insurance arrangements tend to evolve over time, extending to additional populations and encompassing additional benefits, but they build off initial structure, which should be carefully developed. The key initial considerations in designing that structure are determining who will be covered (the breadth of coverage) and what benefits will be included (the depth of that coverage).

Breadth of Coverage: Who Is Covered?

European social insurance programs generally began by covering narrow swathes of the population. As late as 1950, the German social insurance program covered only 70 percent of the working population. This narrow program became the base of the later expansion to the full population. Programs initially aimed at a narrow base offer the opportunity to develop credible and functioning administrative structures. These narrow programs do not, however, address the needs of much of the population or redistribute income and may not be politically acceptable.

The narrowest social insurance program (arguably not a social insurance program at all) limits participation to civil servants. The compensation package offered government employees (financed through other forms of taxation) often takes the form of both wages and benefits such as health insurance.

The first type of expansion from a civil service base would be to employees of firms in the formal economy. In effect, this was the form taken by Bismarck's original program. In this context, *formal sector employment* may be defined as work situations in which employees are already likely to be subject to taxes (payroll or income). Formal sector employees could be required to participate in the mandatory health insurance pool, paying premiums through the workplace.

The next natural extension to this population is to dependents of formal sector employees. A further extension would be to retirees and those on temporary layoff from the formal sector.

Finally, a mandatory health insurance system could permit voluntary opt-in by other sectors. Informal sector workers could choose to participate in the system, paying premiums and joining the risk pool.

Further expansions of the SHI model tend toward universal health insurance systems. The notable difference between a social insurance–based and universal health insurance system is that SHI models continue to rely on payroll taxes or quasi-premiums as a major source of revenue.

Insights on Breadth of Coverage from Economic Theory

Economic theory suggests that the choice of whom to cover through a mandatory health insurance program depends on preferences about health insurance, the nature of the risk pool, and the nature of the labor market, as well as on the administrative feasibility of financing and governing the system. Targeting the program to those who value it most highly reduces deadweight losses. However, targeting also narrows the extent of redistribution.

Demand for Health Insurance

In theory, the relation between the demand for health insurance and income is ambiguous, depending on (among other things) the marginal utility of wealth and the relation between income and losses when sick. Therefore, the income elasticity of demand for insurance is mainly an empirical question. Findings reported in Phelps (1997) suggest that empirical estimates of the income elasticity of insurance are generally positive, though probably smaller than 1. This unexpected result—that the demand for insurance rises with income—occurs, in part, because of the nature of demand for health care services.

The demand for health care services (and for higher-quality health care services) is likely to be increasing with income and, particularly, with wages, so that private health care spending is likely to rise as wages rise. Following the theoretical work of Grossman (1972), health status can be written as a function of a set of inputs including medical care or other market inputs that improve health and time spent on health-improving activities. Other factors, such as education, are not direct inputs into health but can affect individuals' ability to use inputs in the production process. The general production function for health status would therefore take the following form:

Health status = f (medical inputs, time spent on health; education, other factors).

Health status is a capital good with both a stock and a flow. Individuals purchase health and spend time maintaining their health when healthy and when sick. Sickness can be viewed as a negative shock to the stock of health capital. In times of sickness, more investment in medical care and time spent on health-improving activity is required to maintain a given level of health stock. It is generally assumed that the inputs to health exhibit diminishing returns, that is, increases in the inputs to health have larger effects at low levels of health stock than at high levels of health stock.

As with any good, the demand for medical inputs depends on the price of medical care (in the absence of insurance coverage), the price of time spent on health, and the individual's income and earnings. In this conceptual model of health production, higher levels of resources result in higher spending on all "normal" goods, including medical care. The amount of time spent on health depends on the opportunity cost of time (usually defined as the person's wage) and the degree to which time can substitute for direct spending on medical care.

Higher income is also likely to affect the quality and nature of health care demanded. Publicly available health care services are likely to be less attractive to middle- and higher-income people. Lower-income people may not be willing to pay premiums to obtain access to care that is superior (in some respect) to freely available, publicly financed care.

Empirical evidence from the RAND Health Insurance Experiment (Manning et al. 1987) and elsewhere confirms individuals' responsiveness to the price of medical care. The findings from the experiment show that the use of medical services responds to changes in the out-of-pocket cost of care. The findings also confirm the positive correlation between income and the use of any health care services, although low-income individuals were found to use more inpatient services. Health status was also found to be a strong predictor of expenditure levels, although there were no differential responses to changes in the out-of-pocket price by health status.

In sum, theory suggests that the demand for health insurance services is likely to be greatest among individuals with a high price of time and high income. Their high price of time means that this group will likely prefer the use of medical care services to sick time. High income suggests that they will be able and willing to pay for this care. This is the group most likely to be willing to trade wages for health insurance benefits.

Risk Pool

Health insurance programs operate most efficiently when relatively few people need expensive care and many people not ultimately needing expensive care buy insurance. In a voluntary program, the critical issue is the expected future health status of the insured. As the discussion of selection suggests, voluntary insurance will not work effectively if risk pools contain an unexpectedly high share of sicker people. A mandatory insurance program can force healthy people to pool risks with less healthy people, but even a mandatory insurance program works best if it includes many healthy people and a minority of people with health problems. This skewed distribution allows redistribution from the healthy to the sick to take place. If most of the insured have health problems, mandatory coverage will provide neither affordable insurance protection nor redistributive benefits.

Private insurers use various methods to address the nature of the risk pool. They often base coverage rates on age, gender, and pre-existing conditions. They may require a waiting period before coverage takes effect. Some offer benefits that will attract healthy patients more than sick ones. These strategies are unlikely to be available in a publicly regulated mandatory health insurance program. As long as participation in the program is limited to those who are mandated, these tools are not needed to discourage adverse selection. However, since the public insurer generally does not charge risk-based premiums or impose waiting periods on participants, the potential for significant adverse selection and program failure is high if nonmandated groups are permitted to opt voluntarily into the insurance pool.

Labor Market

Most social insurance programs operate through the workplace. Workplace-based mandates offer some (though not complete) protection again the adverse selection problems described above, as well as offering administrative simplicity.

The cost of offering coverage through the workplace is possible impairment of labor market mobility. The extent of such "job lock" is disputed, but some

U.S. studies suggest that it may reduce mobility by between 10 percent and 25 percent. Job lock is likely to be higher in a system with mandatory insurance in some sectors and no coverage at all in most others. Job lock within a social insurance system is minimized when all interconnected sectors participate in the insurance program.

Job lock will exist in a program targeted to one sector, to the extent that workers often move from that sector to other sectors of the economy. If most workers move from the informal to the formal sector to stay, job lock may not be important. Conversely, if transitions from formal employment to entrepreneurship are important, a characteristic element of the informal sector, job lock may have substantial negative effects on the functioning of the economy.

Household Effects

Economic models of the family (Becker 1973) suggest that benefits eligibility, including health insurance eligibility, may affect marriage or fertility decisions or both, particularly among low-income households where the value of the benefits can be large relative to income. For example, if health insurance for mothers and children is targeted to single-parent families, the cost of marriage (including the potential loss of benefits eligibility) may increase sufficiently on the margin to change family decision making. Health care systems in which benefits eligibility is based on the family head's work status or that differentiate by marital status are at the most risk for such (undesirable) incentive effects.

The empirical literature on the effects of benefits on family decisions has been heavily concentrated in the U.S. welfare literature. Moffitt (1998) summarizes much of the literature in this area and concludes that there are strong effects of welfare, which is heavily biased toward female-headed households, on marriage and fertility rates, as predicted in the theory.

Enforcement of the Mandate

The inability to routinely collect and process health insurance payments is a substantial impediment to the development of private insurance systems in developing countries (Pauly et al. 2006). The same factors may stall the development of a mandatory health insurance scheme.

Mandates are only as good as their enforcement. As enforcement becomes more difficult, the mandatory program will become subject to adverse selection. Only firms that benefit disproportionately from participating in the risk pool will comply with the payment mandate.

Governance

Social insurance programs have advantages in governance over universal, general revenue–funded programs. As long as there is a strong connection between premiums paid and benefits received, program beneficiaries have a direct interest in ensuring that costs remain under control and, conversely, that benefits remain adequate. The same connection between payments and benefits that reduces the deadweight losses associated with mandatory nonuniversal insurance can improve program governance.

When workers are insulated from the costs of the health insurance program, these governance advantages do not exist. Workers will prefer more generous coverage, but will not be mindful of the additional cost.

Implications of Theory for Coverage Options

Policy makers usually prefer social insurance options that cover large segments of the population, but these are likely to be costly and to intrude deeply on fiscal space. The economic framework we have described has several implications for the range of coverage options, between civil service–only and nearly universal coverage.

Higher-income, higher-wage workers in the civil service and formal sector are likely to have the greatest demand for health insurance coverage and be the most willing to trade wages for benefits. Most are likely to be healthy, so the risk pool will contain an appropriate mix of high- and low-cost cases. Mandating coverage only in the context of formal employment arrangements will also facilitate collection of premiums and enforcement of the mandate.

Civil service–only arrangements are the easiest to implement but are likely to encounter problems of governance. Government managers often face a soft budget constraint. If increases in health care spending buy services that civil servants would not be willing to offset with lower wages, managers may simply use general revenues to support the health insurance plan. Extension of the program to formal sector employees may help offset the governance inefficiencies associated with soft budget constraints in the public sector.

Expanding a formal sector employment-based program to cover workers' dependents retains the basic structure of coverage. Workers should be willing to accept lower wages in exchange for health insurance participation for their family members. Expansion to dependents, however, substantially increases complexity and may interfere with household formation, as regulations must define the treatment of, for example, two-worker households, divorced families, and widows. Dependent coverage also introduces an element of cross-subsidization from smaller to larger families. Moreover, such expansions are likely to raise the proportion of unhealthy to healthy people within the risk pool.

An expansion to retired or laid-off workers also fits with the general social insurance scheme. Here, workers pay, through lower wages today, for benefits they will or may receive in the future. Problems with these arrangements arise if health care costs increase. In that situation, payments made into the system do not cover current costs, and new revenues must be generated for ex-workers. Current workers are likely to treat these additional payments as new taxes.

Expansion to other populations, while increasing redistribution, reduces the low-deadweight loss, low-selection advantages of mandatory insurance. A voluntary opt-in program, in which individuals or firms in noncovered sectors may participate in the risk pool, is likely to generate substantial selection against the risk pool. This adverse selection will be exacerbated by the limits on risk rating that are likely to exist under social insurance arrangements. Expansions to unrelated individuals who are not employed will necessitate grafting a substantial income redistribution component onto the social insurance program (discussed below).

Depth of Coverage: What Services Are Covered?

The next issue to be considered in designing a social insurance program is the depth of coverage: what services will be covered? Designing a benefits package is a problem in all types of insurance. All insurance arrangements must consider, for example, whether to cover only catastrophic costs or to include preventive and routine services (discussed below). Here the focus is on the relation between social insurance arrangements in particular and the general nature of covered benefits.

In virtually all contexts, social insurance coexists with other government financing of health services. The scope of benefits covered by social insurance may substitute for, supplement, or complement the range of government-financed services. Social insurance may provide primary coverage (it may be the only coverage held by the insured) or it may provide duplicate coverage (including services already covered under coexisting public financing). Coverage for public health services, including those associated with the treatment of endemic diseases (such as HIV and malaria) and those associated with the Millennium Development Goals might substitute social insurance payments for public financing. Likewise, social insurance might cover services provided by publicly financed hospitals or physicians. Coverage of much medical treatment and of income replacement would likely supplement existing government financing. In contexts in which governments finance some tertiary care, coverage of diagnostic services often complements existing government financing. Finally, social insurance could be designed to provide complementary "front-end" coverage, with maximum benefit limits, while public financing might offer further protection against catastrophic costs.

Social insurance arrangements often operate with only one benefits package, but beneficiaries could be offered choices of benefits. Social insurance arrangements might also coexist with private insurance. In many developed countries, supplemental private insurance is offered to social insurance beneficiaries, offering insurance for noncovered services, protecting them against large copayment costs, or offering coverage out-of-country for services that are not available locally.

Insights on Depth of Coverage from Economic Theory

The choice of benefits must take into account the value beneficiaries obtain from coverage (which determines their willingness to pay for it), and the implications for the government-financed system of decisions made by social insurance beneficiaries.

Substitute Services

Governments concerned about budgets find social insurance most attractive when it leads beneficiaries to substitute private dollars for existing government spending. Unfortunately, social insurance participants are unlikely to be willing to pay premiums for services they could otherwise receive at no cost. Requiring payment for undervalued services transforms a portion of the social insurance premium into a tax, simply substituting one form of public financing for another. This relationship limits the extent to which social insurance benefits should be designed to cover publicly provided services.

Governments may also wish to use the social insurance program to generate positive health-related externalities. For example, social insurance programs could be required to cover measures for the prevention of infectious disease. The social insurance arrangement does not, however, inherently subsidize the provision of positive externalities. If governments wish to subsidize such activities, they will need to use tax-based revenues to do so.

A final means of using social insurance to substitute for general revenue financing is through mandatory coverage of services provided in publicly financed facilities or by publicly financed providers. If beneficiaries would otherwise receive services in these facilities free of direct charge, they are unlikely to be willing to pay premiums for identical access.

The situation is somewhat different if beneficiaries would otherwise be required to pay fees for publicly financed services or facilities. In that case, social insurance premiums offer the benefit of limiting costs associated with these fees. Governments may be tempted, however, to use social insurance payments as a substitute both for out-of-pocket costs and for public funds. They may, for example, set fee schedules for social insurance payments that substantially exceed the schedules that would otherwise prevail. This strategy undermines social insurance and is also likely to lead to poor governance of the publicly financed facilities themselves.

Supplemental Services

The most economically efficient set of services to cover through social insurance are those that supplement services already provided through government financing. Supplementary services may be services that would otherwise be purchased through out-of-pocket spending, services that would be highly valued but out of reach without insurance, or improved access to publicly financed services. For example, social insurance could afford people greater choice of providers within the public system or quicker access to public services.

Decisions about which supplemental services to include should consider standard insurance principles. In general, insurance is most useful when it covers substantial, unanticipated, and relatively rare events. Health insurance is most efficient when the services covered have a low price elasticity of demand, so that insurance does not induce excess utilization. Health insurance is also efficient for services that are very costly but also very valuable in poor-health states (where the state-contingent income elasticity of demand is high).

Another important category of supplemental "service" that might be included in a social insurance arrangement is coverage for lost work time. Indeed, Bismarck's original insurance arrangement covered sick pay only, not the cost of medical treatment. In most developing countries, formal insurance against lost earnings due to illness does not exist, although some general-revenue or voluntarily financed health care services may be available.

Complementary Services

Establishing a social insurance arrangement is (in part) intended as a way of expanding access to health care services without costing additional general revenue. Under the wrong benefit design, however, social insurance may increase demands on general revenue–financed health services. This can occur if benefits under social insurance complement those provided by the public sector. In this case, the social insurance scheme diverts funds otherwise available for redistributive purposes. Paradoxically, social insurance in this circumstance can move public financing in a pro-rich direction.

This pattern occurs most frequently when social insurance benefits include improved access to outpatient services, while the public system finances care in hospitals. Increased access to outpatient services leads to more diagnosis of medically responsive conditions. These additional diagnoses generate a demand for more hospital care. This care is financed through general revenues, however, rather than through the social insurance system.

Substantial evidence of these negative externalities of complementary insurance exists in the developed-country context. In Canada, people with private pharmaceutical coverage buy more prescription drugs (financed through the private insurance premium) and also make more visits to physicians (financed through general revenue). Controlling for health status and other characteristics, people with pharmaceutical coverage in Canada use about 5 percent more physician visits than do those without such coverage (Stabile 2001). In the U.S. Medicare system, supplemental "Medigap" policies cover coinsurance for services obtained in the public system. People with Medigap coverage have public expenditures that are about 6 percent higher than those of people without such private coverage (Atherly 2002).

Optional Benefits

Some social insurance arrangements allow choice among benefits. Choice of benefits packages helps to ensure that people with diverse preferences can obtain coverage that they are willing to pay for. Such choice can also generate risk-based selection among benefits packages, however, segmenting the risk pool. Ultimately, risk-based selection of benefits can lead to the disappearance of insurance coverage for chronic disease benefits and other benefits where selection pressure is strong.

Implications of Theory for Benefits Package Options

The simplest design for social insurance benefits is to cover only services people would otherwise pay for out of pocket, and perhaps to compensate for earnings lost due to illness. Expanding benefits to include externality-producing public health services, or public health and treatment services already financed through general revenues, will reduce beneficiaries' willingness to pay social insurance premiums.

At the same time, it is critical that social insurance benefits packages mandate the inclusion of the full scope of health care services. If benefits packages fail to mandate coverage of costly services that complement those included in the package, social insurance can increase the drain on general revenues. Moreover, because coverage of social insurance arrangements is likely to begin with more highly paid workers, failure to cover the full scope of services can lead government policy to become more pro-rich, diverting resources from services poorer populations need most.

FINANCING MECHANISMS

As the preceding discussion suggests, the narrowest form of social insurance program covers only formal sector employees and insures only services not currently (or well) provided under general revenue financing. Like all insurance arrangements, this social insurance scheme generates redistribution from those who had good years to those who had bad years. It does not, however, incorporate any additional redistribution. Most plans for social insurance go beyond these bare-bones models and therefore require supplementary financing. Next, financing options are considered.

The most basic financing arrangement for social insurance is to replicate a private insurance model and charge a per person premium. Some element of redistribution can be added to a premium-based model by using a capped payroll tax. A more redistributive arrangement uses an open-ended payroll tax. General revenue financing can supplement or substitute for employment-based financing, although the availability of such funding may be very limited in a low-income country context. Premium or tax financing can be complemented by coinsurance or out-of-pocket payments. Such payments can be used to control utilization and also to reduce the level of premiums needed. External donor funding may be available to establish a program in the short run but is unlikely to be a stable source of long-term supplemental funding. Revenues generated in any of these ways can be earmarked for the use of the health care system. Revenues can flow to a single pool or be divided into subpools by industry or region.

Insights on Financing from Economic Theory

Most social insurance programs finance benefits primarily through the workplace. Workplace financing takes the form of premiums, payroll taxes, or capped payroll taxes. In each case, the formal incidence of workplace-financed health insurance may be split between employers and employees. The economic incidence of these payments depends on the nature of social insurance, elasticities of labor supply and demand, and the extent of redistributive payments. The economic incidence of employer payments is also affected by the existence of binding minimum wage laws. If social insurance is combined with a binding minimum wage, payments made by employers may not be offset by reductions in wages paid to employees. In this case, social insurance programs may generate involuntary unemployment. The choice among workplace-based financing approaches depends on financing efficiency, administrative complexity, and governance considerations.

Premiums

Premiums are a fixed amount charged in each insurance (or pay) period. A flat premium collected by the government and required as a condition of participation in the system will not distort labor supply. The premium does not change the relative price of working. The income effect of paying the premiums is offset by the income effect of receiving the health insurance benefit. Premiums are not connected to actual usage and therefore should not alter the demand for health services.

Premium financing of social insurance can become administratively complex if workers are employed part-time or work multiple jobs simultaneously. Premium payments for family members can also generate administrative complexity, particularly in the case of two-earner families. Most systems that use premiums charge a higher amount for individuals with dependents, although these amounts generally do not vary with family size, so that larger families are subsidized.

The economic incidence of nonredistributive premium financing of valuable, nonuniversal, social insurance benefits falls entirely on workers. If premium financing is extended beyond the cost of insurance obtained by the covered employee, it acts as a regressive tax. The amount of the premium does not vary with income and consumes a larger share of income for lower-wage workers.

Capped Payroll Taxes

Capped payroll taxes are a blend between premiums and payroll taxes where the total amount levied on an individual through the payroll tax is capped at a fixed level of salary. In principle, the product of the payroll tax and the salary cap level generate a premium amount. People with earnings below this premium amount are subsidized through general revenue financing of the social insurance system. Alternatively, the cap level can be set above the premium amount, so that redistribution occurs within the administrative structure of the social insurance system itself.

Capped payroll taxes generate at least as much administrative complexity as premiums. Earnings over the year must be aggregated to determine whether an individual has exceeded the cap amount or not. Caps for multiple-earner families should incorporate family, rather than individual, income, which is often impossible for an employer to assess.

Capped payroll taxes incorporate an element of redistribution (especially if financing is kept within the social insurance system). The redistributive component of the payroll tax acts like any other tax, generating deadweight loss. The incidence of the payroll tax component depends on labor supply and demand elasticities. If supply is inelastic, workers pay the tax. If demand is inelastic, firms bear part of the tax.

Open-Ended Payroll Taxes

Payroll taxes are levied on employers or their employees based on either individual worker salaries or the firm's total wage bill. Although the tax can be levied on either employers or employees, many payroll taxes are statutorily split between employers and employees.

Open-ended payroll taxes levied on workers in the formal sector are administratively simpler than premiums or capped payroll taxes. Information about the total wage bill (rather than individual worker earnings) is sufficient to generate the taxable amount. Payroll taxes can be levied on multiple-job holders or workers who move in and out of the labor market. It is difficult, however, to adjust a payroll tax to reflect the number of dependents covered under a policy. Thus, single workers subsidize larger families. By design, payroll taxes are more redistributive and more progressive than either premium or capped-premium financing.

Payroll taxes also make more difficult linking benefits received with payments made. Many workers pay far more through a payroll tax than they expect to receive in benefits. Thus, payroll taxes may provide less incentive to control public costs than would capped or premium-based systems.

General Revenue Financing

General revenues are used to finance part of most social insurance systems. These funds come from income and sales taxes. They are frequently used to top up payments from premiums and payroll taxes, particularly as the scope of coverage extends beyond the workplace. As with a payroll tax, these taxes are distortionary and, like both payroll taxes and premiums, have no effect on individual use of the health care system.

General revenue financing has some advantages over payroll tax financing. Even in a developed country, the tax base for general revenue is broader than payrolls. In developing countries, only a small segment of the population is employed in a formal payroll-based sector, and the small payroll tax base is an especially important consideration. The broader tax base for general revenue financing means that the tax rate imposed on the base can be lower, leading to smaller deadweight loss.

Broader-based taxes can also target more equitably than payroll taxes. For example, payroll taxes favor capital over labor. Households that generate income through sales or through rents will be favored over formal sector workers.

Intergenerational Financing

Health care systems financed through payroll taxes or premiums paid or administered through the workplace need to consider how coverage for nonworkers and retirees is financed. Premiums should include a component insuring an individual's coverage if he or she retires or is displaced from the workplace. If insurance plans are stable over long periods of time, and the working population is a relatively constant share of total population, these premium payments transfer funds from current workers to current retirees and do not generate distortions. However, to the extent that the share of the working population shrinks, or costs increase faster than inflation, or programs are not politically stable, intergenerational transfers increasingly differ from savings. In practice, health care costs routinely rise more quickly than general inflation, so that payroll tax rates or premiums must rise in real terms over time. This raises issues of fairness and stability in the financing structure, with future generations of retirees facing heavier financing burdens or reduced benefits.

Coinsurance/Copayment

The bulk of the financing for any publicly funded health care system is likely to come through one of the mechanisms outlined above, but additional funding can be generated through charges at the point of service. These charges are usually in the form of *coinsurance* (with the patient paying a set percentage of the costs of care) or *copayments* (with the patient paying a set amount of the costs of care).

Coinsurance serves three purposes. First, it raises additional funds from people who use the most care (a true benefit tax), unlike the premiums or payroll taxes, which are determined independently of the amount of care used. Second, by imposing a cost at the time of use, coinsurance dampens demand. Evidence from the RAND Health Insurance Experiment (Manning et al. 1987) shows that copayments or coinsurance decrease demand for health care for most of the population, even when these payments are relatively small. Finally, coinsurance and other user fees deliver payments directly to health care providers, rather than to intermediaries. This may be a valuable feature in situations with high transaction costs or weak insurer governance.

These functions of coinsurance may increase revenues, improve access to providers, or reduce costs, but the revenue, provider access, and forgone care are not distributed evenly across the population. Sicker individuals naturally use more care and therefore pay more coinsurance. Since health and income are highly correlated, the sick individuals are also more likely to be lower income.

Financing and Governance

Social insurance programs that tie benefits received to premiums paid should help to contain the costs of the system. The degree to which social insurance programs generate these governance advantages depends on the structure of the financing system.

The more closely a financing system ties revenue received to benefits paid out, the more likely is cost containment to emerge from the system. This logic dictates the use of earmarked premiums that flow into multiple restricted pools. Beneficiaries can compare premium rates (or payroll tax rates) for their pool to those of other pools. Managers can be held accountable for high costs.

While the use of multiple pools and transparent financing generates governance advantages, it also has costs. Multiple pools are likely to differ in composition (especially over time). Higher-cost pools may not be less efficient in procuring health care services—they may simply serve sicker populations. A close connection between payments and benefits also makes redistribution much more apparent and costly. Larger, more heterogeneous pools permit more internal redistribution and avoid selection problems.

Cross-Subsidization/Risk Equalization within Social Insurance Systems

A key function of insurance is the pooling of resources and risks across individuals. Without enough healthy members, insurance pools, regardless of whether they are public or private, cannot cover the costs of care for individuals who get sick. In systems with multiple pools or plans, formal risk-equalization or public reinsurance programs can help shift resources from healthier groups to sicker groups.

Public insurance programs also have other redistributional goals. One likely goal of a publicly established insurance system is to protect individuals who cannot afford to cover the full cost of insurance themselves. Such redistribution requires pooling resources across incomes. Health insurance programs that contain only sick and low-income individuals will be hard-pressed to be self-sustaining.

Public insurance programs with mandatory participation cross-subsidize costs from rich to poor. When public programs are not mandatory and superior private alternatives exist, individuals with strong preferences for medical care and the resources to exercise those preferences may exit the public program for the private tier (Flood, Stabile, and Kontic 2005). Many jurisdictions with both public and private insurance programs require tax contributions to the public program regardless of the level of participation in order to maintain cross-subsidization across incomes.

Most public financing mechanisms cross-subsidize from young to old, from individuals to families, and often from wealthy to poorer regions. However, depending on the financing mechanism used and the extent of tax-based redistribution, programs can have varying degrees of cross-subsidization. Payroll taxes are levied only on people who work, thereby cross-subsidizing those who do not work, and those with multiple dependents. Premiums generally vary by dependent status (though not generally by age or region), but the difference in premiums does not generally account for the difference in utilization. Thus, public premium-based programs generate redistribution from the currently healthy to the currently sick.

Implications of Economic Theory for Social Insurance Financing

Social insurance arrangements can operate almost like private insurance—using premium financing, with premiums rising for coverage of dependents and with revenues directed to multiple pools organized by region or industry. This type of arrangement is economically efficient (and may even be a Pareto improvement), has high accountability, and is likely to generate good governance. It will, however, generate very little redistribution.

Most systems are likely to use financing arrangements that incorporate an additional degree of redistribution. Additional redistribution could come from the social insurance financing mechanism (through a capped or open-ended payroll tax) or through general revenue financing.

In most cases, a social insurance system, organized around the workplace, offers the greatest benefits to formal sector employees and their dependents. This group generally constitutes a relatively well-off segment of the total population. Once a social insurance system is in place, the payroll tax (or premiums) imposed on this population could be increased to progressively finance additional redistribution.

A broad-based "social insurance" system can evolve into a national health insurance system with payroll-tax financing. Since payroll taxes depend on a narrower revenue base than more broad-based revenue sources, these arrangements are likely to be inefficient. Thus, economic theory suggests that narrow social-insurance arrangements should eventually be supplemented with general revenue (consumption or income) financing as the population covered broadens away from the formal sector labor market. Expanding the social insurance system too broadly, however, will eliminate the efficiency and governance gains that accrue to narrower social insurance arrangements. There may be less of a check on health care spending and on the power of health care provider interest groups once spending is no longer linked directly to payroll tax rates.

NOTES

1. For an overview, see Hsiao and Shaw (2007).

2. The reduction in adverse selection that can be achieved through mandatory risk pooling can also be accomplished through mandatory systems of side payments within the context of a private health insurance system. Such risk equalization arrangements cross-subsidize health insurance premiums from the healthy to the sick.

REFERENCES

Atherly, Adam. 2002. "The Effect of Medicare Supplemental Insurance on Medicare Expenditures." *International Journal of Health Care Finance and Economics* 2 (2): 137–62.

Becker, Gary S. 1973. "A Theory of Marriage: Part I." *Journal of Political Economy* 81 (4): 813–46.

Flood, Colleen M., Mark Stabile, and Sasha Kontic. 2005. "Finding Health Policy 'Arbitrary': The Evidence on Waiting, Dying, and Two-Tier Systems." In *Access to Care, Access to Justice: The Legal Debate over Private Health Insurance in Canada*, ed. Colleen M. Flood, Kent Roach, and Lorne Sossin, 296–322. Toronto: University of Toronto Press.

Grossman, Michael. 1972. "On the Concept of Health Capital and the Demand for Health." *Journal of Political Economy* 80 (2): 223–55.

Hsiao, William C., and Paul R. Shaw. 2007. *Social Health Insurance for Developing Nations*. WBI Development Studies. Washington, DC: World Bank.

Manning, Willard G., Joseph P. Newhouse, Naihua Duan, Emmett B. Keeler, and Arleen Leibowitz. 1987. "Health Insurance and the Demand for Medical Care: Evidence from a Randomized Experiment." *American Economic Review* 77 (3): 251–77.

Moffitt, Robert A. 1998. "The Effect of Welfare on Marriage and Fertility: What Do We Know and What Do We Need to Know?" In *Welfare, the Family, and Reproductive Behavior*, ed. Robert A. Moffitt, 50–97. Washington, DC: National Research Council.

Pauly, Mark V., Peter Zweifel, Richard M. Scheffler, Alexander S. Preker, and Mark Bassett. 2006. "Private Health Insurance in Developing Countries." *Health Affairs* 25 (2): 369–79.

Phelps, Charles E. 1997. *Health Economics*. 2nd ed. New York: Addison-Wesley.

Stabile, Mark. 2001. "Private Insurance Subsidies and Public Health Care Markets: Evidence from Canada." *Canadian Journal of Economics* 34 (4): 921–42.

Summers, Lawrence H. 1989. "Some Simple Economics of Mandated Benefits." *American Economic Review* 79 (2): 177–83.

CHAPTER 5

Binding Constraints on Public Funding: Prospects for Creating "Fiscal Space"

Peter S. Heller

Never has there been a time when the visibility of the health problems of low-income countries (LICs) has been so prominent in the world's policy circles. Industrial governments have scaled up their aid for spending on HIV/AIDS treatment and prevention programs; major foundations are providing major financing of immunization and vaccination programs as well as research efforts to develop vaccines and cures for pervasive LIC diseases; nongovernmental organizations (NGOs) have intensified their involvement in the delivery of health services; and government leaders now speak to the worry of a global flu pandemic. Overall spending in the health sector has increased dramatically in some cases, and countries are now grappling with how to staff clinics, hospitals, and vaccination programs. These efforts in the health sector are occurring in the context of the wider global concern about the financial costs of meeting the Millennium Development Goals (MDGs), since these will involve spending on education, water, sanitation, and housing, as well as the physical infrastructure needed to foster rapid economic growth.

In this environment, concerns have emerged as to how to find the fiscal resources (or "fiscal space") required to finance the required spending on health. Will macroeconomic constraints prove an independent limiting factor on what governments can spend? In what follows, I will try to clarify the issues that are involved in the fiscal space debate—describing how fiscal space can be created, indicating the macro- and microeconomic factors that may limit a government's capacity to expand health sector spending, and underscoring the importance of budget sustainability as a factor that needs careful consideration as governments elaborate scaling-up plans. I will use the cases of Malawi, Zambia, and Tanzania to illustrate some of the issues involved.

WHAT ARE THE SOURCES OF "FISCAL SPACE"?

In the broadest sense, *fiscal space* can be defined as the capacity of government to provide additional budgetary resources for a desired purpose without any prejudice to the sustainability of its financial position. The desire is to make additional resources available for some form of meritorious government spending (or tax reduction). In principle, there are different ways in which a government can create fiscal space. Additional revenues can be raised through tax measures or by strengthening tax administration.

Low-priority expenditures can be cut in order to make room for more desirable ones. Resources can be borrowed, either from domestic or from external sources. Fiscal space may also be obtained if a government receives grants from outside sources. And, finally, governments can use their ability to print money to finance public programs.

Raising the revenue share in gross domestic product is an obvious option for countries with low tax burdens. For LICs, raising the tax share to at least 15 percent of GDP should be seen as a minimum objective. Thus, in the case of Tanzania, with a tax ratio below 13 percent, some fiscal space from this source would appear possible. But for countries that have higher tax burdens (for example, Zambia and Malawi at 17 and 21 percent of GDP, respectively), further increases may prove difficult. Often, raising the burden requires efforts to strengthen tax administration or reduce politically popular exemptions, since tax rates are already high (for example, in Malawi and Zambia, the value added tax [VAT] rate is 17.5 percent, and in Tanzania, it is even higher at 20 percent). Even the most ambitious African countries have taken a number of years to raise their tax ratios to GDP by several percentage points. Mobilization of revenues for earmarked purposes (for example, earmarking gasoline excises to road maintenance programs) may be seen as an important vehicle for expanding fiscal space, but such earmarking also creates rigidities. It could result in resources being made available for purposes which may be less critical for growth or poverty reduction than other possible uses (for example, primary education or health care). Earmarking may thus have the effect of crowding out other expenditures such that the fiscal space that is created may, in net terms, be significantly reduced.

Reprioritization of expenditure, by reducing unproductive expenditures, should be the first option for a government seeking to expand meritorious programs. In principal, this would appear appropriate for countries that already have high spending ratios to GDP (for example, Malawi's spending ratio exceeds 40 percent of GDP and Zambia's is above 25 percent of GDP). But finding such fiscal space in this way is also difficult, as governments have significant shares of the budget which are of a largely nondiscretionary character, for example, high interest and wage bills. Reprioritizing expenditure may require a change in subsidy programs, cutbacks in spending on defense and internal security, reduced foreign travel or embassy expenses, and actions to address overstaffing or to weed out ghost workers.

International Monetary Fund (IMF) programs often confront the dilemma that overall wages and salaries of a government have reached an unsustainable level, and yet there is a high return to employing additional staff in certain key sectors, for example, education and health. In principle, this can be reconciled through reduced spending on wages and salaries in nonkey sectors at the same time as spending for critical policy programs is increased. In practice, realizing such a strategy may prove politically difficult to implement quickly.

Fiscal space can also be created by an increase in the efficiency with which services are delivered or transfers targeted. Such strengthening would be appropriate even in favored sectors (for example, rationalizing the approach to delivering medical care). Policies that reduce corruption and improve governance also can create fiscal space. In a similar vein, the donor community increasingly recognizes the fiscal potential that can come from greater "alignment and harmonization" of donor resources. If external resources can be used more efficiently (reducing donor conditionality, eliminating aid-tying, cutting administrative overheads, achieving greater consistency in the meshing of donor spending in a sector, and reducing the administrative overload imposed on recipient country program managers), the more fiscal space can be created.

Government policies that foster significant improvements in the efficiency through which it allocates resources may also facilitate higher and more effective spending in both the public and private sectors. For example, if a government can improve the quality of its own health services, households, even if required to pay user fees, may be able to save resources by reducing spending on inefficient private sector health providers. Conversely, not spending enough in a sector such as health may weaken the sector to the extent that it would, in the future, be costly and time consuming to "rebuild" it. Creating fiscal space by allowing cutbacks in a sector may ultimately be more costly in fiscal space over time.

External grants can clearly provide fiscal space, in contrast to borrowing (which implies the obligation for future debt-service payments). But a sustained and predictable flow of grants is essential, since it reduces the uncertainty as to whether the grant is simply of a one-time character and creates the potential for a scaling-up of expenditure to be maintained in the future. Regrettably, few donors now are willing to make external assistance commitments for more than one or two years. Moreover, the experience of many countries is that grants can prove highly volatile, as a consequence not only of donor decisions and bureaucratic processes but also due to policy slippages by recipient governments. Thus, the fiscal space entailed by additional grants (or concessional loans) may be less than is apparent on the surface.

Expanding programs that entail a "permanent" employment of workers is subject to the risk that further assistance may not come or that the additional fiscal space from any growth-engendered increase in domestic revenues is insufficient. It is risky for government policy makers to assume there is scope for an easy downsizing of a program or cutbacks elsewhere. Temporary employment contracts or the design of programs that may facilitate flexible downsizing may be desirable, but they are often precluded by labor legislation or political economy pressures. Note the difficulties encountered by Zambia in transferring contracts from the public service commission to hospital boards (a shift strongly opposed by the public service union). Perhaps more relevant, when programs are implemented that have high costs of downsizing (for example, antiretroviral treatment of AIDS patients), finance officials may be cautious about exploiting readily available, but only short-term, assistance.

Some have argued that external grants and loans may also reduce the incentive of governments to improve their revenue mobilization efforts and may create dependency and rent-seeking effects within government bureaucracies (Gupta et al. 2004 or Moss, Pettersson, and van de Walle 2006). Assessments of fiscal sustainability necessarily must gauge such disincentive effects, particularly given uncertainties on the long-term sustainability of external assistance inflows. In effect, the fiscal space created in the short term may have a negative impact on available fiscal space in the future if it reduces domestic resource mobilization efforts.

Borrowing represents another option for the financing of additional expenditure. But borrowing, whether domestic or external, implies the need to repay, thus raising the question of whether the return on the expenditure justifies the cost of borrowing, and perhaps even more relevant, whether the spending will enhance future government revenues that can be used to finance the repayment of the loan. Governments may borrow to finance an overall fiscal deficit, rather than a specific project or expenditure program. But such borrowing must then be considered in the context of an assessment of the overall sustainability of a government's debt obligations, in terms of its capacity to service interest and principal repayments. Such assessments typically need to consider, among other things, an economy's prospective growth rate, its potential for exports and remittances, the prospective interest rate environment, the elasticity of revenue to growth, the composition of existing debt (in terms of interest rate, maturity, currencies of borrowing), and the terms of any new debt being considered (IMF 2004) (that is, whether new borrowing is on concessional or at market terms). Certainly, borrowing to finance the recurrent cost of programs, particularly in the health sector, is unlikely to be a reasonable strategy, since it would quickly build up the debt that would then need to be serviced, generating an increased interest burden on the budget.

Domestic borrowing must be managed with particular care, since it can quickly lead to government budgets' being overburdened with debt-service obligations. No possibility exists for such borrowing to be forgiven by external donors through debt-cancellation initiatives. And, as can be illustrated in the cases of Malawi and Zambia, thin domestic capital markets can quickly result in high real interest rates that can prove a heavy burden on a government budget in terms of debt service. Thus, in Malawi and Zambia, domestic debt as a share of GDP has risen sharply in recent years to around 20–25 percent, which, in view of the limited degree of monetization, has resulted in high interest rates of around 20 percent. In contrast, in Tanzania, domestic debt has halved in recent years, with a concomitant drop in the treasury bill rate, thus creating fiscal space by the reduction in the overall interest bill.

Printing money to finance additional government spending, that is, seigniorage, offers only limited room for the creation of fiscal space and should be subordinated to the broader objectives of monetary policy, namely, the creation of sufficient liquidity to support an economy's real growth, preferably on a relatively noninflationary basis. In the normal course of growth, seigniorage consistent with a modest single-digit rate of inflation, perhaps in the order of 0.5–1.0 percent of GDP, is created annually, with the associated resources flowing to the government, usually in the form of the profit remittances from the central bank (IMF 2005b). Some NGOs have advocated that higher rates of monetary creation, even at the cost of higher inflation, should be explored as a mechanism for financing increased health outlays. But there are dangers to this approach. Not only does an inflation rate above 10–12 percent of GDP disproportionately hurt the poor (because they are least able to adjust for the loss in their real income), but high inflation is also a deterrent to efficient investment policies.[1] Except in situations where inflation is being gradually brought down from hyperinflationary levels, it would be unusual for the IMF to endorse a program that explicitly targets an inflation rate above 10–12 percent. Thus, in the cases of Malawi and Zambia, the task remains to bring inflation rates down to single digits.

ISSUES THAT ARISE IN THE CREATION OF "FISCAL SPACE"

The foregoing discussion merely lays out the possibilities for how fiscal space can be created. But there are a number of issues that bear on the usability of the resources thereby created.

The Role of Macroeconomic Constraints

Are there limits to the amount of grants and loans that a country can or should absorb? The finance ministry and central bank must contend operationally with judging the macroeconomic impact of higher grant flows on the exchange rate (the so-called "Dutch Disease" concern that higher foreign exchange inflows lead to an appreciation of the currency). The government's financial authorities may be wary about such an appreciation because of its adverse effect on the competitiveness and profitability of export industries. Such an appraisal is not easy, since the extent of the impact is affected by how the grants are used—whether for imports or what economists call "nontraded" goods and services. In this regard, these financial sector officials may have a different perspective than a minister of education or health on the relative benefits of higher grant flows. While the empirical evidence is mixed as to whether higher grants would lead to an appreciation of the currency, two points are worth noting. First, many countries act as if the Dutch Disease issue is a potential problem, as witnessed by their efforts to use monetary policy tools to prevent a currency appreciation (with adverse consequences in terms of domestic interest rates) (IMF 2005a). Secondly, the likelihood of Dutch Disease problems can be minimized if grants are used to finance the purchase of imports or for investments that relax key bottlenecks, particularly in sectors where absorptive capacity constraints cannot be easily overcome simply by imports. So it would be a mistake to assume that higher external grants necessarily must create difficulties for a country's export industry. Coherent and well-thought-out policies can address many potential obstacles.

Moreover even if, with all best efforts, the Dutch Disease issue remains a relevant concern, its consequences must be weighed against the long-term benefits of the spending that can be financed by higher foreign aid inflows, namely, investments that address key deficiencies in human capital or physical infrastructural bottlenecks that limit the capacity of a country's economy to escape from a low-level poverty trap. The short-to-medium cost of some erosion of competitiveness may be thus worth accepting if the long-run benefits are large enough.

Fiscal Sustainability

Explicit in the definition of fiscal space is the link to the concept of fiscal sustainability. This relates to the capacity of a government, at least in the future, to finance its desired expenditure programs as well as service any debt obligations (including those that may arise if the created fiscal space arises from government borrowing).[2] This has a number of implications. First, it suggests that exploitation of fiscal space requires a judgment that higher expenditure in the short term, and any associated future expenditures, can be financed from current and future revenues. If an expenditure project is debt financed, it should be assessed in terms of its impact on the underlying growth rate or by its effect on a country's capacity to generate the revenue needed to service that debt.

Secondly, the definition forces attention on the medium-term implications of the spending programs for which fiscal space is created in a given year. Are the expenditures for which fiscal space is created likely to be concentrated in the immediate term? Or are the desired expenditures likely to require future expenditures, in which case some fiscal space will be needed in the future as well? To illustrate, budgetary room could be made available in a given budget year to finance a meritorious objective—say, a one-time training program for government civil servants. Yet there are many types of government expenditures—particularly in the health sector, where the initial spending will have implications for subsequent spending on operations and maintenance that would require the availability of future budgetary resources. In particular, for many of the programs for which fiscal space is now being advocated in the health sector, the desire is for higher expenditures that can be sustained over a long period of time, for example, antiretroviral treatment programs for AIDS patients. In either case, it would be insufficient to create fiscal space in the first year without ensuring the creation of similar fiscal space in future years to cover these requirements.

Thirdly, this last point underscores that any consideration of fiscal space must be made in the context of at least a medium-term expenditure framework that has a comprehensive perspective on the government's expenditure priorities. If there is a possibility that the fiscal space that allows for today's additional expenditure will not be replicated in the future, governments may find that they are forced to either underfund the new initiative or cut back on other expenditure programs in the future. Thus, fiscal space should not be seen strictly as an issue associated with a specific sector. It is necessary to assess the scope for higher spending within the context of a comprehensive and forward-looking fiscal and budgetary framework (Foster 2005; World Bank–WHO 2005). Governments have an obligation to weigh the relative merits of spending across different sectors, since initiatives in one sphere may ultimately have crowding-out effects on others.

Competition for Fiscal Space

A critical fact of life with regard to fiscal space is that there are multiple competitors for it. And while there are many who advocate the exceptionality of the health sector, there are others who would also attach a higher priority to investments that will facilitate rapid economic growth. Even those who are motivated by health concerns recognize the importance of investments in water, sanitation, agriculture, and other income-creating sectors. Also, in assessing the overall fiscal framework, a government must take account of the possibility that a higher level of spending in a sector, even if financed from external grant flows, may have ripple effects on spending in other sectors. Thus, an effort to improve the financial compensation of health workers can create irresistible pressures for wage increases in other parts of the public sector for which external grant flows are not available. Finding the financial resources to fund these other programs may bump against overall fiscal resource ceilings.

Absorptive Capacity, Governance, and Other Factors Limiting the Exploitation of Fiscal Space

The issue is often raised of whether a government can "absorb" a higher level of external resource inflows for spending in a sector. The term "absorptive capacity" can be interpreted in many ways, extending to separate concerns ranging from the availability of the required skilled workforce to deliver services, to the availability of managerial staff to organize the scaling-up of programs, to the existence of critical physical infrastructure, to the governance capacity of a government to use resources well, to the strength of public expenditure management systems. Ultimately, these are less issues of fiscal space, and more ones of the potential inefficiencies associated with a rapid scaling-up of expenditure, and the implied reduced cost-effectiveness of such spending. But these various factors may preclude the effective utilization of fiscal space, and may need to be dealt with either before, or at least pari passu with, the efforts to scale up the delivery of services.

The Impact of Sound Macroeconomic Policy Management

Fiscal space can also be created by the pursuit of consistent and effective macroeconomic policies. Some of the volatility in external assistance experienced by many countries has arisen from the failure to implement agreed macroeconomic policy programs. This has resulted in a cessation of donor assistance, with the effective cutbacks in fiscal space dramatically weakening a government's ability to maintain the financing of its level of services. Malawi and Zambia illustrate this problem, where there was high volatility of grants during the period 1990–2003 as a result of macroeconomic policy slippages.

The Effects of the 2005 Debt-Cancellation Initiative

A number of LICs will benefit from the effects of the 2005 G8 initiative in Gleneagles, Scotland, to cancel all debt obligations to the multilateral financial institutions. In the cases of Zambia, Malawi, and Tanzania, the nominal debt-to-GDP ratios will fall sharply (from 65, 82, and 57 percent, respectively, to 10, 20, and 22 percent, respectively). Obviously, there will be some additional fiscal space afforded and this is important, particularly because it is a permanent, predictable stream of resources. But because much of the debt was already on concessional terms, and because much of the debt service was "effectively" financed by new loans from the multilateral agencies, the annual additional resources available on a flow basis to these countries as a consequence of the debt-cancellation initiative will not dramatically enhance the capacity of countries for new spending programs.[3] This initiative will also significantly reduce the net present value of existing debt relative to such economic aggregates as GDP, exports, or government revenues.

Governments will now also have the opportunity to use the fiscal space for creating fiscal infrastructure that can enhance growth prospects, achieve the MDGs, and break out of poverty traps. But past experience with borrowing for unproductive projects highlights the need for any new projects to be financed by borrowing to be carefully appraised in order to ensure they realize high rates of return. Otherwise, these LICs may quickly find their future borrowing capacity to be once again compromised.

CONCLUDING REMARKS

Judgments on fiscal space are inherently country specific, requiring detailed assessments of a government's initial fiscal position, its revenue and expenditure structure, the characteristics of its outstanding debt obligations, the underlying structure of its economy, the prospects for enhanced external resource inflows, and a perspective on the underlying external conditions facing an economy. The basic message of this chapter is that, for most LICs, much of the fiscal space for increased health spending, particularly in the short-to-medium term, is likely to require external financing, with a strong preference for grants. This underscores the importance of greater predictability and longer-term financing by donors if countries are to be enabled to expand employment comfortably in the health sector. Competition for such fiscal space can be anticipated, as countries confront many urgent needs across sectors. While macroeconomic policy constraints are unlikely to be encountered by expanded health sector programs alone, such issues as inflation or the prospect of a real exchange rate appreciation may become relevant if higher aid levels enable a country to scale up spending programs across a wide range of sectors.

NOTES

ACKNOWLEDGMENT: Reprinted, with orthographic and stylistic changes, by permission of Oxford University Press, from "The Prospects of Creating 'Fiscal Space' for the Health Sector," *Health Policy and Planning* 21 (2)(2006): 75–79.

1. Moreover, as inflation increases, the likely fall in the demand for money actually reduces the amount of fiscal space that can be created through seigniorage for any given level of inflation.

2. In considering fiscal sustainability, it is necessary to consider issues of debt sustainability (as noted earlier), the nature of a government's expenditure structure in terms of constructive budget obligations (continuing recurrent expenditures of high priority, such as education, medical care, national security, and so on; implicit social insurance obligations associated with civil service pensions, public pensions), a government's exposure to other contingent fiscal risks (for example, from government guarantees, public-private partnerships), and the elasticity of government revenue to economic growth (Baldacci and Fletcher 2003).

3. On average, relief of debt service to Zambia would amount to US$97 million a year, about US$20 million a year more than the projected flow of budget support grants. In Tanzania, the implementation of the initiative would save on average about US$80 million a year in government external debt-service payments, equivalent to about 10 percent of current annual grant inflows to the budget. In Mali, the average annual debt-service savings through 2015 amount to about US$57 million, or about 1 percent of GDP.

REFERENCES

Baldacci, E., and K. Fletcher. 2003. "A Framework for Fiscal Debt Sustainability Analysis in Low-Income Countries." In *Helping Countries Develop: The Role of Fiscal Policy,* ed. S. Gupta, B. Clements, and G. Inchauste, 130–61. Washington, DC: International Monetary Fund.

Foster, M. 2005. "Fiscal Space and Sustainability—Towards a Solution for the Health Sector." Background paper, High-Level Forum on the Health MDGs, Paris, November 14–25. http://www.hlfhealthmdgs.org/Documents/FiscalSpaceTowardsSolution.pdf.

Gupta, S., B. Clements, A. Pivovarsky, and E. Tiongson. 2004. "Foreign Aid and Revenue Response: Does the Composition of Aid Matter?" In *Helping Countries Develop: The Role of Fiscal Policy,* ed. S. Gupta, B. Clements, and G. Inchauste, 385–406. Washington, DC: International Monetary Fund.

IMF (International Monetary Fund). 2004. "Debt Sustainability in Low-Income Countries—Proposal for an Operational Framework and Policy Implications." Washington, DC: IMF. http://www.imf.org/external/np/pdr/sustain/2004/020304.htm.

———. 2005a. *The Macroeconomics of Managing Increased Aid Inflows: Experiences of Low-Income Countries and Policy Implications*. Washington, DC: IMF.

———. 2005b. "Monetary and Fiscal Policy Design Issues in Low-Income Countries." Washington, DC: IMF.

Moss, T., G. Pettersson, and N. van de Walle. 2006. "An Aid-Institutions Paradox?" Working Paper 74, Center for Global Development, Washington, DC.

World Bank–WHO. 2005. "Fiscal Space and Sustainability from the Perspective of the Health Sector." Background paper, High-Level Forum on the Health MDGs, Paris, November 14–25. http://www.hlfhealthmdgs.org/Documents/FiscalSpacePerspective.pdf.

CHAPTER 6

Universal Coverage: A Global Consensus

Guy Carrin, Inke Mathauer, Ke Xu, and David B. Evans

In 2005, the member states of the World Health Organization (WHO) adopted a resolution encouraging countries to develop health financing systems capable of achieving or maintaining universal coverage of health services—where all people have access to needed health services without the risk of severe financial consequences. In doing this, a major challenge for many countries will be to move away from out-of-pocket payments, which are often used as an important source of fund collection. Prepayment methods will need to be developed or expanded but, in addition to questions of revenue collection, specific attention will also have to be paid to pooling funds to spread risks and to enable their efficient and equitable use. Developing prepayment mechanisms may take time, depending on countries' economic, social, and political contexts. Specific rules for health financing policy will need to be developed, and implementing organizations will need to be tailored to the level that countries can support and sustain. In this chapter a comprehensive framework is proposed, focusing on health financing rules and organizations that can be used to support countries in developing their health financing systems in the search for universal coverage.

INTRODUCTION

Out-of-pocket payments create financial barriers that prevent millions of people each year from seeking and receiving needed health services (Preker, Langenbrunner, and Jakab 2002; Hjortsberg 2003). In addition, many of those who do seek and pay for health services are confronted with financial catastrophe and impoverishment (Xu et al. 2003; Xu et al. 2005; Wagstaff and Van Doorslaer 2003). People who do not use health services at all, or who suffer financial catastrophe, are the extreme. Many others might forgo only some services, or suffer less severe financial consequences imposed by user charges, but people everywhere, at all income levels, seek protection from the financial risks associated with ill health.

A question facing all countries is how their health financing systems can achieve or maintain universal coverage of health services. Recognizing this, in 2005 the member states of WHO adopted a resolution encouraging countries to develop health financing systems aimed at providing universal coverage (WHO 2005a).

This was defined as securing access for all to appropriate promotive, preventive, curative, and rehabilitative services at an affordable cost. Thus, universal coverage incorporates two complementary dimensions in addition to financial risk protection: the extent of population coverage (who is covered) and the extent of health service coverage (what is covered).

In some countries, it will take many years to achieve universal coverage according to the above-mentioned dimensions. This chapter addresses a number of key questions that countries need to address and considers how the responses can be tailored to the specific country context. In addition, it highlights the critical need to pay attention to the role of institutional arrangements and organizations in implementing universal coverage.

SHIFTING TO PREPAYMENT

A first important observation is that many of the world's 1.3 billion people on very low incomes still do not have access to effective and affordable drugs, surgeries, and other interventions because of weaknesses in the health financing system (Preker, Langenbrunner, and Jakab 2002). Investigation of 116 recent household expenditure surveys from 89 countries allowed calculations of the consequences of paying for health services by those who do use them. Up to 13 percent of households face financial catastrophe in any given year because of the charges associated with using health services, and up to 6 percent are pushed below the poverty line. Extrapolating the results globally suggests that around 44 million households suffer severe financial hardship and 25 million are pushed into poverty each year simply because they need to use, and pay for, health services (Xu et al. 2007). Households are considered to suffer financial catastrophe if they spend more than 40 percent of their disposable income—the income remaining after meeting basic food expenditure—on health services. They are often forced to reduce expenditure on other essential items such as housing, clothing, and the education of children to pay for health services. Households are considered impoverished if health expenses push them below the poverty line.

Inability to access health services, catastrophic expenditure, and impoverishment are strongly associated with the extent to which countries rely on out-of-pocket payments as a means of financing their health systems. These payments generally take the form of fees for services (levied by public and/or private sector providers), copayments where insurance does not cover the full cost of care, or direct expenditure for self-treatment often for pharmaceuticals. A major challenge, therefore, to the achievement of universal coverage is finding ways to move away from out-of-pocket payments toward some form of prepayment. Solutions are complex, and countries' economic, social, and political contexts differ, moderating the nature and speed of development of prepayment mechanisms (Mills 2007).

POLICY NORMS IN HEALTH FINANCING

Health financing policy cannot, however, afford to focus solely on how to raise revenues (WHO 2000). It requires concomitant attention to three health financing functions and related specific policy norms (Kutzin 2001; Savedoff and Carrin 2003; Carrin and James 2005b; Schieber et al. 2006): (1) revenue collection, whereby financial contributions should be collected in sufficient quantities, equitably and efficiently; (2) pooling of contributions so that costs of accessing health services are shared and not met only by individuals at the time they fall ill, thus ensuring financial accessibility; and (3) purchasing and/or provision, with contributions being used to purchase or to provide appropriate and effective health interventions in the most efficient and equitable way. Efficiency includes considering the type of services to fund and who should provide them. In addition, and also anticipating the need for cost-containment measures, the identification of an appropriate mix of provider payment methods is warranted.

Active consideration of the policy norms discussed above should steer the development of a universal coverage policy. Some form of legislation or regulation is generally needed to consolidate these norms. For example, revenue collection legislation will usually specify the funds to be raised from taxes or from health insurance contributions, if any vulnerable population groups are exempt, and whether contributions vary by income. In pooling, norms establishing the extent of solidarity are described showing who can benefit from the pooled funds and when. The definition of a detailed health services benefits package may be a response to the norm defined for purchasing, while ways of paying providers will usually require some form of legal agreement.

KEY QUESTIONS

Before initiating reform, policymakers need to address four questions:

- Do political will and stewardship exist?
- Should payment be tax based or covered by health insurance?
- How can we pay?
- How long will reform take?

Do Political Will and Stewardship Exist?

Before a reform toward universal coverage can be initiated, governments need to have the political will and the capacity to exercise good stewardship. Most will also need to consider the extent of diverse preferences within their society. An important case of stewardship is from the Republic of Korea, where it has been suggested that universal coverage implementation benefited from the strong leadership of President Park Jung-Hee in 1977 (Yang and Holst 2007). Thailand is an example of political stewardship that was helped by popular support. A network of civic groups pushed for the introduction of a universal coverage policy. After the elections of January 2001, a policy was introduced that rapidly ensured coverage of the entire population, although this was but the last step of a process that had begun in 1975 with the establishment of free health services for low-income people (WHO 2005b). Some Sub-Saharan African countries are also moving toward universal coverage, including Zambia, whose president declared the abolition of user fees in rural health facilities in April 2006 (MOH, Zambia 2006). Prepayment of health services is being enhanced there due to an increase in government funding supported by external donors. Other countries use an alternative path. For example, Ghana has passed a health insurance law (NHIS, Ghana 2003), and Lesotho has explored the feasibility of social health insurance reform (Mathauer et al. 2007). Kenya's National Hospital Insurance Fund has been examining ways of extending coverage to the informal sector (Mathauer, Schmidt, and Wenyaa 2008), requiring strong political will and stewardship.

Tax-Based or Social Health Insurance?

Often the initial discussions revolve around these two broad choices that, in fact, have a number of common features. Prepayments are compulsory and are generally set according to income. All people make payments (through taxes or through contributions) whether they are sick or not, although people on very low incomes or other vulnerable groups might be exempt. People at low risk are not allowed to opt out although they might be able to take out insurance coverage for services that are not included in the tax or social health insurance funded packages. All people who are sick can draw from the pooled funds, thereby spreading the financial risks of ill health.

In both types of systems, there are substantial differences across countries in the institutional and organizational arrangements used to ensure funds are raised, pooled, and used to purchase or provide services. It is the combination of institutional arrangements and legislation relating to revenue collection, pooling, and purchasing/provision that determines how equitable and efficient a system is, rather than the name that is used to describe it. In fact, the authors have been unable to find evidence that implementation of universal coverage either via tax-based funding or social health insurance is more important to the final outcome (Xu et al. 2007; Carrin et al. 2004).

How Can We Pay?

Many low-income countries are unlikely to be able to finance universal coverage from domestic sources in the short to medium term. In 2003, 48 of 59 low-income countries spent less than US$30 per capita on health. This includes the expenditure derived from external assistance. In 12 of these countries, total health expenditure was less than US$10 per capita. Even a very basic set of services for prevention and treatment would cost in excess of US$34 per year at year 2000 prices (Commission on Macroeconomics and Health 2002).

In most countries with low levels of spending, the bulk of government health expenditure is derived from taxes of various types. Tax-financed domestic financing would have to remain prominent, even if they chose to develop a universal health insurance scheme. In the feasibility analysis of social health insurance in Kenya and Lesotho, for example, maintaining government subsidies was seen as imperative, given that contributions from the formal sector were not able to fully cross-subsidize the informal sector and the poor (Mathauer et al. 2007; Carrin et al. 2007). External donor funding will also be needed to supplement the resources that can be raised domestically. Indeed, if universal coverage is to be achieved, substantial increases, with improved predictability, are still needed in external funding.

How Long Will Reform Take?

International evidence shows that most reforms toward universal coverage have been gradual. Social health insurance systems, for example, usually start by covering formal sector employees and slowly expand to other population groups, often starting with employees' dependents. In most European countries that have achieved universal coverage, the transition took place over many decades, often taking more than 50 years (Barnighausen and Sauerborn 2000; Carrin and James 2005a). More recently, in Costa Rica, the Republic of Korea, and Thailand, reform took between 20 and 30 years.

During the transition process, population coverage often remains incomplete and sometimes may even become more unequal, with the poorest groups the least likely to be protected and often the last to benefit from extended coverage. It is here that existing community, cooperative, and enterprise-based health insurance, as well as other forms of private health insurance, might have a role to play, protecting as many people as possible (Jacobs et al. 2008). Such forms of protection will coexist with compulsory health insurance coverage for particular population groups and with other forms of tax-based funding for particular types of health interventions (for example, prevention and promotion) or for particular population groups (for example, self-employed people and those on very low incomes). Eventually, however, the various forms of health insurance and tax-based funding need to be combined, although this last step can be difficult to achieve if some population groups have better coverage during the transition than others. Figure 6.1 illustrates some of the key health financing options at different stages of the evolution toward universal coverage. Detailed standard paths and timelines for universal coverage, however, are difficult to prescribe.

FIGURE 6.1   Key Health Financing Options at Different Stages of the Evolution toward Universal Coverage

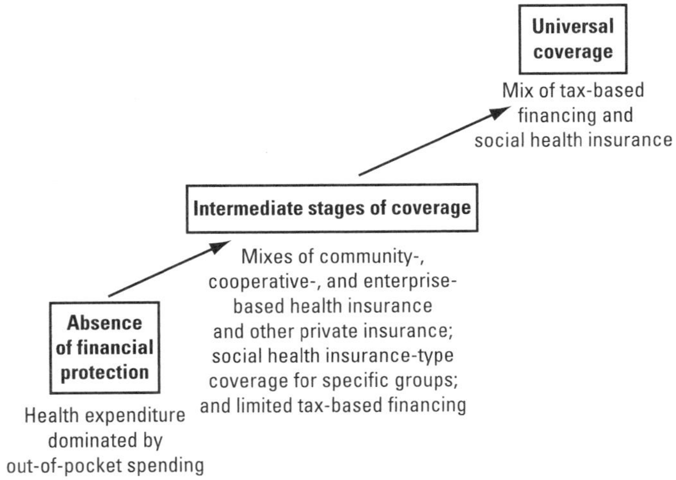

Universal coverage

Mix of tax-based financing and social health insurance

Intermediate stages of coverage

Mixes of community-, cooperative-, and enterprise-based health insurance and other private insurance; social health insurance-type coverage for specific groups; and limited tax-based financing

Absence of financial protection

Health expenditure dominated by out-of-pocket spending

Source: Carrin, James, and Evans 2005.

FACTORS TO CONSIDER

Countries at various stages of economic development and in different social and political contexts have diverse problems and require tailored solutions. Health financing options will be shaped by what countries can sustain. Economic constraints linked to the general state and structure of the economy as well as the size and skill distribution of the labor force will be important to consider, the latter also influencing a country's ability to administer the process. For example, managing a financing system capable of delivering universal coverage requires capacities in accountancy, actuarial analysis, banking, and information processing. The whole process of health financing reform also needs to be monitored and guided, a task that falls naturally on the government. This imposes costs associated with the task of monitoring the process and enforcement of legislation for health financing policy (North 1990).

Broad policy norms and values, which may also be relevant beyond health financing, also codetermine the nature of the implementing organizations and their required tasks. First, it may be stipulated that communities at village or district level be given a voice in health financing. This may then explain the establishment of community-based health insurance schemes in a voluntary setting or the existence of district-level mutual health insurance funds in a compulsory framework. Second, the extent of private sector involvement in the three health financing functions must be decided and appropriate legislation developed.

In India, for example, formal insurance companies are required to expand their activities to the rural and social sectors so that the private sector also offers insurance coverage to parts of the low-income population (Ahuja and Guha-Khasnobis 2005).

Third, the degree of solidarity that can be achieved in health financing is an important factor. An effective system of financial protection for the population as a whole requires a significant amount of cross-subsidization, both from rich to poor and from people at low risk of illness (for example, the young) to people at higher risk (for example, the elderly). Cross-subsidization must be greater, the broader the extent of income inequality in a country, and each country needs to define the appropriate level of solidarity for its own setting. This will have an important impact on the type of organizations that are developed and their tasks. Smaller, geographically based insurance pools allow for more local autonomy but involve less risk pooling across the country as a whole. More extensive pooling arrangements may be established along with an increased acceptance of risk sharing across society's population groups. Finally, health financing policy toward universal coverage is not isolated from national politics, pressure groups, and lobbies. Governments have an important role to play in interacting with stakeholders and guiding the overall public interest as health financing systems develop (Saltman and Ferroussier-Davis 2000). Nevertheless, it is also this political pressure from civil society that may stimulate governments to manifest political will and to exercise good stewardship.

TOWARD A COMPREHENSIVE FRAMEWORK

Achievement of the goal of universal coverage is contingent on the underlying institutional design of the three health financing functions (collection, pooling, and purchasing/provision). The authors propose to integrate the concept of institutional design into a conceptual framework for assessing health financing system reform toward universal coverage. As conceptualized by North (1990), institutions can be understood as "the rules of the game" that guide human and organizational interaction. These rules are the specification of the three health financing functions, as found in legislation and regulations; they are expected to reflect the specific and broad policy norms and values referred to earlier in this chapter.

However, the existence of appropriate rules will not be sufficient to ensure high performance of the health financing system and the attainment or maintenance of universal coverage. Equally important is the way these rules are implemented by organizations, that is, how these rules are carried out and put into practice. Organizations involved in the health financing functions of revenue collection, pooling, and purchasing as well as stewardship may include political bodies (for example, Ministry of Health, regulatory agencies), economic bodies (for example, private health insurance, cooperatives), social bodies (for example, social health insurance agencies, faith-based organizations), and educational bodies (for example, training centers) (North 1990).

Rules and organizations are very much interconnected. In fact, the established rules can restrain or induce people and organizations to do certain things. In other words, rules set incentives and disincentives and as such influence behavior of organizations and individuals and ultimately the outcomes of organizational activities. In many instances, the prevailing rules in a health financing system may not represent the most efficient institutional design to achieve or maintain universal coverage. Hence, when countries seek to move toward universal coverage, there are many explicit institutional design choices to be made, far beyond the question of whether a predominantly tax-based system, social health insurance, or a mixed system is preferred. Table 6.1 illustrates some of the possible rules and organizations that may specify a country's health financing functions and norms in revenue collection, pooling, and purchasing.

TABLE 6.1   Rules and Organizations That May Influence a Country's Health Financing Functions

Type of rule	Legislation and other regulatory provisions of rules	Organizations
Revenue collection		
Taxation rules	Income tax rates range from 15 to 40 percent.	MOF or revenue-collection authority
SHI contribution rules	6 percent contribution rates to be shared 50-50 by employer/employee; informal sector workers with an annual household income of more than US$1,200 pay a flat yearly amount of US$40.	For payroll deductions: SHI fund and MOF For informal sector: NGOs, district authorities, microfinance institutions
Membership/ registration rules	All formal sector employees and civil servants are mandatory members of the SHI scheme; informal sector workers can join voluntarily in a group of more than 20 workers in the same professional area.	SHI fund/registration department; NGOs involved in outreach activities
MOH schedule of user fees	The noninsured pay the established user fees at public and private health facilities.	Public and private health service providers
Pooling		
Pooling across MOH and SHI fund	1 percent of SHI income is transferred to the MOH to subsidize services rendered to the uninsured.	MOH, MOF, SHI fund
Risk equalization rules among SHI funds	Additional resources are provided to SHI funds with high health risk by those SHI funds with low health risks, based on a specific risk-adjustment formula.	Risk-equalization agency
Pooling within the SHI scheme	Contribution rates are income related and not risk related; access is based on need.	SHI fund
Purchasing		
SHI rules on purchasing	The SHI can purchase from both public and private facilities; the SHI must contract all facilities that meet the accreditation standards.	SHI fund/contracts department, health providers associations or health providers, accreditation agency
SHI rules on type and rate of provider remuneration	The SHI remunerates providers on the basis of a case-payment, with predefined rates that vary according to the facility level.	SHI fund/remuneration department, health providers

(continued)

TABLE 6.1   Rules and Organizations That May Influence a Country's Health Financing Functions *(continued)*

Type of rule	*Legislation and other regulatory provisions of rules*	*Organizations*
MOH rules on type and rate of provider remuneration	MOH allocates global budgets to subnational levels based on rational criteria (population characteristics, epidemiological profile, poverty rates within that subnational unit).	MOH, subnational MOH units such as health districts, MOF
Rule on MOH benefits package	MOH provides an essential health services package with services at the primary, secondary, and tertiary levels.	MOH
Rule on benefits package definition of MOH	Services are included based on cost-effectiveness, analysis results, and considerations of disease burden equity. The benefits package is reviewed every two years.	MOH or a national benefits package committee

Source: Authors.

Note: MOF = Ministry of Finance; MOH = Ministry of Health; NGO = nongovernmental organization; SHI = social health insurance.

FIGURE 6.2   Basic Components of the Framework to Guide Health Financing System Reform

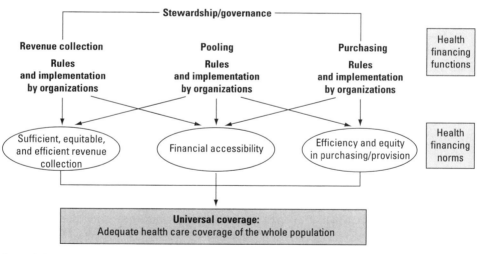

Source: Authors.

Ultimately, it is the combination of specific rules in revenue collection, pooling, and purchasing, as well as the effectiveness of organizations in implementation, that will determine the efficiency and equity of a health financing system. However, before the rules and organizational arrangements can be optimized, it is necessary to assess and understand the existing situation. WHO is developing a framework for doing this, building on North's (1990) concept of institutions and rules and some of the applications that have already been made in the area of health and social protection (Mathauer 2001, 2004). Figure 6.2 outlines the fundamentals of this framework; it focuses on the rules and organizational arrangements currently in force, either explicitly or implicitly, and assesses how they contribute to or detract from the achievement of universal coverage. This forms the basis of plans to modify rules and organizations or to introduce new ones. An example of this framework's application can be found in Mathauer, Cavagnero, and Vivas (2008); Mathauer et al. (2009); and Antunes et al. (2009).

CONCLUSION

The WHO member states have endorsed universal coverage as an important goal for the development of health financing systems but, to achieve this long-term solution, flexible short-term responses are needed. There is no universal formula. Indeed, for many countries, it will take years to achieve universal coverage, and the path is complex. The responses each country takes will be determined partly by their own histories and the way their health financing systems have developed to date, as well as by social preferences relating to concepts of solidarity.

Formulating and implementing health policy toward universal coverage require a multitude of interrelated decisions. The proposed framework links the overall policy goal of universal coverage to the nuts and bolts of health financing policy—the rules and organizational arrangements. This framework can help countries undertake the detailed institutional-organizational analysis required to assess the need for different kinds of change. This assessment should consider fund collection, pooling, and purchasing/provision separately and should also consider the links between the three functions. This will enable a clear assessment of what rules need to be modified or developed and where organizational capacity should be strengthened.

NOTE

ACKNOWLEDGMENT: Reprinted by permission, with stylistic changes, from the *Bulletin of the World Health Organization* 86 (11): 857–63, November 2008, under the title "Universal Coverage of Health Services: Tailoring Its Implementation."

REFERENCES

Ahuja, R., and B. Guha-Khasnobis. 2005. "Micro-Insurance in India: Trends and Strategies for Further Extension." Working Paper 162, Indian Council for Research on International Economic Relations, New Delhi.

Antunes, A., P. Saksena, R. Elovainio, et al. 2009. *Review and Institutional Analysis of the Rwandan Health Financing System.* Geneva and Kigali: WHO, Department of Health Systems Financing, and Ministry of Health, Rwanda.

Barnighausen, T., and R. Sauerborn. 2000. "One Hundred and Eighteen Years of the Ger-man Health Insurance System: Are There Any Lessons for Middle- and Low-Income Countries?" *Social Science in Medicine* 54: 1559–87.

Carrin, G., and C. James. 2005a. "Social Health Insurance: Key Factors Affecting the Transition towards Universal Coverage." *International Social Security Review* 58: 45–64.

———. 2005b. "Key Performance Indicators for the Implementation of Social Health Insurance." *Applied Health Economics and Health Policy* 4: 15–22.

Carrin, G., C. James, M. Adelhardt, O. Doetinchem, P. Eriki, M. Hassan, H. van den Hombergh, J. Kirigia, B. Koemm, R. Korte, R. Krech et al. 2007. "Health Financing Reform in Kenya: Assessing the Social Health Insurance Proposal." *South African Medical Journal* 97: 130–35.

Carrin, G., C. James, and D. Evans. 2005. "Achieving Universal Health Coverage: Developing the Health Financing System." Technical Briefs for Policy-Makers, WHO, Geneva.

Carrin G., R. Zeramdini, P. Musgrove, J.-P. Poullier, N. Valentine, and K. Xu. 2004. "The Impact of the Degree of Risk-Sharing in Health Financing on Health System Attainment." In *Health Financing for Poor People*, ed. A.S. Preker and G. Carrin, 397–416. Washington, DC: World Bank.

Commission on Macroeconomics and Health. 2002. *Macroeconomics and Health: Investing in Health for Economic Development.* Report of the Commission on Macroeconomics and Health. Geneva: WHO.

Hjortsberg, C. 2003. "Why Do the Sick Not Utilise Health Care? The Case of Zambia." *Health Economics* 12: 755–70.

Jacobs, B., M. Bigdeli, M. van Pelt, P. Ir, C. Salze, and B. Criel. 2008. "Bridging Community-Based Health Insurance and Social Protection for Health Care—A Step in the Direction of Universal Coverage?" *Tropical Medicine & International Health* 13: 140–43.

Kutzin, J. 2001. "A Descriptive Framework for Country-Level Analysis of Health Care Financing Arrangements." *Health Policy* 56: 171–204.

Mathauer, I. 2001. *Institutional Analysis Toolkit for Nutrition Programs: Institutional Assessment, Institutional Design, Institutional Capacity Strengthening.* Washington, DC: World Bank.

———. 2004. "Institutional Analysis Toolkit for Safety Net Interventions." Social Protection Discussion Series, no. 0418, World Bank, Washington, DC.

Mathauer, I., E. Cavagnero, and G. Vivas. 2008. *Evaluación institucional del sistema de financiamiento de salud nicaragüense.* Geneva and Washington, DC: WHO and Pan American Health Organization.

Mathauer I., O. Doetinchem, J. Kirigia, and G. Carrin. 2007. "Feasibility Assessment and Financial Projection Results for a Social Health Insurance Scheme in Lesotho." WHO, Geneva.

Mathauer, I., J.-O. Schmidt, and M. Wenyaa. 2008. "Extending Social Health Insurance to the Informal Sector in Kenya: An Assessment of Factors Affecting Demand." *International Journal of Health Planning and Management* 23: 51–68.

Mathauer, I., K. Xu, G. Carrin, and D.B. Evans. 2009. "An Analysis of the Health Financing System of the Republic of Korea and Options to Strengthen Health Financing Performance." WHO, Department of Health Systems Financing, Geneva.

Mills, A. 2007. "Strategies to Achieve Universal Coverage: Are There Lessons from Middle-Income Countries?" Literature review commissioned by the Health Systems Knowledge Network, Commission on the Social Determinants of Health, WHO, Geneva.

MOH (Ministry of Health), Zambia. 2006. "Guidelines on Removal of User Fees in Public Health Facilities in Zambia." Lusaka, MOH.

NHIS (National Health Insurance Scheme), Ghana. 2003. National Health Insurance Law, Act 650. Parliament of Ghana, Accra. http://www.parliament.gh/files/imce/National_Health_Insurance_Act__2003.pdf (accessed September 26, 2008).

North, D.C. 1990. *Institutions, Institutional Change, and Economic Performance*. Cambridge, UK: Cambridge University Press.

Preker, A.S., J. Langenbrunner, and M. Jakab. 2002. "Rich-Poor Differences in Health Care Financing." In *Social Reinsurance: A New Approach to Sustainable Community Health Care Financing*, ed. A.S. Preker and D.M. Dror, 21–36. Washington, DC: World Bank.

Saltman, R.B., and O. Ferroussier-Davis. 2000. "The Concept of Stewardship in Health Policy." *Bulletin of the World Health Organization* 78: 732–39.

Savedoff, W., and G. Carrin. 2003. "Developing Health Financing Policies." In *Health System Performance Assessment: Debates, Methods and Empiricism*. Geneva: WHO.

Schieber, G., C. Baeza, D. Kress, and M. Maier. 2006. "Health Financing Systems in the 21st Century." In *Disease Control Priorities in Developing Countries*, ed. D. Jamison, J. Breman, A. Measham, G. Alleyne, M. Claeson, D. Evans et al., 225–42. 2nd ed. New York: Oxford University Press.

Wagstaff, A., and E. Van Doorslaer. 2003. "Catastrophe and Impoverishment in Paying for Health Care: With Applications to Vietnam 1993–1998." *Health Economics* 12: 921–34.

WHO (World Health Organization). 2000. *The World Health Report 2000: Health Systems: Improving Performance*. Geneva: WHO.

———. 2005a. *Sustainable Health Financing, Universal Coverage and Social Health Insurance*. Geneva: WHO.

———. 2005b. "Social Health Insurance: Selected Case Studies from Asia and the Pacific." New Delhi and Manila: WHO Regional Offices for the Western Pacific and for South-East Asia.

Xu, K., D. Evans, G. Carrin, and A.M. Aguilar-Rivera. 2005. "Designing Health Financing Systems to Reduce Catastrophic Health Expenditure." Technical briefs for policy-makers 2, WHO, Geneva.

Xu, K., D. Evans, G. Carrin, A.M. Aguilar-Rivera, P. Musgrove, and T. Evans. 2007. "Protecting Households from Catastrophic Health Spending." *Health Affairs* 26: 972–83.

Xu, K., D. Evans, K. Kawabata, R. Zeramdini, J. Klavus, and C. Murray. 2003. "Household Catastrophic Health Expenditure: A Multicountry Analysis." *Lancet* 362: 111–17.

Yang, B., and J. Holst. 2007. "Implementation of Health Insurance in Developing Countries: Experience from Selected Asian Countries." In *Extending Social Protection in Health*, ed. J. Holst and A. Brandrup-Lukanow, 158–67. Eschborn, Germany: Deutsche Gesellschaft für Technische Zusammenarbeit (GTZ).

PART 2

From Theory to Practice: Evidence From the Ground

CHAPTER 7

The French Connection in Francophone Africa

Yohana Dukhan, Alexander S. Preker, and François Diop

T he development and current status of health insurance and health financing in Francophone Sub-Saharan African (FSSA) countries are described in
this chapter. The economic, social, political, and institutional factors that
have hampered the development of health insurance are examined, together
with its future prospects. Comparative analyses of different options tested in
these countries (public and private financing, mandatory and voluntary insurance) are also presented in the hope of contributing to the growth of a more
insurance-based financing system.

INTRODUCTION

Health system financing in FSSA and other low-income countries has been characterized by three major trends over the last 30 years.

In the first phase until the 1980s, health care was free and publicly funded and
delivered. Public social security systems developed in most countries between
the 1950s and 1970s, but few of them specifically covered sickness because
health care was already free. Sometimes special provisions were made for family and work injury care but under very specific conditions. Hence, free health
care did not constitute an enabling environment for the development of health
insurance. Beginning in the 1980s, budgetary and macroeconomic difficulties
confronted governments with growing problems of financing, declining quality
of care, mounting inequality in coverage, and proliferating informal payments.
There were no arrangements to make health care available to the poorest people
(Audibert, Mathonnat, and de Roodenbeke 2003).

The second trend, cost recovery (resulting from the Bamako Initiative of
1987), led to user participation in the cost of care. Direct payments by users were
to provide health care facilities with additional resources (to cover all or part
of operating costs), complementing budgetary allocations. These resources were
to be managed at the local level and by the community, in concert with health
care personnel. It was expected that health care centers would operate more efficiently and that the quality of care would improve. However, the problem of
access to care for the poorest persisted: the issues surrounding access to care were
not adequately addressed.

Finally, the third trend, which surfaced in the 1990s, emphasized the development of insurance instruments to protect individuals against health risks

by pooling resources, to mobilize additional resources for the health sector, and to improve the efficiency and quality of care through formal contractual arrangements.

Figure 7.1 shows the main trends in health financing, institutional frameworks, and health coverage since the Independence period in Francophone Africa. It shows that insurance-type mechanisms have emerged fairly recently in Francophone Africa. Two major groups of mechanisms have been tested: mandatory health insurance (MHI) systems and community-based voluntary health insurance (VHI) (mutual health organizations [MHOs] and similar systems). Despite recent MHI reforms in some countries (Côte d'Ivoire, Mali, Rwanda) and movements to extend the mutualist trend in other countries (Mali, Rwanda, Senegal), health insurance coverage remains sparse, and its contribution to financing weak, in the subregion.

Even if experience in developed countries shows that the development of health insurance is a very long process, the literature tends to highlight major economic, social, political, and institutional cultural constraints that account for the low level of implantation and the relatively slow development of health insurance systems in developing countries (Letourmy 2003, 2005; Carrin 2002; Ensor 1999; Griffin and Shaw 1996).

CURRENT STATUS OF HEALTH FINANCING AND HEALTH INSURANCE

The current health financing and health insurance situation in 18 FSSA countries[1] is summarized in this section. These countries share a common history marked by French and Belgian colonial influences and French as the national language. This section shows the heterogeneity among countries in patterns of scaling up health financing and health insurance, also reflected in differences in demographic, social, and economic characteristics (annex table 7A.1).

Health Financing

Public and private health expenditure amounted to US$8.2 billion in FSSA in 2009, an average per capita expenditure of US$35 and a median of US$30. Within the subregion, per capita spending on health varied considerably between the Democratic Republic of Congo, the lowest (US$16), and the Republic of Congo, the highest (US$70). Generally, this spending is below the US$34 threshold recommended by the Commission on Macroeconomics and Health (CMH) as necessary to provide people with essential health services (CMH 2001). Only Burkina Faso, Cameroon, Chad, the Republic of Congo, Côte d'Ivoire, Mali, Rwanda, and Senegal attained the CMH threshold in 2009 (table 7.1).

More than half of the low expenditure is privately financed (average 55 percent). Direct payment by users at the time of service accounts for more than 90 percent of private health expenditure in three quarters of the countries studied.

FIGURE 7.1   Health Insurance and Health Coverage in Francophone Sub-Saharan Africa, 1950 to Present

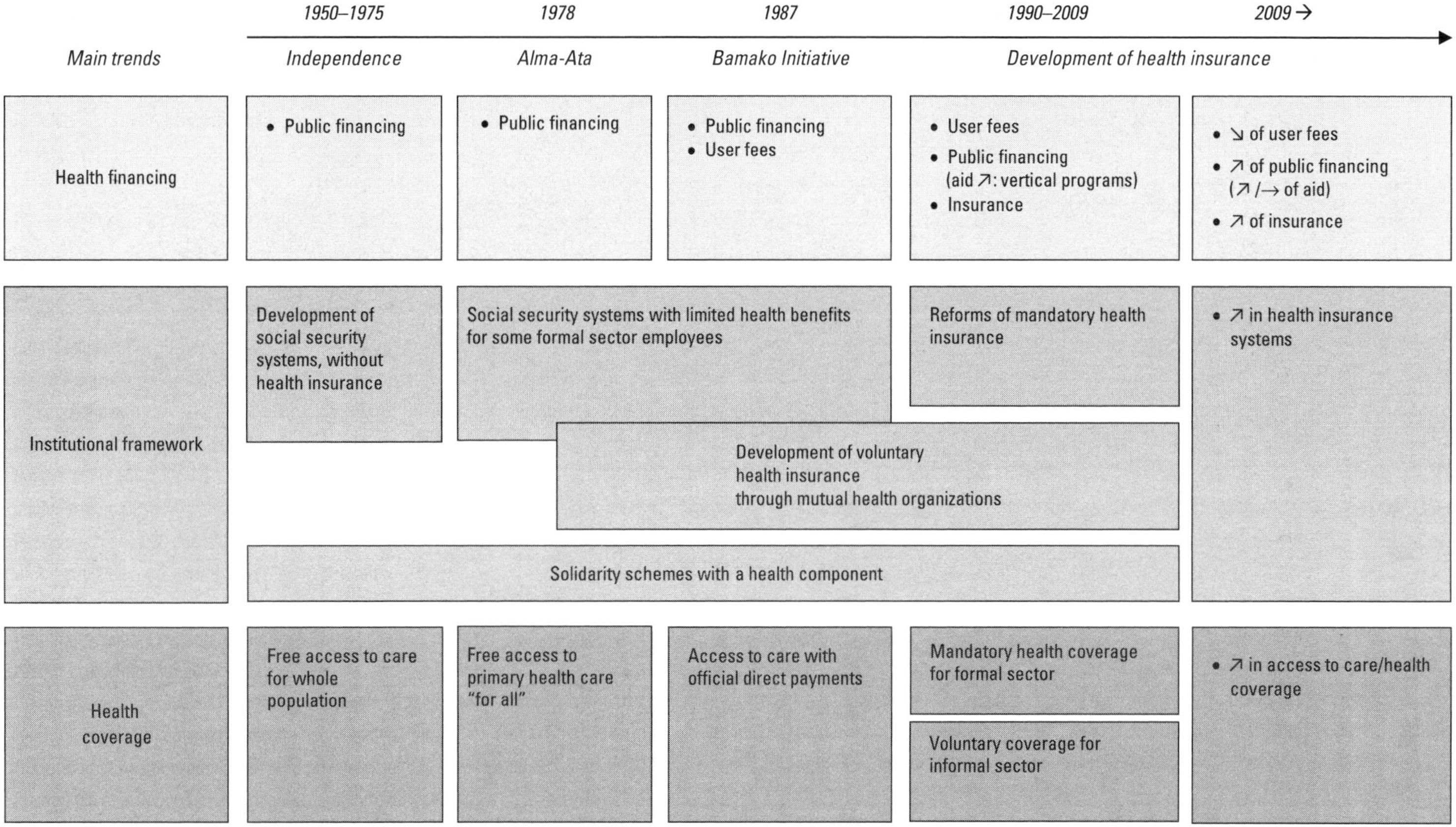

Main trends	*Independence* 1950–1975	*Alma-Ata* 1978	*Bamako Initiative* 1987	*Development of health insurance*	
				1990–2009	2009 →
Health financing	• Public financing	• Public financing	• Public financing • User fees	• User fees • Public financing (aid ↗: vertical programs) • Insurance	• ↘ of user fees • ↗ of public financing (↗ / → of aid) • ↗ of insurance
Institutional framework	Development of social security systems, without health insurance	Social security systems with limited health benefits for some formal sector employees	Development of voluntary health insurance through mutual health organizations Solidarity schemes with a health component	Reforms of mandatory health insurance	• ↗ in health insurance systems
Health coverage	Free access to care for whole population	Free access to primary health care "for all"	Access to care with official direct payments	Mandatory health coverage for formal sector Voluntary coverage for informal sector	• ↗ in access to care/health coverage

Source: Authors.

TABLE 7.1 Health Expenditure in Francophone Sub-Saharan Africa, 2009

Country	GDP/capita (current US$)	Total health expenditure/capita (current US$)	Total health expenditure (% GDP)	Public health expenditure (% THE)	Out-of-pocket spending (% THE)	Social security health expenditure (% THE)	Private prepaid health plans (% THE)	External health expenditure (% THE)	Public health expenditure (% total public expenditure)
Benin	744.9	31.9	4.2	55.2	41.6	0.3	3.3	22.6	8.5
Burkina Faso	516.7	38.1	6.4	61.7	35.6	0.2	1.3	21.9	16.3
Burundi	159.6	19.8	13.1	46.0	34.9	7.5	0.1	44.2	11.8
Cameroon	1,136.5	60.6	5.0	27.1	68.9	1.3	—	8.2	7.8
Central African Republic	453.6	19.3	4.3	38.7	58.3	—	—	40.4	11.0
Chad	610.3	41.8	7.0	55.2	43.3	—	0.1	6.9	13.8
Comoros	832.6	27.8	3.4	61.6	38.4	0	0	15.3	8.0
Congo, Dem. Rep.	160.2	15.6	2.0	23.9	37.4	0	0.1	35.8	5.3
Congo, Rep.	2,600.9	70.1	3.0	53.8	46.2	0	—	7.2	5.1
Côte d'Ivoire	1,105.8	56.5	5.2	20.7	78.4	—	1.0	10.4	1.7
Guinea	407.5	18.8	5.7	15.2	84.3	0.2	0	15.6	4.3
Madagascar	461.2	18.0	4.1	67.1	22.3	—	5.0	28.3	15.1
Mali	691.6	38.4	5.6	47.9	51.8	—	0.3	25.6	9.3
Mauritania	921.0	21.9	2.5	62.6	37.4	0	0	25.6	4.9
Niger	352.1	20.9	6.1	57.6	40.8	0.7	1.4	32.6	14.5
Rwanda	506.5	48.2	9.0	43.2	25.2	2.0	5.8	53.2	16.8
Senegal	1,023.0	58.9	5.7	55.6	34.9	2.3	7.9	14.0	11.6
Togo	431.3	27.3	5.5	23.9	64.1	3.7	3.3	18.5	6.4
Average	728.6	34.5	5.4	45.4	46.9	1.0	1.6	23.7	9.6
Median	563.5	29.9	5.4	50.9	41.2	0.1	0.2	22.3	8.9

Sources: WHO National Health Accounts 2011a; World Bank World Development Indicators 2010.

Note: — = not available; THE = total health expenditure. Private health expenditure is broken down into direct payments, contributions to prepayment systems and risk sharing, and expenditures by nongovernmental organizations (NGOs). NGO expenditures are not presented in this table. This explains why the sum of public expenditure, direct payments, and insurance is not equal to 100 percent in some countries.

For one tier of the country sample (Cameroon, the Central African Republic, Côte d'Ivoire, Guinea, Mali, and Togo), they even exceed 50 percent of total health expenditure (THE) for the sector, reflecting the thin financial protection of individuals against health risks, with potentially disastrous consequences for the poorest. Moreover, in most cases, these revenues do not accrue to the public health sector. Poor quality of care in the public sector as well as household health care preferences (traditional medicine, self-medication) account in part for the volume of private financing outside the public sector.

These figures also confirm the low contribution of insurance to funding the sector. Insurance expenditure accounts for no more than 4 percent of total expenditure except in Madagascar, Rwanda, and Senegal, where insurance amounts to between 6 and 8 percent. Nevertheless, these data have to be interpreted cautiously. The national authorities are not always familiar with the units and ratios of health expenditure, and information is not available in many countries.

Finally, the share of public financing in total health financing is relatively low (45 percent on average). The wide disparity in the countries surveyed is noteworthy, even if it does not seem to be related to revenue levels in the countries. In some very low-income countries (Burkina Faso, Madagascar, Niger), public funding is significant (more than 50 percent of total health expenditure), but much lower in higher-income countries (Cameroon, Côte d'Ivoire, Senegal). In general, the low level of public financing is explained in part by governments' insufficient commitment to the health sector. In 2009, according to National Health Accounts (WHO 2011a), only Burkina Faso, Madagascar, and Rwanda[2] attained the Abuja target of allocating 15 percent of the state budget to health.

Finally, several countries are highly dependent on external aid, which for some of them covers up to 50 percent of their total health expenditure. With such heavy dependence on external aid, aid volatility and disbursement unpredictability are serious problems (Celasun and Walliser 2008).

This was already the setting when the discussions on expanding insurance-type arrangements in Africa began in the 1990s. The development of health insurance is a promising way of financing health care because it is supposed to not only mobilize additional resources but also promote efficiency through the pooling of resources, reduce the number of cases in which lack of cash poses a barrier to health care access, stimulate demand, and reduce inequality, with resources being redistributed under coverage of contributions. The quality of health care is also expected to improve as the payer puts pressure on suppliers. However, after a decade of attempts to enlarge mandatory or optional insurance arrangements, health insurance does not seem yet to have significantly facilitated health financing; its contribution to total financing remains extremely low.

The same observation can be made for access to care and health coverage. Current arrangements and ongoing reforms in some countries are reviewed in the next two subsections.

Medical Coverage and Health Insurance

Medical coverage systems in FSSA vary in form and content from country to country. Mandatory and voluntary coverage systems coexist with varying degrees of functionality. In most countries, health risks are covered by noncontributory[3] as well as contributory schemes. The two dimensions of coverage are measured by breadth, the percentage of the population benefiting from health coverage, and by depth, the type and number of services covered, generally measured by the actuarial value of the benefits package per insured person.

Information about coverage rates under these different schemes is hard to come by, and all data should be interpreted very cautiously. First, coverage rates are not always comparable because they relate to ranges of benefits and health care modalities that differ significantly across countries (table 7.2). Second, most coverage rates are theoretical rather than real, which could mean that the scope of coverage is overestimated, particularly with respect to civil servants. In many countries, the regulations establishing the services are not applied effectively. Finally, the rates do not provide any information on availability of care, capacity of caregivers to provide care, or quality of care. Despite these limitations, table 7.2 presents an estimate of the percentage of population covered in 12 countries. Six countries do not appear in the table, either because no information was identified or because the data were unverified or unrealistic compared with other sources. In theory, the population covered varies by country between 3 percent

TABLE 7.2   Health Insurance Coverage in Francophone Sub-Saharan Africa, 2004

Country	Population with health coverage (percent)	Population with mandatory coverage[a] (percent)	Population with voluntary coverage (percent)
Benin	9.1	6.9	2.2
Burkina Faso	3.1	3.0	0.1
Burundi	—	10.0	—
Chad	5.3	3.9	1.4
Côte d'Ivoire	9.1	6.0	3.1
Guinea	9.6	8.4	1.2
Mali	12.1	11.8	0.3
Mauritania	13.5	13.3	0.2
Niger	3.8	3.4	0.4
Rwanda	91.0[b]	91.0[b]	n.a.
Senegal	20.1[b]	16.1[b]	4.0
Togo	—	—	0.6

Sources: Authors, from CES/ESPAD 2004; Rwanda, Ministry of Health 2007; Senegal, Ministry of Health and Medical Prevention 2008; Dussault, Fournier, and Letourmy 2006; Concertation 2004.
Note: — = not available; n.a. = not applicable.
a. Mandatory coverage includes contributory and noncontributory schemes.
b. 2008.

and 91 percent of total population. The countries with the broadest coverage are Rwanda (91 percent) and Senegal (20 percent). In other countries the coverage rate is low, for example, 3 percent in Burkina Faso, and 4 percent in Niger.

Mandatory Health Insurance

Many developed countries have established the principle of universal coverage through mandatory health insurance. Most African countries see universal coverage as the last stage of a gradually expanding transition. In the process, they expect to improve the performance of their health system, particularly through expanded access to care and better financial protection for their people. However, only a few FSSA countries have embarked on reforms along these lines.

Before presenting the mandatory health insurance systems that have been developed in recent years, the principal criteria used to identify countries working toward MHI are discussed (McIntyre 2007; McIntyre, Doherty, and Gilson 2003; Letourmy 2005; Carrin and James 2005). First, MHI is required by law, and affiliation is compulsory. It usually applies first to the segment of the population working in the formal sector and is progressively expanded to other groups. Second, contributions are equally compulsory. Salaried workers, independent workers, enterprises, and government contribute to the MHI fund. Normally, the contributions of salaried workers and enterprises come from the salary. The contribution of independent workers is either a lump sum or is calculated on the basis of revenue forecasts. The government may provide assistance to people who cannot pay, such as the unemployed and low-income workers in the informal sector. Finally, a package of minimum care is defined. To guarantee it, the MHI scheme has its own network of health care providers, works with accredited public or private providers, or does both. Management functions (registration, collection of contributions, contracting, and provider reimbursement) may be carried out by a paragovernmental or nongovernmental institution, often known as a Medical Fund.

Most countries have centralized social security systems with one or two social security agencies covering family, old-age, invalidity, and professional risks, but few of them cover health risks. However, there are exceptions to the rule. Senegal for example has a fragmented social security system in which the Institution de Prévoyance Retraite du Sénégal (IPRES) deals with old-age and invalidity, while the Institutions de Prévoyance Maladie (IPM) handle health, and the Caisse de Sécurité Sociale deals with family and professional risks. Some countries have integrated the health branch into the already existing social security agencies in order to cover certain segments of the population. Such is the case of the Caisse Nationale de Sécurité Sociale (CNSS) in Guinea and the Rwandaise d'Assurance Maladie (RAMA) in Rwanda. In Côte d'Ivoire, where mandatory coverage for the formal sector was promoted, enterprises and salaried workers take insurance policies with private insurance companies. Finally, since 2006, Rwanda decided to expand mandatory health insurance and include workers in the informal sector in an innovative way by compelling them to join a health mutual fund.

Table 7.3 presents the main characteristics of the MHI schemes as developed or envisaged in five FSSA countries. Most of them lean toward the progressive institution of MHI for the formal sector (Guinea, Mali, and Rwanda). Only Côte d'Ivoire[4] envisages putting in place mandatory insurance systems for the entire population.

Voluntary Health Insurance

Most voluntary health insurance schemes were developed to compensate for the inadequacies of mandatory systems. Two main types of VHI emerged in Africa (Letourmy 2005): federated mutual health organizations and unrelated private voluntary systems resulting from experimentation (micro-insurance, isolated mutual societies, health insurance systems tied to supply or to a financial institution). Usually they are run professionally, but with the insured participating (micro-insurance and isolated mutual societies). Private insurance companies operate alongside these systems, generally serving less than 1 percent of the population. The private nonprofit sector is usually more developed than the commercial insurance sector.

Mutual health organizations have developed significantly in Africa in recent years, according to the censuses of micro-insurance systems in 11 African countries done by the Concertation[5] in 1998, 2000, 2003, and 2007. The number of functional health insurance systems increased from 76 in 1998 to 366 in 2004, with an estimated 886,000 to 1.7 million beneficiaries (Concertation 2004). However, following a change in the counting method used in the 2007 census, the data on the number of systems are not comparable with those of previous inventories.[6] Nonetheless, the movement seems to have progressed considerably in countries such as Burkina Faso, Mali, and Senegal since the 1998 census. Conversely, in other countries, these insurance systems have developed relatively slowly (Cameroon, Chad, Mauritania, Niger, and Togo).

Waelkens and Criel (2004) identified 349 mutual financial systems covering health risks in 21 African countries (303 of them in 13 FSSA countries) and developed a typology for identifying their characteristics. They found that most organizations were "community based," that is, covered a geographical region (village, neighborhood, town) and were run by members. Next are the "corporatist" type mutual organizations of salaried workers, usually in the public sector (e.g., teachers' mutual society of Mali). The third type of insurance system is most often organized by managers of a district hospital. But another model is gaining ground, the systems organized at district level by the Ministry of Health, which is often the major care provider.

Mutual health organizations (MHOs) are receiving much attention and heavy support from the international community these days. Most of these MHOs seem to have emerged with this external support.[7] Nevertheless, the role of local initiative should not be underestimated. Some insurance systems were developed entirely by local care providers.[8] Other initiatives were created by the users of health services.[9] In West Africa the emerging trend is the development of partnerships between

TABLE 7.3   Mandatory Health Insurance Systems, Selected Francophone Sub-Saharan African Countries

Country	Mandatory health insurance	Law (year)	Description	Managing agency	Sources of financing	Population coverage (percent)	Benefits package	Provider choice	Provider-payment mechanism
Côte d'Ivoire	Yes	2001	Mandatory health insurance for entire population, Universal Health Insurance	Caisse Sociale Agricole (CSA), Caisse Nationale d'Assurance Maladie (CNAM), Fonds National de Régulation (FNR)	Contributions by beneficiaries, varying in range, amount, and modalities according to individual's personal situation and parafiscal resources	100[a]	Consultations, dental care, biological tests, medication, surgery, hospitalization	—	—
Guinea	In planning	Social Security Code (1963/ 1994)	Mandatory health insurance for salaried workers (private sector, public enterprises, state contractual staff)	Caisse Nationale de Sécurité Sociale (CNSS)	Medical contribution of 6.5% of gross salary, shared by employer (4%) and employee (2.5%)	3[b]	Consultations, hospitalizations, medication	Yes	Rates negotiated between CNSS and health care facilities
Mali	In planning	—	Mandatory health insurance for formal sector (civil servants and private sector workers)	Institut National de Prévoyance Sociale (INPS) for the private sector and Caisse des Retraites for civil servants	Proposed medical contribution of 7.65% of salary, shared by the employer (state and enterprises) and employee	14 to 15[a]	—	—	—
Rwanda	Yes	2001	Health insurance scheme for state employees; possibility of coverage for private sector employees since 2003	Rwandaise d'Assurance Maladie (RAMA)	Medical contribution of 15% of salary, shared by employer (7.5%) and employee (7.5%)	2[b]	Prevention and cure, including dental services, hospitalization, and surgery, radiology, laboratory, generic medicines, eyeglasses	Yes	Fee for service at end of every month; reimbursement of 85% cost of services by RAMA and copayment of remaining 15% by beneficiaries

(continued)

TABLE 7.3 Mandatory Health Insurance Systems, Selected Francophone Sub-Saharan African Countries *(continued)*

Country	Mandatory health insurance	Law (year)	Description	Managing agency	Sources of financing	Population coverage (percent)	Benefits package	Provider choice	Provider-payment mechanism
Rwanda (cont.)		2006	Compulsory membership in mutual health organizations	Ministry of Health, Cellule technique d'appui aux mutuelles de sante	Premium: about RF 1,000 (US$1.80) per person per year	85[c]	Minimum package of activities at health center and complementary package of activities at district hospital (consultations, hospitalizations), and medications on national essential drugs list	Yes	Payment to health center at end of every month: 90% of costs (10% of copayment, RF 100 to RF 250)
Senegal	Yes	Labor Code (1975)	Mandatory health insurance for private sector employees, pensioners, and noncivil servant state employees	Institutions de Prévoyance Maladie (IPMs)	Contribution fixed at 6% of salary, shared by employer (3%) and employee (3%)	10[c]	Consultations, hospitalizations, medication, evacuations (degree of involvement varying from one IPM to other: 40 to 80% of the costs)	Yes	—

Sources: Authors, from CES/ESPAD 2004; Rwanda, Ministry of Health 2007; Senegal, Ministry of Health and Medical Prevention 2008; Dussault, Fournier, and Letourmy 2006.

Note: — = not available.

a. Target.

b. 2004.

c. 2008.

different actors. States have begun to promote the initiative actively, and support organizations are being set up.

Despite these developments, the role of mutual health organizations in health financing and health coverage remains modest. Mobilization of resources by mutual health organizations appears relatively low. There are at least two main explanations for this. First, the quality of care and guarantees offered do not always correspond to peoples' needs and therefore do not make membership attractive to many individuals, even when they can afford to pay. Often the guarantees do not cover medication, even when those costs are a very substantial part of direct payments. The second has to do with poor management. The mutual organizations' internal difficulties reveal the need to train managers in specific organizational matters: calculating and collecting premiums, pooling and allocating resources, determining the benefits package, negotiating contracts with service providers, using oversight administrative follow-up measures, and managing funds.

The guarantees offered vary significantly from one mutual organization to the next. Most of them cover primary health care, normal delivery, caesareans, and minor hospitalizations at a moderate cost of about 30 percent paid by the patient. Contributions average CFAF 500 (less than US$1) per family every month. However, mutual societies do little to further equity because contributions are usually not proportionate to a member's income, and no discounts are given to the poor and indigent.

The system characteristics for the four countries in which voluntary insurance is the most highly developed are summarized in table 7.4.

Ongoing Reforms

This subsection provides a more detailed overview of the design of existing or planned health insurance arrangements in selected countries. Among them, only Côte d'Ivoire envisages universal coverage by putting in place a mandatory health system for the whole population. The other countries are targeting an extension of the coverage through the promotion of both systems, mandatory and voluntary.

The Quest for Universal Coverage through Mandatory Health Insurance

Côte d'Ivoire. For private sector salary earners in Côte d'Ivoire, collective agreements guarantee systems financed mainly by employers under the enterprise medical care system. However, because employers' contributions do not amount to enough to deliver high-quality health care, big enterprises often choose private insurance companies for their employees' medical coverage. For its civil servants, Côte d'Ivoire has one of the biggest mutual organizations in Francophone Africa, the Mutuelle Générale des Fonctionnaires et Agents de l'Etat (MUGEF-CI). MUGEF membership is automatic and complementary to the public health, dental, and eye care system. This insurance gives beneficiaries access to the private

TABLE 7.4 Voluntary Insurance Systems, Selected Francophone Sub-Saharan African Countries

Country	Law (year)	Description/system type	Amount of premium	Population coverage (percent)	Benefits package	Provider choice	Provider-payment mechanism
Guinea	Decree on social mutualization (1994)	Mutual health organizations from early 1990s:					
		Professional mutual organizations	—		—	—	—
		Mutuals covering pregnancy- and childbirth-related risks (MURIGAs)	GF 6,000 to GF 8,000 per year in urban area	1.2	Antenatal care (ANC), delivery, obstetric complications, transport in case of referral	—	—
		Traditional mutual health organizations: Mutuelles Communautaires d'Aires de Santé (MUCAS)	—		—	—	—
		Private insurance companies	—		Coverage of health care provided by the private sector or abroad	—	—
Mali	Law on mutualization (1996) Support agency: Union Technique de la Mutualité (UTM) (1998)	Mutual health organizations from 1990s; schemes based on the product of the Union Technique de la Mutualité Malienne: Voluntary health insurance since 1999	UTM product: 440 CFAF (US$1) per person and per month (family membership compulsory); CFAF 5,000 per person and per month for access to private clinics and hospitals	3.0	Primary health care and essential drugs	Yes, in public sector	Copayment: 40% for outpatient care, 25% for hospital care

126

Rwanda	Decree on the organization and functioning of mutual societies (1958) Legislation on mutual health organizations being voted	Mutual health organizations since the end of the 1990s—compulsory membership in the proposed system in 2006	n.a.	n.a.	n.a.	n.a.	n.a.
		Commercial insurance companies: Société Rwandaise d'Assurance (SORAS), Compagnie Rwandaise d'Assurance et de Réassurance (CORAR), Africa Air Rescue (AAR)	—	<1	—	—	—
Senegal	Law on mutual health organizations (2003)	Mutual health organizations from the early 1990s	Premium varies according to type of mutual society	4	Varies according to type of mutual society, primary health care generally favored by community-based mutual organizations	No, under most systems	—
		Private insurance companies under the Inter-African Insurance Market Code [Code interafricain du marché des assurances (CIMA)]	—	0.1	—	—	—

Sources: Authors, from CES/ESPAD 2004; Rwanda, Ministry of Health 2007; Senegal, Ministry of Health and Medical Prevention 2008; Dussault, Fournier, and Letourmy 2006; Concertation 2004.
Note: — = not available; n.a. = not applicable.

sector, but the plan is poorly structured. Since 2001, Côte d'Ivoire has launched an ambitious mandatory health insurance project covering the entire population (universal health insurance[10]). The country plans to establish three new agencies: the Caisse Nationale d'Assurance Maladie (CNAM) for the private sector and the self-employed, the Caisse Sociale Agricole (CSA) for the agricultural sector to be financed by levies on the sale of produce, and the Fonds National de Régulation (FNR) to manage the common treasury. They will cover a broad range of services: medical consultations, dental care, diagnostics, medicines, surgery, and hospitalization. The law stipulates that the insurance companies, mutual organizations, or social security institutions must provide complementary coverage for risks. The effective date of mid-2003 had to be deferred to an unknown date due to the political events of September 2002, which divided the country into two and slowed down the economy.

The Quest for Gradual Health Coverage Extension through Mandatory and Voluntary Insurance

Senegal. Senegal's *compulsory contributory system* is unlike those of other countries in the subregion and is somewhat dysfunctional because it lacks a legal and regulatory framework. Since 1975 the Institutions de Prévoyance Maladie (IPMs) have been taking care of private sector employees and members of their families. Any enterprise with more than 100 employees must establish an IPM; those employing fewer persons must come together in an interenterprise IPM or join an already approved one. Coverage for medical care varies considerably from one IPM to another (between 40 percent and 80 percent of the charges). For several years, IPM and the need for reform have been debated.[11] Three hypotheses have long been promoted: establishment of a national health insurance scheme (Caisse Nationale d'Assurance Maladie, CNAM) supported by the CNTS (labor union); institution of an organization known as Union Technique des IPM (UTIS) as an umbrella organization with supervisory powers over the IPM; or establishment of a health unit managed by the National Social Security Fund (Caisse Nationale de Sécurité Sociale, CNSS). The debate on dismantling the IPM is an important one because, although 60 percent do not work smoothly, they account for 50 percent of the income of the liberal private sector (Boyer et al. 2001). Today the vast majority of employers and employees favor the option of creating the UTIS as an autonomous organization, but implementing this reform is taking a long time (Senegal, Ministry of Health and Medical Prevention 2008).

To attain universal coverage, Senegal also wishes to promote *voluntary health insurance*, particularly self-financed, community-based insurance with mutual health organizations. The development of mutual health organizations in Senegal has taken place in three major phases, reflecting the role played by local and external actors: the inception phase of the first mutualist experiments pre-1994, the dissemination phase between 1994 and 1998, and the commitment phase since 1998 when more and more national and international actors became involved in the promotion and development of mutual health organizations (Senegal, Ministry of Health and Medical Prevention 2008). This intention materialized in the 2003 law on mutual health organizations defining their legal framework.[12]

Mali. Since late 1995, Mali has been working on setting up a *mandatory health insurance* scheme for salary earners in the formal sector, state contract workers, and civil servants (13.7 percent of the population). The country also plans to cover 3 percent of the population through social and solidarity insurance schemes[13] (e.g., mutual societies, solidarity funds).

With regard to *voluntary insurance,* Mali has been one of the strongest supporters of the mutualist movement: a law on mutuality was passed in 1996, and a mutuality development agency, the Union Technique de la Mutualité (UTM), was established in 1998. This agency functions at three levels: strategic, to give direction to development by defining relevant projects within the national context; technical, to support mutual organizations being established; and political, as representative of member mutual societies. The UTM also manages the Assurance Maladie Volontaire (AMV), an insurance product, and assists mutual organizations wishing to define and manage their own guarantee, designed for their members' needs. Moreover, in February 2011, the government adopted a national strategy for scaling up health coverage in the rural and informal sectors through MHOs. The main innovations of the strategy include the reorganization of MHOs through an alignment of target population to townships, the implementation of MHO unions at the *cercle* and regional levels to support risk pooling on a bigger scale, and the contribution of the state to MHO funding through subsidies in order to support extension of the benefits package. The implementation of the pilot phase of the strategy is underway in the regions of Segou, Sikasso, and Mopti.

Guinea. There are *contributory schemes* for private sector employees, public enterprises, and state contract workers. The latter are covered by the Caisse Nationale de Sécurité Sociale (CNSS), which receives a medical contribution of 6.5 percent of gross salary (4 percent from the employer, 2.5 percent from the employee). Operational problems, however, limit real care under the CNSS. The CNSS has trouble collecting contributions and is deep in arrears to its health care providers. In coming years, Guinea wishes to develop mandatory health insurance for formal sector employees. Of the several organizational options (centralized or decentralized systems) none has emerged the definite favorite, given the environment and certain external constraints the country has to address. Moreover, political unrest has slowed down the process.

There are several subsets of *voluntary insurance*: private insurance companies, professional mutual societies approved by the Ministry of Social Affairs,[14] mutual societies covering pregnancy- and childbirth-related risks (MURIGAs)[15] established by the Ministry of Public Health in collaboration with UNICEF and the World Bank, and the traditional mutual health organizations called Mutuelles Communautaire d'Aire de Santé (MUCAS). The mutualist movement appears to be relatively fragmented despite the encouragement of the Ministry of Public

Health and the enactment of a decree on mutuals in 1994. Most mutual societies were started by local NGOs and financed by international and bilateral partners (Centre International de Développement et de Recherche [CIDR]; Nantes-Guinea Association; and the German aid agency, GTZ).

Rwanda. In 2001 Rwanda established the *mandatory health insurance* scheme Rwandaise d'Assurance Maladie (RAMA) to take care of state employees' medical needs. Since 2003, it has begun to cover private sector salary earners, too. RAMA is a financially autonomous legal entity; its resources come from employer and employee contributions (refer back to table 7.3). RAMA has signed contracts with all district health centers and referral hospitals as well as with several private health care facilities and several pharmacies. This configuration guarantees members' freedom of choice. Coverage of the MHI scheme RAMA is about to be extended more broadly to private sector employees, retirees, and their dependents. To expedite this policy direction, RAMA and social security will be consolidated under the Rwanda Social Security Board.

In *voluntary health insurance*, Rwanda has distinguished itself in the rapid development of mutual health organizations. Its experience mutualizing health risks at the grassroots level dates to the 1960s. However, most of the mutualization mechanisms did not survive the events of 1994, which also destroyed all health infrastructure. Mechanisms for mutualizing health risks started to emerge again in 1998–99 when the government initiated a pilot phase of health care prepayment systems in three health districts to serve as a platform for the development of mutual health organizations (Ndakingaka 2004). Since then, population coverage has expanded, from 27 percent in 2004 to 44 percent in 2005 and 75 percent in 2007 (Rwanda, Ministry of Health 2007). The number of mutual societies went from 54 in 1999, 226 in 2004, to 403 in 2007. They are different from other systems in Africa because their organizational structure is relatively well suited to the institutional framework put in place for the 2002 decentralization reforms. These mutual health organizations are based at district level, but each of Rwanda's 410 health centers has a mutual unit located in it. They have grown rapidly as a result of the commitment by government and external partners to promote and support the development of mutual health organizations. The rapid expansion of coverage is also explained by the fact that the government, in 2006, made membership in a mutual health organization mandatory. The development of mutual health organizations has benefited from a relatively favorable institutional environment, in that the government's Vision 2020 and all other key national programs have made mutual health organizations an important pillar of efforts to enhance access to health care for the Rwandese. The main reforms of the mutual health insurance system are related to contribution policy and provider-payment mechanisms. At first, annual contributions to MHOs were based on a per capita lump sum. Starting in 2010, to strengthen resource mobilization and improve equity in financing, households have been classified into three socioeconomic categories, and their contributions to MHOs have been related to their capacity to pay. Moreover, Rwanda is planning to extend capitation mechanisms for health center reimbursement at the primary level.

Burkina Faso. In 2008, the government of Burkina Faso began to create a national health insurance system. A national steering committee and a permanent secretariat were formed to supervise the venture. In 2011, the first phase of a *mandatory health insurance* scheme for formal sector workers began (Ministère du Travail et de la Sécurité Sociale 2009). A second phase is planned for 2012–14 to extend health insurance to people in the informal and rural sectors through existing MHO networks, microfinance institutions, and cooperatives.

Various voluntary health insurance initiatives have been developed in the informal and rural sectors over the past two decades in several parts of the country. They include MHOs, solidarity funds, prepayment systems, or joint microhealth insurance and microfinance schemes. In 2007, there were 136 mutual initiatives across the country with a high concentration in the Hauts-Bassin region and Center-North (32). As a result of the economic characteristics of their target populations, the evolving political environment, and their relative newness, the MHOs have several weaknesses. So far, no strategic framework for support has been developed to transform the emerging mutual strategy into a deliberate development strategy.

KEY FACTORS IN THE DEVELOPMENT OF HEALTH INSURANCE

After a decade of attempts and experiments to expand health insurance in Francophone Africa, the results are spotty. The process is a long one that has taken developed countries quite a few years to navigate from start to universal coverage. In Francophone Africa, the small contribution of insurance to health care financing and the low rate of coverage of the population are explained by institutional, structural, and cultural difficulties, according to the literature.

The Institutional and Political Environment

Governance and Political Stability

Considering the institutional and political environment in African countries, the question arises about the extent to which they can embark upon health insurance reforms or implement and monitor them after passage of the enabling laws. The institutional environment needs improvements in four main aspects: the legal framework, regulatory instruments, administrative procedures, and customs and practices, formal and informal (Preker and Velenyi 2006). But most countries record poor results in terms of quality of policies and institutions when measured by the World Bank Country Policy and Institutional Assessment (CPIA)[16] and the governance indicators of Kaufmann, Kraay, and Mastruzzi[17] (2010; table 7.5, this chapter). The same group of countries shows up in country classifications by regional average and for each indicator. The countries with the best results in terms of the reference point are Rwanda, Senegal, Madagascar, Mali, Burkina Faso, and Benin, listed in descending order; the ones with the worst results, Côte d'Ivoire, Guinea, Togo, and Chad.

TABLE 7.5 Political and Institutional Factors Influencing Health Insurance in Francophone Sub-Saharan Africa

Country	Quality of policies and institutions				Mobilization of resources by state government revenues (% GDP, 2007)
	CPIA[a] (2010)	Government effectiveness[b] (2010)	Control of corruption[b] (2010)	Political stability/ absence of violence[b] (2010)	
Benin	3.5	−0.54	−0.75	0.31	18.6[d]
Burkina Faso	3.8	−0.58	−0.37	−0.11	13.4[d]
Burundi	3.1	−1.09	−1.08	−1.54	18.7
Cameroon	3.2	−0.89	−0.98	−0.58	18.9
Central African Republic	2.8	−1.40	−0.78	−2.15	10.2
Chad	2.4	−1.50	−1.32	−1.53	8.7[c]
Comoros	2.5	−1.74	−0.74	−0.43	12.7
Congo, Dem. Rep.	2.7	−1.72	−1.38	−2.20	13.2[c]
Congo, Rep.	2.9	−1.24	−1.14	−0.25	19.6[c]
Côte d'Ivoire	2.7	−1.33	−1.15	−1.55	18.9
Guinea	2.8	−1.15	−1.19	−1.81	14.3
Madagascar	3.4	−0.82	−0.27	−1.13	11.9
Mali	3.6	−0.88	−0.68	−0.25	15.5
Mauritania	3.2	−0.93	−0.68	−1.25	15.7
Niger	3.4	−0.71	−0.66	−1.14	11.7
Rwanda	3.8	−0.05	0.48	−0.11	13.9
Senegal	3.7	−0.51	−0.68	−0.39	20.9
Togo	2.9	−1.39	−0.97	−0.19	16.9[c]
Average	3.1	−1.03	−0.80	−0.91	15.0
SSA average	3.2	−0.84	−0.69	−0.57	—

Sources: World Bank CPIA 2011a; World Bank Worldwide Governance Indicators (WGI) 2011b; IMF country reports 2008.
Note: — = not available.
a. CPIA, Country Policy and Institutional Assessment. The indicator takes values ranging from 1 for low results to 6 when they improve.
b. The indicators take values ranging from −2.5 (low) to 2.5 when results improve.
c. 2006; d. 2008.

These results are also influenced by the political environment, character-ized by political instability and violence in many countries, as measured by the Kaufmann, Kraay, and Mastruzzi indicator,[18] as well as by the many conflicts in recent years. These conflicts diverted scarce resources from the health sector and slowed down insurance development projects. Such was the case in Côte d'Ivoire and Guinea.

Institutional Environment and Mobilization of Internal Resources

In this context, the capacity of the state to mobilize resources is also seriously hampered, and this constitutes a source of instability for several countries. In countries such as Chad, for example, the public levy rate was lower than 10 percent of GDP in 2006; in others, this rate was between 10 and 15 percent (Burkina Faso, Guinea, Niger, Rwanda), and between 15 and 21 percent (Benin, Cameroon, Côte d'Ivoire, Mali, Senegal) (table 7.5). Although important macro-economic difficulties limit resource mobilization, a number of countries seem to be below their fiscal potential[19] due to ineffective fiscal mobilization policies (Chambas 2005).

The State's Role in Funding the Health Sector

The state's commitment to the health sector is an equally decisive factor in the success or failure of efforts to develop health insurance. It boils down to the strength of its commitment as reflected in funding and the organization and regulation of the health insurance systems.

Although some countries have made significant efforts to fund the health sector, the portion of their budgets earmarked for health often remains insufficient. In many countries, it is very low, and it has decreased since 2000 in nearly half of them (figure 7.2). Apart from the additional resources from economic growth and debt cancellation, the state will have to make a significant financial commitment to the health sector, particularly to attain the US$34 target set by the Commission on Macroeconomics and Health (CMH 2001) or the target of allocating 15 percent of the total budget to health, a goal set by African leaders at their summit meeting in Abuja, Nigeria, in April 2001. Nonetheless, according to an optimistic scenario on health expenditure trends to 2015 (Preker et al. 2008),[20] most African countries will not reach this threshold. Only Benin, Cameroon, the Republic of Congo, Côte d'Ivoire, and Senegal might attain it. Thus, even if the

FIGURE 7.2   Public Health Expenditure in Francophone Sub-Saharan Africa

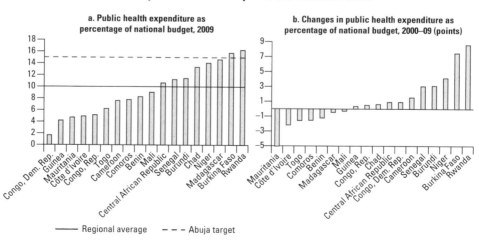

Source: WHO, National Health Accounts 2011a.

states increase the share of the budget devoted to health to 15 percent, expenditure will remain relatively low.

With regard to financing of health insurance, the state, or more generally the public sector, sometimes jeopardizes the viability of mandatory insurance systems by not paying its contributions regularly, running up arrears in payments to social welfare agencies. This tactic reduces the state's immediate expenditures but weakens health insurance and ruins public confidence in the system.

The State's Role in the Development of Health Insurance

The state is also a key player in the process of health insurance development. Its role varies according to the form of organization of insurance chosen. Letourmy (2005) identifies three main roles. First, the state could play a role in creating and designing the configuration of schemes, especially when they are mandatory or cover specific segments of the population. Second, the state may support the setting up of schemes, particularly by improving the legal and regulatory framework for health insurance. This amounts to enacting a law providing the scheme with legal personality and recognizing its right of establishment. Indeed the legislative framework is an essential prerequisite for instituting a scheme. It sets forth the respective rights and responsibilities of the insured and insurers. For a mandatory scheme, it could be a law establishing the MHI, as in Côte d'Ivoire. In the case of voluntary schemes, it could be the provision of a legislative and regulatory framework such as an insurance code, or special provisions such as the mutual society code in Mali. To date, only a few countries have laws on mutual societies or formal contract policies between insurance agencies and health care professionals and facilities. In practice, the Association Statutes are used to approve or register new groups. In certain countries (Mali, Rwanda, Senegal), the state has supported the drive to develop mutual organizations, whereas in others (Benin, Burkina Faso, Guinea), the support came from NGOs or external agencies. Finally, the state may play a major role in the functioning of schemes as regulator, supervisor, and enforcer. Enforcement is particularly important to avert the risks of free riders, moral hazard, adverse selection, cost increases, fraud, and corruption.

The role of the state is equally decisive in complementary reforms to the health insurance system. On the supply side, these reforms pertain mainly to quality of care, availability of medicine in health care facilities, and the presence of trained staff. Indeed, the quality of care is a decisive element for the development of mandatory or voluntary insurance. It shapes peoples' confidence in a state-organized mandatory insurance project and the breadth of membership. The perceived quality of care is also important for African households deciding whether or not to join a mutual health organization (Criel, Blaise, and Ferette 2006). At another level, the growth of mutual schemes is expected to improve the quality of care by increasing both financial resources and stability for providers (Atim 1998). In the long term, mutual health organizations can benefit from heightened competition in supply to influence the quality of care (Bennett,

Creese, and Monasch 1998). Finally, mutual health organizations could constitute a counterweight to health professionals, thereby putting pressure on them to improve their responsiveness and quality of care, although this hypothesis has not been proven by studies.

On the demand side, arrangements have to be made to provide care for the poorest segments of society (e.g., by subsidizing their premiums). To some extent it is up to the state to define how this care will be provided, for example, through the creation of a fund as in Mali or by direct premium subsidies as in Rwanda. In Rwanda the government first put an effective system in place for identifying indigent citizens (Musango 2005) and then saw to their care through mutual health organizations. Other mechanisms for sectoral budgetary aid (SWAP-type) could be used to take care of the poor and ensure free access.

Finally, the development of health insurance depends very much on the relationship between management and labor or between the actors involved in the development of insurance (ministerial departments, insurers, care providers, unions, and associations). Insufficient involvement of the state in the definition, support, functioning, and regulation of insurance systems explains in part the lukewarm participation of many actors in insurance projects and the conflicts among them. At the central level, for example, the ministries involved in mandatory health insurance often do not talk to each other. The Ministry of Labor is usually the supervisory ministry for compulsory schemes; the Ministry of Health, for health care delivery and rates in the public sector. They do not spontaneously set up a negotiation system that would promote improvements in the quality of care for the insured. The lackadaisical involvement of the state in the process of establishing formal contractual arrangements between insurance agencies and health care professionals and formations is partly responsible for conflicts. The state often lets tensions or conflicts fester between mutual societies and public health facilities, making contract awards and the establishment of conventions between them difficult (Bennett 2004).

The Economic and Social Environment

The successful implementation or expansion of a health insurance system, be it mandatory or voluntary, also depends on structural factors related to the economic and social environment. Among the factors involved are incomes and income distribution, the economic growth rate, population and labor market structures, geographical distribution of the population, and different groups' capacity to contribute to insurance.

The experience of developed countries and countries in transition shows that the income level of the population as well as stable economic growth account for the success of health funding reforms and measures to expand insurance-type arrangements. In particular, this experience provides an answer to the first function of health system funding—sustainable public and private resource mobilization. Africans' capacity to contribute to an insurance program or health funding is still limited by low per capita income. In more than three quarters of the countries, the per capita GDP growth rate was below 2 percent in 2009 and negative in some cases (Chad, Mauritania, Niger, and Guinea).

The way the population is distributed over the land also affects the effectiveness of the insurance system. Attempts to expand health insurance are often successful when urbanization and population density are high, facilitating both subscriber recruitment and collection of their contributions, thus benefiting from economies of scale. However, this observation should be qualified insofar as voluntary insurance is concerned because a breakdown of social relations between individuals often accompanies urbanization.

The size of the formal sector and the structure of the labor market are important givens. Insurance is easier to introduce or refine in countries with a high proportion of formal sector employment. It is easier for the state to collect resources through taxation, employer contributions, membership dues, premiums, or contributions for private or community insurance than it is in places with large informal sectors. In Francophone Africa, however, the informal sector predominates. The proportion of the population employed in agriculture—dependent on irregular income—ranges between 20 percent and more than 45 percent. In most countries, the dependency ratios are above 0.8, reflecting limited contribution capacity. This slows down the growth of mandatory health insurance in many countries.

Solidarity within a society is another important factor for the setting up of health insurance. People often have trouble accepting the premise of health insurance, the guarantee of similar health care for all who have similar health needs, irrespective of the amount each individual contributes. The problem is more acute when incomes are disparate. Pooling resources is complicated in a nonegalitarian society (Carrin 2002). The greater the inequality within a society, the more likely are decisions to favor the dominant class.

Cultural Factors and Practices

The success of an insurance system is also determined by the extent to which the population subscribes to it and is the key factor in the ability to meet demand for increased coverage. This element is particularly important in Africa, where the population has little confidence in the state, particularly its officials. In most countries, even where arrangements exist to care for the sick, services are of poor quality. Consequently, people do not readily accept state reforms to mandatory insurance.

A further complication is the scant knowledge of insurance principles among the target populations, especially the poor. A result not only of cultural factors but also of educational shortcomings, it inhibits membership in voluntary schemes. Finally, insurance is hard to institute in Africa because of the peoples' health care–seeking practices, often opting for traditional care over Western medicine.

PROSPECTS FOR THE DEVELOPMENT OF HEALTH INSURANCE

The prospects for mandatory or voluntary health insurance in Africa depend on answers to some questions related to three functions of health funding (revenue collection, pooling of resources, and allocation of resources).

Mandatory Health Insurance

Mandatory health insurance is often considered an effective instrument for mobilizing resources and reducing the financial burden of health coverage. However, in light of the needs to be covered, the resources that can be mobilized will almost certainly not suffice. Usually, mandatory health insurance involves only a small part of the population (formal sector workers). Funding health through MHI therefore needs to be complemented by other funding mechanisms provided as subsidies by the state and by external partners. In view of many countries' low resource mobilization capacity, the development of insurance should be accompanied by fiscal policy reform (increase in the ratio of public revenue to GDP) and by improved governance.

With regard to resource pooling, the development of MHI calls for choices about the design and administration of pools, risk-sharing arrangements, and mechanisms for managing guarantees. Most countries opt for centralized systems run along the lines of principles used by social security systems (e.g., Côte d'Ivoire, Mali). That sort of organization is greeted with skepticism, however, because it does not usually make for effective functioning. Another possibility is to organize MHI through a decentralized system (e.g., Ghana, Nigeria).

Finally, resource allocation raises questions about the target population, range of services offered, choice of health care providers, and provider payment mechanisms. With regard to target population and range of services, when resources are scarce, countries should decide between expanding breadth of coverage (number of persons covered) and depth of coverage (range of benefits). With respect to the target population, the question of care for the poorest arises. Two major approaches are common (Preker and Velenyi 2006).

The first is to introduce or expand MHI for the small part of the population that can help pay for it through payroll deductions by their employers. These are generally civil servants and formal sector employees. If that choice is made, poor and informal sector workers will have access to subsidized public hospitals and outpatient clinics. Although this formula benefits the richest citizens and public sector employees in the first instance, it nonetheless enables release of public funds as subsidies for the care of the poorest citizens and informal workers. This way, limited budgetary resources are stretched.

The second approach consists of introducing mandatory health insurance for most of the population by paying or subsidizing premiums for indigents and low-income, informal sector workers. When funding becomes available, coverage can be expanded by drawing on the resources paid in by the people who can afford to pay in order to subsidize premiums for those who cannot. This approach helps reach poor households more directly than the subsidized offer option described above.

Determinants of the success and viability of MHI schemes are their operating efficiency and control over expenditures against the risks of adverse selection and moral hazard. These considerations argue strongly for developing strategies for formal contractual arrangements.

Voluntary Health Insurance

Mutual health organizations look like an interesting solution with great potential for enhancing access to quality health care, mobilizing funds, improving efficiency, and encouraging dialogue and democratic governance in the health sector. Voluntary insurance could play an effective role during the transition to universal coverage through its ability to mobilize communities, its proximity, and its priority in the social coverage process. The project supporting the construction of a regional framework for the development of mutual health organizations in the Economic Community of West African States (ECOWAS), supported by the French Foreign Ministry and the ILO/STEP,[21] should help speed up the process of developing mutual health organizations. This project seeks to answer demand from the ECOWAS countries for the creation of a legal environment that is conducive to the development of mutual companies. In June 2009, the ECOWAS ministry council adopted the law No. 07/2009/CM/ECOWAS concerning mutual health regulation within ECOWAS. The law provides a harmonized legal framework for mutual companies, including mutual health organizations in the ECOWAS countries. The innovations of the law include, in each country: the implementation of an organization in charge of the regulation of mutual companies; a national registry for mutual companies; a guarantee fund for social mutual companies; and opportunities for numerous stakeholders to give subsidies to mutual health organizations. The ECOWAS commission is currently enacting the law and the rules of execution in the ECOWAS countries in order to develop a plan of action for implementation.

Mutual health organizations could be developed in Africa without exorbitant investments, but first their ability to mobilize internal resources needs to be improved. More internal and external resources should also help finance or subsidize people's insurance premiums, especially those of the indigent. Funds from debt cancellation in the framework of the Heavily Indebted Poor Countries (HIPC) Initiative could also be used in this way. Indeed, although some countries have reintroduced some types of free care (Mali, Senegal), using these resources to subsidize premiums might be more effective and efficient. Mauritania has achieved some impressive results since the introduction of the obstetrical lump-sum payment in 2002. In the framework of a program to improve maternal care, an innovative arrangement was put in place to prevent maternal and perinatal mortality. The principle is based on pooling of obstetrical risks:

every patient who joins the obstetrical lump-sum scheme (by paying a contribution of about US$15) receives medical coverage during pregnancy, delivery, and the post-natal period (antenatal tests, ultrasound scans, normal delivery, caesarean, post-natal care). Mauritanian authorities and all partners consider the lump-sum scheme a true success story. Maternal mortality is now estimated at 747 for 100,000 live births for uninsured women but 100 per 100,000 for insured women (IFC 2007).

Resource pooling also raises the problem of structuring mutualist regimes (unions or federations). In most countries, their isolation endangers their viability. Two main configurations may be envisaged. The first derives from a bottom-up approach (Letourmy 2005), with the creation of a network of mutual societies as in Guinea (union of mutual societies in the forest zone), Benin (alliance of mutual health organizations of Borgou), or Senegal (geographical coordination of mutual health organizations in the Thiès region). The second possibility, a top-down approach, consists of creating a central structure for the development of mutual societies. This is the situation in Mali with the UTM, a private mutualist entity, independent of government authorities. One formula consists of the state's playing the role of development agency as in Rwanda where the state and the decentralized authorities sensitize the population and help them create and manage mutual societies. The first type of organization takes time, and problems of relations with other projects could arise. The second approach gives structure to the movement and homogeneous political representation, but it is more costly and requires sustained external financial support.

CONCLUSIONS

After experimenting with health insurance mechanisms for more than a decade, Francophone Sub-Saharan African countries are only now beginning the transition to universal coverage. Some countries have yet to start this process; others have taken but the first few steps. Overall, the population coverage rate and the insurance contribution to funding the sector remain low. The difficulties encountered in the subregion illustrate the key factors involved in the transition toward universal coverage, which include economic, political, institutional, and cultural dynamics. The evidence highlighted in this chapter suggests that the Francophone Sub-Saharan African countries will not follow the same development pattern as industrial countries.

Indeed, the Francophone countries are trying different formulas to effect the transition toward universal coverage. Some countries want to reach the objective by means of mandatory insurance mechanisms; others opt for progressive implementation of universal coverage through a grassroots approach. But none of these approaches seems to stand out as an exemplary mechanism to be promoted on a national scale within the subregion. Considering the scarcity of resources, both human and material, one of the major challenges for these countries is to expand the insurance gradually while simultaneously helping the various forms of health financing meld in a coherent framework. There are indeed prepayment formulas, communitarian funding formulas, social assistance and social insurance formulas through taxes or social contributions, and commercial insurance. With all these mechanisms, the state should ensure that there is no overlapping coverage, which could result in double taxation.

Despite these challenges, Francophone Sub-Saharan African countries seem to be increasingly aware that health insurance constitutes an instrument for financing effective health care by mobilizing additional resources and protecting individuals against financial risks due to illness. Although the financial resource increases for the sector remain modest, countries could have some margin in the future by increasing the amounts of public, private, and external resources devoted to developing insurance-type mechanisms. Governments will also have to continue trying to expand public resources in general through an enlargement of fiscal space, and resources for the health sector in particular. The development of health insurance needs to be integrated into a global strategy for financing the health sector. It becomes essential that governments take the measure of the challenges raised by the introduction of health insurance, especially if it is intended to achieve universal coverage, a goal espoused by ever more countries. Indeed, insurance cannot develop sustainably in an unfavorable institutional environment.

The role of external partners will also be decisive in terms of new resources brought into the sector and in terms of transferring knowledge and technical assistance. The role of such "new aid" should be addressed because funds mobilized by new actors could be an important financial lifeline for the development of health insurance. Today these funds are used mainly as subsidy and are not enough for insurance.

ANNEX 7A   STATISTICAL ANNEX

TABLE 7A.1   Overview of Francophone Sub-Saharan African Countries, 2009

	Demography and social conditions					Economy			Health status and health service coverage					
Country	Population, total (million)	Age dependency ratio (dependents to working-age population)	Rural population (% of total)	Literacy rate, adult total (% of people ages 15 and above)	Improved sanitation facilities (% of population with access)[f]	GNI per capita, Atlas method (current US$)	GDP growth (annual %)	Inflation (annual %)	Life expectancy at birth (years)	Under-5 mortality rate (per 1,000 live births)	Prevalence of HIV/AIDS (% of 15–49 year-olds)[b]	Immunization, DTP3 (% of children ages 12–23 months)	Physicians (per 1,000 people)[a]	Births attended by skilled health staff (% of total)
Benin	8.9	0.86	58.4	40.8[e]	12	750	3.8	2.2	61.4[e]	118.0	1.2[d]	83	0.06[e]	74.0[c]
Burkina Faso	15.8	0.94	80.0	28.7[d]	11	510	3.5	3.1	53.0[e]	166.4	1.6[d]	82	0.06[e]	53.5[c]
Burundi	8.3	0.70	89.3	65.9[e]	46	150	3.5	13.6	50.4[e]	166.3	2.0[d]	92	0.03[a]	33.6[b]
Cameroon	19.5	0.80	42.4	75.9[e]	47	1,190	2.0	−3.4	51.1[e]	154.3	5.1[d]	80	0.19[a]	63.0[c]
Central African Republic	4.4	0.80	61.3	54.6[e]	34	450	2.4	3.9	47.0	170.8	6.3[d]	54	0.08[a]	43.7
Chad	11.2	0.94	72.9	32.7[e]	9	—	−1.6	−12.4	48.7[e]	209.0	3.5[d]	23	0.04[a]	14.4[a]
Comoros	0.7	0.70	71.9	73.6[e]	36	870	12.3	−2.8	65.3[e]	104.0	0.1[d]	83	0.15[a]	—
Congo, Dem. Rep.	66.0	0.97	65.4	66.6[e]	23	160	2.7	30.2	47.6[e]	198.6	—	77	0.11	74[d]
Congo, Rep.	3.7	0.79	38.3	—	30	2,080	7.6	−20.4	53.6[e]	128.2	3.5[d]	91	0.20	83.4[b]
Côte d'Ivoire	21.1	0.80	50.6	54.6[e]	23	1,070	3.6	1.3	57.4[e]	118.5	3.9[d]	81	0.12	56.8[c]
Guinea	10.1	0.85	65.1	38.0[e]	19	370	−0.3	5.2	57.8[e]	141.5	1.6[d]	57	0.11	38.1[b]
Madagascar	19.6	0.85	70.1	70.7[e]	11	—	0.4	9.1	60.3[e]	57.7	0.1[d]	78	0.29	43.9
Mali	13.0	0.87	67.3	26.2[c]	36	680	4.3	4.3	48.4[e]	191.1	1.5[d]	74	0.08	49[c]
Mauritania	3.3	0.73	58.8	56.8[e]	26	960	−1.1	−6.1	56.7[e]	117.1	0.8[d]	64	0.11	—
Niger	15.3	1.08	83.4	28.7[b]	9	340	1.0	5.0	51.4[e]	160.3	0.8[d]	70	0.02	32.9[e]
Rwanda	10.0	0.81	81.4	70.3[e]	54	460	5.3	12.1	50.1[e]	110.8	2.8[d]	97	0.05	52.1[e]
Senegal	12.5	0.85	57.4	41.9[c]	51	1,040	2.2	−0.5	55.6[e]	92.8	1.0[d]	86	0.06	51.9[b]
Togo	6.6	0.77	57.3	64.9[e]	12	440	2.5	1.3	62.5[e]	97.5	3.3[d]	89	0.05[e]	47.3[d]
SSA average	840.3[f]	0.81	60.9	68.7	33.8	1,987.4	2.7	7.1	54.8	114.7	5.8	76.9	0.21	45.1

Sources: World Bank 2010; WHO 2011b.

Note: — = not available.

a. 2004; b. 2005; c. 2006; d. 2007; e. 2008; f. sum of total population in Sub-Saharan Africa.

NOTES

ACKNOWLEDGMENT: The authors are grateful to Alain Letourmy, Marianne Lindner, Eric de Roodenbeke, Martine Audibert, and Jacky Mathonnat for their insightful comments on the initial drafts of this chapter.

1. Benin, Burkina Faso, Burundi, Cameroon, Central African Republic, Chad, the Comoros, the Democratic Republic of Congo, Côte d'Ivoire, Guinea, Madagascar, Mali, Mauritania, Niger, the Republic of Congo, Rwanda, Senegal, and Togo. Rwanda is reviewed in this chapter although it officially became an Anglophone country in October 2008. Gabon is not included in the analysis because it is an upper-middle-income country.

2. But Rwanda's external resources represented close to 53 percent of total health expenditure in 2009.

3. Noncontributory schemes are schemes that do not fall within the principle of insurance. They are mainly intended for civil servants and the poorest citizens. They are often financed directly by the state through an annual budgetary allocation.

4. In 2006, Gabon also adopted a law on generalized medical coverage, based on mandatory health insurance to which all the active population contribute while those with low earning power do not.

5. The Concertation between development actors of mutual health organizations in Africa is a network for sharing experiences, competencies, and information on the development of mutual health organizations in West and Central Africa. Web site: http://www.concertation.org.

6. The 2007 census identified 127 micro-insurance systems in 13 African countries. This census is now updated every year instead of every two years as previously. The Concertation seeks to empower mutual health organizations which are invited to register, if necessary with the assistance of support agencies. The census method will take time to be refined and adapted to make it more comprehensive.

7. The development of mutual health organizations in Francophone Africa has been promoted and supported by numerous external partners such as the Centre International de Développement et de Recherche (CIDR), the BIT/STEP project, the German, Belgian, French, and Netherlandic cooperations, and so on (Waelkens and Criel 2004).

8. For example, the Nkoranza Community Health Insurance Scheme was created by the Nkoranza Catholic Hospital in Ghana. Since the introduction of cost recovery in 1984, patients had payment difficulties. Therefore, in 1989, the hospital established a health insurance scheme. Under this scheme, the priority community is a rural population of farmers in the district. The insurance is integrated into the hospital administration, which owns and manages the scheme. The insured do not participate in management of the scheme (Letourmy 2005; Atim 1998).

9. The mutual Famille Babouantou from Yaounde, Cameroon, is a mutual company created in 1992 at the initiative of the Babouantou community. Before proposing a health guarantee, the mutual provided other types of insurance (birth, death, or funerals). In return for an annual fee, members receive a lump sum of CFAF 20,000 covering all hospitalizations exceeding seven days, and surgery or injury resulting in an inability to work at least fifteen days (Letourmy 2005).

10. Loi No. 2001–636 du 09 octobre 2001 concerning the creation, organization, and function of the universal health insurance.

11. Already in the 1990s, many reports and publications were urging reorganization of the IPM (Letourmy 1995).

12. Decrees spelling out the modalities of application of the law have not yet been enacted.

13. The third element of this reform is the setting up of a Medical Assistance Fund, Fonds d'Assistance Médicale (FAM), to cover 5 percent of the population (indigents).

14. These are the Compagnie de Bauxite de Guinée (CBG) at Kamsar, the Guinean Customs mutual, the mutual of scientific research teachers at Rogbané, and the AGPG-MS health mutual.

15. The health department began setting up these agencies in 1997 in the framework of the national strategy for the reduction of maternal and neonatal mortality. They propose a targeted guarantee (CPN, delivery, obstetrical complications, and transportation in case of referral) for a minimum contribution. For example, in urban areas, the contribution is between GF 6,000 and GF 8,000 a year. In general, membership is always open.

16. The World Bank CPIA helps evaluate countries according to 16 criteria in four categories: macroeconomic management, structural policies, social policies, and institutions.

17. Government effectiveness is a measure of perceptions of the quality of public services including the civil service and its degree of independence from political pressures, the quality of policy formulation and implementation, and the credibility of the government's commitment to such policies. Control of corruption is a measure of perceptions of the extent to which public power is exercised for private gain, including both minor and major forms of corruption, as well as "capture" of the state by elites and private interests.

18. Political instability and violence is a measure of perceptions of the likelihood that the government will be destabilized or overthrown by unconstitutional or violent means, including politically motivated violence and terrorism.

19. The Union Economique et Monétaire Ouest Africaine (UEMOA, West African Economic and Monetary Union) recommends a tax revenue rate of 17 percent of GDP as a rate its members could reasonably achieve. UEMOA member countries are Benin, Burkina Faso, Côte d'Ivoire, Guinea Bissau, Mali, Niger, Senegal, and Togo.

20. The scenario is based on the assumption of a 5 percent annual economic growth rate between 2005 and 2015 and on a ratio of public health expenditure to total public expenditure attaining the Abuja target in 2015. It also assumes that 60 percent of direct payments to health are captured in an insurance program, inducing an "insurance effect" equivalent to a 25 percent increase in direct payments.

21. International Labor Organization/Strategies and Tools against Social Exclusion and Poverty.

REFERENCES

Atim, C. 1998. *The Contribution of Mutual Health Organizations to Financing, Delivery, and Access to Health Care: Synthesis of Research in Nine West and Central African Countries.* Bethesda, MD: Abt Associates Inc.

Audibert, M., J. Mathonnat, and E. de Roodenbeke. 2003. "Le financement de la santé dans les Pays d'Afrique et d'Asie à faible revenu." Paris: Karthala Editions.

Bennett, S. 2004. "The Role of Community-Based Health Insurance within the Health Care Financing System: A Framework for Analysis." *Health Policy and Planning* 19 (3): 147–58.

Bennett, S., A. Creese, and R. Monasch. 1998. "Health Insurance Schemes for Poor People outside Formal Sector Employment." Discussion of Analysis, Research, and Assessment, Paper 16, WHO, Geneva.

Boyer, S., C. Delesvaux, J.P. Foirry, and C. Prieur. 2001. *Le risque maladie dans les assurances sociales: Bilan et perspectives dans les PVD*. Study by the Centre de Recherches et d'Etudes en Economie de la Sante (CREDES). Paris: French Ministry of Foreign Affairs.

Carrin, G. 2002. "Social Health Insurance in Developing Countries: A Continuing Challenge." *International Social Security Review* 55 (2): 57–69.

Carrin, G., and C. James. 2005. "L'Assurance maladie obligatoire: transition vers la couverture universelle et evaluation de la performance." In *L'Assurance maladie en Afrique francophone: Améliorer l'accès aux soins et lutter contre la pauvreté*, ed. G. Dussault, P. Fournier, and A. Letourmy. Washington, DC: World Bank.

Celasun, O., and J. Walliser. 2008. "Managing Aid Surprises." *Finance and Development* 45 (3): 33–37.

CES/ESPAD (Collège des Economistes de la Santé/Economie de la Santé dans les Pays en Développement). 2004. Country reports from the conference "The Improvement of Health Services Access in Francophone Africa: The Role of Insurance," Paris, April 28–29. http://www.ces-asso.org/PagesGB/defaut_gb.htm.

Chambas, G. 2005. *Afrique au Sud du Sahara: Mobiliser des ressources fiscales pour le développement*. Economica: Paris.

CMH (Commission on Macroeconomics and Health). 2001. *Macroeconomics and Health: Investing in Health for Economic Development*. Geneva: WHO.

Concertation. 2004. *Inventaire des mutuelles de santé en Afrique: Synthèse des travaux de recherche dans 11 pays*. Dakar: La Concertation. http://www.concertation.org.

Criel, B., P. Blaise, and D. Ferette. 2006. "Mutuelles de santé en Afrique et qualité des soins dans les services: Une interaction dynamique." In *L'Assurance maladie en Afrique francophone: Améliorer l'accès aux soins et lutter contre la pauvreté*, ed. G. Dussault, P. Fournier, and A. Letourmy. Washington, DC: World Bank.

Dussault, G., P. Fournier, and A. Letourmy. 2006. *L'Assurance maladie en Afrique francophone: Améliorer l'accès aux soins et lutter contre la pauvreté*. Washington, DC: World Bank.

Ensor, T. 1999. "Developing Health Insurance in Transitional Asia." *Social Science and Medicine* 48: 71–79.

Griffin, C., and P.R. Shaw. 1996. "Health Insurance in Sub-Saharan Africa: Aims, Findings, and Policy Implications." In *Financing Health Services through User Fees and Insurance: Case Studies from Sub-Saharan Africa*, ed. P.R Shaw and M. Ainsworth. Washington, DC: World Bank.

IFC (International Finance Corporation). 2007. *The Business of Health in Africa: Partnering with the Private Sector to Improve People's Lives*. Washington, DC: IFC, World Bank Group.

IMF (International Monetary Fund). 2008. Country Information. http://www.imf.org /external/country/index.htm.

Kaufmann, D., A. Kraay, and M. Mastruzzi. 2010. "The Worldwide Governance Indicators: Methodology and Analytical Issues." Policy Research Working Paper 5430, World Bank, Washington, DC.

Letourmy, A. 1995. "Vingt ans d'assurance maladie au Sénégal." In *Innover dans les systèmes de santé: Expériences d'Afrique de l'Ouest*. Paris: Karthala Editions.

———. 2003. "L'Etat et la couverture maladie dans les pays à faible revenu." Paper prepared for delivery at the XXVIèmes Journées des Economistes Français de la Sante, "Santé et Développement," Centre d'Etudes et de Recherches sur le Développement International (CERDI), Clermont Ferrand, France, January 9–10.

———. 2005. "Assurance maladie: Un cadre général d'analyse en vue de son implantation dans les pays d'Afrique francophone." In *L'assurance maladie en Afrique francophone: Améliorer l'accès aux soins et lutter contre la pauvreté*, ed. G. Dussault, P. Fournier, and A. Letourmy. Washington, DC: World Bank.

McIntyre, D. 2007. *Learning from Experience: Health Care Financing in Low- and Middle-Income Countries*. Global Forum for Health Research, Geneva. http://www.globalforumhealth .org.

McIntyre, D., J. Doherty, and L. Gilson. 2003. "A Tale of Two Visions: The Changing Fortunes of Social Health Insurance in South Africa." *Health Policy and Planning* 18 (1): 47–58.

Musango, L. 2005. "Les axes stratégiques développés pour le renforcement des mutuelles de santé au Rwanda." Paper presented at the Conference on Health Financing in Developing Countries, Centre d'Etudes et de Recherches sur le Développement International (CERDI), Clermont Ferrand, France, December 1–2.

Ndakingaka, J. 2004. *Etude de cas sur les rôles des acteurs dans le développement des mutuelles de santé au Rwanda*. Bethesda, MD: Abt Associates Inc.

Preker, A.S., and E. Velenyi. 2006. "Expansion des programmes gouvernementaux d'assurance maladie obligatoire en Afrique de l'Ouest: Possibilités et contraintes." In *L'assurance maladie en Afrique francophone: Améliorer l'accès aux soins et lutter contre la pauvreté*," ed. G. Dussault, P. Fournier, and A. Letourmy. Washington, DC: World Bank.

Preker, A.S., M. Vujicic, Y. Dukhan, C. Ly, H. Beciu, and P.N. Materu. 2008. *Scaling Up Health Education Opportunities and Challenges for Africa*. Geneva: Global Health Workforce Alliance. http://www.who.int/workforcealliance/documents/Global_Health%20 FINAL%20REPORT.pdf.

Rwanda, Ministry of Health. 2007. *MOH Annual Report 2007*. www.moh.gov.rw.

Senegal, Ministry of Health and Medical Prevention. 2008. *Elaboration d'une stratégie nationale d'extension de la couverture du risque maladie des sénégalais*. Draft report, March, Dakar.

Waelkens, M.P., and B. Criel. 2004. "Les mutuelles de santé en Afrique Sub-Saharienne: Etat des lieux et réflexions sur un agenda de recherche." HNP Discussion Paper 28907, World Bank, Washington, DC.

WHO (World Health Organization). 2011a. National Health Accounts (NHA). Country Information. http://www.who.int/nha/en/.

————. 2011b. WHO Statistical Information System (WHOSIS). http://www.who.int /whosis/en/index.html.

World Bank. 2010. World Development Indicators (WDI). Washington, DC: World Bank.

————. 2011a. Country Policy and Institutional Assessment (CPIA). http://web.worldbank .org/WBSITE/EXTERNAL/TOPICS/ENVIRONMENT/EXTDATASTA/0,,contentMDK:21 115900~menuPK:2935553~pagePK:64168445~piPK:64168309~theSitePK:2875751,00 .html.

————. 2011b. Worldwide Governance Indicators (WGI) 1996–2011. http://info.worldbank .org/governance/wgi/index.asp.

CHAPTER 8

"Big-Bang" Reforms in Anglophone Africa

Caroline Ly, Yohana Dukhan, Frank G. Feeley, Alexander S. Preker, and Chris Atim

Anglophone African countries pursuing mandatory health insurance are at various stages of implementation, from stalled reforms to catalyzed expansion of insurance coverage. The political and socioeconomic characteristics of the countries in the loosely aggregated region called Anglophone Africa help explain these variations in implementation and provide insight into opportunities for scaling up.

INTRODUCTION

"Anglophone Africa" (AA) refers to the former British colonies in Africa that use English as their national language. In reality, although these countries all inherited some common national institutions fashioned after the British system at the time of independence, they are in fact characterized by diversity in culture, local languages, geography, socioeconomic and political systems, and, for the purpose of this chapter, trajectory toward a mandatory health insurance system.

Most AA countries inherited public health care systems from their colonial days, in addition to a disconnected group of mission-based and other modern and traditional health care providers. Modeled after the British National Service, the public systems were predicated on the belief that government-provided health care was a universal right. General revenues from taxes or exports were used to finance public networks of health care providers. In the decades after their independence, economic and political conditions deteriorated in many of these West and East African countries, and their health systems typically bore the brunt. Publicly funded systems could not provide quality health care to all in their diminishing resource environments. Patients increasingly sought health care outside the public system; and the public health care system turned to user fees to make up for funding shortfalls. As a way to solve the dilemma of limited public resources, high financial barriers to access, costly disease burdens, and inefficient public systems, some countries started to experiment with alternative forms of health care financing.

As a result, throughout AA countries today, there is a mix of public and private providers and sources of financing. Alongside their publicly funded systems, countries have experimented with community-based health insurance (CBHI) and have developed private insurance industries. Southern countries such as Namibia, South Africa, and Zimbabwe have a long history of private health insurance. Many AA countries allocate social security expenditures to health.

Ghana, Kenya, Nigeria, and Tanzania have mandatory health insurance (MHI) programs.[1] Other countries in the region are considering following the paths set by those with MHI programs. Countries with MHI programs for a select portion of the population or with limited benefits want to find a sustainable way of expanding coverage.

This chapter does not attempt to argue the merits of mandatory health insurance over tax-funded systems or any other configuration of health care financing mechanism. Instead, it seeks to update previous reviews of the state of health insurance in AA countries and the constraints and opportunities for increasing coverage through MHI programs. It combines political science and economic perspectives to provide insight into the various stages of and potential solutions to scaling up health insurance.

Health Financing Context

The level of economic development varies greatly among AA countries, from competitive middle-income countries in the south such as South Africa and Namibia to poor and largely agrarian economies in Uganda and Tanzania and post-conflict countries such as Sierra Leone and Liberia. Given the positive relationship between per capita wealth and per capita health expenditure, it is not surprising that wealthier countries in the region tend to spend more public resources on health and rely less on out-of-pocket expenditures than do poorer countries. The mostly poor countries struggle with inadequate financial resources and instruments to meet their health care needs.

Few countries in the region have reached either the Abuja target of spending 15 percent of their government budgets on health care or the Commission on Macroeconomics and Health (CMH) target of spending US$34 per capita on basic health services. Even leaving out the post-conflict countries, the remaining countries fall short of the Abuja target. Moreover, even if the Abuja target were met, Kenya, Tanzania, and many other countries would still not be able to meet the CMH target (table 8.1). Middle-income countries like Ghana and Namibia and low-income countries such as Uganda come closest to the Abuja target, spending more than 10 percent of their government budgets on health, while surpassing the CMH target.

Poorer countries obviously have more difficulty meeting both targets. Some countries, such as Kenya, Tanzania, and Nigeria have actually decreased their public health expenditures despite political pledges to increase their commitment to the health sector. Nigeria is one of the furthest from meeting the Abuja target. Despite using oil revenues to finance its public health system, it spends only 5.9 percent of its government budget on health and a total of US$67 per capita on health (table 8.1). The Health Bill passed by the Nigerian House of Representatives and the Senate and now awaiting presidential approval, however, promises to

TABLE 8.1 Social and Economic Characteristics, Selected AA Countries, 2009

	Sub-Saharan Africa	Ghana	Nigeria	Kenya	Tanzania	Uganda	Namibia	South Africa	Zimbabwe
Demography									
Population, total (million)	840.3	23.8	154.7	39.8	43.7	32.7	2.2	49.3	12.5
Population ages 0–14 (% of total)	42.6	38.4	42.5	42.8	44.7	48.9	36.9	30.5	39.9
Population growth (annual %)	2.5	2.1	2.0	2.6	2.9	3.3	1.9	1.1	0.5
Fertility rate (number of births per woman)	5.1[a]	4.0[a]	5.7[a]	4.9[a]	5.6[a]	6.3[a]	3.4[a]	2.5[a]	3.4[a]
Rural population (% of total)	63.1	49.2	50.9	78.1	74.0	86.9	62.6	38.8	62.2
Economy									
GNI per capita, Atlas method (current US$)	1,135.5	1,190.0	1,190.0	760.0	500.0	460.0	4,270.0	5,760.0	360.0[d]
GDP growth (annual %)	1.7	4.7	5.6	2.6	5.5	7.1	–0.8	–1.8	–6.3[c]
Inflation (consumer prices, annual %)	7.1	19.3	11.5	9.2	12.1	12.7	8.8	7.1	24,411.0[b]
Social and infrastructure									
Literacy rate, adult total (% of people ages 15 and above)	62.6[a]	65.8[a]	60.1[a]	86.5[a]	72.6[a]	74.6[a]	88.2[a]	89.0[a]	91.4[a]
Improved sanitation facilities (% of population with access)	31.3[a]	13.0[a]	32.0[a]	31.0[a]	24.0[a]	48.0[a]	33.0[a]	77.0[a]	44.0[a]
Health status and health care									
Life expectancy at birth (years)	52.1[a]	56.6[a]	47.9[a]	54.2[a]	55.6[a]	52.7[a]	61.0	51.5	44.2
Infant mortality rate (per 1,000 live births)	80.8	46.7	85.8	54.8	68.4	79.4	33.6	43.1	56.3
Prevalence of HIV/AIDS (% of 15- to 49-year-olds)	5.0[b]	1.9[b]	3.1[b]	7.8[b]	6.2[b]	5.4[b]	15.3[b]	18.1[b]	15.3[b]
Immunization, DPT (% of children ages 12–23 months)	70.2	94.0	42.0	75.0	85.0	64.0	83.0	69.0	73.0
Physicians (per 1,000 people)	0.19[a]	0.11[a]	0.40[a]	0.14[e]	0.01[c]	0.12[d]	0.3[e]	0.77[e]	0.16[e]
Births attended by skilled health staff (% of total)	44.4	57.1[a]	38.9[a]	43.8	43.4[d]	41.9[c]	81.4[b]	91.2[f]	60.2
Health financing									
Health expenditure per capita (current US$)	78.4	54.5	66.6	33.3	27.1	44.1	296.7	520.6	—
Health expenditure, total (% of GDP)	6.3	5.0	6.1	4.3	5.1	8.5	7.2	9.2	—
Health expenditure, public (% of total government expenditure)	10.2	12.4	5.9	7.3	12.9	13.6	12.1	11.4	—
Health expenditure, private (% of total health expenditure)	51.0	43.3	64.9	56.7	33.9	78.2	45.0	56.2	—
Out-of-pocket health expenditure (% of private expenditure on health)	75.3	66.6	95.6	76.7	41.7	63.6	17.9	29.6	—
Private health insurance (% of private expenditure on health)	7.8	6.2	3.1	9.3	10.1	0.2	61.2	66.1	—
Social security expenditure on health (% of public health expenditure)	4.8	27.1	0.0	10.8	5.5	0.0	2.6	2.5	—
External resources (% of total health expenditure)	21.7	14.4	5.1	34.0	53.4	20.4	12.6	1.8	—

Sources: WHO 2008; World Bank 2010.

Note: — = not available.

a. 2008; b. 2007; c. 2006; d. 2005; e. 2004; f. 2003.

make significant additional resources available by devoting 2 percent of federal government revenues to primary health care in the country.

With such limited public spending on health, private expenditures are a significant, if not the major, component of the total health expenditures in the region. More troublesome is the large role of out-of-pocket (OOP) spending, the most regressive form of health care financing. OOP spending, a major barrier to health care access, accounts for more than 50 percent of private expenditures in the poorer AA countries of West and East Africa. Households burdened with high OOP expenditures are at greater risk of incurring catastrophic health expenditures than well-insured households (Xu et al. 2003).

In the wealthier countries of Southern Africa, the private health insurance industry is more robust, diminishing the role of OOP spending (figure 8.1). Prepaid plans account for more than 60 percent of private health spending in Namibia and South Africa. Although East and West African countries have started to explore alternatives to OOP spending through community-based health insurance schemes, they fail to reach the levels found in Southern Africa, pooling less than 8 percent of their private funds.

Heavy dependency on donor aid is prevalent in this region. External resources account for more than 20 percent of total health expenditures (THE) in Kenya, Tanzania, and Uganda (table 8.1). While donor involvement has helped focus

FIGURE 8.1   Health Financing Structure, Selected AA Countries, 2009

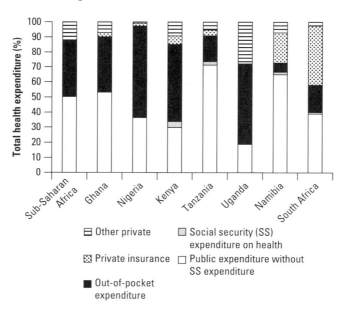

Source: World Bank 2010.

resources on critical health issues, it can be a volatile and inconsistent source of funding that potentially destabilizes health systems through "Dutch Disease," inflationary and other economic effects, and the deterioration of national control.[2]

Like the sources of financing, health care resources suffer from inefficient and inequitable allocation. Public resources tend to be biased toward curative tertiary-level care based in urban centers that favor the better-off (Castro-Leal et al. 2000). Some policies promote the private sector as an alternative to the constrained and inefficient public sector. After all, service delivery in the private sector accounts for a significant portion of spending. Data from the National Health Accounts show spending on private providers accounted for 40 percent of THE in Kenya in 2001–02 and 84 percent of THE in Nigeria in 1998 (Soyibo 2005; Kenya Ministry of Health n.d.). Incentives to promote efficient and equitable use of private resources, however, are still limited. In South Africa, for example, medical schemes acting as passive purchasers fail to constrain high medical inflation. Expenditures on private hospitals per beneficiary increased at three times the rate of inflation between 1997 and 2005 (McIntyre et al. 2007). In addition, in countries with already high rates of inequality, private financing through insurance mechanisms is typically spent by the financially better-off minority. Medical schemes, which cover 17 percent of the population in South Africa, account for 46 percent of THE (McIntyre and Thiede 2007).

It is within a context of limited resources from the public sector, regressive financing, high donor dependency, and inefficient and inequitable use of existing resources that countries have considered policies to scale up health insurance to meet objectives such as increasing sources of funding for the health sector, improving equity in revenue collection and spending, and improving technical and allocative spending efficiency. The implementation of a national health insurance program, by itself, is not seen as the panacea for achieving these objectives. In some cases, a mandatory health insurance program when poorly designed can actually exacerbate inequities in health care and lead to wasteful spending (Dahlgren 1994). The next section summarizes the ways that governments have arranged the use of insurance mechanisms to address some of these problems.

HEALTH COVERAGE AND INSURANCE ARRANGEMENTS

The AA countries are either in an intermediate stage of coverage or lack financial protection (figure 8.2 and annex 8A).

Both mandatory and voluntary health insurance schemes cover a small fraction of the populations in the AA countries (figure 8.3), varying from less than 1 percent in Uganda through CBHI schemes to 25 percent in Kenya's National Hospital Insurance Fund. While voluntary health insurance (VHI) figures most prominently in Southern Africa, mandatory health insurance has progressed further as a politically feasible model in East and West Africa.

Legislation to implement mandatory health insurance has been discussed since the 1960s. Kenya was the first to introduce a mandatory scheme, in 1966.

FIGURE 8.2   Stages of Coverage and Organizational Mechanisms

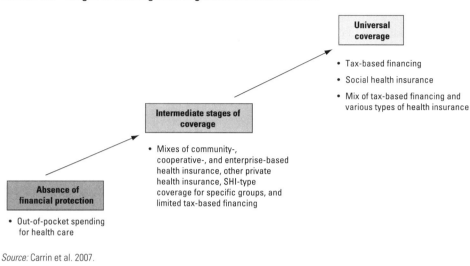

Source: Carrin et al. 2007.

FIGURE 8.3   Health Insurance Coverage, Selected AA Countries

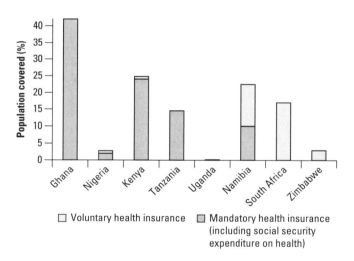

Sources: ILO 2007; NHIA 2008.

Nigeria followed with a version in the 1980s. Experiences with community-based health insurance in this region, namely in Uganda, Tanzania, and Ghana, had prompted governments to explore the possibility of expanding and reforming their health systems on the CBHI model into a nationalized system. In South Africa, MHI has been discussed since the 1990s (table 8.2).

TABLE 8.2 Health Insurance Arrangements, Selected AA Countries

Feature	Ghana	Nigeria	Kenya	Tanzania	Uganda	Namibia	South Africa	Zimbabwe
Mandatory health insurance	Yes	Civil service only	Civil service and all formal sector workers Proposed universal system	Civil service only	2008 National Health Insurance Bill	No, but subsidy for civil servants voluntary; tax-funded public system	Ministerial task team proposal for social health insurance	SHI proposed by MOHCW in 1998, recently revived for discussion
Year legislation passed	2003	1999	1966; 2004 proposal	1999	Pending with first scheme to start mid-2009	1980	2002 proposal tabled	Strong trade union objections derailed first attempt
Revenue collection Sources of financing	2.5% VAT; 2.5% Social Security transfer (SSNIT); premiums	10% employer and 5% employee contributions for formal sector program	Payroll tax Proposed: mix of general revenues, payroll tax, and contributions	NHIF collects 3% from employers and 3% from employee salaries	Payroll tax of 4% from employers and 4% from employee salaries	Ministry of Finance (tax revenues)	Social security tax on all taxpayers, plus voluntary contributions	n.a.
Pooling								
Parastatal agency and/or fund	National Health Insurance Agency (NHIA) and National Health Insurance Fund (NHIF)	National Health Insurance Scheme (NHIS)	National Hospital Insurance Fund (NHIF); proposed National Social Health Insurance Fund	Social Security; National Health Insurance Fund (NHIF)	National Social Health Insurance Scheme	Government medical aid scheme (PSEMAS)	n.a.	n.a.
Insurance administrators	159 District Mutual Health Insurance Schemes	Private sector health management organizations (HMOs)	23 NHIF branches	NHIF	National Health Insurance Scheme	Private sector administration (see below)	Private medical schemes	n.a.
Risk-equalization fund	Yes	No	No	No	No	In private sector for HIV/AIDS	Yes	n.a.
Population covered (%)	32% with ID cards but nearly 55% registered	2%	25%	14.5% (4% through NHIF)	Initial target of 500,000 (public sector)	6%	n.a.	n.a.

(continued)

TABLE 8.2   Health Insurance Arrangements, Selected AA Countries (*continued*)

Feature	Ghana	Nigeria	Kenya	Tanzania	Uganda	Namibia	South Africa	Zimbabwe
Expansion beyond civil service or formal sector	Yes. Aims at universal coverage	No. Aims at universal coverage but only covers civil service now with voluntary	No Proposed: yes	No	Gradual expansion to provide universal coverage starting with civil servants, then formal private, organized informal, and then national	No	Gradual expansion toward mandatory universal	n.a.
Resource allocation and purchasing								
Benefits package	Covers wide services for 95% of disease burden including costs of treatment and drugs	Covers wide IP and OP services including costs of treatment and drugs	Covers IP stay but not treatment or drugs Proposed system to be comprehensive	OP, IP, drugs and basic diagnostic tests	Comprehensive OP, IP, drugs	IP, OP, preventive care, and drugs	Comprehensive with option to "top up"	n.a.
Provider choice	Yes	Yes	Yes—400 hospitals and specialized providers	Yes—government and mission/ religious facilities	Yes	Yes	Yes—choice for private medical scheme members	n.a.
Provider payment mechanism	DRGs for services and at-cost for drugs	Mix of capitation, FFS, per diem, case payment	Per diem "rebates" for hospital stay	FFS with plans to move to capitation	Mix of FFS, capitation	FFS with 1 HMO	Unclear future but currently FFS system	n.a.
Voluntary health insurance								
Year started	1990s. But most, if not all, CBHIs have since joined NHIS	1990s (around Lagos)	1984	1995/6—Igunga CHF started	1996—first CBHI scheme	Namibian Medical Aid Funds, regulatory body established 1995	1889	Public Servants Medical Aid Society (PSMAS, now Premier Aid Medical Aid Society) started before WWII, and Commercial and Industrial Medical Aid Society, now just CIMAS, begun in 1945 for whites, opening its doors to all races from 1961

	Some commercial schemes	18 health insurance companies	60 private insurance firms	Community health funds for agricultural workers; micro-insurance; private health insurers	~13 CBHI and other private schemes	Not-for-profit medical aid schemes with potential for-profit private administration	Mostly nonprofit medical schemes and some limited commercial private related activities	30 nonprofit Medical Aid Societies, with PSMAS and CIMAS by far the two largest
Types of schemes	Some commercial schemes	18 health insurance companies	60 private insurance firms	Community health funds for agricultural workers; micro-insurance; private health insurers	~13 CBHI and other private schemes	Not-for-profit medical aid schemes with potential for-profit private administration	Mostly nonprofit medical schemes and some limited commercial private related activities	30 nonprofit Medical Aid Societies, with PSMAS and CIMAS by far the two largest
Population covered (%)	<1	1	<2	<1	<1	7	17	10
Premium levels (income-based or risk-rated)	Varied; flat rate	Risk-rated with some subsidies	n.a.	Flat rate	n.a.	n.a.	Community-rating	Community-rating
Benefits package	IP, OP, OP drug	IP, OP	IP, OP, preventive, and drugs	Basic package plus curative services	IP, OP, preventive, and drugs	IP, OP, preventive, and drugs	Comprehensive minimum benefits package among medical schemes	CIMAS has primary packages for all members plus different additional, optional packages
Provider payment	FFS	Some capitation, HMO	FFS	n.a.	n.a.	Mixed per diem	Mix of FFS, capitation	For CIMAS and other MAS, tariffs negotiated with providers reflected in Zimbabwe Relative Value Schedule
Administrative expenses (% of total)	20–30	n.a.	n.a.	n.a.	n.a.	35	38	n.a.

Sources: Berman et al. 2001; Humba 2005; ILO 2007; Vogel 1993; Marek, Eichler, and Schnabl 2004; CIMAS 2007; McIntyre and van den Heever 2007; Ladi Awosika, Nigeria NHIS, pers. com., e-mail, Dec. 15, 2008; Ian Kluvitse, pers. com., e-mail, Dec. 2, 2008; NAMFISA 2005; Medical Schemes Council of South Africa 2005.

Note: IP = inpatient; OP = outpatient; FFS = fee-for-service; VAT = value added tax; DRGs = diagnostic-related groups; n.a. = not applicable.

Today, MHI exists to varying degrees in Ghana, Nigeria, Kenya, Tanzania, and Namibia. But it provides coverage mostly for civil service and some formal sector employees. Ghana is the only one of these countries that legislates mandatory enrolment from all its residents. The other MHI countries mentioned mandate health insurance enrolment only for their civil servants and their dependents. Ghana, Kenya, Nigeria, and Tanzania have public parastatal agencies that regulate the risk-pooling functions. Namibia, Nigeria, and South Africa provide government support to privately administer insurance schemes for their civil servants. Uganda and Zimbabwe have been considering the implementation of MHI programs (table 8.2).

FACTORS UNDERLYING RESISTANCE TO REFORM AND IMPLEMENTATION

The minimum prerequisites for a mandatory health insurance system are social solidarity and capable political institutions. Even with these in place, a groundswell of demand for reform toward an MHI system is often lacking due to the limited willingness to trade off between complacency with the status quo and the uncertainty of major health care reform. Many of these countries already have a mix of publicly funded health care systems and gradually expanding private insurance schemes—and stakeholders vested in those arrangements. Thus, the conditions for reform must be such that the benefits of reform can outweigh the status quo. In Ghana, the public was so frustrated with the system of high user fees that the New Patriotic Party was able to come into power on a platform of introducing a mandatory system on the backbone of existing CBHI schemes and, in its brief period of implementation, has increased enrolment to more than 40 percent of the population (Rajkotia 2007). In Tanzania, however, user fees are not high enough to feed public discontent and expand enrolment beyond 15 percent in its district-level Community-Based Fund despite government premium subsidies of 50 percent (Hsiao and Shaw 2007; ILO 2007). In this regard, legislation to promote mandatory health insurance faces political resistance to change. Where legislation has already been implemented, efforts to expand coverage through mandatory health insurance encounter the difficulties of addressing constraints to governance and economic capacity.

Stakeholder Constraints to Reform

One of the underlying conditions of MHI is the notion of solidarity, and the willingness to pool risks in groups organized along communal or employment-based characteristics. In Kenya, for example, the concept of *harambee* ("let's pull together") has been used to raise funds to pay hospital bills (Musau 1999). For their membership base, the CBHI schemes in East and West Africa leveraged preexisting networks based on social solidarity. The Engozi societies in southwestern Uganda formed a ready population base for developing the Kisiizi hospital scheme (Musau 1999). Typically, insurance groups, much like the first schemes of the Bismarck era, are organized around employment. The Land O'Lakes company has helped organize health insurance schemes for their dairy co-ops in Uganda over the last 20 years (Halvorson 2007). Long before that, in 1889, the first private health insurance scheme was started for employees of the de Beers diamond mines in South Africa (Kruger n.d.).

Private insurance has since expanded across Southern Africa covering mainly whites and wealthy blacks. How to expand insurance beyond the existing membership has been widely debated and plagued with problems. In the post-apartheid era, Southern Africa has been struggling to overcome high rates of inequality (for Gini coefficients, see table 8.4, discussed under the subhead "Constraints to Implementation: Institutional and Economic Realities"). These rates can serve as an indicator of the political resistance to pooling together whole populations into a larger MHI scheme, particularly one that involves income cross-subsidization from the organized urban middle class to the poor (Thomas and Gilson 2004). Design elements of MHI, such as the type of financing mechanism, threaten certain stakeholders. Such health financing reforms are politically contentious because they determine who pays for and benefits from the reform (Thomas and Gilson 2004).

A test of national solidarity is the ability to build consensus among the key actors in the policy process involving the scaling up of health insurance. Although the specific actors, their position on the health insurance reforms, and the extent of their influence in the policy process are country-specific, this section highlights some of the key actors that have been involved in previous health insurance reforms and broadly categorizes how they have impeded or supported reform toward scaling up health insurance (table 8.3).

TABLE 8.3   Potential Stakeholders in Scaling Up Mandatory Health Insurance

Sphere	Actors	Common perspective and concerns
Government	Ministry of Finance	Revenue collection: sustainability of sources of funding, tax burden, and impact of taxation on labor markets and economy's competitiveness
	Ministry of Health	Focused on increasing resources to struggling public systems and maintaining policy influence on new governance arrangements
	Public providers	Concerned with provider payment mechanism and increasing resources to public system; sustainability of public funding as opposed to user fees
	Social security agency	Concerned with arrangement of administration housed in larger social security agency or, in case of separate health insurance agency, that it might compete for resources
	Health insurance agency	Concerned with governance arrangements, degree of autonomy, overall sustainability of financing
Social	Labor unions, civil servants, and other formal sector employees	May oppose MHI because this group typically already receives health care through subsidized public system or insurance. But would have to pay more through additional payroll tax used to cross-subsidize other enrollees without any improvement in personal health care coverage.
	The public	Skeptical of government capacity and corruption and may not value the benefits of the health insurance at, or more than, the cost of the benefits, and even when they may desire something different from reliance on OOPs, they are often unmobilized and passive during the reform debates and design stage.

(continued)

TABLE 8.3   Potential Stakeholders in Scaling Up Mandatory Health Insurance (*continued*)

Sphere	Actors	Common perspective and concerns
Social (continued)	The poor	Though typically unempowered and lacking access to health care, this group would be concerned about whether or not they would gain insurance through this system; often NGOs pose as their advocates.
	Donors, technical partners, and external NGOs	Inconsistent views on NHI, which are informed by donor countries' own health system; sustainability concerns
	Academics and other technical experts	Concerned with technical design but often overlooked in the policy process
Private	Employers	Depends on employer's investment in workers' health. Some already provide substantial coverage through in-house programs and would therefore gain from public coverage. Others may oppose it because of increased burden of taxation.
	Private providers including mission sector	Concerned with the monopsonistic purchasing power of a concentration of public or private insurance funds and its consequent effect on provider payment mechanism and decision-making autonomy over patient care
	Private health insurance schemes	Concerned about whether or not MHI will leverage existing schemes or create mechanism competing with private schemes. If MHI leverages existing schemes, what design features will dictate how private schemes manage risk and financial sustainability?

Source: Authors.

Role of State in Health Sector

The state consists of actors with various and sometimes conflicting interests and responsibilities. As steward of the public health sector, it is typically the largest single collector of revenues, and purchaser and provider of health services. A balance of these interests can promote productive reforms, as the state has the critical leadership role of driving the reform process. But often there is an imbalance leading to stalled reforms, unless this leadership role is assumed by one of its agencies such as the MOH.

Ministry of Finance

The Ministry of Finance focuses on the funding mechanisms proposed in an MHI program and its effect on the government budget and overall economy. Payroll taxes typically finance MHI programs, but a mix of additional financing mechanisms, including general tax revenues and premiums, can also feed MHI revenues. The structure of the financing mechanism could increase the tax burden on the public or the formal sector and negatively affect labor markets and the country's economic competitiveness. In South Africa, for example, the national Treasury opposed initial proposals for social health insurance primarily because it would increase the tax burden on the already overburdened middle class (McIntyre and van den Heever 2007).

Ministry of Health and Public Providers

Ministries of Health typically exercise stewardship over most of a country's health infrastructure, including hospitals, clinics, and health professionals. Faith-based or mission hospitals, the next largest group of health facilities, often receive government subsidies or seconded staff. Many civil servants moonlight as "private" practitioners. South Africa and Namibia have a "private medical" sector made possible, in part, by public sector support for comprehensive medical scheme benefits.

Because public or quasi-public facilities dominate health institutions, Anglophone African governments are in a very different position from the European governments that sought to broaden insurance to pay fees in a private health market. Ministries of Health often lead the agenda on developing MHI programs with the expectation that the creation of a dedicated funding source in the form of payroll taxes would sustain an increase in revenues to the chronically underfunded and overworked public health system. Even in South Africa, with a substantial private health industry separate from the public system, one of the goals of insurance regulation is to prevent private insurers from "dumping" patients in public hospitals.

However, a natural tension arises when, as part of the design of an MHI program, a new and possibly independent entity such as a National Health Insurance Agency is created that also lays claims to health sector funds. In new organizational structures, Ministries of Health and public providers would have to cede control over certain responsibilities and funds.

Social Security Agency

The development of MHI arrangements are typically viewed within the context of the country's larger social security program. Pension programs in much of Sub-Saharan Africa already face high liabilities, verging on collapse. Many of the problems that plague pension programs would also constrain MHI programs (Bonnerjee 2003 [draft]). The state of the labor market, unfavorable demographic characteristics, high administrative costs, and even a high incidence of HIV/AIDS burden pension programs and potential MHI programs' financial sustainability and ability to expand (Bonnerjee 2003 [draft]). The problems in many countries' pension programs are fodder for opponents who believe that a new MHI program would follow the same fate. Pension reforms go hand in hand with MHI reforms.

Therefore, through the development of MHI programs, social security agencies would have to share their already small revenue base to provide health insurance coverage. Like mandatory health insurance, revenues for social security typically come from a share of workers' incomes. In addition, some configurations of MHI programs call for a new parastatal health insurance agency to collect revenues through similar mechanisms or to leverage pension arrangements to provide social security expenditures on health. A separate program would compete with social security for the same revenues. In the case of Ghana, the social security fund had to transfer 2.5 percent of its funds to the newly created National Health Insurance Fund. Ghana's pensioners and trade unions had opposed the national health insurance program because of this arrangement. However, the Government placated these opponents by guaranteeing the future solvability of the pension fund. In Uganda, the National Social Security Fund opposed the development of the parastatal Uganda Social Health Insurance Corporation in favor of expanding its own management duties to provide health insurance coverage (Bwogi 2007). In the proposed HI scheme for Sierra Leone, the social security agency has offered to lead the design and implementation as well as to house and "incubate" the new HI agency proposed, thus ensuring it would be able to effectively control this potential rival for resources.

Health Insurance Agency

Most mandatory health insurance arrangements create new health insurance organizations with responsibilities, accountability, and authority that, though laid out in legislation, are de facto unclear for the health insurance organizations. Thus, throughout the process of reform, health insurance agencies are primarily concerned with resolving these issues in a manner that expands their stewardship over health care resources. Experience with health insurance agencies in Sub-Saharan Africa is limited. Recent evidence from Kenya's National Hospital Insurance Fund is not favorable, demonstrating that 25 percent of funds go to administrative costs and 53 percent go to investment projects such as costly new headquarters (Hsiao and Shaw 2007).

Social Sphere

The social sector in this context represents a counter group to the state, a collection of stakeholders that either provide financing (taxes, premiums, or donations) or are the benefactors of the health care system (patients).

Labor Unions, Formal Sector or Civil Service Employees

Most MHI programs collect revenues through payroll taxes. Civil service and other formal sector employees make up the most identifiable tax revenue base within Anglophone African countries where the informal sector dominates. These formal sector workers, most likely already covered by health care insurance, would have to shoulder the major part of the financial burden in any MHI scheme. Although their contributions would increase, they would likely either not gain or would lose some of their health care coverage, as in Ghana. In South Africa, trade unions opposed a 1997 initiative to provide health insurance reform because it did not appear to offer uninsured members any better access to public hospitals than they already had (McIntyre, Doherty, and Gilson 2003). In Tanzania and

Nigeria, workers resisted payroll deductions to cover a share of health insurance premiums. They did not see any improvement in health care access. Support among civil servants for the fledgling National Health Insurance Fund (NHIF) in Tanzania has not been unanimous. In 2005, teachers in the Kwimba District of the Mwanza Region threatened to take the NHIF to court if it continued deducting contributions from salary. The protesting teachers claimed that they did not get proper treatment at hospitals and health centers enrolled with the NHIF.[3] Employees of the Morogoro Municipal Council also threatened to terminate their membership in the NHIF because it provided no benefit to them. They claimed that NHIF-registered providers avoided treating NHIF beneficiaries who had expensive diseases. The complaint also suggests that some enrollees were not clear on the concept of risk pooling and insurance, with protesters asking for an analysis of the fund because not all employees and their dependents fall sick, and the care used does not tally with their monthly deductions.[4]

Despite high out-of-pocket expenditures, constitutional guarantees of "free medical care" in these countries have made it difficult for governments to collect employee contributions for national health insurance. However, where employees do not have health insurance coverage and the underfunded public medical system provides inadequate care, there is strong demand from formal sector employees for some form of government-supported insurance or health care. In Uganda, civil servants had long demanded that government provide them with free care through the public system. Often, MHI programs start with health care coverage for civil servants and formal sector employees because they are the most identifiable group in an informal sector–dominated economy. Once these people receive health care, however, they have little immediate incentive to support further expansion of coverage.

The Public

Even more common are the public's concerns about government's capacity to implement a health insurance reform. Many AA countries rank low in governance indicators (table 8.4). The public, whose opinions are vocalized through civil society organizations, is wary of MHI proposals to create new institutions when the existing institutional capacity is so poor. The Kenyan government's corrupt and inefficient administration of its National Hospital Insurance Fund gave opponents cause for concern over the proposal for universal coverage through the creation of a new National Social Health Insurance Fund (Carrin et al. 2007). The National Hospital Insurance Fund not only fails to pay as intended for outpatient services and drugs, but also devotes only a small portion (22 percent) of its funds to pay benefits (Hsiao and Shaw 2007). One purpose of Kenya's proposed National Social Health Insurance Fund is to replace the existing scheme with a more transparent and accountable agency. It would add to its governance arrangements a Board of Trustees that includes a fraud and investigation unit (Carrin et al. 2007).

TABLE 8.4   Governance and Economic Capacity Indicators, Selected AA Countries

	Ghana	Nigeria	Kenya	Tanzania	Uganda	Namibia	South Africa	Zimbabwe
Governance and stability								
Gini coefficient	42.8[d]	42.9[b]	47.7[c]	34.6[a]	42.6[c]	74.3	57.8[a]	50.1
CPI (2007)	3.7	2.2	2.1	3.2	2.8	4.5	5.1	2.1
Political stability/no violence (percentile rank 0–100) (2006)	54.8	3.8	15.4	40.4	13.5	75.5	44.2	13.9
CPIA public sector management and institutions cluster average (1 = low to 6 = high) (2009)	3.8	2.9	3.3	3.5	3.3	n.a.	n.a.	2.0
CPIA transparency, accountability, and corruption in the public sector rating (1 = low to 6 = high) (2009)	4.0	3.0	3.0	3.0	2.5	n.a.	n.a.	1.5
Economics								
GNI per capita, Atlas method (current US$, 2009)	1,190.0	1,190.0	760.0	500.0	460.0	4,270.0	5,760.0	n.a
Poverty head count ratio at US$1.25 a day (PPP) (% of population)	30.0[d]	64.4[b]	19.7[c]	88.5[a]	51.5[c]	n.a.	26.2[a]	n.a.
Age dependency ratio (2009)	0.73	0.84	0.83	0.92	1.06	0.68	0.54	0.79
Urban population as % of total (2009)	50.8	49.1	21.9	26.0	13.1	37.4	61.2	37.8
Female labor force participation rate (% of 15- to 64-year-olds)	75.2[f]	39.5[f]	77.6[f]	88.8	80.5	53.5	51.0	60.8
Informal labor (%)	80.4[b]	n.a.	32[c]	35[d]	85.9[a]	n.a.	17[e]	n.a.
Informal economy (% of GNP for 1999/2000)	38.4	57.9	n.a.	58.3	43.1	n.a.	28.4	59.4
Government revenues (excluding grants, % of GDP, 2009)	26.9[f]	n.a.	19.5[f]	n.a.	17.0[f]	29.1[e]	30.7[f]	n.a.
General government final consumption expenditure (% of GDP, 2009)	9.6	n.a	16.3	16.2[d]	11.4	24.2	21.0	27.2[c]

Sources: World Bank 2010; UN 2006; Transparency International 2007; Ghana Statistical Service 2007; Republic of Kenya 2003; Tanzania National Bureau of Statistics 2002; Schneider 2002; Statistics South Africa 2007; Uganda Bureau of Statistics 2003. *Note:* Informal sector definitions and years may vary based on household surveys: Ghana data are the percentage of employed; Kenya's household survey separates out self-employed from informal sector; Tanzania data are the percentage of households engaged in informal sector activity; Uganda's labor market is the percentage of self-employed people ages 10 years and above of total employed. CPIA = Country Policy and Institutional Assessment (World Bank); n.a. = not applicable; PPP = purchasing power parity. a. 2000; b. 2004; c. 2005; d. 2006; e. 2007; f. 2008.

Other concerns such as the limited realized value of the benefits, the low willingness to cross-subsidize risks and income levels across disparate groups, and the weak ability to pay for premiums also influence public opinion.

However, since the burden of high OOPs falls mostly on the public, they are also often eager for alternatives, and in a few cases, this has been manifested through the electoral process, although channeling such public frustrations into successful health financing reforms has not so far been the norm.

Donors, Technical Partners, and External NGOs

Through a number of often-disconnected initiatives, donors, technical partners, and external NGOs have a significant role in health care financing policy in Sub-Saharan Africa. User fee policies, for example, have generated disagreement within the donor community over how to increase access to health care for the poor while providing steady funding for health care expenses. Over a decade ago, the World Health Organization in its *World Health Report 2000* (WHO 2000: 85) highlighted the importance of prepayment as a way of protecting the poor from catastrophic health expenditures, but the debate over the specific mechanism (tax-financed public health systems or social health insurance or any number of nuanced approaches) is far from being resolved. The evidence on which financing mechanism has the most beneficial impact in meeting equity, efficiency, and improved outcomes is largely inconclusive in OECD countries. Donor perspectives for or against the use of specific public financing arrangements for health have been largely informed by the donor countries' own experiences with their health system. Many donors have been involved in supporting CBHI schemes and targeting subsidies for insurance to the poor. But this same enthusiasm for CBHI schemes rarely translates into support for MHI arrangements. Donors share the same reservations held by other stakeholders over the government's economic and institutional capacity to implement a national insurance program that meets equity and efficiency objectives. But for MHI programs that aim to target the poor with subsidies, donor support would be crucial. It would be difficult to replace the nearly 50 percent of THE financed from civil servants' out-of-pocket spending and other government revenues in AA countries with just health insurance contributions and no external funding.

Private Sector Stakeholders

Private sector stakeholders refer to the collective group of organizations and individuals whose business is impacted by the potential health insurance reforms.

Employers

Employers' positions are closely related to what they spend on health care to retain and attract skilled workers. In Africa, notably mining companies directly provide health care for their workers, particularly when alternative care is too far away or of poor quality. The more employers spend, the greater are their incentives to keep costs down through mandatory health insurance coverage for their workers, national pooling of the population, and subsidies to firms to provide care. Smaller firms and those with a high turnover of low-skilled workers are less likely to provide care, although some pay cash allowances for medical expenses. Part of the growth in private health insurance in Africa has come from employers who wish to transfer management, risks, and administration of medical benefit payments to a professional insurer. However, insurance may not give workers at isolated sites access to other providers. Employers who have ignored their workers' health needs would be disinterested in a new health insurance benefit or would oppose programs that would increase their tax burden. Such employers, especially in middle-income countries, would be concerned about the impact of these higher costs on their global competitiveness.

Nevertheless, employers are the most likely route to independent expansion of private health insurance in Africa. Moving down-market with policies to cover lower-income workers, as is happening in Namibia, could lead to the expansion of the insured population. Broad coverage of the working population could then become a building block for a still broader national health insurance plan. The role of employment-based insurance will be limited in the near future by the relatively small size of the formal sector of the economy. Employers who have never contributed to employee medical costs may provide coverage only if it is mandated. And because the formal sector is small, large tax or donor subsidies will be necessary to provide coverage for the rest of the population at a level equal to traditional employee coverage.

The Medical Profession: Professional Groups and Provider Businesses

Many medical practitioners are concerned about the effect of health insurance on their own revenues and their decision-making autonomy in patient care. They can be a vocal opponent when the specter of reform means they would have to bear an increased burden of payment risk. The introduction of a new payer, like a health insurance scheme, might move from fee-for-service, where the payer bears payment risk, to a payment system designed to limited supplier-induced demand that shifts some of the risk to the provider. In Tanzania, the medical profession fought the introduction of managed care when Kenya- and South Africa–based HMOs entered the Tanzanian market. In 2002, the Tanzanian Medical Council warned medical practitioners against engaging in transactions with HMOs and consequently, 10 major hospitals terminated their HMO contracts, claiming breach of medical ethics.[5] But health care providers have also provided support for insurance schemes. Examples include the Nkoranza scheme, a hospital-based scheme that was also the largest informal sector CBHI scheme in Ghana. In Ghana, hospitals were known to detain patients who did not pay for the delivered services. The introduction of health insurance ensured that hospitals would receive payment for treating insured patients. For providers, particularly in public tax–funded systems, the introduction of an insurance scheme can mean more and sustainable financing (Kutzin 1998).

Private and Community-Based Insurance Schemes

Existing health insurance schemes can be threatened by an MHI reform program. MHI programs could decide to leverage existing health insurance schemes as financial intermediaries or create a single or multiple government-run financial intermediaries. At a minimum, the MHI arrangements would increase competitive pressures for existing health insurance schemes, while bringing them under greater regulatory scrutiny as they are forced to comply with requirements such as offering minimum benefits packages, collecting set premiums, or paying providers according to specific payment mechanisms or fee schedules. Some MHI programs allow members to opt out of MHI plans as long as they have private insurance or "top up" their benefits packages by purchasing private plans that offer services beyond what is in the prescribed minimum benefits package. These options would allow private insurance schemes to continue running. At the other extreme, MHI arrangements may act as a de facto public monopoly in the insurance industry by resurrecting high barriers for commercial insurance companies.

Constraints to Implementation: Institutional and Economic Realities

Not only has the willingness to reform been hampered by public cynicism of government capacity as in Kenya, but implementation in countries where reform legislation has passed has also been slow due to weak institutional capacity. Many of the Anglophone countries have poor budget management, poor administrative and enforcement capacity, weak accountability systems, and corruption (refer back to table 8.4). For example, a World Bank review found that Nigeria's health sector, like other parts of its bureaucracy, had been subject to politicization and rent-seeking during years of military rule. Few funds for non-salary recurrent expenditures were being disbursed to local areas, and politics determined budget design (World Bank 2005b). Parastatal health agencies like the National Health Insurance Scheme were designed to deliver health care services directly, particularly primary health care. But the report also found that their effectiveness was dampened by inconsistent funding, management problems, political interference, and poor coordination with state and local governments (World Bank 2005b). The Nigerian government had already been forced to delay the collection of employee contributions to the national health insurance fund to ensure timely rollout among federal employees.[6]

A significant problem is the failure to design health insurance agencies that act with sufficient autonomy to manage key health insurance functions and have clear accountability mechanisms and other key institutional attributes. The challenges of solving the problems of a broken system are among the motivating factors in creating a new separate agency. Kenya's new National Social Health Insurance Fund (NSHIF) starts with a clean slate and governance arrangements designed to prevent waste and corruption. But people are rightly skeptical to question whether or not a new agency would be able to resolve the problems that other public agencies have failed to address. Health insurance is administratively complex, and its potential for mismanagement is dependent on the design of revenue collection, risk pooling, and resource allocation

---

BOX 8.1   HEALTH INSURANCE ARRANGEMENTS AND CONSTRAINTS

Revenue collection mechanisms

- The tax base is small, given the large informal sector.
- Government revenue-collection capacity is weak.
- The mechanism chosen can adversely affect equity, labor markets, and global economic competitiveness.
- High premiums are weak incentives to comply.

Pooling revenues and sharing risks

- Small, fragmented risk pools are insufficient to equalize risks and protect from high-cost risks.

Resource allocation and purchasing (RAP)

- The purchaser has limited influence to control costs through provider payment mechanism, fee-setting, and contract enforcement.
- The disease burden is costly.
- Supply constraints cannot keep up with demand. The shortage of human resources for health is a serious constraint.

Source: Authors.

---

and purchasing arrangements (box 8.1). These are important to the success of MHI programs not only in meeting their equity and efficiency objectives, but also in sustaining an expanded coverage of the population. The next section describes the limited economic and institutional capacity that has constrained the expansion of MHI programs.

Revenue Collection

Designing the revenue collection mechanism is complicated by the large informal sector, small tax base, weak government capacity for tax collection, and economic sensitivity to increasing the tax burden. Many low-income Anglophone governments already have weak capacity to enforce tax collection. Indicators like government revenues as a percentage of GDP reflect this weakness. High-income countries' government revenues account for 26 percent of GDP, as compared with 13 percent in low-income countries. In the Anglophone group, government revenues in Uganda and Kenya are low relative to government expenditures. This limited capacity to collect general tax revenues bodes ill for governments' attempts to collect revenues for MHI, even if it focuses on collecting from civil servants. For example, a study in 1993 found Kenya's National Hospital Insurance Fund received less than 70 percent of its expected revenue (Berman et al. 2001).

Because of the large informal sector, most taxes from general revenues come from indirect taxes on sales. But most health insurance programs collect revenues by levying taxes on wages. Payroll taxes would place the burden of financing on civil servants and other formal sector employees, the most easily identifiable segment of the tax base. But payroll taxes have some potentially negative economic consequences. Payroll taxes have to be set at a level that not only meets the financing needs of the MHI program but also avoids severely distorting the labor market and reducing the country's economic competitiveness. If the formal sector feels more overburdened with taxes than the informal sector does, formal sector employees may have incentives to move to the informal sector. Further study into the effects of a payroll tax on employment would need to be done. Strong economic growth should theoretically create an expanding formal tax base for health insurance revenues. Not all of these countries have experienced growth in the size of the formal sector, however, which could indicate the limited potential of payroll taxes as an expanding source of revenue. Furthermore, increasing the costs to employers who do not include health insurance as part of their labor costs could impair a country's immediate economic competitiveness. One of AA's global comparative advantages is its relatively low labor cost. Middle-income countries may be most concerned about the effect a payroll tax would have on labor costs of goods or services produced to compete in the global market.

Moreover, revenue collection systems should be designed to meet equity goals while maximizing tax obligation compliance. Most of the described payroll tax mechanisms (as in Kenya, Nigeria, Tanzania, and Uganda) are proportional tax systems, which tax a set percentage of wages. This arrangement could be regressive because the better-off usually have additional sources of income and wealth that are not captured by payroll taxes. Alternatives to taxes include support from general revenues primarily to subsidize the poor and income-based premiums. Ghana uses an earmarked value added tax (VAT), transfers from the social security program, and income-based premiums to fund its MHI program. The income-based premium might offer a more progressive form of financing than a flat tax. However, Ghana's program still has problems attracting poor informal sector workers who cannot afford even the lowest premium.

Many voluntary health insurance programs have failed to design revenue collection mechanisms that create incentives for users to fully substitute the expectation of out-of-pocket payments for prepayment. One of the reasons given for the failure of community-based health insurance mechanisms to take off in Uganda and Tanzania was that user fees in the public system were too low to attract members.

To attract the poor, the government and/or donors often provide subsidies to exempt the poor from paying insurance contributions. But where governments have demonstrated weak capacity in implementing user fee exemptions for the poor, well-designed premium subsidies would be just as likely to fail to reach the poor. A survey in rural Ethiopia found no relation between poverty level and exemption status.

The high dependency ratios in the region also limit the potential financial contributions from the population. Already, more than half of the members enrolled in Ghana's MHI are exempt from paying premiums because they are under 18 years old, retired civil servants, or over the age of 70 (NHIA 2007). Covering exempt categories still requires additional public financing or external donor resources. While the International Labour Organization (ILO) projected that Ghana's health insurance fund will remain solvent over the next 10 years, it recommends that Ghana revise its current revenue collection system and provider payment mechanism (ILO 2005).

For long-term viability, MHI programs have to make sure long-term financial obligations can be met. In doing so, they have to be immune to political pressures to redirect their revenues toward other programs or to expand their benefits beyond affordability. Thus, the financial realities of mandatory health insurance are closely tied to government capacity and governance. Governance structures have to be strong enough to ensure that public funds for health insurance are not poached by other interests and that they can perform the designated tasks of collecting revenues and distributing benefits.

Risk Pooling

Determining the size, number, and composition of risk pools is important to the sustainability of a health insurance scheme. With the large size of the informal sector, many countries with an MHI program limit their coverage to civil servants or other formal sector employees in the short term. Income and health risk cross-subsidization is limited in this narrow group, which tends to represent the better-off population segment. In restricting inclusion to this better-off population, MHI programs fail to achieve equity objectives. Health insurance tends to draw the limited health care resources (e.g., providers, drugs) to the insured population.

The practicalities of reaching the informal sector, however, make expanding health insurance coverage difficult. Ghana, for example is struggling to enroll informal workers, who constitute 80 percent of the workforce. During this transitional phase to enroll all Ghanaians, the mandatory enrolment requirement has been relaxed. Many of the MHI schemes that focus on compulsory enrolment only for civil servants allow voluntary enrolment from the informal sector. Nigeria and Tanzania mandate civil service enrolment but allow voluntary enrolment for other sectors. This feature opens the financial health of the insurance schemes up to adverse selection problems in which costlier, high-risk individuals will be the most likely to enroll voluntarily while low-risk individuals opt out.

In forming risk pools for an MHI program, pre-existing financial intermediaries could be used as the backbone of health insurance schemes and risk pools for a new MHI, as in Ghana and Nigeria. These pre-existing risk pools may be a fragmented, disconnected, small group. Systems that also allow multiple-tier systems in which members can opt out of the publicly run health insurance in favor of more comprehensive private insurance could further fragment risk pools. A common problem in voluntary health insurance arrangements is that fragmented risk pools will either cream skim to avoid high risks and/or be subject to financial instability from the large expenses of high-risk members and limited collective bargaining power to control costs. MHI programs can create mechanisms to address this problem. They could, for instance, create a single large pool like Tanzania's pool of civil servants, a reinsurance mechanism like Ghana's that protects district schemes from financial deficits, or a risk-equalization fund as proposed in South Africa to redistribute health risks across existing private medical aid societies.

Ghana's National Health Insurance Fund, financed predominantly through general revenues and social security transfers, provides subsidies for the poor and reinsures District Mutual Health Insurance Schemes that run deficits. The use of the fund only partially reduces the risk pool fragmentation problem, and the reinsurance mechanism does not create a disincentive for the district schemes to run financial deficits. Instead, a risk-equalization fund, as proposed in South Africa, would unify the fragmented risk pools and reduce disincentives to cream skim.

Resource Allocation and Purchasing

Resource allocation and purchasing in health insurance are affected by limitations on potential revenues, the high disease burden, and the organizational design of the health insurance scheme(s) as a purchaser of services. In contrast to governments' budgetary process for resource allocation and purchasing, health insurance arrangements could separate the functions of public service provider and public service purchaser. Because most health systems today are publicly run, the impulse would be to provide health insurance for use only in public facilities. But this has not been the case in any of the MHI countries where these are discussed. Health insurance, both public and private, is associated with the expansion of private providers. Kenya's National Hospital Insurance Fund reimburses its members' stay in both public and private hospitals. Because the private sector is a significant provider of health care services, to exclude them from government-run health insurance programs would be impractical.

A new entity tasked with purchasing services could be designed to be either a passive or an active purchaser. A passive purchaser would have little influence over resource allocation and purchasing decisions whereas a strategic purchaser would be able to leverage its bargaining power to negotiate the prices and payment methods for the insurance-covered health care services and commodities used. Allowing MHI agencies to act as strategic purchasers would promote efficient use of resources.

One of the impacts on cost is the high disease burden in Sub-Saharan Africa. Many countries are experiencing a demographic shift and therefore have to pay for services to treat both communicable and chronic diseases. The Uganda feasibility study pointed out that the high costs and unpredictable expenditures of the country's recurring malaria epidemics would strain the insurance system (Berman et al. 2001). MHI countries are struggling to design benefits packages that not only satisfy their countries' health needs but are also affordable. Out-of-pocket payments include drugs purchased from unlicensed drug sellers, fees to moonlighting practitioners, and sometimes under-the-table payments in public facilities. By their very nature, these expenses are not covered as benefits in a health insurance program. For the sake of financial sustainability, benefits packages often exclude *uninsurable risks,* risks that are frequent and expected. Chronic or preventable diseases are difficult to insure. Examples can range from immunizations to pregnancy.

The high prevalence of HIV/AIDS (especially in Southern Africa), complications from opportunistic infections, and drug costs have typically made treatment too expensive for health insurance coverage. Private insurance schemes in Namibia, however, have offered an innovative example of inclusion of HIV/AIDS coverage in the benefits package. Although there is no mandated minimum benefits package, medical schemes have covered HIV/AIDS treatment for both the public and private sectors. However, premium costs have put this option beyond the reach of many private employers and employees. In 2004, some low-cost plans that include antiretroviral therapy began to develop with premiums less than half of those of traditional medical schemes.[7] Other low-cost schemes include broader benefits with a low annual ceiling. These types of policies now provide HIV/AIDS coverage for about 4 percent of the insured population, most of them previously uninsured. A risk-equalization fund reinsures AIDS treatment costs for participating medical schemes. The National Business Coalition on AIDS (NABCOA) encourages employers to address the national AIDS epidemic and supports marketing of the new low-cost insurance plans. Foreign donors, notably PharmAccess International, have provided support for these innovations, including a targeted premium subsidy for low-cost plans. A willingness-to-pay survey showed that 87 percent of uninsured respondents in Namibia were willing to join such a scheme and that the poor are willing to pay up to 5 percent of their income as premiums (Van der Gaag and Gustafsson-Wright 2007).

Design of the benefits packages is intimately linked to not only who will provide services but also how to pay for services. Reforming the provider payment mechanism is politically difficult, as mentioned above. All the MHI programs discussed have a fee-for-service payment component that does little to control costs and gives way to potential supplier-induced demand problems. Fee-for-service payment mechanisms also provide disincentives to focus on preventive care. Many health systems are biased toward providing hospital curative care and are overwhelmed by a burden of diseases that are preventable. Some of the MHI programs include or are moving toward other types of provider payment mechanism. These types of reforms in the insurance and the provider payment mechanism are moving along in parallel to public health programs or other health sector reforms such as strategies to decentralize and provide more autonomy to public health care providers. The reforms are intended to increase a sense of ownership and improve decision making, while creating payment incentives to which providers would respond. There are limitations, however, to the way these new health care resources can be invested to improve health care quality. While health insurance for the poor is supposed to help solve the problem of health care underutilization, the supply of health care services cannot keep up with the resulting increased demand. Many AA countries have a shortage of human resources for health and cannot scale up the supply of services rapidly enough to handle the increase in demand.

South Africa has been waffling on MHI reforms, partly because of the cost. Successive reform proposals narrowed both the target group and the benefits package. Its private medical schemes, which act as passive purchasers, have been experiencing cost explosions due to increases in unit costs and utilization. For example, medical scheme expenditure on hospitals per beneficiary increased 66 percent, three times faster than inflation between 1997 and 2005 (McIntyre et al. 2007). In Nigeria, a feasibility study for health insurance found that Nigerians were willing to provide altruistic subsidies to provide health insurance to the poor. To support a system that could incorporate poorer members, however, altruistic donations from Nigerians would not be enough; it would require sustainable grants from governments and donors (Onwujekwe and Velenyi 2010).

Once political will to develop MHI has been ascertained, countries still have to face the challenges of designing and implementing programs that provide strong governance and sustainable economics. As the Uganda feasibility study cautiously recommended, any decision to develop a mandatory health insurance system would require careful financial analyses to assess its long-term sustainability and careful design of revenue collection, risk pooling, benefits packages, provider payment, and other key features. The state of institutions helps explain the underlying reasons for the current stage of insurance reform and development, but what does this mean for the future of MHI in this region? Box 8.1 on page 166 summarizes some conclusions from the mixed bag of experience with health insurance in Africa.

TARGETED AREAS FOR SCALING UP HEALTH INSURANCE DEVELOPMENT

Historically, health insurance has developed along two axes—horizontally extending outward to a broader segment of the population and vertically expanding the depth of the services covered. Where mandatory health insurance exists today, the path toward broad coverage and depth of services has not been one of constant, gradual expansion. Health insurance reform can fall victim to external economic and political factors that can halt or even reverse progress in scaling up. Zimbabwe, with its once relatively large private insurance base and high per capita income, was the Sub-Saharan African country with the most potential for expanding health insurance coverage (Shaw and Griffin 1995). But the country's recent economic contraction has had adverse consequences for its health insurance industry, which has been struggling to keep up with its hyperinflationary economic and medical cost environment.

Other AA countries, backed by political stability and the momentum of relatively strong economic growth, are pushing for greater government involvement in providing health insurance coverage. Governments have been encouraging health insurance coverage of poorer and/or informal sector groups where their publicly funded health systems have failed either through the expansion of private insurance mechanisms as in the Low-Income Medical Scheme (LIMS) in South Africa, subsidies for Community Health Funds in Tanzania, and the gradual expansion of coverage to the informal sector in Ghana's National Health Insurance Fund.

Early signs of success and failure of these initiatives indicate the nature of the prerequisites for scaling up. Income level is clearly not the sole predictor of a country's ability to provide MHI coverage. Demand-driven reform has strengthened the government's will for scaling up. Small-scale schemes have blossomed into larger ones, and newly created risk pools have succeeded because of the way health insurance arrangements have been designed to fit into the larger health financing context and health system infrastructure. One example is the way prepayment fees (versus cost-recovery fees) have been set to create incentives for certain population groups to join. Ghana, South Africa, and Tanzania offer contrasting experiences. Ghana was able to reach the broadest portion of the population because the prospect of user fees outweighed the cost of insurance. South Africa's private insurance attracts mainly the wealthy, who buy insurance to have access to higher-quality private facilities than the free public facilities. Tanzania's user fees for public facilities were still relatively low compared with the Community Health Fund's subsidized premiums.

In the foreseeable future in Africa, the depth of coverage will have to be thin if the population coverage is to be broad or vice versa. The health systems have fragmented and mixed public and private sources of financing and providers. So far, insurance arrangements in the region have provided coverage mainly for the better-off formal sector and civil service and some targeted subsidies for the poor. Although mandatory health insurance is not advanced in the Anglophone African countries, other insurance arrangements such as community-based health insurance and commercial private insurance schemes can increase demand for insurance and prepare the supply environment for the organizational requirements of insurance. In their quest to expand health insurance coverage, governments have been trying to figure out how to strengthen insurance mechanisms and leverage them to increase health insurance coverage. But AA countries are at varying stages of health insurance development. Many of their scaling-up strategies have tried to apply different approaches to target certain population segments (civil servants, formal sector employees, identifiable groups within the informal sector, the poor) or to cover certain priority services (usually MCH).

Mandates such as those requiring compulsory enrolment or a minimum benefits package are only as effective as the incentives and enforcement apparatus that are in place to promote compliance. To even begin to move toward this, the government should, where the capacity exists, encourage the development of the necessary health insurance infrastructure. This infrastructure should include risk pools among the various social segments by the use of demand-side subsidies as a counterweight to cost-recovery mechanisms in public and private health care service delivery and supply-side support to strengthen health insurance mechanisms such as risk-equalization.

Strategies for the Formal Sector and Employment-Based Health Insurance

Schemes to mobilize risk pools among formal sector employees—whether public or private—should be encouraged. Private health insurers have shown considerable ability to innovate throughout the continent. The Namibian example shows that health insurers can play a role in innovations that would broaden coverage to formally employed populations at low cost. They have responded to the AIDS epidemic by incorporating antiretroviral treatment into their benefits packages.

To run low-cost health insurance schemes, new methods of provider payment may be necessary. The fee-for-service payment system used by traditional medical schemes in South Africa and Namibia contributes to the high cost of these plans. The first low-cost scheme in Namibia with good AIDS benefits was based on capitation of primary care. Nigeria has seen the development of a small but growing managed care industry. These firms serve as intermediaries in the national health insurance plan which capitates primary care. But because of their payment mechanism, managed care schemes and capitation have also been met with strong provider opposition, as in Tanzania.

There is still plenty of room to expand health insurance coverage among formal sector workers. For health insurance coverage to expand, it will be necessary to craft products that are much less expensive than the traditional medical schemes or health insurance on offer in Africa. This can be done. The experiment in Namibia with low-cost schemes (including good AIDS coverage) and with the new spectrum of Government Employee Medical Schemes (GEMS) for South African civil servants should be watched closely. If health insurance can move from 40 percent of the formal sector (as in Namibia) to 70 percent or 80 percent, and if the formal sector of the economy expands with development, employment-based health insurance will play a role more similar to the one it played in more developed countries.

One barrier to broader uptake of health insurance coverage through employment is the existing structure of health care financing in Africa. Unlike Europe or the United States in the 19th and early 20th centuries, or Latin American in the

20th century, there is an extensive, though inadequate and underfunded network of government-run or government-subsidized health institutions in most African countries. A potential "safety net" exists, and thus workers with low wages may see little benefit in payroll deductions that promise coverage for future health expenses. Although quality may be inadequate, fees have traditionally been low or nonexistent in the public system and modest in mission hospitals. Thus, employment-based health insurance has not been at the top of the workers' collective bargaining agenda. In South Africa, public hospitals do provide services to both the insured and uninsured, and charge income-based fees. One way to make health insurance more affordable would be to provide inpatient services in public facilities, while offering more accessible outpatient benefits through private facilities. This is being tried in Namibia together with the low-priced GEMS. Enforcing payment of reasonable user charges by the nonpoor in public hospitals could expand the demand for health insurance but would be politically difficult.

Getting prices and benefits into a range that is affordable for most African employers and employees will address part of the problem, but marketing problems will persist. In several countries, employees have resisted payroll deductions for statutory insurance schemes. In Nigeria, the government was forced to declare a "holiday" on employee contributions in order to start enrolment of federal workers, the first element of the planned national health insurance system. In South Africa, the government made the lowest cost GEMS option free for low-wage employees in order to accelerate enrolment of uninsured civil servants.

Where typical incomes are too small to support the premium for a full private sector benefits package, what other options are available? One is donor subsidy. Because health insurance is seen as a benefit for the wealthy in Africa, there has been little donor support, except for some community health schemes. But health insurance could be a conduit for donors to support improved medical care. The Dutch Health Insurance Fund has embarked on this experiment in Nigeria,[8] and a small donor subsidy is available for the new low-cost plans in Namibia.

Can private, employment-based health insurance go further, to become the basis for protecting a large segment of the population? The biggest barrier remains the small portion of the labor market that works in the formal sector of the economy. With formal employment, risk can be pooled in employment groups and premiums collected through formal payroll systems. Some income cross-subsidy is created if premiums are collected as a percentage of salary. Data quantifying the size of the formal sector are difficult to obtain. In 1999, the formal economy was estimated to employ 80 percent of the labor force in South Africa, but this is probably an overestimate because many of the unemployed sustain themselves through informal economic activity. Elsewhere, the proportion of the labor force in the formal economy is less than 50 percent and probably below 30 percent in many AA countries. Because there are no efficient mechanisms for collecting mandatory premiums from peasant farmers or the informally employed, extending national health insurance programs to the full workforce will require "voluntary" contributions or government "buy ins" using general tax revenue. The history of voluntary enrolment in national health insurance elsewhere is not encouraging. However, Ghana is now trying to collect premiums in the informal sector (and subsidize individuals deemed too poor to pay). This innovation should be carefully watched, although concurrent plans to start a one-time premium payment could, if successful, undermine this innovation.

Economic development should theoretically lead to the expansion of formal sector employment, which could in turn lead to the expansion of employment-based insurance. From this base, and using general taxes, insurance could then be expanded to the broader population. This has been the pattern in much of the OECD. The performance of the insurance industry should be carefully monitored. Can the GEMS in South Africa and low-cost health insurance in Namibia significantly expand the proportion of covered workers? To assess the best strategy for integrating private insurers into a national health insurance plan, the performance of insurance companies (HMOs) as intermediaries in Nigerian national health insurance should be compared with the Ghanaian approach, which creates administrative bodies at the district level that have characteristics of both local governments and the community health plans they are supplanting.

Strategies for CBHI

CBHI schemes do not necessarily depend on the expansion of the formal sector of the economy. Successful small schemes have been developed for employment groups such as farmers and the self-employed that have not been readily captured as part of the formal sector and for social groups such as schools and women's groups without employment affiliation. The literature shows that the plans can be effective in reducing the financial impact of illness and expanding health care access and in generating additional funding for health care (Preker et al. 2001). However, problems of scale and transitional problems in moving from individually successful schemes to national systems based on community health financing have not yet been addressed. In Rwanda, the government and donors were heavily involved in setting up the district schemes. Yet there are still opportunities for governments and donors to target enrolment by the groups that normally have the greatest difficulty accessing other types of formal health insurance or health care, while providing a reinsurance or risk-equalization mechanism that supports the financial sustainability of these schemes. Government and donor support for and interest in CBHI have wavered during its brief history of implementation in Africa. CBHI is by its nature a fragile mechanism for risk pooling and to work, it would require consistent and continuous external support in Africa.

Government Strategies for Universal Health Insurance

The other way to expand health insurance is by moving to the steps taken by developed countries during the latter phases in the evolution of universal health financing—required purchase of private health insurance, or a government-sponsored system of mandatory social insurance. Many of the countries reviewed have considered the mandatory social insurance option, but the approach is either realistically cautious or naïve. Uganda and Zimbabwe seem to be proposing national health insurance without really setting out objectives or considering whether the infrastructure exists to make such a system possible.[9,10] In effect, these two countries seem to be contemplating little more than a "health tax" to supplement tax revenues already flowing to public facilities.

Governments could begin the expansion of health insurance coverage by subsidizing the enrolment premium for individuals who cannot afford the basic health insurance package. Through the insurance program, government funds would follow the patient to the health care provider of his or her choice, but this may mean diverting tax funding from poorly run public health facilities that are major employers. Switching the conduit for health funding will be difficult for governments that depend on the political support of public employees.

Other countries have looked at the financial implications of national health insurance, and pulled back from a commitment. In Kenya, the government refused to expand the formal sector inpatient insurance system to the country as a whole. In both Ghana and Nigeria, the World Bank has warned that the projections of national system costs may be too low and the expectation for revenues too high (Velenyi 2005). Three national health insurance proposals have been introduced in South Africa since majority rule, and none has passed, in part because the nation's cautious (and successful) financial managers do not want to further increase the tax burden or cost of employment when job creation is so essential.

Nigeria has begun to implement a national health insurance plan that was long in incubation. It uses the administrative capacity of private health insurers and is phased according to the employment status of the potential insured. Primary care physicians are paid on a capitation basis in recognition of the inflationary effects of fee-for-service reimbursement. The plan enrolled federal employees first and is scheduled to move on to state government employees now and later to employees of private firms in the formal sector. Still later it will attempt to address the informal sector, a tacit recognition of the difficulties of collecting contributions from this large part of the economy and of diverting tax resources to support coverage for people who cannot pay the premium. Nigeria may have the most realistic of the "national" schemes, but the government was still forced to waive the initial employee premium contribution—not a good sign for the long run. Tanzania also targeted government employees as the first phase of a health insurance system. Here, too, there has been resistance, particularly when the insured see no difference in the services they have traditionally received from government-affiliated institutions.

The future of mandatory health insurance in Africa may rest on the results of the recent insurance experiments in Anglophone Africa. There are many lessons to be drawn from the region for the coming years.

ANNEX 8A   HEALTH INSURANCE ARRANGEMENTS IN ANGLOPHONE AFRICA, BY COUNTRY

This annex provides an overview of the design of current or planned health insurance arrangements in selected countries. The focus is on the different ways countries have organized their proposed and actual revenue collection, risk pooling, and resource allocation and purchasing of mandatory health insurance (MHI) arrangements. The status of scaling up health insurance is discussed in terms of the percentage of the population covered thus far. This measure could broadly indicate how the design of current arrangements has succeeded in meeting health financing objectives while addressing each country's own economic and political constraints. Some of the underlying factors that explain the success or failure of scheme design to attract members are described later in greater detail.

Ghana: Health Insurance for All?

Of the countries studied, Ghana is furthest along in providing an MHI program directed at attaining universal coverage. In 2003 Ghana's National Health Insurance Act passed. In 2004 implementation of the National Health Insurance Scheme began with the creation of a public parastatal agency that regulates a decentralized network of district mutual health insurance schemes. Many of these schemes were built from the backbone of existing mutual health insurance organizations, community-based health insurance (CBHI) schemes that began during the 1990s in response to the burdensome system of user fees. Before the National Health Insurance Act, there were 258 mutual health insurance organization schemes, but they covered only a small portion of the population. Many of these organizations have since been merged with or transformed into district mutual health insurance schemes.

The National Health Insurance Scheme is financed from a combination of sources, primarily a 2.5 percent VAT, a 2.5 percent transfer from the Social Security Fund, and income-based premium contributions from which the indigent, children, the elderly, pensioners, and contributors to the Social Security and National Insurance Trust (SSNIT) are exempt. The central National Health Insurance Fund collects revenues from the VAT and social security, which are used for reinsurance and for subsidies to cover exempt groups.

Risk pools are organized around district schemes, which collect premiums, pay providers, and enroll members. Premium levels and the provider payment mechanism are nationally determined. The main responsibility of the district schemes is administrative. The young scheme has temporarily relaxed its compulsory enrolment requirements as it tries to expand coverage. The new national health insurance plan reports enrolling about 54 percent of the population, but it has distributed health insurance ID cards, which grant health care access, to less than 44 percent of the population (NHIA 2007; World Bank 2005a; NHIA 2008). More than half of the registered members are exempt from paying the income-based premium contributions, which range from the equivalent of US$7 to US$48 a year.

The health insurance benefits are fairly comprehensive and allow access to both public and private providers, who are reimbursed through a mixed payment system of diagnostic-related groups and fee-for-service for drugs (Ghana Parliament, 2003). To maintain the National Health Insurance Scheme's financial sustainability, Ghana is considering adapting policies that would strengthen the central scheme's role as an active purchaser of services to keep costs down. The process of MHI implementation in Ghana demonstrates the necessarily evolving nature of the design of health insurance, as revenue collection mechanisms, risk pooling, and resource allocation and purchasing are adjusted to achieve health system objectives.

Nigeria: Leveraging Health Management Organizations for the Formal Sector

As a federalist state, Nigeria has a decentralized health system with responsibilities divided among different levels of government. Most public funding for health derives from Nigeria's oil revenues, but coordination of activities across the levels of government is limited, regional disparities in quality and access to care are large, and the overall rate of out-of-pocket spending is high. Nigeria has had a small but growing private health insurance sector favoring the better-off. Community-based schemes, both CBHI and savings schemes through community-based organizations, have been tried but are subject to the size limitations of most CBHI initiatives (World Bank 2005b).

In 2005, the government began a process for implementing the National Health Insurance Scheme to cover first federal government employees and their dependents and then state government employees. The legislative act also mandates coverage for employees of large private sector organizations.[11] The scheme is supposed to be financed through a 10 percent employer contribution plus a 5 percent employee contribution. To encourage enrolment, the government has temporarily waived the employee premium contribution of 5 percent of payroll. Nigeria uses its private health management organizations (HMOs) as intermediaries to manage benefit payments. The size of the risk pools varies with HMO member composition, both mandated civil servants and voluntary members. The funds collected from the National Health Insurance Scheme flow to the HMOs, which integrate administratively with their contracted providers. No mechanisms protect HMOs from covering bad health risks, such as a risk-equalization fund that would redistribute health and financial risks across the pool of members.

To control costs, HMOs instead make monthly capitation payments to the primary care provider selected by the insured person. The cost of essential drugs (minus a 10 percent patient copayment) is included in the capitation. The HMO directly pays the limited referral benefits. For primary care, HMOs pay on a capitation basis. For secondary- and tertiary-level care, HMOs pay based on a mix of fee-for-service, per diem, and case payment mechanisms. At the end of 2006, about 2 percent of the national population was enrolled through this scheme, mostly from Abuja and Lagos, where federal ministry offices are located.

Kenya: Replacing a Broken Fund

Kenya has the oldest form of MHI in the region. About 25 percent of the population, consisting of formal sector employees and their dependents, are beneficiaries of its National Hospital Insurance Fund (NHIF). The fund is a minor part of the overall health financing picture, contributing only 4.4 percent to the THE (Kenya Ministry of Health n.d.). Although at its inception in 1966 its purpose was to cover all inpatient services (excluding drugs), now it covers only the cost of inpatient hospitalizations (room and board). The NHIF pays a flat per diem rate based on the hospital's level and accreditation. Members make income-based contributions to the fund but have to pay out-of-pocket for the services and drugs received as inpatients (Hsiao and Shaw 2007).

A more expansive bill that would replace the ineffective National Hospital Insurance Fund proposes to develop a National Social Health Insurance Fund. The new program, to cover all Kenyans for both outpatient and inpatient services, was passed

---

BOX 8A.1   KENYA: SOMETHING HAPPENED ON THE WAY TO SOCIAL HEALTH INSURANCE

Kenya has had a National Hospital Insurance Fund (NHIF) for the formal sector for about forty years. The fund covers a third of the population. In 2001, NHIF accounted for only 2 percent of total health care expenditures in Kenya.[a] The fund pays for inpatient care and is run by a parastatal organization.

In 2003, the government proposed a plan to cover all Kenyans with social health insurance that would pay for both inpatient and outpatient care. The projected annual cost was K Sh 40 billion (US$500 million) a year, to be funded through:

- Formal private sector employment–based contributions, with employers paying twice the payroll deduction for employees

- Contributions collected from workers in the informal sector

- Harmonization of civil servants' and teachers' contributions. These Kenyans receive a regular government medical allowance in cash in addition to membership in the NHIF. The allowances would be paid into the new fund.

- 11 percent of revenue from import and value added taxes

- A US$5 visitor tax.

A bill implementing the proposed National Social Health Insurance Fund (NSHIF) was introduced in Parliament in 2002, but objections to the plan were many. Employers complained that such comprehensive coverage had been achieved only by much more highly developed countries over a long period of time, and never when so large a percentage (an estimated 56 percent of Kenyans) live in poverty.[b] With the Kenyan economy lagging, business leaders and some trade unions worried that additional tax levies would cost jobs. Even if the target revenue were achieved, it would be insufficient. Critics also noted that the new fund would increase demand for services in areas lacking adequate health infrastructure but that no funds were budgeted for the creation of additional facilities. Opponents also challenged the proposal to administer the new NSHIF through the existing NHIF parastatal, saying that the organization had major problems managing the much more limited existing scheme.

The health minister fought hard for the Social Health Insurance Bill. In response to business opposition, proposed employer contributions were reduced from 5.8 percent to 3 percent of payroll.[c] The plan to "harmonize" the medical allowance of civil servants and teachers was dropped, with the expectation that general government revenues would be used to make up the shortfall.

The National Health Insurance Fund commissioned an actuarial study that pegged the annual cost of the Social Health Insurance program at K Sh 70 billion to K Sh 120 billion, two to three times the initial K Sh 40 billion estimate. The K Sh 70 billion estimate was based on utilization patterns of existing NHIF beneficiaries and an assumption that capacity constraints would limit demand. Assuming higher medical need in the poorer population newly served by the NSHIF and an expansion of capacity to meet this demand produced the higher estimate.[d]

The finance minister openly opposed passage, saying that Kenya could not afford the new benefit. The government attempted to withdraw the bill. President Mwai Kibaki announced that, if passed, the NSHIF would have to be implemented in stages. However, parliamentary support was sufficient for the health minister to obtain passage of the act in the closing days of 2004.[e]

Although Parliament passed the Social Health Insurance Act, President Kibaki refused to sign it. The unsigned NSHIF bill lapsed when the Parliament adjourned in 2006.[f] The bill remains politically contentious, with evolving design and implementation details.[g]

Source: Authors.

a. Peter Munaita, "Kenya's $400M Medical Scheme to Cover All," *The East African*, July 21, 2003.

b. "How Social Insurance Will Benefit All Kenyans," *The East African*, n.d.

c. Washington Akumu, "Lobby Puts Forward Proposals to Streamline Costly Health Scheme," *The Nation* (Kenya), September 7, 2004.

d. Jaindi Kisereo, "Proposed Health Scheme's Cost Put at Sh. 121 Billion Yearly in Claims," *The Nation* (Kenya), November 30, 2004.

e. "Kibaki Steps In to Save Health Plan," *The Nation* (Kenya), December 8, 2004.

f. "Several Bills Lapse as House Goes on Recess," *The Nation* (Kenya), December 8, 2006.

g. Dennis Itumbi, "Kenya Parliament Reopens with Busy Agenda," *AfricaNews*, March 5, 2008.

by the Kenyan Parliament in 2004 but rejected by the president, who wanted a phased plan for gradual implementation (Maliti 2005). The future of social health insurance in Kenya remains uncertain. This new bill proposes to provide universal coverage over nine years through the development of a new parastatal agency that would be funded from a combination of income-based and flat-rate contributions and general public revenues (Carrin et al. 2007; Hsiao and Shaw 2007). Many details of the new health insurance program are still evolving, such as the specific level of contributions, method of paying providers, and implementation strategy. There is also a small, private health insurance industry, but it has been troubled by well-publicized insolvencies in the last decade.

Tanzania: Coverage for Civil Servants

Government-supported community health funds, CBHI schemes that focus on providing health insurance to the predominant agricultural sector, have been piloted in Tanzania since 1994 to introduce prepayment as an alternative to user fees while increasing revenues to the constrained public health system (Humba 2005; Shaw 2002). However, coverage through these community health funds and other private commercial schemes represents a small portion of the population. Results from a pilot in Igunga district found that only 5 to 6 percent of households were willing to pay the premiums. Despite the limited success of the CBHI schemes, Tanzania embarked on an MHI program. The National Health Insurance Fund Act in 2001 created a single mandated insurance pool for civil servants and their dependents. At present, it covers about 4 percent of the population with a fairly broad benefits package among mostly public and nonprofit private providers. In comparison, civil servants represent 2 percent of the employed population (Tanzania, National Bureau of Statistics 2002). Tanzania's

---

BOX 8A.2   TANZANIA: PROVIDERS FIGHT MANAGED CARE

Several health insurers, including Kenya-based AAR and South Africa-based MedX, entered the Tanzanian market. But the medical profession reacted strongly to managed care efforts, particularly those of MedX. In 2002, 10 major Tanzanian hospitals terminated contracts with MedX, accusing it of breaching medical ethics. The terminations came following a Medical Council notice that MedX was "conducting a health activity" and therefore should be licensed and supervised by the medical profession body (the Medical Council). The Medical Council also warned medical practitioners and dentists about engaging in transactions with HMOs. The Registrar of the Medical Council stated that "Filling and signing claim forms from HMO's [...] is unprofessional, unethical as well as an offence."

Source: "Major Dar Hospitals Terminate Med-X Deal," *The East African*, May 13, 2002, n.p.

national health insurance is financed primarily through a proportional payroll tax, consisting of 3 percent of income from employees and matched by employers (Tanzania, United Republic of, Parliament 1999). The act does not make provision for expanding beyond the civil service. Although the act lists a comprehensive package of benefits without any description of a copayment requirement, it describes a cap on inpatient costs set by the National Health Insurance Board, above which, members would have to pay the remaining fees. This provision would limit the protection from catastrophic health expenditures offered to the health insurance members.

Uganda: Preparing for Reform

Facing a chronically underfunded public health system, over the last decade Uganda has considered MHI a way of increasing resources for its public system. User fees have been controversial. Community-based health insurance schemes, constrained by small risk-pools, covered only 1 percent of the population. The prospect of developing a single compulsory government health insurance scheme that avoids the problem of fragmented risk pools and increases funds for the health sector while reducing out-of-pocket payments has been seriously discussed. In 2001, Uganda commissioned a mandatory health insurance study that recommended a period of careful preparation through detailed actuarial analyses followed by gradual implementation focused on covering civil servants and employees of large companies and their families.[12] At present, a draft National Health Insurance Bill has put forward provisions for the establishment of a compulsory health insurance program with specific technical features yet to be finalized. The proposed scheme aims to provide universal coverage but through a gradual process beginning with civil servants. A proportional payroll tax on employers and employees would be the primary sources of funds. Specific technical features will be determined after completion of additional actuarial and economic impact studies, but certain general features such as the initial size of the risk pool, the level of contributions, and the provider payment mechanism have been tentatively proposed.

In all the countries discussed thus far, private health insurance plans—both for-profit and community-based—covered no more than 2 percent of the population. The situation in Southern Africa is different. Medical schemes in Namibia reach 13 percent of the population, and in South Africa, about 17 percent. Such insurance pays for a large proportion of private health expenditure. These risk pools give the insured access to private physicians and hospitals and cover a significant portion of private health expenditure—more than three-quarters in Namibia. In general, these schemes have covered only workers (and their families) at the higher end of the wage scale because of the high cost of the premium.

BOX 8A.3   SOUTH AFRICA: NATIONAL HEALTH INSURANCE STIRS MORE DEBATE THAN ACTION

Discussion of the possibility of a National Health Service in South Africa dates back to the development of the British National Health Service after World War II. The Gluckman Commission in 1946 recommended a tax-funded national health system for all South Africans. During the apartheid era, a unified national system was never seriously considered. With majority rule, the national health debate has been joined. Three different proposals have been presented for a national health insurance scheme. None has yet passed.

In 1994, the Health Care Finance Committee proposed a national scheme for all formal sector employees, based on employer and employee contributions. Private insurers could serve as intermediaries. There would be a risk-equalization scheme (McIntyre, Doherty, and Gilson 2003). The benefits package was comprehensive, with the emphasis on public provision—the government was looking for an additional source of revenue for its health institutions.

A more constrained option was suggested in 1995. One of its goals was to address the cost spiral in private health insurance. It would cover all formal sector employees and dependents but would pay only for hospital services. The insured would have a choice between public and private insurance plans, but reimbursements would be based on the cost of service in public hospitals. An even more limited option was proposed by a Department of Health Working Group in 1997. This targeted formal sector employees above the income tax threshold (not the lowest-wage workers) who did not purchase medical scheme coverage. These individuals would be obliged to purchase coverage from a state fund to cover services in public hospitals.

Successive reductions in the scope of proposed reform were driven by opposition from the Treasury, which was concerned about the effects on tax burden and employment. McIntyre and others (2003) give a number of reasons these broader initiatives have so far failed. In addition to the concerns of the Treasury, the medical scheme industry and its current clients reacted negatively to the possible loss of existing options, as has happened with proposed major health insurance reforms in the United States. Trade unions opposed the 1997 initiative because it did not appear to offer currently uninsured members any expansion of the access they already had to public hospitals. McIntyre suggests that many public hospitals did not yet have the billing and financial infrastructure to operate in the proposed insurance environment. And the more limited mechanism proposed in 1997 made no provision for risk equalization or cross-subsidization between existing medical schemes and the proposed government hospital insurance (McIntyre, Doherty, and Gilson 2003).

South Africa: Competing Proposals for Health Insurance

In South Africa, public expenditures on health have remained stagnant while more and more health spending is being funneled through nonprofit private medical schemes that cover a small percentage of wealthier South Africans.

To address health financing problems such as inequitable health spending, rising health care costs in the private sector, and problems created by the public-private mix, different proposals for mandatory health insurance programs have been discussed since the 1990s but without gaining political traction. Instead, a series of implemented measures attempt to promote the gradual expansion of health insurance coverage. The Medical Schemes Act of 1998 sought to regulate the nonprofit, private medical schemes by making risk rating of premiums illegal to prevent cream skimming, increase competition among schemes through open enrolment, introduce financial solvency and governance requirements, and mandate a minimum benefits package to prevent medical schemes from "dumping" beneficiaries on the public hospital system (Picazo 2005; South Africa 1998). This act strengthened the risk pooling mechanisms of the medical schemes but did not increase overall membership (McLeod and Ramjee 2007). Despite a boost through a regressive system that allows tax deductibility of employer contributions, medical schemes have failed to increase insurance coverage because they pass the high inflationary health costs to members in the form of higher contributions and copayments (McIntyre, Doherty, and Gilson 2003). This rising cost to health insurance members, the increasing population, and the stagnant public health expenditures funded from tax revenues continue to exacerbate the health care burden on the public system. Through the GEMS program, South Africa is now trying to enroll the low-income civil servants through specially designed low-cost programs. If this development is expanded to similar private sector workers through the planned Low-Income Medical Scheme (LIMS) program, it could greatly increase the percentage of the formal sector workforce with health insurance. A number of different proposals for a broader national health insurance program share the common task of resolving certain problems. Some elements of the different proposals include the design of a risk-equalization fund, the creation of a social security system to house health insurance coverage, and the continued use of medical schemes as the financial intermediary of an MHI program.

Namibia: Support for the Private Sector

In Namibia, most health insurance is in the form of private nonprofit medical schemes that cater to the wealthier population. No compulsory health insurance exists in Namibia. Instead, a voluntary medical scheme (PSEMAS), heavily subsidized from general taxes, covers government workers. Employees pay only N$60 (US$7) to enroll. Unlike in South Africa, almost all government workers have medical scheme coverage. The plan has broad coverage for outpatient benefits in the private sector but offers inpatient care only in the private wings of government hospitals. Low-income nongovernmental workers have not had access to similar plans until recently. However, since 2005, low-cost plans with extensive coverage of AIDS treatment costs have been started by private medical schemes. Premiums are less than half the traditional medical schemes (table 8.2), and the Namibian innovations could lead to a broadening of the insured population.

NOTES

ACKNOWLEDGMENTS: The authors are grateful to Oscar Picazo, Paul Shaw, and Marianne Lindner for their insightful comments on the initial drafts of this chapter.

1. MHI is characterized as having (1) mandatory contributions for all of its legislatively defined members, who cannot opt out; and (2) a premium or payroll-tax-based funding mechanism which excludes systems that are wholly funded by general revenues.

2. Examples of this: external resources for health in Nigeria accounted for 16.2 percent of THE in 2000 but fell to 5.6 percent the following year. *Dutch Disease* refers to a situation in which donor aid exceeds domestic resources, inflationary effects could be caused by the higher salaries paid to staff of vertical programs, and donor interests in a particular disease could outweigh domestically set priorities on health when donor funds exceed Ministry of Health resources (Garrett 2007; WHO n.d.).

3. Sebastian Gabunga, "Teachers Threaten to Sue NHIF," *Comtex News Network*, May 5, 2005.

4. "NHIF Received Complaint from Council Workers," *Comtex News Network*, April 28, 2005.

5. "Major Dar Hospitals Terminate Med-X Deal," *The East African* (Kenya), May 13, 2002.

6. Onyebuchi Ezigbo, "NHIS: FG Workers to Enjoy Free Service," *This Day Online*, 2005.

7. Some were priced at just N$30 (US$4.75) a month.

8. Fola Laoye, Managing Director, Hygeia Community Health Plan, quoted in "Foreign Investment in Health Receives a Boost," *This Day*, January 25, 2007.

9. Fred Ouma, "Health Officials, Employers Debate Insurance," *New Vision*, February 6, 2007.

10. Dumisani Ndela and Lucia Makamure, "Outcry over NSSA's Health Scheme," *Zimbabwe Independent*, January 19, 2007.

11. "National Health Insurance Scheme," *This Day Online*, 2006.

12. Fred Ouma, "Health Policy in Offing," *New Vision*, August 28, 2006, n.p.

REFERENCES

Berman, Peter, William Hsiao, Paolo Belli, William Bazeyo, Simon Kasasa, and Samuel Atuhurra. 2001. "A Feasibility Analysis of Social Health Insurance in Uganda." Harvard School of Public Health and International Health Systems Group, Cambridge, MA.

Bonnerjee, Aniruddha. 2003. "Pensions in Sub-Saharan Africa: The Urgent Need to Act." Draft. Washington, DC: World Bank.

Bwogi, Charles. 2007. "NSSF Wants to Manage Health Insurance." *The New Vision*. http://www.newvision.co.ug.

Carrin, Guy, Chris James, Michael Adelhart et al. 2007. "Health Financing Reform in Kenya: Assessing the Social Health Insurance Proposal." *South African Medical Journal* 97 (2). http://www.samj.org.za.

Castro-Leal, F., J. Dayton, L. Demery, and K. Mehra. 2000. "Public Spending on Health Care in Africa: Do the Poor Benefit?" *Bulletin of the World Health Organization* 78 (1): 66–74.

CIMAS (Commercial and Medical Aid Society, Zimbabwe). 2007. "History of CIMAS, Operations, and Constitution." http://www.cimas.co.zw (accessed December 27, 2007).

Criel, Bart. 1998. "District-Based Health Insurance in Sub-Saharan Africa." *Studies in Health Services Organisation and Policy*. Tropical Institute, Antwerp, Belgium, G.K.W. Van Lerberghe and V. De Brouwere. http://nzdl.sadl.uleth.ca/cgi-bin/library.

Dahlgren, Goran. 1994. "The Political Economy of Health Financing Strategies in Kenya." In *Health and Social Change in International Perspective*, ed. L. Chen, A. Kleinman, and N. Ware. Boston, MA: Harvard University Press.

Garrett, Laurie. 2007. "The Challenge of Global Health." *Foreign Affairs* 86 (1): 14–38.

Ghana Parliament. 2003. National Health Insurance Act 650 (Ghana). 650.

Ghana Statistical Service. 2007. "Key Social Economic Demographic Indicators 2000." Accra.

Halvorson, George. 2007. *Health Care Co-ops in Uganda: Effectively Launching Micro Health Groups in African Villages*. Oakland, CA: Permanente Press.

Hsiao, William C., and R. Paul Shaw. 2007. "Social Health Insurance for Developing Nations." WBI Development Studies, World Bank Development Institute, Washington, DC.

Humba, Emmanuel. 2005. "Implementing Social Security Health Care: The Experience of the National Health Insurance Fund." Paper prepared for the ISSA Regional Conference for Africa, Lusaka, Zambia, August 9–12.

ILO (International Labour Organization). 2005. "Improving Social Protection for the Poor: Health Insurance in Ghana." Ghana Social Trust Pre-Pilot Project. Geneva: ILO.

———. 2007. "An ILO Strategy towards Universal Access to Health Care." In *Social Health Protection*. Geneva: ILO, Social Security Department. http://www.ilo.org/public/english /protection/secsoc/downloads/healthpolicy.pdf.

Kenya Ministry of Health. n.d. "Kenya National Health Accounts, 2001–2002." World Health Organization, Geneva.

Kruger, Heidi. n.d. "The Second Step towards a Social Health Insurance for South Africa." Board of Health Care Funders of Southern Africa, Johannesburg. http://www.bhfglobal .com/bhf-news/the-second-step-towards-a-social-health-insurance-for-south-africa (accessed December 4, 2007).

Kutzin, J. 1998. "Health Insurance for the Formal Sector in Africa: 'Yes But …'." In *Sustainable Health Care Financing in Southern Africa*," ed. A. Beattie, J.N. Doherty, L. Gilson, E. Lambo, and P. Shaw. Washington, DC: World Bank.

Maliti, John. 2005. "The Flip-Side of Free Health Care." *Inter-Region Economic Network Newsletter* 3.

Marek, Tonia, Rena Eichler, and Philip Schnabl. 2004. "Resource Allocation and Purchasing in Africa: What Is Effective in Improving the Health of the Poor?" Working paper, Africa Region Human Development, World Bank, Washington, DC.

McIntyre, Di, Janne Doherty, and Lucy Gilson. 2003. "A Tale of Two Visions: The Changing Fortunes of Social Health Insurance in South Africa." *Health Policy and Planning* 18 (1): 47–58.

McIntyre, Di, and Michael Thiede. 2007. "Health Care Financing and Expenditure." In *South Africa Health Review 2007*, ed. S. Harrison, R. Bhana, and A. Ntul. Durban, South Africa: Health Systems Trust.

McIntyre, Di, Michael Thiede, Moremi Nkosi, Vimbayi Mutyambizi, Marianela Castillo-Riquelme, Lucy Gilson, Ermin Erasmus, and Jane Goudge. 2007. "A Critical Analysis of the Current South African Health System." *Shield Work Package 1 Report*. Health Economics Unit, University of Cape Town; Centre for Health Policy, University of the Witwatersrand, Johannesburg. http://web.uct.ac.za/depts/heu/publications/SHIELD_WP1_only_report_SA_final.pdf.

McIntyre, Di, and Alex van den Heever. 2007. "Social or National Health Insurance." In *South Africa Health Review 2007*, ed. S. Harrison, R. Bhana, and A. Ntuli. Durban, South Africa: Health Systems Trust. http://www.hst.org.za/publications/711.

McLeod, Heather, and Shivani Ramjee. 2007. "Medical Schemes." In *South Africa Health Review 2007*, ed. S. Harrison, R. Bhana, and A. Ntuli. Durban, South Africa: Health Systems Trust. http://www.hst.org.za/publications/711.

Medical Schemes Council of South Africa. 2005. "2004–2005 Report of the Medical Schemes Council South Africa." Pretoria, Council for Medical Schemes. http://www.medicalschemes.com/publications.

Musau, Stephen. 1999. *Community-Based Health Insurance: Experiences and Lessons Learned from East Africa*. Technical Report 34. Bethesda, MD: Partnerships for Health Reform Project, Abt Associates.

NAMFISA (Namibia Financial Institutions Supervisory Authority). 2005. *2005 Annual Report of NAMFISA*. Windhoek, Namibia.

NHIA (National Health Insurance Agency). 2007. "2007 Mid-Year Operational Report." NHIA, Accra.

———. 2008. "Status Report as at September 30, 2008." NHIA, Accra.

Onwujekwe, Obinna, and Edit V. Velenyi. 2010. "Nigeria." In *Global Marketplace for Private Health Insurance: Strength in Numbers,* ed. Alexander S. Preker, Peter Zweifel, and Onno Schellekens, 349–68. Washington, DC: World Bank.

Picazo, Oscar. 2005. "South Africa Social Health Insurance Proposal: Summary of Issues." Unpublished paper, World Bank, Washington, DC.

Preker, Alexander S., and Guy Carrin, eds. 2004. *Health Financing for Poor People: Resource Mobilization and Risk Sharing*. Washington, DC: World Bank.

Preker, Alexander S., Guy Carrin, Melitta Jakab, William Hsiao, and D. Ahrin-Tenkorang. 2001. "A Synthesis Report on the Role of Communities in Resource Mobilization and Risk Sharing." Background report for the Commission on Macroeconomics and Health. Geneva: World Health Organization.

Rajkotia, Yogesh. 2007. "The Political Development of the Ghanaian National Health Insurance System: Lessons in Health Governance." United States Agency for International Development, Washington, DC.

Republic of Kenya. 2003. *Report of 1998/99 Labour Force Survey.* Nairobi: Ministry of Planning and National Development.

Schneider, Freiderich. 2002. "Size and Measurement of the Informal Economy in 110 Countries around the World." Working Paper, World Bank, Washington, DC.

Shaw, Paul. 2002. "Tanzania's Community Health Fund: Prepayment as an Alternative to User Fees." *World Bank Institute, Flagship On-line Journal on Health Sector Reform and Sustainable Financing.* www.worldbank.org/wbi/healthflagship.

Shaw, Paul, and Charles Griffin. 1995. "Financing Health Care in Sub-Saharan Africa through User Fees and Insurance." *Directions in Development*, World Bank, Washington, DC.

South Africa.1998. Medical Schemes Act No. 31.

Soyibo, Adedoyin. 2005. "National Health Accounts of Nigeria, 1998–2002." World Health Organization, Geneva. http://www.who.int/nha/country/Nigeria_Report_1998-2002 .pdf.

Statistics South Africa. 2007. "Labour Force Survey." http://www.statssa.gov.za/publications /P0210/P0210March2007.pdf.

Tanzania, National Bureau of Statistics. 2002. "Integrated Labour Force Survey, 2000/01." http://www.nbs.go.tz/.

Tanzania, United Republic of, Parliament. 1999. The National Health Insurance Fund Act (Tanzania), 8.

Thomas, Stephen, and Lucy Gilson. 2004. "Actor Management in the Development of Health Financing Reform: Health Insurance in South Africa, 1994–1999." *Health Policy and Planning* 19 (5): 279–91.

Transparency International. 2007. "Corruption Perceptions Index." http://www .transparency.org/policy_research/surveys_indices/cpi/2007.

Uganda Bureau of Statistics. 2003. "Uganda National Household Survey 2002/2003." Published and compiled by the Uganda Bureau of Statistics. http://www.ubos.org/nada/.

UN (United Nations). 2006. *UN Human Development Report 2006.* New York: United Nations Development Programme.

Van der Gaag, Jacques, and Emily Gustafsson-Wright. 2007. "Low-Cost Health Insurance in Africa Provides the Poor with Anti-Retroviral Drugs." Washington, DC: Brookings Institution. http://www.brookings.edu/opinions/2007/1129_aids_van_der_gaag.aspx.

Velenyi, Edit V. 2005. "Nigeria Case Study: Efforts for Designing and Implementing a Comprehensive Health Care Financing Strategy." Unpublished paper, World Bank, Washington, DC.

Vogel, Ronald J. 1993. *Financing Health Care in Sub-Saharan Africa.* Westport, CT: Greenwood Press.

Walt, G., and Lucy Gilson. 1994. "Reforming the Health Sector in Developing Countries." *Health Policy and Planning* 9: 353–70.

WHO (World Health Organization). n.d. "WHO Estimates for Nigeria's NHA Data (1998–2002)." http://www.who.int/nha/country/Nigeria_Report_1998-2002.pdf (accessed December 12, 2007).

———. 2000. *World Health Report 2000*. Geneva: WHO.

———. 2008. "Statistical Information System, Mortality and Burden of Disease." http://apps.who.int/whosis/data/Search.jsp?indicators=[Indicator].[HSR] (accessed December 12, 2007).

———. 2010. Global Health Expenditure Database. Geneva: World Health Organization. http://apps.who.int/nha/database/PreDataExplorer.aspx?d=1 (accessed November 22, 2011).

World Bank. 2005a. "Mutual Health Insurance in Ghana." World Bank, Washington, DC.

———. 2005b. "Nigeria Health, Nutrition, and Population Country Status Report." World Bank, Washington, DC.

———. 2010. *World Development Indicators 2010*. Washington, DC: World Bank.

Xu, Ke, David B. Evans, Kei Kawabata, Riadh Zeramdini, Jan Klavus, and Christopher J.L. Murray. 2003. "Household Catastrophic Health Expenditure: A Multicountry Analysis." *The Lancet* 362.

CHAPTER 9

Moving from Intent to Action in the Middle East and North Africa

Bjorn O. Ekman and Heba A. Elgazzar

The Middle East and North Africa (MENA) Region of the World Bank comprises a highly divergent group of countries.[1]

INTRODUCTION

MENA encompasses the lower-income country of the Republic of Yemen in the south, the middle-income countries of Morocco in the west, the Islamic Republic of Iran in the east, and the oil-producing high-income countries of the Arabian Gulf. In addition to these groups of countries, the MENA Region also contains two conflict-affected countries or territories, Iraq and the West Bank and Gaza. This wide variation in economic and social contexts is reflected in the health financing systems of the Region. In broad terms, the Gulf countries provide universal coverage of health services funded by general revenues while the poorer countries struggle with providing basic services financed by foreign aid. The large group of middle-income countries all display varying degrees of mixed public and private provision of health services funded by multiple sources, the largest of which is frequently private out-of-pocket (OOP) spending by individuals and households at the point of service. Attempts to reform the existing systems or to expand mandatory health insurance coverage to people without formal prepayment coverage are being considered by most governments of the Region. Challenges to the successful implementation of these reforms include limited fiscal space for health, weaknesses in the governance structure of the health system, and ineffective systems for allocating resources to health service providers.

The MENA Region faces difficult demographic and epidemiological transitions over the coming decades. As life expectancy increases, many countries will see their population age with increasingly larger dependency rates. More acutely, the burden of disease is changing drastically in the Region. Many countries are experiencing increasingly higher prevalence rates of noncommunicable and chronic diseases. In particular, the Region has some of the highest prevalence rates of obesity, diabetes, and cardiovascular conditions. These challenges will have a profound impact on the countries' attempts to expand mandatory health insurance in a fiscally sustainable manner.

HEALTH FINANCING IN MENA: TRENDS AND PATTERNS

A useful starting point toward understanding the health financing system's contribution to overall health system performance is to look at some broad health financing statistics over the past decade. The most recently available data and statistics on health spending are used in this section for a comparative review of the nature of health spending in the MENA Region and in other parts of the world.[2] The focus is on the following health financing indicators: total health expenditure as a share of gross domestic product, total government/public health expenditure as a share of total health expenditure and as a share of total government expenditure, total per capita health expenditure in real international U.S. dollar terms, and OOP expenditure as a share of total health expenditure.[3]

To provide a coherent analysis, the countries of the MENA Region are divided into three separate income groups: low-income countries (LICs; the Republic of Yemen), a large group of middle-income countries (MICs) of the Maghreb and Mashreq, and the high-income countries (HICs) of the Gulf Cooperation Council (GCC). These groups of countries are then compared with the global averages of the corresponding income groups. Organizing the countries by income makes for relatively consistent international comparisons. However, the actual context of a particular country may render such a division less useful as, for example, parts of some of the middle-income countries may have more in common with a low-income country when it comes to health service delivery and resource constraints. To capture both trends and overall patterns of health financing in the Region, three separate time points: 1995, 2000, and 2008 are examined.

Health Expenditure as a Share of GDP

Globally, there is a clear trend of health spending becoming a larger share of the total economy as countries grow richer. Understanding how a country compares with the global average of the income group provides a first impression of the nature of the country's health system. However, also important are changes over time because the level of health spending may change due to absolute levels of health expenditure and to changes in gross domestic product (GDP). Table 9.1 shows total health expenditure as a share of GDP for the MENA countries and the global averages for the groups of comparison countries.

As can be seen from the table, the Republic of Yemen spends considerably less on health as a share of GDP than do most other low-income countries. In addition, in contrast to the global trend, increasing over the 1995 to 2008 period, the Republic of Yemen actually spent a smaller share of GDP in 2000 and 2008 than in the mid-1990s. Moreover, looking at per capita health expenditure in real

TABLE 9.1   MENA: Total Expenditure on Health as Percent of GDP, 1995, 2000, 2008

Country/class	Year		
	1995	2000	2008
Low-income countries			
Yemen, Rep.	4.49	4.46	3.67
Global low-income countries average	4.52	4.61	5.16
Middle-income countries			
Egypt, Arab Rep.	3.86	5.54	6.38
Iran, Islamic Rep.	4.65	5.90	6.30
Iraq	—	1.36	2.70
Jordan	8.27	9.82	8.49
Lebanon	10.67	10.87	8.76
Libya	3.66	3.67	2.80
Morocco	3.90	4.18	5.33
Syrian Arab Republic	5.52	4.82	3.23
Tunisia	6.15	5.95	5.95
MENA middle-income countries average	5.19	5.79	5.55
Global middle-income countries average	5.52	5.96	6.18
High-income countries			
Bahrain	4.58	3.95	3.58
Kuwait	3.92	3.01	1.99
Oman	3.65	3.07	2.40
Qatar	3.66	2.29	3.30
Saudi Arabia	2.28	3.74	3.99
United Arab Emirates	4.05	3.21	2.42
MENA high-income countries average	3.69	3.28	2.93
Global high-income countries average	6.63	6.71	7.23

Source: WHO-WHOSIS.
Note: — = not available.

terms shows that over the period 1995 to 2007, health spending decreased in the Republic of Yemen, from US$46 to US$41 per capita per year.

In the middle-income group larger variation would be expected because income levels in these countries differ significantly. Overall, the middle-income MENA countries seem to spend a smaller share on health as a percent of GDP that do other similar countries. In addition, while the trend in the global average is one of increasingly larger health spending, this share has varied over time in the MENA middle-income countries, showing a negative trend for about five years. Finally, the table shows that Jordan and Lebanon are both spending a considerably larger share of GDP on health compared with the other MENA countries and with the global average for MICs.

As noted, there is a relatively strong relationship between economic growth as measured by the annual change in gross domestic product and the level of health spending both over time and across countries. Indeed, in many countries, the annual rate of increase in health spending has outpaced the rate of economic growth. Available data also show only a weak relationship between economic growth and health spending. For some countries (the Syrian Arab Republic, Lebanon, and the Republic of Yemen), despite having had positive economic growth over the period of analysis, the share of GDP going to health has decreased. With the exception of Djibouti, all other middle-income MENA countries display relatively high rates of economic growth, but modest increases in health spending as a share of GDP.

The last group of countries is the high-income GCC countries. There are several things to note in the table. First, the GCC countries spend a significantly smaller share of their total resources on health compared with other high-income countries. The fact that the GCC countries as a group have seen rapid rates of income growth over the past decades as the price of oil has gone up is one explanation for this result. Second, looking across the time period, the share of health spending has gone down in the GCC countries while it has increased in other HICs. Finally, while there is some variation in this indicator across the GCC region, the pattern is relatively uniform. The comparison group is much larger than the number of GCC countries, which in itself makes for larger in-group variation, but there is only one other comparator with a similarly low number, namely Equatorial Guinea, also an oil-exporting country.

Overall, the MENA countries display some noteworthy trends and patterns compared with other comparator groups of countries with respect to health expenditure as a share of total GDP. However, these variations differ across the separate groups and suggest that particular determinants are at play in the various groups and countries.

Public Health Expenditure as a Share of Total Health Expenditure

Understanding the government's role in health financing is relevant for several reasons. First, public funding involves the critical aspects of prepayment and pooling of resources, which, in turn, enables the health financing system to provide the important insurance function for health. Second, a significant share of public funding is one key characteristic of high-performing health systems as seen in several countries around the world. Public finance theory suggests that public financing is warranted for certain types of goods and services for which there is no or only poorly functioning private markets, including public goods and where there are externalities in the production or consumption; health care typically contains several such types of goods and services. And finally, the public role in health financing can be seen as an indication of the willingness of the government to attempt to address some of the inherent market failures associated with private health financing.

Table 9.2 shows government health spending as a share of total health expenditure in the MENA countries compared with the global averages for the comparison groups of countries.

The table shows that both in the Republic of Yemen and in low-income countries more generally the share of public health spending has varied over time, though in different directions. In 2000, the government of the Republic of Yemen spent significantly more on health as a share of total health expenditure than did other low-income countries. By 2008, the situation had reversed.

The main issue emerging from the table is the fact that on average the governments of the MENA middle-income countries spend some five percentage points

TABLE 9.2   MENA: General Government Expenditure on Health as Percent of Total Expenditure on Health, 1995, 2000, 2008

Country/class	Year		
	1995	2000	2008
Low-income countries			
Yemen, Rep.	31.46	53.82	40.65
Global low-income countries average	42.72	39.97	44.93
Middle-income countries			
Egypt, Arab Rep.	46.50	39.63	38.27
Iran, Islamic Rep.	49.90	37.01	45.72
Iraq	—	28.70	81.21
Jordan	62.09	48.91	62.20
Lebanon	28.32	30.01	48.99
Libya	51.86	61.70	75.88
Morocco	32.23	29.42	34.97
Syrian Arab Republic	39.68	40.45	45.13
Tunisia	51.69	54.93	49.57
MENA middle-income countries average	44.31	44.24	52.79
Global middle-income countries average	57.07	55.95	59.68
High-income countries			
Bahrain	69.58	67.54	69.67
Kuwait	82.60	77.50	76.77
Oman	83.92	81.75	73.21
Qatar	62.22	68.80	70.14
Saudi Arabia	67.79	81.70	64.93
United Arab Emirates	78.97	76.57	67.27
MENA high-income countries average	74.18	75.64	70.33
Global high-income countries average	71.77	71.09	72.17

Source: WHO-WHOSIS.
Note: — = not available.

less on health compared with the MIC global average. The variation over time in public health spending in the MENA countries seems to correspond with the global trend as the share of public spending has been rising for the past five years after a reduction during the previous period.

There is considerable variation within MENA middle-income countries with both increases and decreases over time across countries and within countries. For example, in the two countries that spend the most on health, Lebanon and Jordan, the governments seem to have taken on a larger share of total health spending. This is broadly in line with these countries' recent policy efforts to increase coverage of health services by providing uncovered groups with free or subsidized health care at the expense of the Ministries of Health. Finally, it is also clear from the table that there are large variations within the MENA Region with respect to this health financing indicator, which goes from a low of around 35 percent in Morocco to over 80 percent in Iraq.

The trend toward a larger role for government health funding is found in all high-income countries and groups. There are, however, some exceptions as, for example, Bahrain and Saudi Arabia both display public funding as a share of total health spending below 70 percent. By way of comparison, the corresponding estimates for 2008 are for the United States 45 percent, Switzerland 60 percent, the Netherlands 81 percent, and Singapore 33 percent, the lowest of all HICs.[4] It is also clear from the table that over time the relationship between public funding for health between these groups of countries has changed as the GCC average displays a negative trend over the past five years while the opposite is true for the global average.

An important concern with respect to public health spending is the issue of who benefits from public health care subsidies. There is little evidence available to shed conclusive light on this question, but several studies of the health sectors in the MENA Region suggest that public health spending predominantly benefits the relatively well-off and urban residents (e.g., World Bank 2008c). This general pattern is broadly in line with evidence from other regions and suggests that also in the MENA Region governments may want to consider options for making public health spending more effective and equitable by targeting public funds to the socially excluded and particularly vulnerable groups.

Out-of-Pocket Spending as a Share of Total Private Health Spending

The extent to which individuals and households pay for health care out of pocket at the point of service is an important indicator of health financing efficiency and equity. The global pattern is clear: as countries become richer with more advanced health systems, the share of OOP payment goes down, both as a percent of total private spending and of total health expenditure; correspondingly public and private prepayment goes up. Table 9.3 shows OOP spending as a share of total private health spending in the countries of the MENA Region and the global average for the group of comparators.

TABLE 9.3   MENA: Out-of-Pocket Expenditure as Percent of Private Expenditure on Health, 1995, 2000, 2008

Country/class	Year		
	1995	*2000*	*2008*
Low-income countries			
Yemen, Rep.	95.59	94.52	97.74
Global low-income countries average	87.45	85.20	83.93
Middle-income countries			
Egypt, Arab Rep.	89.64	94.10	95.14
Iran, Islamic Rep.	92.41	95.89	95.22
Iraq	—	100.00	100.00
Jordan	64.24	74.94	88.37
Lebanon	77.16	80.08	78.32
Libya	100.00	100.00	100.00
Morocco	77.81	76.58	86.31
Syrian Arab Republic	100.00	100.00	100.00
Tunisia	78.37	80.27	84.32
MENA middle-income countries average	82.93	85.31	89.55
Global middle-income countries average	83.70	82.30	81.55
High-income countries			
Bahrain	71.32	68.65	65.01
Kuwait	93.80	93.92	91.57
Oman	63.24	64.39	63.55
Qatar	92.68	84.48	88.75
Saudi Arabia	47.48	41.27	61.84
United Arab Emirates	71.00	69.41	67.62
MENA high-income countries average	73.25	70.35	73.06
Global high-income countries average	76.75	75.60	74.68

Source: WHO-WHOSIS.
Note: — = not available.

In the Republic of Yemen out-of-pocket expenditures constitute almost all (98 percent) of total private spending. This suggests that there is very little private health insurance in the Republic of Yemen. Moreover, private spending is a relatively large source of health financing in that country, inasmuch as it accounts for almost 60 percent of all health spending. This situation may also suggest some important equity concerns. OOP spending is generally seen as an inequitable way of paying for care in that it may push households into catastrophically high health spending.

For the middle-income MENA countries, the share of OOP payments for health increased steadily over the study period. From 1995 to 2008, the share of

OOP health spending in total private health expenditure increased from around 83 percent (similar to the global average at that time) to almost 90 percent, significantly larger than the corresponding global average of around 82 percent. One possible explanation for this is the inability to introduce and develop private health insurance markets in the MENA Region. With the exceptions of Lebanon and Saudi Arabia, these markets are comparatively small. Another possible explanation is the inability of public systems to provide some of the services included in the benefits packages. For example, several studies have shown that individuals are being asked to purchase drugs and similar inputs from private vendors as public providers' inventories are depleted.

In the high-income GCC countries, out-of-pocket spending as a share of total private spending has varied over the period of analysis. The share of OOP payments in total private health expenditure is on average around 74 percent in both GCC and globally. However, while the negative global trend is evident from the table, the GCC region has displayed a more varied trend since the mid-1990s. In individual HICs this decline is considerably more pronounced; Croatia and Estonia, for example, went from 100 percent to 93 percent during this period.[5] The variation across the GCC region is seen in the table together with indications that this group of countries spends a somewhat lower share out of pocket on health compared with other high-income countries.

An important finding from this analysis is that OOP health expenditure as a share of total health expenditure has been going down for the past few years in some countries, such as Lebanon. For example time series data analysis shows that OOP spending fell from almost 60 percent of total health spending to below 40 percent in 2008. Some possible explanations for this development will be discussed in the next section.

Overall, OOP spending in the MENA countries has varied considerably over the past decade. In contrast to the global trend, the data show no clear reductions on average in the Region, but with important exceptions of both increases (the Arab Republic of Egypt, the Islamic Republic of Iran, Jordan, Morocco, and Tunisia) in the share of OOP in total health spending and decreases (Djibouti and Syria). Some of the underlying forces behind these changes are discussed below.

Per Capita Health Spending

The significant variation in health spending also comes across when looking at per capita health expenditure (annex table 9A.3). Compared with other low-income countries the Republic of Yemen spends more on health in per capita terms than do other similar countries. In real terms, however, per capita health spending has been decreasing in Yemen over the study period.

On average, the MENA middle-income countries spend significantly less on health than do similar countries in other regions. There are, however, important exceptions to this overall pattern, such as Lebanon, which spends more than twice the global average for this group of countries. While Iraq may be considered something of a special case with its recent history of prolonged conflict, Syria, Morocco, and to some extent Egypt would be considered low-spenders in this regard. With the exception of Qatar, the GCC countries spend significantly smaller amounts on health than do most high-income countries. In absolute terms, per capita health spending in Qatar has almost doubled.

Main Findings

This section has provided an overview of health expenditure trends and patterns in the MENA Region. Using the most recently available data on aggregate health spending, the MENA countries were divided into three separate income groups and compared with the corresponding global averages. It was noted that compared with other regions, the MENA countries seem to spend less on health care as a share of GDP. These results were particularly strong for the high-income countries, but, with some notable exceptions, were evident also for the middle-income group. At around 50 percent, the share of public spending in total health expenditure is somewhat lower in the MENA Region than in other parts of the world. Furthermore, governments in the MENA Region devote a smaller share of total public spending to health than do governments elsewhere.

With respect to private health spending, the MENA countries have a larger share of household out-of-pocket expenditure than do other regions. There is also a suggestion that, with a few exceptions, the markets for private health insurance in the MENA Region are smaller because only between 6 percent and 7 percent of total private health spending on average is in the form of insurance. Contrary to other parts of the world, this share has gotten smaller over the past decade.

Some evidence on the nature of health care costs in the MENA Region was then presented, both with respect to the type of care and by projections for health spending and increases in demand for care. The discussion demonstrated several potential cost drivers, including relatively high unit costs of care, the supply of private care, relatively expensive inputs, and the demographic transitions in progress across the MENA Region. To further extend the analysis of the MENA countries' readiness to meet these challenges, the next section provides an overview of the health financing systems of selected MENA countries with a particular focus on their organization and overall performance.

HEALTH INSURANCE IN MENA

This section extends the analysis from the previous quantitative assessment by presenting an overview of the health insurance schemes within the framework of broader financing systems in MENA countries in terms of organization and overall performance. The discussion is based on a review of various country-level health sector studies and reports that have been conducted over the past five to seven years by the countries themselves or in collaboration with the World Bank or other development partners. Because sufficient evidence is not available for all MENA countries, the analysis is limited to the group of countries where the required information is accessible, including at least one country from each income group. The purpose of the assessment is to improve qualitative understanding of some key health financing options and challenges currently facing the MENA countries.

To provide a systematic and coherent analysis across the countries, the analytical matrix used for the assessment includes a set of key health financing indicators and parameters pertaining to the organization of the systems and their particular functions, including resource mobilization, risk pooling, purchasing of services, service delivery system, the role of the private sector, and any other issue of particular relevance. For each country these areas are assessed with respect to their current profile and future reforms. Annex 9B contains the various country cases in summary format. Following on from the previous section, the MENA countries are divided into four general groups based on both income and country context: low-income or International Development Association (IDA) countries, middle-income countries, conflict-afflicted countries, and high-income countries.

Health Financing in the Low-Income or IDA Countries

Yemen and Djibouti are the most resource-scarce countries of the MENA Region, and they share some of the typical characteristics of low-income and IDA countries from other regions.[6] In particular, they face multiple burdens of disease (both communicable and noncommunicable), relatively high levels of maternal and child mortality and morbidity, and comparatively widespread malnutrition. In combination with an underdeveloped infrastructure for health services, high level of dependence on development assistance for health (DAH), and shortages of human resources for health, the Republic of Yemen and Djibouti face somewhat different challenges from those of the middle- and high-income MENA countries. Annex 9B presents a summary of the health financing systems of the Republic of Yemen and Djibouti using the analytical matrix.

A particular constraint in the Republic of Yemen and in Djibouti is the limited fiscal space for health.[7] In all likelihood, they will continue to depend on external assistance for funding basic health services and strengthening the health care infrastructure. Ensuring that these funds are effectively channeled and allocated will be of high policy importance in both countries. Significant challenges are access to health services for particularly isolated populations in the Republic of Yemen, revenue generation at the national level, and the strategic allocation of public resources to vulnerable groups. Options may include exploring criteria for programmatic allocation, for example, to ensure priority health conditions such as prenatal care and child health. Current voucher programs supported by a number of donor agencies are one such example of introducing specific demand-side incentives and coverage for certain priority health conditions.

Health Financing in the Middle-Income Countries

The large and diverse group of middle-income countries in the MENA Region contains both lower- and upper-middle-income countries, some with substantial oil and natural gas revenues. This variation is reflected also in the countries' health financing systems, which range from integrated public health service–type systems to multiple-payer systems relying on a wide range of funding sources and pooling mechanisms. To facilitate the analysis, the presentation of countries is divided into the following broad categories: Mashreq (Egypt, Jordan, Lebanon, and Syria); Maghreb (Libya, Morocco, and Tunisia); and conflict-affected countries (Iraq and West Bank and Gaza).[8]

Health Financing in the Mashreq Region

The Mashreq region contains a group of countries whose health systems have evolved over the past decades to encompass both social health insurance (SHI) programs and more integrated National Health Service–type systems. Among the SHI group, frequently several separate insurance programs cater to different employment groups, such as public civil servants or formal private sector workers. In Lebanon, for example, there are six different public health insurance programs in addition to some 20 private health insurance companies and a number of mutual societies and self-funded schemes (Ammar 2009). Consequently, health resources are mobilized from several different sources and pooled at various levels within the systems. The multiplicity of these risk-pooling arrangements creates especially demanding regulatory requirements in addition to clear risks of segmentation of the health service delivery systems, and impairment of quality, efficiency, and equity of care. Annex 9B shows the summary table for some of these MENA countries where adequate information on the key health financing indicators is available.

For historical and political reasons, Lebanon has allowed the private sector a larger role than other countries in health financing and in service delivery. The share of private insurance expenditure in total private health spending is around 17 percent, somewhat larger than in other Mashreq countries. This share has, however, been falling, suggesting that the role of private health insurance is also relatively limited in Lebanon and may be becoming even more so.

A policy challenge in Lebanon and other MENA countries is to ensure that any reduction in public or private prepayment is not allowed to spill over into larger out-of-pocket spending. As noted in the previous section, this does not seem to be happening in Lebanon, as the share of OOP payments has been dropping for about a decade. Among the reasons for this development is the enlarged share of public spending and more determined role taken on by the Ministry of Public Health (MOPH) to provide health care to previously uncovered groups. Additional reasons may be related to the recent efforts of the MOPH to strengthen its purchasing function by developing beneficiary records and introducing price ceilings at contracted hospitals (Ammar 2003, 2009).

Health Financing in the Maghreb Region

Several countries in the Maghreb region have to various extents inherited the overall structure of the French health financing system with its emphasis on social health insurance schemes covering various population groups and emphasis on civil or private sector formal employees. Yet populations such as the unemployed, informal workers, or dependents have only recently begun to be integrated into these schemes through governmental subsidies, although the success of integration has varied across countries. Over time, also in this part of MENA, the Ministries of Health or corresponding bodies have assumed a larger role for providing financial coverage for different groups, including the poor and workers in the informal labor sector. Annex 9B presents the analytical matrix for Libya, Morocco, and Tunisia.

Similarly to Lebanon, but in contrast to the situation in Libya, both Morocco and Tunisia have a relatively well-established social security system that extends to health insurance, although private health insurance in the Maghreb is far less widespread than in Lebanon. Private health insurance coverage in these countries, though limited, is largely supplementary to other forms of coverage and complementary to, for example, employment-based health insurance programs. In addition, nearly 10 percent of the Tunisian population reports having multiple types of health insurance coverage. In the absence of complete health management information systems with unique identifiers, this multiplicity of coverage may leave room for fraudulent behaviors by both patients and providers. Libya is in the initial stages of embarking on health financing and system reform with a view to strengthening service quality and efficiency, and it is likely that the health financing system can play a role in achieving such goals. Tunisia has gradually succeeded in extending social health insurance coverage to informal workers and low-income individuals, currently covering approximately 33 percent of the Tunisian population in addition to 66 percent who are enrolled through formal employment; 10 percent of the population are still uninsured. By contrast, Morocco has incrementally achieved some gain in pilot health card–based subsidy schemes for specific regions of the country, in part due to challenges in scaling up these schemes and integrating them into broader governmental health insurance policy.

As can be seen from the table in annex 9B, there is considerable variation across this group of countries in the way resources are raised, how funds are pooled, and the mechanisms by which services are purchased and providers paid. Notwithstanding these differences, there are a number of common features that to a very large extent characterize the health financing systems in this group of MENA countries. For example, despite efforts by these countries' governments to provide their citizens with health services either directly or through some type of social health insurance program, out-of-pocket spending by both poor and nonpoor households is often a large source of health funding. In some other instances government does not provide complete coverage or protection against financial risk, but private health insurance then is usually used to supplement publicly provided services. In the MENA Region, the market for private health insurance is limited and, in several instances, shrinking.

Another issue becomes apparent when looking at the way health funds are mobilized and pooled: the relatively high degree of "fragmentation" in the health financing systems (and, as a result, in the health services delivery systems) in many MENA countries. For instance, in the same country, one particular social health insurance scheme may cover public employees while another performs the same services for the privately employed individuals and their dependents. Members of the armed services often have a health program of their own with its own associated delivery infrastructure that may or may not connect in some way to the civil health system. Moreover, some professionals may have access to private health insurance for partial or full access to health services. For people without any formal coverage, the government, through the Ministry of Health or corresponding body, is charged with providing health services as "the insurer of last resort."

There are several important implications of a health system characterized by multiple, largely independent risk pools. First, the benefits may vary considerably from scheme to scheme, which may suggest unequal treatment across population groups. Second, since membership depends on, for instance, labor market status, the average health risk may vary across schemes. For example, all else equal, it is reasonable to assume that the gainfully employed have better health status than the retired, which means that employment-based social health insurance programs may not be required to spend as much per member as some other prepayment schemes. Consequently, there may be a need to introduce some form of risk equalization across the various programs. Today, there is little by way of risk equalization in any of the countries of the MENA Region. Third, health insurance schemes based on employment status may lead to inefficiencies in the labor market because individuals may be reluctant to move from a well-insured part of the market (e.g., the public sector) to a less-well-covered part of the market (e.g., the private sector). The extent to which this is so is an empirical issue which is likely to vary across different contexts.

The fourth issue often raised in discussions of multiple-payer systems is the (aggregate) administrative cost of running several insurance programs. As noted elsewhere, operating several independent insurance programs is likely to be more costly than running a single-payer system. And last, fragmentation may lead to less-than-optimal use of health resources because some programs may limit the choice of care to particular providers. A multiple-payer system may thus lead to overall fragmentation of the health system and suboptimal use of resources. The impact of all these issues depends crucially on the particular context in which they operate.

In addition to these various insurance schemes and mandates, several MENA countries have introduced some type of "special" health care funding scheme using discretionary funds to provide health services inside and outside the country for various individuals and population groups. Although these programs look somewhat different from one country to another, the seemingly ad hoc nature in the allocation of the funds and absence of technical protocols regulating their application contribute to the overall fragmentation of the health financing system and make strategic planning difficult. For example, in Egypt, Jordan, and the Republic of Yemen, these sources of financing have grown substantially over the past decade and now account for between 20 percent and 30 percent of total health expenditure.

Health Financing in the Conflict-Affected Countries

Iraq and West Bank and Gaza in several ways constitute special cases with particular challenges for health financing and service delivery. Even so, the two countries in this group face very different outlooks, with Iraq potentially being able to prosper from substantial oil revenues, a source of funding not present in the West Bank and Gaza.[9] This, among other things, will affect the scope for fiscal space that these countries can create to strengthen services. Annex 9B summarizes the main features of the health financing systems and key issues of these two countries.

The particular political circumstances in both of these countries will undoubtedly affect the policy space over the coming years. In Iraq, a period of reconstruction and overall redevelopment will take place, the pace and scope of which will be largely determined by the extent to which financial resources can be effectively mobilized under improved security conditions. Key policy issues relate to the design of the future Iraqi health financing system, including the number and type of risk pools and the provider reimbursement method.

In the West Bank and Gaza, any prolonged deterioration of relations with Israel will continue to negatively affect the health sector by curtailing available fiscal resources and impairing access to health services.

Health Financing in the High-Income GCC Countries

The high-income GCC countries are different from other MENA countries in many ways. They have extensive natural resources (oil and liquid natural gas, LNG) and, with the exception of Dubai, substantial fiscal space to provide health services to their citizens and nonnational inhabitants. The critical question facing this group of countries is how to do this most effectively, efficiently, and equitably. Annex 9B presents the health financing matrix for Kuwait and Saudi Arabia, the two GCC countries for which sufficient data and information on the key policy variables of the matrix are available.

Although contexts and country-specific conditions vary across the GCC region, in general, these countries' health systems are predominantly government funded, and free or heavily subsidized services are provided for all citizens. A particular issue in the GCC countries is how to provide health services to the relatively large groups of expatriates living and working there. Both Kuwait and

Saudi Arabia have achieved this in two different ways. In Kuwait, all expatriates have access to a broad benefits package for a small nominal user fee paid at the point of service. To obtain a work permit, an individual's employer is required to pay an annual fee that is unrelated to the actual cost of care. The individual then receives a health card to be shown when seeking care. The cost of health care for expatriates in Kuwait is therefore subsidized by general government revenues.

In contrast, Saudi Arabia has developed special legislation mandating private sector employers, many of them foreign, to buy private health insurance for their employees. The private health insurance market is regulated by a special independent public body, the Council for Cooperative Health Insurance (CCHI), which oversees the functioning of the market and ensures adherence to the law. Current policy discussions in this area focus on how to expand coverage to individuals and households outside of large and medium-size private companies.

Coverage of Health Insurance and Health Services

This discussion has demonstrated that most MENA countries have multiple health insurance programs that cover different population groups. Obtaining exact estimates of the coverage rates of these various programs is difficult due to incomplete data systems and issues related to the definition of different types of insurance programs. Table 9.4 provides an overview of the various types of health insurance systems that exist in some MENA countries where information is available.

TABLE 9.4   Health Insurance Coverage, Selected MENA Countries (latest available year)

Country	Directly provided government health services (complete or partial)	Social health insurance schemes	Estimated percent of civil population enrolled in social health insurance	Private health insurance
Yemen, Rep.	Yes/complete	No	—	No
Libya	Yes/complete	No	—	No
Lebanon	Yes/partial	Yes	31.0	Partial
Iran, Islamic Rep.	Yes/complete	Yes	69.3	No
Egypt, Arab Rep.	Yes/partial	Yes	45.0	Limited
West Bank and Gaza	Yes/partial	Yes	48.5	No
Tunisia	Yes/partial	Yes	78.0	Partial
Jordan	Yes/partial	Yes	44.0	Modest
Morocco	Yes/partial	Yes	30.0	Partial
Kuwait	Yes/complete	No	—	Limited
Saudi Arabia	Yes/partial	No	—	Partial

Sources: Authors' estimates of current situations. See annex 9A for details on spending rates.
Note: — = not available.

As can be seen, one group of countries provide universal coverage through the public health services with no social health insurance fund, but in some cases with private health insurance for some groups. Other countries, in particular the middle-income countries, have a mix of publicly provided services combined with one or several social health insurance funds. Finally, most MENA countries have a mix of all different types of health insurance approaches, public provision of health services, social health insurance, and different types of voluntary and mandatory private health insurance options. Although a multiple-payer system is in principle congruous with the aim of universal coverage of equitable and efficient health services, such a system requires a comprehensive regulatory framework and the necessary oversight (World Bank 2009d).

Assessment of Health Financing

The preceding subregional and country-level review of some of the key issues of health financing for most countries in the MENA Region further illustrates the wide intraregional variation in health spending and the organization of these functions. The analysis addresses many issues, three of which would seem to be of particular general importance: data availability, resource allocation and purchasing, and the role of the private sector. A critical weakness in the underlying basis for effective health policy development and health financing reform is the general lack of systematically collected and disseminated health data and statistics. The dearth of key socioeconomic data in the MENA Region has been highlighted in several recent reports, and the health sector is a case in point: little exists in the way of regular health survey data, case register data, or firmly institutionalized national health accounts. To be able to strengthen the performance of their health systems and to enable the health financing system to contribute to this process, many MENA countries will need to improve their health management systems.

The second general finding of the review is the almost universal approach to allocating health resources by means of input-based methods, such as line-item budgeting. Although this way of allocating resources to providers may be effective for keeping spending under control, it offers providers limited or no incentives to focus on performance, for example to achieve agreed output or outcome results against payment. Furthermore, the use of input-based methods makes it difficult to hold providers accountable for the quality of their services or their efficiency in delivering them. Broadening the use of strategic allocation of health resources is most likely one of the most important areas for health financing reform in the Middle East and North Africa Region over the coming years.

A related concern is the extent of discretionary health funding programs in several MENA countries, both rich and poor. These special programs, which serve different purposes, from much needed out-of-country care in the West Bank and Gaza to largely untargeted public subsidies for health care in other countries, have become significant sources of health spending. The discretionary nature and size of many of these special programs suggest that they may become fiscally unsustainable and sources of concern from an equity and efficiency perspective.

Finally, the review shows that the private health sector in many, if not most, MENA countries is either highly underdeveloped or is expanding in a largely unregulated manner with potentially dire efficiency and patient-safety repercussions. The private health sector is an important contributor to equitable and efficient health services of high quality in most countries of the world. However, given the information constraints related to health care, there is a need to regulate private—and public—health care providers in an effective way that allows them to play this role. This is an important area of policy attention in the MENA Region in the years to come.

Although providing advice at the level of individual countries is beyond the scope of this discussion, the following issues are noted with respect to the various country groups. In the Republic of Yemen and Djibouti, the most resource-scarce countries in the MENA Region, fiscal space for health is highly compromised and is likely to continue to be so over the short and medium term. Development assistance for health, out-of-pocket payments, and general government resources will remain the dominant sources of health funding, and finding the most effective ways to channel these resources to ensure basic services will be the overarching policy concern over the coming decade.

A key health financing concern also in many middle-income countries of the Region is the prospect of continued fiscal limitations for scaling up health coverage to currently uncovered groups in a sustainable manner. Over the coming decade, these countries will continue to rely on a broad range of funding sources. Although multiple-payer systems are common in, for example, Australia, Europe, and Japan, they all operate within a regulatory framework that ensures efficiency and equity. Failure to provide such a structure may lead to inadequate financial protection, inefficiencies in the allocation and utilization of resources, and difficulties in controlling costs. Thus, one critical challenge for this group of countries is to ensure that this multitude of health financing mechanisms can be harmonized to ensure broad, effective, equitable, and efficient coverage of basic health services.

Conflict-affected Iraq and the West Bank and Gaza face very different outlooks in terms of health financing. Iraq has substantial oil resources for export, which can be used to ensure fiscal space for health over the medium term, but the West Bank and Gaza are likely to see continued fiscal limitations for health. Their situation is further compromised by the small size of the formal private sector employment from which social contributions can be mobilized. Reliance on external support will continue to be an important source of health financing for the West Bank and Gaza over the short and medium term. Finally, the GCC countries mobilize general revenues for health and provide most of their citizens with free or heavily subsidized services delivered by largely integrated public health care systems. One key issue in these countries will be how to ascertain quality and efficiency of service provision.

The quantitative analysis of key health financing trends and patterns in the MENA countries presented in the previous section and the more qualitative review conducted here provide a sound basis on which a set of key messages and recommendations can be developed. This is done in the final section of this chapter.

CONCLUSIONS AND RECOMMENDATIONS

The first two parts of this chapter provided a comprehensive analysis of critical health financing issues in the MENA Region. The initial part looked at some key health financing indicators over the past decade and a half to obtain an understanding of the broad trends and patterns in health financing in this Region compared with those in other parts of the world. In addition, drawing on the available evidence from two middle-income countries to make projections for health expenditure, the analysis provided an indication of what may occur over the coming decades as a result of the demographic transition that is taking place.

The review then presented a more detailed discussion of some qualitative aspects of the health financing systems in a selection of both rich and poor countries. The discussion addressed the way health resources are mobilized in the MENA Region, how they are pooled, and the way resources are allocated.

The picture that emerges from these analyses is one of both opportunities and shortcomings with respect to the extent to which health financing systems in the MENA Region are optimally prepared to address the challenges to continued provision of quality health services in an equitable manner while ensuring fiscal sustainability. The next section summarizes the main conclusions of the discussion, and the final part presents some recommendations for strengthening health financing systems in the various countries of the Region.

Conclusions

The quantitative analysis in the first section showed that, although health spending levels vary considerably across the MENA Region, most countries spend less as a share of GDP on health than do other similar countries and income groups. Furthermore, although public spending in some countries seems to have stabilized, households and individuals pay increasing amounts of money out of pocket to see a health provider and to buy medicines. This trend is causing many people in the MENA Region to face catastrophic health expenditures and is also pushing some households into poverty when health care costs have to be borne directly without sufficient financial protection. It is unlikely, however, that continuing this trend of keeping aggregate public spending down is an effective and sustainable approach and that more innovative ways of mobilizing funds, pooling resources, and purchasing services are called for.

The analysis then highlighted three issues of general importance. First, there is an almost complete absence of timely and high-quality data on key health system dimensions in the MENA Region. This finding is in line with that of other reviews suggesting that this issue goes beyond the health sector. For effective health policy making, solving this data deficit is of critical importance.

Second, most countries in the MENA Region continue to rely on input-based methods to allocate financial resources to providers. This report has demonstrated that most MENA countries in the Region have done exceptionally well in reducing mortality and morbidity rates. The input-based approaches to resource allocation have most likely served these countries well in providing large groups in society with access to basic services to meet population health challenges related to communicable diseases, maternal and child health, and nutrition. However, in light of the changing disease pattern with the growing prevalence of noncommunicable chronic diseases, accidents, and injuries, finding more strategic approaches to resource allocation is likely to help in meeting these new population health challenges.

Finally, the MENA countries would do well to develop strategies for how the private sector can be made to contribute to providing financial protection and high-quality services in ways that are conducive to equity and cost control. In line with the situation in most other parts of the world, the private sector is a real presence in both health financing and in service provision. However, it is also clear that much more can be done to harness the contributions of these sectors. In many MENA countries, the private health care sector operates all but independently from the public sector. Identifying the most appropriate mechanisms through which the private sector can be an equal and responsible part of the overall health sector is a critical policy issue in the MENA Region.

Recommendations

Based on the findings in this and other chapters of this book, countries in the MENA Region may want to consider the recommendations presented below when designing health finance reform to improve the performance of the health systems by offering providers and patients positive incentives and holding the actors of the system accountable for their actions. The three general recommendations—related to health data systems, strategic resource allocation, and role of the private health sector in finance and service delivery—are noted in the next subsections. The section concludes with recommendations addressing concerns related to the specific country groups.

Improving Health Data Systems for Policy Development

To be able to develop effective health finance reform options and to conduct evaluations to assess their effectiveness, most MENA countries need to strengthen their data collection systems. Modern health systems require access to many different types of data, including regular individual and provider survey data, epidemiological and utilization data, and data for particular diseases. These data need to be widely disseminated and made available to a broad range of stakeholders. Depending on the context, these efforts look different from one country to the next, given the complexities involved in designing and implementing effective data systems.

Strategic Resource Allocation Mechanisms for Better Incentives and Accountability

A decent health management information system is a basic necessity for introducing more advantageous approaches to resource allocation, the second general recommendation. Recent policy discussions address the many different ways of allocating health resources under the heading of "strategic purchasing" of health services (Langenbrunner, Cashin, and O'Dougherty 2009; Preker and Langenbrunner 2005).

The idea behind strategic purchasing is that the way resources are allocated influences the performance of providers and the health-seeking behavior of individuals. Two main questions are pertinent to strategic purchasing: (1) which services should be purchased and (2) how should providers be paid. Concerning services, the benefits package should reflect the burden of disease of the population, including the poor and socially excluded. The package should also contain services that provide value for money in the sense that they are cost-effective. Which services are included in the benefits package, however, is usually the outcome of a complicated process that includes medical, economic, and political considerations.

Providers can be paid in many different ways, each with its own set of performance incentives. Depending on the particular design of the health financing system, there may be multiple or single purchasers of health services. For these markets to work effectively, the health management information system (HMIS) connects purchasers and providers to ensure efficient transactions and payments (Langenbrunner, Cashin, and O'Dougherty 2009; Streveler 2009). The HMIS thus becomes a key tool for effective management of relationships between the systemic partners.

Although detailed country recommendations for provider reimbursement are outside the scope of this discussion, strategic purchasing is most likely one of the most effective tools that policy makers can have for using incentives to both providers and consumers to achieve policy goals related to the quality, efficiency, and equity of health services. Given the current context in most of the MENA countries, one general approach to hospital payment reform would be to move gradually away from line-item budgeting to some type of case-based hospital payment system. Paying public and private hospitals a fixed amount for each case presents hospitals with very different quality and efficiency incentives. A critical issue here is to set the reimbursement rate to reflect the true cost of treatment, an exercise that depends heavily on accurate data and information on the patient. A move toward case-based hospital reimbursement would also imply a need to widen individual hospitals' autonomy in order to reap the full benefits of such a reform initiative. This, however, may require political decisions that go beyond the domains of the health sector.

Similar provider reimbursement changes can also be made at the level of individual physicians and clinics for primary health care. For example, paying doctors a fee-for-service (FFS) is a useful way of increasing production, but it provides little incentive for cost containment and quality improvement. Instead, providers can be reimbursed through some case-based system or through a capitation system, which alters the incentives drastically. Again, reforms in this area will most likely require additional organizational and regulatory measures the scope and nature of which need to be assessed case by case.

Private Partners for Population Health

The third general recommendation relates to the role of the private sector in health financing and service provision. The ability to bring in the private sector as a contributing partner for health rests critically on the two previous recommendations. With respect to private health insurance, for such a market to play any significant role in providing effective and equitable financial protection requires access to timely high-quality data gathered at the level of individuals. As noted above, only a well-developed HMIS can deliver such data.

On the provider side, implementing strategic purchasing through which a public health fund can contract with private providers for specific health services is one effective way of harnessing the private sector and creating a level playing field for health care. Several MENA countries have introduced contracting with the private sector for certain clinical and nonclinical services. Although the impacts of these initiatives are yet to be evaluated, it is likely that scaling up similar efforts would constitute one critical component in strengthening the health systems of the MENA Region.

While these are three of the most important general recommendations for how countries in the Region may strengthen their health financing systems, contextual differences warrant a more specific assessment for what may be the most strategic approaches to effective health finance reform in the MENA Region.

Low-Income and IDA Countries

The Republic of Yemen and Djibouti are the two smallest economies in the MENA Region. They both face particular economic and institutional challenges that to considerable extent will determine the scope for future health financing and systems reform. With respect to resource mobilization, both countries will continue to rely on external funding for significant parts of their health service delivery capacity. Ensuring that these funds complement domestic resources will therefore be of high policy relevance. With respect to risk pooling, it is likely that these countries will continue to rely on public and private not-for-profit providers for delivery of primary health care services and hospital care. Key challenges here include ensuring access to these services also by the poor and socially and geographically excluded population groups.

Both the Republic of Yemen and Djibouti face several institutional constraints with respect to the scope for strategic purchasing. Nonetheless, international experience suggests that low-income countries can make use of performance-based contracting with public, private, and nongovernmental providers of core services. Efforts in this area would include identifying a basic benefits package, including maternal and child health care, and ensuring the provision of core public health and disease prevention programs such as nutrition and vaccinations.

Much evidence from low-income countries shows that the demand is low among the poor and socially excluded groups for preventive and curative health services, including maternal and child health care. Consequently, actual utilization of basic health services is depressed despite service availability. Demand for many health services is low for several reasons, including knowledge and cultural norms. To strengthen demand for key services among particular groups, LICs may want to introduce special interventions, such as community outreach programs and health information, communication, and training (ICT) programs targeted at key local decision makers.

Middle-Income Countries

The previous sections of this chapter have demonstrated the particular challenges that this large group of countries face with respect to fiscal sustainability, fragmentation of the financing and delivery systems, and inequities caused by significant out-of-pocket payments. Although contexts vary considerably, addressing these and other concerns will require sustained reform efforts focused on a set of priority areas in which the returns from reform are largest. In addition to what has already been noted with respect to data collection and strategic purchasing, some middle-income countries may want to consider ways to harmonize their health financing systems, in particular with respect to the pooling function. A number of measures can be implemented to achieve this, including stronger regulation with respect to the benefits packages of the various prepayment programs, enhanced portability across programs when individuals transfer from one state to another, and importantly, more comprehensive data systems to ensure effectiveness in utilization.

Several middle-income countries in the MENA Region face severe fiscal constraints for health care. As recently reported, the fiscal space in many countries is compromised due to the substantial food and energy subsidies on which governments spend public funds. Disregarding for a moment the targeting effectiveness of these subsidies, many MICs in the Region will continue to face fiscal constraints when undertaking health system reform. It would therefore seem particularly important that these countries find ways to improve the effectiveness and efficiency of their health systems so that more care can be delivered to larger groups at smaller unit costs.

One especially relevant issue on the revenue side for all middle- and high-income countries in the MENA Region is the option of introducing excise taxes, in particular on tobacco products. Smoking rates are generally high in this Region, in particular among men, but increasingly also among women. One proven way to mobilize additional funds for health and at the same time reduce smoking prevalence is to increase the consumer price of tobacco products by introducing or raising taxes on all tobacco-related products.[10] The impact of any tobacco tax needs to be assessed case by case and will depend on the price elasticity of demand for tobacco in the particular market. Finally, the equity impact of tobacco taxes needs to be analyzed because tobacco consumption may vary by socioeconomic group.

To improve the overall performance of their health systems, middle-income countries have several options, three of which would appear particularly relevant. First, all countries should review the type of services included in the benefits package to ensure that these are cost-effective and address the most pressing health needs of the population. This seems particularly important in light of the epidemiological transitions that most MENA countries of the Region are going through.

Second, while international comparisons have shown that the number of poor households is smaller in the MENA Region compared with some other parts of the world, these studies have also demonstrated that many individuals and households in this Region live just above the official poverty lines. In other words, there are many near-poor households in the MENA Region. This is a particularly important fact from a health financing perspective because many studies have shown that an increased risk of falling into poverty is one impact of large out-of-pocket payments by households (Wagstaff and van Doorslaer 2003). Providing the necessary financial protection to the poor and the near-poor in the MENA countries may therefore require the introduction of specially targeted programs for particularly vulnerable groups.

Finally, as discussed earlier, most middle-income countries of the Region would do well to introduce reform with respect to the way resources are allocated, including the purchasing function of their health systems. Some countries have initiated changes in this area. Sustaining and scaling up these attempts would seem advisable because they would strengthen incentives to providers to focus on delivering efficient care, engage in quality improvements that would lead to cost savings, and improve overall performance. Furthermore, as discussed earlier, introducing contracting would open up the possibility for creation of more efficient markets for health care where private providers can operate and provide mandatory services along with public providers. This would increase the supply of core services that can meet the increasing demand as incomes grow and disease patterns change.

Many countries in the MENA Region, including high- and middle-income countries, are considering introducing some type of social health insurance (SHI) system. This process would look different depending on each country's own situation, but the overall aim would be to organize the health financing system around an independent health insurance agency that would purchase services on behalf of its members. One driving motivation for moving toward an SHI system is the ability to mobilize additional resources for health without jeopardizing the fiscal position of the government because such an agency is usually financed by means of social contributions levied on employees and employers in the formal public and private labor markets. Although a single-payer system offers important advantages—in particular compared with the current situation in many MENA countries—international experience shows that the actual scope for raising additional funds for health is limited for several reasons. First, countries that have moved in this direction have often seen the social contributions merely replace existing sources of financing, leading to a situation in which little or no additional funding is actually mobilized.

Second, the resource base for SHI is highly dependent on the existence of a large and stable formal labor market, not least a sustainable private sector, to provide the necessary funds. And third, it is likely that the government would have to provide subsidies for the poor and others who would be exempted from paying the full premium. An additional concern about SHI systems and the associated social contributions is that they may impair a country's international competitiveness. All of these issues need careful consideration by any country contemplating introducing a health insurance system based on social contributions.

Conflict-Affected Countries

The particular political and security circumstances in Iraq and in the West Bank and Gaza will continue to have an impact on the nature and scope of health financing reform in the short and medium term. Both countries therefore constitute special cases whose particular challenges require specific attention.

Although both countries have and continue to experience widespread conflict, their circumstances differ substantially in terms of economic and geographic conditions. Iraq has large oil resources that can provide significant fiscal space for health over the medium term. Despite the difficult political situation in West Bank and Gaza, several reform initiatives will pave the way for making the overall health system more effective and equitable. Some of these initiatives include contracting for health services with the private nonprofit sector and the continued production of both household survey data and national health accounts data.

High-Income Countries

The high-income countries of the Gulf share some of the characteristics with some other countries in the MENA Region, but they also differ in important ways. For example, while they have mostly ample fiscal space for health, there is nonetheless a need in most of the Gulf countries to focus on service quality and efficiency. As stressed throughout this chapter, the health financing system can be made to contribute to such aims.

Traditionally, the GCC countries have relied on general revenues to fund a large package of health services delivered through public providers in a largely integrated manner. Previous sections of this chapter noted that, even in such types of systems, changing the way services are purchased can help make providers more accountable for the quality of their services and their efficiency in delivering them.

GCC countries and others may also want to introduce changes on the demand side (see annex 9B for details). Contrary to low- and lower-middle-income countries, for example, such changes may look at options to strengthen cost sharing and thereby provide individuals with the incentives to make changes in their health care–seeking behaviors. Public health policy makers in the GCC countries may also want to consider introducing financial incentives to affect the behavior of individuals to address lifestyle-related diseases and conditions, such as diabetes, high blood pressure, and obesity, which are all on the increase in this Region. Examples of such policies include excise taxes on especially harmful products.

Also noted in an earlier section were the particular circumstances in the GCC countries regarding the need to identify prepayment options that provide all population groups with effective coverage, including nonnationals. The fact that all GCC countries have large groups of expatriates, and that their presence is closely related to the labor markets in these countries, suggests that options for financing health care for these groups would involve the employers of these groups. The discussion earlier also provided two examples of how that may be achieved.

Health Financing Reform in MENA: Options and Challenges

The recommendations put forward in this chapter aim to enhance the performance of the health systems of the MENA Region. Implementing the interventions will come at a cost, and the impact on the quality, efficiency, and equity of health services is not certain. Developing an effective, modern health management information system is a costly process, and it is likely to take several years to get up and running. The payoffs, however, are likely to be significant, all the more so in an environment that has little by way of a health data system already in existence. Furthermore, an HMIS of acceptable standard is in many ways a critical prerequisite for moving the health systems of the Region to the next level of development.

Introducing more strategic approaches to resource allocation is also costly, including linking provider payment to performance and output. However, the costs associated with such interventions are most likely more "political" than pecuniary, while the potential benefits may be significant. There is considerable evidence that paying providers by some of the methods discussed in this chapter has led to reductions in the unit cost of care, increased utilization of services while keeping overall expenditure constant, and achieved savings in overall resource use. For example, introducing capitation in one region in Brazil led to a 100 percent increase in utilization of services with the same overall expenditure ceiling and a 25 percent reduction of physicians who could be relocated to other areas with less supply of doctors. In Hungary, paying hospitals through a case-based payment system led to increased admissions, fewer beds, and shorter lengths of stay (Langenbrunner et al. 2009).

This chapter has highlighted the many impressive improvements in people's health across the MENA Region. These achievements are due to many factors, including investments in education, water and sanitation, and in health care systems. However, a number of challenges have also been identified that may undermine the ability to further improve population health outcomes. These challenges include demographic and epidemiological transitions, quality and efficiency issues in health service delivery, and an excessive reliance on the ability of the state to provide health care effectively. Introducing changes in how the health system is financed (i.e., how resources are mobilized, funds are pooled, and services are purchased) can contribute to making the health sector address some of these challenges more effectively. Based on the experience in middle-income countries in which a mix of social health insurance and governmental subsidies operate, such as Egypt, Morocco, and Tunisia, ensuring that targeting mechanisms are well functioning and sufficiently integrated into national insurance systems will help to bridge gaps in coverage.

Looking at the international experiences of health sector reform it is clear that this is a long and complicated process that requires resources, political attention, and strong management capacities (Gottret, Schieber, and Waters 2008). For the MENA countries to be able to realize the policy objectives of efficient, equitable universal coverage of high-quality health services, health policy makers would benefit from focusing on a set of critical issues. If left unresolved, it will be difficult to achieve the policy aims. Given the experience in MENA of having introduced a broad array of financing tools, future success will lie in expanding these tools comprehensively.

TABLE 9A.1   Government Health Expenditure as Percent of Total Government Expenditure, 1995–2008

	1995	1996	1997	1998	1999	2000	2001	2002	2003	2004	2005	2006	2007	2008
Low-income countries														
Yemen, Rep.	6.92	5.42	6.45	7.83	8.49	8.30	8.37	7.71	7.62	6.24	4.80	4.87	4.47	4.47
Low-income mean (global)	7.89	—	—	—	—	7.90	—	—	—	—	9.31	—	—	9.60
Middle-income countries														
Algeria	10.03	10.08	9.75	9.61	9.44	8.96	9.51	8.09	8.81	8.91	9.90	12.00	10.66	10.65
Egypt, Arab Rep.	5.34	5.46	6.28	6.40	7.20	7.34	7.69	7.61	7.66	7.15	7.15	7.13	7.14	7.14
Iran, Islamic Rep.	9.30	9.66	10.68	10.91	9.68	9.59	11.21	11.28	11.92	11.53	11.52	11.52	11.52	11.40
Jordan	14.30	14.31	14.23	14.25	12.10	11.31	11.38	11.59	10.47	11.00	10.54	10.24	11.36	11.35
Libya	6.08	6.08	6.08	6.08	5.55	7.23	6.30	15.01	9.06	5.38	5.38	5.38	5.38	5.38
Morocco	3.78	4.41	3.89	4.16	4.13	3.98	4.43	5.04	5.04	5.14	4.65	5.93	6.17	6.17
Syrian Arab Republic	7.71	7.18	6.63	6.53	6.46	6.54	6.52	6.49	6.31	6.06	6.80	6.01	6.01	6.01
Tunisia	8.20	7.67	7.61	7.77	7.89	8.11	8.41	8.07	9.07	8.71	9.21	9.43	9.11	8.90
Lebanon	9.80	9.45	9.17	10.43	9.59	7.79	10.34	9.01	9.60	11.13	11.87	11.27	11.69	12.39
Djibouti	6.24	10.69	7.82	9.61	13.33	11.97	11.85	10.75	11.49	9.30	13.41	12.57	14.15	14.15
Iraq	—	1.94	1.94	1.94	1.21	1.28	1.15	0.61	4.40	3.41	3.34	3.06	3.06	3.06
Middle-income mean	8.08	7.90	7.64	7.97	7.87	7.64	8.07	8.50	8.53	7.97	8.52	8.59	8.75	8.78
Middle-income mean (global)	9.82	—	—	—	—	10.24	—	—	—	—	10.68	—	—	10.59

(continued)

TABLE 9A.1 Government Health Expenditure as Percent of Total Government Expenditure, 1995–2008 *(continued)*

	1995	1996	1997	1998	1999	2000	2001	2002	2003	2004	2005	2006	2007	2008
High-income Gulf countries														
Bahrain	11.27	11.59	11.19	11.20	11.18	10.23	10.26	9.47	9.64	9.43	9.03	9.46	9.78	9.78
Kuwait	6.26	6.29	7.01	7.18	7.18	6.73	7.02	6.81	6.76	6.74	6.15	6.94	5.41	6.28
Oman	6.89	7.69	7.26	7.28	7.62	7.07	6.61	6.99	6.86	6.09	6.05	5.41	5.21	4.70
Qatar	5.02	5.02	5.02	5.02	5.02	5.02	5.98	6.12	10.99	9.72	9.72	9.72	9.72	9.72
Saudi Arabia	4.73	4.82	4.89	5.60	9.20	9.16	8.76	9.36	9.07	8.72	8.80	9.48	8.38	8.76
United Arab Emirates	8.09	7.13	8.76	7.93	7.94	7.57	7.73	7.91	8.27	8.13	8.62	8.88	8.86	8.90
GCC/high-income mean	7.04	7.09	7.35	7.37	8.02	7.63	7.73	7.78	8.60	8.14	8.06	8.31	7.89	8.02
High-income mean (global)	11.56	—	—	—	—	12.51	—	—	—	—	13.50	—	—	14.09

Source: WHO-WHOSIS.
Note: — = not available.

TABLE 9A.2 Out-of-Pocket Expenditure as Percent of Total Health Expenditure, MENA and Global Averages, 1995–2008

	1995	1996	1997	1998	1999	2000	2001	2002	2003	2004	2005	2006	2007	2008
Low-income countries														
Yemen, Rep.	65.51	54.18	52.10	49.54	47.53	43.65	44.29	46.23	52.12	57.75	59.33	56.08	59.09	58.01
Low-income mean (global)	50.03	—	—	—	—	50.87	—	—	—	—	—	—	—	45.77
Middle-income countries														
Algeria	23.90	21.57	24.80	25.48	26.34	25.79	21.67	23.02	20.95	24.87	22.87	17.83	17.42	15.30
Egypt, Arab Rep.	47.95	53.86	57.66	61.79	56.70	56.80	57.08	57.50	57.89	59.39	59.27	56.01	58.89	58.73
Iran, Islamic Rep.	46.30	50.55	52.54	53.32	59.34	60.40	55.18	54.14	50.41	53.81	48.59	47.65	50.78	51.68
Jordan	24.35	26.91	28.50	29.70	33.42	38.29	37.64	38.37	39.12	37.43	37.63	38.12	34.79	33.40
Libya	48.14	48.95	52.65	45.71	49.80	38.30	33.36	22.68	25.80	33.66	34.69	33.72	28.20	24.12
Morocco	52.73	52.78	55.55	54.35	54.57	54.05	51.83	60.51	59.97	59.07	57.65	58.00	57.18	56.13
Syrian Arab Republic	60.32	64.47	64.56	61.73	61.63	59.55	55.79	54.23	51.75	52.03	49.50	52.36	54.11	54.87
Tunisia	37.86	40.08	40.50	40.57	40.37	36.17	37.13	38.03	37.98	40.28	40.87	40.93	41.70	42.52
Lebanon	55.31	55.30	56.31	59.61	58.14	56.05	52.45	50.63	46.88	42.44	41.75	42.81	42.92	39.95
Djibouti	39.30	30.52	37.85	35.33	28.75	31.71	34.59	34.98	30.70	35.49	27.12	26.72	23.04	23.60
Middle-income mean	43.62	44.50	47.09	46.76	46.91	45.71	43.67	43.41	42.15	43.85	41.99	41.42	40.90	40.03
Middle-income mean (global)	35.38	—	—	—	—	35.56	—	—	—	—	—	—	—	32.23
High-income Gulf countries														
Bahrain	21.70	22.02	21.40	21.70	22.19	22.28	22.77	22.74	22.46	22.72	22.28	22.45	20.55	19.71
Kuwait	16.32	19.29	18.83	19.25	19.89	21.13	24.89	21.11	21.47	20.83	22.56	20.89	20.61	21.27
Oman	10.17	10.15	10.76	11.89	11.94	11.75	11.28	10.15	10.60	11.15	10.86	11.89	13.04	17.02
Qatar	35.02	30.13	28.25	29.86	29.00	26.36	24.79	27.14	16.60	19.41	19.57	23.60	21.53	26.50
Saudi Arabia	15.29	13.63	12.43	13.24	9.15	7.55	7.36	7.55	7.32	7.21	6.46	5.99	6.61	6.34
United Arab Emirates	56.07	54.64	55.28	54.04	53.63	53.15	54.35	50.88	50.87	46.51	45.49	45.54	45.78	45.49
GCC/high-income mean	25.76	24.97	24.49	25.00	24.30	23.70	24.24	23.26	21.55	21.30	21.20	21.73	21.35	22.72
High-income mean (global)	22.08	—	—	—	—	21.82	—	—	—	—	—	—	—	20.84

Source: WHO-WHOSIS.
Note: — = not available.

TABLE 9A.3   MENA: Per Capita Health Spending, 1995, 2000, 2008 (US$)

Country/class	Year		
	1995	2000	2008
Low-income countries			
Yemen, Rep.	71.40	86.67	103.57
Global low-income countries average	43.45	51.48	75.90
Middle-income countries			
Egypt, Arab Rep.	107.23	195.81	332.95
Iran, Islamic Rep.	245.13	382.33	721.76
Iraq	0.00	37.45	93.76
Jordan	233.13	311.97	431.68
Lebanon	693.45	801.05	1,000.13
Libya	—	384.96	401.27
Morocco	83.11	108.87	228.57
Syrian Arab Republic	168.99	158.88	143.24
Tunisia	222.09	290.21	474.25
MENA middle-income countries average	158.06	185.99	282.02
Global middle-income countries average	218.80	286.25	417.40
High-income Gulf countries			
Bahrain	794.97	800.49	1,241.45
Kuwait	1,048.13	736.02	795.42
Oman	483.54	619.05	592.14
Qatar	1,470.91	1,453.21	2,837.40
Saudi Arabia	364.61	647.06	935.71
United Arab Emirates	920.42	804.71	942.58
GCC countries average	847.10	843.42	1,224.12
Global high-income countries average	1,294.67	1,702.37	2,406.71

Source: WHO-WHOSIS.
Note: — = not available.

ANNEX 9B MENA: HEALTH FINANCING AND INSURANCE, SELECTED COUNTRIES

TABLE 9B.1 Low-Income and IDA Countries, the Republic of Yemen and Djibouti

Item	Republic of Yemen		Djibouti	
	Country profile	Key reforms or issues	Country profile	Key reforms or issues
Revenues	Household resources, general governmental revenues, external resources	Low total spending on health; possibility for more efficient/focused resource allocation mechanisms to prioritize public spending and reduce household burden	Household resources, general governmental revenues, external resources	Despite increases in share of GDP going to health, public spending as percentage of total health spending, and per capita health expenditures the country remains highly dependent on donor assistance. Continued high burden of out-of-pocket spending. No transparency on information on health spending
Risk pooling and payer organization	Largely single, MOF transfer to MOH, but other governmental payers as well; decentralized responsibilities for spending recurrent budgets, centralized responsibility for capital investment	MOH role as integrated provider; feasibility recently conducted regarding introduction of social health insurance schemes on limited basis; implementation unclear	Social health insurance provided to government employees and workers in formal sector	Limited social health insurance coverage; examine expanding to other population groups and ensure sustainability of programs
Strategic purchasing	Global transfers from MOH and other governmental authorities to providers	Introduction of separation of provider and payer functions and gatekeeping/referral system will be beneficial; introduction of strategic purchasing unknown	MOF transfers line-item budgets to MOH and other line ministries. No evidence of strategic purchasing	Consider moving to performance-based budgeting
Role of private sector	Active private market and de facto private market through vertical programs managed by multiple nongovernmental organizations/donors for basic health services	Future role of private sector to be defined; integration of vertical programs and coordination among multiple donors to be determined	Active private market especially for pharmaceuticals; cross-border utilization of health services; HIV/AIDS, malaria, and TB will put strain on health system	Strengthen planning and management capacity of health systems; future role of private sector to be defined
Other issues	Increasing revenues for health sector and sustainability in midst of macroeconomic and civil instability, travel abroad for health care	Strategy to plan more efficiently supply of health services to reach underserved populations in mountainous regions	Active private market especially for pharmaceuticals	Future role of private sector to be defined

Source: Authors.

TABLE 9B.2 Middle-Income Countries, Mashreq Countries

Item	Syrian Arab Republic		Arab Republic of Egypt	
	Country profile	Future reforms	Country profile	Future reforms
Revenues	Household resources; general governmental revenues; limited external resources	Declining trend in percent of GDP and share of government budget going to health. Out-of-pocket spending remains single largest source of financing. No transparency in public spending	Household resources; general governmental revenues; contribution by employers to social health insurance program; limited external resources	Declining percentage of GDP and government budget going to health; high burden of out-of-pocket spending
Risk pooling and payer organization	No evidence of social health insurance; some evidence of very limited private insurance market	Number of studies to examine feasibility of social health insurance. Need to design and pilot schemes	Fragmented social health insurance scheme with separate laws covering different population subgroups; generous benefits package that covers most outpatient, inpatient, and drug costs; social health insurance scheme runs deficits; small private health insurance market	Harmonize and reduce fragmentation in social health insurance scheme; ensure financial viability of social health insurance scheme; more clearly define role of private health insurance
Strategic purchasing	MOF transfers line-item budgets to MOH and other line ministries; no real budgeting in public hospitals; governorates and districts have one lump-sum budget covering both hospitals and health centers; spending is not linked to performance; no incentive to focus on either revenue generation or efficient use of existing funds	Need to consider linking payments to performance	Line-item budgets from MOF to MOH and other ministries providing health services; limited experimentation with performance-based incentives; social health insurance scheme does limited contracting with private providers	Strengthen capacity at both MOH and social health insurance scheme for strategic purchasing; move to performance-based budgeting
Delivery system	There is a large and growing private sector. The government permits dual employment: physicians working in public sector can also work after office hours in private sector. The phenomenon of dual employment coupled with high out-of-pocket spending has fueled the growth of the private sector. Thriving pharmaceutical industry meets domestic needs and exports to other countries.	Need to develop specific policies toward dual employment; accreditation of facilities	Spending at private clinics and pharmacies accounts for half of all health expenditures; government does not recognize and exploit private market to increase access to health care; government action of directing public spending to public providers stifling growth of private market	Future role of private sector to be defined; independent accreditation authority needed to ensure quality of services

Item	Lebanon Country profile	Lebanon Future reforms	Jordan Country profile	Jordan Future reforms
Role of private sector	Continued high burden of out-of-pocket expenditures; it is impossible to break down budgets and spending by facility; no real incentive to follow good management or accounting practices	Strengthen capacity to better plan and manage health systems	Large government-managed discretionary fund to pay for health care distorts markets; inequity in health care use and expenditures; lack of transparency in public spending by program or interventions; dual employment of physicians; increased spending on secondary and tertiary care	Strategy to plan more efficient supply of health services to reach underserved populations to increase access and reduce inequities; improve efficiency and transparency in public spending
Other issues	Household resources; general governmental revenues; limited external resources	Declining trend in percent of GDP and share of government budget going to health. Out-of-pocket spending remains single largest source of financing. No transparency in public spending	Household resources; general governmental revenues; contribution by employers to social health insurance program; limited external resources	Declining percentage of GDP and government budget going to health; high burden of out-of-pocket spending

	Lebanon		*Jordan*	
Item	*Country profile*	*Future reforms*	*Country profile*	*Future reforms*
Revenues	General revenues (MOPH); social security contributions; private insurance	Expansion of formal health insurance coverage and contribution through issuance of national health insurance card	General revenues (MOH); social security contributions (Social Security Corporation); private insurance; special treatment funded by the Royal Court	High percentage of GDP and government budget going to health; continued high burden of out-of-pocket spending; high levels of health expenditures that may not be sustainable given the changing demographic and epidemiologic changes
Risk pooling and payer organization	Multiple social insurance funds (NSSF, civil service, army, security) and MOPH as "insurer" for uninsured	Proposed harmonization of rules and regulation across public insurers under a high-level Health Insurance Committee	MOH, Royal Medical Services, SSC, private insurance	Harmonize and reduce fragmentation in social health insurance scheme; move to universal coverage; more clearly define role of private health insurance

(continued)

TABLE 9B.2 Middle-Income Countries, Mashreq Countries *(continued)*

	Lebanon *(continued)*		Jordan *(continued)*	
Item	*Country profile*	*Future reforms*	*Country profile*	*Future reforms*
Strategic purchasing	Introduction of utilization management in NSSF, coordination with	Introduction of new provider payment methods (flat rates, case adjusted), harmonization of medical tariffs and utilization review process across all payers	Central budget transfers, salaried staff	Strengthen capacity at both MOH and social health insurance scheme for strategic purchasing; move to performance-based budgeting
Delivery system	Predominantly private, some government hospital and primary care services; MOPH, NSSF, and private insurers contract private hospitals and clinics.	Improved efficiency and accountability of hospital services, expansion of primary care services and preventive public health programs	Multiple delivery system: RMS, MOH, private	Improve efficiency and transparency in public spending; contain and rationalize spending on pharmaceuticals
Role of private sector	Large role for private sector in service provision and in financing, including pre-payment	None planned or announced	Large role for private pharmacists and other providers	None planned or announced
Other issues	Overall, considerable fragmentation of health system	Efforts to expand coverage to currently noninsured	Significant discretionary funding program	None planned or announced

Sources: WHO 2006b, 2006c.

Note: MOH = Ministry of Health; NSSF = National Social Security Fund; SSC = Social Security Corporation; RMS = Royal Medical Services.

TABLE 9B.3 Middle-Income Countries, Maghreb Countries

Item	Tunisia		Morocco		Libya	
	Country profile	Key reforms or issues	Country profile	Key reforms or issues	Country profile	Future reforms
Revenues	Payroll contributions (to national insurance fund) and general revenues (Treasury to MOH, social subsidy budget for government-subsidized insurance)	Optimized tariffs schedule	Payroll contributions (multiple social security agencies) and general revenues (MOH)	Very low public spending on health; possibility of performance-based budget to strengthen accountability	General governmental revenues	Optimized resource allocation mechanisms to prioritize investments
Risk pooling and payer organization	Social health insurance unified under the national insurance fund; MOH remaining as an integrated provider	Expanding enrolment of eligible beneficiaries for subsidized insurance	Insurance regulator established, multiple social security agencies for different categories of beneficiaries	Phased expansion of free insurance coverage for poor	Single payer	MOH role as integrated provider
Strategic purchasing	Budget transfers to MOH, global transfers from social security to MOH providers; CNAM-"certified" providers	Reforms planned to introduce shift from line-item to programmatic budgeting; introduction of strategic purchasing unknown	Budget transfers to MOH, global transfers from social security organizations to MOH facilities	Reforms planned to introduce shift from line-item to programmatic budgeting; introduction of strategic purchasing unknown	Global transfers from MOH to providers	Separation of provider and payer functions; gatekeeping and referral system
Role of private sector	Growing market for private sector providers funded through insurance plus copayment if insurance-"certified" providers; or OOP payment	Role of private sector to be strategically developed	Growing private health insurance market and private sector delivery system	Future role of private sector to be defined	Limited market	Proposals to invest substantially in private sector
Other issues	Government priority: expanding medical tourism	Improvement in quality assurance standards	Proposed decentralization of public health services to regional authorities	Unclear relationship between regional authorities and financing agents	Travel abroad for health care	Strategy to develop domestic market

Sources: CHUM/Université de Montréal n.d.; World Bank 2005b, 2006, 2008b, 2008c.

TABLE 9B.4   Conflict-Affected Countries, Iraq and West Bank and Gaza

	Iraq		West Bank and Gaza	
Item	Country profile	Future reforms	Country profile	Future reforms
Revenues	Household resources; general governmental revenues; high dependence on donor assistance	Two conflicts have greatly weakened health system; little transparency in public spending; high donor dependence	Substantial development assistance in health for capital investments; social contributions; general revenues, and private OOP payments	Efforts to strengthen social health insurance and reduce private OOP payments
Risk pooling and payer organization	No risk pooling	Consider introducing social health insurance for certain population groups	Social health insurance for formally employed	Expansion of social risk pooling
Strategic purchasing	No known strategic purchasing; line-item budget transferred by MOF to line ministries	Little scope for strategic purchasing until stability is restored	Predominantly input-based resource allocations, some contracting with hospital providers	Ambitions to strengthen strategic purchasing through contracting with providers
Delivery system	Little information on private market; anecdotal evidence to suggest growing private market	Future role of private sector to be defined	Predominantly public and private not-for-profit provision of tertiary and hospital services; mixed public and private provision of ambulatory and primary health care; UNRWA for large group of refugees status households	Continued dependence on large voluntary and philanthropic sectors and UNRWA
Role of private sector	High spending on hospital-based care; fragmented governance and management of health system; little or no information on spending	Improve efficiency and transparency in public spending; try to reduce dependence on donor funding; increase focus on primary health care	Largely unregulated for-profit and not-for-profit private sectors; some interconnection between public and private	Little scope for change over short and medium terms
Other issues	Household resources; general governmental revenues; high dependence on donor assistance	Two conflicts have greatly weakened health system; little transparency in public spending; high donor dependence	Significant impacts on health sector from general political and security situation, including access to care and fiscal space for reforms	Ambitious medium-term strategy to strengthen health financing, improve primary health care, and enhance focus on public health; significant needs for referrals abroad at high cost

Source: WHO 2006a.
Note: UNRWA = United Nations Relief and Work Agency; OOP = out-of-pocket.

TABLE 9B.5   High-Income Countries, Gulf Cooperation Council

Item	Kuwait		Saudi Arabia	
	Country profile	Key reforms or issues	Country profile	Key reforms or issues
Revenues	Predominantly general government revenues	Continued general revenue funding with possibly increasing role for contributions	General governmental revenues; private insurance premiums; some OOP spending	Role of private contributions
Risk pooling and payer organization	Universal coverage; allocated to public providers by line-item budgeting	Gradual separation of purchaser-provider; expanding role of health insurance	Universal coverage; allocated to public providers by line-item budgeting	MOH role as integrated provider
Strategic purchasing	Little or no role for strategic purchasing	Increased scope for strategic purchasing with separation	Limited role for strategic purchasing	Role of strategic purchasing depends on organization of purchaser function
Service delivery	Predominantly public integrated system of service delivery; autonomous private sector of office-based practitioners and tertiary care	Introduction of two-tier system of service delivery; larger role for private providers	Integrated public health service delivery	Strengthen primary health care and referral system
Role of private sector	Small role for private health insurance; increasing role for private provision	Goal of expanding role of private sectors for financing and provision	Some role for private provision and relatively large role for private insurance	Plans to expand mandatory private insurance
Other issues	Concerns about quality and efficiency of current system; coverage of expatriates	Overall economic reforms will affect health sector; significant spending on treatments abroad	Perceptions of low service quality and efficiency; coverage of expatriates	Enhance performance of sector

Sources: WHO 2006d; World Bank 2003, 2005a.

NOTES

1. The MENA Region includes the following (in alphabetical order): Algeria, the Arab Republic of Egypt, Bahrain, Djibouti, Iraq, the Islamic Republic of Iran, Jordan, Kuwait, Lebanon, Libya, Malta, Morocco, Oman, Qatar, Saudi Arabia, the Syrian Arab Republic, Tunisia, the United Arab Emirates, West Bank and Gaza, and the Republic of Yemen.

2. The main source of data is the WHO-WHOSIS data system; see www.who.int/whosis for details.

3. Annex 9A contains additional tables.

4. The United States, Switzerland, and the Netherlands all have a relatively large share of private health insurance, although, as can be seen from these numbers, public spending on health care is still a large or even dominant source of health funding. Singapore is an exception in this case, partly explained by a relatively large share of private spending by way of individual health accounts.

5. During the same period, the share of OOP in total private health spending went up in some high-income countries, including OECD countries like Germany, Italy, Japan, and Portugal. Some of these changes are due to policy changes in the area of pharmaceutical coverage rates.

6. IDA countries include the world's poorest countries that are eligible for grants or highly concessional loans from the World Bank; see www.worldbank.org/ida for details.

7. Broadly, fiscal space refers to the extent to which a country can increase health expenditure without risking its fiscal position. For a discussion of fiscal space for health see Heller (chapter 5, this volume).

8. Even within these country categories there is significant variation. The Libyan health system, for example, differs from those of other Maghreb countries in important ways. Similarly, Lebanon is somewhat special among the Maghreb countries because of its reliance on private health insurance for some 7 percent of the population, 17 percent of total private health expenditure (Ammar 2009 based on 2005 survey data).

9. Oil and liquid natural gas have been found in the sea off the Gaza Strip, although it remains to be seen whether and when any substantial proceeds from exploration of this find will have a real effect on the economy.

10. Including cigarettes, water pipes, and loose tobacco for pipe smoking.

REFERENCES

Ammar, W. 2003. *Health System and Reform in Lebanon.* Beirut: World Health Organization Eastern Mediterranean Regional Office.

———. 2009. *Health Beyond Politics.* Beirut: World Health Organization Eastern Mediterranean Regional Office.

Brinkerhoff, Derick W. 2004. "Accountability and Health Systems: Toward Conceptual Clarity and Policy Relevance." *Health Policy and Planning* 19 (6): 371–79.

CHUM/Université de Montréal. n.d. "Performance of Tunisia's Public Health Establishments." Executive Summary, Montreal, QC.

Gottret, Pablo, and George J. Schieber. 2006. *Health Financing Revisited: A Practitioner's Guide.* Washington, DC: World Bank.

Gottret, Pablo, George J. Schieber, and Hugh R. Waters. 2008. *Good Practices in Health Financing: Lessons from Reforms in Low- and Middle-Income Countries.* Washington, DC: World Bank.

Hediger, Viktor, Toby M.H. Lambert, and Mona Mourshed. 2007. "Private Solutions for Health Care in the Gulf." *McKinsey Quarterly* (March). http://www.mckinseyquarterly.com/Private_solutions_for_health_care_in_the_Gulf_1947.

Langenbrunner, John C., Cheryl Cashin, and Sheila O'Dougherty. 2009. *Designing and Implementing Health Care Provider Payment Systems: How-To Manuals.* Washington, DC: World Bank and USAID.

Langenbrunner, John C., and X. Liu. 2004. "How to Pay? Understanding and Using Incentives." HNP Discussion Paper, World Bank, Washington, DC.

Lewis, Pettersson. 2009. "Governance in Health Care Delivery: Raising Performance." Policy Research Working Paper 5074, World Bank, Washington, DC.

Loevinsohn, B. 2008. *Performance-Based Contracting for Health Services in Developing Countries: A Toolkit.* Washington, DC: World Bank Institute.

OECD (Organisation for Economic Co-operation and Development). 2009. "Achieving Better Value for Money in Health Care." OECD Health Policy Studies, Paris.

Preker, Alexander S., and John C. Langenbrunner, eds. 2005. *Spending Wisely: Buying Health Services for the Poor.* Washington, DC: World Bank.

Preker, Alexander S., Richard M. Scheffler, and Mark C. Bassett. 2007. *Private Voluntary Health Insurance in Development: Friend or Foe?* Washington, DC: World Bank.

Preker, Alexander S., Peter Zweifel, and Onno P. Schellekens. 2010. *Global Marketplace for Private Health Insurance: Strength in Numbers.* Washington, DC: World Bank.

Roedl, Meyer-Reumann, Middle East Ltd. n.d. *Lex Arabiae* newsletter on health insurance in the Middle East; accessed April 7, 2010.

Shaw, R.P. 1999. *New Trends in Public Sector Management in Health: Applications in Developed and Developing Countries.* Washington, DC: World Bank Institute.

Streveler, D. 2009. "Health Management Information Systems: Linking Payers and Providers." In *Designing and Implementing Health Care Provider Payment Systems: How-To Manuals*, ed. John C. Langenbrunner, Cheryl Cashin, and Sheila O'Dougherty. Washington, DC: World Bank and USAID.

Wagstaff, A. 2009. "Social Health Insurance vs. Tax-Financed Health Systems: Evidence from the OECD." Policy Research Working Paper 4821, World Bank, Washington, DC.

Wagstaff, A., and E. van Doorslaer. 2003. "Catastrophe and Impoverishment of Paying for Health Care: With Applications to Vietnam 1993–1998." *Health Economics* 12: 921–34.

WHO (World Health Organization). 2006a. "Health System Profile: Palestine." Regional Health Systems Observatory. http://gis.emro.who.int/HealthSystemObservatory/Profile/Forms/frmProfileSelectionByCountry.aspx.

———. 2006b. "Health System Profile: Jordan." Regional Health Systems Observatory. http://gis.emro.who.int/HealthSystemObservatory/Profile/Forms/frmProfileSelectionByCountry.aspx.

———. 2006c. "Health System Profile: Lebanon." Regional Health Systems Observatory. http://gis.emro.who.int/HealthSystemObservatory/Profile/Forms/frmProfileSelectionByCountry.aspx.

———. 2006d. "Health System Profile: Saudi Arabia." Regional Health Systems Observatory. http://gis.emro.who.int/HealthSystemObservatory/Profile/Forms/frmProfileSelectionByCountry.aspx.

———. 2006e. "Health System Profile: Kuwait." Regional Health Systems Observatory. http://gis.emro.who.int/HealthSystemObservatory/Profile/Forms/frmProfileSelectionByCountry.aspx.

WHO-WHOSIS. WHO database. www.who.int/whosis; accessed January 15, 2011.

World Bank. 2003. "Kuwait: Health Sector Study." World Bank, Human Development Sector, Middle East and North Africa Region, Washington, DC.

————. 2005a. "Kingdom of Saudi Arabia: Health Financing and Health Insurance: Issues, Options, Recommendations." *Policy Note*, World Bank, Washington, DC.

————. 2005b. "Republic of Tunisia: Health Sector Study Report." MNSHD, World Bank, Washington, DC.

————. 2006. *People's Democratic Republic of Algeria: Assuring High-Quality Public Investment: A Public Expenditure Review*. 2 vols. Washington, DC: World Bank.

————. 2008a. *Islamic Republic of Iran: Health Sector Review*. 2 vols. Washington, DC: World Bank.

————. 2008b. "Libya: Review of Public Expenditure in the Health Sector." Draft, February 14, World Bank, Washington, DC.

————. 2008c. "Kingdom of Morocco: Towards a More Equitable and Sustainable Health Care System: Policy Challenges and Opportunities." *Policy Note*. World Bank, Washington, DC.

————. 2009a. "West Bank and Gaza Health Policy Report: Reforming Prudently Under Pressure: Health Financing Reform and the Rationalization of Public Sector Health Expenditures." MNSHD, World Bank, Washington, DC.

————. 2009b. "From Privilege to Competition: Unlocking Private-Led Growth in the Middle East and North Africa." MENA Development Report, World Bank, Washington, DC.

Yemen, Republic of. 2006. "Health Systems Profile: Regional Health Systems Observatory." Cairo: WHO-EMRO.

————. 2009. "Health Sector Review: Health Financing Modalities in Yemen: Possibilities for Results-Based Financing and Social Health Insurance." World Bank, Washington, DC.

CHAPTER 10

One-Step, Two-Step Tango in Latin America and the Caribbean

Ricardo Bitrán

C ountries in Latin American and the Caribbean (LAC) have developed their health systems according to broadly similar paths. Much of the development started in the early to mid-20th century, and significant changes occurred at the end of that century and continue into the new millennium.

INTRODUCTION

With the notable and recent exception of Brazil, which in 1993 abolished social health insurance (SHI) and unified public health into a single national health system (Jack 2000), most countries in the World Bank LAC Region have chosen the SHI approach to give their people access to health services and financial protection. Coverage began with self-financed formal sector workers through wage-based contributions and then was extended to informal workers and low-income populations through public subsidies. Most LAC countries have begun—and still maintain—segmented systems, where different organizational and financial arrangements have been put in place to serve the health needs of different population groups. In particular, contributory social security has been available for public and private formal sector workers, while a publicly financed Ministry of Health (MOH), operating a broad network of own providers, offers subsidized health services to the large, low-income population. Private health insurance coexists with those two systems, but it has generally covered only the small, high-income segment. Decentralization of financing and health service delivery has, in some cases, been an integral part of the reform process.

This chapter reviews the evolution of health systems in several LAC countries, with a focus on their efforts to expand SHI coverage. The scaling up of SHI denotes here the qualitative step that these countries have taken to move from SHI schemes covering only formal workers to SHI schemes with universal coverage. The countries were selected to document different approaches chosen by reformers in their quest for universality. The evidence indicates that nations in this part of the world present a similar approach in the early stages of development but exhibit considerable variation and ingenuity in their later approaches. The policies adopted, the problems that have arisen, and the solutions found may offer useful examples to reformers in other parts of the developing world, including those in Africa.

According to the OECD (2004), health insurance is a mechanism for distributing the financial risk associated with variations in individuals' health care expenditures by pooling the costs of health care over time (prepayment) and over people (pooling). It differs from out-of-pocket payment (OOP), which does not provide for pooling of risks or prepayment, while medical savings accounts provide for prepayment but not pooling across risks although they are often coupled with an insurance scheme.

As noted, LAC countries rely on an array of health insurance arrangements in their health systems. For example, Chile's SHI system mandates enrolment in health insurance, but leaves it to the individuals to select their insurer—either the single public insurer known as the National Health Fund or one of the many competing private insurers known as ISAPREs. Mexico relies on health social security to cover about one-half of its population. Financing comes from workers, employers, and the federal government; and tax-based financing subsidizes part of the premium for the other half of the population through Popular Health Insurance.

Efforts to reform health insurance systems in the LAC region have been plagued by a strong ideological and political debate, one often driven by interest groups defending the status quo. For example, initiatives to improve efficiency among public health care providers, or to promote private participation in provision and insurance, have been characterized or discarded by some as neoliberal or privatizing in nature. Government health workers' unions and medical associations have generally been behind these claims. Likewise, efforts to strengthen the regulation of private health insurers have been attacked by the insurers themselves as central planning. Initiatives to improve the quality of health care through the implementation of diagnostic and treatment protocols have been rejected by the medical profession on the basis that they threaten their professional independence. This debate, still ongoing, has slowed progress.

The remainder of this chapter presents an overview of the LAC region and discusses the challenges countries face in their quest for universal health insurance coverage through mixed health systems. Next, five LAC countries' approaches to universal coverage are described with their achievements to date and their challenges ahead. The countries are Mexico, Chile, Costa Rica, Colombia, and Ecuador. The last section presents lessons learned and some concluding remarks.

OVERVIEW OF THE LAC REGION

The LAC region comprises 45 countries and territories totaling 542 million people (9 percent of the world's population) and extending over 20 million square kilometers (18 percent of the world's land surface area; table 10.1). In 2005 LAC

TABLE 10.1 World Bank Regions: Selected Economic and Development Indicators, circa 2005

Region	Population, total		Population growth (annual %)	Life expectancy at birth, total (years)	GNI per capita, Atlas method (current US$)	Surface area	
	Million	%				Million square kilometers	%
Latin America and Caribbean	542	9	1.3	73	4,157	20.4	18
East Asia and Pacific	1,869	29	0.9	71	1,628	16.3	14
Europe and Central Asia	460	7	0.1	69	3,968	24.2	21
High-income countries	1,016	16	1.0	79	34,962	34.5	30
Middle East and North Africa	300	5	1.8	70	2,223	9.0	8
South Asia	1,447	23	1.6	63	693	5.1	5
Sub-Saharan Africa	735	12	2.3	47	743	24.2	21
World	6,369	100	1.0	68	7,016	113.4	100

Region	Primary school completion rate (%)	Girls to boys in primary and secondary school (%)	Improved water source (% of population with access) (2004)	Prevalence of HIV, total (% of population ages 15–49) (2003)	Health expenditure per capita (US$)	U-5 mortality rate (2005) (per 1,000)
Latin America and Caribbean	98	99	79	0.2	272	31
East Asia and Pacific	92	96	92	0.7	238	33
Europe and Central Asia	—	—	100	0.0	3,687	—
High-income countries	89	92	90	0.1	104	32
Middle East and North Africa	82	87	84	0.7	27	53
South Asia	58	86	56	5.8	45	83
Sub-Saharan Africa	—	—	—	—	—	163
World	—	—	—	—	—	—

Source: Author, from www.worldbank.org.

Note: U-5 = under 5 years of age; — = not available.

233

per capita income of US$4,157 was similar to that of Europe and Central Asia and the highest of all regions in the developing world; it represented, however, just 12 percent of the average per capita income in high-income countries (US$39,962). Whereas per capita health spending in LAC, equal to US$272 in 2004, was the highest of all developing regions, it was equivalent to just over 7 percent of the corresponding indicator in high-income countries.

In LAC, health systems are as varied as the countries themselves and often reflect a colonial influence in their design. Barbados has a system similar to the U.K. National Health Service, with the government assuming nearly two-thirds of health financing out of general revenue sources, while managing the bulk of the delivery system.[1] Suriname's health system is similar to the Netherlands': large hospitals are either public or private nonprofits, and primary health care in the interior is in the hands of nongovernmental organizations (NGOs). Mexico relies heavily and increasingly on social security financing with publicly subsidized coverage for enrolment by the poor. Brazil has, since the late 1990s, adopted a tax-financed, decentralized national health system.

Health expenditure per capita in LAC varies as much as income. Haiti, the region's poorest country, with a per capita GNI of US$480 in 2006, spent on average only US$33 per person on health services. At the other end of the spectrum, Mexico, the region's richest country, with per capita GNI of US$7,870, devoted US$454 per citizen to health care.

Overall, health financing in LAC is evenly split between public and private sources, although this average hides considerable variation among individual countries. Colombia, which is seeking to achieve universal coverage through social health insurance, initiated a major legal reform to its health system in 1994, which demanded massive public financing during its implementation in the initial years. Consequently, by 2004 over 85 percent of all health financing in Colombia was considered public. In contrast, public financing of health care in the Dominican Republic accounted for only one-third of all funding. A more detailed depiction of the health financing structure reveals the different policy approaches taken by some LAC countries. Colombia and Costa Rica are two countries that have actively sought to achieve (and succeeded in Costa Rica's case) universal health insurance coverage through SHI.

POLICY CHALLENGES THAT ARISE WHEN EXTENDING COVERAGE

Countries in LAC that are introducing or expanding SHI face many challenges. Some of them are inherent to social insurance while others arise from the coexistence of SHI and a tax-financed MOH—two systems operating with different mandates and rules.[2] This section defines and illustrates those problems; it serves as a conceptual framework to examine the country experiences that follow in the subsequent section.

Adverse Selection

SHI systems in LAC typically mandate enrolment by all workers, both formal and informal, but many workers—especially the younger and healthier with a low self-perceived probability of facing catastrophic health events—often prefer not to enroll, thus not paying the legal contribution and hence maximizing their short-term take-home income. In contrast, older individuals, and those with an otherwise lower perception of health status, are more likely to enroll. This phenomenon, whereby the propensity to enroll in insurance is positively linked with people's self-perceived health risk, is known as adverse selection. Adverse selection presents SHI systems in the LAC region with a formidable challenge, especially in countries with a large fraction of the active labor force engaged in informal employment.

Whether enrolment is compulsory or voluntary, evidence shows that enrolling informal sector workers in SHI is difficult, and the LAC region presents a high share of informality in its labor markets (figure 10.1).

The existence of a tax-financed health system that offers health care to all at subsidized prices may limit informal sector workers' interest in joining the SHI. Some policy measures may help overcome this, however. For example, the imposition of barriers to access to the tax-financed MOH system, based on an individual means test or otherwise, may provide an incentive for some informal workers—particularly the older and the sicker ones—to join the SHI. Similarly, when the tax-financed system delivers deficient services some nonpoor informal

FIGURE 10.1   Share of Informal Workers, Selected LAC Countries, 1990–2005

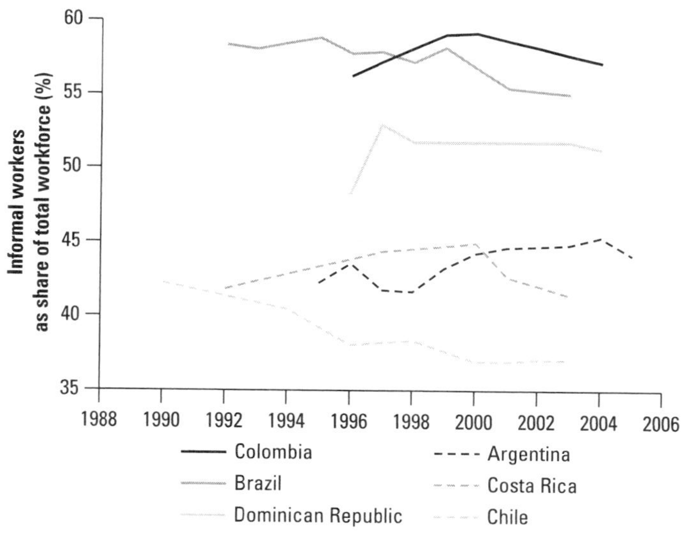

Source: Author, from Gasparini and Tornarolli 2007.

workers may prefer to obtain coverage through the SHI. Even in the presence of mandatory enrolment laws for the informal sector, no developing country has been successful in enrolling that entire population. High-income countries also face this problem. For example, despite heavy public subsidization of enrolment in the United States, a large number of informal sector workers, especially young, self-employed individuals, prefer to remain uninsured (see box 10.1). In Indonesia, attempts at enrolling informal workers have to date been largely unsuccessful. A report by IHSD (1999: 8) notes:

> International experience has shown that whilst achieving cover for employees in the formal sector is fairly straightforward, it is very difficult to establish schemes that collect contributions from the informal and self-employed and rural sectors. The latter make up over two thirds of Indonesia's workforce. Even for the formal sector, Indonesia has achieved low coverage with compulsory social insurance. There is, therefore, a major risk of relatively little funding being collected to finance JPKM [Jaminan Pemeliharaan Kesehatan Masyarakat, a community health insurance scheme] and hence the managed care will be under-funded and disappoint the members.

BOX 10.1   INSURING THE INFORMAL SECTOR: LESSONS FROM THE INTERNATIONAL EXPERIENCE

Low insurance coverage of the informal sector is a universal problem, present even in industrial countries. For example, one out of six Americans is without health insurance today (Kahn and Pollack 2001). For many reasons, achieving high insurance coverage of informal sector workers has proven infeasible to date. These are formidable policy challenges, and whether they can be solved is unclear. Below is a list of these challenges.

Inelastic demand for health insurance. The international evidence shows that demand for health insurance among the informally employed remains low even in the presence of high public subsidies for enrolment. A study by the Urban Institute about the demand for health insurance in the United States concluded that offering insurance enrolment subsidies had only a marginal impact on enrolment. For example, a subsidy covering 10 percent of the premium led to only a 1 percent increase in enrolment, while a subsidy covering as much as 75 percent of the premium led to a modest 13 percent rise in enrolment. The U.S. states of Tennessee, Hawaii, Minnesota, and Washington adopted mechanisms to enroll their population to subsidized state health insurance. When the premium represented as little as 1 percent of the families' income, 57 percent of the families would enroll; if the premium represented 3 percent of family income, only 33 percent of the families would enroll.

Adverse selection. This is a major problem in countries trying to implement insurance schemes for the informal sector. Workers in the informal sector tend to seek affiliation when they are sick or when they anticipate health problems in the near future. Once the health problem is solved, they tend to drop out of insurance. In Madras (India) for example, an insurance scheme for informal sector workers allowed them freely to enroll and drop out of insurance at any time. Less than one-fourth of all those affiliated renewed their annual enrolment. Others became affiliated upon becoming ill and dropped out of insurance with recovery. The scheme quickly went bankrupt. Making health insurance mandatory for informal sector workers is obviously not a solution. Weak institutions and frail enforcement systems together with the specific characteristics of informal sector workers (unsteady work, irregular income, and geographic mobility) mean that adverse selection is likely to remain a problem. To work, mandated enrolment must be accompanied by other measures, such as collective enrolment, to prevent adverse selection. For example, in the Republic of Congo an insurance scheme managed by an NGO required that, to become operational, at least 75 percent of the town's population had to enroll.

Low capacity to contribute. Informal workers tend to have a limited capacity to contribute to regular social security schemes. For example, in Colombia, 80 percent of informal sector workers earn less than the national minimum wage. This limitation, combined with the requirement that informal workers contribute on their own as much as formal sector workers and their employer contribute together, makes it unlikely that high levels of enrolment will occur.

High administrative costs. Enrolling, monitoring, and controlling small groups of affiliates with low and unstable incomes are administratively expensive. In the United States, high administrative costs have been identified as key factors leading to the low supply of health insurance for informal sector workers. The use of group, instead of individual, insurance contracts is one way to help reduce administrative costs.

Reluctance to enroll. For example, in Colombia a study was carried out to examine the determinants of people's willingness to affiliate in health insurance. The study showed that at any given income level, informal workers are less likely to want to insure themselves than are formal sector workers. This situation may be explained by the fear that enrolment in a health insurance scheme may have other, adverse consequences for them (such as paying taxes).

Source: Author.

A design feature of the health system seen in more than one country (e.g., Colombia) may in part contribute to the low enrolment rates of informal workers. In Colombia the Contributory Component of SHI requires a 12 percent contribution of which 8 percent comes from the employer and 4 percent from the worker. Yet informal workers willing to enroll must contribute the full 12 percent themselves. Thus, informal workers are expected to devote a higher proportion of their income to SHI than are formal workers, in what is a clearly regressive situation given their relatively lower incomes.

Intergenerational Cross-Subsidies

SHI systems typically provide benefits not only to active contributing workers but also to formerly contributing but currently retired workers. This may give rise to an intergenerational subsidy from the young to the old. With a stable ratio between the populations in both groups, such a subsidy may not pose financial equilibrium problems but, with an aging workforce and a dropping ratio of active workers to retired beneficiaries, disequilibrium takes place. This disequilibrium is reached sooner with a pay-as-you-go financing approach, where current SHI benefits are financed with current revenue from contributions. Using data from the World Bank, Gertler (1998) discusses the financial implications of an aging workforce in selected Asian countries. Rodríguez (2006) discussed the likely consequences of an aging workforce on the financial sustainability of Costa Rica's SHI system. Chile will likely face similar problems: the proportion of Chileans under 15 or over 64 years is expected to rise from 48 percent in 2007 to 63 percent by 2050. In SHI systems, where the retirees are not required to make SHI contributions, the burden will fall increasingly on active workers. This situation may lead to unsustainably high labor costs and loss of international competitiveness, thus making SHI financially infeasible.

Small Risk-Pools

Effective health insurance requires the existence of large enough risk pools to ensure that the risk related to financing health interventions is spread across a large enough number of pool members (Smith and Witter 2001). Sometimes SHI systems are composed of fragmented risk pools, some of them too small to be capable of financing as little as a single catastrophic health event of one of their members. Nicaragua's Providence Medical Enterprises (PMEs), which are contracted out by that country's social security institute (known as INSS) to cover its affiliates, make up an atomized market. Officials with INSS report PMEs with as few as 2,500 members and therefore with very limited ability to withstand expensive health events (Ubilla, Espinoza, and Bitrán 2000).

Evasion and Elusion of SHI Contributions

The avoidance by workers or employers of their legal obligation to contribute the specified share of the worker's salary to SHI is known as evasion (if the avoidance is through illegal means) or elusion (if legally done). While the boundary between legal and illegal avoidance of contributions is sometimes blurry, the avoidance or minimization of SHI contributions is a significant problem in developing countries. Two examples of this from the LAC region are Argentina and Colombia. In Argentina's SHI system, made up of union-owned welfare agencies (Obras Sociales), individuals who lose their employment may preserve regular SHI benefits over long periods of time, even though technically such benefits should be discontinued shortly after contributions cease. In Colombia until a few years ago, it was common for workers and their employers to collude to underreport income, or to pay only the minimum wage while paying the rest of the compensation under the table or via nonmonetary benefits to minimize their SHI contributions. That behavior has been curbed through a measure that links workers' contributions to their pension funds with their contributions to health. Colombia's case is common in that the benefits obtained by an affiliate from the SHI are independent of his or her contributions, hence the incentive to minimize payment (Bitrán & Asociados 2001).

Benefits Packages Offering Insufficient Financial Protection and Few Cost-Effective Services

Many SHI systems around the developing world offer their beneficiaries limited financial protection. When faced with expensive health events, beneficiaries of those systems have to shoulder a significant part of the bill, and thus remain effectively exposed to financial catastrophes despite their coverage. Nicaragua's PMEs fail to offer catastrophic coverage because the INSS-defined basic benefits package excludes many forms of expensive hospital care. PME beneficiaries needing expensive hospital care can always obtain such services in MOH hospitals for free or with modest user charges. Another problem with some benefits packages is that they offer little coverage for cost-effective services. Chile's ISAPREs cover some preventive care, but few of them actively promote or have succeeded in promoting use of preventive services. The long-term nature of health benefits for prevention, coupled with beneficiary mobility, are thought to be two chief reasons behind this behavior: in a competitive health insurance market, insurers may be reluctant to invest in prevention for fear of not being able to capture the return on their investments before their beneficiaries switch to a competing insurer. Investments in prevention are seen by insurers as a public good. This failure can be corrected through policy measures such as compensatory payments among insurers for their past investments in keeping their beneficiaries healthy.

Moral Hazard Leading to Cost Escalation

Moral hazard denotes the phenomenon by which the quantity of health care demanded by individuals goes up once they are insured because health insurance lowers or removes out-of-pocket payments for covered services. Copayments and deductibles are some of the tools insurers use to protect themselves against moral hazard. Gertler (1998) argues that the introduction of SHI in two Asian countries, the Republic of Korea and Taiwan, China, led to cost escalation, or a rapid increase in overall health care spending, yet the timing of the introduction of SHI coincided with a period of significant economic growth in both countries. Thus, economic growth was able to absorb the rising health care expenditures. In the LAC region, Chile's private health insurance system has also experienced rapid cost escalation. Bitrán and Vergara (2001) analyzed the components of this increase in spending, distinguishing between three root causes: changes in the price of health services; changes in the per capita utilization of services; and changes in the structure of the portfolio of beneficiaries (older people, women of fertile age, and people with poor health status consume more services do than other groups). They found that over a five-year period, average annual spending of an ISAPRE on a beneficiary went up by 66 percent, 10.7 percent a year. Two-thirds of the increase in this spending was attributable to an increase in the utilization of health services (moral hazard); just over one-fourth of the increase was due to rising prices of health care;[3] and only 7 percent of the increase was the result of a change in the structure of the portfolio of beneficiaries. In Chile's case moral hazard was sizable.

Leakage of Public Subsidies to SHI Beneficiaries

When the tax-financed health system maintains its doors open to all patients, a leakage of public subsidies may occur. Even when insured through SHI, higher-income individuals have a greater ability to capture public subsidies from the universal provision system whose role, instead, is the provision of health care for the uninsured poor. World Bank (2000) shows how MOH services are used more by higher-income individuals than by the poor—the MOH intended beneficiaries.

Not all countries with coexisting SHI and publicly subsidized health care systems exhibit this pattern of regressive cross-subsidies. For example, Chile's public insurer has over time developed efficient individual-targeting mechanisms to keep people who are privately insured through ISAPREs from using publicly subsidized health care intended for the poor. A study conducted in 1995 by Bitrán and others showed that the leakage of public health care subsidies to individuals with private insurance accounted for only 2.5 percent of all public subsidies. Much of this leakage was for inpatient care. At the root of the leakage was a system of public sector prices for the privately insured that underestimated the true cost of care.

Disaffiliation from SHI in Times of Economic Crisis

When SHI beneficiaries lose their jobs they may also lose with it their ability to contribute to SHI. In times of economic crisis, massive unemployment may lead to massive disaffiliation from SHI or loss of benefits and thus loss of health insurance coverage. The newly uncovered may therefore become beneficiaries of the tax-financed health system, competing for resources with the poor and other regular target beneficiaries of that system. Whether or not they will be able to draw benefits depends on the barriers that the tax-financed system imposes on them. In this case, massive loss of SHI benefits for the unemployed may rather result in increased competition for limited resources and in constrained access to care by the poor and other groups that regularly rely on the tax-financed system. In some other SHI systems, in contrast, the loss of employment does not lead immediately to the loss of benefits. (In the case of Argentina in the LAC region, the lack of a performing beneficiary information system keeps the SHI agencies for months from detecting when the unemployed continue to draw benefits from the system.) This may cause problems of financial sustainability to the SHI agencies.

STRATEGIES FOR EXTENDING HEALTH SYSTEM COVERAGE: SOCIAL INSURANCE AND OTHER APPROACHES

The evolution of health systems in five LAC countries is reviewed in this section: Mexico, Chile, Costa Rica, Colombia, and Ecuador.[4] The countries were selected to document different approaches chosen by reformers in their search for universality. For example, some countries have chosen to implement mandatory health insurance arrangements while others rely partially on voluntary components. In some countries, health insurance covers services of both public and private providers; in others it covers only services of public providers. One characteristic that all countries share is the order in which different groups of people were incorporated: first (and mostly during the 1940s), formal workers were covered and, more recently, informal workers and the poor were added to the pool of active beneficiaries. Each country case has three sections: background, which presents the historic developments of health insurance schemes; achievements, which describes the results that these developments have had on expanding health insurance; and challenges ahead, which examines outstanding problems on the way to universal health insurance coverage.

Mexico

Mexico's health system was shaped through three waves of reform.[5]

Background

The first wave of reform in Mexico started in 1937, when "the federal government formally assumed responsibility for the care of the needy with the creation of the Secretary of Public Assistance" (Haddad, Baris, and Narayana 2007: n.p.). In 1943, three institutions were created: the Ministry of Health, the Mexican Institute for Social Security (IMSS), and the Children's Hospital. In 1959 the Institute of Social Services and Security for Civil Servants (ISSSTE) began to cover government employees and their families. Before this first wave of reform, "during the colonial period, after independence and into the 1930s, health care institutions were built either to cater to those who could pay, or in charitable response to the needs of the poor. Private medical care dominated, with care of the needy and destitute undertaken principally by Catholic charities" (Haddad, Baris, and Narayana 2007: n.p.).

A second reform wave started in the late 1970s to extend coverage of basic services to low-income populations in urban and rural areas. A constitutional amendment was passed granting all Mexicans the right to health protection, and a new, progressive health law replaced an old-fashioned sanitary code. Health services for the uninsured began to be decentralized to state governments, and a new program expanded coverage of primary health care services, including oral rehydration, childhood immunizations, potable water supply, improved access to education for women, and a campaign to reduce the transmission of HIV/AIDS. As a result, Mexico experienced a considerable drop in mortality and a decreasing gap in health inequalities, despite growing income inequality.

The third wave of reforms began in the 1990s with the decentralization of health services, strengthening of the financial base and improvement in health service quality at IMSS, and design and provision of a basic package of 12 essential health care interventions targeted to the poor in rural areas. An incentive-based welfare program, PROGRESA, was also introduced, delivering cash subsidies to the poor conditioned on the recipient's adherence to several education, health, and nutritional interventions. Prior to the adoption of a new reform in 2003, Social Protection in Health (SPH), about 47 percent of Mexicans were covered by social security (40 percent by IMSS and 7 percent by ISSSTE), while no more than 2 to 3 percent were covered by private health insurance. Thus, about half of the population, 45 million people not covered by SHI, relied on a network of poorly funded MOH providers and on private providers. Under SPH, a newly established system seeks to provide universal health insurance for the poor and hence to improve access to basic health care and financial protection against large health expenditures. The SPH system explicitly separates financing for personal and nonpersonal health services. Its operating arm, known as Popular Health Insurance (PHI), seeks progressively to enroll over seven years about 11 million families, 45 million people. PHI guarantees access to more than 100 interventions, including more than 90 percent of all ambulatory services and 70 percent of all hospital admissions.

The health system that has resulted from these reform waves is marked by segmentation, particularly between the insured in the formal sector of the economy and the mostly informal sector of uninsured, poor individuals (figure 10.2).

Financing for the PHI program is tripartite, and similar in structure to the other two major SHI systems, IMSS and ISSSTE (table 10.2). The federal government's contribution to PHI, equal for all families, was set at 15 percent of the mandatory minimum wage, an annual amount equivalent to US$230 per affiliated family.

Achievements

Until 2000, the population coverage of SHI in Mexico depended mainly on formal labor rates. In 1959, for example, estimates by the National Statistical Institute (INEGI) indicate than 17 percent of the population had formal work and IMSS coverage. In the next 40 years, formal labor rates increased steadily, and SHI coverage reached 47 percent. The number of Mexicans enrolled in SHI increased progressively since 2002 to reach 11.5 million in the first quarter of 2006. Further, Gakidou et al. (2007) show that PHI preferentially reaches the poor and marginalized communities; hence, it is exhibiting good targeting. To sustain this growth, public spending on health has increased as well, both in absolute terms and as a percentage of GDP. As a result, and also partly owing to a concurrent increase in private spending, total health spending in Mexico grew from 5.6 percent of GDP in 2002 to 6.4 percent in early 2006.

FIGURE 10.2   Mexico's Health Care System Prior to the SPH Reform of 2003

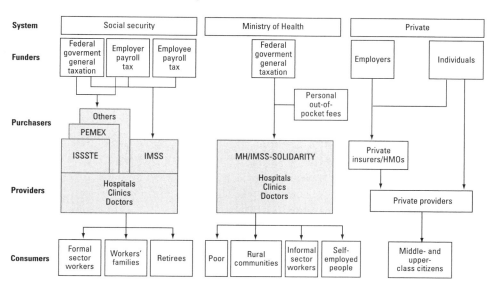

Source: Frenk et al. 2003.

Notes: IMSS = Mexican Social Security Institute; ISSSTE = federal civil servants and the armed forces; PEMEX = employees of the national oil company; MH/IMSS-SOLIDARITY = special branch of the Ministry of Health managed through the existing social security system; HMO = health maintenance organization.

TABLE 10.2   Mexico: New Financial Architecture of SHI

Institution	Population group covered (and percentage of country's population)	Source of financing			
		Worker or family	Employer or public subsidy		Social quota
IMSS	Private sector formal workers and their families (40%)	Worker	Employer		Federal government
ISSSTE	Civil servants and their families (7%)	Worker	Federal government as employer		Federal government
Popular Health Insurance	Informal sector workers and the indigent (50%)	Families	State government	Federal government	Federal government

Source: Adapted from Salud Pública de México 2004.

Note: An estimated 2 percent to 3 percent of Mexicans have private health insurance coverage.

Utilization of health services during this period increased as well. Gakidou et al. (2007) showed that between 2000 and 2005–06 utilization rates went up for 11 selected primary health care interventions. The same study showed that the propensity to perceive a need for health care was higher among those covered by PHI than among those without any coverage, and it was similar between those with PHI and the beneficiaries of other social security institutes (IMSS and

ISSSTE). In addition, the study found that the propensity to obtain health care among those with a perceived need was lowest among the uninsured, followed by the beneficiaries of PHI and by the beneficiaries of IMSS and ISSSTE. Thus, PHI seems to have increased access to health care among its beneficiaries relative to the uninsured, although their utilization levels are not yet as high as those of other social security institutes.

Challenges Ahead

Covering all the uninsured with PHI will require a sustained political commitment and substantial additional public financing. In 2006, three quarters of the PHI target population was not yet enrolled. Covering this population will pose difficulties to Mexico's government. First, the 11.5 million beneficiaries who have been enrolled so far have been mostly classified in the poorest income quintile. As such and in accordance with law, they are not required to make any payments for their coverage. The population still to be enrolled is relatively richer and therefore applicants will by law be required to pay a contribution. This may bring about a natural resistance from those prospective enrollees, entailing higher administrative costs. Also, contributors will feel more entitled to demand higher-quality services, posing a new challenge. Second, among the populations not yet enrolled are the poorest of the poor. As Gakidou and others (2007) show, individuals living in the poorest decile and in the highest decile of community marginalization have a lower probability of enrolling in PHI than do individuals living in the second poorest and second highest community marginalization deciles. Reaching these populations may entail higher administrative costs. Third, many of the communities not yet enrolled are in places with less health infrastructure and human resources relative to the communities enrolled between 2002 and 2006. Thus, the higher demand induced by PHI may be offset by the limited local supply of services. Although the new resources collected with PHI (in the form of public subsidies or contributions) can be used to finance improvements in infrastructure and human resources, implementing these changes quickly and efficiently will also be challenging. Finally, the size of the public subsidy required to finance PHI universal coverage is substantial. Between 2002 and 2005, public health expenditure as a percentage of GDP increased from 2.7 to 3.0 percent, and it is estimated that it may increase by an additional 1 percentage point when universal coverage is reached (Gakidou et al. 2007).

Chile

Chile relies on SHI to provide health insurance coverage to most of its population.[6]

Background

Until 1887 in Chile, public health was the responsibility of local authorities, and there was no responsible national institution or plan. Since the 16th century, most health services had been entirely financed privately by households or provided by different charity or philanthropic institutions, for example, the church. Several public initiatives dating to 1887 are behind the development of Chile's SHI system. The creation in 1887 of the National Health Junta, an arm of the Ministry of the Interior, superseded in 1892 by the Higher Body of Hygiene, were the first formal involvements of government in health policy. They were followed in 1918 by the enactment of the Sanitary Code and the creation of the General Health Directorate. Until then, government involvement in health was mainly as a regulator of health delivery. The Ministry of Hygiene, Assistance, and Social Services, created in 1924–25, became the Ministry of Health (MOH). Three social security institutions were also created: the Mandatory Workers' Insurance (SOO), the Public Employees National "Caja," and the Private Employees Providence "Caja." These entities served as a mechanism through which government began implementation of health social security policies. A law passed in 1938 mandated these three social security entities to oversee the health of their affiliates and dependents and to prevent chronic conditions such as tuberculosis, syphilis, rheumatic fever, and cardiovascular disease. Other vulnerable segments of the population were also entitled to free health care through these institutions: peasants, artisans, domestic personnel, their children under 2 years of age, and their spouses.

In 1942 government created the Workers National Health Service (Sermena), the public entity responsible for managing health benefits to public and private sector formal workers previously covered by the separate social security entities already mentioned. The creation of the National Health Service (SNS) in 1952 merged several health care delivery institutions. Together with Sermena, it was the pillar of Chile's modern health system, allowing government to implement health policies in an orderly manner and to expand health coverage. Government was able to implement several public health initiatives through the SNS, including nutritional programs, social assistance for children and the elderly, vaccination campaigns, and two national health programs, one under the Eduardo Frei government and another under Salvador Allende's. Estimates indicate that by the mid-1960s two-thirds of Chile's population had regular access to government-delivered health care. By the mid-1970s, Sermena covered formal sector employees and their families, accounting in total for about one-fifth of the country's population. Toward the end of that decade, 85 percent of the population had regular access to health care either through the SNS or Sermena, 10 percent obtained coverage from private providers, and 5 percent were beneficiaries of the Armed Forces health systems.

A series of reforms under the military government of Augusto Pinochet between 1979 and 1981 assigned the MOH a policy steering role; decentralized the public health delivery system through the National Health Services System (SNSS); transferred management responsibility of primary health care provision to municipalities; split public financing from provision, assigning a financing role to the newly created FONASA (National Health Fund) and a provider role to the SNSS; and created the private health insurers known as ISAPREs (health providence institutions), as an alternative to FONASA. The creation of ISAPREs allowed well-off individuals to opt out of public health insurance, using their mandatory contribution to pay for their ISAPRE. Pinochet's government also awarded a public subsidy equal to 2 percent of a worker's salary to allow him or her to switch from FONASA to an ISAPRE.

The most significant health sector reform that followed was passed in 2005 under the Ricardo Lagos government. It became known as AUGE, and its most noteworthy component was the mandate to FONASA and the ISAPREs to provide explicit coverage guarantees for 56 priority health problems. The AUGE reform was aimed at reducing the significant differences in coverage, quality, and access to health services that existed between the nation's lower-middle class and the poor, covered by FONASA, and the upper-middle class and the rich, covered by ISAPREs. The reform called for equal health benefits for all citizens, irrespective of their income or insurance status, to prevent and treat the priority health problems. This equity-enhancing reform defines four explicit guarantees for insurance beneficiaries: (1) *access*: anybody wishing to prevent or treat any of the 56 medical problems can obtain the care defined in AUGE's benefits package; (2) *quality*: health care for the 56 medical problems is strictly regulated through medical protocols; (3) *opportunity*: time limits are imposed for beneficiaries to obtain health care in the benefits package; (4) *financial protection*: upper limits are set, relative to the insured's income, on the amount of out-of-pocket expenses that he or she may have to incur annually. Facing fierce resistance from the Medical Association, the ISAPREs, and some members of the congress, President Lagos astutely maneuvered to secure the political backing he required for the passage of the reform.

Achievements

Until 1980, SHI population coverage in Chile was determined mainly by formal labor rates, as in Mexico. In 1942, coverage was about 20 percent, and as formal labor rates increased, coverage reached a maximum of 67 percent right before the reform of 1980. With the incorporation of the indigent regime of FONASA, coverage increased to the rates observed today.

The country's SHI system thus comprises both public and private insurers (figure 10.3). FONASA, the single public insurer, is by far the system's largest, covering over two-thirds of the national population at the end of 2003. Several ISAPREs compete to offer coverage to about 16 percent of the nation's population.[7] Other systems, such as those of the Armed Forces, cover up to 5 percent of the remaining population, while another 5 percent is presumed to have commercial insurance coverage or no coverage. Market concentration has been growing for ISAPREs. In 1990, the three largest ISAPREs captured 43 percent of the total ISAPRE market; by the end of 2005, that share had grown to just over two-thirds.

Chile's SHI system has both mandatory and voluntary components. By law, formal workers are required to contribute a health insurance premium, equal to 7 percent of their income, up to a monthly income ceiling of about US$1,500 per

FIGURE 10.3   Chile's Health System

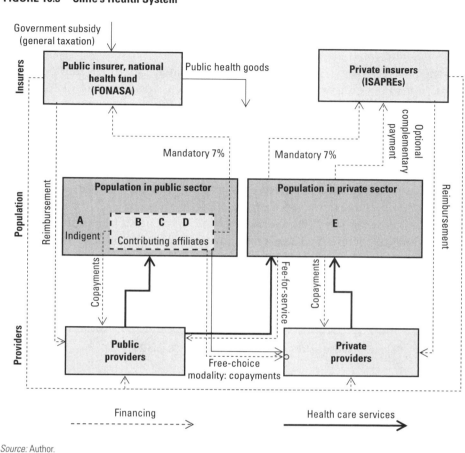

Source: Author.

worker. Formal workers can choose to enroll with FONASA or with one of the many competing ISAPREs. In addition, the law allows ISAPRE affiliates to make voluntary premium contributions above the mandatory 7 percent in exchange for better coverage. Informal workers are free to buy health insurance if they so desire and to select the insurer of their choice, either public or private. The choice of insurer, however, is driven by the individual applicant's income. If an individual wishing to purchase health insurance coverage has too low an income to purchase the levels of coverage he or she expects from an ISAPRE, the individual has no other choice but to insure with FONASA. In practice, only the middle-, upper-middle-, and high-income individuals can actually exert their choice of insurer; most, if not all of them, select an ISAPRE in exchange for their mandatory 7 percent as a rational strategy for buying better coverage. Both FONASA and ISAPREs have set copayments. FONASA's copayments are rather small overall and increase with the affiliate's income. FONASA covers the nation's indigent, who are required neither to contribute a premium nor to make any copayments. Most health care covered by FONASA is delivered by public providers, although this insurer has a program, referred to as Free Modality Choice, which grants a modest subsidy for health care in the private sector. Most services covered by ISAPREs are delivered by private providers.

In the past few years ISAPREs have faced a considerable growth in their medical loss ratio (the cost of medical claims over total costs) as a result of rising medical care prices and increasing per capita consumption of services by beneficiaries. In response, ISAPREs have been forced to increase their premiums year after year. This increase in the cost of private insurance, combined with improvements in FONASA coverage, has brought about a drop in demand for ISAPRE coverage. Demand being less elastic among the better-off, the drop in ISAPREs' market share has been characterized by a growing concentration of their portfolio on higher-income beneficiaries (figure 10.4).

FONASA's coverage, unlike coverage by ISAPREs or other indemnity insurers, is somewhat independent of the premium level. This encourages low-income individuals to enroll in FONASA, because their 7 percent contribution is too low to pay for better coverage in an ISAPRE. Conversely, higher-income individuals prefer ISAPREs, where they can buy better coverage with their 7 percent premium.

FIGURE 10.4   Chile: Enrolment in SHI, by Income Quintile, 1990 and 2005

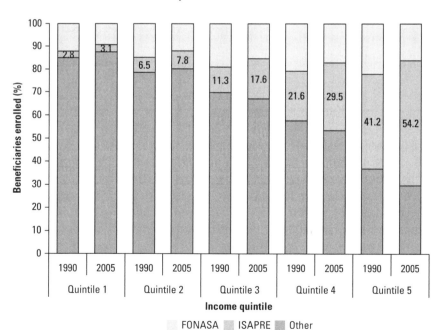

Source: Chile Health Superintendence, www.supersalud.cl.

The novelty of the AUGE reform in the LAC context is twofold. First, it forces the public insurer to offer explicit guarantees for health and financial coverage, as well as for waiting times and quality of care. Prior to this reform, FONASA functioned much like many other public health insurers in the LAC region, or like Ministries of Health. In other words, if FONASA did not make its coverage explicit, it rationed benefits through waiting lines or by offering low-quality services.[8] Second, private insurers are also required to provide at least the same coverage as FONASA. Thus, by defining this common benefits floor, the reform effectively promotes equity in access to health services throughout the country.

The establishment of priorities under AUGE was eclectic in the sense that technicians used multiple criteria to set priorities. They included: the significance of a health problem in terms of its share in the nation's burden of disease; the social preferences obtained through household surveys; experts' opinions; and cost-effectiveness.

The incremental costs of FONASA under the AUGE reform were financed with revenue from a 1 percent increase in the value added tax (VAT), from 18 percent to 19 percent. While there is ample evidence in Chile showing that the VAT is a regressive tax, all other financing options were discarded by the reforms for reasons involving political and technical feasibility. In the case of ISAPREs, AUGE is financed by an increase in insurance premiums.

The AUGE reform comprised other changes beyond the establishment of treatment priorities. Through the Sanitary Authority Law, the reform created the Health Superintendence, affirmed the MOH's role as a policy-making public entity, and gave greater administrative autonomy to public hospitals.

Challenges Ahead

With time, the number of medical problems with treatment guarantees under AUGE is expected to grow. Michelle Bachelet, M.D., who was Chile's president when the AUGE was enacted, said that before the end of her term in 2010, 26 additional problems would be added to the AUGE priorities list. In the end, she added only 10 new problems. The expansion of the list will likely demand considerable additional financial resources. It is unclear, however, where those resources will come from. Still, Chile devotes in total only 6 percent of its GDP to health, a small percentage when compared with other countries in the region with similar per capita GDP (e.g., Argentina 10 percent; Brazil 9 percent; Colombia 8 percent). Thus, there seems to be room for growth in the proportion of national resources spent in the health sector, even if the origin of the financing remains unclear. A recent reform proposal developed at the request of President Sebastián Piñera in late 2010 recommended that the health social security payroll contribution be increased from 7 percent to 8 percent, with 6 percentage points being earmarked for health services and 2 percent to maternity and sick leaves. This increase may help finance part or all of an expanded set of health services. The new reform proposal also recommended that the benefits package to be financed by FONASA and the ISAPREs be expanded to include also preventive services and catastrophic health care (Presidential Health Reform Committee 2010).

The AUGE reform was to be accompanied by an information system and by studies to assess compliance monitoring and impact assessment. Yet, in the first five years of the reform, the monitoring of the system has been deficient. Some argue that this deficiency responds to the government's reluctance to uncover possible failures in compliance with the guarantees on the part of FONASA. Others attribute the deficiency to limited technical capabilities by the new Health Superintendence. Improving the monitoring system should be a priority, one that as of early 2011 had not yet been addressed, to assess the system's compliance with the AUGE guarantees both by FONASA and the ISAPREs.

A final key challenge is the implementation of the hospital autonomy policy. By law it was expected that by the end of 2009 all public hospitals should have become autonomous. To do so, hospitals must meet a series of criteria defined in the law. As of early 2011, there has been little progress on this front, however, and most public hospitals remain unprepared to become autonomous. Enabling them to become eligible for autonomy should be a policy priority as well.

Costa Rica

Costa Rica's Caja Costarricense de Seguro Social (CCSS) continues to stand out in the region as the sole example of a unified health system that has relied exclusively on SHI to seek, and nearly achieve, universal coverage, with excellent health outcomes.

Background

A further noteworthy characteristic of Costa Rica's health system is the dominance by government. As Clark (2002) notes:

> A single institution [the CCSS] monopolizes health insurance and provides most of the curative and preventive services available in the country. The health sector reforms of the 1990s are unusual among Latin American cases because Costa Rican authorities rejected key aspects of the regional reform agenda, such as privatization and decentralization. Instead, Costa Rican health reforms have sought to improve the public system by completely overhauling the primary care network and deconcentrating administrative responsibility.

As of 2004, 87.8 percent of Costa Rica's population was legally covered by SHI through the CCSS, while half a million people, out of the country's 4.18 million, remained uninsured (figure 10.5). The extension of SHI coverage in Costa Rica has had several milestones, as shown in table 10.3. Before the CCSS initiated public health insurance in 1941, "citizens had to pay for health care out of pocket, work for a company that had its own doctor, or beseech the few charity clinics" (Clark 2002).

FIGURE 10.5   Costa Rica: Population, by Employment Status and SHI Coverage through CCSS, 2004

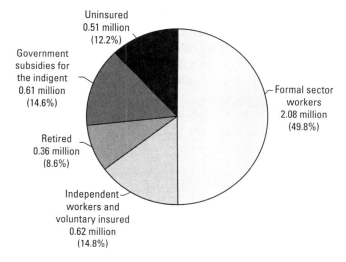

Uninsured
0.51 million
(12.2%)

Government
subsidies for
the indigent
0.61 million
(14.6%)

Formal sector
workers
2.08 million
(49.8%)

Retired
0.36 million
(8.6%)

Independent
workers and
voluntary insured
0.62 million
(14.8%)

Source: Author, from Rodríguez 2006.

TABLE 10.3   Costa Rica: Policy Milestones for Promoting SHI Enrolment through CCSS

Year	Policy milestone
1941	Mandatory health insurance coverage of salaried workers in urban areas
1947	Mandatory health insurance and maternity coverage of salaried workers in urban areas
1962	Extension of coverage to rural areas
1965	Extension of coverage to the entire family group
1974	Creation of noncontributory disability, old age, and death regime
1975	Mandatory coverage of nonsalaried workers
1975	Creation of voluntary enrolment program
1976	Establishment of mandatory contribution for health insurance regime by pensioners
1984	Creation of publicly financed health insurance regime for the indigent
1984	Introduction of mechanism to allow group enrolment
1995	Mandatory pension coverage effective for health coverage applicants
1996	Creation of student health insurance
2005	Health insurance coverage becomes mandatory for all independent workers

Source: Rodríguez 2006.

During the 1990s Costa Rica's health sector underwent a significant reform which comprised the following three main elements:

- *Transfer of the primary health care (PHC) system from the MOH to the CCSS.* Until the reform, the MOH operated a nationwide array of health centers. With the reform, the ownership and management of those facilities was transferred to the CCSS which, as owner and operator of the public hospitals, became the sole operator of the public system's health care network. The national territory was divided into seven health regions, each with a Support Health Team and several Basic Integrated Health Systems Teams (EBAIS). The EBAIS operate out of clinics or health centers, and are staffed with a general practitioner, a nurse assistant, and a primary health care technical assistant. They serve a population of 3,500 to 7,000 people. Through the EBAIS the CCSS delivers a basic benefits package of services for children, adolescents, women, adults, and the elderly. Since the transfer of the PHC system to the CCSS, the budget share of PHC has risen considerably, from 18.8 percent in 1997 to 23.8 percent in 2004. This increase is said to have been behind the recent drops in infant mortality and the improvements in other health status indicators in the country.

- *Specialization by the MOH in policy steering and regulatory capacities.* Until the reform of the 1990s, the MOH regulatory role was limited to food and drug safety. Starting in 1998, the MOH was assigned new roles, including policy steering, legislation and regulation of environmental health and of health services and quality, health surveillance, and promotion of health research and development.

- *Adoption of a new payment and budget allocation system.* The most controversial reform initiative, it ended up integrating into the CCSS the three functions of financing, purchasing, and hospital network management.[9] A payment system was adopted by which each hospital, under its management agreement (*convenios de gestión*), would negotiate its budget with the CCSS, thus linking hospital budgets with performance and moving away from historic budgets.

Despite the achievements of the CCSS, recent data signal a stagnating affiliation and a drop in use of services by middle- and upper-income beneficiaries. Likewise, failure by government to fulfill its legally mandated financial contributions to SHI further threatens the viability of this otherwise noteworthy system.

SHI financing comes from contributions by workers, employers, the retired, and government. For all beneficiaries, government subsidizes enrolment from general revenue. The largest public subsidy per beneficiary, in percentage terms, is directed to the indigent, whose affiliation is entirely subsidized by government.[10] Formal sector workers, despite having the highest relative incomes of all groups, also benefit from a legal public subsidy, equal to 0.25 percent of their salary. So do the retired. Self-employed workers and the voluntarily insured obtain a much larger government subsidy intended to replace the employer's contribution for formal workers (table 10.4).

A review of the literature and the CCSS Web site suggests that CCSS health benefits are only partly explicit. The health services that beneficiaries can obtain, both at the ambulatory and hospital levels, are explicitly named, and so are the copayments they are required to make, but the conditions under which those

TABLE 10.4   Costa Rica: Legal Contributions to SHI (percent)

Group covered	Worker/individual	Employer	Government	Total
Formal sector workers	5.50	9.25	0.25	15.00
Independent workers	4.75	0.00	5.75	10.50
Voluntary insured	4.60	0.00	5.75	10.35
Retired	5.00	8.75	0.25	14.00
Indigent	0.00	0.00	14.00	14.00

Source: Rodríguez 2006: 50.

services are provided are not fully defined. In particular, CCSS has not set time limits for delivering care once a beneficiary requests services.

Starting in 1996, the delivery system reform, through the EBAIS model described earlier, seems to have boosted access to outpatient care (table 10.5). The observed drop in the rate of specialty care use may be a positive sign, suggesting an improvement in the ability of general practitioners (GPs) to resolve medical problems at the primary level. In contrast, the considerable increase in emergency care visits signals a serious problem. It may be that the uninsured requesting an appointment with a GP during the day are required to establish SHI eligibility, a requirement they can bypass by seeking services at night in the emergency care service.

The hospitalization rate has dropped considerably, from 9.59 percent in 1990 to 8.04 percent in 2004. Concurrently, hospital efficiency has improved somewhat as measured by a reduction in average length of stay (ALOS), and increases in the bed turnover and utilization rates. Two drawbacks seem to be the slight increase in the rate of C-sections and in the days of presurgical hospitalization.

A major source of concern is the drop in two indicators of quality of care (not shown in table 10.5) in 1990–2004: intrahospital maternal mortality increased from 1.8 percent to 2.2 percent and post-surgery mortality doubled from 0.35 percent to 0.72 percent.

Achievements

A major achievement of Costa Rica's reform has been the high level of SHI coverage reached by the CCSS (table 10.6). Costa Rica was able to achieve in only 40 years what took Austria and Germany a much longer time (figure 10.6).

In addition, this high population coverage seems to have resulted in equitable access to health care at all levels. Rodríguez (2006) found no significant differences in health services utilization rates per capita when comparing the country's five most highly developed cantons with the five least-developed cantons.[11] That was a remarkable finding given the considerable difference in socioeconomic status between the two groups, as seen through the Human Development Index (HDI).

TABLE 10.5   Costa Rica: Ambulatory and Inpatient Care Utilization Statistics

Indicator	1990	1995	1996	1997	1998	1999	2000	2001	2002	2003	2004
Outpatient	2.20	2.20	—	—	—	—	2.43	2.49	2.61	2.70	2.75
General medicine	1.19	1.23	—	—	—	—	1.38	1.39	1.49	1.53	1.56
Specialty	0.72	0.69	—	—	—	—	0.61	0.62	0.64	0.63	0.64
Dental	0.21	0.20	—	—	—	—	0.35	0.39	0.40	0.44	0.46
Other	0.07	0.08	—	—	—	—	0.08	0.09	0.09	0.09	0.09
Emergency	0.51	0.63	—	—	—	—	0.85	0.88	0.88	0.90	0.95
Total	2.71	2.83	—	—	—	—	3.28	3.37	3.49	3.60	3.70
Hospital discharges per 100 insured	9.59	8.60	8.40	8.38	8.23	8.26	8.38	8.34	8.23	8.21	8.04
Average length of stay (days)	6.01	5.84	6.11	5.91	5.50	5.80	5.46	5.33	5.22	5.73	5.29
Bed turnover rate	44.5	49.94	49.93	51.31	51.55	53.06	55.49	56.23	56.83	57.65	58.08
Bed occupancy rate	76.76	80.28	81.09	81.18	79.61	80.54	81.67	82.37	81.29	81.65	80.91
Presurgery stay (days)	1.58	1.61	1.49	1.05	1.34	1.28	1.86	1.94	1.90	1.88	—
Cesarean deliveries per 100 births	19.52	21.21	21.25	18.16	21.23	21.99	21.28	22.18	21.95	22.02	—

Source: Rodríguez 2006: 33.

Note: — = not available.

TABLE 10.6   Costa Rica: Evolution of SHI Coverage

Year	Population coverage (percent)	Real GDP per capita (constant prices, US$)
1941	0	2,215
1962	21	4,377
1965	30	4,921
1975	52	6,360
1984	62	6,202
2004	88	8,739

Sources: Population coverage for the period 1962–1984 from Carrin and James 2004 and Rodríguez 2006; GDP per capita 1950 to 2004 from Penn World Table Version 6.2; GDP per capita before 1950 based on author's estimation.

Challenges Ahead

The growing preference for private providers and cross-subsidies are emerging challenges.

The preference for private providers. The preference for private, paid-for hospital providers grows with income among CCSS beneficiaries and may signal quality problems in the CCSS network. This may be a source of concern because, as is shown next, much of the financing available for the CCSS actually comes from cross-subsidies provided by the higher-income affiliates. If these affiliates were

FIGURE 10.6   Costa Rica, Austria, and Germany: Time Required to Achieve Near-Universal SHI Coverage

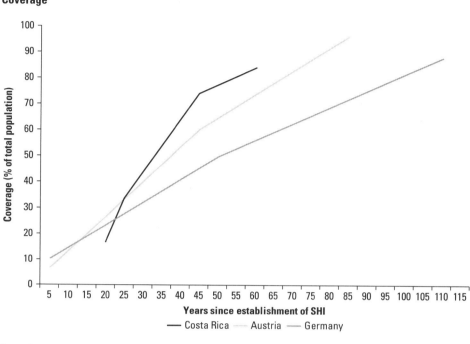

Source: Bitrán 2005 from data presented in Carrin and James 2004.

to see their contribution increasingly as a tax in return for which they receive limited benefits, their willingness to contribute may weaken. Whereas affiliation will remain mandatory, they may find ways of evading or eluding contributions.

Cross-subsidies. Formal sector workers bear a major share of the financing burden in Costa Rica's SHI system. In 2004 more than three-fourths (78.2 percent) of all CCSS financing came from contributions from formal sector affiliates. Yet only about one-half of their contributions went to finance their own benefits. The excess contributions over the value of their benefits were used by the CCSS to subsidize the benefits of independent and voluntary workers and the retired. While by law government should fully subsidize coverage for the indigent, in practice that has not been the case.

Formal sector beneficiaries derived the most benefits (US$393.5 million) and paid for them in full. Independent workers and voluntary affiliates contributed only US$43.1 million out of the US$114 million they received in benefits; formal sector affiliates subsidized the gap of US$71.3 million. Likewise, retirees paid in US$57.6 million, only about one-third of their benefits. Again formal sector affiliates came up with the difference of US$97.9 million. Finally, had the government contributed the US$62.4 million it was supposed to contribute (it only contributed US$5 million), it would have barely covered about a fourth of all benefits delivered by the CCSS to the indigent; again, the formal sector contributors picked up the difference of US$205.8 million. Such a high level of cross-subsidies may not be politically sustainable.

Colombia

Like in other countries in the region, Colombian health care before the 20th century was provided mainly by private medical doctors and traditional healers for those who could afford it, and by church-run charity institutions for those who could not.

Background

The first social insurance scheme, the Caja Nacional de Provisión (CNP), was created in 1945 to provide health services for civil servants. In 1946, the Institute for Social Insurance (ISS) was created to provide health services for formal workers in the private sector (Hanratty and Meditz 1988). In 1953, the current Ministry of Health was created, providing informal workers and low-income individuals, as well as any other citizen, health care free of charge in a system of universal provision consisting of government-run ambulatory and inpatient facilities.

In 1994 Colombia's congress passed a comprehensive health reform package, whose aim was to develop the Generalized Health Social Security System (SGSSS, box 10.2). Starting that year affiliation in SGSSS became mandatory for all citizens, irrespective of location, income, employment, or other individual characteristics. The nonpoor, including formal and informal sector workers, were required to enroll in the Contributory Regime.

Members of the CR could choose their own insurer among a pool of competing public and private insurers, the Health Promoting Enterprises (EPSs). Enrolment was conditional on payment of a monthly contribution equal to 12 percent of their payroll. For formal workers the contribution would be split between the employer (8 percent) and the worker (4 percent). Informal workers, instead, were required to contribute the full 12 percent. The contribution of 12 percent was broken up into two parts. Eleven percentage points would finance health benefits from the CR while the remaining 1 percent would be used as a cross-subsidy to finance enrolment in SGSSS by the poor. The 11 percent contribution went to a risk pool managed by an institution called Solidarity and Guarantee Fund (FOSYGA) and would be used to compensate ex post EPSs on the basis of the risk of their portfolio of beneficiaries. Risk assessment was based on age and gender only.

The poor would be enrolled in the Subsidized Regime (SR). Enrolment of the poor would take place on a decentralized basis by municipalities, using a means-testing procedure carried out at the household level using a standardized instrument. Financing of the SR came from FOSYGA. This entity, in turn, drew its financing from two sources: the already mentioned 1 percent solidarity contribution from the CR and a supplemental subsidy from the country's treasury.

BOX 10.2   MAIN DESIGN FEATURES OF COLOMBIA'S GENERALIZED HEALTH SOCIAL SECURITY SYSTEM

- Mandatory enrolment for all citizens

- Two SHI regimes: the Contributory Regime (CR) for the nonpoor and the Subsidized Regime (SR) for the poor

- Self-financing of the CR with a 12 percent payroll tax (8 percent worker, 4 percent employer)

- Subsidization of the SR, with funding coming from the treasury and from a 1 percentage solidarity point out of the CR's 12 percent payroll tax

- Regional allocation of subsidies on the basis of size of enrolled population

- Decentralized management of SR subsidies by municipalities through individual targeting using standardized means testing

- Competition among insurers responsible for enrolment in both regimes

- Ex post risk adjustment among insurers

- Initially differentiated benefits packages for each regime were expected to converge by the year 2000, but they are still different today

- Competition among public and private health care providers

- Reduction of supply-side financing for public hospitals replaced by growing demand-side financing from their sale of health services to the two SHI regimes.

Source: Author.

Every municipality would receive a budget from FOSYGA proportional to the expected number of poor individuals in its population. Municipalities would then target the subsidy to the poor by applying a means test at the household level. Individuals qualifying as poor could then enroll with the health insurer of their choice from a pool of competing private and public insurers known as ARS (Managers of the Subsidized Regime).

A comprehensive health benefits package, the Mandatory Health Plan (POS), was designed, combining cost-effectiveness and financial protection criteria. The package contained both cost-effective ambulatory and inpatient health services, and high-cost tertiary procedures with a low cost-effectiveness ratio. Members of the Contributory Regime were entitled to all benefits in POS. A less comprehensive package the Subsidized POS (POS-S) was defined for the members of the Subsidized Regime. The less costly POS-S was deemed necessary to achieve full coverage of the poor through the Subsidized Regime within the limited financial envelope available at FOSYGA. Reformers envisioned that, with time, the POS-S would become increasingly more comprehensive in coverage, equaling the POS package by the year 2000. That did not happen, however. To this day the benefits package of the contributory regime covers more services than that of the subsidized regime.

Achievements

Colombia's health reform of 1994 may well be one of the most comprehensive reforms of its kind in a developing country. It completely reshuffled the health system, creating new institutions, abolishing old ones, and changing the logic of this country's health system (figure 10.7). Substantial financing was required to make it possible, and substantial additional financing will be required to achieve universality. This reform has had many detractors, both in Colombia and in the international community, and there have been numerous political initiatives in the country to defeat it in order to return to the conventional health system that Colombia had prior to 1994. Whereas some of the reform's achievements seem unambiguous, such as the increase in coverage, accessibility, and utilization of health services by the poor, many problems lie ahead, and their solutions appear elusive. Still, Colombia's reform was a pioneer in Latin America, and some of

FIGURE 10.7   Colombia's Reformed Social Health Insurance System after Law 100

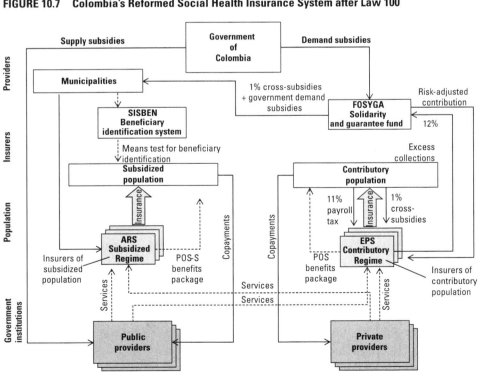

Source: Author.

its design features have inspired many other reform initiatives in the region, including those in Chile, the Dominican Republic, Mexico, and elsewhere.

Since the passage of Law 100, health insurance coverage in Colombia has grown considerably; overall, it went from less than one-fourth of the population in 1993 to just under two-thirds in 2003 and to about 88 percent by 2005 (table 10.7).

More notably, insurance coverage experienced relatively greater growth in lower socioeconomic groups than in upper groups. For example, whereas in 1993 it was a mere 6.1 percent in the lowest quintile, in 2003 it was 46.5 percent (table 10.8). In 2003 insurance coverage still increased with socioeconomic status, but the differences across socioeconomic groups were significantly smaller than in 1993.

Total health financing for health care, as a percentage of GDP, has increased in Colombia to sustain the development of SHI. It went from 6.2 percent of GDP in 1993 to 7.8 percent of GDP in 2003. In 1997 it reached 9.6 percent of GDP. The structure of health financing has changed as well, as seen in figure 10.7. Public financing for the Subsidized Regime of social security reached 11 percent of total health financing, while private financing of the Contributory Regime reached 44.5 percent of total health financing. These two sources combined, equaling

TABLE 10.7   Colombia: Evolution of SHI Coverage and Per Capita GDP

Year	Population coverage (percent)	Real GDP per capita (constant prices, US$)
1946	0	2,309
1993	24	5,596
1994	32	5,725
1997	57	6,186
2003	62	6,095
2005	88	6,171

Sources: Population coverage from CASEN Survey 1993; LSMS Surveys 1997 and 2003; MPS Statistical Report 2005 and author's estimation; GDP per capita 1950 to 2004 from Penn World Table Version 6.2; GDP per capita before 1950 and after 2004 based on author's estimation.

TABLE 10.8   Colombia: Health Insurance Coverage, by Socioeconomic Group, 1993, 1997, and 2003 (percent)

Quintile	1993	1997	2003
1	6.1	43.4	46.5
2	16.5	48.7	52.5
3	27.5	59.0	58.2
4	35.3	65.7	69.3
5	43.1	76.7	82.7
Total	23.8	57.1	61.8

Sources: Escobar 2005 based on CASEN survey (1993) and LSMS (1997, 2003) household surveys.

55.5 percent of all health financing, sustained Colombia's new health social security regime. Over the period covered in the figure, out-of-pocket financing of health care dropped steeply, from 43.7 percent in 1993 to only 7.5 percent in 2003.

The incidence of financing for Colombia's social security SR compares favorably with other publicly subsidized social programs. Nearly three-quarters of the subsidy reaches the two poorest quintiles, while slightly more than a tenth of it reaches the two richest quintiles.

As noted above, the demand-side subsidies channeled through the SR were expected progressively to replace supply-side public subsidies to public health care providers. Bitrán and associates (2004) examined the incidence of the demand-side subsidies of the SR with that of the supply-side subsidies to public providers and found that supply subsidies were poorly targeted, with a Gini coefficient of –0.06. Demand subsidies, instead, were progressive, with a positive Gini coefficient of 0.10. Both subsidies combined were only proportional, not progressive as they should be.

Consistent with the preceding information, an analysis of affiliation with Colombia's health social security system shows highest affiliation with the SR in the poorest socioeconomic groups and vice versa. This is shown in figure 10.8, which presents information on affiliation by socioeconomic group. The groups themselves are those defined through the means-testing instrument used by municipalities to enroll the poor with the SR. The instrument classifies households into six socioeconomic groups, known as SISBEN 1 (poorest) through SISBEN 6 (richest). Figure 10.8 also shows that as of 2005 nearly as many poor individuals were enrolled in the SR as there were poor individuals without any coverage. The high proportion of uncovered, low-income Colombians is a consequence of the lack of financing available to subsidize the SR such as to achieve universal coverage.

Giedion (2007) examined the consequence that Colombia's health reform had on access to health services and health status. Using different methodologies, she found consistent evidence that the subsidized health insurance scheme improves access to and utilization of health services, especially among the rural and the poorest population. The impact of health insurance on health status is less clear, but this may be due to data limitations.

Challenges Ahead

Colombia's ambitious reform has faced and continues to face major challenges, including the following: (1) The benefits package of the SR has not yet become equal to that of the CR, and this is a source of systemic inequity; (2) The large number of successful legal suits ("*tutelas*") by SGSSS beneficiaries to obtain health services not included in the benefits package is defeating the purpose of prioritization and threatening the financial viability of the reform; (3) Public hospitals have been unable to convert fully from a supply-side to a demand-side financing regime, and it looks as if a substantial proportion of supply-side financing will be required indefinitely to keep these facilities going.

FIGURE 10.8   Colombia: Affiliation Status, by Income Group, 2005

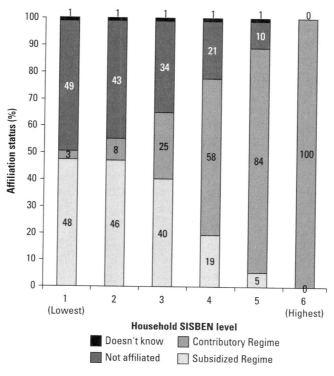

Source: Giedion 2007.

Ecuador

Ecuador is similar to most other countries in the LAC region in its large disparities in health status. This section reviews the history and prospects of Ecuador's Rural Health Insurance (RHI), a policy initiative that has sought to scale up health insurance to reach universality and hence to improve access to health services for the nation's rural poor.

Background

In 1985–95 infant and child mortality rates among indigenous children were twice as high as among nonindigenous children, while mortality rates among the extremely poor were two to three times higher than among the nonpoor. Mortality rates dropped significantly for all population groups during that 10-year period, but the relative gap between groups remained just as high or widened. For example, in the five-year period between 1985 and 1990, the child mortality rate among the indigenous population was 142 deaths per 1,000 live births, 2.0 times as high as among nonindigenous children. In the following five-year period it fell to 91 for indigenous children and to 39 for the nonindigenous, with the ratio between the two increasing to 2.3.

Ecuador is also similar to several other LAC countries in that it has a social security institute that provides health, pension, and other benefits mostly to formal sector workers. The Ecuadorian Social Security Institute (IESS), created in 1928, originated with a series of laws protecting public servants passed beginning in 1905.

As of 2007, the IESS covered 1.5 million people, about 11 percent of the country's population. Likewise, Ecuador has a Ministry of Health, created in 1967, offering universal access to health services through a nationwide network of publicly financed ambulatory and inpatient facilities. Concerns about the welfare of the nation's majority of low-income peasants led in 1935 to the passage of a Supreme Decree (Decreto Supremo No. 18) establishing that social security should also be made available to that group. But the creation of the RHI had to wait another 40 years to become a reality. In 1968 the National Providence Institute set up a pilot test incorporating 611 rural families to the social security institute. Today, the RHI covers 840,000 people, just over 6 percent of the population (table 10.9).

The sources of social security financing in Ecuador vary by regime. The regular social security regime, also known as the Mandatory General Insurance component of IESS, was designed to be cofinanced by employers, workers, and government. However, several legal loopholes and failure by government to contribute its dues have resulted in a system financed solely by employers, who contribute a legal 3.41 percent of the payroll (figure 10.9).

In contrast, RHI has four sources of financing: IESS employers and workers must each provide a cross-subsidy to finance RHI equal to 0.35 percent of the worker's salary. Government must add an amount equivalent to 0.30 percent of the worker's salary, and peasants must contribute 1 percent of the minimum wage. In practice, the peasants' contribution is nominal and represents a negligible part of total RHI financing. Thus, RHI is a subsidized health insurance

TABLE 10.9   Ecuador: Coverage of Social Security System, by Beneficiary Population, 2007

Social security institution	Beneficiary population	Population coverage (%)
Mandatory General Insurance of Ecuadorian Social Security Institute (IESS)	1,511,319	11.0
Social Security for Peasants (RHI)	838,293	6.1
Social Security for Armed Forces	264,512	1.9
Social Security for Police Force	251,085	1.8
Total	2,865,209	20.8

Source: Vallejo 2007.

FIGURE 10.9   Ecuador: Social Security for Urban Workers and Peasants, 2007

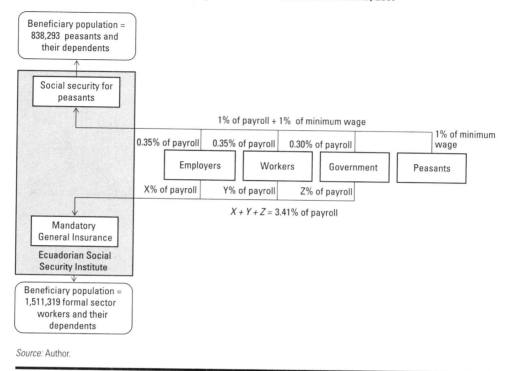

Source: Author.

program financed with a cross-subsidy equal to 1 percent of the urban IESS affiliates split in nearly equal parts between the employers, workers, and government
(PAHO 2001).

Achievements

Of the five countries in this study, Ecuador has achieved the lowest SHI population coverage. Only 21 percent of the population is enrolled in one of the available social health insurance schemes—this is one-third of the coverage achieved
by Mexico, which has the second lowest population coverage rate. It seems para-
doxical that Ecuador was also the first country that started implementing social
health insurance arrangements. It was the first to implement civil servants social
insurance, in 1905; to enroll formal workers, in 1928; and to begin expanding
social insurance to rural poor populations, in 1968. Although it was a precursor
in these initiatives, Ecuador has failed to increase SHI coverage. This modest
coverage may be explained by low rates of formal employment and by a lack of
financing to cover the rural poor (see below).

Challenges Ahead

Throughout its four decades of life, the RHI has suffered from chronic shortages
of financing. Whereas its budget in current U.S. dollars grew by a factor of 3.60

TABLE 10.10   Ecuador: Total Public Health Expenditure (Actual), 2000–2003 (current US$, million)

Organization	2000	2001	2002	2003	Ratio 2003/ 2000	Health spending structure 2003 (%)	GDP 2003[c]	Total population covered (millions)	Expenditure per capita 2003 (US$)[d]
Ministry of Public Health	103.2	188.6	259.0	325.1	3.15	64.1	1.2	12.66	25.68
IESS[a]	56.6	83.6	114.1	168.3	2.97	33.2	0.6	1.51	111.47
RHI[b]	3.8	5.1	7.8	13.7	3.60	2.7	0.1	0.84	16.31
Total	163.6	277.3	381.0	507.1	3.10	100.0	1.9	12.66	40.06

Source: Adapted by author from data in Vallejo (2007).

a. Includes IESS administrative budget weighted according to participation of General Health Insurance within the total IESS budget.

b. Includes IESS administrative budget weighted according to participation of SSC medical units within the total IESS budget.

c. GDP for 2003 was US$26,745.83 million.

d. Reference population for 2003 was 12.66 million according to INEC projections.

between 2000 and 2003, a higher growth than that of IESS and the MOH, its total budget amount per beneficiary remains only a fraction of the IESS budget. In 2003, RHI spent only US$16.31 per beneficiary, about 14 percent of what IESS spent per person, $111.48 (table 10.10).

SUMMARY AND CONCLUSIONS

Mandatory health insurance has been part of public health systems in the LAC region for several decades. In many LAC countries, organized public health sprung in the first half of the 20th century, with the simultaneous creation of Bismarckian mandatory health insurance schemes for formal workers, and Beveridgean national health systems for the rest of the population. Before the creation of this mixed system in the early to mid-20th century, health services were provided by private practitioners or traditional healers. People who could not afford their fees could go to charity institutions, most of them run by the Catholic Church. Under the mixed system, formal workers, only a small part of the population, were covered by a relatively well-funded SHI institution. The rest of the population, composed of informal workers and the indigent, had two choices: they could either purchase private health services through out-of-pocket payments or they could go to a public MOH facility. MOH services were free or much less expensive for patients than private practitioners but were also less funded and of lower quality than SHI-covered care. In many cases, poor informal workers and the indigent had to rely exclusively on public MOH facilities.

At the beginning, most public health systems in LAC were dominated by their Beveridgean component because most of the population worked informally, and poverty was deep and widespread. During the second half of the 20th century, many LAC countries developed a more formal economy, which facilitated the expansion of SHI. However, a large part of the population still remained dependent on the MOH, which was persistently unable to provide the population with good-quality, timely services. As a consequence, at the end of the 20th century many LAC countries started scaling up SHI to incorporate poor informal workers and the indigent. They achieved this by relying on government subsidies to finance the participation of this less-favored population segment in SHI. Table 10.11 summarizes the evolution of health financing in these countries, in three phases: (1) until the first half of the 20th century, when there was little or no organized public health, (2) the second half of the 20th century, when the mixed systems were predominant, and (3) the end of the 20th century to today, when SHI systems that seek universal coverage are replacing national health systems.

This study reviewed the case of five LAC countries, Mexico, Chile, Costa Rica, Colombia, and Ecuador, that implemented SHI (table 10.12). Notwithstanding the general tendencies noted in that table, each country has chosen different ways to implement SHI, with different degrees of success. These countries also vary in their income level and formalization of employment, important enabling factors for the scaling-up of health insurance. Other LAC countries that followed similar tendencies are Honduras, Bolivia, Dominican Republic, Peru, El Salvador, Guatemala, Nicaragua, and Panama.[12]

Figure 10.10 shows the chronology of the main SHI phases shared by the five LAC countries reviewed in this chapter. The first phase is the pre-SHI era, when health services were provided by private practitioners, traditional healers, and charity institutions. The second phase corresponds to the first public SHI initiatives, which sought to provide civil servants with health benefits. The third phase can be considered the actual beginning of mixed systems. Some countries like Mexico, Costa Rica, and Colombia went directly from the first to the third

TABLE 10.11   Evolution of Health Financing in Many LAC Countries

| Population group | *Time* | | |
	Until first half 20th century	*Second half 20th century*	*End 20th century to today*
Formal workers	Out-of-pocket payment with private practitioners or healers	Mandatory health insurance (contributive)	
Nonpoor informal workers		Out-of-pocket payments and voluntary private health insurance	
Poor informal workers and the indigent	Charitable institutions	National health systems (general tax funded)	Mandatory health insurance (subsidized)

Source: Author.

TABLE 10.12   Paths Chosen to SHI, Selected LAC Countries

Country	Main SHI institutions	Target population	Starting date	Percent of population covered	Compulsory/ voluntary	Single/ multiple	Public/ private	Financing	Choice of providers
Mexico	ISSSTE	Civil servants	1959	7	Compulsory	Single	Public	Subsidy/ contributions	Public
	IMSS	Private sector formal workers	1943	40	Compulsory	Single	Public	Subsidy/ contributions	Public
	PHI	Informal workers and the indigent	2000	13	Compulsory	Single	Public	Subsidy/ contributions	Public
Chile	FONASA B/C/D	Formal workers	1980	47	Compulsory	Single	Public	Contributions	Public/ private
	ISAPREs	Formal workers	1980	16	Compulsory	Multiple	Private	Contributions	Public/ private
	FONASA A	The indigent and poor informal workers	1980	24	Voluntary	Single	Public	Subsidy	Public
Costa Rica	CCSS	Universal	1941	88	Compulsory	Single	Public	Subsidy/ contributions	Public
Colombia	Contributory Regime	Nonpoor	1994	38	Compulsory	Multiple	Public/ private	Contributions	Public/ private
	Subsidized Regime	Poor	1994	45	Compulsory	Multiple	Public/ private	Subsidy	Public/ private
Ecuador	Mandatory Gen. Ins.	Formal workers	1928	11	Compulsory	Single	Public	Subsidy/ contributions	Own
	RHI	Rural	1968	6	Mix	Single	Public	Subsidy/ contributions	Own

Source: Author.

phase, simultaneously enrolling civil servants and private formal workers in SHI. The fourth phase corresponds to the scaling-up of SHI to incorporate poor informal workers and the indigent. The beginning of the third phase occurs at practically the same time in all countries (1941–45), except in Ecuador (1928). However, the beginning of the fourth phase, SHI scaling-up, occurs at different points in time, somewhere between 1968 and 2000.

Between 1946 and 1968, these five countries had relatively similar SHI systems, consisting of single public institutions. However, differences began to appear. For example, in Mexico and Colombia, civil servants were separated from private sector workers, while in Chile, Costa Rica, and Ecuador both types of workers were in the same insurance funds. Also, in Colombia, small public or private prepaid health programs began to appear spontaneously after the creation of the CNP and the ISS, in response to their lack of effective coverage.

FIGURE 10.10   Chronology of Main SHI Phases in Mexico, Chile, Costa Rica, Colombia, and Ecuador

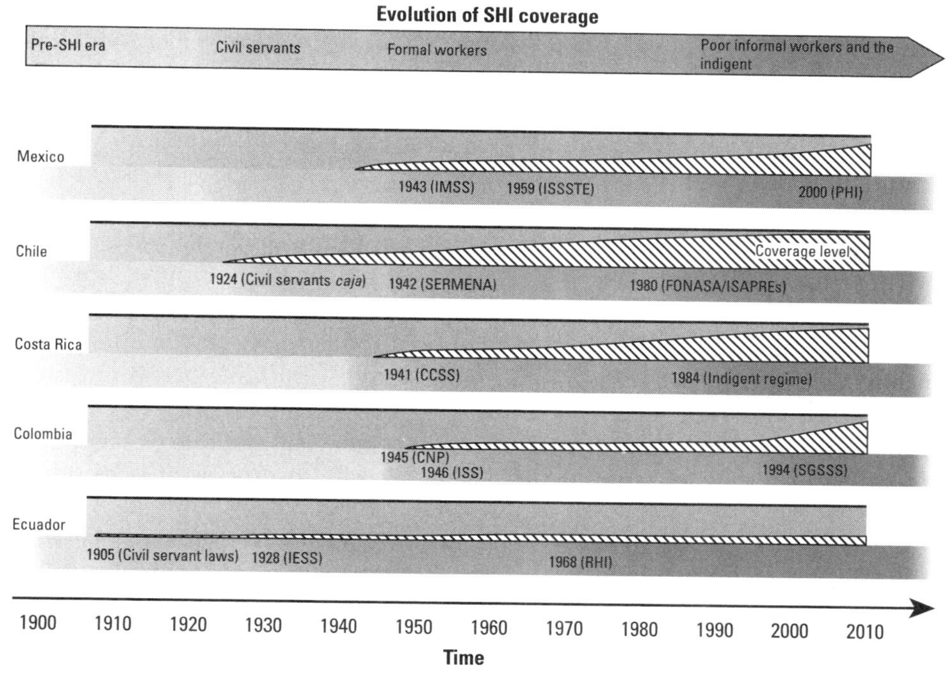

Evolution of SHI coverage

Pre-SHI era	Civil servants	Formal workers	Poor informal workers and the indigent

Mexico

1943 (IMSS)   1959 (ISSSTE)   2000 (PHI)

Chile

Coverage level

1924 (Civil servants *caja*)   1942 (SERMENA)   1980 (FONASA/ISAPREs)

Costa Rica

1941 (CCSS)   1984 (Indigent regime)

Colombia

1945 (CNP)
1946 (ISS)   1994 (SGSSS)

Ecuador

1905 (Civil servant laws)   1928 (IESS)   1968 (RHI)

1900   1910   1920   1930   1940   1950   1960   1970   1980   1990   2000   2010

Time

Source: Author.

Population coverage of SHI was relatively low and depended mostly on countries' formal employment rates.

Today, SHI is structured much more heterogeneously between the five countries (see table 10.12 for an overview of SHI institutions today). All countries have carried out efforts to scale up SHI to reach poor informal workers and the indigent but have done so in different ways. Some, like Chile and Colombia, have entirely changed their old SHI structures. Chile abolished SERMENA and created FONASA and ISAPREs instead. Colombia replaced CNP and ISS with the Contributory and Subsidized Regimes. Others, like Mexico and Ecuador, have kept their old SHI institutions, but have built new ones to scale up. Mexico kept ISSSTE and IMSS but created the PHI to scale up. Ecuador kept the Mandatory General Insurance, but created the RHI to scale up (although both actually operate under the same institution, IESS). Costa Rica, in contrast, relied on its old SHI institution, the CCSS, to scale up. This illustrates how these countries began with similar health systems and shared a common SHI evolution until scaling-up occurred. But to scale up SHI, these countries chose different timings, strategies, and models.

One important differentiating characteristic in today's SHI institutions is whether enrolment is compulsory or voluntary. Some countries, like Mexico, Costa Rica, and Colombia, have designed compulsory insurance schemes for scaling up. In Mexico, for example, enrolment of informal workers and the indigent is mandatory, although implementation is being phased in by locality over seven years. In contrast, Chile implemented a voluntary enrolment scheme, called FONASA, targeted exclusively to the indigent (however, in practice many poor informal workers manage to enroll by declaring no income). In Ecuador, enrolment is also mandatory for selected communities, although peasants from elsewhere can enroll voluntarily if they wish.

In scaling up, some countries chose to have a single insurer, whereas others chose to implement multiple insurers, in the hope of promoting efficiency through competition. Mexico, Costa Rica, Ecuador, and Chile used a single public insurer scale-up. However, Colombia opted for multiple public and private insurers. Although Chile has ISAPREs, consisting of multiple private insurers, they are not important actors in scaling up SHI to the poor and the indigent. In this case, FONASA, a monopolistic public insurer, had the role of scaling up. Colombia, instead, used multiple public and private insurers in the Subsidized Regime, which is responsible for scaling up.

The degree of success in scaling up SHI population coverage varies between countries. Figure 10.11 shows the difference in SHI coverage between 1946–68 and today (coverage rates in 1946–68 are approximate because of fluctuations during that period and lack of reliable information). Most countries have been

Figure 10.11   SHI Population Coverage, 1946–68 and Today

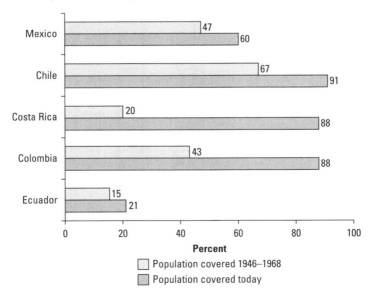

relatively successful to date. Mexico has increased SHI coverage from 47 percent to 60 percent and is quickly moving toward universal coverage. In 1980, Chile reached practically universal coverage with the creation of FONASA. In 1984, Costa Rica also achieved nearly universal coverage with the creation of the indigent regime. In 2006, Colombia achieved similar rates of SHI coverage.

In contrast, Ecuador has not had the same success, and SHI coverage remains low. Although Ecuador was the first to try to scale up SHI, it lagged behind the other four countries, notably because it is a poorer and more politically unstable country. Comparing Ecuador and Costa Rica, similar SHI coverage rates under the old system can be observed, but in Costa Rica there has been a much more successful scaling-up. This can be explained by the higher levels of formal employment and income attained by Costa Rica in the second half of the 20th century, which contrast with the poorer situation of Ecuador.

Colombia and Mexico present a similar situation. They had similar SHI coverage rates in the old system and were also the last to try to scale up SHI. Mexico decided to scale up gradually, over a period of seven years, which is why it has not attained the same coverage rates as Colombia. However, it is expected that Mexico will reach similar coverage rates in the next few years.

Chile presents a different case, because its SHI coverage rates in the old system were relatively high to begin with (67 percent). Thus, less effort was required to scale up than in the other countries.

All five countries share one common challenge to scale up SHI sustainably: availability of resources to finance subsidized SHI. As experience in these five countries shows, expanding SHI to lower-income populations seems impossible without additional public subsidies. Mexico estimates an increase of 1.3 points in public health expenditure as a percentage of GDP. In Chile, about half of FONASA's expenditure comes from public subsidies. In 2002 in Colombia, the path toward universal coverage under the Subsidized Regime was interrupted because of insufficient government subsidies. Ecuador is proof of the financial vulnerability of scaled-up SHI systems because one of the main reasons for the lack of success of Ecuador's RHI is the government's failure to honor its financial commitments.

NOTES

ACKNOWLEDGMENTS: I thank Alexander S. Preker of the World Bank and Marianne Linder of PharmAccess Foundation for their helpful guidance and comments on earlier versions of this chapter. Maria Luisa Escobar of the Brookings Institution and Cristian Baeza of the World Bank also provided valuable feedback. Rodrigo Muñoz of Bitrán & Asociados helped revise the chapter for this final version and draw conclusions and lessons from the case studies.

1. Unlike the United Kingdom, however, Barbados exhibits considerable private financing for health care. In 2005, 37 percent of all health financing was private, a figure that contrasts with the much lower 13 percent in the United Kingdom.

2. Gertler (1998) and Bitrán (2005) discuss some of those problems in the Asian context, which shares many similarities with the LAC context.

3. Health care prices faced by ISAPREs increased on average by 3.3 percent per year between 1995 and 2000, while average annual inflation was 5.1 percent. Thus, real prices fell by about 2 percent per year.

4. In descending order of per capita GNI in 2005 current U.S. dollars.

5. This section draws on Frenk et al. 2003.

6. This section draws mostly on Bitrán and Urcullo (2007) and Olavarría (2005).

7. There are two basic kinds of ISAPREs, open and closed. Open ISAPREs compete with each other for beneficiaries from the general population, and most are for-profit. Closed ISAPREs belong to large companies in the mining, oil, steel, and other industries and admit as beneficiaries only their respective companies' employees and dependents. By December 2005, the entire ISAPRE market had 2,673,409 beneficiaries, 94.6 percent of them from open ISAPREs and the remainder from closed ones.

8. Colombia's Law 100 health reform also makes health benefits explicit.

9. Reportedly, the World Bank sought to promote a model in which those three functions would belong to three separate institutions, a view that the CCSS opposed and won.

10. Government's subsidy for enrolment of the indigent is set at 14 percent of the minimum income required for contributory enrolment. By early 2005 that monthly income was about US$220.

11. Costa Rica's political division comprises 7 provinces, 81 cantons, and 463 districts. The average population of a canton is 50,000 people.

12. During part of Manuel Noriega's government in the late 1980s and early 1990s, Nicaragua temporarily implemented a socialized national health system similar to Cuba's.

REFERENCES

Bitrán, R. 2005. "Health Insurance Issues in East Asia." Report prepared for the World Bank, Santiago, Chile.

Bitrán & Asociados, Econometría S.A. (ESAP). 2001. "Evaluación y Reestructuración de los Procesos, Estrategias y Organismos Públicos y Privados Encargados de la Afiliación. Pago y Recaudo de Aportes al Sistema—Lineamientos de una Propuesta de Fiscalización y Modificación al Proceso de Recaudo." Consultants report prepared for the Government of Colombia, Bogotá, Colombia.

Bitrán, R., R. Muñoz, U. Giedion, and G. Ubilla. 2004. "Equidad e igualdad en los sistemas de salud con aplicación al caso de Colombia" (translation). Monograph presented at the Eurolac conference, Recife, Brazil.

Bitrán, R., and G. Urcullo. 2007. "Good Practice in Expanding Health Care Coverage—Lessons from Reforms in Chile." Report prepared for the World Bank, Santiago, Chile.

Bitrán, R., and C. Vergara. 2001. "Evolución y Determinantes de los Costos Técnicos de las ISAPREs Abiertas." Report prepared for Salud y Futuro, Santiago, Chile.

Bustos, R. n.d. "La Reforma de La Salud en América Latina ¿Qué Camino Seguir? (la experiencia chilena)." Publication of Colegio Médico de Chile, Santiago, Chile.

Carrin, G., and C. James. 2004. "Reaching Universal Coverage via Social Health Insurance: Key Design Features in the Transition Period." Health Financing Policy Issue Paper, World Health Organization, Geneva.

Clark, M. 2002. "Health Sector Reform in Costa Rica: Reinforcing a Public System." Paper prepared for the Woodrow Wilson Center Workshops on the Politics of Education and Health Reforms, Washington, DC.

DANE (Departamento Administrativo Nacional de Estadística). 1993. Encuesta de Caracterización Socioeconómica de la Población Colombiana—CASEN 1993. Bogota, Colombia.

———. 1997. Encuesta de Calidad de Vida 1997. Bogota, Colombia.

———. 2003. Encuesta de Calidad de Vida 2003. Bogota, Colombia.

Escobar, M.L. 2005. "Health Sector Reform in Colombia." 2005. *Development Outreach*. World Bank Institute. http://www.devoutreach.com/may2005/SpecialReport /tabid/1325/Default.aspx.

Frenk, J.J. Sepúlveda, O. Gómez-Dantés, and F. Knaul. 2003. "Evidence-Based Health Policy: Three Generations of Reform in Mexico." *Lancet* 362 (9396): 1667–71.

Gakidou, E., R. Lozano, E. González-Pier, J. Abbott-Klafter, J.T Barofsky, C. Bryson-Cahn, D.M. Fehan, D.K. Lee, H. Hernández Lamas, and C.J.L. Murray. 2007. "Evaluación del impacto de la reforma Mexicana de salud 2001–2006: Un informe inicial." *Salud Pública de México* 49 (Supplement 1): n.p.

Gasparini, L., and L. Tornarolli. 2007. "Labor Informality in Latin America and the Caribbean: Patterns and Trends from Household Survey Microdata." Center for Distributional Labor and Social Studies. Universidad Nacional de La Plata, Argentina.

Gertler, P. 1998. "On the Road to Social Health Insurance: The Asian Experience." *World Development* 26 (4): 717–32.

Giedion, U. 2007. "The Impact of Subsidized Health Insurance on Access, Utilization and Health Status: The Case of Colombia." Monograph prepared for the World Bank, Washington, DC.

Haddad, S., E. Baris, and D. Narayana. 2007. "Safeguarding the Health Sector in Times of Macroeconomic Instability: Policy Lessons for Low- and Middle-Income Countries." Africa World Press. International Development Research Center [/CRDI 2007; http:// books.google.com.pe/books?id=ZyCWEMMszH4C&pg=PA252&lpg=PA252&dq=Hadda d.+Baris.+and+Narayana+2007&source=bl&ots=eG2JL3uEe6&sig=PS8Yid4B-z4WmDO csav2GK3GU90&hl=en&ei=ZfxjTbWfB8P78AbAv9CVDA&sa=X&oi=book_result&ct=r esult&resnum=3&ved=0CB0Q6AEwAg#v=onepage&q=Haddad%2C%20Baris%2C%20 and%20Narayana%202007&f=false.

Hanratty, D., and S. Meditz. 1988. "Colombia: A Country Study." Washington, DC: Library of Congress, Federal Research Division.

IHSD (Institute for Health Sector Development). 1999. *Health Sector Financing in Indonesia*. London: IHSD.

Jack, W. 2000. "Health Insurance Reform in Four Latin American Countries: Theory and Practice." Policy Research Working Paper 2492, World Bank, Washington, DC.

Kahn, C.N., and R.F. Pollack. 2001. "Building a Consensus for Expanding Health Coverage." *Health Affairs* 20 (1): 40–48.

MPS (Ministerio de la Protección Social de Colombia). 2005. "Informe Estadístico." Bogota, Colombia.

OECD (Organisation for Economic Co-operation and Development). 2004. "Proposal for a Taxonomy of Health Insurance." *OECD Study on Private Health Insurance*. OECD: Paris.

Olavarría, M. 2005. "Pobreza, Crecimiento Económico y Políticas Sociales." Editorial Universitaria.

Páez, R., P. Lozada, and M. Villalobos. 1999. "Políticas de Salud y Reforma Sectorial: La Opinión de los Actores de la Salud en el País." Centro de Estudios y Promoción para el Desarrollo Social. CEPAR. Quito, Ecuador.

PAHO (Pan American Health Organization). 2001. "Perfil del Sistema de Servicios de Salud de Ecuador." n.p.

Presidential Health Reform Committee. 2010. "Informe Comisión Presidencial de Salud Diciembre 2010." Report submitted to the President of Chile.

Rodríguez, A. 2006. "La Reforma de Salud en Costa Rica." Unidad de Estudios Especiales Secretaría Ejecutiva de Cepal y GTZ.

Salud Pública de México. 2004. Debate. "Seguro Popular de Salud." *Siete perspectivas* 46 (6): n.p.

Smith, P.C., and S.N. Witter. 2001. "Risk-Pooling in Health Care Finance." Report prepared for the World Bank, Washington, DC.

Superintendencia de Salud. 2005. "Boletín Estadístico 2005." Santiago, Chile.

Ubilla, G., C. Espinoza, and T. Bitrán. 2000. "The Use of Capitation Payment by the Instituto Nicaragüense de Seguridad Social and the Empresas Médicas Previsionales." Bitrán y Asociados and Partnerships for Health Reform Project. Abt Associates Inc. Cambridge, Mass.

Vallejo, M.C. 2007. "Retos de la Seguridad Social. El Caso de Ecuador." Presentation at the workshop "El Futuro de la Protección Social en América Latina." Government of Chile and International Labor Organization, Santiago.

World Bank. 2000. "Ecuador Poverty Assessment." World Bank, Washington, DC.

———. 2006. "Costa Rica Social Spending and the Poor." World Bank, Washington, DC.

CHAPTER 11

Orient Express in South, East, and Pacific Asia

William C. Hsiao, Alexis Medina, Caroline Ly, and Yohana Dukhan

Despite the diversity across the Asian continent, two dominant paths toward achieving universal coverage through health insurance have emerged. Industrial states such as China, Japan, the Republic of Korea, and Taiwan, China, have followed a traditional path like the one in Western Europe—starting with the formal sector workers then expanding to informal sector workers and the poor. These countries' relative wealth and broad formal sector employment make social health insurance (SHI) viable. Developing countries, notably China, the Philippines, and Thailand, have followed a new path, shaped by their own circumstances, targeting and subsidizing hard-to-reach informal sector workers and the poor from the outset. A particular feature has been the establishment of community-based insurance in several nations, covering the rural population first and then serving as a base for universal coverage later.

The evolution of social health insurance in the Asia region and the successes and failures of selected nations to move toward universal coverage are analyzed in this chapter. The low- and lower-middle-income countries selected for this analysis hold the most valuable and relevant lessons for other developing nations.

INTRODUCTION

Rich diversity characterizes the Asia region, comprising in this discussion the South, East, and Pacific Asia subregions.[1] The region encompasses more than 40 nations where annual per capita incomes range from US$500 in Cambodia to US$38,000 in Singapore; populations range from 21,000 in Palau to 1.3 billion in China; and dominant religions vary from Islam in Indonesia, Hinduism in India, Buddhism in Thailand, and Christianity in the Philippines and Korea. It is a vast region of 3.6 billion people, more than half of the world's population. Two of the continent's nations, China and India, have more than 1 billion people each. Yet many of Asia's nations pursue a common method in financing health care—social health insurance. Only a few nations in the region rely mainly on general tax revenue to finance health care.

Four Asian nations have achieved universal coverage through health insurance in a relatively short period of time, as compared with the histories of Western

European SHI countries (figure 11.1). Japan, the first industrialized nation in the region, adopted Germany's Bismarckian social health insurance system. It set an example for other Asian countries. Most of them embarked on limited mandatory health insurance for civil servants and employees of large companies. When nations such as Korea and Taiwan, China, developed into newly industrialized states, they were able to use this mandatory insurance base to expand health insurance for other groups to achieve universal SHI. Developing countries like Thailand, which has achieved nearly universal coverage, and China and the Philippines, which have successfully expanded coverage to more than 80 percent of their populations, are following a different paradigm from their industrial neighbors. Besides these three nations, other low-income Asian countries experienced serious barriers to scaling up health insurance.

Particular attention is given to Thailand, which has achieved close to universal coverage, and China, which has achieved nearly universal coverage for its 800 million rural dwellers and for more than half of its 500 million urban population. Experience in those countries is contrasted with those in another populous nation, India, which has great difficulty in scaling up its health insurance coverage. The last section in this chapter offers some lessons and conclusions.

FIGURE 11.1   Years to Achieve Universal Health Insurance Coverage, Selected Asian Countries

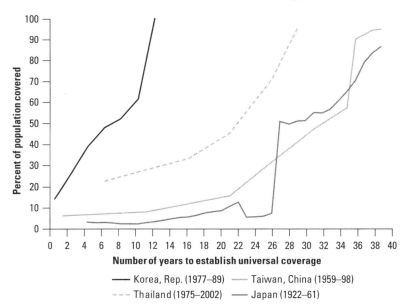

Sources: Tangcharoensathien et al. 2007; Hughes and Leethongdee 2007; Japan Ministry of Internal Affairs and Communications 2008; Yang 2001; Chiang 1997.
Note: Japan's reported insurance data do not include enrolment in schemes for seamen, public servants, and private school teachers and staff. According to these enrolment figures, Japan achieved universal coverage in 1961.

OVERVIEW OF SOCIOECONOMIC, DEMOGRAPHIC, AND HEALTH CONDITIONS

This section describes the socioeconomic, demographic, and health character-istics that are relevant to understanding the challenges and opportunities for scaling up health insurance systems. Although having strong fundamentals can create a favorable environment for scaling up SHI, not all of the necessary pre-conditions such as good governance and strong political will can be as easily captured by quantitative measurements.

Table 11.1 presents summary statistics for selected nations in Asia. It shows the diversity in socioeconomic, demographic, and health conditions.

Economic Growth

Economic growth is a key determinant of ability to scale up health insurance schemes. Asia has experienced overall rapid growth in the past few years, led by China's and India's average annual expansion of 9 percent in the past five years. This growth has not been monolithic. A number of smaller countries (with pop-ulations of less than 1.5 million people) experienced average negative economic growth in the same period.

Overall, the region's economic growth creates favorable conditions for scaling up health insurance in certain countries. Gottret and Schieber (2006) identified some preconditions for scaling up SHI, common to most of Asia, such as increas-ing political stability, high administrative capacity, space for increasing taxation and labor costs, and rapid growth of formal sector employment. The size of the informal sector and quality of the health care infrastructure vary widely, how-ever, not just across the region but within countries. Health issues range from lack of access to care and poor sanitation problems endemic among the poor to chronic diseases such as diabetes and heart disease more common among the wealthy.

The World Bank's income categories provide a means to illustrate commonali-ties found among the countries' socioeconomic, demographic, and health condi-tions. As expected, categorizing Asian countries by income group reveals trends in health status and socioeconomic characteristics similar to other non-Asian countries within the same income category (table 11.2). But there are further differences between the South Asia (SA) and East and Pacific Asia (EAP) Regions.

Social indicators can indicate the degree to which certain preconditions for scaling up health insurance can be met. For example, the overall adult literacy rate is high across Asia. However, some low-income countries such as Papua New Guinea and in South Asia have a less than 60 percent literacy rate. A high degree of education provides a foundation not only for the health workforce but also for the administrative capacity to run an SHI program.

Inequalities within countries affect the disease burden, readiness to income cross-subsidize insurance premiums, and overall health care financing struc-ture. For example, Cambodia has a high rate of poverty, with 66 percent of the

TABLE 11.1 Socioeconomic, Demographic, and Health Conditions, Selected Asian Countries

	East Asia and Pacific Region	China	Indonesia	Japan	Korea, Rep.	Philippines	Taiwan, China	Thailand	South Asia Region	India
Demography (2006)										
Population, total (million)	1,898.9	1,311.8	223.0	127.6	48.4	84.6	22.8	64.7	1,499.4	1,109.8
Population ages 0–14 (% of total)	23.5	20.9	28.0	13.9	18.1	34.6	—	23.5	33.4	31.6
Population growth (annual %)	0.77	0.6	1.1	–0.2	0.3	1.8	0.2	0.8	1.6	1.4
Fertility rate (number of births per woman)	2.0	1.8	2.2	1.3	1.1	3.3	1.1	1.8	2.8	2.5
Rural population (% of total)	57.6	58.7	50.8	34.0	19.0	36.6	—	67.4	—	71.0
Economy (2006)										
GNI per capita, Atlas method (current US$)	1,863	2,010	1,420	38,410	17,690	1,420	17,230	2,990	766	820
GDP growth (annual %)	9.4	10.7	5.5	2.2	5.0	5.4	4.6	5.0	8.6	9.2
Inflation (annual % CPI)	—	1.5	13.1	0.2	2.2	6.2	0.4	4.6	—	5.8
Social and infrastructure (2004)										
Literacy rate, adult total (% of people ages 15 and above)	91 (2005)	—	90	—	—	93 (2003)	—	—	58 (2005)	61 (2001)
Improved sanitation facilities (% of population with access)	50.6	44	55	100	—	72	—	99	37.2	33
Health status and health care (2005)										
Life expectancy at birth (years)	70.7	71.8	67.8	82.1	77.6	71.0	76.5	70.9	63.5	63.5
Infant mortality rate (per 1,000 live births)	26.4	23	28	3	5	25	—	18	62.0	56
Prevalence of HIV/AIDS (% of 15–49 year olds)	0.20	0.08	0.13	0.10	0.10	0.10	—	1.40	0.72	0.92

Immunization, DTP3 (% of children ages 12–23 months)	83.7	87	70	99	96	79	—	98	65.1	59
Physicians (per 1,000 people) 2004	—	1.06 (2001)	0.13 (2003)	—	1.57 (2003)	0.58 (2000)	—	0.37 (2000)	0.6	0.6
Births attended by skilled health staff (% of total)	86.9	97.3 (2004)	71.5 (2004)	—	—	—	—	—	37.2	—
Health financing (2004)										
Health expenditure per capita (current US$)	61.6	70.5	32.5	2,831.1	787	36.1	—	88.1	27.3	31.4
Health expenditure, total (% of GDP)	4.4	4.7	2.8	7.8	5.6	3.4	—	3.5	4.6	5
Health expenditure, public (% of total government spending)	—	10.1	5	—	10.3	6.3	—	11.2	—	2.9
Health expenditure, private (% of total health expenditure)	60.2	62.0	65.8	19	48.6	60.2	—	35.3	81.2	82.7
Out-of-pocket health expenditure (% of private expenditure on health)	87.6	86.5	74.7	93.4	76	77.9	—	74.7	93.6	93.8
Prepaid plans and risk pooling (% of private health spending)	—	5.5	5.9	1.9	7.1	12.1	—	16.5	—	0.8
Social security expenditure on health (% of public health spending)	—	55.2	10.8	80.0	79.2	23.8	—	10.2	—	5.6
External resources (% of total health expenditure)	—	0.1	1.3	0	0	3.6	—	0.3	—	0.5
Kakwani index	—	0.0404 (2000)	0.1729 (2001)	0.0688 (1998)	0.0239 (2000)	0.1631 (1999)	0.0119 (2000)	0.1972 (2002)	—	—

Sources: WHO 2002a; World Bank 2008a.

Note: — = not available.

TABLE 11.2   Income Groups, Selected Asian Countries, 2006

Low-income (<US$935)	Lower-middle-income (US$936–US$3,705)	Upper-middle-income (US$3,706–$US11,455)	High-income (>$11,455)
Bangladesh	Bhutan	Malaysia	Australia
Cambodia	China	Palau	Brunei Darussalam
India	Fiji		Hong Kong SAR, China
Kiribati	Indonesia		Japan
Lao PDR	Maldives		Korea, Rep.
Mongolia	Marshall Islands		Macao SAR, China
Nepal	Micronesia, Fed. Sts.		New Zealand
Pakistan	Philippines		Singapore
Papua New Guinea	Samoa		
Solomon Islands	Sri Lanka		
Timor-Leste	Thailand		
Vietnam	Tonga		
	Vanuatu		

Source: World Bank 2008a.

population living on less than US$1 a day. This large, impoverished population could not be expected to pay into an SHI system. The degree of inequality, as measured by the Gini coefficient, increases with income in developing Asian countries (table 11.3), perhaps due to the associated high economic growth rates experienced across the lower-middle-income countries such as China.

Economic Development and Health Financing

Even after controlling for income, differences persist between the SA and EAP Regions (table 11.4). EAP has a relatively high life expectancy, considering its low expenditures on health and income, compared with wealthier Regions such as Eastern Europe and Central Asia (ECA), Middle East and North Africa (MENA), and Latin America and the Caribbean (LAC). The SA Region comprises fewer countries, all of them in the low- and lower-middle-income categories.

Burden of Disease

The disease burden varies by income and region.[2] Each country has to decide, in the light of its particular disease burden, how its health financing system should pay for treatment and promote prevention. Broadly, SA experiences higher overall death rates and lost disability-adjusted life years (DALYs) than does EAP; and the absolute burden of diseases in both regional groups lightens with rising income. Noncommunicable diseases, such as heart and cerebrovascular diseases, are the leading causes of morbidity and mortality in EAP and SA, accounting for

TABLE 11.3   Urbanization, Poverty, and Inequity Rates, by Income and Region

Item	Low-income		Lower-middle-income		Upper-middle-income	High-income
	EAP	SA	EAP	SA	All	All
Literacy rate (%)	85.5	59.2	91.0	90.8	88.7	89.4
Population living below the poverty line (% living on < US$1 per day)	49.7	34.9	9.5	5.6	—	—
Gini coefficient	30.6–41.7		34.3–46.9		—	—
Revenues as a percentage of GDP	9.7	12.6	10.4	16.4	—	24.5

Source: World Bank 2008a.
Note: Population-weighted averages. EAP = East and Pacific Asia; SA = South Asia; — = not available.

TABLE 11.4   Broad Comparison of Developing-Country Regions

Item	EAP	SA	SSA	ECA	MENA	LAC
GDP per capita, 2006 (constant 2000 US$)	1,358.2	564.3	560.7	2,529.1	1,802.3	4,155.1
Life expectancy at birth, 2006 (years)	70.7	63.9	49.0	69.0	69.5	72.7
Health expenditure per capita, 2005 (current US$)	70.3	30.9	49.3	279.0	122.9	328.6

Source: World Bank 2008a.
Note: EAP = East and Pacific Asia; ECA = Eastern Europe and Central Asia; LAC = Latin America and the Caribbean; MENA = Middle East and North Africa; SA = South Asia; SSA = Sub-Saharan Africa.

more than half of deaths in those Regions. Communicable, maternal, perinatal, and nutritional conditions are most prevalent in low-income countries and afflict SA more than EAP. But unlike noncommunicable diseases, the burden of these conditions drastically improves as income rises (table 11.5).

There are wide differences not only between the EAP and SA Regions but within the Regions, particularly in low-income EAP, which consists of Pacific islands, poor Southeast Asian nations, and Mongolia. There is a wide variance in the disease burden in EAP low-income countries. For example, Cambodia and the Lao People's Democratic Republic face some of the Region's highest rates of morbidity and mortality due to HIV/AIDS and diarrheal disease, respectively. But neighboring Vietnam experiences the lowest morbidity and mortality rates within the low-income country group. Mongolia, although characterized as a low-income country, maintains a different trend in disease burden from its EAP cohort. It has the lowest death rate from respiratory infection and highest death rate due to cancer.

Inequalities within country health outcomes persist, which help explain how developing countries in EAP and SA have the range of diseases associated with low- and high-socioeconomic groups. Table 11.6 shows wide differences in mortality outcomes in children under 5 (U-5) years of age for selected countries, where data are available.

TABLE 11.5   Age-Standardized Death Rates, by Income Group and Region, 2000

Causes	Low-income		Lower-middle-income		Upper-middle	High-income
	EAP	SA	EAP	SA		
All	1,093	1,290	883	921	832	679
Communicable, maternal, perinatal, and nutritional conditions	299	426	137	125	156	58
Noncommunicable diseases	717	751	668	714	625	552

Source: Authors.
Note: Deaths per 100,000 people, population weighted averages. EAP = East and Pacific Asia; SA = South Asia.

TABLE 11.6   Intracountry U-5 Mortality Inequality

Country	Absolute difference between lowest-highest wealth quintile in U-5 mortality
Bangladesh	49.6 (2004)
Cambodia	91.2 (2000)
India	95.8 (1998/9)
Indonesia	54.9 (2002/3)
Nepal	62.2 (2001)
Philippines	45.7 (2003)
Vietnam	37.1 (2002)

Source: Gwatkin et al. 2007.
Note: U-5 = under 5 years of age.

Health Financing

Resources for the health sector and mechanisms to target resources for health insurance increase with income (table 11.7). There are, however, still variations in health expenditures between the EAP and SA Regions (figure 11.2). Low-income countries in EAP allocate more public resources to the health sector and are less reliant on out-of-pocket (OOP) expenditures than are low-income countries in SA. These differences are less stark in the lower-middle-income countries where SA countries provide more public resources for the health sector. Donor aid provides greater resources for health in the low-income countries such as Cambodia, where aid accounts for 29 percent of total health expenditures (THE). As income increases, external resources become less significant. Other health financing mechanisms such as private pre-paid mechanisms and social health insurance contribute an increasing amount to the total health expenditures as income rises. This is the case in the EAP countries where, in low- and lower-middle-income groups, private insurance and SHI contribute more to their THE than in SA countries. However, the degree of equity in revenue collection for health is less clear.

TABLE 11.7   Health Expenditures, by Income Group and Region

Item	Low-income		Lower-middle-income		Upper-middle-income	High-income
	EAP	SA	EAP	SA		
Health expenditure per capita, 2005 (current US$)	34.9	30.7	72.2	54.9	222.4	2,356.5
Health expenditure, public (% of GDP)	1.8	0.9	1.7	2.0	1.9	5.5
Health expenditure, public (% of government expenditure)	6.4	3.6	2.2	7.9	7.0	15.3
Health expenditure, total (% of GDP)	5.9	4.5	4.2	4.2	4.2	7.4
OOP expenditure (% of THE)	57.7	74.9	48.8	45.5	41.8	20.4

Source: World Bank 2006b.
Note: Weighted average. EAP = East and Pacific Asia; SA = South Asia; OOP = out-of-pocket; THE = total health expenditure.

FIGURE 11.2   Health Financing Structure, Selected Asian Countries, 2004

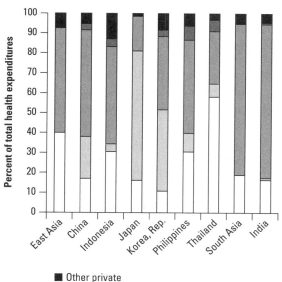

■ Other private
■ Private pre-paid plans
▨ Out-of-pocket expenditures
▢ Social security expenditures on health
□ Public expenditures without social security

Sources: WHO Statistical Information System; World Bank World Development Indicators.
Note: "East Asia" and "South Asia" aggregate social security expenditures with public expenditures.

In an analysis of the equity in revenue collection of health systems across Asia, O'Donnell and others (2008) examined the different revenue sources (direct taxes, indirect taxes, social insurance, private insurance, and out-of-pocket expenditures) across 13 Asian countries. They found a general progressivity in the health financing systems primarily in low- and middle-income countries. High-income countries, primarily Japan, Korea, and Taiwan, China, had a somewhat regressive system because of greater reliance on social insurance which, as found in European systems, tends to be less progressive than general revenue financed systems. Out-of-pocket payments are made mostly by better-off households in low- and middle-income countries either because of policies that targeted the poor, as in Indonesia and Thailand, or because of the exclusion of the poor from health services utilization due to high costs of out-of-pocket payments.

ROLE OF PRIVATE INSURANCE IN SCALING UP

Private insurance, differentiated by commercial and nonprofit organizations, is considered in terms of its relationship with SHI programs in this chapter. It provides health care financing, in addition to occasionally administering SHI.

Commercial insurers have not played a dominant role in financing health care in developing countries—for obvious reasons. First, only a very small portion of the population in low- and lower-middle-income nations can afford to buy individual or group health insurance from commercial insurance companies. The purchasers are usually society's most affluent members and employees of banks and multinational corporations. Second, commercial insurance companies find operating in developing countries very difficult because of poor licensing standards and regulations for practitioners, clinics, and hospitals and therefore the high risk of overtreatment of patients and fraudulent claims that can undermine the insurer's financial viability. Usually, when commercial insurance plans do exist, they operate like closed-panel health maintenance organizations (HMOs) with their own clinics and hospitals (or contract with only the few best hospitals in the country), insure only medical services abroad, or pay a fixed sum per day of hospitalization.

Commercial insurance companies have served as third-party administrators for SHI in a few Asian countries. Governments, when their capacity to administer SHI is weak, turn to commercial companies. This is the case in India.

Nonprofit insurance organizations usually operate as community-based, rather than nationwide, plans. These nonprofits have played an important role in scaling up SHI in some nations. China's previous form of community-based plan—the Cooperative Medical System (CMS) helped scale up the current Chinese rural health insurance scheme. The CMS educated people about risk pooling and enabled the current insurance plan to scale up quickly. The history of Japan's community-based plans illustrates the critical role nonprofits have in scaling up insurance.

The Japanese Jyorei system, a community-based financing scheme, played a major role in extending SHI to Japanese farmers. The Jyorei system began in 1835 in the village of Kamisaigo. After a succession of poor harvests threatened doctors' livelihoods because patients were unable to pay for care, doctors petitioned their village leaders to intervene to protect their incomes. The leaders responded by creating the Jyorei system. Under this system, villagers pre-paid a contribution in rice, depending on the size of their income. In return, they were entitled to free basic health care, including consultations, curative services, disease control and prevention, and drugs, with no copayments. Providers signed a contract agreeing to a fixed salary to be paid in rice and were given free lodging in the village. The Jyorei system was an immediate success, and by 1897 this type of mechanism had spread to more than half of the neighboring villages in Kamisaigo's district and neighboring districts (Ogawa et al. 2003).

The success of the Jyorei system can be largely attributed to three factors. First of all, villages already had a detailed tax collection system in place, and the revenue was earmarked for specific purposes, creating a system of accountability. This familiarity with a tax system and trust in the government made it easy to levy and earmark an additional tax for health. Village leaders had full authority over the scheme and had demonstrated their capacity to administer programs similar to the Jyorei. Second, social capital such as social norms, reciprocity, and mutual assistance in the villages was strong enough to curb any major problems of moral hazard. Even without copayments to discourage excess spending, health expenditures remained low after the program began. Third, all stakeholders benefited from the Jyorei system. Doctors were given a stable and generous salary, and villagers received the health care from their usual providers and were comfortable with the idea of subsidizing their neighbors through redistribution. Moreover, the collection of the rice premium took place at times of the year when households traditionally had a large supply of rice on hand (Ogawa et al. 2003).

The Jyorei system underwent several changes throughout the 19th and early 20th centuries, including the introduction of a household consulting fee in addition to the rice premium, a gradual shift to cash payments instead of rice payments, and an expansion of the benefit to include discounts on some hospitalization fees (Ogawa et al. 2003).

In 1938 when Japan passed the National Citizen's Health Insurance Law, the Jyorei system formed the basis for covering farmers and informal sector workers on a voluntary basis while the government subsidized the premiums for the poor. Enrolment became mandatory in 1948 (Ogawa et al. 2003).

BARRIERS TO SCALING UP

To overcome barriers to health insurance coverage for all individuals, different nations have devised different approaches. The traditional path, developed in Europe and Latin America, starts by insuring government workers then expands to include formal sector workers. As a nation industrializes and most workers become employed in the formal sector, SHI then expands to cover informal sector workers, farmers, and the poor by having the government subsidize their enrolment premiums.

The first two steps are straightforward: civil servants and formal sector workers are easy to reach because they are associated with large companies or organizations that have employment and earnings records that can be used for enrolment and premium collection. Formal sector workers are also among society's better-paid and better-educated workers and can thus afford insurance premiums and understand the benefits of joining an insurance scheme. Once these two groups are covered, however, countries are faced with the challenge of extending insurance to informal sector workers, the elderly, the poor, and the unemployed. These groups are much more difficult to insure. They are usually not affiliated with any organization that would enroll them and collect their premiums. Each individual has to be reached. Moreover, they likely have low incomes and cannot afford to pay the insurance premiums. As a result, two of the most basic factors affecting the expansion of health insurance coverage are the size of the informal sector and the incentives that government offers to ensure enrolment in the insurance plan.

Prior to 1990, most Asian countries followed the traditional European path. Since then, Asian nations have been following a different paradigm. Their primary goal is first to expand the number of people covered, and poor and informal sector workers often receive a smaller benefits package than formal sector workers during this stage. Later, the benefits packages are gradually equalized.

The National Context

The national context in which a health insurance program will operate intrinsically affects the plan to attain universal coverage and establish sustainable SHI. The factors described in this section are not directly related to health or government but are part of each country's economic and social landscape.

Economic Development and Growth Rate

A nation's economic capacity and growth rate are good predictors of its ability to scale up an SHI program. Both Japan and Taiwan, China, were able to achieve universal coverage only after their per capita GDPs had reached US$11,900 and US$7,900,[3] respectively. Meanwhile, Indonesia, with one of the lowest coverage rates in Asia at 41 percent, also has one of the lowest per capita GDPs in the region. One of the most effective ways of extending coverage beyond civil servants and formal sector workers is for the government to subsidize premium payments for low-income, informal sector workers. In developing countries like China and Indonesia, such workers account for more than half of the total population. Consequently, specific targeting of these workers can allow them to be covered as quickly and easily as civil servants and formal sector workers. Whether such targeting is financially and administratively possible, however, largely depends on economic conditions within the country and the government's capacity to collect tax revenues and manage complex programs. Thus, it is not surprising that few of the low-income Asian countries have achieved nearly universal coverage. Many that are attempting it are facing a number of barriers related to their economic capacity.

Indigenous Medicine

Before the introduction of Western medicine in the late 19th century, most Asians relied on indigenous medicine such as traditional Chinese medicine in China, Taiwan, Korea, and Japan and Ayurvedic medicine in Bangladesh, India, and Pakistan. These indigenous medicines, developed over thousands of years, relied largely on herbal medicines, nutritional supplements, massage, meditation, acupuncture, and other treatments. Many Asians still rely on traditional medicine for primary care treatment of minor and chronic illnesses.

Indigenous medicine had a strong influence on the way governments would finance health care. Historically, the government played little role in financing health care dominated by indigenous medicine. Traditional medicine involves few formal standards for herbal drugs or licensing requirements for practitioners upon which insurance plans rely, inhibiting the development of health insurance. Also, herbal medicine is usually inexpensive—farmers can grow herbs on their own land. When the colonial powers brought Western medicine to Asian countries to treat their expatriate staff, they financed their medical services. As these Western clinics and hospitals opened their services to local patients, the local patients had to pay out of pocket. However, Western drugs and procedures tended to be more expensive than traditional medicine. Subsequently, colonial powers established primitive forms of their own countries' health financing methods in their colonies. For examples, the United Kingdom established a primitive National Health Service in India, Hong Kong, and Malaysia, financed by tax revenues. The Netherlands established health insurance for civil servants in Indonesia, financed by premium income. However, these organized financing methods funded only Western medicine. It seems that unless a nation rich in indigenous medical practices can standardize and formally organize its indigenous medicine into its health care delivery system (as China and Taiwan have done), scaling up health insurance for primary care would encounter major difficulties.

Political Commitment and Government Capacity

Political commitment to providing universal coverage may well be the most important factor in scaling up. The political environment, of course, varies among nations. Some political leaders choose universal SHI as a political strategy to gain popular support, as in China and Thailand. In Thailand, a candidate for prime minister promised universal SHI to gain the support of rural voters. Once elected, he delivered on his campaign promise and quickly enacted the National Health Insurance Act. This mandated enrolment in a health insurance scheme, with the government paying the premium for pensioners, the poor, farmers, and informal sector workers. Thailand has since achieved nearly 100 percent coverage, proving that swift and firm government action can lead to real results. Similarly in China, increased social unrest precipitated the government to introduce a new, local government–managed voluntary health insurance scheme in 2002 called the New Cooperative Medical Scheme (NCMS). Within five years, NCMS had grown to cover more than 90 percent of China's rural population. In contrast, in Indonesia, legislation for the creation and implementation of a new universal health insurance scheme was drafted in 2004. Since then, it has stagnated in the legislature, as government infighting prevents it from being passed into law. The lesson, perhaps, is that the political leaders must be fully convinced of the importance of SHI before effective political action will be taken. Passive or indifferent governments will not succeed in pushing through the necessary legislation or implementing it effectively.

Government capacity is another important factor in the expansion of a universal SHI plan. Unstable or weak governments as in Cambodia, India, Lao PDR, and Pakistan do not have the prerequisites in place to attempt universal SHI. They not only suffer from lack of economic resources but they also have limited government capacity to set up the critical organizations for an SHI system. Success depends on a competent administration to define the parameters of the scheme, such as the scope of the benefits package and the design of a means-testing system. The administration also needs to be able to set and enforce regulations. Administrative capacity and regulatory capacity are the two critical facets to overall government capacity.

Administrative capacity is an indicator of how well the government is able to design and operate the health insurance program. A government that already operates one or more social security programs is likely to be experienced in the challenges posed generally by health insurance schemes, such as how to identify and define those eligible for government subsidies and assistance. For example, when Japan began its community health financing schemes, it already had an effective tax collection system in place with collected funds earmarked for specific public services. As a result, it was easy for the government to begin to collect insurance premiums and earmark them for health.

Administrative capacity is also determined by the skill set of the labor force. A labor force that possesses the tools, such as bookkeeping and banking, needed to operate an insurance program is likely to be able to keep the program running smoothly. Thailand's creation of a new health insurance scheme is an excellent example of the importance of an educated and experienced labor force. Thailand was able to learn from the means-testing failures of its old Medical Welfare Scheme and went on to create a new and improved information system for its 30 baht scheme in 2001. Moreover, an administration composed of technically skilled workers will also be able to conduct the actuarial estimates that are essential for the long-run sustainability of the insurance scheme. In Indonesia, for example, a lack of government employees skilled in actuarial analysis led HMOs to set premiums well below cost, thus threatening their financial sustainability and severely lowering their quality of care. India is another country in which the government lacks the capacity to administer SHI. Consequently, India turned to commercial insurers for urban health insurance and to nongovernmental organizations (NGOs) for rural health insurance.

Regulatory capacity refers to the government's ability to pass and enforce laws and regulations. To survive, a health insurance scheme must have a funding base that is broad enough to support the health costs of its insured. A mandatory scheme is theoretically guaranteed a funding base composed of everyone in the eligible population, regardless of age and health status. If, however, the government is unable to enforce its mandate, adverse selection becomes a serious problem. Individuals expecting low health costs will not enroll in the scheme. This erodes the funding base while constant health expenditures threaten the plan's long-run sustainability. Low regulatory capacity has crippled the Jamsostek insurance scheme for private, formal sector employees in Indonesia. Jamsostek is a mandatory scheme, with one exception: if an employer can prove it offers its employees alternative enrolment in a private scheme of equal or better quality, it can opt out of the scheme. Because this rule is not enforced, however, many employers opt out without offering alternative coverage, thus cutting labor costs and maintaining a higher profit margin. Jamsostek has been unable to scale up, and currently it covers only 3 percent of the population.

Capacity to regulate health practitioners who provide services for the insurance scheme is also critical. The compliance—or lack thereof—of health care providers, the ground-level executors of insurance schemes, can determine the success of the scheme. If a scheme offers demand-side subsidies by, for example, reimbursing patients for a fixed amount of their health expenses, providers might raise their fees and balance bill the patients to cover costs or earn additional profits, as in the Philippines' Medicare scheme. Doing so harms patients not only from higher costs but also from loss of the intended financial protection under SHI. In the Philippines, so few of the Medicare benefits reached patients that enrolment as a percentage of the employed population began to decline, even though Medicare was a mandatory scheme. In addition to defeating the purpose of health insurance, such unfettered provider behavior threatens the long-run financial sustainability of the insurance scheme. Government monitoring and regulation can help curb such harmful practices.

Administration of Social Health Insurance

Bureaucracy is often one of the main barriers to change, and the case of social health insurance is no exception. How the government is organized, especially in the health sector, has an enormous effect on the success or failure of plans for a new or expanded insurance scheme.

One important organizational factor is the institution created or appointed to manage the social health insurance scheme. Both public and private institutions can be plagued by agency problems, in which they do not act, as they should, as an agent for the government, but instead pursue their own interests. The government may wish to achieve equal health care for all, while the institution is simply looking to build up its funds. This has happened in China with the Ministry of Labor and Social Security (MOLSS), which controls the social insurance fund for formal sector workers in urban areas. The MOLSS is supposed to contract with the best-qualified and most efficient providers, but in reality cares only about balancing the books. In other cases, the institution may be influenced by powerful interest groups whose goals conflict with those of the government. Again turning to China for an example, the Chinese Ministry of Health is greatly influenced by public hospitals and physicians and puts their interests ahead of the patients' interests. As a result, the ministry is unwilling to enact and implement policies that may put financial pressure on providers, such as performance-based pay or capitation.

Another crucial organizational factor is how the government chooses to consolidate or unify pre-existing insurance schemes. China, Thailand, and several other Asian countries have stagnated at this stage. For equity and administrative efficiency reasons, SHI should have a uniform benefits package, unified administration, and standardized premiums. Consolidation can be extremely difficult when different schemes offer different benefits packages and provider payment systems. In Indonesia, for example, civil servants are entitled to comprehensive care at public facilities, while private employees are offered a much-narrower benefits package but have a choice of either public or private facilities. Doctors serving informal sector workers are paid by capitation, while doctors serving formal sector workers are paid fees for service. Compare this situation with that of China, which faced the challenge of merging different schemes. But insurance schemes for both formal and informal sector workers in the urban areas offer similar benefits packages, provider payment is the same, and a national guideline emphasizes coverage of outpatient care. China will likely make a smoother transition to a unified social insurance administration than will Indonesia.

The role of the private sector in health can also affect the scaling-up process. Private insurers can play an important role in the expansion of coverage. Both India and Indonesia have been increasing their reliance on the private insurance market as a way of increasing national coverage. Neither country has been particularly successful in its efforts to reach the poor through private insurers. Indonesia's JPKM program has had a particularly dismal experience, with national enrolment under 0.6 percent. This is largely because JPKM plans (HMOs) are tasked with the nearly impossible task of trying to sell insurance to the poor and making a profit at the same time. India has been somewhat more successful, perhaps because of its many, strong, grassroots NGOs. Both countries are characterized by weak governments and lack of national unity on health issues. This may be why they are turning to the private sector more than are other Asian countries with stronger governments and more clearly defined health goals and priorities.

Evasion

One of the basic barriers to scaling up a health insurance scheme is simply that some people do not want to join. As a result, evasion and adverse selection are two of the most critical problems in expanding and sustaining SHI. Evasion can occur for a variety of reasons. Most often, people feel that the expected benefits do not outweigh the costs. This may be because they do not trust the delivery system or government. In China, for example, rural villagers are reluctant to turn their earnings over to local government officials who have a history of corruption. It is therefore unsurprising that 80 percent of the premiums paid by the enrollees for the China rural health insurance scheme are returned to individuals in the form of individual health savings accounts.

Two additional reasons people may choose not to enroll in an SHI scheme are that they are unhappy with the benefits package or they cannot afford the premium. Because the two are closely related, governments and insurance companies must tread carefully to strike a balance between desirability and affordability. Too narrow a benefits package is often seen as "not worth it," while too generous a package is likely to be unaffordable or unsustainable in the long run. The experience of the Thai Voluntary Health Card Scheme is a perfect example of how these two extremes can lead to the failure of an insurance scheme. The health card scheme aimed to enroll informal sector workers by selling them a card that entitled them to certain health benefits, free of charge. In its first incarnation, the benefits offered were so narrow that enrolment was quite low, and the plan was quickly abandoned as a failure. In its second incarnation eight years later, the government tried to create a more attractive benefits package, but the cost of providing these benefits exceeded the price charged for the card, and the scheme went bankrupt. For an insurance scheme to be successful there has to be a dialogue between the government and the people so that individual preferences can be met. A strong civil society can help foster such dialogue.

The social dynamic of an area can also cause people to hesitate before joining a risk-pooling scheme. Higher-income individuals may not want to subsidize the care of their lower-income neighbors by pooling their money in an insurance fund. One of the reasons the Japanese Jyorei system of community financing was so successful was the spirit of social solidarity already prevalent in Japanese villages. Villagers already participated in other community redistribution schemes and were willing to apply the same principle to health care.

Even when health insurance enrolment is mandatory, evasion can still be a serious problem. In the formal sector, employers and workers may underreport salaries in order to pay a lower premium, thus threatening the long-run financial sustainability of a scheme. Workers and employers will also take advantage of weak enforcement and not enroll in the scheme at all, as in

Indonesia. In that country, an estimated 86 percent of those eligible for coverage in the national scheme have taken advantage of an opt-out clause in the legislation. This can lead to problems of adverse selection, whereby the young and healthy evade enrolment while the elderly and sick enroll. Because care for the latter groups is more expensive, the scheme may quickly fall into bankruptcy. This was a problem under the Thai Voluntary Health Card Scheme. Only individuals who expected an expensive health event purchased the card, driving up costs and contributing to the scheme's ultimate failure. Evasion and adverse selection are especially severe when extending insurance to informal sector workers. Because these workers shift jobs frequently and seldom have documented earnings records, it is easy for them to operate under the radar of scheme managers.

FACTORS ENABLING DEVELOPED ASIAN COUNTRIES TO SCALE UP

Three advanced economies in Asia are studied in this section to see how they scaled up. All three attained universal coverage when they became industrialized states with high per capita incomes and small informal sectors, and their governments had enough tax revenues to subsidize the premium for a large part of the population. Japan's experience is especially noteworthy due to its long history.

Japan

The historical development of Japan's social health insurance began with the Jyorei scheme, a community health insurance scheme established in 1835 (table 11.8). The social principles and the strong capacity of Japanese village leaders allowed this scheme to succeed and be replicated in other villages. As the nation became more industrialized in the 1920s, workers in the formal sector demanded greater social security. Japan adopted the Bismarckian SHI model, relying on many private nonprofit insurance funds, including industrial guilds, cooperatives, municipals, and workers' unions. The central government also established an insurance fund for the poor, small employers, and pensioners. Each insurance fund was responsible for enrolling its target population on a voluntary basis. Nonetheless, Japan found its greatest difficulty in achieving universal coverage was in enrolling the poor, pensioners, and the informal sector workers. Although the National Law was passed in 1938, government resources were siphoned off to the war, and the development of SHI languished.

In 1948, while still suffering from the devastation of World War II, Japan passed a new law, mandating health insurance coverage. To attain universal coverage, the government recognized it had to subsidize premiums for informal workers, pensioners, the unemployed, and other similar groups. Thirteen years later in 1961, Japan had the resources needed to subsidize 50 percent of their premiums, and universal coverage was achieved.

TABLE 11.8   Japan: Timeline of Historical Development of Social Health Insurance

Date	Event	Economic indicators
1835	First Jyorei scheme established in one village in Munakata district.	GDP per capita (1990 GK): 669
1891	Introduction of westernized medicine leads to medical cost escalation, exerting pressure on pre-payment scheme. Interest in Jyorei scheme increased.	GDP per capita (1990 GK): 956
1897	Scheme expanded to 37 out of 60 villages in Munakata district and to surrounding districts.	GDP per capita (1990 GK): 1,062
1916	Japan Medical Association established. Physicians supported Jyorei scheme.	GDP per capita (1990 GK): 1,387
1920s	Offshoot schemes developed.	GDP per capita (1990 GK): 1,696–2,026
1938	National Citizen's Health Insurance (CHI) Law and Fund established, incorporating Jyorei scheme. Voluntary enrolment.	GDP per capita (1990 GK): 2,449
1948	National CHI Law, mandating health insurance, was passed after the devastation of WWII. Administration of General Douglas MacArthur encouraged Japanese Parliament to pass the law.	GDP per capita (1990 GK): 1,725
1961	Achieved universal coverage.	GDP per capita (1990 GK): 7,904

Sources: Maddison 2008; World Bank 2008a; Ogawa et al. 2003.
Note: 1990 GK is the International Geary-Khamis dollar, equivalent to the 1990 U.S. dollar in purchasing power.

Currently, a third of Japanese are covered by "society-managed" health insurance funds that insure employees of large companies. Another 27 percent are insured by municipal and other health insurance funds that are responsible for covering government workers and employees of small companies. These groups of workers and their employers pay the full premium without any government subsidy. The other 40 percent of Japanese are covered under a central government insurance plan where their premiums, on average, are subsidized 50 percent (Ogawa et al. 2003).

The Republic of Korea

The Republic of Korea was established as an independent nation after World War II. When Korea became a newly industrialized nation in the early 1970s, workers demanded greater social security. Korea inaugurated a universal SHI scheme in 1976 with a plan to achieve universal coverage in 12 years through a phased process of expanding coverage across different population groups. Beginning with a platform of available voluntary coverage for health insurance, Korea started making health insurance compulsory for formal sector employees for large companies and then gradually expanding the compulsory requirement to harder-to-reach population groups such as the self-employed and unemployed. Like Japan, it relied on many private nonprofit insurance plans (eventually numbering 1,400) to enroll people, including nonprofit community organizations in the rural areas (Yang 2001).

Learning from other nations' experiences, the Korean government decided to achieve equity by providing everyone with a uniform benefits package and subsidizing premiums for farmers and informal sector workers. Korea achieved universal coverage on schedule (table 11.9). However, it found that numerous private nonprofit plans are administratively inefficient and that portability between plans confuses people. Hence, a decade after achieving universal coverage, Korea decided to consolidate all the plans into one government-run plan. However, the president expended significant political capital to overcome the strong resistance from the private plans to merge.

TABLE 11.9   Korea, Rep.: Timeline of Insurance Expansion

Date	Event	Economic indicators
1963	Health Insurance Act of 1963 aims at voluntary coverage.	GDP per capita (2000 USD): 1,204
1976	Korea launches 12-year plan to achieve SHI.	GDP per capita (2000 USD): 2,709
1977	Makes enrolment in health insurance compulsory for firms with more than 500 employees.	GDP per capita (2000 USD): 2,934
1979	Compulsory enrolment for civil servants and schoolteachers.	GDP per capita (2000 USD): 3,322
1980	Expansion to military personnel and pensioners.	GDP per capita (2000 USD): 3,221
1981	Occupational health insurance schemes for organized self-employed workers.	GDP per capita (2000 USD): 3,367
1983	Compulsory insurance extended to firms with more than 16 employees.	GDP per capita (2000 USD): 3,884
1988	Rural regional health insurance for rural farmers and fishermen.	GDP per capita (2000 USD): 5,798
1989	Marks universal coverage with expansion through urban regional health insurance program for remaining self-employed and unemployed.	GDP per capita (2000 USD): 6,130

Sources: Yang 2001; World Bank 2008a.

Taiwan, China

Health insurance barely existed in Taiwan until the Nationalist Government moved from mainland China to Taiwan in 1949 (table 11.10). The government also transplanted the mandatory health insurance programs for civil servants and formal sector workers from the mainland to Taiwan. Labor Insurance and

TABLE 11.10   Taiwan, China: Timeline of Insurance Expansion

Date	Event
1949	Nationalist Government moves to Taiwan from mainland China bringing mandatory health insurance for civil servants.
1950	Labor insurance established.
1959	Government employment insurance established.
1985	Government introduces trial farmer's health insurance.
1993	Taiwan mandatory health insurance law passed.

Source: Chiang 1997.

Government Employee Insurance were established in 1950 and 1959, respectively. When Taiwan became a newly industrialized economy in the late 1970s, the noncovered population demanded extension of the SHI benefit to them. However, the government took no action until Taiwan's legitimacy to represent the whole of China was invalidated, and Taiwan was expelled from the United Nations. This chain of events put pressure on the government to pay closer attention to domestic affairs and to gain political support from its citizens. The general public demanded greater social security. Consequently, SHI was expanded to farmers who benefited from heavily subsidized government premiums. The next step was for Taiwan to achieve universal coverage. The government decided to use a three-pronged strategy. First, the government would pay the premiums for the poor and veterans. Second, formal sector workers could choose to cover their parents and extended family members by paying additional premiums. Last, informal sector workers were encouraged to enroll by paying a modest, standard, lump-sum premium unrelated to income. The premium was not adequate to cover the full costs of the informal sector workers and their families, and the deficiency was made up by a government subsidy. Taiwan passed a mandatory health insurance law in 1993 and fully implemented it. Within a year, Taiwan was able to expand the coverage rate from 57 percent to more than 90 percent. Now, Taiwan covers everyone with the same comprehensive benefits package that includes outpatient and inpatient services, drugs, dental care, Chinese traditional medicine, and home nursing visits (Chiang 1997).

SCALING UP IN FIVE LOW- AND LOWER-MIDDLE-INCOME ASIAN COUNTRIES

Scaling-up experiences in the five countries selected in this section illustrate each country's efforts to establish universal SHI, the barriers they confronted, and their success or failure in overcoming the barriers.

Thailand

Aided by a steadily expanding economy, Thailand followed a progressive path to achieving near-universal health insurance coverage, beginning with a government-funded safety net for the poor (table 11.11). It next rolled out a health insurance scheme for civil servants, followed quickly by a similar scheme for private formal sector employees. Thailand struggled with several experimental schemes to cover informal sector workers, who make up a large portion of the employed—63 percent of the labor force in 2007. To address this problem, Thailand passed the National Health Security Act in 2001, mandating that all Thai citizens be covered by health insurance, and finally achieved near-universal coverage in 2002. The current health financing system is composed of a patchwork of pre-existing plans, with the gaps filled by a new insurance scheme—the 30 baht scheme. Thailand now is confronting the challenges of unifying these

TABLE 11.11   Thailand: Timeline of Historical Development of Social Health Insurance

Date	Event	Target population	Economic indicators
1975	Medical Welfare Scheme is established.	The poor	GDP per capita (2000 USD): 602
1978	Civil Servant Medical Benefit Scheme is established.	Government employees and their families	GDP per capita (2000 USD): 747
1981	Medical Welfare Scheme is expanded.	Elderly, children, veterans, and religious leaders	GDP per capita (2000 USD): 828
1983	Voluntary Health Card Scheme (a community financing scheme) is established. Enrolment rates are low, and plan never gets off ground.	Informal sector workers	GDP per capita (2000 USD): 891
1990	Social Security Scheme is established.	Private, formal sector employees	GDP per capita (2000 USD): 1,462
1991	Voluntary Health Card Scheme is revived, this time offering more comprehensive benefits. Fails due to adverse selection.	Informal sector workers	GDP per capita (2000 USD): 1,568. Informal labor as percentage of employed, 1994: 76.8
2001	National Health Security Act is passed, requiring all Thai citizens to enroll in a health insurance scheme. 30 baht scheme is established.	Individuals not covered by Civil Servant Medical Benefit Scheme or Social Security Scheme	GDP per capita (2000 USD): 2,049
2004	Gatekeeping system is established for the 30 baht scheme.	n.a.	GDP per capita (2000 USD): 2,405. Revenue as percentage of GDP: 19.6
2005	Government begins to merge the administrations of the various national insurance schemes.	n.a.	GDP per capita (2000 USD): 2,496. Revenue as percentage of GDP: 21. Informal labor as percentage of employed, 2005: 62
2008	More than 95% of the population is covered by health insurance.	n.a.	GDP per capita 2006 (2000 USD): 2,713. Revenue as percentage of GDP 2006 (2000 USD): 20.1. Informal labor as percentage of employed, 2007: 63

Sources: World Bank 2008a; Thailand National Statistical Office 1994, 2005, 2006, 2007; Tangcharoensathien et al. 2007.
Note: n.a. = not applicable.

different plans with their different benefits packages and insurance administration, and ensuring long-run sustainability.

Thailand's first financing scheme, the Medical Welfare Scheme, was established in 1975. It was a tax-financed scheme that provided the poor with free basic medical care. It was expanded in 1981 to include the elderly, children, veterans, and religious leaders. Hospitals were reimbursed for the services they provided to beneficiaries, but the reimbursement levels were set below cost. Hospitals thus had no incentive to deliver quality care and would often charge insured patients extra to recoup their losses. Moreover, the means-testing system was unreliable for identifying program eligibility. Estimating the incomes of informal sector workers was especially difficult, and, as a result, people who should have been eligible were excluded and vice versa. These shortcomings compromised program effectiveness.

Next, Thailand established two health financing programs—the Civil Servant Medical Benefit Scheme (CSMBS) for civil servants and the Social Security Scheme (SSS) for private sector employees of employers of at least 20 individuals. Together these programs cover nearly 30 percent of the population.

The CSMBS, established in 1978, had no cost-sharing mechanism until 1998. This generous plan for government employees and their families has a comprehensive benefits package and no premium payment by civil servants. It pays providers through a fee-for-service payment mechanism. As a result, its beneficiaries have a high hospital admission rate and a long length of stay.

The SSS, established in 1990, covers all employees of private enterprises but not their dependents. It is financed through a payroll tax with equal contributions from employees, employers, and the government. The benefits package includes curative care, high-cost care, and preventive care with no copayment, and pays providers through a capitation payment system. All beneficiaries are required to choose a hospital network and are permitted to receive care only from providers within that network. Hospitals are paid capitation based on the number of beneficiaries. To combat problems of adverse selection and underprovision of expensive services, now hospitals receive extra payments for high-cost services, and capitation payments are based on a formula that accounts for age and number of patients with chronic diseases.

With formal sector workers and their families covered by either the CSMBS or the SSS and a health safety net firmly in place for the poor, Thailand turned to enrolling its informal sector workers. In 1983, it experimented with a community-financing scheme, the Voluntary Health Card Scheme. In its original incarnation, people could buy a health card that entitled them to a set of limited benefits such as vaccinations and maternal and child health care. However, the cards did not sell, and the scheme petered out. It was revived eight years later, in 1991, with support from the Ministry of Public Health (MOPH). This time, the benefits package was more comprehensive, including drugs, outpatient care, and inpatient care at local public facilities. The providers who sold the cards were paid a fixed amount based on the number of cards that they sold. Because of adverse selection, however, the expense they incurred per card was greater than the amount reimbursed. This led to the demise of the scheme in 2001.

By this point, Thailand's health insurance coverage had stagnated, with only 70 percent of the population covered. Government officials decided that only an insurance mandate would be able to reach the remaining 30 percent. In 2001, the National Health Insurance Act was passed, requiring all Thai citizens to enroll in a health insurance scheme. The CSMBS and the SSS remain largely untouched for the time being, but a new insurance program was created to fill in the gaps, the 30 baht scheme.

As part of the 30 baht scheme, a National Health Security Fund was established, financed with general tax revenues, to cover persons not already enrolled in one of the two formal sector plans. An autonomous purchasing agency, the National Health Security Office (NHSO), was set up to contract with providers. Beneficiaries register with a provider network, and are then entitled to services from a comprehensive benefits package. They are charged small copayments of B 30 (US$0.80), hence the program's name. Beneficiaries are identified via a new information system created using records from the national registration database. This system is intended to avert the problem faced by the Medical Welfare Scheme, where people who should have been eligible were excluded and vice versa. The Medical Welfare Scheme was absorbed into the 30 baht scheme, ensuring that the poor, the elderly, and children receive the same benefits for free. A temporary alleviation fund was set up to help ease this transition, but the policy still met with significant opposition from providers.

Some of the details of the 30 baht scheme were not fully worked out until after implementation. For example, the switch in hospital payment from global budget to capitation met with significant resistance from providers. They first protested that the level of capitation was too low and lobbied successfully for a higher rate. Next, they asserted their power by effectively stealing control of the capitation funds in both rural and urban areas. In urban areas, large public hospitals were being squeezed by their new capitation-based budgets but refused to make the necessary staff cuts, opting instead to petition the government for more funds from the government budget. The government conceded and allowed the large provincial-level hospitals to control both budgets. With their pre-reform funding thus restored, the impact of the new capitation system was minimized.

The method by which the NHSO contracted with providers also saw some changes. Originally, the fund copied the SSS and only contracted directly with large public hospitals; smaller facilities and private providers were subcontracted. However, this method put a disproportionate focus on inpatient care. To encourage the use of basic preventive care, it was decided in 2004 that both private and outpatient facilities could be contracted directly. The resultant gatekeeping system has been one of the most successful elements of the 30 baht scheme. Outpatient visits at health centers and smaller, district hospitals have increased, while outpatient visits to the larger, general hospitals have decreased.

Nevertheless, Thailand's referral system has seen some setbacks. In rural areas, purchasing power was given to small primary care units that were to act as fund holders, purchasing care from community hospitals. Because the primary care units depend on physicians from these hospitals, however, the community hospitals have been able to leverage their power to control the purchasing behavior of the units. This has affected both the referral system—hospitals hold on to patients to keep the capitation funds—and the quality of care—funds that should have gone to primary care units and district health offices are instead kept for the community hospitals.

Thailand now faces two main hurdles: how to ensure the long-run financial sustainability of the scheme and how to merge the universal scheme with the CSMBS and the SSS. Because of the tax-based nature of the universal scheme, it is subject to the political winds blowing at any particular time. In recent years, leaders have been gradually cutting the funding base, reducing the budget to below cost-recovery levels. Moreover, the needs of an aging population are expected to raise health costs in Thailand. If the scheme is to survive its infancy, funding must be increased. In terms of merging the various schemes into a unified health financing program, Thailand has a long way to go. Each of the three schemes is significantly different in terms of its benefits package, cost, level and source of funding, and provider payment method. In October 2005, the government started to synchronize provider payment administration by merging claims-processing activities, but this is only one step down a long road (Hanvoravongchai and Hsiao 2007; Hughes and Leethongdee 2007; Tangcharoensathien et al. 2007).

China

China has followed a jagged path in its quest to providing health insurance for its population (table 11.12). Before liberalizing its economy in the 1980s, China had already achieved near-universal coverage under its socialist economic system. Despite its low income, China's strong government capacity was able to mobilize health care coverage for a large portion of its population.

Rural dwellers were covered by the Cooperative Medical Scheme, financed primarily by the communes' welfare funds. CMS organized health stations, paid village doctors to deliver preventive and primary care, and provided prescription drugs. It also partially reimbursed patients for services received at higher-level facilities. At its peak in 1978, CMS covered 90 percent of China's rural population. In urban areas, government staff and their dependents were covered by the Government Insurance Scheme (GIS), financed by government budgets, while workers, their families, and retirees of state-owned enterprises (SOEs) were covered by the Labor Insurance Scheme (LIS), financed by each SOE's welfare fund. Together, these schemes covered the majority of urban residents.

All three systems of financial risk pooling disappeared as China began to reform its economy in the early 1980s, leaving more than half of its urban population and 90 percent of its rural population without health insurance of any kind. These liberalizing reforms accelerated economic growth but also pushed many workers into the informal sector, creating a hard-to-reach group for enrollment in a national health insurance program. In the urban areas, the proportion of self-employed in overall employment rapidly increased after 1978, from 0.16 percent to over 10 percent in 2006 (China, National Bureau of Statistics 2007). China has since been gradually working to rebuild its system of health financing. Currently, China is in the midst of rolling out a skeletal system of community health financing for rural residents and is finalizing the details for a new and improved social health insurance scheme in urban areas.

TABLE 11.12   China: Timeline of Historical Development of Social Health Insurance

Rural	Event	Urban	Event	Economic indicators
1952	Land and capital are socialized.	1949–78	The Government Insurance Scheme (GIS) and the Labor Insurance Scheme (LIS) cover the urban population, offering comprehensive benefits through employers.	n.a.
Late 1950s	Community-based financing (CMS) based on commune welfare fund is developed.			1961 GDP per capita (2000 USD): 105
1967	CMS adopted for 90% of rural population.			1967 GDP per capita (2000 USD): 99
1982–84	CMS abolished when communes disbanded and China shifted to household responsibility system. No replacement financing scheme.	1978–98	With the liberalization of the economy, state-owned enterprises (SOEs) begin to go bankrupt. Insurance coverage falls drastically.	1983 GDP per capita (2000 USD): 228 1983 labor force participation percentage of 15–64 year-olds: 84 1978 urban self-employed as percentage of employed: 0.16
1985–2002	Ninety percent of rural population is without public health services; patients pay out of pocket for care.	1995	Pilot experiments making fundamental changes to GIS and LIS are conducted in two Chinese cities.	1995 GDP per capita (2000 USD): 658 1995 revenue as percentage of GDP: 5.4
		1998	GIS and LIS are eliminated. Basic Medical Insurance (BMI) scheme is established to cover both government and private sector employees. It replaces comprehensive coverage with medical savings accounts (MSAs).	1998 GDP per capita (2000 USD): 827 1998 revenue as percentage of GDP: 5.9
2002	New Cooperative Medical Scheme (NCMS) piloted in 300 counties.			2003 GDP per capita (2000 USD): 1,209 2003 revenue as percentage of GDP: 8.8 2005 GDP per capita (2000 USD): 1,451
		2005	Community health centers are established to focus on provision of preventive and outpatient care.	2005 revenue as percentage of GDP: 9.6 2006 self-employed as percentage of employed: 10.6
2008	NCMS is adopted and covers more than 90% of rural population.	2008	BMI expands to cover nonworking urban residents in addition to formal sector workers.	2007 GDP per capita (2000 USD): 1,791

Source: World Bank 2008a.

Note: n.a. = not applicable.

Formal Sector

As China turned to a market economy in the 1980s, the SOEs, the foundational members of the LIS, began to dissolve. The government responded by merging the GIS and LIS into a comprehensive urban social insurance program, administered by the Ministry of Labor and Social Security and financed by premium contributions. All public and private employees in urban areas and all civil servants are covered. Employees contribute 2 percent of their salaries; employers contribute 6 percent of their employees' salaries. Dependents, informal sector workers, and migrant workers are not eligible for enrolment. Only about half of the urban population is covered. Moreover, the benefits offered are less comprehensive than those previously offered by GIS and LIS, the dominant model being a combination of individual medical savings accounts and catastrophe insurance. The MOLSS is responsible for actively contracting with providers on the basis of quality and performance. In reality, however, the MOLSS has been a more passive than active purchaser. It has neither curbed cost inflation nor maintained service quality. Instead, its primary concern has been to ensure that the insurance fund does not run a deficit.

Informal Sector

China's vast rural areas are home to 60 percent of the population, mainly farmers or self-employed. Following the collapse of the commune system, 90 percent of the population was left without any form of financial risk protection. The government has tried to provide low-cost services at public facilities by setting prices for basic services below cost. However, because public facilities are severely underfunded, they have to rely on user fees for financial survival. As a result, induced demand—especially for drugs and high-tech diagnostic services—is a serious problem, exacerbated by the fact that most rural Chinese pay out of pocket for health care. In 2002, in response to growing social unrest, the government unveiled the New Cooperative Medical Scheme, run by local government. This voluntary scheme is funded jointly by the central and local governments, and by small premium contributions from enrollees. The central government sets broad guidelines and minimum requirements on financial solvency, and details of the scheme, including the scope of the benefits package and the exact amount of the premium, are decided by local county governments, with an average population of 350,000, and tailored to local needs. The dominant model combines an individual medical savings account with high-deductible catastrophe insurance. The government hoped that NCMS would cover all rural Chinese by the end of 2008. Rural Chinese seem to be fairly receptive to the plan because the premium is highly subsidized. By the middle of 2008, more than 90 percent of the rural population had enrolled (more than 700 million people).

Despite high rates of coverage, NCMS has not met expectations in terms of providing financial risk protection for rural Chinese. Only a small percentage of the population incurs catastrophic medical expenses, so only they are actually helped by the scheme. Typically, only Y 8 per year is deposited in a beneficiary's medical savings account, a mere drop in the bucket when the average cost of an outpatient visit ranges from Y 20 for a visit to a village health post to Y 128 for a visit to a hospital outpatient clinic. With a high deductible and no outpatient coverage, the average Chinese patient sees few tangible benefits from NCMS. Furthermore, because the program is locally run, the depth of coverage varies substantially according to the socioeconomic conditions of the region.

Looking Ahead: Universal Coverage?

The Chinese government has created a plan for health insurance reform, to be implemented over the next three years. It is to expand coverage in the urban areas to include migrant workers, the unemployed, students, children, retirees, and the disabled. The plan will continue to focus on expensive care such as "hospitalizations and outpatient services for high-cost medical conditions," and will be financed by premiums and budgetary allocations for the poor. In rural areas, NCMS will be expanded to include coverage of outpatient services.

Despite the great strides China has made in recent years toward achieving universal coverage, it still faces a number of significant obstacles. The coverage currently available in both rural and urban areas is shallow, with an emphasis on medical savings accounts and high-deductible coverage for catastrophic inpatient services. Moreover, while the Chinese government has committed to injecting an additional 1 to 2 percent of GDP into health care, it has been having a hard time deciding how best to direct these funds. It is debating between direct government provision of care at public facilities or assigning an independent agency to contract with providers for health care.

The Philippines

The Philippines has had social health insurance since 1969 (table 11.13).

The Philippine health system is financed primarily by out-of-pocket payments, which account for 47 percent of health expenditures (WHO 2008a). By contrast, government health spending accounts for only 38 percent, causing public facilities to be grossly underfunded and provider salaries to be quite low (World Bank 2008a). Out-migration to other countries with higher salaries is a serious problem that has led to a shortage of human resources in the health sector. Public facilities are thus often plagued by long wait times. They lack both personnel and supplies, and their services are generally perceived to be of low quality. Consequently, patients choose private facilities over public ones whenever possible (WHO 2007).

Private sector doctors are paid by fee for service. They set their own fees with little oversight. Drug prices are much higher than prices elsewhere in Asia, and there are few checks on health expenditure inflation. The health care system is decentralized, with most of the power and responsibilities at the local level.

TABLE 11.13   Philippines: Timeline of Health Insurance Development

Date	Event	Target population	Economic indicators
1969	Legislation establishing Medicare is passed. Aims to provide universal coverage of hospital care.	All	GDP per capita (2000 USD): 726
1972	Phase I of Medicare begins.	Public and private formal sector workers	GDP per capita (2000 USD): 770
1993	Medicare reaches peak enrolment, covering 40% of the population.	n.a.	GDP per capita (2000 USD): 873 Revenue as percentage of GDP: 17.4
1995	PhilHealth is established. It is a voluntary scheme that continues Medicare's focus on coverage of inpatient services.	The poor	GDP per capita (2000 USD): 913 Revenue as percentage of GDP: 17.7
2004–5	The "Oplan 5 million" scheme expands enrolment in PhilHealth's indigent program by 4.2 million households.	The poor	GDP per capita, 2004 (2000 USD): 1,087 Revenue as percentage of GDP: 14.6
2005	Health system reform framework Fourmula One is announced. It aims to shift focus from inpatient to outpatient care and is working to incorporate community-financing schemes into PhilHealth.	Remaining informal sector	GDP per capita, 2005 (2000 USD): 1,117 Revenue as percentage of GDP: 15
2007	Health insurance covers 79% of the population.	n.a.	GDP per capita, 2007 (2000 USD): 1,216

Sources: World Bank 2006a, 2008a; Jowett and Hsiao 2007.
Note: n.a. = not applicable.

Formal Sector

The Medical Care Plan (Medicare) introduced in 1969 aimed to provide universal coverage. It covered hospital care with no deductible. The services of patients in private hospitals are covered up to a fixed benefit ceiling. The fee schedule and ceiling are set very low. Private hospitals and their physicians "balance bill" patients for charges not paid by Medicare. These charges are usually large. Hence, Medicare offers patients little financial protection. Many patients transfer from private to public hospitals after reaching their benefit ceiling (Obermann et al. 2006).

Medicare was implemented in two phases. Phase I began in 1972, and mandated the enrolment of both public and private employees (and their dependents) in the formal sector. It was highly successful in achieving coverage for these workers. Phase II targeted informal sector workers but was largely unsuccessful. It was never fully implemented, and the vast majority of the rural poor were without coverage. Near its peak enrolment in 1993, Medicare covered just over 40 percent of the population, falling far short of its stated goal of universal coverage (Beringuela 1993).

Reaching the Poor and the Informal Sector: PhilHealth

In 1994–95, a report commissioned by the Department of Health and the Philippine Institute for Development Studies found that enrolment in Medicare was decreasing as a percentage of the employed population. As a result, in 1995 the Philippines revised its insurance program under the National Health Insurance Act, creating the Philippine Health Insurance Corporation (PhilHealth). PhilHealth aimed to reach the poor and achieve universal coverage by 2010. It is a voluntary scheme and, although so far it only makes up around 9.5 percent of total health expenditures, 70 percent of the population is covered (Obermann et al. 2006).

Contributions are about 3 percent of income for formal sector workers, shared between employers and employees. Informal sector workers are part of PhilHealth's individual paying program; they pay a fixed rate of ₱1,200 (US$30) per year. Retirees who have made at least 120 monthly payments are considered nonpaying members, as their premiums are subsidized by the government. Legal dependents of enrollees are all fully covered.

The poor are eligible for PhilHealth's indigent program, in which government subsidies—funded jointly by local- and national-level taxes—cover all or part of the premium for means-tested indigents. The take-up was low through 2003, due primarily to high copayments and lack of accredited facilities in the rural areas where many indigents live. The "Oplan 5 million" scheme in 2004–5 aimed to increase enrolment and was largely successful, expanding the indigent program by 4.2 million households. Approximately 14.4 percent of the population in 2003 lived on less than US$1 a day. It may have been slightly too generous, however, because PhilHealth also saw a decline in the number of enrollees in the individual paying program, probably because they were newly eligible for the indigent program (World Bank 2006a).

PhilHealth offers first-dollar coverage of services in the benefits package, with a low ceiling. The benefits package is limited and focuses on inpatient care instead of preventive or outpatient services. PhilHealth has been successful in many ways, but also has encountered certain obstacles to its efforts to achieve universal coverage and financial risk protection for the poor.

One of the most serious barriers to expansion of coverage is that PhilHealth simply is not an attractive package for poor or informal workers, as exhibited by the fact that informal sector workers make up only 45 percent of total enrollees. The contribution rates for workers in the informal sector are prohibitively high relative to their income. The contribution scale for PhilHealth is regressive, in that all informal workers must pay a fixed premium, while formal sector workers pay a percentage of their salaries up to a fixed amount. This fixed level is set quite low, so high-salary employees pay a smaller percentage of their earnings than lower-salary employees. Also, because PhilHealth does not have an effective means-testing system, it is difficult to identify which low-income individuals should receive premium subsidies. If PhilHealth does not allocate subsidies to those who should qualify, it increases systemic inequities; if it allocates subsidies to those who should not qualify, it is in danger of becoming financially unsustainable.

Furthermore, many informal sector workers are based in the rural areas, where geographic access to health care services is limited. The shortage of health sector workers is most acute in rural areas, where there are few hospitals. Even those few hospitals are unlikely to be accredited by PhilHealth, and therefore workers cannot be reimbursed for services received there. The accreditation system does not take location into account, and therefore the lower-quality hospitals in the rural areas often do not make the cut.

PhilHealth is also limited in its ability to provide financial risk protection and to control costs. Enrollees typically seek care at private hospitals, where doctors charge a fee for service. Enrollees are then reimbursed for their covered expenses. Because doctors' fee schedules are unregulated, they often charge more for patients with PhilHealth coverage, thus capturing the rents from the insurance program and exacerbating the problem of health expenditure inflation. The losers in this practice are the patients, who bear the burden of these higher costs when their health expenditures exceed the low reimbursement ceiling set by PhilHealth.

An additional weakness of PhilHealth is its focus on inpatient services. Preventive and outpatient services are financed mainly with out-of-pocket payments. As a result, large private hospitals are wealthy, while other services are underfunded. People often delay care until they require hospitalization, unnecessarily inflating health expenditures as people forgo relatively cheap preventive and screening services in favor of more expensive but covered hospital treatments. This behavior also has negative public health consequences.

A private insurance market does exist, but private insurers typically step in only after a patient's health expenditures exceed the PhilHealth reimbursement ceiling. Private insurers now require enrollees to be members of PhilHealth and will reimburse only for services included in the national benefits package.

Looking Ahead

In August 2005, the Philippine Department of Health introduced a health system reform framework, "Fourmula One," with three stated goals: improved health status, enhanced public satisfaction, and increased equity in financing. The department is working to stem the flight of health care workers to other countries by adjusting medical training to meet local needs. It has introduced a national drug list in an attempt to curb drug expenditure inflation and is running a campaign to encourage the purchase of generic drugs. Fourmula One also intends to work more closely with private providers to shift the focus from inpatient to outpatient care. In an attempt to extend coverage to informal sector workers, it is also working to incorporate community-financing schemes into the national program.

Indonesia

The Indonesian health care system lags behind those of other Asian nations. It has one of the lowest levels of total health expenditure in the region, 2.8 percent of GDP. Out-of-pocket payments make up 65.8 percent of private health expenditure. Indonesia's health outcomes are also worse than those of other Asian nations. Life expectancy is only 67.8 years in Indonesia, compared with 70.9 in Thailand and 77.6 in Korea, and the infant mortality rate is 28 per 1,000 births in Indonesia, as compared with around 18 in Thailand (table 11.1).

Indonesia has a number of health care financing plans. The goal of proposed plans is universal coverage (table 11.14).

Currently, the vast majority of Indonesians pay out of pocket for health care at low-cost, low-quality public facilities, while the affluent pay out of pocket at high-cost, high-quality private facilities. Even those with ready access to health insurance typically opt out, do not take advantage of the benefits offered, or refuse to enroll. With as much as two-thirds of the population in the informal sector and little public interest in pre-paying for health care, Indonesia has a long way to go toward finding a sustainable financial risk protection scheme that will offer a desirable and affordable benefits package. The 2004 proposal for a mandatory national health insurance scheme is poorly thought out and has met with significant resistance from certain government departments and interest groups.

For now, Indonesia's health financing system is composed of several government-sponsored schemes and a smattering of private plans catering mainly to the very wealthy.

Civil Servants

Askes was Indonesia's first health financing scheme, established in 1968 to cover civil servants and their dependents. It is a mandatory scheme, funded

TABLE 11.14   Indonesia: Timeline of Historical Development of Social Health Insurance

Date	Event	Target population	Economic indicators
1968	Askes established.	Civil servants and their dependents	GDP per capita in 2000 USD: 211
Late 1970s	Jamsostek established.	Private sector employees	GDP per capita, 1979 in 2000 USD: 372
1970s	Dana Sehat established to provide community-based insurance.	Rural residents	GDP per capita in 2000 USD: 235–372
1992	Passage of Health Insurance Act, allowing private companies to offer health insurance. JPKM established.	Private sector employees	GDP per capita in 2000 USD: 692 Revenue as percentage of GDP: 17.9
2004	Plans announced for new, universal insurance scheme (Jamsosnas).	All	GDP per capita in 2000 USD: 904 Revenue as percentage of GDP: 18.4
2005	Askeskin established as safety net for poor.	The poor	GDP per capita in 2000 USD: 943
2008	Around 41% of population covered by health insurance.	n.a.	GDP per capita, 2007 in 2000 USD: 1,034

Sources: World Bank 2008a; Thrabrany et al. 2004.
Note: n.a. = not applicable.

by a payroll tax made up of 2 percent from employees and 0.5 percent from the government, and managed by a for-profit state-owned insurance company. Copayments are high, at around 30 to 60 percent of total cost. Beneficiaries and their dependents are entitled to comprehensive care at public facilities; however, because of the perceived low quality of services at these facilities, only 7 percent of beneficiaries actually seek care there. The remainder choose to pay extra for services at private facilities, where the service reputedly is of much higher quality. Around 14 million civil servants and their dependents, around 5 percent of the total population, are currently covered by Askes.

Private Sector Employees

Askes was soon followed by Jamsostek in the late 1970s, a mandatory scheme targeting workers at private firms with 10 or more employees. It is funded by premiums from employers, ranging from 3 to 6 percent of base salary. The benefits package is less comprehensive than Askes', excluding catastrophic conditions such as cancer and heart surgery. It does, however, allow beneficiaries to seek care at either public or private facilities. Like Askes, Jamsostek is mandatory, with one significant exception: employers have the option of opting out of the scheme if they provide their employees with better health insurance. Because Jamsostek is unable to ensure that employers adhere to their legal obligations when they opt out, and because Jamsostek is seen as offering only meager benefits, the opt-out rate is high. In 2004 fully 86 percent of those eligible for Jamsostek opted out, and many small and rural firms did not offer their employees a chance to enroll in an alternative scheme. Overall, Jamsostek covers around 3 million employees and their dependents, only 3 percent of the total population.

Informal Sector Workers and the Poor

In addition to the government-sponsored schemes for the formal sector, there are two government-sponsored schemes targeting the informal sector. The informal sector is a significant component of the economy, accounting for 62 percent of Indonesia's jobs in 1999 (ILO 2007). One scheme is Dana Sehat, the small community financing program established in the 1970s. Dana Sehat is managed at the local level, so contribution rates vary by region. Underfunding has led to a very limited benefits package that only covers outpatient services, giving the program limited appeal. Moreover, because it is a voluntary scheme, adverse selection is a problem.

The other is a state-owned organization known as JPKM, which serves as a licensing board for private companies that want to sell HMO-style health insurance. JPKM was established in 1992, with the passage of the Health Insurance Act, which allowed private insurers to enter the health insurance market. JPKM is plagued by problems, one of its most severe being its conflicting goals to simultaneously provide financial risk protection to the poor and make a profit. As a result, although the insurance is financed by premiums, the premiums are set low and without actuarial analysis, leading to underfunding. This, coupled with poor government oversight, has led to a narrow benefits package. The scheme also strictly limits beneficiaries' choice of provider, making it still less attractive. Fewer than 500,000 individuals are currently enrolled in JPKM, less than 0.6 percent of the population.

Since 2005, the government has also offered a social safety net for the poor, known as Askeskin. Administered by Askes, this scheme offers free health care services at public clinics and third-class hospital wards. An estimated 15 percent of the population utilized Askeskin benefits in 2006. There are no premiums or cost sharing. The government pays capitation for outpatient services and a fixed reimbursement rate for inpatient services and drugs. The program is beset by problems that jeopardize its long-run financial sustainability. Because it is fairly simple to obtain the government card and prove eligibility for the program, more people have enrolled than originally expected. Moreover, those who enroll often know they need health services, making adverse selection a serious problem. The combination of more enrollees than expected and higher than expected costs per enrollee has pushed the program into a deficit. Providers also contribute to the high costs. Because providers of inpatient services are paid per service provided, induced demand has become a problem. Though difficult to prove, anecdotal reports abound of unusually high cesarean section rates and outbreaks of mysterious skin allergies.

Looking Ahead: Universal Health Insurance?

Despite the abundance of insurance schemes, only about 27 percent of Indonesia's population is covered by any type of health insurance. As a result, in 2004 the government announced a proposal for the creation of a new universal insurance scheme, to be known as Jamsosnas. This plan is supposed to achieve universal coverage within 25 to 30 years. Workers in the formal sector will pay a premium equal to 3 percent of their salary, matched by an additional 3 percent contribution from their employer. Informal sector workers will pay a premium based on the minimum wage and will receive a reduced benefits package. Eventually, the program will be managed by a nonprofit insurance company, and enrolment will be mandatory. Supplementary private insurance will be permitted. Services will be contracted at negotiated prices, and the benefits package will be comprehensive. Quality and appropriateness reviews will be conducted at regular intervals. Initially, however, Askes and Jamsostek will continue to operate as usual. Their insurance organizations will be converted to nonprofit entities, and they will gradually expand their coverage base. Askes will continue to administer Askeskin, and will expand to cover informal sector workers as well. Jamsostek will continue to focus on formal sector workers (World Bank 2008b).

Since the plan for Jamsosnas was announced, little progress has been made toward making the proposal a reality, or even passing the bill. One of the main problems with the proposal is the lack of critical details. The benefits package is undefined, and how those eligible for government assistance will be identified is unclear. The contribution rates and costs of the program have not been determined by actuarial analysis, so whether Jamsosnas is financially sustainable is unclear. The proposed scheme calls for significant intergovernmental cooperation, which may be a fantasy rather than an achievable goal. These problems, combined with a lack of universal support from involved government departments, no fixed timeline, and the poor reputation of existing schemes, make it doubtful that Jamsosnas in any form will ever become a reality.

India

India has a primitive national health service with all care funded and delivered by the government. However, the scheme is underfunded, and public clinics and hospitals are often poorly managed. Most public hospitals lack drugs and supplies and provide only free professional physician and nursing services. Patients have to buy drugs and supplies from private stores before surgeries are performed. The underpaid public physicians usually have private practices on the side and may only appear in the public hospitals in the mornings, reserving afternoons and evenings for work at their private clinics or hospitals. It is not uncommon for physicians in public clinics to refer wealthier patients to their private practice for higher-quality care. As a result, public facilities are thought of as a last resort and generally provide a low quality of care. This two-tiered system disproportionately affects the poor, who have no choice but low-quality public care when ill.

With a health insurance coverage rate of 25 percent, India's financing system is extremely fragmented (La Forgia and Nagpal 2012). Because local community financing schemes cover the largest number of people, coverage details vary considerably by region. In the urban areas, most Indians receive care through their employers, so high-income, formal sector workers are the primary recipients. In the rural areas, community financing often takes the form of cooperation between local governments and private, nongovernmental organizations. India would like to expand SHI but has not yet developed a formal plan or framework for doing so.

Formal Sector

In the urban areas, insurance is provided through employers. These schemes typically cover basic care for employees and some retirees. Separate schemes cover employees of railways, defense, police, and other national industries. A few state-sponsored insurance agencies offer voluntary health insurance. Private insurers play only a minor role, covering between 4 and 5 percent of the population.

Informal Sector

India has a large informal sector, accounting for approximately 46 percent of the employed nationally and 55 percent rurally in 2000 (ILO 2007).

In rural areas, insurance coverage is provided largely by localized community financing schemes that vary widely from state to state. For example, the state of Karnataka cooperates with nonprofit organizations to provide subsidized insurance coverage for children, farmers, and the poor, while the state of Andhra Pradesh encourages low-income pregnant women to give birth in health facilities by offering them subsidized insurance coverage. Together, these two plans have enrolled more than 70 million Indians. They receive funding from the Ministry of Health and Family Welfare and the National Rural Health Mission (NRHM).

The NRHM is a centrally sponsored program that aims to expand and improve existing schemes as well as establish new ones. It is one of the major policy initiatives created following the government's promise of a 2 to 3 percent of GDP increase in health spending (Berman and Ahuja 2008). In addition to funding the two schemes described above, NRHM is working toward enacting general health financing improvements in rural areas. Not only will funding be increased, but NRHM is also experimenting with pay-for-performance schemes and demand-side subsidies in an attempt to ensure that the benefits of additional funding do not simply end up in providers' pockets. NRHM is also working to improve public facilities and solve the problem of provider absenteeism.

Indigents

On the national level in 2003, the central government introduced a voluntary insurance scheme targeting the poor. About 34 percent of India's population lived on less than US$1 a day in 2004. Any Indian living below the poverty level can join by paying a low premium of Rs 30 (US$0.80) per year. The central and state governments will share the remaining contribution of Rs 750 per year. Coverage is comprehensive, but capped at Rs 30,000 (US$750) per family per year. So far, enrolment rates have been low.

Looking Ahead

Unlike many other Asian countries, India, a decentralized nation, does not have the government capacity to manage and administer health insurance schemes for its large population. It seems to be turning to the private sector to cover its people while providing the subsidy to fund the premium for low-income households. In 1999, private carriers began to be allowed to enter the insurance market. Since then, private carriers have begun to offer health insurance, covering between 4 and 5 percent of the population. A 2007 summit on health insurance specifically addressed how to promote private insurance, sparking new private health insurance offerings. Indeed, the private health insurance market is expected to grow 75 percent annually in coming years. This heavy reliance on private insurers may be due to India's large, diverse population and decentralized system of government, both of which make small, agile private companies ideally suited for quick and efficient expansion of coverage.

LESSONS AND CONCLUSIONS

The Asian experience shows that several key drivers enabled scaling up. Economic development was a key driver that reduced the portion of population in the informal sector, requiring subsidies, and increased government tax revenues. Consequently, the government had the fiscal capacity to expand its enrolment subsidies for low-income households and informal sector workers. How Japan, Korea, and Taiwan, China, achieved universal coverage illustrates this point. The experiences of India, Indonesia, and the Philippines show that their fiscal constraints inhibited them from providing adequate subsidies to achieve universal coverage. Other Asian countries such as Cambodia or Pakistan, though not discussed here, similarly exhibit the limited government and economic capacity in their national contexts that would inhibit scaling up health insurance coverage. China and Thailand showed different patterns. Although both nations are lower-income nations, the governments had political reasons for reallocating resources for universal coverage.

Political demand for universal coverage is another key driver. Grassroots demand and organization generate the political pressure for governments to take action. In China, Japan, and Thailand when people found health care unaffordable, governments took action to scale up SHI. Demand for equal treatment can also generate the necessary grassroots pressure, as in Thailand, the Philippines, and Taiwan, China, where the uncovered population demanded health insurance coverage similar to that of the formal sector workers. However, the timing of top political leaders' (or groups') response to grassroots pressure seems to depend on the leaders' social and equity orientations, as in China and Thailand during the 2001 election.

The government's capacity determines the feasibility of scaling up. A clear case of comparison is China and India. Both countries decided to allocate significant new funds to cover the rural population. China, with a strong and effective government, was able to expand coverage from 10 percent to more than 95 percent of its rural residents in five years. India has hardly expanded coverage. Indonesia and the Philippines also illustrate the way ineffective governance limits the ability to scale up. When governments lack the capacity to enroll and administer SHI, a nation has to rely on NGOs and commercial firms to perform these functions, as India is trying to do. When relying on the private sector, government plays another important role—through regulations of private insurers and providers. Negligent governments (China and the Philippines) may allow private providers to exploit patients, and ineffective government (India) may do the same.

The Asian experience clearly shows that incentives have to be given to farmers and informal sector workers to enroll in an SHI program. To achieve universal coverage, the government has to be willing to subsidize even nonpoor informal sector workers.

Covering farmers and other rural residents has been a vexing problem for most nations. The historical development of SHI in China and Japan offer a valuable lesson. Both nations had developed community-based insurance schemes for rural residents but found it was an effective means of insuring them. When Japan established its SHI, it relied on Jyorei, the community-based insurance scheme, as the basis for covering rural residents and informal sector workers. China is building its current government-managed rural health insurance on the previous foundation of community-based insurance, the Cooperative Medical System, which gave people an appreciation for pooling risks. On the other hand, Indonesia has not relied on its community-based insurance, Dana Sehat, to expand its coverage to the rural residents, and the coverage rate is low.

All Asian countries are struggling with one common challenge—how to transform money into effective and efficient health services. A dual problem coexists for many Asian countries. They may not have adequate financing for health care while waste and inefficiencies undermine their health care systems. The same question confronts nations that have achieved universal coverage or provided adequate financing. Hence, the larger question is not only scaling up, but also how to scale up while using resources efficiently. The answer lies not only in good governance, but also in defining and coordinating the roles of the public and private sectors to transform resources into equitable and efficient services for the people.

NOTES

1. This chapter focuses on the Asian experience. It excludes Australia and New Zealand from the analysis because they carry on European traditions and practices in health care financing.

2. Data on DALYs are from 2002, but income groups use data from 2006. Based on 2002 income data and 2006 income group criteria, Bhutan, Indonesia, and Sri Lanka would fall into the low-income category.

3. In 2000 current U.S. dollars.

REFERENCES

Beringuela, M. 1993. "The Performance of Medicare I: An Economic Evaluation." Discussion Paper Series No. 95–06, Philippine Institute for Development Studies, Manila.

Berman, P., and R. Ahuja. 2008. "Government Health Spending in India: Getting to 2% of GDP," World Bank, New Delhi, India.

Chiang, Tung-Liang. 1997. "Taiwan's 1995 Health Care Reform." *Health Policy* 39: 225–39.

China, National Bureau of Statistics. 2007. *China Statistical Yearbook 2007*. Beijing: China Statistics Press.

Gottret, Pablo, and George Schieber. 2006. *Health Financing Revisited*. Washington, DC: World Bank.

Gwatkin, Davidson, Shea Rutstein, Kiersten Johnson, Eldaw Sulliman, Adam Wagstaff, and Agbessi Amouzou. 2007. "Socio-Economic Differences in Health, Nutrition, and Population within Developing Countries." In *Country Reports on HNP and Poverty.* Washington, DC: World Bank.

Hanvoravongchai, Piya, and William Hsiao. 2007. "Thailand: Achieving Universal Coverage with Social Health Insurance." In *Social Health Insurance for Developing Nations*, ed. W.C. Hsiao and P.R. Shaw. Washington, DC: World Bank.

Hidayat, B., H. Thabrany, H. Dong, and R. Sauerborn. 2004. "The Effects of Mandatory Health Insurance on Equity in Access to Outpatient Care in Indonesia." *Health Policy and Planning* 19 (5): 322–35.

Hughes, David, and Songkramchai Leethongdee. 2007 "Universal Coverage in the Land of Smiles: Lessons from Thailand's 30 Baht Health Reforms." *Health Affairs* 26 (4): 999–1008.

ILO (International Labour Organization). 2007. *Key Indicators of the Labor Market.* 5th ed. Geneva: ILO.

Japan Ministry of Internal Affairs and Communications, Statistics Bureau. 2008. "Social Security." In *Historical Statistics of Japan.* http://www.stat.go.jp/english/data/chouki/23.htm; accessed December 2008.

Jowett, Matthew R., and William C. Hsiao. 2007. "The Philippines: Extending Coverage Beyond the Formal Sector." In *Social Health Insurance for Developing Nations*, ed. W.C. Hsiao and P.R. Shaw. Washington, DC: World Bank.

La Forgia, Gerard, and Somil Nagpal. 2012. *Government-Sponsored Health Insurance in India: Are You Covered?* Washington, DC: World Bank.

Maddison, Angus. 2008."Statistics on World Population, GDP and Per Capita GDP, 1–2006 AD." http://www.ggdc.net/maddison/; accessed 2008.

Obermann, Konrad, Matthew R. Jowett, Maria Ofelia O. Alcantara, Eduardo P. Banzon, and Claude Bodart. 2006. "Social Health Insurance in a Developing Country: The Case of the Philippines." *Social Science & Medicine* 62: 3177–85.

O'Donnell, Owen, Eddy van Doorslaer, Ravi P. Rannan-Eliya, Aparnaa Somanathan, Shiva Raj Adhikari, Baktygul Akkazieva, Deni Harbianto, Charu C. Garg, Piya Hanvoravongchai, Alejandro N. Herrin, et al. 2008. "Who Pays for Health Care in Asia?" *Journal of Health Economics* 27 (2): 460–75.

Ogawa, Sumiko, Toshihiko Hasegawa, Guy Carrin, and Kei Kawabata. 2003. "Scaling Up Community Health Insurance: Japan's Experience with the 19th Century Jyorei Scheme." *Health Policy and Planning* 18 (3): 270–78.

Scheil-Adlung, X. 2004. "Sharpening the Focus on the Poor: Policy Options for Advancing Social Health Protection in Indonesia." Extension of Social Security (ESS) Paper 19, International Labour Office, Geneva.

Tangcharoensathien, Viroj, Phusit Prakongsai, Walaiporn Patcharanarumol, and Ponpisut Jongudomsuk. 2007. "Universal Coverage in Thailand: The Respective Roles of Social Health Insurance and Tax-Based Financing." In *Extending Social Protection in Health: Developing Countries' Experiences, Lessons Learnt and Recommendations*, ed. ILO, GTZ, and WHO. Berlin: Deutsche Nationalbibliografie.

Tangcharoensathien, Viroj, Samrit Srithamrongsawat, and Siriwan Pitayarangsarit. 2002. "Overview of Health Insurance Systems in Thailand." In *Regional Overview of Social Health Insurance in South-East Asia*. New Delhi: WHO.

Thailand National Statistical Office, Ministry of Information and Communication Technology. 1994. Labor Force Survey, Bangkok.

———. 2005. Informal Employed Survey, Bangkok.

———. 2006. Informal Employed Survey, Bangkok.

———. 2007. Informal Employed Survey, Bangkok.

Thrabrany, H., A. Gani, Pujianto, L. Mayanda, Mahlil, and B. Satri Budi. 2004. "Social Health Insurance in Indonesia: Current Status and the Plan for National Health Insurance." In *Regional Overview of Social Health Insurance in South-East Asia,* ed. T. Sein. New Delhi: World Health Organization.

World Bank. 2006a. "Project Appraisal Document on a Proposed Loan in the Amount of US $110 Million to the Republic of the Philippines for a National Sector Support for Health Reform Project," World Bank, Washington, DC.

———. 2006b. *World Development Indicators 2006*. Washington, DC: World Bank.

———. 2008a. *World Development Indicators 2008*. Washington, DC: World Bank.

———. 2008b. "Investing in Indonesia's Health: Challenges and Opportunities for Future Public Spending." In *Health Public Expenditure Review 2008*. Jakarta: World Bank.

WHO (World Health Organization). 2002a. *Health Systems and Information Statistics*. Geneva: WHO.

———. 2002b. *Global Burden of Disease*. Geneva: WHO.

———. 2007. *Country Health Information Profiles: The Philippines*. Geneva: WHO.

Yang, Bong-Min. 2001. *Health Insurance and the Growth of the Private Health Sector in Korea*. Washington, DC: World Bank Institute.

CHAPTER 12

Bismarck's Unfinished Business in Western Europe

Hans Maarse, Alexander S. Preker, Marianne E. Lindner, and Onno P. Schellekens

To extract valuable lessons for scaling up health insurance, some main trends in the historical development and the current state of national health insurance in Europe are reviewed in this chapter. Special attention is given to Belgium, France, Germany, the Netherlands, and Switzerland,[1] five countries that have a national health insurance model in common to protect their citizens against the costs of sickness and ensure their access to basic health care. The main characteristics of this model are: mandatory membership, broad coverage in terms of persons and health services, contributions related to income instead of medical risk, no integration of health care financing and provision of medical services, and strong government involvement (Saltman, Busse, and Figueras 2004).[2]

Neither a detailed description of the historical developments in each of the five countries nor extensive comparison of their current health insurance system is intended.[3] Instead, from the historical paths that emerge from this study, policy lessons are sought. What are the opportunities and threats for scaling up health insurance in low-income countries that have as yet had little experience with it (Bärnighausen and Sauerborn 2002)?

THE "LOGIC" OF HEALTH INSURANCE

Modern national health insurance arrangements are highly complex systems. They rest upon some fundamental notions with not always well-understood implications: joint action, normative-affection, instrumentality, good governance and accepted authority, and selectivity. They imply some important policy lessons for the introduction of health insurance arrangements and share a common theoretical basis: social capital.

National health insurance (or any health insurance arrangement) is based on the principle of *joint action*. The participants pool their risks to protect themselves against the costs of disease. Usually, they cannot afford to pay privately for expensive medical treatments. What people essentially buy when they join a common arrangement is the certainty that, once they are sick, the costs of their medical treatment will be covered by a third party. Joint action also functions as an efficient instrument to collect resources for medical care in a community.

314 Hans Maarse, Alexander S. Preker, Marianne E. Lindner, and Onno P. Schellekens

Health insurance arrangements rest to some extent upon a "moral infrastructure" (Hinrichs 1995) that can be described as a shared notion that members of the community are mutually dependent and must take care of their fellow members who are sick and need medical care. It is regarded as a moral obligation to remove financial barriers to health care. This cultural or *normative-affective* dimension of health insurance provides a moral basis for pooling each other's risks. On the European Continent, the normative-affective dimension of health insurance is often referred to as the solidarity dimension (Ter Meulen, Arts, and Muffels 2001).

Health insurance and solidarity also have an *instrumental* dimension. People join a scheme not only for moral reasons, but also to protect themselves against financial risks. Thus, they are motivated by self-interest as well as altruism. The notion of self-interest corresponds to the Anglo-Saxon concept of fairness, which, much stronger than the concept of solidarity, refers to mutual obligations and rights (Van Oorschot 1999). Fairness is a matter of shared utility based upon contracts ("contractual solidarity") rather than shared identity.

Most normative-affective and instrumental considerations are not strong enough to support solidarity relationships in modern society. Support is neither necessarily spontaneous nor completely voluntary. Furthermore, there may be a problem of free-ridership. To resolve these problems, control and coercion of contributions will be necessary. Hence, health insurance is shaped as a mandatory arrangement. This may be called the dimension of *accepted authority* of health insurance (Van Oorschot 1999).

The notion of accepted authority is closely related to the concept of *good governance*. In fact, good governance functions as a precondition for effective health insurance. The gradual extension of state intervention in health insurance required the state to be politically capable of not only enacting health legislation but also building up an effective administrative organization and fiscal capacity to put the legislation into practice. Kaufmann, Kraay, and Mastruzzi (2004, 2005) define good governance as a multidimensional concept with three main dimensions: the process by which governments are selected, monitored, and replaced; the capacity of the government to formulate and implement policies effectively; and the respect of citizens and the state for the institutions that govern economic and social relations (annex 12C).

The notion of *selectivity* has always played a significant role in national health insurance. Who is covered, and who is excluded? This question leads to the more fundamental question of the structure of society and its criteria for drawing social boundary lines. Bayertz (1999: 26) rightly points out that the concrete meaning of "solidarity is relative to the community." The selection criteria used to draw the dividing line in the five countries studied are seen later in this chapter. Here, it is sufficient to note that over time, health insurance became ever more inclusive in terms of membership. Diminishing selectivity was intimately linked to the expanding state role in health insurance and the transition from voluntary to mandatory arrangements.

So far, five fundamental notions on health insurance have been briefly elaborated. They have a common basis, *social capital*, which in the view of Putnam (1993: 167) "refers to features of social organization, such as trust, norms and networks that can improve the efficiency of society by facilitating coordinated actions." Putnam sees social capital as a public good that functions as a prerequisite for institutional performance and democratic institutions. It creates a socio-cultural basis for joint action and accepted authority. Social capital presumes a minimum level of reciprocity, trust, or mutual confidence in society, based upon notions of normative-affection and instrumentality (Rothstein 2001). Social capital is selective, too, because it is bound to a certain (sub)community. The relationship between social capital and good governance can best be seen as reciprocal. Social capital stimulates good governance (Putnam's claim), and good governance is a precondition for the development of social capital (Levi 1996).

THE SOCIAL ORIGINS OF HEALTH INSURANCE

Health insurance started as a model of voluntary and informal risk sharing. It was a product of self-organizing activity in social life during the 17th and 18th centuries. In Belgium and the Netherlands, guilds initially played a leading role. Because of increasing political problems due to the French Revolution, guilds were either converted to mutual societies or terminated in the 19th century. In the 20th century, many nonguild-related voluntary mutual societies, associations, and nonprofit and commercial companies were also developed as a collective arrangement for covering the costs of medical care and loss of income due to illness, physical ailment, or death (Veraghtert and Widdershoven 2002).

The advent of health insurance arrangements cannot be divorced from the progressive industrialization of economic life in the 17th and 18th centuries. Sickness deprived workers of their income. Therefore, most schemes started as a sick pay arrangement for workers during sick leave. Only later did covering medical care costs become the main function of health insurance.[4] The shifting focus is nicely illustrated by the fact that in Germany social health insurance at its inception provided 1.7 more cash benefits than benefits in-kind. By 1955 this ratio had reversed to 1:4, by 1977 to 1:10, and by 1984 to 1:16 (Bärnighausen and Sauerborn 2002: 1569).

Although local governments in Belgium and the Netherlands did not directly participate in the creation of sickness funds, they soon became indirectly involved. Local governments mostly welcomed the private initiative of the guilds or other social organizations because it lessened the need for public poverty programs. For this reason, they conferred on the funds the right to introduce compulsory membership.

Health insurance in France and Switzerland was also a bottom-up initiative rather than a state-orchestrated process. Only Germany followed a more centralistic path. Some states, in particular Prussia and Bavaria, passed legislation in the 18th century to force or strongly encourage local governments to establish sickness funds and make membership in the company funds compulsory. A political argument for this strategy, which led to the introduction of local funds, was to keep the church out of poverty programs.

In summary, health insurance in Europe started as a voluntary, small-scale, and mostly informal initiative rooted in local communities. In retrospect, it is difficult to determine to what extent this start may be considered a precondition for its success. Yet, it is plausible to conclude that its local and pluralist origins significantly contributed to its effectiveness and legitimacy. The local initiatives also served as useful learning models for the subsequent establishment of large, formal arrangements. The policy lesson in this respect is that countries with some experience in small-scale insurance arrangements may be wise to build their national scheme as much as possible on these local arrangements to increase its effectiveness and legitimacy. Where these small-scale arrangements do not yet exist, it is probably prudent to introduce health insurance by encouraging local community-based initiatives that are subsidized by the government (Bärnighausen and Sauerborn 2002).

THE EXTENSION OF STATE INVOLVEMENT IN HEALTH INSURANCE

The history of health insurance in Europe can be described in terms of continuous state intervention. During the 19th and 20th centuries, the state became ever more involved in health insurance (box 12.1). The extension of state intervention had several important implications (Bärnighausen and Sauerborn 2002). First, health insurance arrangements were gradually converted from voluntary into compulsory arrangements. Second, they were transformed from mainly local or regional arrangements into supraregional or national arrangements. Third, state intervention grew in scope and strength. As a result, health insurance gradually moved from general principles into a system of concrete, detailed regulations.

The extension of state intervention was not taken for granted. It involved many political conflicts (discussed later). Mostly ideology-driven, these conflicts concentrated on the issue of how to shape the state's political responsibility and tasks in health insurance. Although health insurance was increasingly considered an indispensable social arrangement, that conclusion did not automatically imply that the state should assume the lead from the private initiatives organized by social organizations like the guilds, companies, mutual aid societies, and so on. The basic question was how to define the relationship between the state and social organizations. Another key issue concerned the institutional structure of health insurance. Even if the state had to introduce some indispensable hierarchical elements in health insurance, the big question was how to define the functions and responsibilities of the preexisting funds in the newly designed institutional structure. A related issue concerned the representation of interests

BOX 12.1   HIGHLIGHTS IN NATIONAL HEALTH INSURANCE LEGISLATION

Belgium

1851	State officially recognizes mutualities.
1894	Legislation enacted to extend official scope of mutualities' activities and to grant them state subsidies.
1944	Social security introduced for salaried workers.
1963	Law enacted establishing and organizing scheme of compulsory insurance against disease and invalidity (Law of Leburton). New governance system introduced for social health insurance, improving access to insurance coverage for all Belgian residents.
1994	Royal Decree issued to make mutualities more self-responsible for financial management.

France

1930	Law on Social Insurance enacted to create compulsory protection system for employees in industry and business whose earnings fall below a certain level.
1945	Coverage of social health insurance extended in stages by ordinance.
1999	Universal Health Coverage Act (CMU) enacted introducing free coverage of basic and complementary social health insurance to persons on very low incomes.

Germany

1883	First statutory health insurance instituted, making health insurance mandatory nationwide for certain categories of employees.
1911	Imperial Insurance Regulation issued, introducing common framework for social health insurance.
1994	Statutory health insurance instituted for long-term care.

Netherlands

1941	Sickness Funds Decree created compulsory health insurance system for salaried workers whose earnings fell below a certain level. Voluntary scheme for elderly introduced. Voluntary scheme for self-employed workers introduced.
1964	Sickness Fund Act replaced Sickness Funds Decree.
1968	Exceptional Medical Expenses Act enacted to provide universal access to long-term care.
2006	Health Insurance Act introduced universal and mandatory scheme covering curative health services. Act ended traditional dividing line between social and private health insurance.

Switzerland

1911	Federal Law on Sickness and Accident Insurance enacted.
1994	Federal Law revised to introduce mandatory and universal health insurance.

Sources: Belgium, EOHSP 2007; France, EOHSP 2004c; Germany, EOHSP 2004a; Netherlands, EOHSP 2004b; Switzerland, EOHSP 2000.

at all levels of health insurance, including representation of doctors, workers, and employers on the fund boards.

The transition from a voluntary type of health insurance to a national health insurance system proved to be a contested political issue in Belgium in the 19th and 20th centuries. The socialist funds wanted a national model to introduce universality and receive compensation for the overrepresentation of bad risks. The Catholic mutualities advocated a mutual aid society legislation model. Following the Catholic principle of subsidiarity, they fought for a pluralistic model. The laws on the mutualities of 1851 and 1894 explicitly recognized the role of the religion-based funds. The Belgians (and the Swiss, too) found a pragmatic way out of this fundamental conflict by introducing government subsidies to the mutualities. In exchange for these subsidies, the government acquired the right to take some regulatory measures, in particular on the conditions for membership, the financial practice of the mutualities, and the types of benefits they were required to provide.[5] After World War I, the major political parties eventually agreed on the necessity of a national health insurance model, but they could not unite on its institutional structure. Whereas the Socialists called for a neutral national organization, the Catholic mutualities held to a pluralistic model according to the subsidiarity principle. The political compromise in the 1944 law on health insurance eventually combined a national health insurance model with a pluralist institutional structure. The Belgian resolution of "subsidized freedom" still exists.

Germany followed a somewhat different path. Health insurance in Germany has always been more centralistic. The 1883 health insurance legislation enacted by Chancellor Bismarck was a landmark in the development of national health insurance in Germany. Interestingly, Bismarck had clear political intentions with his law, because he was quite concerned about class unrest and the formation of a social democratic party in 1869. His health insurance program, aimed at alleviating the material needs of the growing industrial proletariat and fostering their loyalty to the state, was accompanied by the suppression of the Social Democratic Party (Immergut 1992). Yet, it is important to emphasize the high degree of path dependency in the Bismarck legislation. In fact, it combined three elements of the pre-existing structure: mandatory enrolment of the local funds; self-regulation of employers and employees (*Selbstverwaltung*) of the auxiliary funds; and employer contributions of the company funds (Alber and Bernardi-Schenkluhn 1992). The "Bismarckian model" is a mixture of national health insurance with a corporatist institutional structure. Germany, however, has never developed a purely national health insurance scheme: in 2007 about 11 percent of the German population had private health insurance.

The adoption of national health insurance legislation also turned out to be problematic in the Netherlands (Maarse 2006; De Bruine and Schut 1990). From 1900 to 1940 successive governments did not succeed in implementing a model for health insurance legislation.[6] In a few cases, legislative proposals were withdrawn. This impasse would last until 1941 when the German occupier introduced a compulsory health insurance scheme for employees. The German Sickness Funds Decree, which for pragmatic reasons was not abolished after the war (Okma 1975), was codified with the Sickness Fund Act in 1964. However, not until 2006 did the Netherlands have a purely national health insurance model (Immergut 1992). The fraction of the population affiliated with a sickness fund always fluctuated around 63 percent. In the 1970s and 1980s several proposals to transform the sickness fund scheme into a national health insurance scheme failed. National health insurance has only recently been accomplished with the 2006 health insurance reform (Bartholomée and Maarse 2006).

The road to national health insurance in France was also strewn with political conflicts. The present system is the product of decades of group-interest politics in which mutual funds, employers, the self-employed, farmers, and especially the medical profession constantly sought to influence or block political decision-making. It took for instance eight years to decide on the 1928 Social Insurance Law that introduced compulsory health insurance. Interest-group politics caused the law to be rescinded immediately, but it was reenacted in 1930. The mutual funds protested against the law, which, in their view, was "too statist" because of the proposed introduction of regional public funds. In response to these protests, the mutual funds retained their position as primary insurance carrier. To please the farmers, they were given their own separate scheme, financially supported by the state (Immergut 1992; Wilsford 1991).

The enactment of the 1945 Social Security Ordinances was another political battlefield. These government programs aimed at the introduction of national health insurance legislation by means of *caisses,* administered by boards of representatives delegated by the unions and employers' associations (self-administration). The displaced mutualities would be given a new status by allowing them to provide complementary schemes. Its strong centralizing tendencies led the mutualities and the medical profession to warn of the "nationalization of medicine" and even the "Sovietization of French health care" which would threaten "*la médicine libérale*" (Immergut 1992: 105). Main controversies were the split of the financial burden between employers and employees, the regulation of doctors' fees, and the administrative structure. The reform was eventually realized in 1948, but it was not a great success, as measured against its initial intentions. The concept of universal coverage under a single scheme was abandoned and replaced with a structure of separate social security schemes for specific occupational groups (Wilsford 1991).

Several policy lessons can be drawn from this short history. First, the introduction of national health insurance in every country took many years. The development path can best be described as a process of incremental adjustments over a long period of time. A second lesson is that health insurance legislation and the extension of state intervention in health care proved a source of political conflict. The transition from voluntary arrangements to national health insurance was not easy. There were many conflicts on the power balance between state and local funds (subsidiarity), doctors' fees (see next section), the required degree of pluralism and "uniformism," and the administration of the sickness fund boards. Thus, the present structure of national health insurance was less the result of rational design than political compromise and incremental policymaking. Policymaking was mostly driven by political rationality. The logical result of this observation is that the design of health insurance must be considered a political compromise between conflicting interests (third lesson). A final lesson is that the history of health insurance in Europe can be analyzed in terms of convergence and divergence. Convergence refers to the fact that each country introduced health insurance and gradually moved away from decentralist, voluntary, informal systems, covering only a limited portion of the population, toward more centralist (national), formal, compulsory models with broad population coverage. In each country health insurance also featured some plurality. But there was divergence as well because each country followed its own specific way. Consequently, there is no single historical path toward national health insurance. As a result, the institutional variety of national health insurance in the five countries selected has always been immense (see annex 12B for more details on the present situation).

THE DOCTORS' STRUGGLE

Doctors have always played a prominent role in the development of national health insurance. Health insurance presented them with a fundamental dilemma. On one hand, they had a strategic interest in health insurance because it made financial resources available to treat poor patients. On the other hand, doctors perceived health insurance as a strategic threat because it contradicted the principle of "liberal medicine." In their view, health insurance would compromise professional autonomy because it intruded into the doctor-patient relationship. National health insurance would increase the leverage of the government over health care providers, in particular regarding their revenues (Immergut 1992). At the local level, the doctors' interests also conflicted with those of the funds. Thus, doctors were in conflict both with the funds and with the government. Both organizations became a target in the doctors' political fight over three basic principles: free choice of doctor, control over the funds, and, last but not least, economic independence.

Even in the early days of health insurance, relations between doctors and funds were often far from friendly. To economize, the funds contracted with doctors at a discount. Some funds also employed their own doctors. The doctors fiercely opposed the "closed panel" of doctors and campaigned for a "free choice of doctor." Furthermore, they worried about the power concentration of the funds. For this reason, doctors' associations advocated a pluralistic institutional structure as an effective weapon against power concentration on the funds' side. To break the monopsony power of the funds, in some countries doctors' associations demanded collective contracts on remuneration instead of individual contracts (Immergut 1992).

The struggle over free choice of doctor and control over the funds has been a key obstacle in the history of health insurance legislation in the Netherlands. There were big controversies with the funds (and the government) on the relationship between the funds and the doctors. A central claim of the Dutch Medical Association and the Dutch Association of Pharmacists was that doctors and pharmacists had to have 50 percent of the seats on the funds' boards. To weaken the position of the funds, some members of the Dutch Medical Association (established in 1849) started doctor funds that integrated health care financing with health care provision. They were governed by boards dominated by doctors, pharmacists, and local dignitaries. The association also initiated "association funds" (*maatschappijfondsen*). Doctors used these funds—successfully—as a countervailing power in their struggle with established funds and the government. Their market share on the eve of World War II was 38 percent (De Bruine and Schut 1990).

The gradual transition to national health insurance in the 19th and 20th centuries was, from the doctors' perspective, a complex mixture of threats and opportunities. They feared it would lead to ever more government involvement in health insurance matters. Doctors well understood that, once governments paid for medical services, they would seek to lower their prices. Hence, they perceived the progressive nationalization of health insurance and the centralizing tendencies in the administrative structure as the emergence of a payer cartel between government and the funds.

At the same time, however, health insurance legislation provided the doctors with opportunities to reinforce their position. They successfully campaigned for a pluralistic institutional structure, collective contracting, and free choice of doctor. Sometimes, for instance in Germany, they were supported by worsening economic conditions. The economic crisis at the end of the 1920s and early 1930s brought many funds to the verge of bankruptcy and forced the government to intervene. The 1930 emergency law imposed the obligation on the funds to negotiate collective contracts with the regional associations of the doctors, and doctors were obligated to join the regional association. These associations acquired a monopoly for treating the funds' insured in exchange for a capitation payment. The insured were given free choice of doctor (Veraghtert and Widdershoven 2002; Alber and Bernardi-Schenkluhn 1992). The Nazi-government further favored the doctors' position in health care at the expense of the sickness funds (Webber 1988).

The most intense conflicts were on payment for medical care. Doctors in the Netherlands sought to restrict the percentage of the population covered by national health insurance in order to limit the loss of their privately paying patients. For this reason the Sickness Fund Act covered only persons under a government-set wage ceiling. To secure the income of general practitioners, the Dutch Medical Association claimed a system of subscription fees. At the same time, it successfully fought for a fee-for-service system for the private patients of general practitioners and medical specialists working in hospitals or private practice.

Doctors in Belgium were fiercely opposed to collective bargaining and a benefit in-kind payment system that would place sickness funds as a third party between doctor and patient. After long negotiations, political deadlock, and strikes the doctors eventually accepted collective tariff agreements introducing uniform tariffs ("conventions"), but they retained, with some restrictions, the right to extra billing. Furthermore, they were successful in keeping the fee-for-service payment system unchanged. Another success was that patients had to pay their doctors directly and were remunerated by the funds later (Veraghtert and Widdershoven 2002).

The same issues were also on the political agenda of health insurance policy making in France (Immergut 1992). A particular aspect of the French situation was the existence of ideological and other cleavages among the doctors. Internal conflicts culminated in the 1960s. Eventually, three groups of doctors that had earlier left the Confédération des Syndicats Medicaux Français (CSMF) joined together in the Fédération de Médicine de France (FMF). In 1967–85, they opposed the CSMF on several issues, including fee schedules, social benefits, and cooperation with state authorities (Wilsford 1991).

The most important policy lesson from this short history is that doctors were heavily involved in the development of national health insurance and fought many conflicts with the government and funds over what they saw as major points: freedom of doctor choice, no predominance of the funds, and, last but not least, fee-for-service payment. Health insurance posed a dilemma for doctors. On one hand, they had an interest in health insurance legislation, particularly doctors who served the poor in the rural areas. On the other hand, they correctly understood that health insurance legislation would provide the state with leverage to intervene in their affairs. Hence, national health insurance forced the doctors to play a political balancing act.

BROADENING COVERAGE

The history of the *breadth of coverage* of health insurance—the portion of the population covered by insurance—is a history of gradual extension. Only recently has coverage been provided for the entire population of Belgium (1969), Switzerland (1994), France (2001), and the Netherlands (2006). Germany is the only one of the five European countries discussed where about 11 percent of the population has private health insurance (box 12.2).[7]

The present broad coverage of national health insurance is a relatively recent phenomenon. Insurance funds were selective in the early years of their existence and usually covered only a limited portion of the population. Important social selectivity mechanisms were: membership in a guild or category of workers; employment in a company; religious affiliation; place of residence; socioeconomic status; health status; political affiliation; and ethnicity (racism) during the Nazi regime (Webber 1988). There were also open voluntary funds, but most of them denied access to the very poor. Other funds often followed a similar course of action. Hence, group solidarity meant selective solidarity (Veraghtert and Widdershoven 2002).

BOX 12.2   SOCIAL HEALTH INSURANCE COVERAGE

Belgium

1944	Introduction of universal access to social health insurance for all salaried employees (compulsory)
1964	Extension of coverage to self-employed but for major risks only
1965	Extension of coverage to public workers for both major and minor risks
1967	Extension of coverage to the physically incapable of working
1969	Universal coverage (self-employed only major risks)

France

1900	Coverage 2.5 million persons
1940	Coverage 10 million persons
1945	Social Security Ordinance to introduce universal coverage, which was put into practice in stages; extended to students (1948), career soldiers (1949), farmers (1961), self-employed professionals (1966–70), and medical doctors (1985)
1999	Universal coverage

Germany

1885	Coverage 10%
1913	Coverage 34%
1924	Coverage 51%
1960	Coverage 83%
1987	Coverage 89%
2003	Coverage 89%

Netherlands

1900	Coverage 10%
1937	Coverage 40%
1945	Coverage 60%
2000	Coverage 63%
2006	Universal coverage

Switzerland

1945	Coverage 48%
1960	Coverage 72%
1970	Coverage 89%
1980	Coverage 97%
1995	Universal coverage

Sources: Belgium, EOHSP 2007; France, EOHSP 2004c; Germany, Bärnighausen and Sauberborn 2002; Netherlands, EOHSP 2004b; Switzerland, Alber and Benardi-Schenkluhn 1992.

Generally speaking, national health insurance started as a social security arrangement for the employed. The self-employed and the nonworking parts of the population were admitted later and stepwise. The coverage of the working population in each country was also the result of successive steps. Germany provides a good example of this. The 1883 statutory health insurance law covered various categories of blue-collar workers and persons employed by lawyers, notaries, bailiffs, and industrial cooperatives. Transport workers were covered in 1885, commercial office workers in 1892, agricultural and forestry workers and civil servants in 1911, unemployed in 1917–18, wives and daughters without own income in 1919, all primary dependents in 1930, self-employed workers in nursing and child care in 1938, retirees in 1941, and artists as well as publicists in 1981 (Bärnighausen and Sauerborn 2002). One of the last categories added to the list in France in 1985 was, ironically, physicians (Wilsford 1991).

The elderly and the self-employed often posed specific problems. They are now fully covered in France and Switzerland. National health insurance in Belgium covers the self-employed as well but only for major risks such as hospitalization. During several decades, the Netherlands followed a different, and not particularly successful, route. Because the elderly were not covered by the 1941 Sickness Funds Decree, the government came up with a special scheme in 1957 to cover the elderly living on incomes below a government-set income ceiling. The income-dependent premium could never break even, however, and deficits had to be covered by government subsidies and mandatory transfer payments of the sickness funds. Despite this financial support, the elderly fund could not survive. Its abolishment in 1986 contained an important policy lesson: specific arrangements for insured at risk are doomed to fail if they lack sufficient political and social support.

Another instructive experience concerned the history of the "voluntary" sickness fund in the Netherlands. This state-arranged device was a resort for the self-employed and some other categories who in 1941 could not enroll in the compulsory sickness fund scheme. It would soon develop as the Achilles' heel of health insurance because of rising expenditures and lagging revenues. To tackle this problem, the government used the subsidy instrument. This policy brought no adequate solution, however, particularly after the private insurers, offering low premiums, began to lure away the good risks. The voluntary health insurance scheme was abolished in 1986. The main policy lesson here is again that specific funds with an overrepresentation of bad risks cannot survive financially without a strong political or social will for risk pooling.

From this short description emerges the general conclusion that in every country it took decades to achieve (almost) universal coverage. In the early days, health insurance arrangements were highly selective. In an incremental process, coverage was gradually broadened.

DEEPENING COVERAGE

As for *depth of coverage*—the comprehensiveness of the health services package—the historical path has been more or less identical. In a threefold process, first, the list of covered medical services was lengthened. Second, the benefits packages were gradually extended to additional disease groups and services (e.g., occupational diseases and sexually transmitted diseases). Third, already existing benefits gradually increased in amount and duration (e.g., Germany eliminated the time limit on coverage of inpatient care in 1974) (Bärnighausen and Sauerborn 2002).

The earliest government interventions in depth of coverage date from the time of mutual aid society legislation in the 19th century. For instance, in Belgium and Germany the state introduced a minimum package of services the funds had to cover to receive state subsidies. In the Netherlands, the government always abstained from such measures before the enactment of the 1941 Sickness Funds Decree. The passage of national health insurance legislation provided the government with sufficient leverage to define the package of covered health services. In all countries studied, legislation introduced a centralistic decision-making model in which the government was responsible for defining a standard package of medical services to be covered. The room for autonomous "package decisions" by the funds was limited to what is called complementary health insurance.

The history of deepening coverage of national health insurance can be depicted as one of gradual extension. Yet concerns soon arose over the rising costs of health care. In 1923 Belgium introduced a copayment system to tackle the cost increase (Veraghtert and Widdershoven 2002). Germany had already done so in its *Krankenversicherungsgesetz* of 1883. The economic crisis in the 1970s and 1980s definitely altered the landscape for package decisions. Governments became more critical about further extensions of the standard package and also began to remove some health services from it. But the importance of this development should not be exaggerated. Everywhere, decision making followed an incremental path, and some decisions to remove certain health services from the package were later revoked. In none of the five countries under study is there consensus on the definition of what constitutes a *basic* or standard package of health services (Ham 1997; Ham and Robert 2003). The definition of a standard package has always been colored by political considerations, private interests, and cultural notions. The concept of evidence-based medicine has gained importance over time, but its role should not be overstated (Goddard et al. 2006).

THE STRUCTURE OF THE HEALTH INSURANCE MARKET

A first observation on the *structure of the health insurance market* concerns the number of funds. The development path can be described in terms of two periods: extension and contraction. During the first decades of health insurance, the number of funds grew rapidly. In the next period the number of funds declined. For instance, Germany had 21,342 operating funds in 1913. That number dropped by 4,625 in 1937 and 2,028 in 1960, leaving 1,200 operating funds by 1992. Consolidation has continued since then, and the number of sickness funds in 2004 was 250 (Alber and Bernardi-Schenkluhn 1992). In Switzerland, the number of sickness funds grew from 453 in 1914 to its peak of 1,160 in 1935 (Alber and Bernardi-Schenkluhn 1992). Since then the number has continuously declined, dropping to 92 in 2004. In the Netherlands, after the enactment of the Sickness Funds Decree in 1941, many sickness funds had to terminate because they could not fulfill their requirements. Only 291 of the roughly 650 operating sickness funds applied for a license, and 204 were eventually approved by the government (Veraghtert and Widdershoven 2002; De Bruine and Schut 1990). Due to ongoing consolidations, the number of health insurers has further declined.

Another structural aspect of the insurance market concerns the type of funds. In Belgium, most funds have always been closely affiliated with political organizations and the unions (Nonneman and Van Doorslaer 1994). Ideological competition between the mutualities has been and still is a constitutive element of health insurance. In the Netherlands, sickness funds function as neutral organizations without ties to social organizations. Until the early 1990s, they operated as regional monopolists, but now they are exposed to competition.[8] Germany developed a mixed system of local funds, company funds, substitute funds, and a few other fund types. Competition between the funds was introduced in the mid-1990s. Competition has always been a distinctive characteristic of the Swiss health insurance market.

France is the only one of the five countries without freedom of sickness fund choice. Although the French see solidarity as the underpinning concept of their social security system, they did not manage to introduce a single national health insurance scheme. The Caisse Nationale de l'Assurance Maladie de Travailleurs Salariés (CNAMTS) covers about 80 percent of the French population. The rest of the population is covered by specific funds. This fragmented structure is a result of political compromises. During the political debate on the 1945 Ordinance, the self-employed considered having their own fund a matter of prestige and did not want to share the burden of other population segments. The farmers and a few other groups also emphasized the need for social selectivity. To please them and to build enough political support for health insurance reform, they were permitted to have a separate scheme heavily subsidized by the state (Immergut 1992; Wilsford 1991).

A final aspect of the structure of health insurance concerns the governance of the sickness funds. In Belgium, France, and Germany, many funds have always been self-governed by representatives of employer and worker organizations. Sickness funds in the Netherlands were also self-governed, but employer and worker organizations did not play a prominent role.

ECONOMY AND GOVERNANCE

Contextual factors have always influenced the course of the development path of health insurance. Understanding the influence of these factors is critical for the successful introduction of health insurance. Here the economic context and governance are analytically differentiated.[9]

Three observations about the economic context are important. First, the birth of health insurance can be viewed as a social response to the industrialization process in the 18th and 19th centuries. Social security arrangements were necessary to financially protect workers against the loss of income during sickness leave and the costs of medical care. Hence, it is not surprising that health insurance initially concentrated in the cities and that its expansion in nonindustrial life went more slowly. Second, general economic crises sometimes significantly delayed health insurance legislation. For instance, in the Netherlands policymakers on a few occasions in the pre-war period reasoned that the economic crisis made health insurance economically unaffordable. The third factor regards the formalization of the economy. Extending the breadth of coverage of health insurance required a clear definition of the newly admitted groups. It is no coincidence that coverage of the self-employed, including farmers, was often deferred.

The last factor contains an important policy lesson for scaling up health insurance. The presence of a large informal economy is a big obstacle to the implementation of national health insurance schemes. It requires inventive new strategies to collect the revenue for these schemes and to demarcate exactly who is covered. The private sector may be given a leading role in this respect.

The evolution of national health insurance was intimately linked to the development of the welfare state in Europe. An important aspect of this development was that the state gradually started programs to protect its citizens against major problems such as unemployment, sickness, inability to work, and the costs of medical care. Most of these programs started as voluntary activities in the community. After a while, they were taken over by the state, their depth of coverage extended, and made compulsory. The evolution of national health insurance presents a prime example of this historical trend. By no means did this development constitute a single event. It was embedded in wider sociopolitical developments, with social and political impacts that can hardly be overstated. Despite divergent ideological positions and frequent political conflicts about shaping the structure of the social protection arrangements and moving forward, the general trend in Europe toward an active state role in welfare programs had broad support among the people.

The activation of the state's role in welfare programs was accompanied by a strong centralization tendency in governance. The state took on a central role in outlining and implementing social protection programs, including national health insurance arrangements. The state also possessed the legal and political instruments to make these programs compulsory and safeguard their financing. At the same time, however, social protection programs were not completely monopolized by the state. These programs can be understood as a fundamental compromise between an active involvement of the state and an active involvement of societal groups. The resulting institutional arrangement had a three-layer structure: the state at the top, an intermediary layer of societal groups, and citizens at the bottom. This collaborative arrangement made a significant contribution to the effectiveness and legitimacy of national health insurance programs.

The transition from voluntary sickness funds to national health insurance did not mean that the funds were fully downgraded to bureaucratic task organizations of the state. On the contrary, they not only retained a strong position in the implementation of national health insurance but were also given a prominent position in policymaking by their participation in what are often termed corporatist structures. Under corporatism, the state confers upon groups representing major economic or functional interests an officially recognized role, "public status" in policymaking and administration, whereby they share in the state's authority to make and enforce binding decisions. Although there are many variations, organized interests[10] are accorded by the state a privileged place in the policy-making administrative structure (which often implies more than mere consultation) and delegates authority to them to implement public policy on its behalf (Giaimo 2002). Corporatism can be conceptualized as a tool of governance to increase the legitimacy of public policymaking by explicitly including organized interests in public policymaking.

The important policy lesson from this discussion is that the evolution of national health insurance in Europe not only assumed a leading role of the state but also a prominent role of civil society (i.e., social capital). These formed the necessary preconditions for its effectiveness and legitimacy. Without these preconditions, the historical path of national health insurance would probably have been quite different. If the steering capacity of the state fails and a strong civil society is largely absent, it is prudent to develop other routes for scaling up health insurance arrangements. In this case, the private sector may be granted a leading role.

Bärnighausen and Sauerborn (2002) make an interesting observation in this respect. After pointing out that health insurance in Germany was transformed from a voluntary arrangement into a compulsory arrangement, the authors cast some doubt about whether compulsory arrangements are always superior to voluntary arrangements. In particular, they suggest that political contingencies in middle- and low-income countries may make voluntary arrangements a preferable strategy, in particular in the initial stage of health insurance. Compulsion may also prove unenforceable for administrative or economic reasons.

CONCLUSIONS AND POLICY LESSONS

From this analysis of the historical pathway of health insurance in five European countries, the most important concluding observations and policy lessons are summarized in this final section.

Conclusions

(1) There is no single type of national health insurance in Europe. Each country has developed its own version.

(2) There is no single historical path in the development of health insurance. Each country followed its own route. However, despite national variations in pathways, there are also some common elements.

(3) Health insurance started everywhere as a voluntary, bottom-up, risk-sharing arrangement, rooted in communities and groups. It was not a state-orchestrated activity. At the time of ascendance of the funds, the state was not even capable of setting up and running a national scheme. Local governments welcomed these initiatives because they lessened the need for public poverty programs.

(4) The introduction of national health insurance occurred in steps. It was the result of a process of continuous incremental adjustments in a given economic, political, and social context.

(5) A similar conclusion can be drawn for state intervention. It developed in steps and was often contested. National health insurance arrangements run by the state are the present result of a historical development.

(6) National health insurance has developed as a largely public arrangement that, with some exceptions, crowded out private health insurance.

(7) The introduction of health insurance poses a dilemma for doctors. It creates both opportunities (payment of care for the poor) and threats (growing state intrusion into the doctor-patient relationship and unfavorable financial conditions). Doctors in Europe fought over three basic principles: free choice of doctors, no predominance of sickness funds, and economic independence.

(8) Initially, health insurance arrangements were selective in terms of breadth of coverage—they covered only specific groups in society. The personal scope of health insurance arrangements was only gradually extended.

(9) Initially, health insurance arrangements were also very selective about the depth of coverage, the package of health services covered. Their package was expanded gradually in steps. The gradual extension of the benefits package cannot be seen apart from the development of medicine. Financial considerations (limited financial resources) also played a role.

(10) There are wide variations in the structure of the health insurance market. A common element is that the number of funds has declined significantly over time. There is also a wide variety of fund types (see last section and annex 12B).

(11) Successful implementation of health insurance depends on the availability of a minimum level of social capital. Social capital is required to understand mutual reciprocity and is indispensable for joint action and accepted authority. Social capital also implies the existence of a common normative framework stipulating the moral obligation to set up social security programs, including health insurance, for mutual support.

Policy Lessons

(1) National health insurance arrangements must be embedded in each country's wider social, economic, political, and cultural contexts. This may lead to variations: in Europe, there is no single type of health insurance. Neither is there a single European path.

(2) Countries with some experience in small-scale insurance arrangements might be wise to build their national scheme as much as possible on these local arrangements to increase the scheme's effectiveness and legitimacy. Where small-scale arrangements do not yet exist, it is probably prudent to introduce health insurance by encouraging local community-based initiatives that are supported financially by the government.

(3) The evolution of national health insurance in Europe not only assumed a leading role for the state but also a prominent role for civil society. They formed prerequisites for its effectiveness and legitimacy. If the steering capacity of the state fails and a strong civil society is largely absent, it is prudent to develop other routes for scaling up health insurance arrangements. The private sector might be granted a leading role in this respect.

(4) An introductory path in steps may contribute to the effectiveness and legitimacy of national health insurance.

(5) Selective membership may contribute to the effectiveness and legitimacy of health insurance arrangements.

(6) A pluralistic institutional structure may contribute to the effectiveness and legitimacy of national health insurance.

(7) Involve doctors and other providers as early as possible in setting up health insurance arrangements. Beware that their position on health insurance may be ambiguous.

(8) In a large informal economy, inventive strategies will be required to collect the financial resources for these schemes and to demarcate their breadth of coverage. The private sector may be granted a leading role in this respect.

(9) The road to national health insurance is strewn with political conflicts. The present structure of health insurance is less the result of rational design than of political compromise and incremental policymaking. Consultants advising countries on the design of health insurance must be fully aware of the unique elements of the health insurance model in their home country.

(10) The European experience is a reminder that the development of national health insurance may take many years.

ANNEX 12A SOCIOECONOMIC DATA ON HEALTH INSURANCE, SELECTED WEST EUROPEAN COUNTRIES

TABLE 12A.1 The Economy

Country/year	GDP per capita (US$)	Government final consumption (% GDP)	Public revenue (% GDP)	Age dependency ratio[a]
Belgium				
1970	2,729	16.4	39.0	58.7
1980	12,785	22.4	45.5	52.4
1990	20,296	20.0	45.5	49.4
2000	22,529	21.3	49.1	52.5
2004	34,129	22.9	49.4	52.5
France				
1970	2,916	17.0	—	60.5
1980	12,872	21.1	46.0	57.0
1990	21,856	21.7	47.7	52.0
2000	22,424	22.9	50.2	53.4
2004	22,804	23.9	49.9	53.5
Germany				
1970	3,104	15.3	39.6	57.1
1980	13,389	19.9	45.0	50.8
1990	24,283	18.1	42.5	42.9
2000	23,031	19.0	46.4	48.2
2004	33,160	18.6	43.2	50.6
Netherlands				
1970	2,835	19.1	39.9	58.9
1980	13,161	19.1	49.8	51.1
1990	20,468	24.4	47.4	45.1
2000	24,167	22.6	45.6	47.4
2004	37,051	24.3	44.5	47.8
Switzerland				
1970	3,608	8.3	—	53.6
1980	17,244	10.1	—	49.7
1990	35,110	11.1	30.6	46.1
2000	34,224	11.1	36.3	48.3
2004	48,666	11.9	31.7	47.3
United States				
1970	4,999	18.3	30.6	61.4
1980	12,186	16.8	31.8	51.3
1990	23,064	17.0	33.1	52.0
2000	34,603	14.4	35.9	51.1
2004	39,772	15.8	31.7	49.4

Source: OECD 2006.
Note: — = not available.
a. Population 0 to 14 years of age plus population over 65 years divided by population ages 15 to 64 years.

TABLE 12A.2   Health Care Expenditure, 2004

Country	THE per capita (US$)	THE as % GDP	OOP as % THE	Government health exp. as % THE	Social health insurance as % THE	Private prepaid health insurance as % THE	External resources as % THE	Government health exp. as % GDP
Belgium	3,009	10.1	23.5	8.9	62.2	3.4	1.9	0.86
Germany	3,205	10.9	10.4	9.8	68.4	8.8	2.6	1.04
France	3,566	10.5	7.5	3.3	75.0	12.4	1.7	0.35
Netherlands	3,417	9.2	7.8	3.0	59.3	19.1	6.0	0.27
Switzerland	5,645	11.6	31.9	17.0	41.4	8.7	0.9	1.93
United States	6,102	15.3	13.2	32.2	12.5	36.7	5.4	15.34

Source: OECD 2006.
Note: OOP = out of pocket; THE = total health expenditure.

TABLE 12A.3   Health Care Expenditure as Percentage of GDP

Country	1960	1970	1980	1990	2000	2004
Belgium	—	3.9	6.3	7.2	8.6	10.1
France	3.8	5.3	7.0	8.4	9.2	10.5
Germany	—	6.2	8.7	8.5	10.4	10.9
Netherlands	—	6.6	7.2	7.7	7.9	9.2
Switzerland	4.9	5.5	7.4	8.3	10.4	11.6
United States	5.1	7.0	8.8	11.9	13.3	15.3

Source: OECD 2006.
Note: — = not available.

TABLE 12A.4   Health Care Expenditure per Capita (US$, PPP)

Country	1960	1970	1980	1990	2000	2004
Belgium	—	148	636	1,341	2,277	3,044
France	70	205	698	1,532	2,450	3,159
Germany	—	269	960	1,738	2,670	3,005
Netherlands	—	329	755	1,435	2,257	3,041
Switzerland	166	351	1,031	2,029	3,179	4,077
United States	147	352	1,072	2,752	4,588	6,202

Source: OECD 2006.

Note: — = not available; PPP = purchasing power parity.

TABLE 12A.5   Health Indicators, 2004

Country	Life expectancy at birth	Infant mortality rate (%)	Maternal mortality rate (%)	Number of physician consultations per capita/year	Physician density per 1,000	Medical specialists per 1,000	% pop. covered by social health insurance	% pop. covered by private health insurance[a]
Belgium	78.8	4.3	—	7.6	4.0	1.9	99.0	1.0
France	80.3	3.9	8.8	6.7	3.4	1.7	99.3	0.7
Germany	78.6	4.1	5.2	—	3.4	2.4	89.8	10.2
Netherlands	79.2	4.1	5.2	5.3	3.6	0.9	63.0	23.7
Switzerland	81.2	4.2	5.6	3.4	3.8	2.5	100.0	0
United States	77.5	6.9	12.1	3.9	2.4	1.4	26.6	—

Source: OECD 2006.

Note: — = not available.

a. Estimated percentage of the population covered by substitute private health insurance. Complementary health insurance schemes have been left out of consideration.

ANNEX 12B   OVERVIEW OF HEALTH FINANCING AND SOCIAL HEALTH INSURANCE, SELECTED WEST EUROPEAN COUNTRIES

TABLE 12B.1   Overview of Health Financing/Social Health Insurance Scheme, Selected West European Countries

Item	Belgium	France	Germany	Netherlands, until 2006	Netherlands since 2006	Switzerland
Insurance type	Compulsory	Compulsory	Compulsory under income ceiling	Compulsory under income ceiling	Compulsory	Compulsory
			Opt-out arrangement for persons above income ceiling	Persons over income ceiling must buy private health insurance		
Population covered by social health insurance (%)	99.0	99.3	89.0	76.3	99.0[a]	100
Number of schemes	Single	Single with small variations	Single with small variations	Single	Single	Single
Number of sickness funds, 2002	94 (organized in 7 associations)	17	355	22	32 (2007)	93
Starting date	1944	1945 (social security ordinance)	1883 (Bismarck legislation)	1941 (sickness fund decree)	2006	1911
Benefits package, size	Comprehensive	Comprehensive	Comprehensive; separate scheme for long-term care	Comprehensive; separate scheme for long-term care	Comprehensive; separate scheme for long-term care	Comprehensive
Standard basic benefits package	Yes	Yes	Yes with small variations	Yes	Yes with variations	Yes with variations
Complementary health plans	Yes	Yes	Yes	Yes	Yes	Yes
Percentage of population covered	30–50	94	9	95[b]	95	30
Year	2000	2000	2000	2005	2007	2000
Contribution type	Uniform income-related premium rate (7.4%) plus nominal premium rate per capita varying per fund	Income-related premium rate varying per fund (mean 14.1%)	Uniform income-related premium rate (13.6%) plus social security tax (7.5%) plus social debt tax (0.5%)	Income-related premium rate (8.45%) plus nominal premium rate per capita varying per fund	Income-related premium rate (6.5%) plus nominal premium rate per capita varying per fund Children <18 free Government subsidies to low-income people	Income-related premium rate plus nominal premium rate per capita varying per fund. Children <18 free Government subsidies to low-income people

(continued)

TABLE 12B.1   Overview of Health Financing/Social Health Insurance Scheme, Selected West European Countries *(continued)*

Item	Belgium	France	Germany	Netherlands, until 2006	Netherlands since 2006	Switzerland
Ceiling on contributory income	Only for self-employed	Yes	Only for self-employed	Yes	Yes for income-related premium Not applicable for nominal premium	Not applicable
Employer-employee split	52–48	50–50	94–6	80–20	100–0 income-related part 0–100 nominal premium rate	0–100
Access to providers general practitioner	Yes	Yes	Yes	Yes (gate-keeper)	Yes (gate-keeper)	Partly yes[c]
Ambulatory specialist	Yes	Yes	Yes	Yes	Yes (preferred provider possible)	Partly yes[c] (preferred provider possible)
Hospital	Yes	Yes	Yes	Yes	Yes (preferred provider possible)	Partly yes[c] (preferred provider possible)
Sickness fund	Yes	Yes	No (occupational)	Yes	Yes	Yes
Major health insurance reforms since 1990	Introduction of financial responsibility of sickness funds by risk-based capitation formula (1995)	Free choice of sickness fund for most of insured (1993) Introduction of statutory insurance for long-term care (1996)	Law on health care financing: part of social health insurance financing shifted from salary-based contributions to generalized income tax (1998) Introduction of free complementary health plan provided to poorest part of population (about 4.5 million people)	Sickness free to set per capita nominal premium rate (1991) Free choice of sickness fund (1992)	Introduction of new health insurance law (2006)	Revision of federal law on health insurance (1996)

Sources: Saltman, Busse, and Figueras 2004; Mossialos and Thomson 2004; Bartholomée and Maarse 2006.
a. Under 100 percent because of uninsured.
b. Under social health insurance.
c. People, in principle, have no free access outside their canton of residence.

ANNEX 12C   THE CONCEPTUALIZATION OF GOOD GOVERNANCE

Kaufmann, Kraay, and Mastruzzi (2005) conceptualize governance as multidimensional. They distinguish between three main dimensions, each consisting of two subdimensions.

1. Process of Selecting, Monitoring, and Replacing Governments

(a) *Voice and accountability*

Some indicators are the extent to which citizens are able to participate in the selection of governments, exercise democratic accountability and civil (political) rights (e.g., freedom of speech, assembly, demonstration, religion, press), benefit from respect for minorities, and enjoy equal opportunities.

(b) *Political instability and violence*

Some indicators are likelihood that government will be destabilized or overthrown by unconstitutional means including domestic violence; frequency of armed conflicts, violent demonstrations, political killings, disappearances, torture, extremism, and ethnic tensions; scale of political terrorism; and security risk rating.

2. Government's Capacity to Formulate and Implement Policies Effectively

(a) *Government effectiveness*

Some indicators are quality of public service provision; quality of bureaucracy, competence of civil servants; independence of civil service from political pressures; public spending composition; public debt; credibility of government's commitment to policies; trust in government; policy consistency; focus on input required for the government to formulate and implement good policies and deliver public products.

(b) *Regulatory quality*

Some indicators focus on content of policies; absence of market-unfriendly policies including price controls, excessive protection; unfair competition practices, discriminatory tariffs; adequacy of bank supervision; excessive burdens due to excessive regulation, taxes; price stability; access to capital markets.

3. Respect of Citizens and the State for Institutions Governing Economic and Social Relations

(a) *Rule of law*

Some indicators are the extent of confidence in the rules; compliance with rules; effectiveness and predictability of the judiciary; measure of society's success in developing an environment in which fair and predictable rules form the basis for economic and social interactions and the extent to which property rights are protected.

(b) *Control of corruption*

Some indicators are corruption as "exercise of public power" for private gain; "petit corruption"; "grand corruption" (state capture).

NOTES

ACKNOWLEDGMENTS: The authors are grateful for the comments of Dr. K. Okma and Dr. K. Companje on an earlier draft of this chapter.

1. Other West European countries with a national health insurance model are Luxembourg and Austria. The model has also been adopted by some countries in Central and Eastern Europe that had a Semashko-type of health care system before the fall of the Berlin Wall in 1989.

2. A single national health insurance model does not exist. Hence, countries differ in the extent to which each of these basic characteristics is fulfilled. For instance, a national health insurance scheme may cover a substantial part of the population, but not all, as in Germany and, until 2006, in the Netherlands. Similarly, government involvement may be very strong (e.g., in France) or less strong (e.g., in Germany).

3. For the convenience of the reader, basic information on health care expenditures and health systems of the countries studied are presented in annexes 12A and 12B, respectively.

4. The Netherlands followed a different path. Covering the costs of medical treatment has always been the core business of sickness funds. The coverage of income risk to sickness was organized by small, local mutual societies.

5. By 1938 about 32 percent of the mutualities' revenues were government subsidies.

6. The Sickness Benefit Law providing protection against the loss of income during illness was implemented in 1929.

7. However, Germany has an opt-out system. Persons who pass the income threshold may opt out but are not compelled to do so, as was always the case in the Netherlands before the 2006 health insurance law.

8. The 2006 Health Insurance Reform also put an end to the traditional dividing line between sickness funds and private health insurers. The term sickness fund has been abolished and replaced with health insurer.

9. See annex 12A for some basic background information on Belgium, Germany, France, the Netherlands, Switzerland, and the United States.

10. Here, the representative associations of health insurers and health care provider agents.

REFERENCES

Alber, J., and B. Bernardi-Schenkluhn. 1992. *Westeuropäische Gesundheitssysteme im Vergleich: Bundesrepublik Deutschland, Schweiz, Frankreich, Italien, Grossbritannien.* Frankfurt, Germany/New York: Campus Verlag.

Bärnighausen, T., and R. Sauerborn. 2002. "One Hundred and Eighteen Years of the German Health Insurance System: Are There Any Lessons for Middle- and Low-Income Countries?" *Social Science and Medicine* 54: 1559–87.

Bartholomée, Y., and J. Maarse. 2006. "Health Insurance Reform in the Netherlands." *Eurohealth* 12 (2): 7–9.

Bayertz, K. 1999. "Four Uses of Solidarity." In *Solidarity*, ed. K. Bayertz, 3–28. Dordrecht, Germany: Kluwer Academic Publishers.

Colombo, F., and N. Tapay. 2004. *Private Health Insurance in OECD Countries: The Benefits and Costs for Individuals and Health Systems*. Paris: OECD.

De Bruine, M., and F. Schut. 1990. "Overheidsbeleid en Ziektekostenverzekering." In *Beleid en Beheer in de Gezondheidszorg,* ed. J. Maarse and I. Mur-Veeman, 114–119. Assen/Maastricht, Netherlands: van Gorcum.

EOHSP (European Observatory on Health Systems and Policies). 2000. *Health Care Systems in Transition: Switzerland*. Copenhagen: World Health Organization.

———. 2004a. *Health Care Systems in Transition: Germany*. Copenhagen: World Health Organization.

———. 2004b. *Health Care Systems in Transition: Netherlands*. Copenhagen: World Health Organization.

———. 2004c. *Health Care Systems in Transition: France*. Copenhagen: World Health Organization.

———. 2007. *Health Care Systems in Transition: Belgium*. Copenhagen: World Health Organization.

Giaimo, S. 2002. *Markets and Medicine: The Politics of Health Care Reform in Britain, Germany, and the United States*. Ann Arbor: University of Michigan Press.

Goddard, M., K. Hauck, A.S. Preker, and P. Smith. 2006. "Priority Setting in Health—A Political Economy Perspective." *Health Economics, Policy and Law* 1: 79–90.

Ham, C. 1997. "Priority Setting in Health Care: Learning from International Experience." *Health Policy* 42: 49–66.

Ham, C., and G. Robert, eds. 2003. *Reasonable Rationing: International Experience of Priority Setting in Health Care*. Buckingham, UK: Open University Press.

Hinrichs, K. 1995. "The Impact of German Health Insurance Reform on Redistribution and the Culture of Solidarity." *Journal of Health Politics, Policy and Law* 20: 653–83.

Immergut, E. 1992. *Health Politics: Interests and Institutions in Western Europe*. Cambridge: Cambridge University Press.

Kaufmann, D., A. Kraay, and M. Mastruzzi. 2004. *Governance Matters III: Governance Indicators for 1996, 1998, 2000, and 2002*. Washington, DC: World Bank.

———. 2005. *Governance Matters IV: Governance Indicators for 1996–2004*. Washington, DC: World Bank.

Levi, M. 1996. "Social and Unsocial Capital: A Review Essay of Robert Putnam's *Making Democracy Work*." In *Politics and Society* 24: 45–55.

Maarse, J. 2006. "Report on Mandatory Health Insurance in the Netherlands." Report prepared for the World Bank, Maastricht, Netherlands/Washington, DC.

Mossialos, E., and S. Thomson. 2004. *Voluntary Health Insurance in the European Union.* Geneva: World Health Organization.

Nonneman, W., and E. Van Doorslaer. 1994. "The Role of the Sick Funds in the Belgian Health Care Market." *Social Science and Medicine* 39 (10): 1483–95.

OECD (Organisation for Economic Co-operation and Development). 2006. *Health Data 2006.* Paris: OECD.

Okma, G.H. 1975. "Studies on Dutch Health Politics, Policies and Law." Dissertation, Rijswijk.

Putnam, R.D. 1993. *Making Democracy Work: Civic Traditions in Modern Italy.* Princeton, NJ: Princeton University Press.

Rothstein, B. 2001. "Social Capital in the Social Democratic Welfare State." *Politics and Society* 29 (2): 207–41.

Saltman, R., R. Busse, and J. Figueras, eds. 2004. *Social Health Insurance Systems in Western Europe.* Maidenhaid, UK: Open University Press.

Ter Meulen, R., W. Arts, and R. Muffels, eds. 2001. *Solidarity in Health and Social Care in Europe.* Dordrecht, Germany: Kluwer Academic Publishers.

Van Oorschot, W. 1999. "The Legitimacy of Welfare: A Sociological Analysis of the Motives for Contributing to Welfare Schemes." Paper 99.11.02, Work and Organisation Research Centre, Tilburg, Netherlands.

Veraghtert, K., and B. Widdershoven. 2002. *Twee eeuwen solidariteit: De Nederlandse, Belgische en Duitse ziekenfondsen tijdens de negentiende en twintigste eeuw.* Amsterdam, Netherlands: Aksant.

Webber, D. 1988. "The Politics of German Health System Reform: Successful and Failed Attempts at Reform from 1930–1984." Paper prepared for the European Consortium for Political Research Workshop on policy change in perspective, Bologna/Rimini, Italy.

Wilsford, D. 1991. *Doctors and the State: The Politics of Health Care in France and the United States.* Durham, NC: Duke University Press.

CHAPTER 13

From Cradle to Grave in the United Kingdom, Canada, Australia, and Elsewhere

Alexander S. Preker and Mark C. Bassett

INTRODUCTION

The introduction of universal access to health care is reviewed in this chapter in a select group of OECD countries—the United Kingdom, Canada, Australia, New Zealand, the Scandinavian countries, Greece, Spain, Italy, and Portugal. All these countries moved beyond the insurance model to general taxation funding to finance health care.

Universal or near-universal coverage of health care has been the topic of health care reform in many countries, first in the more advanced market economies and more recently in low- and middle-income countries. The Declaration of Alma-Ata was adopted at the International Conference on Primary Health Care (PHC) of 1978 (WHO 1978).[1] It expressed the need for urgent action by all governments, all health and development workers, and the world community to protect and promote the health of all people. It was the first international declaration underlining the importance of primary health care. Since then, the primary health care approach has been accepted by member countries of the World Health Organization (WHO) as the key to achieving the goal of "Health for All."

Universal coverage is defined as "a situation where the whole population of a country has access to good quality services (core health services) according to needs and preferences, regardless of income level, social status or residency." (Nitayarumphong and Mills 1998: 1)

Such universal access may be financed through taxes or through contributory insurance schemes. And it may be organized through a national health insurance service or a more fragmented delivery system. There are two major paths to achieve this goal of universal health care coverage, undertaken by most developed and developing countries. One is through compulsory or social insurance (known as the Bismarck model), and the other is through taxation (the Beveridge model). Chapter 12 described the experience of countries that chose the Bismarck model. This chapter describes what the countries that chose the Beveridge model encountered. In reality, as will be seen in this chapter, there is a significant overlap between these two approaches.

At the end of the 20th century, most western countries relied mainly on direct out-of-pocket payment and unregulated markets to finance and provide health care. In 1938, New Zealand became the first country with a market economy to introduce compulsory participation and universal entitlement to a comprehensive range of health services, financed largely through the public sector (the United Kingdom followed a similar path when—10 years later—it established the National Health Service [NHS], in 1948).

Universal access to health care in many East European countries—Albania, Bulgaria, the Czech Republic, the Slovak Republic, Hungary, Poland, Romania, and the former USSR—was achieved through similar legislative reforms. A number of other middle- and low-income countries have followed a similar path.

Today, the populations in most OECD countries (with the exceptions of Mexico, Turkey, and the United States) enjoy universal access to a comprehensive range of health services that are financed through a combination of general revenues, social insurance, private insurance, and user charges. In 13 of the OECD countries, universal access was achieved through landmark legislative reforms that guaranteed their population such benefits, while most other OECD countries achieved similar coverage through voluntary and regulatory mechanisms. The focus of this chapter is mainly on the countries that achieved universal access through specific landmark legislative reforms and a single-payer financing mechanism rather than through incremental expansion of multiple payers through voluntary and regulatory mechanisms.

PAST ACHIEVEMENTS

The experience of the United Kingdom, Canada, Australia, and other countries that have already achieved universal access for their population can usefully be placed in the context of recent improvements in health and growth in health expenditure.

Improvements in Health and Shifts in Priorities

The previous century witnessed greater gains in health outcomes than at any other time in history. These gains are partly the result of improvements in income with accompanying improvements in health-enhancing social policies (housing, clean water, sanitation systems, and nutrition) and greater gender equality in education. They result also from new knowledge about the causes, prevention, and treatment of disease, and from the introduction of policies, financing, and health services that make such interventions accessible in a more equitable manner.

Parallel to these developments, the disease patterns of the past century are changing high mortality and fertility to low mortality and fertility. The share of the global disease burden due to noncommunicable diseases (mainly cardiovascular and neuropsychiatric diseases, and cancers) is expected to increase from 36 percent in 1990 to 57 percent in 2020, while the burden due to infectious diseases, pregnancy, and perinatal causes is expected to drop from 49 to

22 percent. Even with effective prevention, this epidemiological shift will have a profound impact on the health care institutions needed to treat the resulting illnesses.

Growth in Financial Resources

Fortunately, the resources available to the health sector have grown. Global GDP was expected to be around US$57 trillion in 2012. Global spending on health care was expected to reach a record US$6.0 trillion, US$660 billion of it in developing countries alone. Donor spending has also grown in the past decade from less than US$5 billion to over US$30 billion.

Although spending on health care in the most impoverished regions such as Africa has reached more than US$30 billion, it continues to lag behind the per capita spending of other regions, and reliance on out-of-pocket spending remains high (between 50 and 80 percent of spending), not unlike the situation observed in Europe and North America a hundred years ago. Figure 13.1 illustrates the relationship between per capita GDP and the share of GDP spent on health.

FIGURE 13.1   Relationship between Per Capita Income and Health Spending

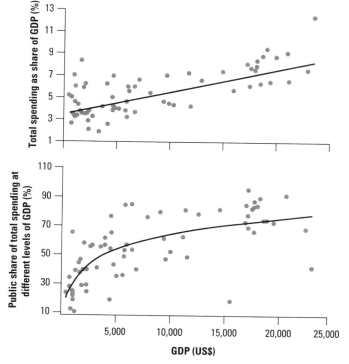

Source: World Bank 1993.

MAJOR OUTSTANDING ISSUES

Despite these achievements, low- and middle-income countries throughout the world face many difficult challenges in meeting the health needs of their populations, mobilizing sufficient financing in an equitable and affordable manner, and securing value for scarce resources spent on preventive and curative health services.

This is not unlike the situation in Western Europe and North America a century ago. Throughout most of history, people used home remedies, private doctors and other health care workers, and nongovernmental hospitals when they were ill. Often, only the rich could afford such care, and the range of effective treatment was limited. Today, in low-income countries—where public revenues are scarce (often less than 20 percent of GDP) and institutional capacity in the public sector is weak—the financing and delivery of health, nutrition, and population (HNP) services are largely in private hands. In many of these countries, large segments of the poor still have no access to basic or effective care for a variety of reasons discussed below.

In most developed countries—and in many middle-income countries—governments have become central to social policy and health care. This involvement by the public sector is justified on both theoretical and practical grounds to improve: (a) equity, by securing access by the population to health, nutrition, and reproductive services; and (b) efficiency, by correcting for market failures, especially when there are significant externalities (public goods) or serious information asymmetries (health insurance).

The main actions taken by governments to correct for such market failures, from least to greatest intervention, include: providing information to encourage behavioral changes needed for long-term improvements in health, nutrition, and population outcomes; enforcing regulations and incentives to influence public and private sector activities; issuing mandates to indirectly finance or provide services; financing or providing subsidies to pay for services or influence prices; and direct public production of preventive and curative health services.

One of the clearest cases for strong government intervention in the HNP sector can be made when there are large externalities (the benefits to society are greater than the sum of benefits to individuals). This is true in the case of clean water, sanitation services, vector control, food safety measures, and a range of public health interventions (e.g., immunization, family planning, maternal and perinatal health care, control of infectious diseases, and control of tobacco, alcohol, and illicit drug abuse). Medical education and R&D are two other areas for active government intervention.

A second area for strong government intervention is health care financing because private voluntary health insurance is particularly prone to a number of market imperfections, many of which relate to information asymmetries. While insurance may succeed in protecting some people against selected risks, it usually fails to cover everyone willing to subscribe to insurance plans, and it often excludes those who need health insurance the most or who are at greatest risk of illness. This happens because insurers have a strong incentive to enroll only healthy or low-cost clients (risk selection or cream skimming). Private insurers also have incentives to exclude costly conditions or to minimize their financial risk through the use of benefit caps and exclusions. This limits protection against most expensive and catastrophic illnesses.

Because of these factors, individuals who know they are at risk of illness have a strong incentive to conceal their underlying medical condition (adverse selection). Individuals who are healthy—or think they are—often try to pay as low premiums as possible. This prevents insurers from raising the funds needed to cover the expenses incurred by sicker or riskier members. Worse, the healthy may deliberately underinsure themselves, in the hope that free or highly subsidized care will be available when they become ill (free-riding). When third-party insurers pay, both patients and providers have less incentive to be concerned about costs, and some may even become careless about maintaining good health. This leads not only to more care being used (the reason for insurance), but also to less-effective care, or care that would not be needed if people maintained good health (moral hazard).

This chapter focuses on a group of countries in which policy makers decided to replace insurance coverage with state funding and a mix of public and private provision of services as a way of mobilizing financial resources equitably and efficiently instead of trying to fix existing market failures observed in health insurance-based systems (chapter 12).

Issues relating to health status and improving the performance of the health care providers (public and private) are not discussed, although the interlinkages between these three systems (figure 13.2) are important to the impact of health care financing reforms.

TWO DIFFERENT REFORM PROCESSES TO UNIVERSAL ACCESS

The OECD experience in introducing universal health care can be regarded as taking place in two phases: the policy formulation phase; and the implementation phase (figure 13.3).

During the policy formulation phase, the design of the reform needs to consider both the financing and service delivery aspects. Without access to health services, legislation that mandates universal financing is little more than a paper law. After the design of a successful system of financing universal access, a major stumbling block in most countries has been the political economy of policy formulation and dealing with various stakeholders with vested interests that may resist such reforms for a variety of reasons, to be discussed later.

In the OECD, this policy formulation phase was, however, only the first phase in the introduction of universal access. An equally important phase during

FIGURE 13.2   Health Financing

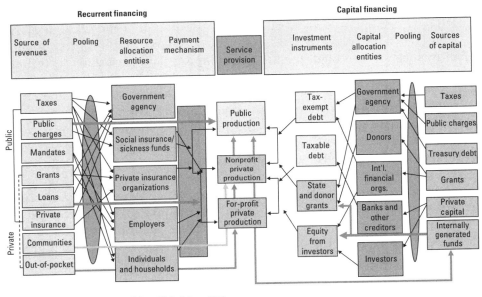

Source: Adapted from Preker, Zweifel, and Schellekens 2010.

FIGURE 13.3   Phases in the OECD Experience

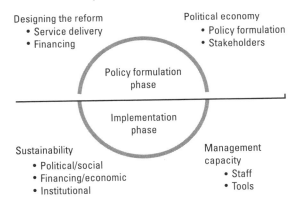

Source: Preker 1998.

which the reforms were sometimes derailed was the implementation phase. During this phase, both management capacity (staff, resources, and administrative tools such as information systems) and sustainability factors (financial resources, political commitment, and institutional infrastructure) played critical roles in securing the success of the reforms.

FIGURE 13.4   Different Approaches to Universal Coverage

Entitlement	1 Restricted	4 Universal
Participation	2 Voluntary	5 Compulsory
Financing mechanisms	3 Multipayer	6 Single payer

Group I

Australia	– – – + + +
Canada	– – – + + +
Denmark	– – – + + +
Finland	– – – + + +
Greece	– – – + + +
Iceland	– – – + + +
Italy	– – – + + +
New Zealand	– – – + + +
Norway	– – – + + +
Portugal	– – – + + +
Spain	– – – + + +
Sweden	– – – + + +
United Kingdom	– – – + + +

Group II

Austria	+ – + – + –
Belgium	+ – + – + –
France	+ – + – + –
Germany	+ – + – + –
Ireland	+ – + – + –
Japan	+ – + – + –
Luxembourg	+ – + – + –
Netherlands	+ – + – + –
Switzerland	+ + + – – –

Group III

Mexico	+ + + – – –
Turkey	+ + + – – –
United States	+ + + – – –

Source: Preker 1990.

The OECD countries that enjoy universal access to health care can be separated into two groups (figure 13.4) based on

- The extent of legal entitlement and physical access offered to the population under public schemes (universal versus restricted)

- The nature of participation in the public or privately mandated schemes (compulsory versus voluntary membership)

- The number of financing sources (single-payer versus multipayer).

Political Economy of Reform Process

The political process in the Group I countries was often painful. Legislation was often introduced only after years of public debate on the pros and cons of the reforms, with stakeholders on both sides having entrenched positions. In any reform that involves sharing of risks and the financial burden of illness, there are both winners and losers. While the social benefits were great, the political cost was high. Most governments that introduced the major legislative reforms needed to introduce universal coverage ended up losing during the subsequent election for office. In this respect, the 2012 reelection of President Barack Obama in the United States after having introduced the draft Affordable Health Care Act of 2009 was an exception to this historical trend. Although the draft act was never passed into law, the related Health Care and Education

Reconciliation Act passed in 2010, closing an important gap in coverage in the Unites States.

Different Dimensions of Universality

Group I countries listed in the left column of figure 13.4 are characterized largely by compulsory participation and universal entitlement to comprehensive services financed through a single payer. Group II countries listed in the right column lack one or more of these characteristics. The health insurance countries discussed in chapter 12 belong mainly to Group II. These different dimensions of entitlement, participation, and financing mechanisms are explored briefly in the sections that follow.

LEGAL ENTITLEMENT AND DIMENSIONS OF ACCESS

Universal entitlement implies that the whole population is eligible for benefits, irrespective of income, health status, membership in good standing, or other constraints. All Group I countries have passed legislation that provides such benefits, while Group II countries restrict entitlement to a targeted portion of the population such as low-income earners, children, pensioners, and other groups of the nonemployed. Many Group II countries, such as Belgium, France, Germany, Japan, and the Netherlands, achieved almost universal coverage through extensive membership in different sickness funds and other insurance organizations. Most of the Nordic countries and the United Kingdom passed through a similar historical phase before extending coverage to the whole population under a single legislative act. Because most Western countries offer supplemental health insurance to cover higher standards of care, private accommodations in hospitals and other health facilities, entitlement is a question of degree and open to interpretation. The dates of the legislative reforms that introduced universal entitlement in the Group I countries are provided in table 13.1.

Legislative Reforms Leading to Universal Entitlement

Universal entitlement is meaningful only to the extent that there is reasonable access to services. In practice, a lag often occurs between the time that policies are formulated, legislation prepared, and laws passed, and the date on which programs are implemented, services offered, and entitlement exercised. This is a particular problem in many low- and middle-income countries where entitlement is often restricted to publicly provided services and where such services are either of a low quality or absent altogether.

Where geographic, financial, cultural, or functional barriers exist, legal entitlement may lose some of its significance. This issue remains a topic of ongoing

TABLE 13.1   Landmark Dates in Introduction of Universal Coverage

Country	Coverage date
New Zealand	1938
England/Wales	1949
Sweden	1953
Norway	1956
Finland	1963
Canada	1966
Demark	1971
Iceland	1972
Australia	1974
Portugal	1978
Spain	1978
Italy	1980s
Greece	1980s
United States[a]	2010

Source: Preker 1990.

a. The United States has a policy of universal coverage and has passed legislation, but has not completed implementation.

debate on equity in most of the OECD. In most of the countries that have achieved universal access, measures had to be introduced to mitigate such problems after the initial legislation was passed. For example, compulsory universal health insurance in Sweden led to universal entitlement to health services in 1955. But it was the Seven Crowns Reform of 1969 that reorganized the health service and expanded access to the whole population.

Likewise, compulsory universal health insurance was introduced in Finland in 1964, but it was the Public Health Act of 1972 that extended access to the whole population. The range of services offered through various forms of entitlement has changed greatly over time and varies from one country to another. The minimum standards for health care provided through social security advocated by the ILO (ILO 1952) were much more limited in scope than the more comprehensive requirements needed to satisfy the WHO (WHO 1985).

Even the core contents of many programs, such as health promotion, prevention, curative treatment, rehabilitation, and chronic care, have changed over time. One of the most clear-cut cases of segmentation into a limited range of services occurred in Canada. The National Hospital and Diagnostic Services Act of 1957 called for compulsory participation and universal entitlement to hospital care only. Treatment by doctors was not included until 1967 under the Medical Care Act. Even this act excluded most ambulatory services not provided by doctors. Most other ambulatory services, dental care, chronic care, pharmaceuticals, and so on were not included under either piece of legislation. Today, many low- and middle-income countries are pursuing a similar strategy by restricting universal access to a limited range of essential health services (the basic package).

NATURE OF PARTICIPATION

The meaning of voluntary and compulsory participation has been equally open to interpretation. Denmark has been credited for having achieved a remarkably high membership with the "voluntary sickness funds" prior to the 1970s. However, only the upper echelons of a means-tested population could afford to opt out. Medium- to low-income workers did not really have this choice, since failure to be a member in good standing in a sickness fund meant automatic loss of eligibility for a number of other social benefits such as pensions and unemployment benefits.

Canadian participation still depends largely on provincial compliance because the federal government has no real direct jurisdiction over most aspects of health care. When the federal government introduced its Medical Care Act in the late 1960s, Ontario was allowed to qualify for federal cofinancing once the province had achieved a 90 percent rate of voluntary participation, even though the law called for 100 percent participation. All other countries have been classified as having compulsory participation.

Group I countries offer some voluntary programs through supplemental or private health insurance to cover above-standard services provided by both the private and public sectors. Only Australia and Denmark have allowed participants in these programs to opt out of their public programs. Likewise, all the countries that have been classified in Group II have compulsory participation for part of their populations.

In most OECD countries, the nature of participation in a particular scheme has been heavily influenced by the interests of a few major stakeholders. For example, during the early 20th century, when doctors and hospitals had a difficult time making ends meet, there was little objection to extending membership in the friendly societies or sickness funds to ensure participation of low-income earners. Later, when compulsory participation attempted to extend such coverage to high income groups, it was seen as state interference in the doctor-patient relationship. Similar arguments are often seen in low- and middle-income countries that are trying to introduce compulsory schemes.

FINANCING MECHANISMS

The actual source of financing used to achieve universal access varies greatly in the OECD, relying on a combination of general revenues, social insurance, private health insurance, and direct charges. Today, Group I countries rely

FIGURE 13.5   Effect of Reform on Health Care Expenditure and Economic Sustainability

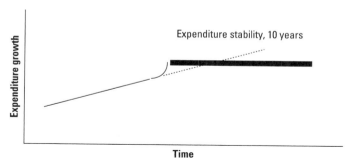

Source: Based on Preker 1990.

more heavily on general revenue financing, while Group II countries rely more heavily on a mix of general revenues, social insurance, and private insurance. Group I countries use a single-payer mechanism, and all the Group II countries use multiple-payer mechanisms.

Despite the doomsday prediction of many critics, almost all the OECD countries that passed major legislative reforms to introduce universal access to health care experienced a decade-long period of stability in health care expenditure following the reform (figure 13.5).

Health Expenditure

Several explanations can be provided for this leveling off of health care expenditure after the introduction of universality:

• Greater policy control over expenditure

• Elimination of the inflationary pressures created by private health insurance

• Saturation of the service delivery system even when entitlement increased

• Near-universal coverage in some countries prior to the reforms.

RELEVANCE OF OECD EXPERIENCE TO THE DEVELOPING WORLD

In health care financing, blind faith in the market is no more likely to resolve the complex problems that face the health sector than is a naive belief in government. A central lesson from the OECD experience, which is equally applicable to developing countries, is that whereas the private sector plays an increasingly prominent role in service delivery, strong government will be needed in most countries to secure adequate risk pooling, sustainable financing, cost containment, and equitable resource allocation.

Pooling of Risks

Some people are much sicker than others. Sharing of risks across population groups is a fundamental aspect of social protection in the HNP sector. Furthermore, people use health care most during childhood, the childbearing years for women, and old age—when they are the least productive economically. Income smoothing across the life cycle can, therefore, also contribute to social protection in the HNP sector.

Yet, as in 19th-century Europe when health care was still in a primitive stage of development, direct out-of-pocket health expenditure continues to be a distinctive feature of many low- and middle-income countries (figure 13.6).

Household payments can account for as much as 80 percent of total health expenditures because of: nontrivial user fees charged in public facilities (official and unofficial); high copayments required in health insurance schemes; and use of private health services (hospitals, clinics, diagnostics, medicines, and health care providers). This undermines the social protection that could be provided by the HNP sector even in low-income settings.

Experience has shown that strong action is needed by the public sector to take advantage of the substantial resources that can be mobilized through private channels, while at the same time ensuring social protection for vulnerable groups. Because of cost and the pronounced market failure that occurs in private health insurance, this is not a viable option for risk pooling at the national level in low- and middle-income countries. Figure 13.7 shows the pattern of risk pooling in the OECD and selected developing countries.

FIGURE 13.6   Financing Pattern for Health Care in Developing Countries

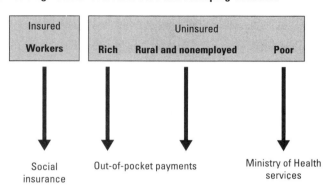

Source: Preker 1998.

FIGURE 13.7   Degrees of Risk Pooling

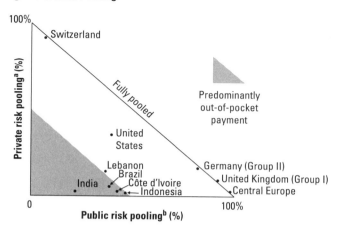

Source: Preker 1998.

a. For example, private insurance.

b. Through social insurance and general revenues.

Securing Adequate Financing

Strong, direct government intervention is needed in most countries to finance public health activities and essential health, nutrition, and reproductive services, as well as to provide protection against the impoverishing effects of catastrophic illness. In low-income countries, total government revenues may constitute 20 percent or less of GDP (figure 13.8). Although it is impossible to define a lower threshold precisely, a country with a per capita income in the range of US$300 to US$800 would have to spend in the range of 1.5 to 3 percent of GDP (equivalent to 7.5 to 15 percent of government revenues) to finance a minimum level of preventive and essential clinical services. Many low-income countries spend less than this, and have weak capacity to mobilize further tax revenues. Governments in these countries may need to mobilize additional financing from community sources and international donors to pay for public health interventions with large externalities and essential programs for the poor.

In middle-income countries with per capita incomes above US$800, even at low tax collection rates, governments may choose to spend as much as 3 to 5 percent of GDP on health care. This is usually sufficient to pay for care that goes well beyond essential preventive and clinical services for the poor.

In these countries, other considerations become important, such as tailoring the mix of broad-based financing instruments to each country's individual circumstances. Critical factors in this respect would include equity and efficiency in collection mechanisms, administrative simplicity, budget mechanisms, cost

---

FIGURE 13.8   Tax Capacity, by Country GDP per Capita

- Governments in many countries often raise less than 10% of GDP in public revenues

- Tax structure in many low-income countries is often regressive.

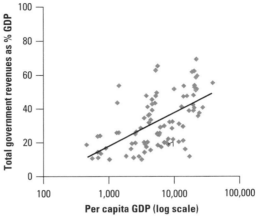

Source: Preker et al. 2004.

---

containment, willingness to pay, affordability of the benefits package, and stability in the underlying macroeconomic environment. Countries must also ensure that a large share of financing derives from a prepaid source of revenues (risk pooling through general revenues, and social or community-rated mandated health insurance, or both) to avoid the equity and efficiency problems associated with extensive reliance on user charges.

Containing Costs and Fiscal Discipline

Even in low- and middle-income countries, a significant share of national product and public resources is spent on health care. Although there are no fixed upper limits, fiscal concern may be warranted if total health spending is greater than 6 to 7 percent of GDP or if it is rising rapidly, since public funds are often involved. In too many countries, high expenditure levels involve public money spent on ineffective services that benefit only a few, while large segments of the population still do not have adequate access to essential care. In cases where expenditure control becomes an issue, governments have recourse to three broad types of policies:

- Policies that contain costs in the public sector through supply, demand, and price control strategies

- Policies that regulate the private sector, discourage the use of indemnity insurance, and encourage capitation payments rather than fee-for-service

- Policies that strengthen monitoring and tracking of health expenditure patterns (using health accounts).

Improving Budget Practices and Resource Allocation

Unfortunately, in a large number of low- and middle-income countries, one of the key issues relating to health care financing is neither lack of adequate resources nor runaway expenditures. Rather, problems in health care financing often result from poor budget practices, including a habit of deficit financing and a misallocation of scarce resources on ineffective care.

Three policies help countries balance their budget:

- Avoiding unfunded mandates (ensuring that financing is available to cover such expenditures)

- Ensuring that income from all sources exceeds expected aggregate expenditure levels by a margin (often 3 to 5 percent) that is sufficient to cover capital depreciation, and maintenance

- Setting clear sanctions against budget overruns and the accumulation of irreducible debt

- Allocating a large part of the budget envelope to effective interventions that improve outcomes.

REVISITING UNIVERSAL ENTITLEMENT

Most of the governments in the Group I set of countries have during the past few years revisited their universal entitlement reforms, flirting with some aspect of Group II characteristics. For example, some have considered restricting universal entitlements to a defined package of services, with the rest being available on a voluntary basis outside the mandatory package. And some have introduced a second tier of voluntary and supplementary health insurance.

Ironically, while many Group I countries have considered such changes, several Group II countries are doing the exact opposite. Most have slowly expanded their mandate to universal and compulsory coverage. And among Group II countries, debate has been active about the benefits of simplifying the financial arrangements under a single-payer system.

The recent debate on the role of markets and managed competition in the United Kingdom and compulsory universal coverage mandated under the Affordable Care Act in the United States highlight that the health financing debate in both Group I and Group II countries is likely to continue being revisited periodically in most countries, with a possible convergence on a middle ground.

NOTE

1. The conference was held in Almaty (formerly Alma-Ata), Kazakhstan (formerly Kazakh Soviet Socialist Republic), September 6–12, 1978.

REFERENCES

ILO (International Labour Office). 1952. "Social Security (Minimum Standards) Convention." No. 102. Geneva: ILO.

Nitayarumphong, S., and A. Mills, eds. 1998. *Achieving Universal Coverage of Health Care: Experiences from Middle- and Upper-Income Countries*. Bangkok: Ministry of Public Health.

Preker, Alexander S. 1990. *Universal Health Care in the OECD*. London: London School of Economics and Political Science (LSE).

———. 1998. "The Introduction of Universal Access to Health Care in the OECD: Lessons for Developing Countries." In *Achieving Universal Coverage of Health Care: Experiences from Middle- and Upper-Income Countries*, ed. S. Nitayarumphong and A. Mills, 85–104. Bangkok: Ministry of Public Health.

Preker, Alexander S., Guy Carrin, David Dror, Melitta Jakab, William C. Hsiao, and Dyna Arhin-Tenkorang. 2004. "Rich-Poor Differences in Health Care Financing." In *Health Financing for Poor People: Resource Mobilization and Risk Sharing*, ed. Alexander S. Preker and Guy Carrin, 3–51.Washington, DC: World Bank.

Preker, Alexander S., Peter Zweifel, and Onno P. Schellekens. 2010. *Global Marketplace for Private Health Insurance: Strength in Numbers*. Washington, DC: World Bank.

WHO (World Health Organization). 1978. *Declaration of Alma Ata*. International Conference on Primary Health Care, Alma-Ata, USSR, September 6–12.

———. 1985. Regional Office for Europe (ROE). *Targets for Health for All: Targets in Support of the European Regional Strategy for Health for All*. Copenhagen: WHO, ROE.

World Bank. 1993. *Investing in Health: World Development Report 1993*. New York: Oxford University Press.

CHAPTER 14

Great Post-Communist Experiment in Eastern Europe and Central Asia

Adam Wagstaff and Rodrigo Moreno-Serra

T he post-Communist transition to social health insurance in many of the Central and East European and Central Asian countries provides a unique opportunity to try to answer some of the unresolved issues in the debate over the relative merits of social health insurance and tax-financed health systems. This chapter employs regression-based generalizations of the differences-in-differences method on panel data from 28 countries for the period 1990–2004. The authors find that, controlling for any concurrent provider-payment reforms, adoption of social health insurance increased national health spending and hospital activity rates, but did not lead to better health outcomes.

INTRODUCTION

All but two of the OECD's 30 countries—Mexico and the United States—finance most of their health spending publicly, with half operating broad-based "tax-financed" health systems (e.g., Canada and the United Kingdom) and half operating payroll-based "social health insurance" (SHI) systems (e.g., Germany and Japan).[1] Outside the OECD, the fraction of countries financing the greater part of their health spending publicly is smaller (56 percent), and only one-fifth of these countries finance most of their government spending through SHI.[2]

The relative merits of SHI and tax finance is an old debate, but one that has recently resurfaced. In part this is due to the fact that three of the world's oldest SHI countries—France, Germany, and the Netherlands—are in the process of reducing their reliance on payroll contributions in favor of a broader financing base.[3] But the renewed interest in the SHI versus tax-finance debate also stems from the current interest in SHI in the developing world.[4] Many developing countries that have relied largely on general revenues (and out-of-pocket payments) to finance their health systems have introduced SHI, or are thinking about doing so.[5] And countries that have a fledgling SHI scheme in place are redoubling their efforts to expand its reach, especially to the informal sector.[6]

Despite the topicality and vibrancy of the SHI versus tax-finance debate, the evidence base is surprisingly thin. Some comparisons have been undertaken, especially on distributional issues: payments for health care tend to be more progressive or less regressive in tax-financed systems than in SHI systems; and tax-financed systems seem to be more successful at ensuring universal coverage within a single health system.[7,8] But on aggregate systemwide differences, there appears to be no rigorous evidence. We do not know whether SHI systems spend more on health care, and if they do whether this translates into higher levels of throughput and better health outcomes.

Getting at these questions through a cross-country econometric analysis where some systems are financed through SHI contributions and others are financed through general revenues would be problematic because there are likely to be unobservable variables that would be correlated with the type of financing system in place and the outcomes of interest (i.e., SHI is likely to be endogenous). A more promising strategy would be to look for *changes* in the way countries finance their health care, exploiting the variations in changes across countries to eliminate (time-invariant) unobservable variables. The difficulty with this approach is that in the group of countries that have the best data (those in the OECD), there have been very few switches between the SHI and tax-financed camps (six "old" OECD countries abandoned SHI in the 1970s and 1980s: Denmark, Greece, Iceland, Italy, Portugal, and Spain), and the transitions occurred some time ago, so the available data are very limited.

This chapter looks instead to a (mostly) different group of countries where transitions have occurred with greater frequency and more recently, namely the countries of (central and eastern) Europe and Central Asia (ECA).[9] Of the 28 ECA countries, 14 abandoned tax-finance and adopted SHI at some stage between 1990 and 2004 (and 4 other countries had adopted SHI prior to 1990). These countries are also data-rich countries, having inherited and largely maintained the Communist tradition of extensive data-gathering, and falling under the most data-rich regional office of the World Health Organization.[10] One dimension in which the database we have been able to assemble is especially rich is health outcomes; we have been able to assemble extensive information on mortality and disease incidence *by disease*. The fact that a sizeable fraction (perhaps 70–80 percent) of mortality is not amenable to medical care (cf. Nolte and McKee 2008) probably helps explain why many cross-country regression studies have been unable to find a strong relationship between health spending and health outcomes (cf., e.g., Martin, Rice, and Smith 2008). The same fact might—in the absence of disease-specific mortality data—have made it hard for us to credibly establish whether, by increasing health spending or by raising the efficiency of health spending, countries that switched to SHI have been able to improve health outcomes.[11] The ECA health financing experiment thus affords a valuable "laboratory" to try to shed light on the question of how SHI systems fare compared with tax-financed systems in spending, throughput, and health outcomes.

To shed light on these issues, we use regression-based generalizations of the differences-in-differences (DID) method, with data from (up to) 28 countries for

15 years (1990–2004). We pay particular attention to the issue of the possible endogeneity of SHI, since it seems likely that there may be events that occurred around the time SHI was introduced that we implicitly lump into our error term but which may affect outcomes. We employ three different approaches to allowing for this possible endogeneity. The first is a simple individual-specific effects model estimated along the lines of the classic DID model. This allows for the endogeneity of SHI only insofar as the unobservables that are correlated with SHI adoption and with our outcomes are time-invariant. This is the parallel trends assumption that is often considered the Achilles' heel of the DID approach (cf., e.g., Blundell and Costa Dias 2000). Because our database spans a relatively long period of time, we can explore two more flexible—and more robust—approaches to controlling for the potential endogeneity of SHI. The first is a random (linear) trend model: this allows for a country-specific unobserved linear time trend whose growth rate could be correlated with SHI status (i.e., whether the country operates an SHI system in the year in question). The second is a differential trend model: this allows SHI and tax-financed systems to have different trends in unobservables that are not necessarily linear but do depend only on SHI status. This is not the first analysis to employ the random trend regression model.[12] But it is—to our knowledge—the first to propose and employ a regression version of the differential trend generalization of the DID model.[13] We are able, using the two generalizations of the DID approach, to shed light empirically on the validity of the parallel trends assumption. In the event, we find that for most outcomes the data are reasonably consistent with the assumption. We also test for reverse causality in all three models, and find little evidence of it.

The organization of this chapter is as follows. The second section provides a brief history of the SHI reforms in the post-Communist ECA region and discusses the hypothesized effects of SHI adoption on health spending, throughput, and health outcomes. The third section outlines our methods, the fourth section our data, and the fifth section our empirical results. The sixth section presents our conclusions.

EUROPE AND CENTRAL ASIA'S SHI REFORMS AND HYPOTHESIZED EFFECTS

Under Communism, health care in almost all of the ECA countries (the former Yugoslavia was the exception) was financed out of general revenues and out-of-pocket payments.[14] Health care was delivered through a centrally planned "Semashko" model consisting of a tiered system of health providers, each allocated budgets according to population-based norms, with health workers paid by salary. In the early 1990s, as most countries shifted away from Communism, several looked to SHI to solve several emerging problems and improve the performance of the health sector.

Transitions to SHI

Of the 28 ECA countries, 14 introduced payroll taxes earmarked for health care at some stage between 1990 and 2004, and 4 others had already done so prior to 1990 (Bosnia and Herzegovina, Croatia, Serbia and Montenegro, and Turkey). Early SHI adopters in the 1990s included Estonia, Hungary, Lithuania, the former Yugoslav Republic of Macedonia, and Slovenia; all adopted SHI in the period 1990–92. Some countries adopted much later: Bulgaria, for example, adopted SHI as late as 1999. Often, both the employee and employer are liable, though of course there may be wide difference between who is legally liable for what and who ends up bearing the incidence of the payroll tax, the latter depending on conditions in the labor and product markets. Contributions are mandatory, and in exchange for them the contributing employee is entitled to receive health services under the terms of the SHI scheme. Groups other than formal sector workers usually have some coverage. Contributions are required from the self-employed in all SHI countries, and from pensioners in some. Other groups are financed out of general revenues, but often the contributions are not specified, and insufficient funds are provided in respect to these groups, who sometimes have inferior de facto coverage.

SHI does not always raise more than 50 percent of revenues, though in some countries its importance has increased over time and has gradually grown to 50 percent or more. This is clear from figure 14.1 (derived largely from WHO's *Health Systems in Transition* [HiTs] series[15]), which shows the timing of the introduction of SHI in different countries and the share of SHI in total health spending. In central and eastern Europe, SHI shares have tended to be higher, and payroll tax rates have tended to be higher there as a result. In the first group of countries, payroll tax rates are normally between 10 percent and 15 percent of earnings, while in the countries of the former Soviet Union, they are less than 10 percent, often considerably so (Langenbrunner, Sheiman, and Kehler 2008). Two countries (Latvia and Poland) introduced earmarked taxes for health care, but the tax base is income, not earnings, so from a financing perspective these are not "pure" SHI systems.

Hypothesized Benefits of the Transition to SHI

The most pressing problem that SHI aimed to tackle was the decline in health spending caused by a decline in government revenues as a share of GDP. This in turn was caused by a variety of factors, including the growth of the private and informal sectors where tax compliance was lower, a shrinking of traditional tax bases such as state-owned enterprises, and pressures for tax cuts from a population experiencing declines in real income. With falling GDP and revenues falling as a share of GDP, health sectors experienced substantial cuts in government spending. For a number of reasons, SHI was seen as a way of protecting spending in the health sector if not facilitating increases in spending: it was thought that people

FIGURE 14.1   SHI as a Share of Total Health Spending, 1990–2003

Country	90	91	92	93	94	95	96	97	98	99	00	01	02	03
Albania														
Armenia														
Azerbaijan														
Belarus														
Bosnia and Herzegovina	M	M	M	M	M	M	M	M						
Bulgaria														
Croatia														
Czech Republic														
Estonia			M	M	M									
Georgia														
Hungary	M		M		M									
Kazakhstan														
Kyrgyz Republic														
Latvia														
Lithuania		M	M	M										
Macedonia, FYR		M	M	M	M									
Moldova														
Poland														
Romania														
Russian Federation														
Serbia and Montenegro	M	M	M	M	M	M	M							
Slovak Republic														
Slovenia			M	M										
Tajikistan														
Turkey	M	M												
Turkmenistan														
Ukraine														
Uzbekistan														

☐ SHI share = 0%   ▦ 0% < SHI share < 50%

M = SHI in place but SHI share data missing   ■ 50% < SHI share

Source: Authors.

would be more willing to pay SHI contributions than (other) taxes because under SHI the revenues are earmarked for health services, and contributions confer entitlements to use them; it was argued that earmarking would help ensure that the health sector did not have to compete with other sectors in government spending allocation decisions; and it was thought that earnings in the economy as a whole would fall less than government revenues and be more stable. Providers were especially enthusiastic about SHI which they saw as a way to increase their incomes.

The reality has been rather different. Contributions in SHI systems have often fallen well below "theoretical" levels because of nonreporting and underreporting of earnings and nonenrolment. In Kazakhstan, for example, only 40 percent of expected revenues were actually collected (Gottret and Schieber 2006). In the Russian Federation, similar problems have been reported, with considerable variation geographically.[16] The scale of the evasion problem reflects the fact that in most SHI systems, access to health care does not increase with contributions, and may not actually require making any contributions at all. In most Latin American countries, noncontributors are often able to fall back on the health delivery system financed and operated by the health ministry; in the ECA countries, evidence of contributions is rarely required when accessing the health system. Furthermore, as countries have switched to SHI, tax financing has often been reduced by finance ministries, often in line with "theoretical" SHI revenues rather than actual revenues. In Kazakhstan, for example, the finance ministry reduced the allocation of tax revenues to the health sector as SHI contributions were introduced, regarding them as a substitute for tax revenues not a complement (Langenbrunner, Sheiman, and Kehler 2008). And in SHI systems, contributions are linked to earnings through a formula and typically subject to ceilings that may change infrequently, with the result that at times of rapid growth SHI revenues may not keep pace with per capita incomes, and a tax-financed system might produce higher revenue growth.[17]

Tax-financed systems in the ECA countries have had their own problems raising revenues, though in many cases informal out-of-pocket payments have plugged at least part of the gap (Lewis 2007). These problems included the aforementioned growth of the private and informal sectors where tax compliance was lower, and a shrinking of traditional tax bases such as state-owned enterprises. A priori, it is not obvious, then, whether SHI systems have fared better or worse than tax-financed systems in protecting health spending levels.

It was not just the idea that SHI would allow health spending to be better protected that attracted the ECA countries to SHI. It was also felt that SHI would permit a more efficient health system. It was thought that SHI would allow for a loosening of the grip of finance and health ministries over the finance and delivery of health care, the vision being that payroll tax contributions could flow automatically to an SHI agency that would sit at arm's length from both the finance and health ministries and that would develop a capacity to engage in strategic purchasing. The SHI agency, it was argued, would implement provider-payment reform, engage in selective contracting, and foster competition between public and private sector providers for SHI contracts. This would make government (and private) providers more accountable for their performance. Autonomization of providers was seen as a logical part of this process, which was seen as necessary for better performance and greater accountability.

Again, the reality has been somewhat different. SHI countries now typically have an SHI agency, but so, too, do Poland and Latvia that rely on income taxes or general revenues rather than on payroll taxes. These agencies are indeed typically independent of the ministry of health and have responsibility for administering the SHI scheme or at least some functions, such as collecting contributions, setting or recommending contribution rates and ceilings, pooling contributions, and so forth. Where it exists, the SHI agency pays providers, but some funds still flow from the health ministry (allocations for capital spending, for example, but also sometimes other items of spending, too). Where there is an SHI agency, it typically has explicit contracts with providers, although this has not always been the case, and has become common only in recent years. Moreover, the contracting is not always selective, although this, too, has become more common recently. Often there is no contracting with the private sector, and where it does occur, it is typically in primary care.

Most SHI countries have indeed shifted from budgets as a way of paying hospitals (the biggest spenders in a health sector) to either fee-for-service (FFS) or a patient-based payment method (PBP), such as diagnosis-related groups (DRGs). We have used information contained in WHO's HiTs series to classify a country's predominant hospital payment method in a given year as (1) fixed budgets/ block grants (the prevailing method under the Communist Semashko system), (2) fee-for-service/payment by bed-days, or (3) patient-based systems (mainly DRG-based) (cf. Ellis and Miller 2008). Of the 18 countries that adopted SHI, 12 switched from the use of budgets, though in four cases the switch occurred with a lag, and in one case the switch occurred prior to SHI adoption. Some switched to FFS and stuck with it, while others switched subsequently to a PBP. A few switched immediately to PBP.[18]

The switch to SHI has in practice, then, led to some changes in the purchasing and delivery of health care, and may therefore have led to improvements in the efficiency of the health system. It seems plausible that any such improvements will have been reflected to higher rates of throughput and lower rates of mortality and morbidity, even in the absence of any impact of SHI on spending levels.

There are, however, a couple of caveats. First, not all of the changes in purchasing and provider-payments hinged on a switch to SHI. For example, some ECA countries that did not adopt SHI (namely Latvia and Poland) switched away from budgets anyway. It is of some interest, therefore, to know how far any impact of SHI adoption is due to the shift to payroll finance and the setting up of an SHI agency, rather than to provider-payment reforms which could have occurred (and in the cases of Latvia and Poland did occur) even without the adoption of SHI. The lag between SHI adoption and provider-payment reform, the fact that different countries opted for different payment methods and sometimes switched a second time after SHI adoption, and the fact that some non-SHI countries also switched from budgets during our period all help create an opportunity to shed light on this question.

Second, the fact that the changes mentioned above occurred does not necessarily mean that the efficiency of the system necessarily increased. An SHI agency is likely to add a new layer of bureaucracy and cost to the health system. In several countries, the demarcation of responsibilities between the SHI agency and the pre-existing government health departments was blurred; and in most countries, risk pools were fragmented which meant economies of scale in health insurance administration were sacrificed (Kutzin et al. 2009). The purchasing and provider-payment reforms are also likely to have been costly to design and implement. Furthermore, putting aside the possibility of higher administrative costs in an SHI system, it is by no means automatic that the purchasing and provider-payment reforms seen in these systems will necessarily have led to lower health care costs and better health outcomes. Budgets and salaries do, of course, have their limitations; but FFS and PBP have their drawbacks too

(Ellis and Miller 2008). And while selective contracting is widely advocated, the evidence on its impact is thin.

METHODS

Let y_{it} be the health sector outcome of interest in country i at time t. In the empirical analysis below, the outcomes studied include health spending, throughputs, and health outcomes. Let X_{it} be a vector of covariates thought to potentially influence both outcomes and the SHI adoption decision, and SHI_{it} be a dummy variable taking on a value of 1 if country i has an SHI health financing system at time t. Consider the model:

$$y_{it} = X_{it}\gamma + \delta SHI_{it} + e_{it}, \tag{1}$$

where the e_{it} capture unobservable variables and noise. Our interest is in the coefficient δ which gives the impact of SHI on the outcome y_{it}. Estimating Eq. (1) by pooled ordinary least squares (OLS) would run the risk that the estimate of δ would be biased because of a correlation between SHI_{it} and e_{it}, i.e., SHI status might be endogenous. It could be that countries with unobserved characteristics that led to higher-than-expected levels of, say, health spending deliberately chose not to adopt SHI in the belief that it might be less easy to control spending in an SHI system. Or it might be that certain changes or events occurred broadly around the same time that SHI was introduced; if we do not capture these in our model but instead lump in the error term, and if they affect the outcomes of interest, our estimate of δ will be biased.

The Differences-in-Differences Model

The simplest way to allow for such a correlation is to let:

$$e_{it} = \alpha_i + \theta_t + \varepsilon_{it}, \tag{2}$$

where θ_t is a period-specific intercept, α_i is a country-specific effect which captures time-invariant unobservables that are potentially correlated with SHI status, and ε_{it} is an idiosyncratic error term (iid over i and t). Substituting Eq. (2) in Eq. (1) gives

$$y_{it} = X_{it}\gamma + \delta SHI_{it} + \alpha_i + \theta_t + \varepsilon_{it}. \tag{3}$$

In the special case where the X_{it} are omitted, Eq. (3) collapses to the standard differences-in-differences (DID) estimator (cf., e.g., Wooldridge 2002: 284). Eq. (3) can be estimated as a fixed effects model, or via first differences. In the latter case, the estimating equation can be expressed as

$$\Delta y_{it} = \Delta X_{it}\gamma + \delta \Delta SHI_{it} + \xi_i + \Delta\varepsilon_{it}, \tag{4}$$

which can be consistently estimated by pooled OLS if the endogeneity of SHI adoption is adequately captured by the error term specified in Eq. (2).

Care needs to be taken to get accurate standard errors in this type of analysis. Bertrand, Duflo, and Mullainathan (2004) have shown that many outcome variables used in published policy impact analyses generate positive serial correlation in the ε_{it}. If ignored, and the model is estimated as a fixed-effects specification, this positive serial correlation results in standard errors that are too small, and t-statistics that are too large—possibly dramatically so. In such a case, first differences may be preferred. Of course, if the ε_{it} in Eq. (3) are serially uncorrelated, the error term in the first-differenced version may well be subject to negative serial correlation, in which case the standard errors would be overestimated. An obvious strategy is to report standard errors that are robust to any type of serial correlation (and heteroskedasticity), whether one uses fixed effects or first differences. This is what we do below in all our models. The Monte Carlo results reported by Bertrand, Duflo, and Mullainathan (2004) suggest that with a sample of 28 countries the rate of rejection of the null hypothesis of no impact ought to be close to the right one.[19]

This generalized DID estimator assumes a parallel or common trend: the θ_t do not depend on the value of SHI_{it}, and therefore the "treated" health systems (i.e., those that switch to SHI) and the "untreated" ones exhibit the same trend. In reality, there may be time-varying unobservables that are correlated with both y_{it} and SHI status. We explore two approaches to relaxing the parallel trend assumption (PTA).

The Random Trend Model

The first approach is through the somewhat misleadingly named "random trend" (RT) model (cf., e.g., Wooldridge 2002: 316). The assumption in Eq. (2) is replaced by the assumption

$$e_{it} = \alpha_i + \theta_t + k_i t + \varepsilon_{it}. \tag{5}$$

This allows for the possibility that different countries have different trends, as reflected in different values of k_i. Substituting Eq. (5) in Eq. (1) gives

$$y_{it} = X_{it}\gamma + \delta SHI_{it} + \alpha_i + \theta_t + k_i t + \varepsilon_{it}. \tag{6}$$

One way of estimating this model is differencing Eq. (6) to get

$$\Delta y_{it} = \Delta X_{it}\gamma + \delta\Delta SHI_{it} + \xi_t + k_i + \Delta\varepsilon_{it} \tag{7}$$

and using a fixed effects estimator on this differenced equation.[20] If the k_i are jointly insignificant, Eq. (7) collapses to Eq. (4), which would provide some evidence in support of the PTA. However, directly testing this hypothesis through a least-squares dummy variables approach in the present context is unfeasible due to the incidental parameters problem.[21] Even if the k_i were jointly significant in Eq. (7), the PTA would still be a reasonable assumption if the k_i are uncorrelated with SHI_{it}. This can be tested through a single-variable, generalized version of the Hausman test of fixed versus random effects which takes into account the clustered nature of our data and is implemented by estimating an auxiliary quasi-demeaned regression (cf., Wooldridge 2002: 290). For each health sector outcome, we implement this test by estimating an augmented version of Eq. (7) using a random effects estimator—adding the within-country panel means of the original covariates which vary over i and t as regressors—and testing the null hypothesis of insignificance of the additional SHI term (with cluster-robust standard errors). Nonrejection of this hypothesis would suggest that the k_i are uncorrelated with SHI_{it} and thus provide evidence in favor of the PTA.[22]

The Differential Trend Model

The RT model is less restrictive than the standard DID model (the latter is nested in the former), but two objections might be raised against it: the assumed trend is linear; and the trend is specific to the country and assumed not to be modified by the treatment (i.e., the introduction of SHI). The second approach we employ to relaxing the PTA is a regression operationalization of the "differential trend" (DT) model of Bell, Blundell, and Van Reenen (1999). They assume:

$$e_{it} = \begin{cases} \alpha_i + k_s m_t + \varepsilon_{it} & if\ SHI_{it} = 1 \\ \alpha_i + k_n m_t + \varepsilon_{it} & if\ SHI_{it} = 0, \end{cases} \tag{8}$$

where m_t is an unobserved trend, the influence of which on y_{it} is allowed to differ between SHI and non-SHI systems. Incorporating this assumption into Eq. (1) gives:

$$y_{it} = X_{it}\gamma + \delta SHI_{it} + \alpha_i + k_n m_t + (k_s - k_n)m_t SHI_{it} + \varepsilon_{it}, \tag{9}$$

which can be estimated as a fixed-effects model including year dummies (*YEAR*) and year dummies interacted with the SHI dummy:

$$y_{it} = X_{it}\gamma + SHI_{it} + \alpha_i + \sum_{\tau=2}^{T} \tau YEAR_\tau + \sum_{\tau=2}^{T} \varphi_\tau YEAR_\tau SHI_{it} + \varepsilon_{it}. \tag{10}$$

In this model the impact of SHI varies over time, but one can estimate the average impact of SHI over time:

$$MEAN\ SHI\ IMPACT = \hat{\delta} + \sum_{\tau=2}^{T} \hat{\varphi}_\tau / T - 1. \tag{11}$$

The PTA assumption in this model implies $k_s = k_n$. This can be tested indirectly by testing the nonlinear restriction:

$$\frac{\sum_t m_t(k_s - k_n)}{\sum_t m_t k_n} = \frac{(k_s - k_n)\sum_t m_t}{k_n \sum_t m_t} = \frac{\sum_{\tau=2}^{T} \varphi_\tau}{\sum_{\tau=2}^{T} \beta_\tau} = 0. \tag{12}$$

An alternative to the fixed-effects model would be a first-differenced model:

$$\Delta y_{it} = \Delta X_{it}\gamma + \delta\Delta SHI_{it} + k_n\Delta m_i + (k_s - k_n)\Delta(m_t SHI_{it}) + \varepsilon_{it}. \tag{13}$$

In the estimation, the Δm_t would be replaced by first differences of year dummies and the $\Delta(m_t SHI_{it})$ would be replaced by first differences of interactions between year dummies and the SHI status dummy:

$$\Delta y_{it} = \Delta X_{it}\gamma + \delta\Delta SHI_{it} + \sum_{\tau=2}^{T}\beta_\tau \Delta YEAR_\tau + \sum_{\tau=2}^{T}\varphi_\tau \Delta(YEAR_\tau SHI_{it}) + \Delta\varepsilon_{it}. \tag{14}$$

This model can be estimated by pooled OLS. The estimates from this first-differenced model could also be used to compute an average SHI impact via Eq. (11) and to test the PTA via Eq. (12).

Testing for Reverse Causality

Although our DID, RT, and DT models all allow for some correlation between SHI and the original error term e_{it}, they entail specific assumptions and may not adequately capture the endogeneity of SHI. An informal yet intuitive test of reverse causality based on that proposed by Gruber and Hanratty (1995) in a similar modeling exercise is to include in each of our three models a lead dummy variable indicating whether SHI will be adopted the following year. If causality goes from SHI to the outcome variable, the coefficient on the lead dummy will be zero. A nonzero coefficient would point toward causality running the other way or some other type of endogeneity that cannot be captured by the model in question.

DATA

We use annual data on SHI status and health sector outcomes for the 28 ECA countries, from 1990 to 2004. Our dataset has been constructed using a variety of sources; the description in this section begins with our independent variable of interest, SHI status, and then continues for the dependent and other independent variables included in the health models. In our sample, data are generally available for most country-year combinations.[23]

Social Health Insurance Status

We define our SHI dummy SHI_{it} as taking a value of 1 if in country i at time t earmarked payroll taxes for health care were collected from formal sector workers and there was an SHI agency in place.[24] Our SHI status indicator follows the pattern in figure 14.1.[25] Our strict definition means that we end up classifying as non-SHI some country-year combinations that are often—we believe, erroneously—classified as SHI (such as Latvia and Poland). Further-more, we classify Romania as SHI only after 1998; despite the fact that payroll taxes were used somewhat before then, it was not until 1998 that SHI was fully set up with an SHI agency and with payroll contributions making up the major part of health care revenues. We explore the sensitivity of our results to not classifying these as SHI countries by rerunning our models with the three of them classified as SHI for certain years.[26] Our SHI status dummy is equal to 1 in about half (218 observations) of the 442 country-year combinations for which we have nonmissing values of the indicator.

Outcome Variables

Our outcome measures include: per capita health spending (total, public, and private) and the share of spending going on salaries; population health status; hospital activity rates and capacity utilization; and quality-of-care indicators. Our variable definitions and sources are briefly described below, and the descriptive statistics for them—for the full sample and disaggregated by SHI status—are presented in table 14.1.[27]

We measure per capita health spending as total health care expenditures per capita expressed in constant 2000 dollars adjusted for purchasing power parity (PPP; deflated using the United States GDP deflator), to allow comparisons in real values between countries and over time (Gerdtham and Jonsson 1992). The source for these figures is the World Bank's World Development Indicators (WB-WDI) database. The WB-WDI database is the primary World Bank database for development data, obtained from recognized international sources. It contains an expanded set of the economic, health, and other time-series indicators published in the Bank's *World Development Reports*. Average health spending for the period 1990–2004 was US$403 PPP per capita. The Czech Republic, Hungary, and Slovenia are the countries with highest spending levels (each with an average of at least US$857 PPP per capita between 1990–2004 and at least US$1,225 PPP per capita in the last year), whereas Azerbaijan, the Kyrgyz Republic, Tajikistan, and Uzbekistan have the lowest spending levels in our sample (at most US$132 PPP per capita on average for 1990–2004 and US$163 PPP per capita in the last year). On average, government health spending accounted for almost 70 percent of a country's total health spending over the period of analysis and 60 percent in the year 2003. Armenia and Tajikistan exhibited the smallest shares of government health spending in 2003—less than 21 percent—while in the Czech Republic and the Slovak Republic the share was higher than 88 percent in the same year.

We also include among our indicators health sector salaries as a percent of total health spending. Data on this—like the data on many of the remaining health sector outcome indicators—are taken from the World Health Organization's Health for All Database (WHO-HFA). This database, maintained by the European Office (Copenhagen) of the WHO, contains data for all European

TABLE 14.1 Descriptive Statistics for Outcome Variables

Item	Full sample			SHI = 1			SHI = 0		
	Mean	SD	Obs	Mean	SD	Obs	Mean	SD	Obs
Health expenditures, total	402.83	296.92	359	536.16	325.16	186	259.47	172.88	173
Health expenditures, government	295.87	249.61	324	404.22	281.52	167	180.62	136.89	157
Health expenditures, private	101.26	71.77	324	123.91	72.54	167	77.16	62.69	157
Salaries (percent)	39.41	12.67	167	40.24	16.62	69	38.82	8.95	98
Physicians	2.98	0.93	342	2.72	1.01	158	3.20	0.79	184
Life expectancy	70.49	2.91	379	71.52	3.03	181	69.55	2.45	198
Life expectancy (male)	66.40	3.51	376	67.53	3.76	178	65.39	2.92	198
Life expectancy (female)	74.63	2.66	376	75.64	2.61	178	73.73	2.36	198
Under-5 mortality rate (TransMONEE)	21.60	13.08	382	15.95	8.19	179	26.58	14.51	203
Under-5 mortality rate (WHO)	21.13	13.07	365	15.37	7.73	167	25.99	14.61	198
Infant mortality rate (World Bank)	20.24	19.74	229	13.25	11.10	127	28.95	24.25	102
Infant mortality rate (TransMONEE)	17.10	9.54	393	13.24	6.57	181	20.40	10.42	212
Infant mortality rate (WHO)	16.93	9.59	377	14.31	9.29	179	19.29	9.25	198
Perinatal mortality rate	12.40	4.74	352	10.91	5.25	161	13.64	3.87	191
Neonatal mortality rate	7.77	3.00	295	7.35	3.34	154	8.24	2.51	141
Postneonatal mortality rate	7.32	6.29	294	4.89	3.18	154	9.99	7.66	140
Maternal mortality rate	28.51	21.79	382	23.05	23.01	178	33.27	19.51	204
Maternal mortality rate (3-year)	28.68	18.91	348	21.94	17.12	156	34.16	18.55	192
Caesarean sections	92.77	50.10	331	118.53	43.52	154	70.35	44.43	177
Standardized death rate, all causes	1,146.30	185.03	365	1,081.83	182.81	167	1,200.68	169.12	198
Standardized death rate, infectious diseases	17.17	15.33	362	11.81	10.25	167	21.77	17.37	195
Standardized death rate, tuberculosis	9.84	8.03	360	7.57	8.23	167	11.80	7.33	193
Standardized death rate, diarrhea (under 5)	31.47	67.38	353	11.82	22.38	166	48.92	86.59	187
Standardized death rate, acute respiratory infection (under 5)	105.73	145.51	341	46.61	66.83	167	162.47	175.26	174

(continued)

TABLE 14.1 Descriptive Statistics for Outcome Variables (continued)

Item	Full sample			SHI = 1			SHI = 0		
	Mean	SD	Obs	Mean	SD	Obs	Mean	SD	Obs
Standardized death rate, heart disease	303.44	129.63	362	239.05	109.83	167	358.58	119.68	195
Standardized death rate, liver diseases	29.45	21.38	320	26.16	18.02	151	32.39	23.66	169
Standardized death rate, diabetes	14.91	8.60	362	14.35	6.91	167	15.39	9.81	195
Standardized death rate, circulatory diseases	623.84	125.44	362	576.83	120.03	167	664.11	115.85	195
Standardized death rate, cerebrovascular diseases	175.49	53.25	362	171.89	55.21	167	178.57	51.46	195
Standardized death rate, neoplasms	172.82	47.62	362	190.83	45.72	167	157.40	43.72	195
Standardized death rate, female breast cancer	21.60	6.68	362	24.52	5.70	167	19.11	6.46	195
Standardized death rate, respiratory diseases	68.38	34.95	362	54.13	27.91	167	80.59	35.80	195
Standardized death rate, bronchitis	31.01	19.59	349	25.36	19.93	161	35.85	17.99	188
Standardized death rate, digestive diseases	48.13	22.92	362	44.73	20.10	167	51.03	24.76	195
Standardized death rate, alcohol causes	135.08	57.16	320	123.72	57.61	155	145.75	54.78	165
Standardized death rate, smoking causes	543.11	166.82	320	466.26	131.64	155	615.31	164.40	165
Tuberculosis incidence rate	52.76	31.92	414	50.41	33.97	201	54.98	29.76	213
Hepatitis incidence rate	141.48	171.15	319	67.66	83.37	148	205.37	199.84	171
Hepatitis B incidence rate	17.26	19.31	383	10.38	9.61	178	23.24	23.26	205
Measles incidence rate	13.34	27.02	413	10.33	23.45	200	16.17	29.76	213
Mumps incidence rate	54.81	76.57	389	37.95	58.73	182	69.63	86.83	207
Syphilis incidence rate	31.86	52.20	380	28.21	55.82	180	35.14	48.61	200
Congenital syphilis incidence rate	0.16	0.30	217	0.23	0.40	88	0.11	0.18	129
Pertussis incidence rate	4.05	5.62	412	4.33	6.78	199	3.78	4.27	213
Diphteria incidence rate	1.32	5.20	413	0.67	2.94	200	1.93	6.61	213

	Full sample			SHI = 1			SHI = 0		
	Mean	SD	Obs	Mean	SD	Obs	Mean	SD	Obs
Tetanus incidence rate	0.09	0.11	406	0.11	0.12	196	0.07	0.09	210
Cancer incidence rate	245.01	147.37	335	318.21	159.21	138	193.72	113.47	197
Tuberculosis immunization rate	93.17	10.14	414	93.10	10.39	201	93.24	9.93	213
DPT immunization rate	91.88	9.11	414	91.90	7.67	201	91.87	10.31	213
Polio immunization rate	92.39	8.25	414	91.94	7.76	201	92.82	8.69	213
Mumps immunization rate	82.48	22.48	226	88.63	16.39	127	74.59	26.50	99
Rubella immunization rate	88.41	18.42	189	90.05	15.52	124	85.29	22.78	65
Length of stay (total)	12.75	3.04	397	11.23	2.93	193	14.19	2.39	204
Bed occupancy rate	72.78	14.80	277	74.85	9.82	149	70.36	18.78	128
Hospital beds	8.11	2.91	341	6.72	2.59	155	9.28	2.64	186
Inpatient admissions	16.20	5.99	396	15.51	6.02	194	16.86	5.90	202
Acute care admissions	15.18	5.38	276	15.17	5.50	150	15.20	5.26	126
Hospital discharges, infectious	826.10	444.11	353	658.64	352.78	170	981.66	464.08	183
Hospital discharges, cancers	809.34	588.59	346	1,068.85	643.08	163	578.19	417.81	183
Hospital discharges, heart	669.00	468.43	343	684.00	425.49	163	655.41	504.97	180
Hospital discharges, circulatory	1,904.45	1,099.73	354	2,092.45	1,152.72	170	1,730.76	1,021.10	184
Hospital discharges, cerebrovascular	339.11	240.51	350	394.82	243.94	168	287.68	226.04	182
Hospital discharges, respiratory	2,088.68	1,014.24	351	1,737.75	778.42	170	2,418.28	1,098.08	181
Hospital discharges, digestive	1,623.59	626.99	354	1,544.75	579.86	170	1,696.44	660.83	184
Hospital discharges, musculoskeletal	776.92	508.15	354	809.35	536.77	170	746.96	479.71	184
Standardized death rate, appendicitis	0.30	0.18	346	0.23	0.14	158	0.36	0.19	188
Standardized death rate, hernia and intestinal	2.23	0.75	349	2.34	0.74	161	2.14	0.74	188
Standardized death rate, adverse effects	0.19	0.31	182	0.19	0.33	116	0.19	0.28	66
Surgical infection rate	1.09	1.22	74	0.92	0.82	42	1.30	1.59	32

Source: Authors, based on data sources and analysis detailed in text.

Note: Mean, standard deviation (SD), and number of observations (Obs) for the full sample and for the subsamples of observations with the SHI dummy equal to one (SHI = 1) and zero (SHI = 0).

countries plus the former USSR republics in Central Asia on about 600 health indicators, including annual information on morbidity and disability; hospital discharges; and health care resources, utilization, and expenditure. The original sources of information are mainly WHO itself, country statistical offices, and other international organizations. In our attempt to get a comprehensive, general picture of the (potential) SHI impact on population health conditions, we include dependent variables related to life expectancy, group-specific mortality rates, disease-specific standardized death rates and incidence rates, and measures of utilization of services such as caesarean sections and immunization. We used the same database for obtaining data on hospital indicators, which include measures of average length of stay, bed occupancy, number of hospital beds (from the WB-WDI database), admissions, and disease-specific discharges. We also include in our analysis a few indicators of avoidable deaths—such as standardized death rates for appendicitis and hernia and intestinal obstruction—as proxies for the average quality of hospital care. Finally, alternative infant mortality and under-5 mortality rates were obtained from WB-WDI and the TransMONEE 2006 Database, a UNICEF database which contains data for ECA countries except Turkey on 146 economic and social indicators divided into 10 different topics and ranging from 1989 to 2004.

Simple comparisons of the average outcomes presented in table 14.1 indicate that SHI countries tend to spend more on health care, both in the public and private sectors, and a higher fraction of the government health spending seems to be absorbed by salaries. On the other hand, there is some indication that mortality and disease incidence rates are generally lower in SHI countries, while no clear pattern emerges for immunization rates. As far as hospital indicators are concerned, total length of stay, inpatient admissions, and beds tend all to be lower in SHI countries; most of our diagnosis-specific hospital discharges indicators are higher for SHI countries, and there is no clear pattern concerning our quality-of-care proxy measures. Visual comparisons of the evolution of SHI adoption in our sample relative to two health outcomes, average total health expenditures per capita and WHO's average infant mortality rate (figure 14.2 and figure 14.3, respectively), show somewhat clear patterns: average health spending slightly decreased during the first period of growing SHI adoption by ECA countries (1990–93) but experienced a sustained increase during and after the second period of SHI growth (1995–98, when SHI prevalence reached more than 50 percent in our sample), while the average infant mortality rate tended to remain stable around 22 per thousand births during the first period but continuously decreased during and after the second period, when SHI prevalence reached half of the countries. Determining whether the differences and patterns described above are due to SHI adoption (that is, a *causal* effect) or whether they merely reflect preexisting differences—observable and/or unobservable—between countries that eventually adopted SHI and those that did not (a *selection* effect) is the main task of our empirical work.[28]

FIGURE 14.2   Evolution of SHI Adoption and Average Health Expenditure per Capita in ECA Countries, 1990–2004

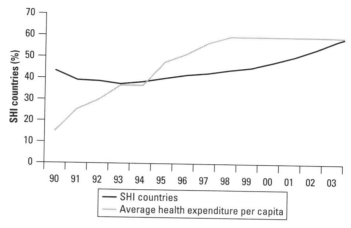

Source: Authors, based on data sources and analysis detailed in text.

FIGURE 14.3   Evolution of SHI Adoption and Average Infant Mortality Rate in ECA Countries, 1990–2004

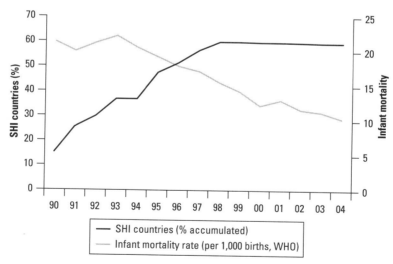

Source: Authors, based on data sources and analysis detailed in text.

Covariates in the Estimating Equation (the X-Vector)

We are not attempting to estimate a complete model of our health sector outcomes, but rather to estimate the impact of SHI adoption. The criterion for including a variable in our X_{it} vector is whether its omission would bias our estimate of δ, our SHI impact parameter. We want to include in X_{it}, therefore, variables that are correlated with both our outcomes and SHI adoption.

Although evidence on the determinants of SHI adoption is scarce, it has been indicated that SHI schemes emerged first in countries with higher initial (i.e., pretransition) per capita income levels, while tax-based funding prevailed in countries with lower initial per capita income (Preker, Jakab, and Schneider 2002). This positive correlation between income levels and SHI status is also present in our data; thus, we include GDP per capita (measured in constant 2000 dollars adjusted for purchasing power parity) in our X_{it} vector. We also include among the X_{it} the share of the population age 65 or above and the urban population as a fraction of the total. Data on these three covariates come from the WB-WDI database.

These three variables comprise the X_{it} vector in our basic model. We also estimate a second model where we control for the ways hospitals are paid in order to establish how far any SHI impacts in our basic model are attributable to provider-payment reforms. In this second model, we add to the X_{it} vector dummy variables for FFS and PBP ("fixed budgets/block grants" is the reference category).[29]

RESULTS

We begin this section with the results of our specification tests, and then present the estimates of the models.

Specification Tests

Figure 14.4 reports the results of our parallel trend assumption tests for the first-differenced versions of our random-trend and differential-trend models, i.e., Eqs. (7) and (14), and figure 14.5 reports the results of our reverse-causality tests for our differences-in-differences model (Eq. (4)) and our first-differenced random-trend and differential-trend models. In the random-trend model, the generalized Hausman test of the null hypothesis that the k_i are uncorrelated with SHI_{it} is rejected in only 9 out of 69 outcomes (13 percent) at the 10 percent level, suggesting that the parallel trends assumption is for the most part highly consistent with the data. This is reinforced by the results of the nonlinear restriction test in the differential trend model: the null hypothesis that there is a common trend in unobservables between the SHI adopters and nonadopters is rejected in only 12 outcomes at the 10 percent level. For the most part, then, the data seem consistent with the parallel trends assumption of the basic diffs-in-diffs model. The results of the reverse causality test suggest that in all of our three models, reverse causality is also not an issue: the lead SHI dummy is significant at the 10 percent level for only two outcomes in the diffs-in-diffs

FIGURE 14.4   Frequency Distributions of Probability Values for Tests of Parallel Trends Assumption

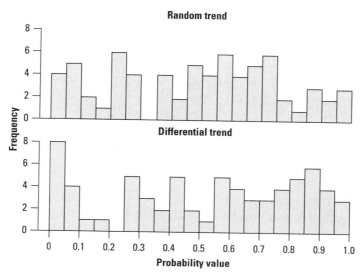

Source: Authors, based on data sources and analysis detailed in text.
Note: Frequency distributions of probability values for the parallel trend assumptions for the 69 models estimated.

FIGURE 14.5   Frequency Distributions of Probability Values for Tests of Reverse Causality

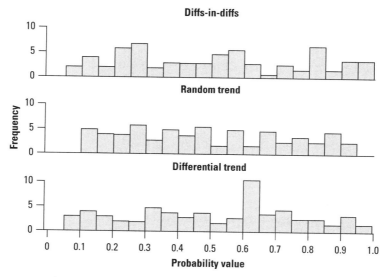

Source: Authors, based on data sources and analysis detailed in text.
Note: Frequency distributions of probability values for *t*-tests of reverse causality on lead SHI dummy variable for the 69 models estimated.

model, for none of the outcomes in the random-trend model, and in only three outcomes for the differential-trend model.

Basic Estimates

Overall, then, our test results suggest that the simple diffs-in-diffs model provides a reasonable approach to modeling the impacts of SHI. We focus therefore on these estimates, which are reported in columns 1–3 of table 14.2.[30]

The most noteworthy result is that the SHI impact is insignificant in the vast majority of outcomes. SHI has a significant impact (at the 10 percent level) in only 16 percent of outcomes (cf. the top panel of figure 14.6). Furthermore, the impact is typically small in magnitude when expressed in percentage terms: in very few cases is the impact larger than 10 percent (see the distribution of estimates in figure 14.7).

The significant impacts are largely confined to two sets of outcome variables: the spending variables and the basic set of hospital variables. Our main results suggest that SHI has increased government health spending by 15 percent, equivalent to around US$45 per capita in 2000 prices. Private spending does not seem to have been affected by SHI adoption, by contrast. The overall effect has been to raise total health spending by around 11 percent.[31] Whether the additional spending resulting from a transition to SHI is a good or bad thing cannot be said without seeing what the extra resources buy. The results in table 14.2 suggest that SHI may have increased the share of health spending going on wages and salaries, with the impact being of the order of around 11 percent, equivalent to a mean increase in the share of spending going on wages and salaries of around 4 percentage points. We must interpret this result with caution, however, due to the reduced number of changes in our SHI dummy used to identify the SHI impact in this case. The results in table 14.2 also suggest that SHI adoption reduced mean length of stay (by about 3 percent), increased the bed-occupancy rate (by around 3 percent or 2 percentage points), and increased both inpatient admissions in general (by almost 3 percent) and acute inpatient admissions in particular (by around 4 percent). It is noteworthy that the percentage impact on admissions is a good deal smaller than the percentage impact on spending. Among the other hospital variables, there is less evidence of SHI adoption having an impact, and the significant effects are confined to just three variables: hospital discharges for patients treated for infectious diseases (an 11 percent increase); discharges for patients treated for cerebrovascular diseases (a 4 percent increase); and surgical infection rates, though the large estimated negative effect needs to be interpreted with caution due to the limited number of switches of the SHI dummy in the subsample used to obtain this particular parameter estimate.

SHI adoption thus seems to have increased (government) health spending and to have increased (albeit by a lesser percentage) inpatient admissions. What is striking about table 14.2 in the light of these results is that SHI adoption does

TABLE 14.2 SHI Impact Estimates

	(1)	(2)	(3)	(4)	(5)	(6)	(7)	(8)	(9)	(10)
	Basic diffs-in-diffs model			Basic model with provider-payment variables added			SHI share model			
Dependent variable	Coef.	p-value	SHI impact	Coef.	p-value	SHI impact	Impact at mean first-year share for adopters	Impact at mean share for adopters	p-value	# shifts
Health spending										
Health expenditures, total		0.114	11.3%	21.25	0.360	5.3%	28.71*	58.77*	0.058	11
Health expenditures, public	45.57**	0.036	15.0%	36.32**	0.038	12.1%	25.72*	52.64*	0.076	11
Health expenditures, private	0.61	0.965	0.6%	−15.90	0.323	−15.90%	2.87	5.87	0.446	11
Salaries percent	4.35**	0.012	11.1%	6.87*	0.074	17.2%	2.39**	4.89**	0.036	3
Physicians	0.04	0.322	1.3%	0.05	0.205	1.7%	0.04	0.09	0.265	13
Health outcomes										
Life expectancy	−0.21	0.370	−0.3%	−0.36	0.141	−0.5%	0.15	0.32	0.347	13
Life expectancy (male)	−0.24	0.371	−0.4%	−0.42	0.154	−0.6%	0.18	0.36	0.355	13
Life expectancy (female)	−0.15	0.374	−0.2%	−0.26	0.135	−0.3%	0.09	0.18	0.462	13
Under-5 mortality rate (TransMONEE)	0.10	0.911	0.5%	0.00	0.998	0.0%	−0.13	−0.27	0.762	14
Under-5 mortality rate (WHO)	0.92	0.195	4.5%	0.67	0.367	3.2%	0.06	0.12	0.881	13
Infant mortality rate (World Bank)	1.03*	0.068	9.2%	1.02	0.183	9.1%	0.03	0.05	0.904	7
Infant mortality rate (TransMONEE)	0.25	0.667	1.5%	0.25	0.692	1.5%	0.01	0.03	0.957	14
Infant mortality rate (WHO)	0.40	0.429	2.4%	0.25	0.704	1.5%	0.12	0.24	0.647	14
Perinatal mortality rate	0.39	0.244	3.2%	0.35	0.437	2.8%	0.04	0.09	0.822	13
Neonatal mortality rate	0.56	0.158	7.5%	0.31	0.583	4.0%	0.06	0.12	0.577	10
Postneonatal mortality rate	−0.46*	0.099	−6.5%	−0.54*	0.074	−7.6%	−0.12	−0.24	0.596	10

(continued)

TABLE 14.2 SHI Impact Estimates *(continued)*

	(1)	(2)	(3)	(4)	(5)	(6)	(7)	(8)	(9)	(10)
	Basic diffs-in-diffs model			Basic model with provider-payment variables added			SHI share model			
Dependent variable	Coef.	p-value	SHI impact	Coef.	p-value	SHI impact	Impact at mean first-year share for adopters	Impact at mean share for adopters	p-value	# shifts
Maternal mortality rate	2.59	0.225	9.1%	2.39	0.351	8.3%	2.33**	4.78**	0.037	13
Maternal mortality rate (3-year)	1.31	0.198	4.5%	1.34	0.277	4.6%	−0.79*	−1.62*	0.096	13
Caesarean sections	−0.27	0.761	−0.3%	−1.17	0.320	−1.2%	0.36	0.73	0.794	10
Standardized death rate, all causes	5.96	0.777	0.5%	20.26	0.352	1.8%	−11.69	−23.92	0.364	13
Standardized death rate, infectious diseases	1.38	0.447	7.8%	1.15	0.552	6.4%	−0.12	−0.24	0.876	13
Standardized death rate, tuberculosis	1.63	0.282	15.7%	1.68	0.279	16.0%	−0.10	−0.21	0.862	13
Standardized death rate, diarrhea (under 5)	4.09	0.442	13.4%	3.23	0.454	10.1%	2.15	4.40	0.248	13
Standardized death rate, acute respiratory infection (under 5)	1.63	0.747	1.6%	1.34	0.815	1.3%	−2.53	−5.18	0.641	12
Standardized death rate, heart disease	−0.36	0.953	−0.1%	4.46	0.529	1.5%	−5.75*	−11.77*	0.100	13
Standardized death rate, liver diseases	−0.53	0.659	−1.7%	−0.38	0.766	−1.2%	−0.73	−1.50	0.220	10
Standardized death rate, diabetes	0.66	0.615	4.4%	1.33	0.189	8.7%	−0.62	−1.28	0.144	13
Standardized death rate, circulatory diseases	−2.00	0.889	−0.3%	9.69	0.496	1.5%	−6.69	−13.69	0.369	13
Standardized death rate, cerebrovascular diseases	0.88	0.856	0.5%	4.95	0.321	2.8%	−1.15	−2.35	0.685	13
Standardized death rate, neoplasms	2.23	0.320	1.3%	2.47	0.338	1.4%	0.65	1.34	0.430	13
Standardized death rate, female breast cancer	0.06	0.883	0.3%	0.24	0.566	1.1%	0.17	0.35	0.262	13
Standardized death rate, respiratory diseases	2.03	0.283	2.9%	3.12	0.200	4.5%	−0.38	−0.78	0.822	13
Standardized death rate, bronchitis	3.68	0.300	11.8%	5.37	0.237	17.5%	2.22	4.55	0.250	13
Standardized death rate, digestive diseases	−0.32	0.773	−0.6%	−0.29	0.785	−0.6%	−0.97	−1.99	0.113	13

Health outcomes

Standardized death rate, alcohol causes	-1.27	0.731	-0.9%	0.18	0.975	0.1%	-7.23*	-14.80*	0.096	11
Standardized death rate, smoking causes	1.65	0.905	0.3%	10.03	0.544	1.8%	-0.31	-0.64	0.970	11
Tuberculosis incidence rate	-2.63	0.342	-4.8%	-5.28	0.191	-9.7%	-2.66	-5.44	0.233	14
Hepatitis incidence rate	34.08	0.203	26.4%	20.89	0.417	15.9%	10.19	20.86	0.389	14
Hepatitis B incidence rate	1.69	0.127	10.4%	1.19	0.329	7.2%	0.81	1.65	0.262	12
Measles incidence rate	-5.09	0.507	-43.1%	-3.83	0.656	-32.0%	-6.27	-12.84	0.380	14
Mumps incidence rate	4.68	0.603	8.1%	14.07	0.467	25.4%	-0.09	-0.19	0.988	14
Syphilis incidence rate	7.38	0.457	20.1%	5.73	0.496	16.7%	0.81	1.65	0.853	14
Congenital syphilis incidence rate	-0.01	0.704	-5.3%	-0.02	0.549	-11.6%	0.00	-0.01	0.807	7
Pertussis incidence rate	1.05	0.333	25.8%	1.58	0.243	38.7%	0.49	1.01	0.198	14
Diphteria incidence rate	-0.05	0.936	-3.7%	-0.02	0.985	-1.1%	-0.21	-0.43	0.539	14
Tetanus incidence rate	0.02	0.287	20.8%	0.01	0.516	11.5%	0.01	0.02	0.520	14
Cancer incidence rate	2.37	0.447	1.0%	-0.29	0.934	-0.1%	5.54**	11.35**	0.007	14
Tuberculosis immunization rate	0.92	0.520	1.0%	-1.03	0.575	-1.1%	-0.17	-0.35	0.901	14
DPT immunization rate	-0.40	0.738	-0.4%	-1.79	0.406	-1.9%	-0.21	-0.42	0.784	14
Polio immunization rate	1.25	0.381	1.3%	0.99	0.546	1.1%	0.65	1.33	0.321	14
Mumps immunization rate	9.69	0.155	11.6%	5.50	0.356	6.7%	1.31	2.68	0.511	14
Rubella immunization rate	13.90	0.212	15.3%	12.14	0.223	13.4%	-1.26	-2.58	0.537	10
Length of stay (total)	-0.32*	0.063	-2.6%	-0.18	0.342	-1.4%	-0.13	-0.27	0.127	6
Bed occupancy rate	1.91*	0.085	2.6%	2.01	0.118	2.8%	0.50	1.02	0.230	9
Hospital beds	-0.17	0.371	-2.1%	-0.04	0.825	-0.5%	0.01	0.02	0.890	13
Inpatient admissions	0.44**	0.015	2.7%	0.27*	0.076	1.7%	0.24**	0.49**	0.021	14
Acute care admissions	0.63**	0.004	4.2%	0.47**	0.022	3.1%	0.29**	0.60**	0.001	10
Hospital discharges, infectious	90.63*	0.060	11.0%	75.28*	0.051	9.2%	25.31*	51.81*	0.084	13
Hospital discharges, cancers	25.18	0.160	3.0%	24.20	0.251	3.0%	39.62**	81.11**	0.000	13
Hospital discharges, heart	11.65	0.279	1.7%	0.05	0.996	0.0%	-3.13	-6.41	0.808	13

Hospitals

(continued)

TABLE 14.2 SHI Impact Estimates (continued)

	(1)	(2)	(3)	(4)	(5)	(6)	(7)	(8)	(9)	(10)
	Basic diffs-in-diffs model			Basic model with provider-payment variables added			SHI share model			
							Impact at mean first-year share for adopters	Impact at mean share for adopters		
Dependent variable	Coef.	p-value	SHI impact	Coef.	p-value	SHI impact			p-value	# shifts
Hospital discharges, circulatory	37.40	0.125	1.9%	−28.93	0.624	−1.6%	36.68**	75.09**	0.010	13
Hospital discharges, cerebrovascular	12.45*	0.073	3.6%	8.20	0.128	2.5%	−1.76	−3.60	0.847	13
Hospital discharges, respiratory	96.49	0.121	4.7%	58.86	0.293	3.0%	68.19**	139.58**	0.017	13
Hospital discharges, digestive	20.08	0.263	1.2%	−1.76	0.921	−0.1%	30.20**	61.81**	0.008	13
Hospital discharges, musculoskeletal	17.74	0.107	2.2%	7.63	0.546	1.0%	13.48	27.59	0.125	13
Standardized death rate, appendicitis	−0.04	0.436	−14.1%	−0.04	0.427	−14.5%	−0.02	−0.04	0.306	13
Standardized death rate, hernia and intestinal	−0.16	0.172	−7.1%	−0.14	0.293	−6.1%	0.02	0.04	0.563	13
Standardized death rate, adverse effects	0.00	0.931	2.1%	0.00	0.979	−0.8%	0.02	0.05	0.621	6
Surgical infection rate	−1.32**	0.013	−142.7%	−1.62**	0.006	−175.3%	−1.16**	−2.38**	0.000	3

Hospitals

Source: Authors, based on data sources and analysis detailed in text.

Note: Results are for diffs-in-diffs models estimated through first-differences, i.e., Eq. (4). Results refer to the coefficient (Coef.) and p-values from two-sided t-tests with cluster-robust standard errors. The symbols * and ** denote p-values lower than or equal to 0.10 and 0.05, respectively. SHI percentage effects implied by the corresponding δ coefficients are calculated over the mean outcome variable in the corresponding estimating subsample. For the SHI share model (model 3 in table), impacts are calculated by multiplying δ initially by the mean of the SHI share among adopters in the first year of adoption (32 percent) and then by the mean of the SHI share among adopters for the whole study period. In the last column, number of shifts refers to the number of transitions between tax-funded and SHI systems in the subsample used to estimate the corresponding coefficients.

FIGURE 14.6   Frequency Distributions of Probability Values for Estimate of SHI Impact

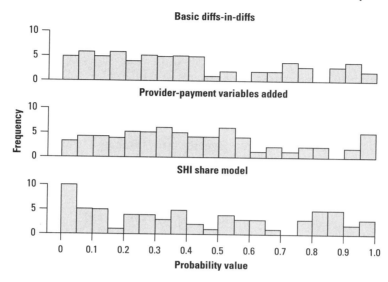

Source: Authors, based on data sources and analysis detailed in text.

FIGURE 14.7   Distribution of SHI Impact Estimates from Diffs-in-Diffs Model

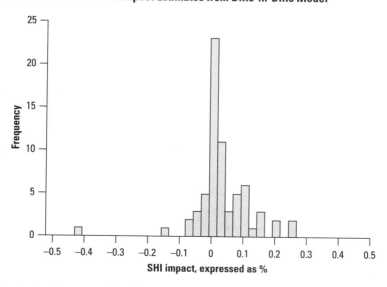

Source: Authors, based on data sources and analysis detailed in text.

not appear to have had any perceptible impact on health outcomes. This is despite the fact that we are not controlling for health spending in our regressions and the fact that we have over 40 different health outcome variables, including detailed cause-specific data on both mortality and disease incidence. In only two outcomes (infant mortality and postneonatal mortality) is there any evidence of a significant impact of SHI in our preferred diffs-in-diffs model, and here the evidence is not altogether compelling. Interpreted literally, SHI increased (though not significantly) neonatal and perinatal mortality, significantly reduced postneonatal mortality, and significantly increased infant mortality, but only for one of our three infant mortality variables. It would seem unwise to read too much into these results, however. Overall, our estimates suggest that SHI adoption resulted in neither health improvements nor adverse effects on population health status.

Robustness of Estimates to Model Specification

We undertake two robustness tests. The first is to include dummy variables—alongside the SHI dummy—that capture provider-payment reforms. As noted in the second section, SHI adoption was often (though not always) associated with a change in the way hospitals are paid, from budgets to either FFS or PBP. From an empirical point of view, it might be argued that our estimates of the impacts of SHI adoption in columns 1–3 of table 14.2 are simply picking up the effects of provider-payment reforms rather than the impact of SHI adoption per se. Because payment reforms can be effected in non-SHI systems—and were in some of the ECA countries over the study period—it is important to try to isolate the impacts of SHI adoption per se from the impacts of concurrent provider-payment reforms.[32]

Columns 4–6 of table 14.2 present the results for our preferred diffs-in-diffs model with the hospital payment dummies included.[33] These results contain somewhat fewer significant SHI effects (see the middle panel of figure 14.6). However, our earlier finding that SHI adoption increased per capita health spending is robust to the inclusion of the provider-payment dummies. Even with these additional variables included, we find that SHI led to an increase in annual government health care expenditures per capita of around 12 percent or US$36 PPP in the "adopter" countries, compared to what would have occurred had these countries not switched to SHI. This estimated effect is only 3 percentage points smaller than that obtained from our original diffs-in-diffs specification (i.e., without the payment dummies) and is significant at the 5 percent level. The results suggest, in other words, that SHI adoption *of itself* increases government health spending.

As far as hospital indicators are concerned, the results in columns 4–6 of table 14.2 suggest that our initial impact of SHI on mean length of stay reported in columns 1–3 may have been largely due to contemporaneous provider-payment reforms: the point estimate is reduced considerably in the fuller specification, and is no longer significant. The estimate of the impact on the bed-occupancy rate is slightly increased by the addition of provider-payment dummies and is still borderline significant at the 10 percent level even in the fuller specification. By contrast, the evidence on the impact of SHI on inpatient admissions survives the inclusion of provider-payment dummies in the model, although the point estimates are reduced. Our earlier impacts of SHI on infectious disease discharges and surgical infection rates also survive the inclusion of the provider-payment dummies. As far as health outcomes are concerned, there was little evidence in our original specification of SHI adoption having any impact, and this remains the case even after including provider-payment method dummies.

Overall, then, our basic empirical conclusions seem fairly robust to the inclusion of changes in hospital payment methods as potential confounders of SHI impacts. In particular, SHI adoption per se—that is, without any change in payment methods—has apparently led to higher government health spending and hospital admissions, but has not led to any perceptible improvements in population health indicators.

Our second robustness check is to replace the SHI dummy variable (which treats SHI adoption as an on-off process) by a variable capturing the fraction of health revenues financed through SHI. This captures, in effect, the intensity of treatment, the hypothesis being that it is not simply whether an SHI system is in place but how much it is relied upon to finance health care. The data on SHI shares are taken from the same sources as the SHI dummy; cf. figure 14.1. We use the basic diffs-in-diffs estimator.

The results are reported in columns 7–9 of table 14.2. In this specification, SHI has a statistically significant impact in a larger fraction of outcomes than in the basic model in columns 1–3 of table 14.2: cf. the top and bottom panels of figure 14.6. Where we previously found a significant impact of SHI, we mostly continue to find a significant impact after switching to the SHI share specification: we continue to find significant effects on government health spending, the salary share in costs, and inpatient admissions; the exceptions are the impacts on length of stay and the bed occupancy rate, which were significantly impacted by SHI in the basic diffs-in-diffs specification but are not in the SHI share specification. To make the results more comparable with those for the SHI dummy we report not the coefficient δ itself but rather δ multiplied by an SHI share. We choose two values: the mean share (among adopters) during the first year of adoption (32 percent); and the mean share (among adopters) for the whole period being studied (65 percent). So, for example, our estimate of δ in the SHI share model implies that annual government health spending has increased by around US$26 per capita when the country reaches an SHI share of 32 percent and around US$53 per capita when the SHI share reaches 65 percent. This specification thus has the merit of allowing the impact of SHI to grow as the SHI share climbs in the years following the adoption of SHI financing.

DISCUSSION AND CONCLUSIONS

The health system reforms that the European and Central Asian (ECA) countries implemented during their transition from socialist economies in the 1990s provide a unique opportunity to assess the impacts of social health insurance (SHI) on the health sector. We took advantage of this highly unusual "experiment" in which many ECA countries unequivocally switched from general tax-funded to SHI systems in a relatively short period of time, and on a staggered basis, so as to shed light on a broad set of currently unanswered questions: How does SHI affect national health spending, the way such resources are spent, and population health outcomes? In order to obtain empirical evidence on these issues, we have used regression-based generalizations of the differences-in-differences approach on panel data from 28 ECA countries for the period 1990–2004. In two of our generalizations, we relaxed the parallel trends assumption that is seen as a major drawback of the differences-in-differences approach. In one we allow for a country-specific unobserved linear time trend that could be correlated with SHI adoption; and in the other we allow for differential (possibly nonlinear) time trends between SHI adopters and nonadopters.

Our tests suggest that the parallel trends assumption is not, in fact, inconsistent with our data. We also find that whichever model we use there is no evidence of reverse causality—SHI adoption being caused by changes in our outcomes. Our estimated SHI impacts are also similar for our three models. Our tests and parameter constancy provide some reassurance that we have identified causal relationships between SHI adoption and health sector outcomes.

Our estimates suggest that SHI adoption per se increased government health expenditure per capita. We also obtain some evidence that part of the extra financial resources available in the health sector due to SHI adoption have served to increase the fraction of salaries as a percentage of government health spending in SHI countries. This result provides quantitative evidence in support of claims about the process of transition to SHI in some ECA countries being favored and accelerated by pressure from health professionals, who expected to have their income levels driven up by the introduction of an SHI system.[34] Our results also suggest that SHI has impacted on how physical resources are used, by reducing average hospital length of stay and increasing bed occupancy rates and hospital admissions. Despite this, our analysis of several mortality and morbidity indicators showed that transition to SHI has *not* caused general improvements in health outcomes for ECA countries. This is despite the fact that we have been able to analyze SHI impacts on over 40 health outcome measures, including cause-specific mortality and morbidity indicators.[35] It might be argued that the absence of any beneficial impacts of SHI adoption—with its associated increase in health spending—on general mortality is not surprising, since, for many mortality causes, it is not reasonable to expect death to be averted by timely or higher quality health care after the condition develops (e.g., many types of malignant neoplasms, heart and circulatory diseases). However, the wide range of mortality measures examined here means that we are not restricted to examining only such "unavoidable" deaths; rather, we have been able to show that SHI adoption did not cause any general improvements in mortality from causes that should not occur in the presence of timely and effective/better quality health care, a concept known as "amenable mortality" which has been used elsewhere to assess the quality of health care systems (Nolte and McKee 2008). Compared to tax-funded health systems, SHI systems do not seem to have reduced amenable mortality when this is measured by a variety of mortality indicators containing an important "avoidable" or preventive component for most age ranges, such as standardized death rates by tuberculosis, female breast cancer, cerebrovascular diseases, diabetes, ischemic heart disease, alcohol-related causes, and the maternal mortality ratio; the same general conclusion arises as far as children-specific amenable mortality is concerned (judged by measures such as death rates by diarrhea and acute respiratory infections). Thus, in this study, we have been able to perform an investigation of the broad population health impacts that could in theory be brought about by a different organization of a national health system—namely, the adoption of social insurance—taking into account both morbidity and amenable mortality indicators.

Our results are mostly robust to the inclusion of dummy variables capturing shifts in provider-payment methods alongside the SHI status dummy; they are therefore pure SHI effects, not provider-payment reform effects. For example, the higher government spending caused by a transition to SHI is not a spurious result attributable to the fact that some countries switched to fee-for-service when they adopted SHI. We are able to estimate separate provider-payment effects because SHI adoption did not always lead to provider-payment reform, and even when it did, it sometimes did so with a lag, because some non-SHI countries reformed the way they paid hospitals as well, and because some SHI countries switched provider-payment methods more than once (some, for example, switched to fee-for-service only to change to a patient-based payment method later on).

The question arises: Why did health outcomes not improve as a result of SHI adoption even though it led of itself to higher government health spending and higher inpatient admissions? One might be tempted to explain our results in terms of lack of statistical power. From table 14.1 it might appear that this is not a major issue. For example, for total health expenditures, we have 186 observations in the "treatment group" (SHI is in place) and 173 in the "control group" (a tax-financed system). The problem is that our observations are clustered at the country level, and we have a relatively small number of countries (28). It is possible that our *effective* number of observations (i.e., allowing for intracluster correlation) may be too small for us to detect effects that in reality exist. So, some of the insignificant results we obtain could in reality be significant effects. The opposite is not true—the significant effects we obtain, despite low power, are (assuming the model is specified and estimated correctly) real effects. Why might we fail to detect significant effects for some variables and not others (when in reality effects do exist)? The obvious explanation is differences in standardized effect size, that is, the effect size standardized by the standard error of the parameter in question (which depends, of course, on the standard deviation and sample size). After all, the other key elements of a power calculation—sample size, which has a direct effect on power in addition to its indirect effect via the standard error, and the significance level chosen—are much the same across models (the sample size does vary but only marginally). With limited power, then, we may be able to detect significant impacts where the impacts are large but not where they are small, and with a larger sample size we might have been able to determine with greater certainty whether the effects of SHI on variables such as the standardized mortality rate and the infant mortality rate are indeed significantly different from zero. But the fact remains that their estimated effect is still likely to be small. Lack of statistical power helps us explain the preponderance of high probability values on the SHI coefficient. But it does not help explain the small estimated impacts on health outcomes; these still need explaining.

One reason for the small impacts of SHI on health outcomes could be that the percentage increase in admissions due to SHI is much smaller than the percentage increase in spending (3 percent compared to point estimates of 11 percent and 15 percent for total and government health expenditures, respectively). Much of the extra spending caused by SHI adoption would appear, therefore, to have resulted in more costly admissions and/or extra spending elsewhere in the health system. Part of the story seems to be the higher salary share of costs as a result of SHI adoption. But it also seems likely that costs were incurred undertaking new activities (e.g., collecting contributions, writing contracts with providers) or that existing activities became more costly (e.g., more tests being administered on inpatients, more expensive drugs being given, and so forth). It is also possible that SHI adoption may have resulted in less comprehensive and less well integrated public health and prevention programs (cf., e.g., Allin et al. 2004), and that the extra admissions and extra costs caused by the transition to SHI were incurred in treating additional patients who would not have otherwise become sick. The fact that SHI adoption appears to have led to increased numbers of infectious disease hospital discharges is consistent with this story. Gaps in coverage may also be part of the explanation. Some groups seem to have fallen through the coverage net, such as the Roma population (cf., e.g., Rechel et al. 2003), and there is anecdotal evidence that some formal sector workers wait to enroll until they get sick. Because of lack of coverage, these groups may use primary care less than they would have otherwise done, increasing the likelihood that illness is left untreated until serious enough to warrant hospitalization. Some of the extra hospital caseload associated with SHI may therefore simply be due to people waiting until they get so sick that they require hospitalization.

Of course, our results do not necessarily imply that SHI adoption everywhere must necessarily raise health spending without improving health outcomes. These results are likely to hinge in part on the fact that SHI was introduced with costly institutional reforms but ones that did little to stimulate the performance of the health system. Nonetheless, the largely negative results in this analysis ought to serve as a warning to those contemplating shifting from general revenue finance to SHI.

NOTES

ACKNOWLEDGMENTS: The authors thank the World Bank's Research Support Budget for financial support; Armin Fidler, Ana Djordjevic, Peyvand Khaleghian, Jack Langenbrunner, Silvia Mauri, and Pia Schneider for information on social health transitions in Europe and Central Asia; and Tom McGuire, a referee, and the participants of seminars at Erasmus University, the Nordic Health Economists Study Group, the University of Oxford, the University of York, and the World Bank for helpful suggestions and comments on earlier versions of this chapter.

1. Figures calculated from data in the *World Health Report* annexes. The Republic of Korea is around 50 percent public-private. Mexico's public share is increasing quickly (OECD 2005).

2. These countries are almost all in Europe and Latin America.

3. France widened the tax base from earnings to include nonwage income, Germany has decided that from 2009 onward it will reduce the emphasis on payroll taxes, while the Netherlands introduced a reform in 2005 where insurers receive only half their income from payroll revenues (albeit channeled through a central fund), the rest coming from flat-rate direct contributions from members (with offsetting income supplements for low-income groups). For further details, see, for example, Gottret and Schieber (2006) and the Health Policy Monitor Web site, http://www.hpm.org/en/index.html. In addition to these changes, it is worth noting that Iceland and Spain both shifted wholesale from SHI to tax-finance in the late 1980s.

4. Two recent conferences focused on SHI in developing and transition economies, one in Berlin in November 2005, the other in Manila in October 2006. Details are to be found at http://www.shi-conference.de/ and http://www.shiconferencemanila.info/.

5. Examples include Vietnam (1993), Nigeria (1997), Tanzania (2001), and Ghana (2005). Discussions are underway in South Africa, Zimbabwe, Cambodia, and the Lao People's Democratic Republic. Malaysia also recently began debating a shift to SHI. See Hsiao and Shaw (2007) on some recent experiences of SHI in the developing world.

6. Examples include Colombia, Mexico, the Philippines, and Vietnam. Cf. Hsiao and Shaw (2007).

7. Wagstaff et al. (1992; 1999) find that SHI is less progressive than tax-financed systems (in fact, is mostly regressive) in the OECD countries. O'Donnell et al. (2008) find the same in Asia.

8. The European SHI countries studied by Carrin and James (2005) (Austria, Belgium, Germany, and Luxembourg) took close to 100 years to achieve universal health insurance (UHI). Costa Rica, Japan, and Korea, which achieved UHI in 1991, 1958, and

1989, respectively, took considerably less time, although Costa Rica's coverage rate in 1991 was still only 85 percent, and Japan and Korea were both at an advanced stage of economic development when they reached UHI.

9. The countries treated as being in central and eastern Europe and Central Asia (the countries in the World Bank's ECA region) are listed in figure 14.1.

10. The European office of the World Health Organization developed and has maintained a huge database to track progress toward its Health for All initiative. In addition, it is home to the European Observatory on Health Systems and Policies, which has produced detailed overviews of the health systems of the member countries (known as *Health Systems in Transition* [HiT] profiles), as well as a variety of volumes that discuss health systems and health policies in the region.

11. The view that only amenable mortality responds to health spending may be overly pessimistic. Martin, Rice, and Smith (2008) actually find that health spending impacts favorably on mortality causes previously considered as being unavoidable and unamenable to better care, such as neoplasms and circulatory diseases.

12. Friedberg (1998) used a random trend model in her analysis of divorce laws in the United States, and found that allowing for state-specific trends is crucial to unearthing the impacts of these laws.

13. The differential trend model was first proposed by Bell, Blundell, and Van Reenen (1999), but their estimation was undertaken using (triple) differencing rather than via regression analysis. In our case, because the date of "treatment" (i.e., adoption of SHI) varies across countries, differencing would not work.

14. This section draws heavily on Langebrunner, Sheiman, and Kehler (2008) and the *Health Systems in Transition* (HiT) series, downloadable from http://www.euro.who .int/observatory/Hits/TopPage.

15. We also relied on World Bank reports and on consultations with World Bank staff to obtain data on countries for which HiTs have not yet been published, and to double-check the information assembled through the HiTs.

16. Russia's Kemerovo region collects 75–78 percent of the money due to it, while in Moscow City the rate is even higher (90 percent); by contrast, in the Volgograd region, only 508 of over 32,000 private enterprises apparently pay into the insurance fund at all (Twigg 1999). The problem is not confined to the ECA countries. In Colombia, evasion in the contributory regime (which covers formal sector workers as well as informal workers not classified as poor) has been estimated to cost US$836 million in forgone revenues (2.75 percent of GDP) (Escobar and Panopolou 2003). Nearly three quarters of this was due to underreporting, the rest being due to nonpayment. In the Philippines, evasion also appears to be a major issue, particularly among small shops and businesses, with one estimate suggesting that 70 percent of those who should be contributing are not doing so (Jowett and Hsiao 2007).

17. See, for example, Lu and Hsiao (2003) on Taiwan, China's, experience in this regard.

18. Full details are available in Wagstaff and Moreno-Serra (2007).

19. We also experimented with (block) bootstrapped standard errors, and obtained broadly similar results.

20. Alternatively, we could use the first differences estimator once again, this time applied to Eq. (7) so as to eliminate the k_i, and estimate the resulting model by

pooled OLS. However, this procedure would mean losing an additional period of time for estimation purposes, which is why we have opted for the fixed effects estimator in the case of the random trend model.

21. Testing the joint insignificance of the k_i for the 28 countries of our sample would mean testing 27 model constraints of the form $k_i = 0$. Since our data are clustered at the country level, there would not be enough degrees of freedom for performing such F tests after the inclusion of the country dummies in addition to the original regressors in the model unless some of these constraints are dropped, thus reducing the appeal of this test in our context. The same problem would arise if we would test for the equality of k_i (that is, $k_i = k$, all i) in Eq. (7) via a least-squares dummy variable estimator.

22. This approach is equivalent to estimating the auxiliary quasi-demeaned regression suggested by Wooldridge (2002) using a pooled OLS estimator and performing a Wald test on the subset of regressors of interest. We can use a chi-square test statistic since, if only one parameter is tested (as in our case), the F statistic is asymptotically equivalent to a chi-square with one degree of freedom under the null hypothesis. We also implemented an alternative version of the Hausman test by directly testing for the equality of the SHI dummy coefficients obtained from estimating Eq. (7) using random and fixed effects estimators with cluster-robust standard errors. Under the null hypothesis of no difference between the coefficients, the test statistic is asymptotically distributed as a chi-square (with one degree of freedom in our case); nonrejection of the null would suggest that the k_i are uncorrelated with SHI_{it} in Eq. (7) and provide support to the PTA in our data. The results obtained from this alternative generalized Hausman test (not shown) were extremely similar to the ones obtained from our main approach, both in terms of the number of rejections of the null hypothesis and the specific outcomes for which rejections were found.

23. In the case of Bosnia and Herzegovina, the period between 1992 and 1996 has been excluded from the analysis due to the lack of data for many dependent variables and the complete disorganization of the health system—which obviously included the SHI scheme—during the war period.

24. Our classification is consistent with that of Langenbrunner, Sheiman, and Kehler (2008).

25. For more information, see Wagstaff and Moreno-Serra (2007).

26. Full details are contained in Wagstaff and Moreno-Serra (2007).

27. The complete list of definitions and sources for our outcome variables can be found in Wagstaff and Moreno-Serra (2007).

28. Moreover, the comparisons of descriptive statistics between SHI and non-SHI countries presented in table 14.1 cannot be strictly interpreted as a preliminary assessment of SHI effects, because eventual SHI adoptions occurred on a staggered basis in our sample.

29. SHI adoption and a change in the predominant hospital payment method have occurred in the same year for some countries, namely Bulgaria, the Czech Republic, Estonia, the Kyrgyz Republic, and FYR Macedonia. For the detailed timing of changes in predominant hospital payment methods for the countries in our sample, see Wagstaff and Moreno-Serra (2007).

30. The results for the other models are available from the authors upon request. Unsurprisingly, in view of the results of the parallel trends assumption and reverse-causality tests, the SHI impact estimates are similar across all three models. We also estimated

fixed-effects versions of the diffs-in-diffs and differential trend models (the results are also available upon request). In general, the results were similar to those obtained for the first-differences estimates. According to the fixed-effects results, SHI has significantly increased government health spending and has had no perceptible beneficial effects on population health (the fixed-effect estimates are in fact more pessimistic on this point than the first-differences results). A positive impact on discharges of patients treated for infectious diseases is also evident in the fixed-effects estimates. Where the results differ somewhat is on the impacts of SHI on hospital length of stay, bed occupancy, and admissions. There are no significant impacts on any in the fixed-effect results, though the point estimates are actually usually somewhat larger.

31. The impacts on government and total health spending are reduced to about 12 percent and 8 percent (respectively) when we switch to the alternative "non-classical" definition of SHI for Latvia, Poland, and Romania, where we classify the first two countries as SHI countries despite the fact they do not meet the strict definition of SHI, and Romania as SHI from 1992 onwards even though it was not until 1998 that Romania set up a formal mandatory SHI system. This reduction of impact when the definition is changed provides additional evidence that SHI—interpreted strictly—does indeed increase health spending. Similarly, for all the remaining models estimated in this analysis, using the alternative definition of the SHI variable does not alter our qualitative results and only marginally affects the size of our parameter estimates in some instances.

32. We would like to have expanded the scope of this part of the analysis to cover other potentially relevant changes that may have been associated with SHI adoption, such as changes to the way physicians were paid, the introduction of a gatekeeping function for primary care providers, and so on. We were unable, however, to get the relevant data, year by year. At best, we could obtain typically only snapshots of the initial (i.e., Communist) and current arrangements, with no information on the *timing* of these changes over the decade.

33. We undertook the same reverse-causality test for this model. In only 4 percent of cases was the coefficient on the lead SHI dummy significant at the 10 percent level.

34. See, for instance, the individual HiTs for the Czech Republic and the Russian Federation.

35. Studies with similar objectives to ours (though not specifically on SHI) have usually been constrained by lack of data on mortality and (especially) morbidity outcomes, thus potentially missing important health benefits arising from public health insurance arrangements. See, for instance, Finkelstein and McKnight (2008), who were only able to investigate Medicare impacts on elderly mortality but could not examine any potential effects on morbidity indicators.

REFERENCES

Allin, S., E. Mossialos, M. McKee, and W. Holland. 2004. *Making Decisions on Public Health: A Review of Eight Countries.* Copenhagen: World Health Organization.

Bell, B., R. Blundell, and J. Van Reenen. 1999. "Getting the Unemployed Back to Work: The Role of Targeted Wage Subsidies." *International Tax and Public Finance* 6 (3): 339–60.

Bertrand, M., E. Duflo, and S. Mullainathan. 2004. "How Much Should We Trust Differences-in-Differences Estimates?" *Quarterly Journal of Economics* 119 (1): 249–75.

Blundell, R., and M. Costa Dias. 2000. "Evaluation Methods for Non-experimental Data." *Fiscal Studies* 21 (4): 427–68.

Carrin, G., and C. James. 2005. "Social Health Insurance: Key Factors Affecting the Transition Towards Universal Coverage." *International Social Security Review* 58 (1): 45–64.

Ellis, F.R., and M. Miller. 2008. "Provider-Payment Methods and Incentives." In *International Encyclopedia of Public Health*, ed. K. Heggenhougen. Waltham, MA: Academic Press.

Escobar, M.-L., and A. Panopolou. 2003. "Health." In *Colombia: The Economic Foundation of Peace*, ed. M. Giugale, O. Lafourcade, and C. Luff, 653–707. Washington, DC: World Bank.

Finkelstein, A., and R. McKnight. 2008. "What Did Medicare Do? The Initial Impact of Medicare on Mortality and Out-of-Pocket Medical Spending." *Journal of Public Economics* 92 (7): 1644–68.

Friedberg, L. 1998. "Did Unilateral Divorce Raise Divorce Rates? Evidence from Panel Data." *American Economic Review* 88 (3): 608–27.

Gerdtham, U.-G., and B. Jonsson. 1992. "International Comparisons of Health Care Expenditure—Conversion Factor Instability, Heteroscedasticity, Outliers and Robust Estimators." *Journal of Health Economics* 11 (2): 189–197.

Gottret, P.E., and G. Schieber. 2006. *Health Financing Revisited: A Practitioner's Guide.* Washington, DC: World Bank.

Gruber, J., and M. Hanratty. 1995. "The Labor-Market Effects of Introducing National Health Insurance: Evidence from Canada." *Journal of Business and Economic Statistics* 13 (2): 163–73.

Hsiao, W.C., and R.P. Shaw, eds. 2007. *Social Health Insurance for Developing Nations.* Washington, DC: World Bank.

Jowett, M., and W.C. Hsiao. 2007. *The Philippines: Extending Coverage Beyond the Formal Sector: Social Health Insurance for Developing Nations*, ed. W.C. Hsiao and R.P. Shaw, xi, 172. Washington, DC: World Bank.

Kutzin, J., S. Shishkin, L. Antosová, P. Schneider, and P. Hroboň. 2009. "Reforms in the Pooling of Funds." In *Lessons of Health Reforms in Eastern Europe and Central Asia*, ed. J. Kutzin, n.p. Brussels: European Observatory.

Langenbrunner, J.C., I.M. Sheiman, and J.C. Kehler. 2008. "Sources of Health Financing and Revenue Collection: Reforms, Lessons, and Challenges." In *Lessons of Health Reforms in Eastern Europe and Central Asia*, ed. J. Kutzin, n.p. Brussels: European Observatory.

Lewis, M. 2007. "Informal Payments and the Financing of Health Care in Developing and Transition Countries." *Health Affairs* 26 (4): 984–997.

Lu, J.R., and W.C. Hsiao. 2003. "Does Universal Insurance Make Health Care Unaffordable? Lessons from Taiwan." *Health Affairs* 223 (May/June): 77–88.

Martin, S., N. Rice, and P.C. Smith. 2008. "Does Health Care Spending Improve Health Outcomes? Evidence from English Programme Budgeting Data." *Journal of Health Economics* 27 (4): 826–842.

Nolte, E., and C.M. McKee. 2008. "Measuring the Health of Nations: Updating an Earlier Analysis." *Health Affairs* 27 (1): 58–71.

O'Donnell, O., E. van Doorslaer, R.P. Rannan-Eliya, A. Somanathan, S.R. Adhikari, B. Akkazieva, D. Harbianto, C.C. Garg, P. Hanvoravongchai, A.N. Herrin et al. 2008. "Who Pays for Health Care in Asia?" *Journal of Health Economics* 27 (2): 460–75.

OECD (Organisation for Economic Co-operation and Development). 2005. *OECD Reviews of Health Systems: Mexico*. Paris: OECD.

Preker, A., M. Jakab, and M. Schneider. 2002. "Health Financing Reforms in Central and Eastern Europe and the Former Soviet Union." In *Funding Health Care: Options for Europe, A.D.E.*, ed. E. Mossialos, J. Figueras, and J. Kutzin, n.p. Buckingham, UK: Open University Press.

Rechel, B., W.C. Hsiao, R.P. Shaw, and M. McKee, eds. 2003. "Healing the Crisis: A Prescription for Public Health Action in South-Eastern Europe." London School of Hygiene and Tropical Medicine, London.

Twigg, J.L. 1999. "Obligatory Medical Insurance in Russia: The Participants' Perspective." *Social Science & Medicine* 49 (3): 382.

Wagstaff, A., and R. Moreno-Serra. 2007. "Europe and Central Asia's Great Post-Communist Social Health Insurance Experiment: Impacts on Health Sector and Labor Market Outcomes." Policy Research Working Paper 4371, World Bank, Washington, DC.

Wagstaff, A., E. van Doorslaer, S. Calonge, T. Christiansen, M. Gerfin, P. Gottschalk, R. Janssen, C. Lachaud, R. Leu, and B. Nolan. 1992. "Equity in the Finance of Health Care: Some International Comparisons." *Journal of Health Economics* 11 (4): 361–88.

Wagstaff, A., E. van Doorslaer, H. van der Burg, S. Calonge, T. Christiansen, G. Citoni, U.G. Gerdtham, M. Gerfin, L. Gross et al. 1999. "Equity in the Finance of Health Care: Some Further International Comparisons." *Journal of Health Economics* 18 (3): 263–90.

Wooldridge, J.M. 2002. *Econometric Analysis of Cross Section and Panel Data*. Cambridge, MA: MIT Press.

PART 3

Implementation Challenges: Staying the Course

CHAPTER 15

Political Economy of Reform

Ashley M. Fox and Michael R. Reich

O ver the last twenty years a growing number of developing countries have sought to transform their health financing mechanisms—with the goal of achieving universal coverage, often through national health insurance. Yet successful reform is the exception rather than the rule. If scaling up health insurance coverage is popular, can greatly improve access to care, and can potentially reduce costs through risk pooling, why is it so hard to adopt and implement?

INTRODUCTION: WHY POLITICAL ECONOMY?

Reforms are difficult because they involve a series of complex political exchanges, any one of which can stop the process short of its goals. To overcome these challenges, different political skills are required at different stages of the reform process. In short, the reform of health financing is difficult because of the political economy challenges embedded in each step of the policy reform process. Politics affects whether reform makes its way onto the national agenda, how the reform proposal is designed, the compromises needed to produce an acceptable agreement, and ultimately the implementation of reform (Reich 2002).

Health financing reform is often treated as a technical matter—designing the right policy to produce the intended effect. However, what is viewed as technically optimal is seldom politically feasible. Interventions often do not work in the intended manner. If reform teams wish to succeed, they need to give more attention to the political dimensions of the policy process together with the technical dimensions of policy development (Gilson and Raphaely 2007).

Health policy analysts and international development organizations are giving increasing emphasis to political economy analysis to provide the missing link between reform processes and policy outcomes. The World Bank has recognized the critical role of political economy for all sectors of development (World Bank 2008) and recently formed a "community of practice" within the Bank to promote political economy knowledge and analysis. This approach involves a deeper understanding of the political, institutional, social, and economic issues at play, the power relations among actors, and the incentives that affect change. Political economy analysis can help answer a series of questions crucial to scaling up access to health insurance, such as: Why have some countries been successful at adopting national health insurance whereas others have failed? Why have leaders preferred particular policy designs over others? Why has the same reform produced the intended effect in certain settings, but not in others? What are the prospects for scaling up health insurance coverage in developing countries?

As this volume shows, few developing countries have adopted national health insurance, although the health insurance model is growing in popularity, and systemic reform is gaining momentum over vertical approaches. Nor is this trend limited to middle-income countries. Although traditionally viewed as a luxury only wealthier countries could afford, low-income countries are beginning to view health insurance as a means of increasing resources for health even in the absence of an expanding tax base. Ghana is perhaps the poorest country to attempt national health insurance. Rwanda's government is working to scale up national health insurance from local community-based financing schemes. Chile, Colombia, and Mexico are middle-income countries with large and enduring informal sectors that have instituted national health insurance. Most East Asian Tigers have adopted national health insurance systems in the context of rapid economic growth and shrinking informal sectors. East European countries have switched from a national health service model financed by general tax revenue and focused on salaried hospital-based specialists to a national health insurance model financed by payroll taxes with providers paid through fee for service (Wagstaff and Moreno-Serra, chapter 14, this volume). All advanced industrial countries (with the exception of the United States) have some form of universal health coverage—either through national health insurance or a national health service—although these systems are coming under increasing pressure for retrenchment. What can be learned from the experiences of scaling up health insurance in developing countries and from the historical experiences of now developed countries? What recommendations should policy makers and technocrats draw from the political economy of health reform?

Analysis of the political economy of health financing reform shows that there is no consensus about what constitutes a "good" reform, because of disagreement about underlying social values (Roberts et al. 2004). Different ethical assumptions result in different reform policies. A full exploration of the ethical underpinnings of health financing reform is not possible in this chapter, however, due to limitations of space and analysis.

This chapter highlights how the political economy of reform affects the agenda-setting, design, adoption, and implementation of national health insurance schemes by drawing on examples of health financing reform in both successful and unsuccessful cases. The challenges specific to scaling up health insurance in low- and middle-income countries that make health reform so difficult to achieve are assessed. It is argued that simply exhorting leaders to commit to national health insurance is insufficient to move countries to scale up coverage and that lack of political commitment to reform is inadequate to explain why some countries have been more successful than others. In addition, problems are explored with several other commonly asserted reasons to explain the failure or success of health insurance scale-up (such as economic growth, democratization, and political culture). Instead, the authors focus on four variables they believe particularly affect the probability of successful reform: institutions, ideas, interests, and ideology. Although a deterministic account of which variables matter most is not provided, concrete examples of health reform are presented to illustrate the effects of each variable on the reform process. In addition, the authors suggest ways that policy makers may find these four variables useful in designing their health reform strategies.

There are many schematics of the policy cycle. For this chapter, the authors adapt the models of Kaufman and Nelson (2004) and Roberts et al. (2004) to distinguish four phases of the policy reform cycle: (1) the initial placement on the policy agenda (agenda setting); (2) technical design of the reform proposal (design); (3) legislative consideration and passage of the reform bill (adoption); and (4) implementation of the adopted policy (implementation). Different elements of political economy come into play at these four stages in the reform process, and different theories of political economy help explain what happens and why some proposals go forward while others founder. The objectives of this chapter are twofold: to introduce key theories of political economy that help explain why health financing reform is difficult and to present practical implications of understanding this perspective.

To illustrate, the authors draw on cases of health reform (Chile; China; Colombia; Ghana; Mexico; and Taiwan, China) as well as cases of nonreform or incremental reform (Canada, South Africa, and the United States). The examples were selected because they are relatively well studied, are known to the authors, and include both successful and unsuccessful cases. Although this chapter draws on evidence from various national contexts, the examples are not intended as a systematic review of countries scaling up health insurance. The authors propose hypotheses about the political economy of health reform and use evidence from country cases to support preliminary conclusions with theoretical and practical applications. The analysis reveals several paradoxes. Sometimes increasing democracy helps the reform process, and sometimes not. Sometimes prosperity drives health reform, and sometimes economic adversity. Sometimes decentralization can help by allowing experimentation, and sometimes it hurts by hindering implementation. These paradoxes lead to a more complex understanding of health financing and the reform process.

AGENDA SETTING: GETTING HEALTH INSURANCE ONTO THE NATIONAL AGENDA

What determines whether health insurance is prioritized on the national agenda and not education, pensions, or some other issue? Policy analysts often attribute low expenditure on health care as a share of GDP to a lack of "political will" to allocate more money to health (Scheil-Adlung, chapter 2, this volume; Hsiao and others, chapter 11, this volume). However, developing-country governments are faced with many pressing challenges and limited resources (Heller, chapter 5, this volume). Some analysts explain the lack of national health insurance as a result of inadequate knowledge about the nature of insurance, inadequate trust in insurance companies, or lack of willingness or ability to pay an insurance premium (van de Ven, chapter 3, this volume). This question is viewed from a political economy perspective in this chapter, with particular attention to theories of agenda setting.

Agenda Setting: Coupling Policies with Political Windows

On its own, the problem of low coverage and limited financial risk protection is insufficient to place health insurance expansion high on the national agenda, due to various factors. According to Kingdon (2003), the process of agenda setting requires a combination of three streams: a window of opportunity in the *political stream*, with a ready-made solution (e.g., health insurance) in the *policy stream*, which addresses a persistent trouble (such as low access to health services) in the *problem stream*. Problems make it to the top of the national agenda for legislative enactment when there is a coupling of a problem window such as a crisis or major focusing event (e.g., an epidemic outbreak) with a political window (elections or some other political upset to the status quo). Whereas interest groups and lobbyists exert ongoing pressure for certain policy platforms, a combination of swings in national mood and elections are thought to be more important in affecting when certain issues are given a high priority (Kingdon 2003).

Problems need to be socially defined and politically supported through processes of mobilization in order to appear on the political agenda and be addressed by policy reform. Policy alternatives are narrowed by the policy process (bargaining and competition among political actors), and hidden participants or specialists (i.e., technocrats) get involved. Skilled politicians and policy entrepreneurs must recognize the potential to bring these three streams (problem, policy, and political) together to take advantage of an opportunity before it passes (Kingdon 2003). This requires attention to the roles of policy windows, the ambiguous effects of economic growth, and the influence of dominant political ideas and ideology, discussed next. The processes of problem definition and agenda setting, thus, are deeply political.

Policy Windows: The Role of Critical Junctures and Exogenous Shocks

In countries that have adopted some form of national health insurance, why did health reform make it onto the national agenda? Some policy analysts assume that if "a problem" exists, reform becomes inevitable once a breaking point is reached. However, experience with health reform shows that, even when patient dissatisfaction and cost inflation are high, reform does not automatically follow (as illustrated by the U.S. experience). Large political or economic shocks are often necessary to open a window of opportunity for change. These critical junctures and exogenous shocks can reshuffle political competition in ways that allow advocates to push more effectively for policy change. Democratization, for example, can open a political window for health reform—allowing increased political competition, giving politicians and policy entrepreneurs new opportunities for change, and creating space for "big-bang" reform. Economic transitions can also open political space for reform.

Democratization and the Political Space for Reform

Several countries, for example, adopted national health insurance in the wake of democratization (e.g., the Republic of Korea; Mexico; and Taiwan, China). Under the prior authoritarian regimes health insurance expansion in Korea and Taiwan, China, moved in a gradual, piecemeal fashion, primarily benefiting economically vital coalitions and sectors. After democratization, increased political competition resulted in a more dramatic expansion of benefits (Wong 2004). In each case, the party in power used universal coverage as a political strategy to gain popular support (Wong 2004). In Mexico, the election of Vicente Fox as president in 2000 ended the 70 years in power of the Partido Revolucionario Institucional (PRI) and brought a new group of technocrats into the Ministry of Health (MOH); they pursued health reform with the president's support and commitment (Lakin 2010). In Ghana, reform emerged out of an electoral strategy of the opposition party (New Patriotic Party) in Ghana's first successfully contested multiparty election, in 2000. To galvanize the support of the rural poor, the New Patriotic Party used health reform as an election platform promising a big-bang approach that would replace the unpopular cash-and-carry system with national health insurance based on ability to pay (Rajkotia 2007; Agyepong and Adjei 2008). These findings are supported by a comparative study of education and health sector reform in eight Latin American countries, which showed that democratization increased the political salience of reform for government decision makers through the logic of political competition (Kaufman and Nelson 2004).

But democratization does not necessarily increase the probability of achieving health insurance coverage in the ways that are most commonly theorized, that is, through popular pressure from newly enfranchised, relatively poor voters (Meltzer and Richard 1981). In Mexico, for example, reform was driven by "insurgent technocrats" in the MOH seeking policy change, not by the popular demands of newly enfranchised voters lacking health insurance (Lakin 2008). Lakin (2008) stresses that a change in the nature of political appointments and a reduction of partisan discipline within the executive branch allowed a reform-focused change team to come to power and created a coincidence of factors that enabled reform from above. In other cases (such as Korea and Taiwan, China), there was more popular pressure from below for reform than in Mexico, but the expansion of health insurance was primarily politician-led (or policy-elite-led) (Lakin 2008; Lin 2002; Wong 2004). In the United States, popular pressure for health reform on its own has been insufficient to catalyze universal health coverage for decades (Steinmo and Watts 1995).

Democratic transitions can also affect the ideological character of the reform, including the role of the state and the market. In Chile, for example, under 18 years of military rule, private health insurance was encouraged to proliferate, which might have been less likely under democratic circumstances. Following the elections of 1989 and Chile's return to democracy, public officials tried to restore equity in the health system. But their efforts were constrained by the "pacted democracy" institutions that were created in negotiations between the military regime and other political actors to end the dictatorship. As a result, reform in Chile has followed an incremental process of strengthening the public sector without directly confronting the political and economic interests opposed to reform (Bossert 2010).

Experience also shows that democratization does not guarantee that health reform makes it onto the legislative agenda. In South Africa, after the end of apartheid in 1994 the African National Congress gave health reform and social health insurance a prominent place on its policy agenda in the transition to multiracial democracy. But these reform ideas were not successfully transformed into national policy for consideration by the legislature (Gilson et al. 2003; McIntyre, Doherty, and Gilson 2003; Marks 1997).

In addition, autocratic regimes sometimes have incentives to provide social risk protection in ways that redistribute benefits. Health financing reform can serve as a political strategy to control social pressure for democratic change. For example, in the Middle East, some oil-rich "rentier" states that provide national health insurance for their citizens are beginning to expand insurance coverage to noncitizens (Ekman and Elgazzar, chapter 9, this volume). In these cases, the state may be using the expansion of social benefits as a carrot to contain popular pressure for greater political participation. Other health systems historically provided more benefits under nondemocratic circumstances. In Eastern Europe and the former USSR, for example, health benefits were more comprehensive under communism than after the fall of the iron curtain.

Nor does democratization always predict the direction or shape that reform will take. In the transitional economies, the move to a less generous social health insurance model occurred in political space created by the disintegration of the USSR (Wagstaff and Moreno-Serra, chapter 14, this volume). Health insurance financed through payroll taxes was introduced as part of a package of reforms aimed at supporting the transition from centrally planned to market-based economies. These reforms reduced public services in order to generate leaner, more liberal welfare states with protection decoupled from provision. This shock-therapy package spilled over into health policy, where 18 out of 28 East European and Central Asian countries adopted national health insurance to replace their faltering national health services and fee-for-service payment systems based on the North American model (Wagstaff and Moreno-Serra, chapter 14, this volume).

Thus, democratization (or the threat of democratization, as in the Middle East) can create a political window of opportunity and can precipitate the expansion of health insurance, but democratization is neither necessary nor sufficient to do so. Democratization does not automatically put health financing reform on the table, but it increases the probability that different reform options will be considered. Increased political competition and structural change in political institutions are what make reform more probable, not popular pressure per se. Nor does democratization necessarily translate into more risk protection; it can also be used as a window for retrenchment.

Economic Growth and Reform

Policy analysts often assume that economic expansion is a key factor in the scale-up of health insurance, as discussed in the chapter on East Asia (Hsiao and others, chapter 11, this volume). In Japan, Korea, and Taiwan, China, the rapidly expanding economies and large formal employment sector facilitated a significant expansion of government-mandated social health insurance—starting with formal sector workers and then including informal sector workers, rural farmers, and the poor.

Functionalist views of welfare state expansion have presented universal social protection as an inevitable by-product of economic growth and an expanded tax base (Wilensky 1975), but recent experience suggests otherwise. In contrast with the East Asian example, in some cases economic contraction can lead policy makers to promote the expansion of coverage to provide more social risk protection. For instance, in many Western countries, large expansions of health coverage came in the wake of the Great Depression of the 1930s (Steinmo and Watts 1995; Immergut 1990). In the United Kingdom, the National Health Service was established during the period of post-war recovery (Fox 1985). The case of the United States, however, provides some counter examples (as well as some support) for this pattern. The failure of health reform to pass in the United States during the New Deal came at a time when citizens were most vulnerable, and this marked the beginning of a series of failures at expansion (Steinmo and Watts 1995). The major expansion in coverage in the United States came with Medicaid and Medicare in the mid-1960s, which occurred during the post-war economic boom. Conversely, President Barack Obama's health reform finally passed in 2010, in the wake of a huge economic crisis.

Cycles of boom or bust can open a political space for reform but do not guarantee the passage of reform nor the direction the reform will take (greater expansion or retrenchment). Economic crisis in Latin America and Africa generated a wave of fiscal austerity measures including the introduction of user fees in the 1980s (Weyland 2004). Economic transitions in the former USSR moved in the direction of greater austerity as economic conditions deteriorated during the transition to a market system.

The recent introduction of national health insurance in several low-income countries further draws into question the notion that expanded health coverage is an inevitable by-product of economic growth and an expanded tax base. Instead of waiting for economic expansion, some low-income countries with large informal sectors are viewing health insurance as a means to raise revenue for health, increase utilization of health services, and improve financial risk protection even for citizens outside the formal sector. A few low-income countries have substantially scaled up health insurance, even with large and enduring informal sectors and resultantly small tax bases. Rather than introducing top-down national health insurance, middle-income East Asian countries with large informal sectors, such as China, the Philippines, and Thailand, have targeted the informal sector and the poor from the outset by expanding community-based insurance, starting with rural populations and then gradually achieving universal coverage (Hsiao and others, chapter 11, this volume). Other lower-middle-income countries like Colombia and low-income countries like Ghana have adopted national health insurance and are finding ways to finance coverage incrementally over a 10-to-20-year period—even in the absence of rapidly expanding public funds generated through economic growth. There remain questions, however, about how to collect health insurance premiums from the informal sector in both low- and middle-income countries (discussed below). Despite these difficulties, health insurance expansion is increasingly on the policy agenda of developing countries over direct expansion of national health services through general taxation. This suggests that a similar political calculus regarding the introduction of health insurance prevails in low-income countries even though they potentially lack sufficient resources to sustain these programs.

This discussion suggests that having adequate economic resources is not a sufficient condition to place health reform on the national agenda, and it may not even be a necessary condition. Indeed, in some situations, financial instability can be a political motivator for the expansion of risk protection and help push insurance expansion onto the legislative agenda. Importantly, it is the shock of rapid economic growth or contraction that changes the political calculus of leaders, which can increase the probability of health reform's making its way onto national agendas, not popular or interest group pressure on their own. Although available economic resources differ, the political process for arriving at national health insurance may not differ substantially among countries at different levels of development.

Narrowing the Policy Scope: Why Some Issues Are Completely Off the Agenda

A country's dominant political ideas and ideology also shape which policy designs are given serious consideration. (Political scientists refer to this set of beliefs and values in a society as "political culture.") While resistance to scaling up social benefits like health insurance is frequently attributed to a country's political culture, this explanation can be circular (Smith 1996). Critics of cultural explanations note the endogeneity of this variable and its lack of explanatory power (Steinmo and Watts 1995). For instance, unequal states produce fragmented welfare states, which feed back into the existing inequality and reinforce the antistatist narrative that the state should play a minimal role in social risk protection (Alesina, Glaeser, and Sacerdote 2001). While cultural explanations alone may have difficulty explaining the adoption of reform, they may help explain why certain design options gain political traction and how the range of possible options becomes narrowed down. As Kingdon (2003) notes, what gets selected for the national agenda depends not only on technical and financial feasibility but also must be congruent with the values of community members and general public acceptability.

Depending on a country's political culture, some policies may simply be "off the agenda." For instance, in the United States, a single-payer system has consistently been off the agenda, in part due to public resistance to "socialized medicine" (as well as opposition from insurance companies and the practical problems of removing private insurance plans from the health system).[1] Social health insurance rests on notions of social solidarity (Ly and others, chapter 8, this volume), suggesting that heterogeneous societies are more likely to resist plans that spread risk and subsidies across diverse social groups (e.g., Alesina, Glaeser, and Sacerdote 2001; Miguel 2004). Popular objections to social solidarity and popular acceptance of individual responsibility are commonly cited reasons for the U.S. failure to adopt national health insurance or a single-payer system or even get these options on the national agenda (Jacobs 1993). By contrast, some scholars argue that East Asian countries are solidaristic and defer to authority (e.g., Moody 1996), making health insurance expansion more culturally acceptable (Doh and Cole 2009).

In sum, the first step in scaling up health insurance is for the issue to make it onto the national policy agenda. Health reform appears on the national agenda when different streams come together at the right moment—a coupling of an ongoing problem with a political window and a policy solution (Kingdon 2003). Social mobilization and lobbying around a problem (like expanding health coverage) will not get far without a political opening that changes the policy equilibrium. Likewise, a political opening may pass unexploited if policy entrepreneurs are not promoting persuasive solutions. The authors' review of cases further suggests that major political and economic shifts can create opportunities for health financing reform, but that both democratization and economic expansion have ambiguous impacts since reform has also reached the national policy agenda in situations of nondemocracy and economic contraction.

TECHNICAL DESIGN: WHAT AFFECTS THE CONTENTS OF THE PROPOSED REFORMS?

During the design phase, policy proposals are hammered out. A complex negotiation process shapes what gets into the legislation and what is left off the table. Although participatory approaches to policy development are sometimes promoted in the policy literature, experience shows that behind-the-scenes advising by technocrats plays an important role at this stage, as during the agenda-setting period (Kaufman and Nelson 2004). During the design stage, the policy space narrows as the preferred proposals of policy entrepreneurs become the focus of debate (Kingdon 2003). Design issues are typically considered to be a technical process of applying economic theory to the problems of health insurance (Glied and Stabile, chapter 4, this volume), but design is actually a profoundly political process as well.

Policy Diffusion and Learning from Foreign Models

As the introduction to this volume suggests (Preker, Lindner, Chernichovsky, and Schellekens, chapter 1), the health insurance model has recently gained momentum over the general revenues finance model of national health service (NHS). Why is this the case? Public policy has been observed to diffuse in a wavelike S-shaped pattern, sweeping across regions of the world and clustering geographically and temporally (Weyland 2005). Scholars of policy diffusion have proposed various explanations for the wavelike diffusion of policy ideas (e.g., Simmons and Elkins 2004):

- *Influence of external pressure.* Countries adopt policies due to pressure from international financial institutions or donors.

- *Symbolic or normative imitation.* Countries imitate trendsetter countries to stay on the frontier of policy experimentation.

- *Rational learning.* Countries learn from other cases where adequate information is available about what has worked.

- *Cognitive heuristics.* Countries adopt policies in the absence of full information and unlimited time to make decisions, by using "boundedly rational" inferential shortcuts and looking at other countries' experiences.

The approach used in deciding on policy design has important implications for a policy's impact, as suggested by the health reform experiences of various countries. The selection of the policy design approach is often conditioned by broader historical and political circumstances.

External pressure for policy design can take various forms. For example, as discussed in the chapter on Anglophone Africa (Ly and others, chapter 8, this volume), most former British colonies adopted Britain's NHS model upon independence, as an institutional carryover from the colonial experience. With a small resource base and a high cost of care, however, these systems were chronically underfunded. In the 1980s and 1990s, in response to economic austerity packages and fiscal crisis, many African countries introduced user fees to make up for funding shortfalls. Critics have pointed to the role of the international financial institutions in pressing countries to adopt these cost-recovery schemes (e.g., Kim et al. 2000). More recently, health insurance is increasingly being advocated by development agencies to overcome the gaps in coverage emanating from underfunded or fragmented national health services and the limited experiments with health insurance that have been undertaken in a number of developing countries.

But the ideas of development agencies are not directly transferred in cookie-cutter fashion to recipient countries; policy diffusion is mediated by domestic political processes. While external pressure is frequently invoked as an explanation for the convergence of policy across diverse countries, a number of studies find continued diversity and innovation in national social policy even amid general convergence (e.g., Murillo 2002). Nelson finds, for instance, that "external attempts to prompt specific actions had a rather limited impact [on health sector reform], despite the substantial influence [...] of broader international intellectual currents on reform debate and government agendas" (Nelson 2004: 32). Countries in very different parts of the world may adopt prevailing models from other parts of the world. For instance, Chile in the 1950s adopted a modified version of the British NHS even though it was not within the British sphere of influence. Whether policy makers are adopting a national health insurance model from external pressure and imitation or from some form of domestic learning (whether rational or bounded) remains for researchers to examine and explain.

In East Asia, the decision to adopt a national health insurance model appears to have occurred more through domestic learning than through external pressure or peer imitation. Japan was the first non-Western country to expand health insurance following the German social health insurance model (Hsiao and others, chapter 11, this volume). In contrast to the first-mover advantage that has been noted in the development literature (Gerschenkron 1962), in social policy late developers like Japan have the advantage of being able to learn from existing models rather than creating policy de novo. The ability to leapfrog existing models has enabled newly industrial countries to introduce universal health systems much more rapidly than *"la longue durée"* that characterized the development of the welfare state in the West (Singh 1999). In considering how to provide health coverage, Japan had foreign models to observe and evaluate. As a result, Japan decided to adopt Germany's Bismarckian model of employee-based social health insurance in 1922, beginning with the coverage of blue-collar workers and then expanding coverage to other population groups (Hsiao and others, chapter 11, this volume).

Japan's policy experience in turn set an example for other East Asian countries like Korea and Taiwan, China, which also adopted a social health insurance model. Korea and Taiwan, China, however, subsequently adopted a single government-run insurance model to provide universal coverage, unlike Japan, which has maintained multiple insurers (Hsiao and others, chapter 11, this volume). Recently, China has followed a rational learning process for health reform, surveying different countries' health systems and experimenting before deciding on a particular model (Blumenthal and Hsiao 2005). By developing after the West expanded welfare protections, newly industrializing countries can learn from these experiences and design their policies accordingly. In Mexico, for example, the design of national health insurance was driven by a technocratic policy assessment of the "evidence-based" merits of health insurance (demand-driven delivery) over a national health service (supply-driven delivery) (Frenk 2006; Lakin 2010).

Policy Entrepreneurs, Technocrats, and Change Teams in Policy Design

Policy diffusion is not simply the process of policy makers' "learning from what works." The role that technocrats and policy entrepreneurs play in diffusing academic ideas has been gaining increasing attention in the policy literature (e.g., Silva 1991; Dominguez 1998; Lee and Goodman 2002). The recent switch toward a health insurance model in developing countries appears to be driven by teams of policy experts or "expert epistemic communities" that endorse particular policy solutions (Dobbin, Simmons, and Garret 2007). According to Kaufman and Nelson (2004: 475), "specific proposals have generally been designed from the top, by reform or 'change teams' within or among the ministries." Change teams of technocrats are the technical entities that design policies and build networks of support within government (Waterbury 1992). The assignment of policy design to technocrats takes some of the political pressure off politicians and allows politicians to claim some plausible deniability if the reform fails. Change teams were crucial to the success of attempted health reforms in Latin America during the 1990s (Bossert and González-Rossetti 2000).

Technocrats alone may lack the political skills needed to get their proposals accepted. The challenge is to make the policy design both palatable to politicians so that the legislation will pass and digestible to bureaucrats so that the policy can be implemented. Successful change teams often include both technocrats, concerned mainly with the technical design of policy, and "technopols," who combine a technocrat's technical expertise and training with a politician's pragmatic expertise on how to produce change (Dominguez 1998).

Chile's health sector reform under President Ricardo Lagos (2000–2006), for example, involved two change teams. The first included technical experts in public health, costing, law, and economics from the Ministries of Health and Finance, responsible for developing the details underlying health sector reform, which enabled the Lagos administration to generate internal support from the Ministry of Finance (MOF). The second change team was more political, with membership from think tanks associated with political parties like the Christian Democrats and right-wing interests. This team's political affiliations enabled it to secure support from the far right in the legislative process (Bossert and Amrock n.d.). In Mexico, a politically astute change team in the Ministry of Health eventually abandoned the strategy of trying to convince the Ministry of Finance to come on board through evidence of cost savings. Instead, in order to pass legislation for national health insurance, the change team sidelined the MOF, misrepresenting the MOF position to other government ministries so that the MOF could not effectively oppose the reform (Lakin 2010).

Good politicians possess practical political knowledge of how the policy process works. Politicians know which interest groups will oppose a particular design and the bargaining chips that may persuade fellow legislators to support an idea. The content of reform is often deliberately shaped to appeal to a particular coalition of actors. A failure to consult with relevant interest groups can lead to a policy design's being dead on arrival. For instance, President Bill Clinton's strategy of extensive consulting with technical experts while excluding groups seen as obstacles later led to legislative gridlock with politicians and resistance from groups he did not include. By contrast, Obama's willingness to negotiate with key interest groups up front helped reduce political obstacles in the legislative process even though it later raised some public concerns.[2]

While technocrats often present an air of value neutrality and objectivity, their ideological orientation is rarely far from the surface. In Chile and Colombia, technocrats pushing managed competition viewed themselves as apolitical, although they were ideologically in favor of changing the role of the state in the social sector through a greater reliance on the private sector by adopting targeting and demand subsidies over more comprehensive social risk protection (Bossert and González-Rossetti 2000). Likewise, Clinton's strategy of linking his reform to managed competition was not driven primarily by his belief in the soundness of Enthoven's theory, but rather by the political calculus that market delivery would synthesize the "liberal ends" of universal coverage with the "conservative means" of provision by private insurers (Oberlander 2007). This compromise, though ultimately unsuccessful, allowed Clinton to reach across the aisle to attract majority support in Congress and avoid antagonizing organized interests (Oberlander 2007). Obama eventually dropped his "public option" as this policy drew opposition from both moderate Democrats and Republicans. In Taiwan, China, the president ultimately decided not to accept the advice of technocrats to replace fee-for-service payment with capitation to control costs, because of anticipated political resistance to the change (Yeh, Yuang, and Hsiao forthcoming). Although some policies may diffuse globally, how the ideas are integrated into national policies is mediated by partisan political competition and domestic political calculations.

Technocrats shape reform, but their ideas still must go into the policy process. Designs are subject to institutional and partisan constraints and what is politically feasible in a given system. The assessment of what is politically feasible requires strategizing between technocrats and technopols who know the political context. Policy makers need to take into account the institutional and partisan landscape in designing reforms—if they wish to make policy.

Distributive Politics: Hard and Soft Budget Constraints and the Role of Finance Ministries

Financing represents one of the most contentious elements of policy design. Ministers of finance typically oppose the expansion of large social programs like national health insurance for fear of breaking the bank. In South Africa, expanding health insurance coverage was stymied by the MOF (McIntyre and van den Heever 2007; McIntyre, Doherty, and Gilson 2003). In many countries, the MOF acts as the gatekeeper of reform. As noted earlier, Mexico's technocratic supporters of health reform (Lakin 2008) purposefully built alliances within the government to work around opposition from the MOF. Similar opposition by the MOF to the expansion of social health insurance has been observed in Israel (Gross, Rosen, and Shiron 2001) and the Arab Republic of Egypt (Nandakumar et al. 2000).

Both Chile and Colombia managed significant budgetary increases for reform initiatives despite resistance from their respective Ministries of Finance. In Chile, the president succeeded in introducing a significant increase in the social security tax on the formal sector, and Colombia imposed a value added tax (VAT) to cover the transitional costs of reform. Sustained presidential commitment to reform and concerted efforts by the change team were necessary to overcome the resistance from the MOF. In Chile, a compromise with the MOF that the increases in the social security tax be accompanied by a ceiling on total government expenses in health ultimately contributed to the fiscal soundness of Chile's reform. In Colombia, however, the transitional costs became permanent, thereby contributing to subsequent fiscal crisis. As Glied and Stabile note (chapter 4, this volume), while MOFs generally oppose expansion of the public budget, politicians face soft budget constraints and incentives to run deficits. In the long term, those deficits can threaten the financial sustainability of a system or necessitate new funding streams, especially for a cost-inflationary good like health care.

Political Battles over Financing: Interests and Ideology

Financing is also contentious because it usually involves compelling the wealthy (who can afford to pay for their own insurance) to contribute resources to subsidize the poor and others who cannot pay for health insurance and compelling the healthy to subsidize the sick. This improves the welfare of the poorest and most vulnerable, while making society as a whole better off. However, as a risk-pooling mechanism, health insurance schemes generate collective action dilemmas—how to compel individuals (especially in high-income groups) to contribute to the pool when it is against their individual interests to do so. While it is often assumed that health insurance is redistributive, the actual design of a financing reform affects the degree of redistribution and the extent to which insurance is regressively or progressively financed (Glied and Stabile, chapter 4, this volume). Certain financing streams are politically more difficult than others, and the politically feasible financing streams may also be more regressive. For example, sales taxes and sin taxes (such as taxes on alcohol and cigarettes) are politically less contentious but are also more regressive. Payroll taxes are easier to implement than income or corporate taxes, since the latter tend to be strongly opposed by business and the wealthy, but payroll taxes can also be more regressive.

If health reform is redistributive, the relevant political question is who benefits and who pays? Even where there is consensus that reform is necessary, political factions may disagree about the specific financing mechanism and its political implications. This disagreement shapes the type of system that is politically feasible to get through the legislature and the degree of redistribution. In short, the design of financing has a profound effect on political support for reform, and the political actors behind reform have a profound impact on the design of financing.

In Taiwan, China, the initial design of social health insurance called for 60 percent of the premium to be covered by the employer and 40 percent by the employee. But after deliberation within the planning commission, the government agreed to pay 10 percent of the premium for public and private sector workers to reduce the burden on workers without increasing costs for industry, and to lower the contribution of workers to 30 percent (Lin 2002; Yeh, Yuang, and Hsiao forthcoming). In addition, the initial plan proposed that family dependents should also have to make contributions to the premium to ensure fiscal soundness. The Council of Labor Affairs objected, arguing that, in the spirit of mutual assistance, dependents should be exempt since employers, who also are required to pay a portion of the premium, would discriminate against workers with many dependents (Lin 2002). A compromise was reached whereby the employer would pay for the average number of dependents and the insured would pay for the actual number of dependents. All of this deliberation took place between the ministries and the Executive Yuan before the bill was sent to the Legislative Yuan for a vote (Lin 2002).

Judging the equity in financing from different financing mechanisms is a complicated question. But taking into account equity in the design of financing is politically important because it affects which factions will support or oppose reform in the legislative phase. Whether the financing of national health insurance in developing countries is regressive or progressive depends in part on the capacity of the state to collect taxes and the size of the informal sector. Financing through general tax revenue, especially income taxes, is thought to be the most progressively redistributive in developed countries (Glied and Stabile, chapter 4, this volume). But due to low government revenues from general taxation in developing countries (and the difficulties of collecting income taxes in these countries), public health services in poor countries tend to be severely underfunded and consequently often low quality. As a result the wealthy may prefer to buy private health insurance (or pay out of pocket) rather than pay more to subsidize a weak system, which can generate separate tiers of care and undermine social risk pooling.

Health insurance financed through payroll taxes depends on an even narrower resource base—those employed in the formal sector—and therefore may still require a large infusion of general tax revenue in poor countries. For premium-based systems, the degree of regressiveness in financing depends largely on the graduated cost of premiums and decisions on who qualifies as exempt. Cost-sharing and coinsurance spread the cost burden and generate a soladaristic notion that "everyone is paying something," creating a "culture of prepayment" (Lakin 2010) that may offset some resistance to other financing mechanisms. However, like sales taxes, cost-sharing is regressive, and even small fees in developing countries can create large barriers to care for the poor.

Financing schemes in developing countries must struggle with how to raise money from a limited tax base while mediating conflict between the small but powerful group of urban elites that work in the formal sector and the large populace in the informal sector with limited ability to pay. In Ghana, the government's attempt to deduct a 2.5 percent contribution from the formal sector pension funds to finance the health insurance scheme was met with sharp resistance by public sector workers during the design phase (Coleman 2010). Ultimately, the largest share of health insurance financing was designed to come from a VAT and the second largest from payroll taxes on formal sector workers and premium contributions from informal sector workers who are not otherwise exempt (Agyepong and Adjei 2008; Witter and Garshong 2009). How and why the New Patriotic Party (NPP) developed its financing scheme remain obscure. However, increasingly exemptions are being extended to additional populations not previously entitled to free care, such as pregnant women (Witter and Garshong 2009). In Mexico, the major opposition to national health insurance came from the left (the opposition Partido de la Revolución Democrática, PRD). The left objected to premium payments, which they saw as regressive, preferring "free" services financed through general tax revenues (Lakin 2010). In Mexico, as in Ghana, with few effective sticks to enforce means testing, the scope of who is considered exempt from premium payment has been widening.

In sum, multiple factors drive the recent popularity of the national health insurance model in the design of health reform. Those factors include the spread of ideas through increasingly global policy networks, change teams of technocrats, and the advice of aid agencies that seek to promote certain policy ideas, including social health insurance. Political institutions constrain the set of potential design options that are politically viable, as politicians anticipate what is possible to get passed, given the institutional and partisan circumstances at a particular political moment. Existing institutions further bind politicians in what is possible, since policy makers have to construct reform on existing institutions. Interest groups also influence the direction of reform to make sure their positions are protected. Policy makers often must act under uncertainty about what the actual impacts of the policy will be. Distributive politics is perhaps the most contentious element of design as the ideological orientations of the left and the right clash over preferences for redistribution, and groups with the most power often have the least interest in contributing.

ADOPTION: POLITICAL BARGAINING AND THE LEGISLATIVE PROCESS

Once on the agenda, there is no guarantee that the reform as designed will be adopted. In general, policy stability is thought to be the norm rather than the exception (Pierson 2004; Tsebelis 2002; Baumgartner and Jones 1993). Radical policy change, such as a large scale-up of a national health insurance program, is rare and difficult to achieve. Health reform is hard because new policy meets resistance from groups that stand to lose from a change in the status quo, and the future potential beneficiaries may not be mobilized or even organized. Policy change in the real world never achieves Pareto efficiency, where everyone is made better off without anyone's being made worse off. Health reform typically involves a complex redistribution of costs and benefits across society, and people who will be made worse off resist change. Inherently, reforms are conditioned by historical influences, and change is subject to increasing returns as interest groups become entrenched, and the relative costs of switching the current activity become higher when compared with once-possible options (Pierson 2004). Further, public policy constitutes an inherent collective action problem—coordination is essential, but the effectiveness of an individual's actions depends heavily on the actions of others. According to some observers, the creation of conditions for collective action is the principal object of political life (Pierson 2004; Stiglitz 1995). For this reason, the policy-making process has been described as unfolding in a "punctuated equilibrium": long periods of stability interrupted by infrequent and sudden upheaval, followed by a return to stasis (Baumgartner and Jones 1993).

Interest Group Influences and Policy Feedback

As recognized in many chapters in this book, interest groups often influence health financing reform via their influence on politicians (Marmor 2000). For national health insurance, these groups include private insurance companies, medical associations, and trade unions, among others. However, to understand the relative impact of different groups on health reform, one must look at how a group's power becomes institutionalized over time and how this power varies across countries. In the United States, the failure of the state to take a leading role at particular critical junctures allowed the insurance industry to assume a dominant position (Steinmo and Watts 1995). Once private insurance companies are established, it becomes increasingly difficult to constrain their power or reform them away. Colombia's health insurance reform institutionalized the power of private insurance companies inspired by Enthoven's "managed competition" model, and expanded a small prepaid private insurance industry into a formidable power that now covers nearly 70 percent of the population. The government's efforts to regulate private insurers, control spiraling health care costs, and equalize benefits packages have been unsuccessful at reducing the influence of private insurance companies (Bossert 2010). Similarly, Chile has not been able to remove private health insurance entities (called ISAPREs), but it has incrementally strengthened the public sector without directly confronting the political and economic interests of the private insurance entities (Bossert 2010).

The legacy of union-based benefits packages can also make reform more difficult to achieve, especially if the goal is to pool previously separate benefit plans. In countries that have established benefits packages for public and private sector unions, introducing a uniform benefits package for all citizens, including the informal sector, can be difficult. Typically, unions have fought hard to win their benefits and legitimately fear losing their gains if public benefits are extended to previously excluded groups. In addition, a uniform benefits package that covers the poor, who may not contribute to the pool, implies higher taxes on the rich, which could place an additional burden on relatively well-off union members. In Mexico, the power of one of Mexico's largest unions, the union of the Instituto Mexicana del Seguro Social (IMSS), and its opposition to being pooled with the previously uninsured, resulted in the establishment of a separate national health insurance system for the uninsured (the Seguro Popular) administered through the Ministry of Health, rather than an integrated system, and has arguably reinforced a two-tiered benefits package (Lakin 2008). Countries with existing private insurers and multitiered health plans face more hurdles in generating a single-payer, uniform benefits plan than do countries without these existing institutions. The result can be the continuation of two-tiered systems, as has occurred in Colombia and Chile (Bossert 2010). One counter example is Japan, which has reduced differences in benefits and copayments among plans over time through incremental changes (Ikegami and Campbell 1999), but still confronts nearly 3,500 social insurance plans with varying premium rates.

Although national health insurance may be hard to introduce, once adopted and institutionalized, it can be even harder to remove or change. Even in a context of general retrenchment of the welfare state, health has been one area that the public has been reluctant to see cut (Kitschelt 2001). The bad news is that certain less desirable health system designs (such as cost-increasing fee-for-service and private, for-profit health insurance) can also become increasingly difficult to regulate or reform because interests become entrenched over time.

Political Institutions and Veto Players

Despite the critical power frequently assigned to interest groups in explaining health reform, health policy analysts have increasingly argued that "we have veto points within political systems and not veto groups within societies" (Immergut 1992: 391; also: Steinmo and Watts 1995; Hacker 1998). In other words, the demands of interest groups are mediated through political institutions that structure the kind of legislative change possible in a given system.

A critical determinant of whether a policy gets adopted is the number of veto players and veto points in the legislative process (Immergut 1992; Tsebelis 1995; Hacker 1998). Veto players are the individuals or collective actors whose agreement is required to make a policy decision (Tsebelis 1995). These include *institutional veto players* such as the president and legislative chambers in a federal system, which have formal veto power, and *partisan veto players* or parties in parliamentary systems, whose veto power can vary depending on electoral outcomes. A greater number of veto players increases the likelihood that policy stability (the status quo) will prevail and militates against radical, big-bang policy changes such as adopting national health insurance. Veto points refer to junctures in the legislative and policy design process where reform can be blocked. For countries with multiple veto points, big-bang reform is difficult, and incremental reform is more likely. Furthermore, as the number of veto points increases, lobbyists and interest groups have more access and control over the policy process (Immergut 1992).

The number of veto points may surpass the influence of interest groups in influencing health reform, and different reform strategies may be necessary in countries with a greater number of veto points. For instance, Immergut (1992) notes that differences in the development of national health systems in Sweden, France, and Switzerland cannot be explained by reference to the mobilization of medical associations, since each country had influential medical professions that had achieved a legal monopoly of medical practice by the outset of the 20th century. Rather, the influence of these political pressure groups operated through their institutionalized access to policy makers. In Switzerland, the political institution of the popular referendum provided a critical access point for the medical association to block reform efforts. At several points in Switzerland's history, health reform legislation was enacted into law by both chambers of parliament but subsequently vetoed through referendum challenges because higher income voters, who stood to lose from national health insurance or other forms of social protection, were far more likely to vote. As a result, even the threat of calling a referendum was enough to make legislators shy away from enacting large-scale reform (Immergut 2002). By contrast, in Sweden, with no institutional veto points and a majority support in parliament, comprehensive health reforms passed without substantial challenge in spite of lobbying by the powerful medical association (Immergut 1992). This example illustrates that the mobilization of interest groups is not sufficient to explain the reform process. In this comparative analysis, institutional differences in veto points better explain why a minority (the medical association) in one case had a more profound influence on policy proposals.

Certain political institutions further militate against large, redistributive social programs where the benefits are diffuse. Representatives elected in single-member majoritarian voting systems that represent small geographic constituencies (as in the United States) have a greater incentive to pass policies that benefit their particular constituent base (pork-barrel politics) rather than support broadly redistributive social policy. The result is a welfare state based on local rather than national public goods provision (Cox and McCubbins 2001; Persson and Tabellini 2003). Majoritarian voting systems, as in the United States, are therefore likely to face more obstacles in adopting national health insurance coverage. The "veto-ridden" political institutions of the United States have been cited as a primary barrier to the adoption of national health insurance and for the country's tendency to spend more on pork-barrel projects that are easily geographically targeted (e.g., schools, roads) than on transfer spending (e.g., unemployment benefits and old-age pensions) (Hacker 1998; Steinmo and Watts 1995; Milesi-Ferretti, Perotti, and Rostagno 2002). As highlighted in this book's chapter on Europe (Maarse and others, chapter 12), in European countries with complex multiparty consensual political systems, such as Germany, social health insurance evolved through prolonged and fierce political battles over health reform. The resulting layered and fractured health system reflects the compromise and appeasement of diverse views and the battle wounds from a greater number of veto points. In addition, the countries that followed this Bismarckian path tend to view social insurance as an entitlement that is paid for rather than a universal right that is guaranteed to all, and free-riding is strictly monitored (Maarse and others, chapter 12, this volume).

Viewed from this perspective, incrementalism is less an approach to reform than a result of institutional design (multiple veto players). Federal states, for instance, with a greater separation of powers and devolution of authority, are more likely to engage in incrementalism. But when health reform in federal states is impossible at the national level, policy experimentation can be lively within subnational units (states or provinces or regions). This decentralized policy experimentation increases the likelihood of health insurance at the subnational level, since it can be achieved without a great deal of additional federal funds or cooperation but may create greater inequality as richer jurisdictions are better placed to experiment with reform without federal support. Decentralized policy success can then create incentives for others to follow, both at the subnational and national levels (Bossert 1998). For instance, in Canada, a federal state, political movements supportive of single-payer health reform first gained a political foothold in western provinces and enacted programs that served as an example, which subsequently spurred other provinces and the federal government to respond (Hacker 1998).

In veto-ridden states, incremental scale-up may at times be more effective than top-down big-bang approaches to reform. But incremental reforms can also create new interest groups that block more fundamental reforms (since those changes would make the groups' services redundant). In the United States, there have been a number of policy innovations to create universal health coverage at the state level, some more successful than others. State-based policy innovation in the United States played an important political role in the debate over reform legislation in 2009–10. However, because the same veto-ridden political institutions are mirrored at the state level as at the national level, incremental state-based reform has so far met with limited success at building universal coverage within states or in furthering universal coverage at the national level (Gray et al. 2005). Further, a number of federal constraints and reliance on federal funding impede experimentation within states, making incremental, bottom-up reform more challenging, even for more politically liberal states (Carter and LaPlant 1997). In recent battles over health reform in the United States, the small left-leaning contingent, after abandoning its hopes for more substantial single-payer reform, turned its energy toward protecting the right of states to experiment with more far-reaching reform options; this, too, however, was ultimately unsuccessful.[3]

Partisan Political Competition and Legislative Bargaining

The adoption of national health insurance is also influenced by the partisan policy preferences of vote-seeking political representatives. Although institutional structures incentivize and constrain politicians in different ways, politicians generally seek to maximize both their chances of reelection and their influence on public policy (Strøm 1990).

Politicians are considered responsive when they "adopt policies that are signaled as preferred by citizens" through "public opinion polls; various forms of direct political action [...] and, during elections, votes for particular platforms" (Przeworski, Stokes, and Manin 1999: 9). In terms of consulting the public at large, evidence suggests that politicians do not directly respond to current public opinion in formulating their preferred policy option or stance. Instead, politicians use informational shortcuts and make prospective judgments. They speculate about what the media will focus on at reelection and the likely positions of their constituents. For instance, in the case of the United States, Gelman, Lee, and Yair (2010) note the surprising disconnect between what politicians' constituents have signaled as their preferences on health reform through polls and politicians' actual voting records on the Obama health reform. Likewise, Shapiro and Jacobs (2010) note a form of "post-hoc representation" in the relationship between public opinion and the policy choices of U.S. representatives for health reform, whereby individual components of the reform are selectively spotlighted, which suggests that public opinion is a two-way street. Citizens do not simply communicate preferences and politicians respond; instead, politicians actively construct the preferences of their constituents through targeted messaging.

Party loyalty and discipline can sometimes determine how politicians vote on health reform proposals, depending on the institutional context. In Mexico, partisan political competition and ideology came into play during the negotiation of the health reform bill in the legislature. As the fate of the bill came down to the number of votes in the Mexican Congress, party discipline became a critical deciding factor in the passage of health reform (Lakin 2008). In 2003, in the absence of a majority for the governing Partido Acción Nacional (PAN), a lack of party discipline among the PRI allowed passage of health reform. The PRI split between legislators associated with the IMSS union who opposed the reform and legislators who backed the reform even though it was spearheaded by the PAN. The left party (PRD), conversely, was fairly united in its opposition to the reform in the Mexican Congress, based on the party's view of the financing mechanism as not progressive enough (Lakin 2008).

During legislative bargaining, politicians may also seek to add personal legislative provisions or riders for their favored policy in exchange for a vote for a bill. This can result in the bill's substance being compromised and criticism if the rider is unpopular. For instance, during the 2010 health reform debate in the United States, pro-life Democrats added an executive order to the bill clarifying the existing law that federal funding would not be used to pay for abortion services. This angered pro-choice legislators and advocates.[4] Further, once the "public option" and amendments for states wishing to adopt single-payer systems were dropped from the legislation, support among left-of-center Democrats waned. In the final vote, however, these Democrats felt pressured to vote in favor of the bill on the argument that some reform was better than no reform.[5] In Mexico, as a deliberate strategy to prevent the passage of Seguro Popular, the MOF (unsuccessfully) attempted to add a fiscal reform rider to the health insurance bill that would have resulted in unpopular tax increases (Lakin 2010).

While parties on the left may seem more likely to propose and support national health insurance, reform does not always come from the usual suspects. When reform is proposed by a party that would not traditionally support a large state-driven fiscal expansion, the public may be more inclined to accept that there is a dire problem, and partisan wrangling may be reduced. This "Nixon-in-China effect" is partly what can account for the success of reform in Mexico where the PAN, a center-right party, put health insurance reform on the agenda and ultimately passed it with support from the traditionally centrist party, the PRI (Lakin 2008). In the United States, while health reform has typically been promoted by Democrats, in the 1970s Nixon put health reform on the agenda, even though it was ultimately defeated in Congress.[6]

This review of the political economy of adoption leads to a number of conclusions. First, a greater number of veto players and veto points makes it increasingly difficult to adopt a major reform. Incrementalism is often a by-product of veto-ridden systems. Reformers either propose an incremental reform, knowing that more thoroughgoing reform will be opposed from the start, or comprehensive reform slowly gets whittled down as it moves through legislative bargaining. In veto-ridden systems, reformers seeking to produce big-bang changes either need to wait for a major upset to the status quo (a critical juncture) or try to scale up reform gradually from more local experimentation. Second, political institutions such as federalism and majoritarianism incentivize politicians against broadly redistributive programs. Third, large-scale policy change is relatively rare because entrenched interests become increasingly "locked in" over time and the costs of policy switching become steeper relative to the political gains from the status quo. Finally, ideology affects partisan competition and political bargaining strategies.

IMPLEMENTATION: OPERATIONALIZING THE REFORM

Implementation is the complex process of putting a policy into practice. In their classic book, Pressman and Wildavsky (1975: xv) define implementation as "the ability to forge subsequent links in the causal chain so as to obtain the desired results." All implementation is hard. The politically attractive parts of the policy cycle are agenda setting, policy design, and adoption. The hard work occurs in implementation and producing tangible results. This is partly due to the large number of "decision points" that implementation has to go through and the "clearances" necessary for its success. A decision point is reached when "an act of agreement has to be registered for the program to continue," and "each instance in which a separate participant is required to give his consent is called a clearance" (Pressman and Wildavsky 1975: xvi). Like veto points, more clearances in a system can generate additional obstacles to implementation.

In this section three dimensions of political economy that affect reform implementation are considered. First, how the structure of political institutions, especially federalism and majoritarianism, and political time horizons affect processes of implementation are examined. Next, the political economy of evaluation and targeting during implementation is explored. Third, how policy choices made in the design and adoption phases can produce unintended consequences in implementation is examined. These factors can shape implementation in ways that affect the ultimate functioning of the health insurance program.

Political Institutions, Delegation, and Executive Time Horizons

Whereas the political battle over adoption and design of reform normally occurs on the national stage, the battle over implementation plays out at the local level (Grindle 1980). The political institutions of federalism and majoritarianism play a key role in affecting implementation by generating a division of power between the central and local governments and by creating incentives for pork-barrel spending. One of the core questions facing the drafters of legislation concerns the degree of detail to include in legislation versus the amount of discretion to grant to implementers (Yeh, Yuang, and Hsiao forthcoming; Huber and Shipan 2002). As Grindle (1980) outlines, the central problem in implementation is that government officials at the top level seek to avoid conflict by trying to appease local elites and politicians responsible for implementation, who often have the most to lose from redistributive programs. This presents a common pool problem (Persson and Tabellini 2003): the beneficiaries who have the most to gain have limited power over implementation, whereas the opponents who have the most to lose have a great deal of power. Whereas corruption is often blamed for implementation challenges, Grindle (1980) stresses that, contrary to the common view, bureaucrats are not inherently corrupt; rather, they face pressures on a number of fronts to avoid conflict.

One way to circumvent problems with government officials at the central level is through delegation, which has both advantages and disadvantages. Delegation can reduce resistance since it can encourage experimentation and innovation, tailoring programs to the diversity of local situations, but it can also increase opportunities for resistance to implementation and patronage (Bossert 1998; Faguet 2001). Delegation can also serve as a means of blame shifting and plausible deniability for implementation failures. In economically or ethnically diverse countries, however, the ability to experiment and adapt national legislation to the local context can also help reduce or avoid conflict (Miguel 2004).

Political systems where a higher degree of discretion is granted to regional and local political actors, such as in federal systems, have the potential to generate greater pressures for patronage through the targeting of public services for political gain. Where public goods can be targeted (as with local public goods), rational reelection-seeking politicians will in theory reward regions or groups of voters that have provided support in the past (Cox and McCubbins 1986), or target concentrations of swing voters that could go either way to maximize future votes (Armesto 2009; Dixit and Londregan 1996). But a problem arises with this kind of targeting if it is connected with the power of the local representative, to the detriment of the poorest regions or individuals within regions. Patronage can highlight the political forces behind unequal patterns of development and distribution that operate through machine politics. Through patronage, supporters of opposition groups may be systematically disadvantaged and punished for their views. But machine politics can also sometimes reward otherwise disadvantaged groups, under certain circumstances.

In Mexico, studies have shown that, in order to win back votes, local spending on the antipoverty program PRONASOL, a precursor to Seguro Popular, was targeted to districts that had defected to the opposition PRD as a reward (Molinar and Weldon 1994). Other studies have shown that spending on PRONASOL was targeted by the incumbent party, the PRI, to punish opposition municipalities by withdrawing resources, diverting resources to reward supporters, and targeting resources to swing municipalities that could vote either way (Magaloni 2006). Analysis of targeting of Seguro Popular benefits has similarly found evidence that its implementation occurred in ways that targeted swing voters in order to shore up support for the incumbent party, the PAN (Lakin 2008).

The effects of scaling up health insurance take a long time to unfold, like many other interventions. Politicians' time horizons, conversely, are short and regulated by election cycles (Pierson 2004). Parties that pass substantial social entitlement legislation often want to create a relatively permanent policy that will endure past the current government—in essence to "tie the hands" of their successors so that reform is not easily undone (King et al. 2007). Furthermore, politicians that oppose reform may nonetheless allow it to pass, banking on the reform's not actually being implemented. This allows them to take credit for its passage, while avoiding the blame if implementation falters.

Electoral timing also affected implementation in Mexico. There, the president and other politicians who backed national health insurance faced a dilemma. They needed to affiliate as many citizens as legally possible to Seguro Popular in a short period to demonstrate the program's political appeal before the next election in 2006 (and build up political support for the program in case of a party change in government), but "opposition from providers and states was incompatible with speedy affiliation" (Lakin 2010). Although the evaluation found in the short term that the reform had increased access and reduced catastrophic expenditures for some people (King et al. 2009), over time questions have been raised about whether Mexico's reform can be considered health insurance and not simply a large infusion of funding into its existing public health service, since only around 5 percent of affiliates pay a premium (Lakin 2010). Thus, Mexico's bold experiment with health insurance has been portrayed as an extension of its previous system during implementation. In addition, the big-bang approach of the change team became increasingly threatened during implementation, as the problems with this tactic became apparent. Lacking the support of the MOH provider union (which saw the reform as producing more work with no pay increase) and with state governors opposing the requirement of state contributions, the central government found itself with limited leverage to enforce the implementation of a top-down reform in a decentralized system (Lakin 2010).

Similarly, within five years of implementation, Ghana faced increasing pressure to overhaul its health insurance system as the program was bordering on insolvency (Siadat 2010). This party, which preferred an incremental approach to national health insurance, lacked enough votes in parliament to oppose the reform at adoption but subsequently forged "horizontal" alliances during implementation, aligning itself with government agencies and organized labor, community-based health insurance schemes, donors, and other opponents of the big-bang reform strategy (Agyepong and Adjei 2008).

Political considerations also affected the timing of the implementation of National Health Insurance (NHI) in Taiwan, China. With legislative elections looming at the end of 1995, the same year that the NHI was adopted, the president ordered the implementation of the NHI within three months of adoption. Within only three months, the newly constituted Bureau of National Health Insurance would have to "enroll nine million people, clarify the insurance benefits, set standards and payment rates, contract providers, and prepare to pay more than twenty million claims per month" (Yeh, Yuang, and Hsiao forthcoming). This hurried roll-out resulted in suboptimal implementation.

Policy implementation thus creates new opportunities for opposition and criticism, even after a bill has been approved and signed into law. Pushing reforms through the legislature may be politically expedient and necessary to meet the short time horizons of election cycles before the political window of opportunity closes. But the compromises made to meet election deadlines can create serious problems in implementation, which can sometimes undermine the objectives of the reform or raise the possibility of reversal.

In both Mexico and Ghana, parties and politicians have been punished at the voting booth in the election following the major reform efforts. Conflicts that existed at the beginning of the reform did not cease after reform. In Mexico, the left opposition (the PRD), which had opposed the introduction of Seguro Popular, continued to attack the program during implementation and substantially increased its number of seats in the 2006 election, nearly winning the presidential contest. In the United States, immediately after the adoption of the Obama reform, calls arose to reverse the new law and challenge its constitutionality.[7] Political competition and deep societal divisions over expanded access do not cease after reform is passed into law and continue to influence the implementation of policy in ways that designers may not anticipate.

The Political Economy of Evaluation and Targeting

Technocrats may wish to evaluate health reforms to assess their impact. Politicians, however, may have mixed feelings about evaluation. Politicians who backed reform have an incentive to claim success even when a program is in serious trouble, and politicians who opposed reform have an incentive to paint the program in a negative light and assign blame. As a result, the truth of success or failure can be difficult (if not impossible) to discern. These processes of credit claiming and problem blaming make evaluation all the more challenging. "Politically robust" evaluations are difficult to achieve since politicians have an incentive to roll out reforms in a politically instrumental rather than scientifically sound manner (King et al. 2007). Furthermore, most politicians are reluctant to allow an arm's-length evaluation, since the political risks are steep and personal. If the evaluation goes well, the payoffs are high, but if it goes badly, the risks are potentially disastrous, at least to one's reputation and legacy and potentially to one's political future as well.

Mexico is one of the few countries where evaluation was designed and conducted to protect randomization from political influence (King et al. 2007). Like many other policy evaluations, Mexico's faced pressure from state-level leaders seeking to more rapidly extend program coverage to their areas. In an attempt to overcome this natural democratic incentive, the evaluation matched areas in pairs on background characteristics so that if one area was contaminated, the other area in the pair could be dropped, rather than contaminate the entire sample (King et al. 2007).

This strategy allowed for a scientifically strong evaluation of impacts. It also reflects the tensions between the evaluation of technical elements of design and an evaluation of the political economy of implementation. Political parties have a political incentive to target social spending to their constituents at the expense of providing broad public goods that benefit a wider set of beneficiaries (Persson and Tabellini 2003). Where this targeted spending harms or distorts the effective roll-out of a program, such as when program benefits are captured by elites, preferred ethnic groups, or political partisans, this democratic incentive may negatively shape the implementation of health programs. In short, competitive politics produces incentives to implement policy in a nonrandom manner, which complicates the design of evaluation.

Although proponents of randomization try to control the roll-out of programs to protect against selection bias (Deaton 2009), it is precisely the nonrandomness or purposive selection in take-up that political economists are interested in understanding. An evaluation of reform that includes political factors would assess why implementation unfolded in the manner it did. Who were the winners and losers from reform? Why were benefits targeted toward certain groups or areas at particular times? In the real world, take-up does not occur in a random manner. For instance, researchers of the welfare state have identified political "business cycles" in the tendency of government expenditure to increase according to the electoral calendar (Nordhaus 1975; Alesina, Roubini, and Cohen 1997). As a result, fiscal policies in electoral democracies are to a significant extent determined by electoral politics.

Governments also may have incentives to target national subsidies to "swing" provinces, in which electoral contests are competitive, to reward supporters or punish opponents. Targeting takes on a different significance from a political economy perspective than its technical meaning. Whether public programs should attempt to target the poor through means testing, or if this effort is more costly and less effective than simply making services available to all households, has been debated in the public policy literature (Besley and Kanbur 1993). In the political economy meaning of targeting, however, the important question is not how to better target the poor, but rather who gets targeted and why. Evidence of political business cycles and the targeting of swing districts and loyal supporters in the allocation of public goods is a pervasive issue considered by students of political economy (Diaz-Cayeros et al. 2002; Armesto 2009; Bardhan and Mookerjee 2006).

The capacity of the state can also affect the processes of implementation and evaluation of reform. The debate over means testing is pertinent to the scale-up of health insurance in developing countries where the state may lack the capacity to successfully implement means-tested targeting. As Hsiao and others (chapter 11, this volume) point out, the greatest difficulty in scaling up social health insurance in weak states (such as Cambodia, the Lao People's Democratic Republic, and Pakistan) is the lack of adequate administrative and regulatory capacity to set up and oversee the organization of such a system. Successful implementation requires a competent administration to define the scope of the benefits package and to enforce a means-testing system. Where capacity is lacking, a larger number of implementation challenges arise.

In Ghana, while health insurance is mandatory de jure, there is no enforcement de facto and nonenrolment is not penalized (Blanchet 2010). Similarly, a graduated, means-tested premium has been abandoned in favor of a low, fixed annual premium for all (the equivalent of about US$7) (Blanchet 2010). While affiliation in Ghana has been growing rapidly, only an estimated 59 percent of the population has registered with the national health insurance service, and there is evidence that enrolment unequally favors the relatively wealthy (Asante and Aikins 2008; Mensah 2009; Sarpong et al. 2010). Yet, in contrast to the typical urban bias in the provision of public goods and services, higher enrolment rates in Ghana occur in poorer, rural regions that are the vote banks of the party that introduced health insurance (Witter and Garshong 2009). With a lack of means testing, however, few members contribute financially through premiums, a trend that may threaten the program's economic sustainability (Blanchet 2010).

Although state capacity is arguably stronger in Mexico, it too has faced challenges to enforcing means testing. One concession won by the MOF was that the program be rolled out gradually (affiliating only 14 percent of the eligible population per year) to make sure the program's budget did not exceed government revenues (Lakin 2010). While this gradual roll-out created an effective laboratory for program evaluation, the voluntary nature of affiliation reduced the social risk-pooling element of insurance and undermined the ability to do means testing. Even though states are required in Mexico's federal structure to subsidize the premiums of the informal sector workers, states have had a difficult time persuading residents to pay their premiums and have not used means testing in deciding on the income level of new members (Lakin 2010). With federal incentives to show progress in affiliation, the states turned a blind eye to residents who declared their incomes in the lower two deciles in the sign-up process so that they would not be required to pay a premium. Consequently, Mexico has a voluntary health insurance program that is in practice free for nearly all members, which has raised questions about the financial sustainability of the program without additional infusions of general tax revenue (Lakin 2010).

The terms "targeting" and "selection" have political connotations that differ from their common technical designations. In keeping with the classic definition of politics as "the social processes that determine who gets what, when, and how" (Lasswell 1936), a political economic analysis of implementation is fundamentally interested in the nonrandomness of public goods distribution and service provision.

Unintended Consequences of Policy Design Choices

Choices made for political reasons at the design and adoption phases can affect the implementation and future sustainability of national health insurance programs. The example of Colombia highlights the unintended consequences of policy reform that can appear in implementation. In adopting a new constitution in 1991 that guarantees Colombians a universal right to health care, Colombia sowed the seeds of a financial crisis for its health insurance system. The tutela (protection writ) system was originally designed to allow citizens to seek redress when they believe a denial of medical services violates their right to health.

However, this appeals process to protect a citizen's right to health has created a substantial burden on the country's health system. Tutela claims allow citizens to demand goods and services that fall outside their limited benefits packages. Much as abuse of the emergency room has become an option of last resort for people without insurance coverage in the United States, the tutela system in Colombia has provided individual patients with a reimbursement strategy for expensive health services, which over time has created financial problems and fairness questions for the health system (Yamin and Parra-Vera 2009).

In Ghana, political incentives to please a broad constituency during the design phase led to the bypassing of cost-control measures in favor of policies that appealed to the incumbent party's political base. As Witter and Garshong (2009) summarize, efforts to appeal to the party's rural base of voters resulted in: (1) NHIA revenues primarily growing with GDP rather than with membership; (2) an overly generous benefits package; (3) exemption schemes covering large population groups, but without a sufficient subsidy to cover exempt members; (4) little oversight of the diagnosis-related group (DRG) tariff or of overprescribing by providers; and (5) no cost-sharing for patients. The economic costs of these design features have become increasingly apparent with expanded implementation.

Implementation generally involves setting up a new institution or agency to administer the program, which can cause problems as each stakeholder jockeys to capture the agency (Yeh, Yuang, and Hsiao forthcoming). There can also be pressure on governments to appoint representatives from a broad group of interests, and institutional appointments may involve patronage rather than a merit-based choice of leader.

In Taiwan, China, heated debates occurred among business leaders and labor and social welfare advocates over whether the agency to administer national health insurance should be a government agency, parastatal, or private nonprofit organization, with pro-government and pro-market groups sharply divided (Yeh, Yuang, and Hsiao forthcoming). Taiwan, China, ultimately decided to create a state-owned, semi-governmental enterprise to administer the NHI. Integration of the existing insurance schemes into a state-owned enterprise in Taiwan, China, was similarly controversial. Separate insurance schemes existed for labor, farmers, and civil servants, each group with a different premium base, different premium rates, and different benefits packages. One strategy the new NHI head adopted to resolve the resistance toward integration was to recruit the key staff from existing insurance programs, offering promotions as an incentive (Yeh, Yuang, and Hsiao forthcoming). Political factions and vested interest groups tried to influence the various appointments to leadership positions to ensure that representatives of their interests would hold positions that would give them political leverage (Hsiao and others, chapter 11, this volume). Ultimately, the president exercised his authority to make a unilateral appointment based on merit.

In Mexico, the development of a separate, single-payer agency to administer a new integrated social health insurance was impossible due to resistance from the powerful social security provider union of the IMSS. Integration could have led to public contracting and competition for the IMSS with the MOH and potentially private providers (Lakin 2010). The IMSS effectively resisted integration during the adoption phase, resulting in a policy to administer Seguro Popular through the MOH, leading to continued fragmentation of coverage.

To summarize, politics influences implementation through the political pressures generated by electoral cycles and the short time horizons of politicians, patronage in local politics, and feedback from groups resistant to change. Countries where these tendencies are more explicitly built into the constitutional structure, such as federal or decentralized states with majority rule, have more institutional pressures to delegate discretion over implementation to the local level, which can increase difficulties in implementation. Likewise, geographic targeting of benefits may reward or punish areas that supported or opposed the incumbent party, or roll-out may be targeted toward swing voters. Interests, institutions, and ideology continue to impact the implementation of reform as different groups, parties, and politicians try to maximize the gains from the roll-out of social programs and distance themselves from the failures.

CONCLUSIONS

While it is well known that formulating, adopting, and implementing social policies occur through political processes, most of the literature on health financing reform focuses on the economic or technocratic design of policy—with little attention paid to how political dynamics affect policy design and outputs. Politics is treated as idiosyncratic, unpredictable, nonacademic, and as a barrier to be overcome in achieving the most technically optimal, utility-maximizing reform. As a result, in citing why so few countries have adopted systemic health reform like national health insurance, researchers often invoke a lack of "political will" or commitment to reform. The assumption seems to be that if leaders were so inclined, reform would be easy (Reich 2002; Roberts et al. 2004).

Politics needs to be viewed as the pathway to reform, the process by which technical plans are adapted to the preferences of different constituents in society. The structure of political institutions has a major influence on the distributive impacts of policy. As discussed, political systems with multiple veto points inhibit policy reform, and some systems are particularly adept at targeting political benefits in a nonrandom manner (Persson and Tabellini 2003; Cox and McCubbins 2001). Furthermore, political goals have a "lumpy" or "winner-take-all" quality to them. Unlike economic markets, where there is usually room for many firms, in politics second place often means no place at the table (Pierson 2004). Thus scaling up national health insurance in developing countries should not be expected to occur in the same way in different contexts. As U.S. politician Tip O'Neill put it, "All politics is local." Nevertheless, trends and lessons can be drawn from studying the political economy of reform cross-nationally, with important implications for future reform efforts.

This chapter concludes by presenting a few practical implications about the political economy of health financing reform, drawing evidence from the chapter's analysis and intended as advice for policy makers and policy analysts. These ideas will not provide a definitive answer to when universal health insurance will be successfully scaled up, but they can help policy makers judge when the timing is ripe for reform and how to design a politically feasible reform.

Health reform is a profoundly political process, and politics plays a role in all phases of the health reform process (Roberts et al. 2004). The specific political strategies and skills at each phase are different, although decisions made at each phase interact with one another. Health reform is not only a technical process. It is a political process characterized by trade-offs and influenced by ideology, ideas, interests, political calculations, bargaining, and strategizing within a particular institutional context. Each technical design component has a political calculation associated with it (table 15.1).

TABLE 15.1   Political Strategies to Manage the Political Economy of Health Financing Reform

Policy cycle	Constraints and facilitators	Strategies
Agenda setting Getting health reform on the policy agenda	• Critical junctures, focusing events, and opportunity windows • Partisan policy cycles • Political culture, ethnic and religious fractionalization, and heterogeneity of preferences	• Recognize a political window of opportunity and exploit that opportunity (and know when the moment is not right). • Work with policy entrepreneurs to create political momentum for health reform. • Understand political culture and package messages accordingly.
Policy design Crafting the technical design of reform in a political context	• Trendsetters, international organizations, and external pressure • Technocrats and policy entrepreneurs • Finance Ministry • Interest group and partisan influences	• Give different groups the feeling of participation while maintaining control. • Balance concerns of different stakeholders to reach a political equilibrium. • Design around major political and institutional obstacles. • Consider distributive consequences of policy and partisan support base.
Adoption Getting health reform through the legislative process	• Interest groups and existing institutions • Number of veto points and veto players • Political leadership and party discipline	• Practice the art of legislative negotiation and bargaining. • Keep certain agreements nontransparent to maintain support of different interests. • Find allies within the legislature.
Implementation Carrying out the reform	• Federalism, decentralization, and delegation • Political time horizons • Existing institutions and positive feedback	• Balance delegation with retention of oversight. • Appoint cabinet members and bureaucrats strategically. • Anticipate and manage partisan politics and the patronage of implementation. • Account for natural "democratic incentive" in the design of policy evaluation.

Source: Authors.

This analysis of health financing reform across the policy cycle identifies four political factors that commonly affect reform strategies and successful scale-up: (1) institutions; (2) ideas; (3) ideology; and (4) interests. The interaction of the four I's at each stage in the policy process is particularly relevant in managing the politics of reform.

- *Institutions.* A country's political institutions—whether they are veto-ridden or veto-few—affect the political calculations for reformers from the beginning. Politicians calculate what is politically feasible given the checks and balances they face and the support/opposition ready to mobilize for or against different reform options. Countries with more institutional and partisan veto points have a more difficult time passing big-bang reforms and may instead have to adopt an incremental approach. Insurgent tactics may also be used to manage the multiple veto points to achieve big-bang reform. However, costs are associated with this strategy as opposed to a more participatory approach. Insurgent tactics can lead to the emergence of more problems during implementation; participatory engagement, conversely, can force more compromises up front during design and adoption of the policy.

- *Ideas.* Health reform is heavily influenced by the prevailing ideas in society. Kingdon (2003) describes the policy-making process as a "primeval soup"— ideas float around, bumping into one another, encountering new ideas, and forming combinations and recombinations. These ideas are circulated waiting to be linked up with political opportunities. Thus, the ideas that are prominent at any given time have a greater likelihood of being taken up by policy makers. This explains why particular policies appear to cluster in time and space. Recently, national health insurance has gained popularity as a means of increasing access to health services and is diffusing rapidly through global policy networks. Technocrats can bring technical ideas to the policy table, but those ideas must be adapted to the local political palate.

- *Ideology.* Ideologically driven partisan competition also affects reform, but it is more mutable than the institutional rules of the game since the composition of political competition changes more frequently. In general, parties on the left of the ideological spectrum support more redistributive social policies, including financing through general tax revenue and publicly rather than privately delivered health services. Parties on the right prefer the status quo or more regressive forms of financing and more involvement from the private sector, often with limited government participation. Likewise, incumbent parties wish to show that their policies are working, whereas the opposition has an incentive to discredit the prior government's reform and propose alternatives. Thus, the content of reform bears the partisan imprint of parties backing the plan and reflects the political competition between different political factions and the constituents they represent. If compromise cannot be reached, the status quo (the present health system) usually prevails, which ironically may satisfy no one. Politicians should consider the political consequences of the policy designs they recommend.

- *Interests.* While policy makers are arguably the mediators of the various stake-holders' interests, the mobilization of these groups has a profound influence on policy makers' decisions and their political calculus. Organized interests, often representing a minority, have a disproportionate influence on policy makers. Medical associations and providers have resisted national health reforms that would limit free choice of doctors and their economic independence. Private health insurers fight tooth and nail to protect their independence and their incomes. Industry generally opposes the increased taxation that more progressive financing measures entail. Influential unions that have fought hard to achieve their benefits resist efforts to extend protection to the uninsured for fear it will compromise their own hard-won gains. Due to existing power structures, countries have frequently had to design reform around them instead of incorporating them into a single system, often further reinforcing inequality in an already fragmented welfare state. This discussion highlights the importance of taking into account the irreversibility of certain policy choices. Some policies are more difficult to undo than they were to do, and the dynamics of reversal may be different from the dynamics of adoption due to the rising costs of reversal over time (Pierson 2004). All policies, once implemented, build up networks of stakeholders and supporters who resist reforms that would reduce their benefits. In adopting policies that may be particularly difficult to undo, the potential unintended (but foreseeable) consequences should be considered.

These four variables—institutions, ideas, ideology, and interests—interact with each other at each stage of the reform process.

What does this mean for policy makers wishing to scale up health insurance in developing countries? This presents a strategic political choice: Should leaders ram through adoption of national health insurance in spite of large informal sectors and insufficient capacity for implementation, or should leaders incrementally scale up health insurance coverage by building on community financing schemes and the formal sector? As the experience of Mexico and Ghana illustrate, even if national health insurance fails to meet all the technical criteria to constitute health insurance, its introduction can infuse needed revenue into an underfunded public health system and expand health benefits for previously disadvantaged people. Further, having this architecture in place can serve as a means of gradually increasing coverage and institutionalizing insurance, making reversal of gains difficult over time. In short, in some situations, political logic trumps economic caution. However, where this big-bang approach is infeasible, either because a window of opportunity does not present itself or because the existence of multiple veto points makes radical reform infeasible, a gradual, bottom-up community health insurance model has worked to substantially expand coverage in Thailand and China, and is being experimented with currently in Rwanda, where the national government is steering the gradual increase in insurance coverage.

Technocrats who design reform are frequently interested in what works in a laboratory setting, but real reform has to work in real societies and requires grounding in both politics and economics. Evaluations of health policy designs (like payroll tax–financed systems versus general taxation) focus on whether one financing design works better than another, while trying to control for existing background conditions or other immeasurables captured in the "error term." Political economy analysis is interested in exploring the immeasurables and unpacking the error term to explain what happens in all phases of the policy reform process. We believe that political economy analysis has both theoretical and practical implications for making health financing reform work better.

NOTES

1. T. Hamburger and T. Marmor, "Dead on Arrival: Why Washington's Power Elites Won't Consider Single-Payer Health Reform," *Washington Monthly*, September 1993, 27–32, http://findarticles.com/p/articles/mi_m1316/is_n9_v25/ai_13276711/?tag=content;col1; Associated Press, "Single-Payer Health Care Plan Dies in Senate: Nixed Amendment to Create Government-Run System Would Not Have Passed," December 16, 2009, http://www.msnbc.msn.com/id/34446325/.

2. P. Krugman, "Not Enough Audacity," *New York Times*, June 26, 2009.

3. J. Zelleny and R. Pear, "Kucinich Switches Vote on Health Care," *New York Times*, March 17, 2010.

4. E. MacAskill, "US Healthcare Reform: Winning Over Anti-Abortionists the Key Step," *The Guardian*, March 22, 2010, http://www.guardian.co.uk/world/2010/mar/22/us-healthcare-reform-abortion-obama.

5. P. Bacon, Jr., and G. Franke-Ruta, "Kucinich Drops Opposition to Health-Care Bill," *Washington Post*, March 17, 2010, http://voices.washingtonpost.com/44/2010/03/kucinich-drops-opposition-to-h.html.

6. P. Krugman, "Missing Richard Nixon," *New York Times*, August 30, 2009.

7. D.M. Herszenhorn and R. Pear, "Health Vote Is Done, but Partisan Debate Rages On," *New York Times*, March 22, 2010, http://www.nytimes.com/2010/03/23/health/policy/23health.html.

REFERENCES

Agyepong, I.A., and S. Adjei. 2008. "Public Social Policy Development and Implementation: A Case Study of the Ghana National Health Insurance Scheme." *Health Policy and Planning* 23 (2): 150–60.

Alesina, A., E. Glaeser, and B. Sacerdote. 2001. "Why Doesn't the US Have a European-Style Welfare System?" *Brookings Paper on Economics Activity* (Fall): 187–278.

Alesina A., and N. Roubini, with G.D. Cohen. 1997. *Political Cycles and the Macroeconomy*. Cambridge, MA: MIT Press.

Armesto, A. 2009. "Governors and Mayors, Particularism in the Provision of Local Public Goods in Mexico and Argentina." Prepared for delivery at the 2009 Congress of the Latin American Studies Association, Rio de Janeiro, Brazil, June 11–14. http://lasa .international.pitt.edu/members/congress-papers/lasa2009/files/ArmestoAlejandra .pdf.

Asante, F., and M. Aikins. 2008. "Does the NHIS Cover the Poor?" Working Paper supported by DANIDA Health Sector Support Office. http://www.moh-ghana.org/Upload Files/nhis/NHIS%20pro-poor%20research090805112429.pdf.

Bardhan, P., and D. Mookerjee. 2006. "Pro-Poor Targeting and Accountability of Local Governments in West Bengal." *Journal of Development Economics* 79: 303–27.

Baumgartner, F.R., and B.D. Jones. 1993. *Agendas and Instability in American Politics.* Chicago: University of Chicago Press.

Besley, T., and R. Kanbur. 1993. "The Principles of Targeting." In *Including the Poor*, ed. M. Lipton and J. Van Der Gaag. Washington, DC: World Bank.

Blanchet, N.J. 2010. "A Review of the Implementation of Ghana's National Health Insurance Scheme." Working Paper, PATH, Seattle, WA.

Blumenthal, D., and W. Hsiao. 2005. "Privatization and Its Discontents—The Evolving Chinese Health Care System." *New England Journal of Medicine* 353 (11): 1165–70.

Bossert, T. 1998. "Analysing the Decentralisation of Health Systems in Developing Countries: Decision Space, Innovation and Performance." *Social Science and Medicine* 47: 1513–27.

———. 2010. "The Role of Private Insurance Institutions in the Policy Process of Health Sector Reform in Chile and Colombia." Paper prepared for the First Global Symposium on Health Systems Research, Montreux, Switzerland, November 16–19.

Bossert, T.J., and S.M. Amrock. n.d. "The Politics of Prioritization: Political Strategies for Achieving Health Reform in Chile, 2000–2006." Unpublished manuscript, Harvard School of Public Health, Boston, MA.

Bossert, T., and A. González-Rossetti. 2000. "Enhancing the Political Feasibility of Health Reform: A Comparative Analysis of Chile, Colombia and Mexico." Latin American and Caribbean Regional Health Sector Reform Initiative Report 36, June.

Carter, L.E., and J.T. LaPlant. 1997. "Diffusion of Health Care Policy Innovation in the United States." *State and Local Government Review* 29 (1): 17–26.

Coleman, N.A. 2010. "Universal Health Coverage: Ghana's Transition to National Health Insurance." Working Paper prepared for the Rockefeller Foundation, New York.

Cox, G.W., and M.D. McCubbins. 1986. "Electoral Politics as a Redistributive Game." *Journal of Politics* 48 (2): 370–89.

———. 2001. "The Institutional Determinants of Economic Policy Outcomes." In *Presidents, Parliaments, and Policy*, ed. S. Haggard and M.D. McCubbins, 21–63. New York: Cambridge University Press.

Deaton, A. 2009. "Instruments of Development: Randomization in the Tropics, and the Search for the Elusive Keys to Economic Development." Working Paper, Center for Health and Wellbeing, Princeton University (CHW WP#70). http://www.princeton .edu/~deaton/downloads/Instruments_of_Development.pdf; accessed July 21, 2010.

Diaz-Cayeros, A., K.M. McElwain, V. Romero, and K.A. Siewierski. 2002. "Fiscal Decentralization, Legislative Institutions and Particularistic Spending." Working Paper, Department of Political Science, Stanford University, Palo Alto, CA. http://politica.itam.mx/english_version/papers/documents/2006-02.pdf; accessed July 21, 2010.

Dixit, A., and J. Londregan. 1996. "The Determinants of Success of Special Interests in Redistributive Politics." *Journal of Politics* 58 (4): 1132–55.

Dobbin, F., B. Simmons, and G. Garrett. 2007. "The Global Diffusion of Public Policies: Social Construction, Coercion, Competition, or Learning?" *Annual Review of Sociology* 33: 449–72.

Doh, S., and B.R. Cole. 2009. "Comparative Analysis of Health Insurance Systems in the United States and South Korea." *World Medical and Health Policy* 1 (1): Article 10. http://www.psocommons.org/wmhp/vol1/iss1/art10; accessed July 21, 2010.

Dominguez, J. 1998. *Democratic Politics in Latin America and the Caribbean*. Baltimore, MD: Johns Hopkins University Press.

Faguet, J.-P. 2001. "Does Decentralization Increase Responsiveness to Local Needs? Evidence from Bolivia." Policy Research Working Paper 2516, World Bank Development Research Group on Public Economics, Washington, DC.

Fox, D.M. 1985. *Health Policies, Health Politics: The British and American Experiences, 1911–65*. Princeton, NJ: Princeton University Press.

Frenk, J. 2006. "Bridging the Divide: Global Lessons from Evidence-Based Health Policy in Mexico." *Lancet* 368: 954–61.

Gelman, A., D. Lee, and G. Yair. 2010. "Public Opinion on Health Care Reform." *The Forum* 8 (1): Article 8.

Gerschenkron, A. 1962. *Economic Backwardness in Historical Perspective*. Cambridge, MA: Harvard University Press.

Gilson, L., J. Doherty, S. Lake, D. McIntyre, C. Mwikisa, and S. Thomas. 2003. "The SAZA Study: Implementing Health Financing Reform in South Africa and Zambia." *Health Policy and Planning* 18 (1): 31–46.

Gilson, L., and N. Raphaely. 2007. "Literature Review: Health Policy Analysis in Lower- and Middle-Income or Transitional Countries (LMIC/TC)." Consortium for Research on Equitable Health Systems. http://web.wits.ac.za/NR/rdonlyres/8B4CCC61-E5CF-44CA-9778-929C6634E328/0/M91.pdf; accessed August 16, 2010.

Gray, V., D. Lowery, E.K. Godwin, and J. Monogan. 2005. "Incrementing Toward Nowhere: Universal Health Care Coverage in the States." Paper prepared for delivery at the 2005 Annual Meeting of the American Political Science Association, September 1–4.

Grindle, M. 1980. "The Implementor: Political Constraints on Rural Development in Mexico." In *Politics and Policy Implementation in the Third World*, ed. M. Grindle, 197–223. Princeton, NJ: Princeton University Press.

Gross, R., B. Rosen, and A. Shiron. 2001. "Reforming the Israeli Health System: Findings of a 3-Year Evaluation." *Health Policy* 56: 1–20.

Hacker, J.S. 1998. "Historical Logic of National Health Insurance: Structure and Sequence in Development of British, Canadian and U.S. Medical Policy." *Studies in American Political Development* 12: 57–130.

Huber, J.D., and C.R. Shipan. 2002. *Deliberate Discretion*. New York: Cambridge University Press.

Ikegami, N., and J.C. Campbell. 1999. "Health Care Reform in Japan: The Virtues of Muddling Through." *Health Affairs* 18: 56–75.

Immergut, E.M. 1990. "Institutions, Veto Points, and Policy Results: A Comparative Analysis of Health Care." *Journal of Public Policy* 10 (4): 391–416.

———. 1992. *Health Politics: Interests and Institutions in Western Europe*. New York: Cambridge University Press.

Jacobs, L. 1993. *The Health of Nations: Public Opinion and the Making of American and British Health Policy*. New York: Cornell University Press.

Kaufman, R., and J. Nelson. 2004. "Conclusions: The Political Dynamics of Reform." In *Crucial Needs, Weak Incentives*, ed. R. Kaufman and J. Nelson, 473–519. Washington, DC: Woodrow Wilson Center Press.

Kim, J.Y., J.V. Millen, A. Irwin, and J. Gershman, ed. 2000. *Dying for Growth: Global Inequality and the Health of the Poor*. Monroe, ME: Common Courage Press.

King, G., E. Gakidou, K. Imai, J. Lakin, R.T. Moore, C. Nall, N. Ravishankar, M. Vargas, M.M. Téllez-Rojo, J.E. Hernández Ávila, M. Hernández Ávila, and H. Hernández Llamas. 2009. "Public Policy for the Poor? A Randomized Assessment of the Mexican Universal Health Insurance Programme." *Lancet* 373: 1447–54.

King, G., E. Gakidou, N. Ravishankar, R.T. Moore, J. Lakin, M. Vargas, M.M. Téllez-Rojo, J.E. Hernández Ávila, M. Hernández Ávila, and H. Hernández Llamas. 2007. "A 'Politically Robust' Experimental Design for Public Policy Evaluation with Application to the Mexican Universal Health Insurance Program." *Journal of Policy Analysis and Management* 26 (3): 479–506.

Kingdon, J. 2003. *Agendas, Alternatives, and Public Policies*. New York: HarperCollins.

Kitschelt, H. 2001. "Partisan Competition and Welfare State Retrenchment: When Do Politicians Choose Unpopular Policies?" In *The Politics of the Welfare State*, ed. P. Pierson, 265–302. New York: Oxford University Press.

Lakin, J.M. 2008. "The Possibilities and Limitations of Insurgent Technocratic Reform: Mexico's Popular Health Insurance Program, 2001–2006," dissertation, Cambridge, MA, Harvard University.

———. 2010. "The End of Insurance? Mexico's Seguro Popular, 2001–2007." *Journal of Health Politics, Policy and Law* 35 (3): 295–334.

Lasswell, H.D. 1936. *Politics: Who Gets What, When, and How*. New York: Wittlesey House.

Lee, K., and H. Goodman. 2002. "Global Policy Networks: The Propagation of Health Care Financing Reform Since the 1980s." In *Health Policy in a Globalizing World*, ed. K. Lee, K. Buse, and S. Fustukian, 97–119. Cambridge, UK: Cambridge University Press.

Lin, C.W. 2002. "The Policymaking Process for the Social Security System in Taiwan: The National Health Insurance and National Pension Program." *Developing Economies* 40 (3): 327–58.

Magaloni, B. 2006. *Voting for Autocracy: Hegemonic Party Survival and Its Demise in Mexico*. New York: Cambridge University Press.

Marks, S. 1997. "South Africa's Early Experiment in Social Medicine: Its Pioneers and Politics." *American Journal of Public Health* 87 (3): 452–59.

Marmor, T.R. 2000. *The Politics of Medicare.* 2nd ed. Hawthorne, NY: Aldine de Gruyter.

McIntyre, D., J. Doherty, and L. Gilson. 2003. "A Tale of Two Visions: The Changing Fortunes of Social Health Insurance in South Africa." *Health Policy and Planning* 18 (1): 47–58.

McIntyre, D., and A. van den Heever. 2007. "Social or National Health Insurance." In *South Africa Health Review 2007*, ed. S. Harrison, R. Bhana, and A. Ntuli. Durban, South Africa: Health Systems Trust. http://www.hst.org.za/publications/711.

Meltzer, A.H., and S.F. Richard. 1981. "A Rational Theory of the Size of Government." *Journal of Political Economy* 89: 914–27.

Mensah, S. 2009. "Status of NHIS and New Strategic Direction." PowerPoint presentation to the Ghana Bi-Annual Health Summit, Accra, November. http://moh-ghana.org /health_summit_N09/present.html.

Miguel, E. 2004. "Tribe or Nation? Nation Building and Public Goods in Kenya versus Tanzania." *World Politics* 56: 327–62.

Milesi-Ferretti, G.M., R. Perotti, and M. Rostagno. 2002. "Electoral Systems and Public Spending." *Quarterly Journal of Economics* 118: 609–57.

Molinar, J., and J. Weldon. 1994. "Electoral Determinants and Consequences of National Solidarity." In *Transforming State-Society Relations in Mexico: The National Solidarity Strategy,* ed. C. Cornelius, A.L. Craig, and J. Fox, 123–41. San Diego, CA: Lynne Rienner.

Moody, P.R. 1996. "Asian Values." *Journal of International Affairs* 50 (1): 166–92.

Murillo, M.V. 2002. "Political Bias in Policy Convergence: Privatization Choices in Latin America." *World Politics* 54 (4): 462–93.

Nandakumar, A.K., M.R. Reich, M. Chawla, P. Berman, and W. Yip. 2000. "Health Reform for Children: The Egyptian Experience with School Health Insurance." *Health Policy* 50: 155–70.

Nelson, J. 2004. "The Politics of Health Sector Reforms: Cross-National Comparisons." In *Crucial Needs, Weak Incentives,* ed. R. Kaufman and J. Nelson, 23–64. Washington, DC: Woodrow Wilson Center Press.

Nordhaus, W. 1975. "Political Business Cycle." *Review of Economic Studies* 42: 1969–90.

Oberlander, J. 2007. "Learning from Failure in Health Care Reform." *New England Journal of Medicine* 357 (17): 1677–79.

Persson, T., and G. Tabellini. 2003. *The Economic Effects of Constitutions.* Cambridge, MA: MIT Press.

Pierson, P. 2004. *Politics in Time.* Princeton, NJ: Princeton University Press.

Pressman, J.L., and A.B. Wildavsky. 1975. *Implementation: How Great Expectations in Washington Are Dashed in Oakland.* Berkeley, CA: University of California Press.

Przeworski, A., S. Stokes, and B. Manin. 1999. *Democracy, Accountability and Representation.* New York: Cambridge University Press.

Rajkotia, Y. 2007. "The Political Development of the Ghanaian National Health Insurance System: Lessons in Health Governance." Bethesda, MD: Health Systems 20/20 Project, Abt Associates.

Reich, M.R. 2002. "The Politics of Reforming Health Policies." *Promotion and Education* 9 (4): 138–42.

Roberts, M.J., W. Hsiao, P. Berman, and M.R. Reich. 2004. *Getting Health Reform Right: A Guide to Improving Performance and Equity*. New York: Oxford University Press.

Sarpong, N., W. Loag, J. Fobil, C.G. Meyer, Y. Adu-Sarkodie, J. May, and N.G. Schwarz. 2010. "National Health Insurance Coverage and Socio-Economic Status in a Rural District of Ghana." *Tropical Medicine and International Health* 15 (2): 191–96.

Shapiro, R.Y., and L. Jacobs. 2010. "Simulating Representation: Elite Mobilization and Political Power in Health Care Reform." *The Forum* 8 (1): article 4.

Siadat, B. 2010. "The Adoption of Ghana's National Health Insurance Scheme." Working Paper, PATH, Seattle, WA.

Silva, P. 1991. "Technocrats and Politics in Chile: From the Chicago Boys to the CIEPLAN Monks." *Journal of Latin American Studies* 23 (2): 385–410.

Simmons, B., and Z. Elkins. 2004. "The Globalization of Liberalization: Policy Diffusion in the International Political Economy." *American Political Science Review* 98 (1): 171–89.

Singh, J.P. 1999. *Leapfrogging Development? The Political Economy of Telecommunications*. Albany: State University of New York.

Smith, A.D. 1996. "Culture, Community and Territory: The Politics of Ethnicity and Nationalism." *International Affairs* 72 (3): 445–58.

Steinmo, S., and J. Watts. 1995. "It's the Institutions, Stupid! Why Comprehensive National Health Insurance Always Fails in America." *Journal of Health Politics, Policy and Law* 20 (2): 329–72.

Stiglitz, J.E. 1995. "The Theory of International Public Goods and the Architecture of International Organizations." Background Paper No. 7, Third Meeting, High-Level Group on Development Strategy and Management of the Market Economy 1-9 UNU/WIDER, Helsinki, Finland, July 8–10.

Strøm, K. 1990. "A Behavioral Theory of Competitive Political Parties." *American Journal of Political Science* 34 (2): 565–98.

Tsebelis, G. 1995. "Decision Making in Political Systems: Veto Players in Presidentialism, Parliamentarism, Multicameralism and Multipartism." *British Journal of Political Science* 25 (2): 289–325.

———. 2002. *Veto Players: How Political Institutions Work*. Princeton, NJ: Princeton University Press.

Waterbury, J. 1992. "The Heart of the Matter? Public Enterprise and the Adjustment Process." In *The Politics of Economic Adjustment: International Constraints, Distributive Conflicts, and the State*, ed. S. Haggard and R.R. Kaufman. Princeton, NJ: Princeton University Press.

Weyland, K. 2004. *Learning from Foreign Models*. Washington, DC: Woodrow Wilson Center Press.

———. 2005. "Theories of Policy Diffusion: Lessons from Latin American Pension Reform." *World Politics* 57 (2): 262–95.

Wilensky, H.L. 1975. *The Welfare State and Equality*. Berkeley, CA: University of California Press.

Witter, S., and B. Garshong. 2009. "Something Old or Something New? Social Health Insurance in Ghana." *BMC International Health and Human Rights* 9 (20): 1–13.

Wong, J. 2004. *Healthy Democracies: Welfare Politics in Taiwan and South Korea*. Ithaca, NY: Cornell University Press.

World Bank. 2008. "The Political Economy of Policy Reform: Issues and Implications for Policy Dialogue and Development Operations." World Bank, Social Development Department, Washington, DC.

Yamin, A.E., and O. Parra-Vera. 2009. "How Do Courts Set Health Policy? The Case of the Colombian Constitutional Court." *PLoS Medicine* 6 (2): 1–4.

Yeh, C.C., C.L. Yuang, and W. Hsiao. Forthcoming. "The Politics and Practice of Implementation." In *Why National Health Insurance? A Primer for Health System Studies*, ed. W. Hsiao, W. Yip, and Y.T. Shih. London: World Scientific/Imperial College Press.

CHAPTER 16

Institutions Matter

Alexander S. Preker, April Harding, Edit V. Velenyi, Melitta Jakab,
Caroline Ly, and Yohana Dukhan

INTRODUCTION

The political economy, policy options, and implementation arrangements for the underlying institutional reforms related to scaling up health insurance are reviewed in this chapter.

A great deal of controversy still surrounds the scaling up of both private voluntary and government-run mandatory health insurance throughout the world. Developed countries are split into three camps—those that still rely on hierarchical funding arrangements, those that rely on an agency arrangement, and those that rely on a more market-based system. Those that rely on general tax-funded National Health Service hierarchical arrangements include the United Kingdom, the Nordic countries, Italy, Spain, Greece, and Portugal. Countries that rely more on a mix of payroll- and tax-funded social health insurance agency arrangements include Germany, France, and the Netherlands. And countries that rely more on premium-funded private health insurance market arrangements include Ireland, Switzerland, and the United States.

Over time, the pendulum has swung back and forth. Most of the Central and East European countries have switched from a general tax-funded hierarchical system to a payroll tax-funded agency arrangement since 1990. Over time, the Scandinavian countries, Canada, and Australia switched from a payroll tax-funded agency arrangement to a general tax-funded hierarchical arrangement. Policy makers in Switzerland and the United States have, on several occasions, tried unsuccessfully to switch from private health insurance to government-run mandatory health insurance.

The international donor community remains equally split. There are some strong advocates for private health insurance, others sit on the sidelines, and still others strongly oppose it. In some instances where private voluntary health insurance has grown, policy makers and some donors have tried to stifle its further development. The same critics often also dislike government-run mandatory health insurance movements. Other donors try to encourage low-income countries to adopt such policies against their will.

Any extreme position in this debate is probably misguided. Both private voluntary and government-run mandatory health insurance could make an important contribution to health care financing at low income levels, even in contexts such as those found in many Sub-Saharan African and South Asian countries.

No one mechanism is likely to succeed by itself in securing all the objectives of health financing systems: mobilizing resources to pay for needed services, protecting populations against financial risk, and spending wisely on providers. A multipillar approach that combines various instruments—including subsidies, insurance mechanisms, contractual savings, and user fees—is more likely to succeed in meeting these objectives in resource-constrained environments with weak institutions, organizational arrangements, and managerial capacity. Such a system includes a public option but one in which private choice remains essential in ensuring the system's responsiveness to patients.

Institutions matter in this story. *Institutions* are the rules (formal and informal) that govern how organizations behave. Changing the institutional structure for health care financing is a long process that can take years, even decades. Old institutions are resistant to change; new institutions, fragile. Many health financing reforms attempt to change the institutional arrangements for financing health services without fully recognizing the complexity of the underlying institutional framework or the time needed to change it.

Not surprisingly, in many low-income African and South Asian countries, the political cycle of governments is much shorter than the implementation timeline for many of the financing reforms they try to introduce. As a result, new governments often give up on recent reforms and try something new, long before the previously planned health insurance reforms have a chance to be implemented.

Getting the underlying institutions to work properly, irrespective of the financing mix used, is often more important than trying to make a single mechanism respond to all the needs of the health system during the long process of scaling up health insurance.

POLITICAL ECONOMY OF HEALTH FINANCING REFORMS

The underlying motives for reform in health financing are a complex array of political and social factors in addition to the usual economic and technical considerations about improving equity and efficiency. There are usually subtle ideological agendas. Health insurance reforms are often part of a broader attempt to rebalance the relative role of the state and nongovernmental actors in a given society. The fact that almost always there are both winners and losers is an inherent part of any reform that involves redistribution from one segment of society to another. Health insurance reforms always involve such redistribution in terms of transfer of financial resources from the better-off to the less-well-off, from healthy individuals who contribute but do not collect benefits to those who are less healthy and need benefits, and from the actively employed who are able to contribute part of their income to inactive segments of the population who may need to rely on temporary to medium-term cross-subsidies. Health insurance reforms also involve major changes in the institutional, organizational, and managerial arrangements for handling the significant flow of financial resources through the health sector. Managing money means power. Such reforms threaten established stakeholders, who controlled such resources under the old system, and give power to the new set of actors who will run the health insurance system. Not surprisingly, such reforms often provoke strong resistance from the established bureaucracy.

Role of the State in Financing Services That Benefit the Public

Before looking at specific policy options for reforming health care financing in low-income countries, a review of the nature of reforms in other public sector domains and state-owned enterprises during the last century might be useful. One way to understand options for public finance reform is to view the different incentive environments for collecting revenue (figure 16.1) (Manning 1998). Budgetary units (government departments), autonomous units, corporatized units, and privatized units are four common organizational modalities that straddle these incentive environments in the health sector (Preker and Harding 2003). The core public sector lies at the center (usually Ministry of Finance or Treasury). Outside this central core public sector, revenue collection can also be carried out in the broader public sector through various agency arrangements

FIGURE 16.1   Continuum in Public and Private Roles

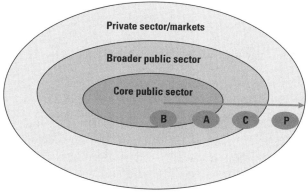

B - Budgetary units   C - Corporatized units
A - Autonomous units   P - Privatized units

Source: Preker and Harding 2003.

FIGURE 16.2   Financing Arrangements and Incentive Environments

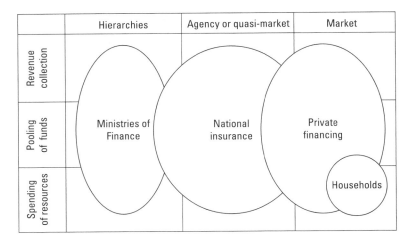

Source: Authors.

such as national insurance funds. Finally, some revenue collection can take place directly through the private sector. Mechanisms used to manage risks and spend funds on services that benefit the public can be viewed in the same manner as these arrangements for revenue collection (figure 16.2).

The core public sector is characterized by rigid, hierarchical, command-and-control processes. The broader public sector is distinguished by the relative flexibility of the financial management regime and by managerial freedom in recruitment and promotion. This sector may include special-purpose agencies, autonomous agencies, and, on the outer limits, state-owned enterprises. Beyond the public sector lies the domain of the market and civil society. Services may be delivered by for-profit, nonprofit, or community organizations. Incentives for efficient production are higher, moving toward the periphery where service delivery is more efficient.

The Public-Private Mix in Health Care Financing

Arrangements for health care financing mirror the picture of public finance in general (figure 16.3). Once again, the core public sector lies at the center. Countries that have financing arrangements that use the core public sector for all three financing subfunctions—revenue collection, risk management, and spending—rely on hierarchical command-and-control processes. Money collected by the Treasury or the Ministry of Finance is then transferred directly to another ministry (Health or Social Affairs). Control is hierarchical and direct. Equity and efficiency in revenue collection reflect the general tax structure and composition of consolidated revenues.

FIGURE 16.3   Application to Health Care Financing

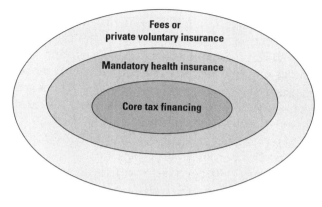

Source: Modified from Preker and Harding 2003.

Under this arrangement, there are usually no specific techniques to manage financial risk. Redistribution relies on indirect cross-subsidies through the consolidated tax system. As a result, countries that have progressive taxation systems have progressive financing of their health sector. Those with regressive taxation systems, as is often the case at low income levels, have regressive financing of the health sector. Sectoral policies are powerless to address the underlying structural inequities in the tax system. The share of general government revenues allocated to the health sector depends on complex political negotiations among the various ministries and public agencies that lay a claim on the overall fiscal space devoted to the public sector. At low income levels, the health sector is often in a weaker negotiating position than the Ministries of Defense, Energy, Agriculture, or Public Enterprises.

In addition to funding through such core public financing mechanisms, the health sector in many countries is also financed through some form of public insurance organized along an agency arrangement under semiautonomous or corporatized health insurance funds. Although payroll taxes may be collected at the same time as income taxes, they are often indicated as explicit categories on the pay stub of formal sector employees and may even have a different contribution structure from that of the general tax system. In many countries, the payroll-tax system for pensions and health insurance is separated completely from the general tax system with a parallel collection system and administration. In some cases, there are explicit cross-subsidies. In other cases, these processes are hidden and not made fully explicit. There is considerable debate about whether such funding should be considered part of or outside the core fiscal space.

Finally, funding may also come from households directly in the form of private health insurance or direct out-of-pocket payments to providers, thus bypassing all intermediate prepayment mechanisms. Mechanisms used to manage risks and spending funds on services can be viewed in the same manner under such arrangements (figure 16.4).

Typically countries that have dominant National Health Service arrangements for their health sector rely more on hierarchical incentives across all three financing functions—revenue collection, risk pooling, and resource allocation/purchasing of services. Funding arrangements that rely on government-run mandatory health insurance tend to incorporate hierarchical, agency, and market incentives across the three financing functions, while private voluntary health insurance relies more heavily on market pressures and to a lesser extent on government mandates that outsource some public sector functions to the private sector. Finally, direct out-of-pocket spending by households is more fully exposed to market pressures although fee structures and some of the behavior of providers may still be under some loose regulatory control by the public sector.

As in the case of reforms in the public sector, recent reform in health care financing have sought to move away from the center of the circle to more arm's-length contracts with public and private organizations in health care financing. Increased autonomy or corporatization—moving from the center of the circle to the outer limits—requires accountability mechanisms that rely on indirect rather than direct control. These indirect control mechanisms often rely on information, regulations, and contracts (figure 16.5). How far countries may go in pushing activities to incentive environments in the outer circles depends on the nature of the services involved and their capacity to create accountability for public objectives through indirect mechanisms such

FIGURE 16.4   Financing Arrangements and Incentive Environments in Health

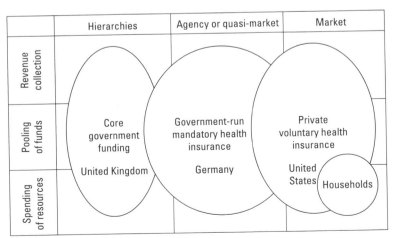

Source: Authors.

FIGURE 16.5   New Indirect Control Mechanisms

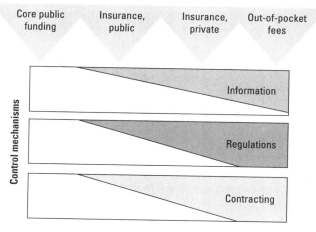

Source: Preker and Harding 2003.

FIGURE 16.6   Public and Private Roles in Exercising Control

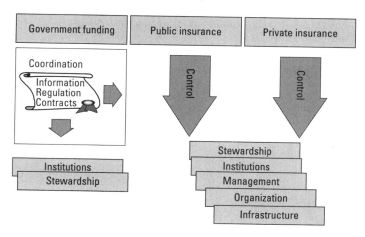

Source: Authors.

as regulation, contracting, and information. Usually the government wants to retain responsibility over strategic decisions that one would usually put under the stewardship function and the institutional environment, while responsibility for deciding on the best organizational structure, management, and infrastructure arrangements can be safely delegated to public agencies or the private sector (figure 16.6).

Swing of Pendulum over Time

This debate and recent changes in views on the appropriate role of the state in health care financing is not new. Since the beginning of written history, the pendulum has swung back and forth between heavy-handed state involvement in health care financing (exclusive core government funding) and minimalist involvement (private sector).

Minimalist Involvement

During antiquity, people used home remedies and private healers when they were ill. Yet there is evidence that as early as the second millennium BC, Imhotep, a physician, priest, and court official in ancient Egypt, introduced a system of publicly provided health care with healers who were paid by the community.

This early experiment in organized health care did not survive the test of time. The *Code of Hammurabi* (1792–1750 BC) laid down a system of direct fee-for-service payment, based on the nature of services rendered and the patient's ability to pay.[1] For the next three thousand years, the state's involvement in health care revolved mainly around enforcing the rules of compensation for personal injury and protection of the self-governing medical guild.[2]

At best, financing, organization, and provision of health care were limited to the royal courts of kings, emperors, and other nobility who might have a physician on staff for their personal use and for their troops at the time of battle. The masses got by with local healers, midwives, natural remedies, apothecaries, and quacks.

Heavy-Handed State Involvement

Unlike the early experience just described, governments during most of the 20th century have played a central role in both financing and delivery of health care. Today, most industrial countries have achieved universal access to health care through a mix of public and private financing and service delivery arrangements.[3]

Proponents of such public sector involvement in health care have argued their case on both philosophical and technical grounds. In most societies, care for the sick and disabled is considered an expression of humanitarian and philosophical aspirations.

But one does not have to resort to moral principles or arguments about the welfare state to warrant collective intervention in health. The past century is rich in examples of how the private sector and market forces alone failed to secure efficiency and equity in the health sector. Economic theory provides ample justification for such an engagement on both theoretical and practical grounds to secure:

- *Efficiency.* Significant market failure exists in the health sector (information asymmetries, public goods, positive and negative externalities, distorting or monopolistic market power of many providers and producers, absence of functioning markets in some areas, and frequent occurrence of high transaction costs)(Evans 1984; Bator 1958; Atkinson and Stiglitz 1980; Musgrave and Musgrave 1984).

- *Equity.* Individuals and families often fail to protect themselves adequately against the risks of illness and disability on a voluntary basis due to short-sightedness (free-riding) and characteristic shortcomings of private health insurance (moral hazard and adverse selection) (Barer et al. 1998; Van Doorslaer, Wagstaff, and Rutten 1993; the classical reference is Arrow 1963).

Largely inspired by the British National Health Service (NHS) and to avoid known failure in insurance markets, many low- and middle-income countries introduce state-funded and vertically integrated health care systems.

Back to the Neoliberalism of the 1990s

During the 1980s and 1990s, the pendulum began to swing back in the opposite direction. During the Reagan and Thatcher era (Young 1986; Vickers and Yarrow 1992), the world witnessed a growing willingness to experiment with market approaches in the social sectors (health, education, and social protection). This was true even in countries such as Great Britain, New Zealand, and Australia—historical bastions of the welfare state approaches to social policy. As in the ascendancy of state involvement, the recent cooling toward state involvement in health care financing and enthusiasm for private solutions has been motivated by both ideological and technical arguments.

The political imperative that has accompanied liberalization in many former socialist states and the economic shocks in East Asia and Latin America contributed to a global sense of urgency to reform inefficient and bloated bureaucracies and to establish smaller governments with greater accountability (Barr 1994; World Bank 1996: 123–32). Yet, it would be too easy to blame ideology and economic crisis for the recent surge in attempts to reform health care financing by exposing public bureaucracies to competitive market forces, downsizing the public sector, and increasing private sector financing (Enthoven 1978a, 1978b, 1988).

In reality, the welfare-state approach failed to address many of the health needs of populations across the world (WHO 1996, 1999; World Bank 1993, 1997; UNICEF 1999). Hence, the dilemma of policy makers worldwide: although state involvement in the health sector is clearly needed, it is typically beset by public sector production failure (Preker and Feachem 1996).

Toward a New Stewardship Role of the State

Today, governments everywhere are reassessing when, where, how, and how much to intervene or whether to leave things to the market forces of patients' demand. The growing consensus is that to address this problem requires a better match between the roles of the state and the private sector, and their respective capabilities—getting the fundamentals rights. In most countries, this means rebalancing an already complex mix of public and private roles in financing for the health sector (Rice 1998; Musgrove 1996; Schieber 1997).

To improve efficiency or equity, governments can choose from an extensive range of actions—from least to most intrusive. These include:

- Disseminating information to encourage behavioral changes needed to improve health outcomes
- Developing policies and regulations to influence public and private sector activities
- Mandating or purchasing of services from public and private providers
- Introducing subsidies to pay for services directly or indirectly
- Providing preventive and curative services (in-house production).

In many countries, for reasons of both ideological views and weak public capacity to deal with information asymmetry, contracting, and regulatory problems, governments often try to do too much—especially in terms of public subsidies for services produced in-house—with too few resources and little capability to deliver in these areas.

Parallel to such excess involvement in the financing and production of public services, the same well-intentioned governments often fail to

- Develop effective policies and make available information about personal hygiene, healthy lifestyles, and appropriate use of health care
- Regulate and contract with available private sector providers
- Ensure that complementary financing is mobilized from other sources
- Provide targeted subsidies to ensure that poor populations are not excluded
- Finance public goods with large externalities where consumer willingness to pay may be suboptimal.

POLICY OPTIONS FOR REFORM

The story in many low-income countries is similar. Escalating financial obligations, triggered by commitments to global agendas, rising medical prices, shortages in systemic inputs, and calls for the elimination of user fees have made current arrangements for financing health services unsustainable. Volatility in donor funding and limited fiscal space contribute to heightened skepticism about excessive reliance on donor aid and central government solutions. There is a sense of urgency about securing more sustainable sources of financing for the health sector (Beattie et al. 1998; World Bank 2004; WHO 2005). Furthermore, most state-run national health services suffer from significant deterioration in consumer quality due to a combination of resource constraints and poor public sector management. The political and socio-economic transformations currently sweeping across Sub-Sahara Africa are making governments sensitive to the negative public relations created by perceptions of poor public service delivery, be it in the health sector or other segments of the economy (WHO 2000; World Bank 2004). In this context, many countries are trying to scale up both voluntary private and government-run mandatory health insurance in the hope that this may somehow lead to better access to needed health services, improved financial protection against the cost of illness, and delivery of health services that are more responsive to public expectations.

In moving through the development process of expanding prepaid financing, no single mechanism is likely to provide the solution to all the policy and implementation challenges faced in health care financing. A multipillar approach that combines different financing mechanisms and operational arrangements is more likely to succeed. Many countries have already been unsuccessful in leapfrogging from no collective financing to universal coverage by promising to pay for everything for everyone under a national health service model. In most instances, this approach has not worked (Abel-Smith 1986). The result is usually that scarce public money is spread around so thinly that in the end no one has access to even minimal basic care.

Two alternative approaches underpin recent efforts to expand coverage through insurance-based mechanisms. Under the first approach, mandatory government-run health insurance is being introduced for a small part of the population that can afford to pay and from which employers can easily collect payroll taxes at source, usually civil servants and formal sector workers (figure 16.7). Under this model, the poor and low-income informal sector workers continue to be covered through access to subsidized public hospitals and ambulatory clinics.

FIGURE 16.7   Progress toward Subsidy-Based Health Financing

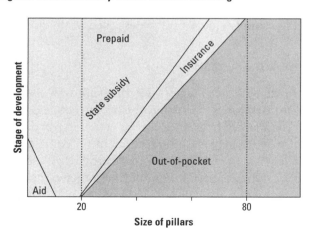

Source: Preker, Zweifel, and Schellekens 2010.

FIGURE 16.8   Progress toward Insurance-Based Health Financing

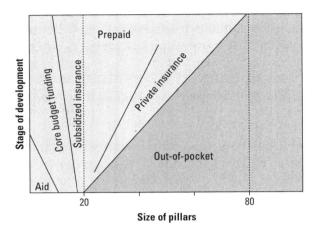

Source: Preker, Zweifel, and Schellekens 2010.

Although at first sight this policy option would appear to be pro-rich, since only people in formal employment who can afford to pay can join the program, in reality such a program can free up public money that can be used to subsidize care for the poor and informal sector workers who may not have the means to pay themselves. It therefore allows indirect targeting of the limited government finances that are available to the Ministry of Health.

Under the second approach, mandatory health insurance is introduced for a broader segment of the population by paying for or subsidizing premiums for the poor and low-income informal sector workers (figure 16.8). Using resources freed up from the contributing part of the population to pay these subsidies rather than the service providers that they use allows a more rapid expansion of coverage. This approach offers the advantage of allowing more direct targeting of poor households than the supply-side subsidies described in the previous example.

Implementation Arrangements

The complex political and social factors described above will determine whether a given country embarks on a reform process to introduce private voluntary or government-run mandatory health insurance or some mix of the two. The success or failure of such a policy is often dependent on constraints during implementation, not the wisdom or lack thereof in introducing such programs in the first place. There are good examples of public and private financing systems that work well. And there are good examples of both public and private financing systems that do not work well. Understanding "what" works well and "why" in different contexts is important, but understanding "how" and "how well" to execute any given program is even more important.

When introducing a new health insurance program or expansion of an existing one, policy makers are faced with a wide range of choices in terms of the underlying policy framework and associated institutional, organizational, and management arrangements. Table 16.1 provides a checklist of some of the key factors that need to be considered during the implementation process.

TABLE 16.1   Implementation Arrangements for Government-Run Mandatory Health Insurance

Functions	Dimensions	
Financing functions	*Revenue-collection mechanisms* Level of prepayment (full vs. partial with some copayment or cost sharing) Degree of progressivity (high vs. flat rate) Earmarking (general vs. targeted contributions) Choice (mandatory vs. voluntary) Enrolment (unrestricted vs. restrictions in eligibility, waiting periods, and switching)	
	Pooling revenues and sharing risks Size (small vs. large) Number (one vs. many) Risk equalization (from rich to poor, healthy to sick, and gainfully employed to inactive) Coverage (primary vs. supplementary, substitutive, or duplicative) Risk rating (group or community rating vs. individual)	
	Resource allocation and purchasing (RAP) arrangement itself For whom to buy (members, poor, sick, other?) What to buy, in which form, and what to exclude (supply question 2) From whom—public, private, NGO (supply question 1) How to pay—what payment mechanisms to use (incentive question 2) At what price—competitive market price, set prices, subsidized (market question 1)	
Institutional environment	Legal framework Regulatory instruments Administrative procedures Customs and practices	
Organizational structures	Organizational forms (configuration, scale, and scope of insurance funds) Incentive regime (from public to private in terms of hierarchies vs. agency vs. market incentives in decision rights, market exposure, financial responsibility, accountability, and coverage of social functions) Linkages (extent of horizontal and vertical integration vs. purchaser provider split or fragmentation)	
Management capacity	Management levels (stewardship, governance, line management, client services) Management skills Management incentives Management tools (financial, human resources, health information)	
	⬇	⬇
Possible outcome indicators	*Efficiency*	*Equity (mainly poverty impact)*
Financial protection		
Coverage		
Household consumption		
Access to health care		
Labor market effects		

Source: Adapted from Preker and Langenbrunner 2005.

Financing Functions

As discussed earlier, revenue collection, pooling, and spending can be carried out by the core public sector, public sector agencies, and the private sector. Several factors make the policy options for financing health care in Sub-Saharan Africa and other low-income areas different from those at middle- and higher-income levels. Policy makers contemplating introducing mandatory government-run health insurance must be prepared to confront these differences during implementation (Carrin, James et al. 2003; Shaw and Ainsworth 1996; Hsiao 1995; Preker and Carrin 2004).

Revenue Collection

Low-income countries often have large rural and informal sector populations, significantly limiting the ability of governments to collect general tax revenues as well as payroll taxes (figure 16.9) (Preker and Carrin 2004). The size of the informal economy varies from 78 percent in rural agricultural societies, to 61 percent in urban areas, to 93 percent in new areas of employment (Charmes 1998). People's willingness and ability to pay for health care—even the poor—are far greater than their government's capacity to mobilize revenues through taxation, including payroll taxes (figure 16.10). Not surprisingly, in much of Sub-Saharan Africa, the relative share of health expenditures financed directly through households can be as high as between 60 and 80 percent (WHO 2002, 2004).

FIGURE 16.9   Limited Taxation Capacity

- Governments in many countries often raise less than 10% of GDP in public revenues

- Tax structure in many low-income countries is often regressive.

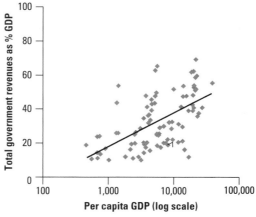

Source: Authors.

FIGURE 16.10   Ability and Willingness to Pay

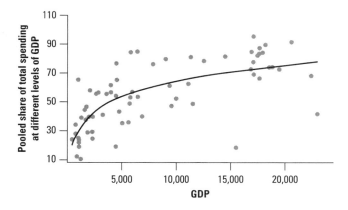

Source: Authors.

Important decisions need to be made in addressing these constraints during the design and administration of the revenue collection system for a government-run mandatory health insurance program. In terms of the pre-payment level, a choice needs to be made between full and partial prepayment with some cost sharing or copayment. Full prepayment provides better financial protection but may be associated with moral hazard and loss of efficiency. Copayments and cost sharing may limit excessive use, but they undermine the financial protection provided by the scheme. Likewise, decisions need to be made in terms of the level of cross-subsidies allocated to low-income populations for a partial or total subsidy of their premiums.

There are also decisions to be made in terms of the progressivity of the contribution level. A highly progressive contribution schedule improves equity but requires information on real income, which is often not available. At the lower end, a progressive scheme may still not be affordable for the indigent or very low-income populations, and it may be excessively punishing at high income levels. For this reason many countries include both a lower and an upper threshold. At the lower level, households with less income are exempted from making contributions (the state can pay on their behalf), and at upper levels there can be a cap. A flat-rate premium is regressive but administratively much simpler. Subsidies and exemptions can be used to ensure the poor are not left out. There is also a policy choice between revenue collection being based on broad nonearmarked general revenues (called a health insurance levy in countries like Australia) or an earmarked payroll tax as in Germany or France.

The degree of choice given to individuals or households in becoming a member or not and the choice among available plans if there are more than one are other important elements that must be considered when designing the revenue collection system. Mandatory membership with premiums deducted at source by employers is one way to force everyone who should pay to contribute. But in countries with a small formal labor force participation the penetration of such mandatory membership can be quite small. Furthermore it relies on employers declaring their employees, something which many do not do because of associated tax liability. Mandatory membership with collection at source therefore does not confer larger coverage at low income levels. Voluntary membership relies on a willingness and ability to pay. Members have to want to belong and the insurance scheme has to prove its worth. It relies on trust that premiums paid today will lead to benefits tomorrow. At low income levels, poor households in rural areas may not trust national insurance programs because of past negative experience or they may be willing to take the risk of not having insurance coverage. Enrolment may be open at all times to everyone who qualifies, or there may be restrictions in eligibility (employee and close family), a waiting period (time lapse after enrolment before claims can be made), or limits on the time and frequency that members can switch plans.

Pooling

Pooling of the collected revenues presents another set of problems at low income levels. At low income levels, the urgency to satisfy temporal needs often outweighs concern for the future (ILO 2002; World Bank 2004). People are more willing to pay for care when they know they will need it in the next few months (predictable or uninsurable risks) than for some uncertain event sometime in the future. Not surprisingly, the percentage of total health care expenditure that flows through some form of prepayment program is small in low-income countries. And low-income households exposed to financial shocks related to the cost of illness often fall below the poverty level. Yet there is evidence in countries such as Ghana, South Africa, and Tanzania that household contributions can be successfully channeled through insurance mechanisms and that government subsidies can be used to help pay premiums for the poor so that they are not excluded in the process.

Important decisions must be made in respect to the design and administration of revenue pooling and arrangements for sharing risks. Risk equalization can be achieved in different ways; three predominate in health care financing—through use of subsidies, insurance, and savings (figure 16.11).

The three financing instruments are not equally good at achieving all policy goals related to risk equalization (figure 16.12). For example subsidies may be better at achieving equity goals, while insurance may be better at protecting against expenditure variance, and saving may be better at providing income smoothing. Policies that aim at achieving equity objectives may

FIGURE 16.11   Policy Options for Risk Equalization

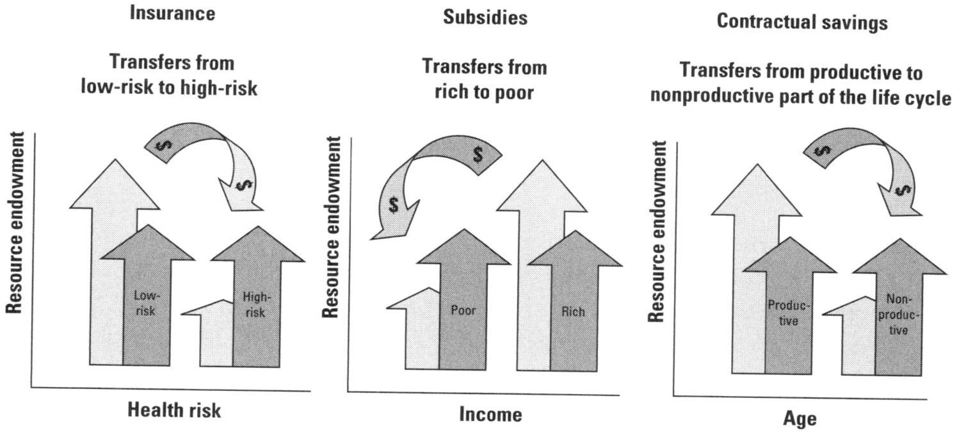

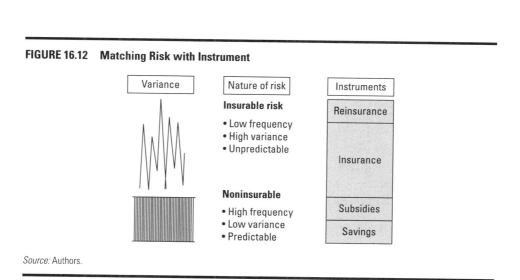

Source: Preker, Scheffler, and Bassett 2007.

FIGURE 16.12   Matching Risk with Instrument

Source: Authors.

be more effectively implemented through subsidies under the revenue collection function than by using insurance and savings under the pooling or spending functions. Policies that aim at achieving financial protection may be more effective at achieving protection against expenditure variance under the pooling function than subsidies and savings under the revenue collection or spending functions. Finally, policies that aim at achieving income smoothing across the life cycle may be more effective using savings than subsidies and insurance under the collection or pooling functions.

Yet in health financing arrangements these financing instruments and financing subfunctions are often merged under the same organizational arrangements. Worse, in some countries, health financing, pensions, and other social protection benefits are all merged into a single social security scheme without trying to match instruments with objectives or distinguishing the financing function under which they are most likely to be effective. Evidence is now emerging that this "one size fits all" approach leads to significant problems during implementation and attainment of specific policy goals. Furthermore, at low income levels where there are significant constraints on the fiscal space available for the health sector, resources that can be used for subsidies may have some significantly binding constraints. Under a multipillar approach to health care financing, households would benefit from several financing mechanisms that together would achieve equity, risk management, and income smoothing objectives (figure 16.13).

The size and number of pools affect the amount of risk equalization that can take place within any given pool and the likelihood of adverse selection and other insurance market problems. A few big pools may therefore be better than many small pools. But a few large pools may also be better than a single monopsonistic pool which often becomes unresponsive to changes in needs or consumer expectations. And the pooling function may provide comprehensive primary coverage. Or it may provide partial supplementary, substitutive, and duplicative coverage. These are important issues since they affect the cost of the benefits package that will be provided and therefore the level of the premium.

Risk ratings may be based on group or community experience or be individual risk profiles. Although in the past there was a preference for group- and community-rated premiums to avoid an excessive financial burden for those with high morbidity profiles or adverse selection by insurers, recently some countries such as the Netherlands are trying to deal with these problems by subsidizing the higher individual risk-rated premiums. This eliminates the incentive for insurers

FIGURE 16.13   Objectives of Different Financing Instruments

Objective	Equity		Risk management			Income smoothing
Financing mechanism	Donor aid	General revenues	Public health insurance	Private health insurance	Community financing	Household savings
Voluntary						
Mandatory						

Sources: Dror and Preker 2002; Preker, Scheffler, and Bassett 2007; Preker, Zweifel, and Schellekens 2010.

to engage in adverse selection and makes the insurance premiums affordable for individuals with chronic and expensive conditions for their higher premiums. Such subsidies for high individual risk-rated premiums do not deal with the problem of moral hazard, but this problem would be no greater under such an insurance arrangement than under a community or group rates program, or, for that matter, access to a free national health service. A disadvantage of this approach in low-income settings is that it is data intensive, and data may not be available.

Spending (Resource Allocation or Purchasing)

How scarce resources are spent is an important part of the health insurance story. Experience has shown that, without clear spending policies and effective payment mechanisms, health insurance mechanisms are not significantly different in achieving underlying objectives from private out-of-pocket or core government funding. The poor and other ordinary people often get left out (Preker and Langenbrunner 2005; Preker et al. 2007; Langenbrunner, Cashin, and O'Dougherty 2009).

Benefit incidence studies of health care spending at low income levels is often pro-rich even in countries in which significant efforts are made to target public spending to the poor (Castro-Leal et al. 2000; Gwatkin 2002; World Bank 2004). Without recourse to insurance, the only means for facilities to increase revenues is through user charges. De facto, this gives higher-income groups better access to publicly subsidized facilities. The Africa region has the most severe pro-rich bias in spending despite its limited public resources (Gwatkin 2001).

The shift from hiring staff in the public sector and producing services "in house" to strategic purchasing of nongovernmental providers—*outsourcing*—has been at the center of a lively debate on collective financing of health care during recent years (Preker and Harding 2000). Goods and services that are characterized by high contestability and measurability such as basic inputs (drugs, equipment, consumables, unskilled labor) can usually be produced more efficiently and at a better quality by the private sector (figure 16.14). Information disclosure and consumer protection are usually sufficient public policy measures (figure 16.15). Services such as clinics, diagnostic centers, hospitals, and health financing systems are more complex. But governments can usually regulate such services and contract nongovernmental entities to produce them. This leaves only activities such as policy making, monitoring and evaluation (M&E), and some public health activities where the case might be compelling for core budget financing and public production.

In moving from passive budgeting within the public sector to strategic purchasing or contracting of services from nongovernmental providers under a government-run mandatory health insurance program, policy makers and managers must ask five fundamental questions: for whom to buy, what to buy, from

FIGURE 16.14   "Make or Buy" Decision Grid

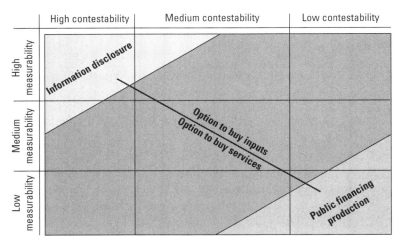

Source: Preker and Harding 2000.

FIGURE 16.15   Policies to Deal with Reduced Contestability and Measurability

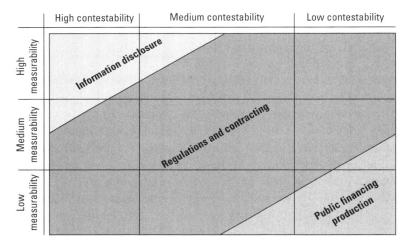

Source: Preker and Harding 2000.

whom to buy, how to pay, and at what price? Private voluntary health insurance programs have to examine these issues (box 16.1). In coming to grips with these questions, policy makers and managers are forced to address many important questions about the role of organizational, institutional, and management issues to the performance of public spending on health care, discussed in the sections that follow (Preker and Langenbrunner 2005).

BOX 16.1   LIMITATIONS OF MAJOR HEALTH CARE FINANCING MECHANISMS

No single financing mechanism is likely to meet all policy goals, hence the need for a multipillar approach:

- *Consolidated tax revenues.* Partly influenced by colonial ideological heritage and partly by post-colonial *étatisme* or socialism, countries in the Africa region between the 1960s and 1980s placed heavier emphasis on publicly provided and financed health care. However, reliance on general taxation has not been successful, given the low level of general revenues in Sub-Saharan Africa (SSA), typically below 15 percent. Notwithstanding increased economic growth and improved health budgets, public financing remains secondary to private expenditures in many African countries.

- *Grants and donor aid.* Foreign assistance to the health sector in the Africa region is already exceptionally high compared with other regions. An average of 35 percent of health sector expenditures are financed by donor aid, with levels reaching 50 percent and above in some case countries. Although such assistance is badly needed in the short run, policy makers have started to recognize the urgent need to begin building the organizations and institutions needed to secure more sustainable financing for the future (Beattie et al. 1998; World Bank 2004; Heller 2005; WHO 2005).

- *Public mandatory health insurance.* Given that MHI is payroll based, revenue streams heavily depend on the share of formal sector employment, which is typically low in SSA (Charmes 1998; Blunc, Canagarajah, and Raju 2001; Djankov 2003). Household surveys from selected case countries between 1997 and 1999 show that the national averages on formal sector employment as a share of total labor force range from 17 percent in Mozambique to 27 percent in Kenya, with stark urban/rural differences (World Bank 1996). In most SSA countries at their present stage, MHI is limited to the public sector and the formal private sector, which may create equity problems (Shaw and Ainsworth 1996; Hsiao 1997; ILO 2001). Payroll deductions, considered another tax burden, typically lead to resistance from labor unions/employees (e.g., Nigeria, Tanzania) (Cutler and Zeckhauser 2000; ILO 2001). Contributions, combined with other taxes, may be distortive or prohibitive. Such excessive tax burden is feared to create incentives for informalization and thus, distortions in the labor market (ILO 2001; World Bank 2006). If not tackled through cost-containment measures and provider-payment mechanisms, MHI is associated with cost escalation and increased curative bias in service delivery. Developing MHI is a resource-intensive process requiring significant institutional, organizational, and management capacity building (Shaw and Ainsworth 1996; World Bank 2004). SSA countries that embarked on MHI reforms have been going through years or decades of preparatory steps to create a environment conducive to the introduction of the scheme. Expanding MHI to universal coverage (national health insurance) is a long-term strategy that

(continued)

BOX 16.1   LIMITATIONS OF MAJOR HEALTH CARE FINANCING MECHANISMS (*continued*)

requires solid technical design, adequate implementation capacity, and a good deal of political salesmanship (Abel-Smith 1986; ILO 2001). Long-term success is dependent on political stability and sensitive to economic growth, which, despite the recent positive trends, leaves this instrument vulnerable to such exogenous shocks.

- *Private health insurance.* The proliferation of community-based financing (*mutuelles*) (e.g., in Ghana, Senegal, and Tanzania) indicates that community-based health financing is considered an important first step toward prepayment and pooling. However, limitations such as low levels of participation, high financial risk, dependence on public subsidies, and the exclusion of the poorest call for the enlargement of risk pools through scaling up or scheme linkage through reinsurance or by connecting them through incentives into the social insurance system (Arhin-Tenkorang 2001; Jakab and Krishnan 2004). Private commercial insurance has been expanding, which implies increased willingness and ability to pay for insurance (Preker, Scheffler et al. 2007; Preker, Zweifel, and Schellekens 2010). This instrument is perceived to have a pro-rich bias and a curative care focus and to exacerbate cost escalation. Private commercial insurance serves both as primary insurance and as complementary to benefits received through other means.

- *User fees.* Excessive reliance on user fees, as high as 70 percent in some cases, has significant impoverishing effects in societies, where between 50 and 70 percent of the population is below the poverty line (World Bank 2001; WHO 2004). High OOP expenditures may have catastrophic effects on the non-poor (Wagstaff, Watanabe, and Van Doorslaer 2001). User fees are a regressive means of resource mobilization. They forgo the benefits of risk sharing, and do not provide incentives for improving the services.

Institutional Arrangements

A range of decisions need to be taken with respect to four aspects of the institutional environment when trying to scale up health insurance. These include: legal framework, regulatory instruments, administrative procedures, and formal or informal customs and practices.

Institutional Environment

The introduction of mandatory health insurance requires not only strengthening existing institutions but also setting up organizational structures not yet in existence. Decisions need to be made in terms of several variables: the organizational form, the incentive regime, and the degree of vertical/horizontal integration versus differentiation of the new system.

The organizational form relates mainly to the number and size of the organizations that will be used (figure 16.16). There are two extreme policy options. First, there may be a single health insurance fund that allocates money to a single

FIGURE 16.16   Market Structure

		Number of financing agencies		
		One	Several	Many
Number of providers	One	1. Monopsony 2. Monopoly	1. Monopoly 2. Purchaser competition	1. Monopoly 2. Purchaser competition
	Several	1. Monopsony 2. Provider competition	1. Partial competition	1. Partial competition
	Many	1. Monopsony 2. Provider competition	1. Partial competition	1. Full competition

Source: Authors.

own-network of providers (sometimes owned by the health insurance system itself). This leads to a monopsony-monopoly arrangement. At the other extreme, there may be many smaller funds that buy services from a wide range of providers (public and private). This leads to a more open competitive environment. There are variations between these extremes with a single purchaser and several providers or several purchasers and a single provider.

In essence, the incentive regime refers to the degree of decision rights of those running the organizations (figure 16.17). Do the managers of the health insurance fund have a right to make decisions concerning, for example, financial management, human resources, infrastructure, and information systems? Are such decisions made centrally in the Ministry of Health or in a line department of another core ministry? Other relevant aspects of the incentive regime relate to the degree of market exposure. If there is more than one fund and provider, are they allowed to compete with each other? Sometimes, even when there are more than one fund and provider, they are not allowed to compete. Who decides what to do with profits, and who is responsible for deficits? What are the accountability arrangements? How are social benefits dealt with (explicitly or indirectly)?

There is a range of ways in which health insurance funds may integrate or fragment the subfunctions of health care financing (box 16.2). At one extreme, in terms of vertical integration, all the health financing functions (collection, pooling, and purchasing) and service delivery may be fully integrated under a single insurance organization. This happens when the insurance system collects its own premiums and employs its own providers. Many national health insurance funds are configured in this way. Such funds behave in a similar way to a unified Ministry of Health or national health service. In other cases, there

FIGURE 16.17   Incentive Environment

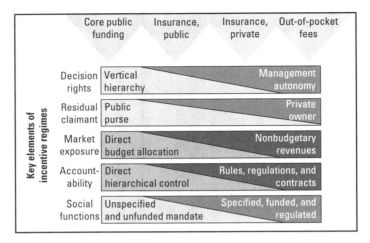

Source: Preker and Harding 2003.

BOX 16.2   SCHEMATIC OF HEALTH FINANCING MODEL TRANSITION

FIGURE B16.2.1   Schematic of Health Financing Model Transition

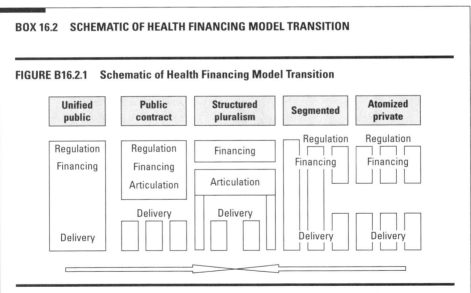

"Structured pluralism" is a centrist model that conveys the search for a middle ground between the extreme arrangements that have hampered the performance of health systems (Londono and Frenk 1997). "Pluralism" avoids the extremes of monopoly in the public sector and atomization in the private sector. "Structured" avoids the extremes of authoritarian command-and-control procedures in government and the anarchic absence of transparent rules of the game to correct market failures.

In this model, *modulation* (i.e., stewardship) is the central mission of the Ministry of Health, which moves out of direct provision of personal health services (financing-provision split). *Financing* is the main function of social security institutes, which is to be gradually extended to protect the entire population (national health insurance). The *articulation* function (Londono and Frenk 1997; Chernichovsky 2002) is made explicit by fostering the establishment of "organizations for health services articulation" (agency creation), which perform a series of crucial activities, including the competitive enrolment of populations into health plans in exchange for a risk-adjusted capitation, the specification of explicit packages of benefits or interventions, the organization of networks of providers so as to structure consumer choices, the design and implementation of incentives to providers through payment mechanisms, and the management of quality of care. Finally, the *delivery* function is open to pluralism (contracting; private-public partnerships) that would be adapted to differential needs of urban and rural populations (Preker, Liu et al. 2007). Such transitions can well be tracked in the case countries discussed thus far.

Source: Based on Londono and Frenk 1997.

are various degrees of separation of the purchasing and provider functions or separation of the revenue collection, pooling, and purchasing subfunctions into different organizations. Health insurance funds modeled on the German or Netherlandic sickness funds often have this type of functional differentiation.

Management Capacity

Finally, there are aspects of managing a health insurance system that are very different from management of a national health service in terms of management level (stewardship, governance, line management, client services), management skills, management incentives, and needed management tools (financial, human resources, health information). In examining the management requirements of a health insurance system, it is useful to distinguish four different management levels and associated leadership/management skills (figures 16.18 and 16.19):

- Macro or stewardship level (management of strategic policies and institutions at the national, provincial/state, or regional level of the health care system) (Saltman and Ferroussier-Davis 2000; WHO 2000)

- Meso or governance level (executive management of large organizations or networks of public health programs, hospitals and clinics)

- Micro or operational level (line management of client services)

- Household or individual level (clinical management of patients).

FIGURE 16.18   Management Levels

Type of management \ Level	Macro Institutional level	Meso Organizational level	Micro Operational level	Household Individual level
Stewardship	★	☆		
Governance	☆	★	☆	
Line management		☆	★	☆
Clinical management			☆	★

Source: Authors.

FIGURE 16.19   Associated Leadership and Management Skills

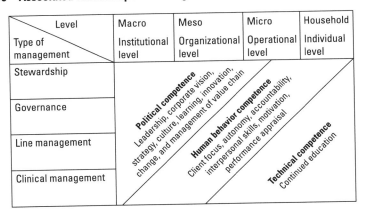

Type of management \ Level	Macro Institutional level	Meso Organizational level	Micro Operational level	Household Individual level
Stewardship				
Governance				
Line management				
Clinical management				

Political competence
Leadership, corporate vision, strategy, culture, learning, innovation, change, and management of value chain

Human behavior competence
Client focus, autonomy, accountability, interpersonal skills, motivation, performance appraisal

Technical competence
Continued education

Source: Authors.

In a well-functioning health insurance system, there is a good deal of interaction and complementarity between these different levels of management, while at the same time a clear division in responsibilities and accountability. This is equally true in low- and middle-income countries. In poorly functioning health insurance systems, there are significant gaps and overlaps. Hence, the categories described in figures 16.18 and 16.19 are not mutually exclusive or necessarily of equal importance at the different levels of the health care system. At the macro level, policy makers of a large national health insurance organization may become overwhelmed with micro-level decisions associated with a large cadre of health workers who are civil servants or with the procurement problems of nationally run supplies and stores. At the micro level, clinicians and directors of local facilities may be overwhelmed by the added tasks imposed by excessive bureaucratic procedures that have little to do with the clinical care they are trying to provide for patients or the local operation of the health care facility in which they work.

As in the case of health services, there are several different approaches to managing health insurance programs:

- Management by hierarchical command and control within the core public sector

- Modern business school management in the private sector

- New public sector management outside the core public sector (broader public sector).

These management styles have their origins in different approaches to the role of the state and private sector described earlier (Preker and Harding 2003). The boundaries between the three management styles are often blurred with the public sector adopting techniques from modern business management and the private sector exercising some command and control.

Good health insurance management practices in today's context rely on a range of management tools that were not available to previous generations. This includes the availability of information technology that allows managers to have access to "real-time" data and information, much better access to reliable data and information, and the use of regulations and contracts as powerful management instruments. Above all, it means the ability to frame problems, think creatively about solutions, and use information and technology rather than be a hostage to it.

NOTES

1. In this famous cuneiform legal code of the first Babylonian Dynasty, 9 of its 282 statutes relate to the services of healers. Statutes 215–17 and 221–23 deal with laws governing the fees to be received for certain services; Statutes 218–20 deal with penalties to be inflicted on healers in case of unsatisfactory therapeutic results and death (Chapman 1984: 4–5).

2. Control of membership and secrecy, reflected in the Hippocratic oath, was characteristic of all trades (BMA 1984: 6).

3. Today, the United States, Mexico, and Turkey are three exceptions in the Organisation for Economic Co-operation and Development (OECD) where universal access has not yet been secured. For a review of the introduction of universality in the OECD, see Preker 1989.

REFERENCES

Abel-Smith, B. 1986. "Funding Health for All: Is insurance the Answer?" *World Health Forum* 7 (1): 3–32.

Arhin-Tenkorang, D. 2001. *Health Insurance for the Informal Sector in Africa: Design Features, Risk Protection, and Resource Mobilization.* Geneva: WHO.

Arrow, K.W. 1963. "Uncertainty and the Welfare Economics of Medical Care." *American Economic Review* 53 (5): 940–73.

Atkinson, A.B., and J.E. Stiglitz. 1980. *Lectures on Public Economics.* Maidenhead, U.K.: McGraw-Hill.

Barer, L., T. Morris, E. Getzen, and G.L. Stoddart, eds. 1998. *Health, Health Care and Health Economics: Perspectives on Distribution.* Chichester, West Sussex, England: John Wiley & Sons.

Barr, N., ed. 1994. *Labor Markets and Social Policy in Central and Eastern Europe.* Oxford, U.K.: World Bank/Oxford University Press.

Bator, F. 1958. "The Anatomy of Market Failure." *Quarterly Journal of Economics* 72 (3): 351–79.

Beattie, A., J. Doherty, L. Gilson, E. Lambo, and P. Shaw, eds. 1998. *Sustainable Health Care Financing in Southern Africa.* EDI Learning Resource Series. Washington, DC: World Bank.

Blunc, N.-H., S. Canagarajah, and D. Raju. 2001. *The Informal Sector Revisited: A Synthesis across Space and Time.* Washington, DC: World Bank.

BMA (British Medical Association). 1984. *Handbook of Medical Ethics.* London: BMA.

Carrin, G., C. James, M. Adelhardt, O. Doetinchem, P. Eriki, M. Hassan, H. van den Hombergh, J. Kirigia, B. Koemm, R. Korte, R. Krech, C. Lankers et al. 2003. "National Social Health Insurance Strategy: Key Findings and Prerequisites for Implementation." Geneva: WHO.

Carrin, G., R. Korte, B. Schramm, and J. van Lente. 2003. "National Social Health Insurance Strategy: Comments and Suggestions of the Joint WHO/GTZ Mission on Social Health Insurance in Kenya." Nairobi: WHO, GTZ, KfW.

Castiglioni, A. 1998. *A History of Medicine.* Trans. and ed. E.B. Krunbhaar. 2nd ed. 1947. New York: Aronson.

Castro-Leal, F., J. Dayton, L. Demery, and K. Mehra. 2000. "Public Spending on Health Care in Africa: Do the Poor Benefit?" *Bulletin of the World Health Organization* 78 (1).

Chapman, C.B. 1984. *Physicians, Law, and Ethics.* New York: New York University Press.

Charmes, J. 1998. *Informal Sector, Poverty, and Gender: A Review of Empirical Evidence.* Washington, DC: World Bank.

Chernichovsky, D. 2002. "Pluralism, Public Choice, and the State in the Emerging Paradigm in Health Systems." *Milbank Quarterly* 80 (1): 5.

Cutler, D.M., and R. Zeckhauser. 2000. "The Anatomy of Health Insurance." In *Handbook of Health Economics,* ed. A.J. Culyer and J.P. Newhouse, 563–637. Amsterdam: Elsevier.

Djankov, S. 2003. *The Informal Economy: Large and Growing in Most Developing Countries.* Discussion Paper, World Bank, Washington, DC.

Dror, D.M., and A.S. Preker. 2002. *Social Reinsurance: A New Approach to Sustainable Community Health Financing.* Washington, DC, and Geneva: World Bank and International Labour Office.

Enthoven, A. 1978a. "Consumer Choice Health Plan: First of Two Parts." *New England Journal of Medicine* 298 (12): 650–58.

———. 1978b. "Consumer Choice Health Plan: Second of Two Parts." *New England Journal of Medicine* 298 (13): 709–20.

———. 1988. *Theory and Practice of Managed Competition in Health Care Finance.* New York: North Holland.

Evans, R.G. 1984. *Strained Mercy.* Toronto: Butterworth.

Gwatkin, D.R. 2001. "Poverty and Inequalities in Health within Developing Countries: Filling the Information Gap." In *Poverty, Inequality, and Health: An International Perspective*, ed. D. Leon and G. Walt. Oxford, U.K.: Oxford University Press.

———. 2002. *Who Would Benefit Most of the Efforts to Reach the Millennium Development Goals for Health? An Inquiry into the Possibility of Progress That Fails to Reach the Poor.* Washington, DC: World Bank.

Heller, P.S. 2005. *Understanding Fiscal Space.* Washington, DC: IMF.

Hsiao, W. 1995. "A Framework for Assessing Health Financing Strategies and the Role of Health Insurance." In *An International Assessment of Health Care Financing: Lessons for Developing Countries*, ed. D.W. Dunlop and J.M. Martins. Washington, DC: World Bank.

———. 1997. "Revenue Sources and Collection Modalities: A Background Paper and Introduction to the Case Studies." EDI/World Bank Flagship Course on Health Sector Reform and Sustainable Financing, Module 3, World Bank, Washington, DC.

ILO (International Labour Office). 2001. *Social Security: A New Consensus.* Geneva: ILO.

———. 2002. "Towards Decent Work: Social Protection in Health for All Workers and Their Families: Conceptual Framework for the Extension of Social Protection in Health." *ILO Socio-Economic Security Programme, Newsletter.*

Jakab, M., and C. Krishnan. 2004. "Review of the Strengths and Weaknesses of Community Financing." In *Health Financing for Poor People: Resource Mobilization and Risk Sharing*, ed. A.S. Preker and G. Carrin, 53–117. Washington, DC: World Bank; Geneva: WHO/ILO.

Langenbrunner, J.C., S. Cashin, and S. O'Dougherty. 2009. *Provider-Payment Systems in Health Care: How-To Manuals.* Washington, DC: World Bank.

Londono, J.L., and J. Frenk. 1997. "Structured Pluralism: Towards an Innovative Model for Health System Reform in Latin America." *Health Policy and Planning* 47: 1–36.

Manning, N. 1998. "Unbundling the State: Autonomous Agencies and Service Delivery." Discussion Paper, World Bank, Washington, DC.

Mason, J.K., and R.A. McCall Smith. 1987. *Law and Medical Ethics.* 2nd ed. London: Butterworths, 4, quoting A. Castiglioni, *A History of Medicine*, translated and edited by E.B. Krunbhaar, 2nd ed., 1947.

Musgrave, R.A., and P.B. Musgrave. 1984. *Public Finance in Theory and Practice*. 4th ed. New York: McGraw-Hill.

Musgrove, P. 1996. *Public and Private Roles in Health: Theory and Financing Patterns*. Washington, DC: World Bank.

Preker, A.S. 1989. *The Introduction of Universality in Health Care*. London: International Institute of Health Services.

Preker, A.S., and G. Carrin, eds. 2004. *Health Financing for Poor People: Resource Mobilization and Risk Sharing*. Washington, DC: World Bank.

Preker, A.S., and R.G.A. Feachem. 1996. *Market Mechanisms and the Health Sector in Central and Eastern Europe*. Technical Paper Series No. 293, World Bank, Washington, DC. [Translated into Czech, Hungarian, Polish, Romanian, and Russian.]

Preker, A.S., and A. Harding. 2000. "The Economics of Public and Private Roles in Health Care: Insights from Institutional Economics and Organizational Theory." HNP Discussion Paper, World Bank, Washington, DC.

———, eds. 2003. *Innovations in Health Service Delivery: Corporatization of Public Hospitals*. Washington, DC: World Bank.

Preker, A.S., and J.C. Langenbrunner. 2005. *Spending Wisely: Buying Health Services for the Poor*. Washington, DC: World Bank.

Preker, A.S., X. Liu, E.V. Velenyi, and E. Baris. 2007. *Public Ends, Private Means*. Washington, DC: World Bank.

Preker, A.S., R.M. Scheffler, and M.C. Bassett. 2007. *Private Voluntary Health Insurance in Development: Friend or Foe?* Washington, DC: World Bank.

Preker, A.S., P. Zweifel, and O.P. Schellekens. 2010. *Global Marketplace for Private Voluntary Health Insurance: Strength in Numbers*. Washington, DC: World Bank.

Rice, T. 1998. *The Economics of Health Reconsidered*. Chicago: Health Administration Press.

Saltman, R.B., and O. Ferroussier-Davis. 2000. "The Concept of Stewardship in Health Policy." *Bulletin of the World Health Organization* 78 (6): 732–39.

Schieber, G., ed. 1997. "Innovations in Health Care Financing." Discussion Paper No. 365, World Bank, Washington, DC.

Shaw, P.R., and M. Ainsworth, eds. 1996. *Financing Health Services through User Fees and Insurance: Case Studies from Sub-Saharan Africa*. Washington, DC: World Bank.

UNICEF (United Nations Children's Fund). 1999. *State of the World's Children*. New York: UNICEF.

Van Doorslaer, E., A. Wagstaff, and F. Rutten, eds. 1993. *Equity in the Finance and Delivery of Health Care: An International Perspective*. Oxford, U.K.: Oxford Medical Publications.

Vickers, J.S., and G.K. Yarrow. 1992. *Privatization: An Economic Analysis*. Cambridge, MA: MIT Press.

Wagstaff, A., N. Watanabe, and E. van Doorslaer. 2001. "Impoverishment, Insurance, and Health Care Payments." World Bank, Washington, DC.

WHO (World Health Organization). 1996. *European Health Care Reforms: Analysis of Current Strategies*, Series No. 72. Copenhagen: WHO Regional Office for Europe.

———. 1999. *World Health Report 1999*. Geneva: WHO.

———. 2000. *World Health Report 2000*. Geneva: WHO.

———. 2002. *World Health Report 2002*, Annex 5. Geneva: WHO.

———. 2004. "Selected National Health Accounts Indicators for All Member States." *World Health Report 2004*, Annex 5. Geneva: WHO.

———. 2005. *World Health Report 2005*. Geneva: WHO.

World Bank. 1993. *World Development Report 1993: Investing in Health*. New York: Oxford University Press.

———. 1996. "Investing in People and Growth." *World Development Report 1996: From Plan to Market*, 123–32. New York: Oxford University Press.

———. 1997. *Sector Strategy: Health, Nutrition, and Population*. Washington, DC: World Bank.

———. 2001. *World Development Report 2001: Attacking Poverty*. Washington, DC: World Bank.

———. 2004. *World Development Report 2004: Making Services Work for the Poor*. Washington, DC: World Bank.

———. 2006. "The Challenge of Extending Risk Pooling to Informal and Non-Salaried Workers." In *Beyond Survival*. Washingon, DC: World Bank.

Young, P. 1986. *Privatization around the Globe: Lessons from the Reagan Administration*. Houston, TX: National Center for Policy Analysis.

CHAPTER 17

Accountability and Choice

Dov Chernichovsky, Michal Chernichovsky, Jürgen Hohmann, and Bernd Schramm

The United States, one of the richest countries on earth, outspends every other country on state-of-the-art medical technology. Yet its health indicators and its people's satisfaction with its health care system compare unfavorably with those of other highly developed countries (Davis et al. 2007; Schoen et al. 2006; D. Chernichovsky 2009). Unlike the United States, these other countries have integrated health care systems that secure access for all their people to socially set medical benefits, funded by mandatory, and usually means-tested, contributions. Though diverse in their health care systems, these countries share the basic health system features termed the "Emerging Paradigm" (EP) (D. Chernichovsky 1995, 2002; D. Chernichovsky et al. 2012).

Indeed, considering epidemiology, socioeconomic factors, and availability of medical and other resources, countries that protect their citizens' health as well as income by the features or principles of the EP show better health results and a more satisfied public than do countries that rely mostly on commercial insurance, let alone out-of-pocket (OOP) payments, to fund medical care. The superior outcomes follow because the countries that adhere to the EP are better able to deal with issues of equity, cost containment, efficiency, and client choice than are countries that do not.

Against this background, many low-income and transitional economies, mainly in Africa, Latin America and the Caribbean (LAC), and Southeast Asia (SEA), may have a great deal of untapped potential for mobilizing private funding for more equitable and productive health systems than they currently have. As highlighted in chapter 1 of this volume, between 70 and 90 percent of their medical care funding is private, mostly out of pocket, whereas in the industrial nations (except the United States) such spending is limited to the 20 percent to 30 percent range. Most of India's population, for example, relies on individual ability to pay for medical care and therefore lacks orderly access to basic quality care (Ellis, Alam, and Gupta 2000; World Bank 2004; Gottret and Schieber 2006).

Although public funding in India and other less-developed and transitional economies in LAC, SEA, and Africa often signifies free access to medical services, possibly with some copay, these services are considered nominal at best, both in terms of population coverage and the scope of benefits, and unresponsive to clients and their needs. The vast majority of the population, relying only on nominal state services, is considered for all practical purposes "uninsured," even if constitutions stipulate the contrary.

Poor and transitional economies cannot be expected either to secure universal access to basic medical benefits or to shape a national integrated health care system using general revenues alone, not even factoring in the substantial foreign aid that is typical mainly of African countries. These economies have relatively low tax revenues because of their large, untaxable informal sectors and their generally low income levels. This realty is associated with a general lack of "fiscal space," jammed with pressing priorities that crowd out medical care (Heller 2005, 2006, and chapter 5, this volume), and with governments not trusted with handling the taxes they collect. Moreover, their medical needs, especially considering HIV/AIDS and Malaria, are costly (Dukhan et al., chapter 7, this volume; Ly et al., chapter 8, this volume).

In addition, expansion of coverage and medical benefits by taxes and other centrally regulated mandated contributions—without a clear view of the overall nature of the expanded system, notably its ability to supply services—can yield unaccountable, inefficient, nonresponsive, and even corrupt services. These contribute to people's unwillingness to contribute toward funding care that is not by out-of-pocket spending.

A lack of fiscal space as well as widespread distrust in the state have led the Russian Federation and other East European and Central Asian nations to fund health care from general revenues instead of with mandated earmarked funding (D. Chernichovsky, Barnum, and Potapchik 1996; Wagstaff and Moreno-Serra 2008, and chapter 14, this volume).

Thus, as suggested in this volume, a new approach is needed, based on the recognition that less-developed and transitional economies must get rid of health care systems funded almost entirely by out-of-pocket payments. At the same time, these nations indeed cannot be expected to achieve almost wholly state-funded systems. That is, solutions between general revenues and private funding, combined with a clear long-term strategy for an integrated and universal system, are both required and possible. These solutions must be based, however, on institutional-economic as well as political realities involving a combination of, on one hand, poor disenfranchised populations, albeit majorities in most cases, that make up the informal sectors, and politically strong, well-organized groups that make up the formal sector, on the other.

Carrin and James (2003) show that most developed countries started medical coverage for only a small part of the population (often 5 to 10 percent of the working population) and gradually extended coverage over many years. Less-developed and transitional economies of today neither have nor need centuries or decades to make this transition, if they decide to do it and have the experience of developed health care systems to follow.

This chapter attempts to bring together and generalize the key economic and institutional issues underlying discussion in the previous chapters that can further understanding of the politics of health care finance (Fox and

Reich, chapter 15, this volume). The pivot of the discussion is the rather fuzzy and often wrongly perceived concept of social health insurance (SHI).

Building on the experience of developed health care systems and theoretical considerations grounded in economics and social anthropology, the goal of this chapter is to articulate SHI as a dynamic concept that offers a path out of a fragmented and failed health care market, based on ability and willingness to pay by large segments of the population, to an integrated, universal system, based on mandated, often means-tested, contributions. The milestones along this path represent economic, social, and institutional realities that translate into political realities that must be surmounted, often with the help of state stewardship (Fox and Reich, chapter 15, this volume).

The chapter is divided into two major parts. The first, in three sections, identifies the parameters that help define SHI, sets its institutional and policy context, and builds a typology of SHI models. This first part provides the different SHI milestones needed to establish an integrated system that secures meaningful universal coverage. The second part, three additional sections, deals with the obstacles to be overcome on the path to universal entitlement to care in an integrated health care system based on SHI.

SOCIAL HEALTH INSURANCE: THE CONCEPT

Social health insurance is commonly defined by what it is not. There is a wide consensus that SHI funding excludes the two basic and diametric forms of health care funding: funding from general state revenues and funding from out-of-pocket payments and individually rated voluntary medical insurance (figure 17.1) (Normand and Weber 1994; Saltman, Busse, and Figueras 2004; GTZ 2004; Gottret and Schieber 2006; WHO 2005).

Invariably SHI involves earmarked contributions mandated by a self-governing group[1] or corporation,[2] the state, or a combination thereof, to fund the medical benefits set by either for its membership or citizenry. This arrangement marks a quid pro quo between the collective and the individual. Earmarking disallows the collective, group, corporation, or state, discretionary use of members' contributions. Mandating denies the individual or the household discretionary use of part of its income, even when contributions are collected

FIGURE 17.1   Domain of Social Health Insurance

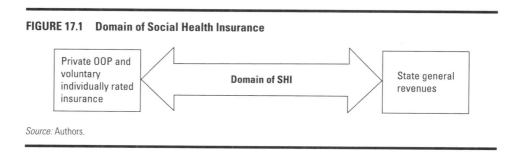

Source: Authors.

by employers. It is noteworthy here that mandating employers to pay for their employees' care is not the defining feature of SHI.

Some exceptions may exist even at the extremes, not considered SHI (figure 17.1). For example, the state may support SHI arrangements from general revenues in order to pay for the indigent who cannot themselves contribute to the system. Alternatively, the state may hand over taxing rights to self-governing closed groups and market-oriented corporations that maintain open enrolment. Additionally, private insurance can be regulated by the state to have SHI features such as community-rated premiums and open enrolment with insurers (D. Chernichovsky 2012).

Mandated contributions mean coercive membership in the group and closed enrolment, to avoid adverse selection or, alternatively, to enforce subsidies from the good risks to bad risks within the collective. An individual's limited right and ability to enter or enroll in, and exit, groups is thus a critical element of SHI. Clearly, groups that share identical contributions and benefits can permit their members to move between such groups. For example, a labor union may allow its members to move among its geographic chapters. This portability of contributions and benefits reaches its maximum potential when the uniform state or federation forms the collective of the ultimate social group for SHI. In this case, membership is automatic and contributions and entitlement/eligibility rules are universal.

SHI can thus be envisioned as a social contract involving the household, a group, or a corporation, and the state (figure 17.2). Mandated contributions and their earmarking, combined with limits on entry and exit from the SHI collective, interlock shared risk and subsidized funding of collective medical benefits (Glied and Stabile, chapter 4, this volume). The nature of the contract, which can be part of a broader social protection contract (chapter 3, van de Ven, this volume), varies by the organization of subsidies as delineated by the subsidy circles in the figure: households can subsidize each other within separate groups, groups subsidize each other within the state framework, and—eventually, with the dissolution of contribution-based groups—households subsidize each other within the state framework. Groups (and households) mandate contributions and participation for their internal arrangements. When the state is the SHI framework, participation is by default by groups, and households rather than groups may demand earmarking.

This organization concerns division of labor between the state and the self-governing group or corporations with regard to

- Fund-raising and fund allocation

- Contracting for care.

The institutional evolution of SHI concerns the assumption of these responsibilities by different group or corporate arrangements and subsequent sharing of the responsibilities with the state, which has been increasing its control over fund-raising and allocation.

FIGURE 17.2   Evolution of SHI by Institutions, Subsidy Circles, Social Quid Pro Quo

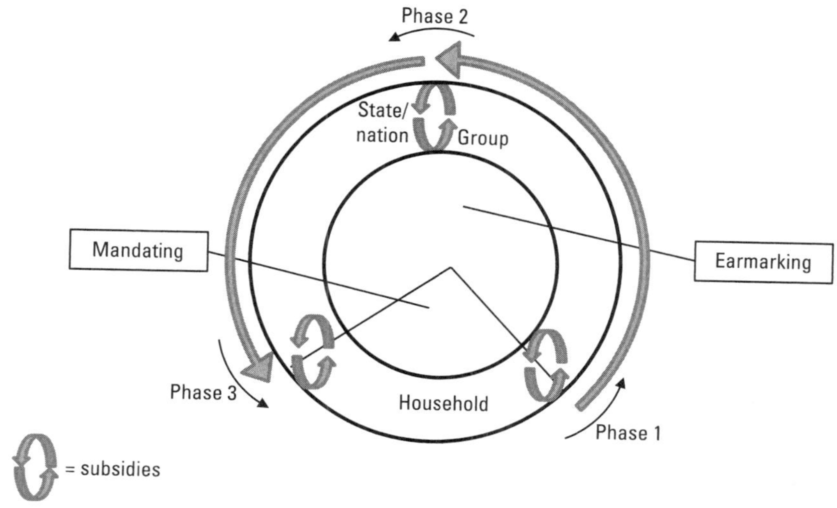

Source: Authors.

A basic institutional feature of SHI is thus the self-governing group or corporation, which has responsibilities, often statutory, with regard to medical benefits and their funding. SHI thus combines the basic principles of public funding—affordable mandated contributions (van de Ven, chapter 3, this volume), and forced participation, with earmarking—the basic principle of private funding, including voluntary insurance.

The functional, institutional, and public-private dimensions of SHI can explain the complexity of defining and implementing it. By recognizing these dimensions and the shapes they can take, however, SHI can be organized by fairly structured institutional variants, each delineating a particular social contract and governance arrangements. It follows that SHI does not conform to a single model but to a family that shares the common features: mandated earmarked contributions, involving cross-subsidies and group responsibility for at least some aspects of care funding and fund holding in ways that keep these aspects sustainable.

SOCIAL HEALTH INSURANCE MODELS: A TYPOLOGY

Social health insurance does not conform to a single model (Scheil-Adlung, chapter 2, this volume). Within the SHI domain delineated by the types of health care funding not considered SHI (figure 17.1), the following major variants or models of SHI can be identified:

- The Informal, Nonuniversal, Nonmarket (INN) Model

- The Formal, Nonuniversal, Nonmarket (FNN) Model

- The Formal, Nonuniversal, Market (FNM) Model

- The Universal Group (UG) Model[3]

- The Universal Pool (UP) Model.

These models are delineated in figure 17.3, expanding on figure 17.1. They are organized, from left to right, by their proximity (on the right) to the basic funding principles of the EP—means-tested mandated contributions, possibly taxes, that fund universal entitlement to effective care, the ultimate goal of SHI (Carrin, Mathauer, Xu, and Evans, chapter 6, this volume). By their general principles, most reforms described in chapters 7 through 14 can be cast in this general framework. The models are not mutually exclusive; several, including those not considered SHI, can coexist in the same health care system. The policy challenge in this general scheme of things is thus to move models rightward while at the same time trying to assemble them.

Generally speaking, the INN Model conforms to mutual aid and microinsurance arrangements where groups assume common health care–related responsibility (semi-)voluntarily on the basis of an innate characteristic: tribe, religion, and so on. Because the underlying group characteristic is innate, enrolment is exclusive.

In contrast, the FNN Model is based on acquired characteristics, most notably profession, place of work, or union. Although the underlying group characteristic is attained, enrolment and exit can still be prohibitive for reasons discussed above, as it was in the European guilds well into the 19th century. This model is probably the most prevalent today in nonnational health systems, notably in Latin America and Africa, as well as in the United States.

FIGURE 17.3   Social Health Insurance Models

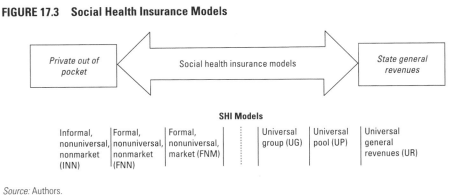

Source: Authors.

The FNM Model is based on market corporations rather than exclusive groups. Enrolment is based on willingness and ability to pay the premium and follow regulations. This model, which delineates private insurance arrangements, might be considered SHI, if there is cross-subsidization among group members, some paying above, others below, their "fair" premiums. Kaiser Permanente in the United States has age-based, community-rated premiums that involve cross-subsidies. Israeli sickness funds have similar arrangements for supplemental insurance for their membership.

The nonmarket models signify imperfect markets where households lack the right to enter or exit self-governing groups. The remaining models signify situations in which individuals have such rights, in consistency with the EP free enrolment principles.[4]

The nonuniversal models denote systems comprising independent SHI schemes or plans, either groups or corporations, alongside uncovered or nominally covered populations. The most common groups are associated with state employees (e.g., Mexico, Tanzania, and the United States). The different schemes in each system do not constitute an integrated national system securing universal entitlement (D. Chernichovsky, Martinez, and Aguilera 2009).

The nonuniversal market arrangements are associated with a formal labor market; the nonmarket arrangements, with the informal labor market. This difference is significant from the SHI perspective. In the formal labor arrangements, employers and unions can provide frameworks for SHI; in the informal markets, other frameworks are needed for the establishment of SHI nuclei.

The last two models signify integrated national systems that secure universal entitlement and, by implication, mandated contributions and free enrolment. These, as well as the Universal General Revenues (UR) Model, not considered SHI, conform to the principles of the EP. In the UG and UP Models, the state secures universal entitlement by regulating the collection of contributions, and their allocation. Any of these three models is considered a strategic objective for developing a health care system, including that of the United States.

In general, the progression to the right by the models presented in figure 17.3 and counterclockwise in figure 17.2 indicates wider and larger social and economic circles of risk pooling and cross-subsidies, culminating at the national level in the UG, UP, as well as UR Models. This progression occurs in a mercurial process in which households transform into groups marked by intragroup subsidies (phase 1, figure 17.2), and groups transform into a national system marked by intergroup subsidies (phase 2, figure 17.2), thus forming a universal national system marked by interhousehold subsidies without group brokerage (phase 3).

The Informal, Nonuniversal, Nonmarket (INN) Model

The INN Model comprises mutual aid, microinsurance schemes, and voluntary community (social) health insurance.[5] These schemas can be considered primeval forms of SHI. Members of a cohesive group pool their resources to compensate for damages some members might incur in situations in which the probability of damage (risk) as well as the claim (benefits) are random.

Microinsurance units normally pay for each benefit (e.g., consultancies, lab fees, hospital bed, drugs) rather than covering specific pathologies. Because the "premium" is not determined in relation to the risk but rather in relation to the member's perceived ability to pay, it is a subsidy. Payments to the provider institution can be made in advance, but need not be. The pooling of resources to fund benefits is thus often of a virtual nature. This follows the group's inability to form an insurance scheme due to insufficient size and lack of appropriate infrastructure.

In the case of wider community social insurance, the system might be more advanced in that members "prepay" to some pool. If members' contributions are neither based on their individual risk nor on their actual income, both difficult to assess in many situations, the contribution could probably be viewed as a rudimentary form of community rating.[6] The pool is more obvious and so, too, is the payment system to providers.

In the general framework advanced here, the group controls both funding and fund holding. It controls the latter also by controlling entitlement and potentially morally hazardous as well as adversely selective behavior by disallowing opting out of the system. Members cannot use subsidized care at will, without due consideration of what the group is willing "to tolerate" and cover financially. The covenant is closed, for joining and leaving. Clearly, there is no scope for competition between groups because group cohesiveness, the foundation of its existence, defies competition. The role of the state in this case might be confined to reinsurance in the more rudimentary arrangements and, in the community arrangements, to some subsidies, in infrastructure, especially these initiated by the state itself.

The Formal, Nonuniversal, Nonmarket (FNN) Model

The FNN Model comprises formal and well-defined self-governing groups that operate independently of each other, at least in funding, fund holding, and provision. This model is most common today in Latin America, for example, in Mexico (D. Chernichovsky, Martinez, and Aquilera 2009), but it also resembles developments in Europe since the mid-20th century.

In the FNN Model, the group or corporation—mainly labor unions and large employers, notably the state—each has its own SHI arrangement along the lines defined above. Due to their considerable size and general infrastructure, such groups can effectively manage even their own supply of care. The dominance of this specific model has promoted the identification of SHI with employer-based arrangements.

Cross-subsidies and risk sharing are group or corporate endeavors, mainly through group-rated or means-tested contributions earmarked for the medical benefits of members.[7] The group governs itself, but may be subject to, and have rights under, general state law.[8]

Usually, membership in the group is based on a nonmedical cause and mandated in the relevant health care plan to prevent adverse selection. Benefits vary across schemes by their contribution base, even when some benefit from state subsidies. The different schemes or plans do not constitute an integrated national system, even if coverage can be almost universal and possibly subsidized by the state.[9]

The Formal, Nonuniversal, Market (FNM) Model

The FNM Model is closely associated with commercial insurers and plans operating as corporations that seek clients or members in a competitive market that does not exist in the context of universal insurance arrangements. Members have the right to enter and exit the groups at will for as long as they pay the required premiums. The FNM Model can exist alongside the other SHI closed-group arrangements within the same health care market. This is the case of the U.S. Kaiser Permanente, which is open to the public and uses community-rated premiums. Simultaneously, there are other programs such as the Federal Employees' Health Benefits Program (FEHB), a closed-group SHI insurance arrangement. Though applicable primarily to the United States, such arrangements are possible elsewhere, especially in the context of regulated private health insurance (D. Chernichovsky 2012). Such corporations might qualify as SHI schemes to the extent that they cross-subsidize between members or enrollees and have a clear form of self-governance. As such, not-for-profit institutions are more likely than for-profit institutions to qualify as SHI schemes.

Young people who are not sick, for example, are a good risk. They may enter such an arrangement, first, for the care of their children and, second, as a way to stay enrolled as they themselves age.

The Universal Group (UG) Model

The UG Model emerged from the Bismarck Model in Germany. It is based on universal, state-mandated contributions, by employers and households, supplemented by government contributions for special groups, notably the unemployed, the aged, and the indigent.

To secure universal entitlement, the state regulates the universal means-tested contribution schedules for raising funds, and the universal risk-adjustment (expected cost) need schedules for allocation of these funds. Contributions of any individual and the money allotted to him or her are now aligned nationally across groups, rather than only within individual groups. Any intragroup surpluses, positive or negative, between state-regulated collection and state-allowed spending are used for equalization across groups; groups that have surpluses subsidize groups that have shortages. The UG Model is thus an extension of the aforementioned models in that it aligns all groups as well as disenfranchised populations along common national and universal benefits and contribution rules.

Because all contributions are virtually pooled, an integrated health care system is formed for all practical purposes. The state secures equity and a measure of cost control by regulating spending. This system is also amenable to a unified health policy.

As the group—now the health care plan—continues to be the fund holder, it may or may not be sanctioned to provide care directly; it may purchase care from free-standing providers and continue to exercise strategic monopsony purchasing in tandem with group preferences about form of care. Supplemental group insurance can accommodate group and individual preferences.

In addition, and key to consistency with the EP, as contributions and benefits are universally or nationally aligned, free enrolment, signifying competition in internal markets, becomes possible. Competition is among self-governing corporations or sickness funds entrusted with the fund-holding function in the first-tier internal market and providers in the second tier (D. Chernichovsky 2002).

The Universal Pool (UP) Model

The emerging UP Model is financed by means-based contributions and taxes that are earmarked, and hence, paid directly into a public national or regional SHI pool rather than into the state revenue system. Similarly to the UG Model, the pool allocates funds to the plans via risk-adjusted capitation. In other words, in contrast to the previous model, employers and groups cease to collect contributions for the group. They collect the contributions similarly to any other tax collection. This system is most pronounced in Israel (D. Chernichovsky and Chinitz 1995), Russia (D. Chernichovsky, Barnum, and Potapchik 1996), the Netherlands and Belgium (van de Ven and D. Chernichovsky 2003), and new systems are emerging in Latin America, namely in Colombia (Londono 2000; Hsiao 2007).

SHAPING THE INSTITUTIONAL AND GOVERNANCE INFRASTRUCTURE FOR SHI

Developed SHI frameworks, these beyond mutual aid and microinsurance, depend thus on self-governing groups and corporations. These, in turn, depend on the existence of a developed democratic civil society, on the one hand, and market insurance—management institutions, on the other. This political-economic infrastructure helped shape SHI in Europe.

Consequently, forming and reforming groups and corporations for advancing SHI (moving toward the right in figure 17.3) is a formidable challenge in the highly centralized state systems (e.g., in Cuba, the Democratic People's Republic of Korea, and in the former socialist countries in Eastern Europe and Central Asia). It is no less challenging in segregated, nonmarket systems involving highly segregated environments such as those in Africa. These two political-economic extremes lack democratic traditions of a civil society, and competitive markets, including insurance-management infrastructure.

The focus of this section is on poor nations, mainly in Africa, and on transitional economies, mainly in Latin America and Southeast Asia, that have wide informal disenfranchised populations that lack any form of credible health care insurance coverage.

The Group

Success in shaping groups and corporations for SHI greatly depends on the individual's incentive and discretionary readiness to become part of a collective, whether it is a socially-based closed group or a market-based open corporation.

Schwartz (1980) sees the group as an enterprise for mutual aid, an alliance of individuals who need each other, in varying degrees, to resolve common problems. A mutual aid group begins to form when a group has a need that lies beyond the original formative feature of the group, commonly, ethnicity and religion. This feature can be an extra need that causes members to create combined social, economic, and psychosocial safety nets to deal with this need to protect themselves (box 17.1).

The group offers an advantage to its members by providing assistance with basic needs, including a secure food supply, self-esteem, and individual empowerment. Groups provide networks and channels for information, and give

---

BOX 17.1   ETHIOPIA: BUILDING ON AVAILABLE INFRASTRUCTURE

Ethiopia's *eders* are indigenous arrangements used originally to assist victims in bereavement and to provide support and funds for funeral activities. They have also begun to provide group health insurance as one of their self-help activities. Their organizational apparatus provides a good, flexible framework for adding such projects because eders are legally constituted entities with functional administrative bodies, proven management practices for mobilizing people, and reservoirs of mutual understanding. Another advantage of the eders establishment is their openness to all people in a locality, regardless of economic standing, religion, gender, or ethnicity, and they specifically provide for those who fall into unfortunate economic circumstances. The logic of the eders groups involves concepts of reciprocity and credit—all members expect to receive benefits at some time during their membership. The group exempts the very poor and the very old from payments, while those who can contribute, do so on a monthly or weekly basis. It is assumed that with even minimal government support and some financial support from donor agencies, these types of rural, community-based systems can increase the efficiency of service delivery as well as pay the local health care unit a capitation fee in advance of service for a basic benefits package for their members (Mariam 2003).

members easier access to goods and services. They are efficient mechanisms for receiving resources from other institutions including government, nongovernmental organizations (NGOs), and development agencies. The groups can reduce the administrative transaction costs of lending and other financial endeavors (e.g., credit associations and unions) and reduce the risk of default through collective risk taking. Finally, groups can be learning laboratories, promoting skills such as enterprise management.

In the context of SHI, the group must provide these fundamental advantages to its members through the organization and management of funding, fund holding, provision, and oversight functions.

Mutual Aid, Group Solidarity, and the Social Quid Pro Quo

Mutual aid can be the most natural arrangement for starting SHI because, beyond the framework of the household or extended family, this arrangement is the basic form of cross-subsidies. Mutual aid grows out of the sharing of people's hardships and suffering. It is further generated by a common concern and belief in the possibility, or rather the random probability, that the plight may occur to anyone and, as such, matters can be improved through a quid pro quo of mutual assistance. The help may take the form of group members' providing services and/or material assistance to each other or advocating that these resources be provided by the broader community. In other words, the group may combine advocacy with provision of service.

Mutual aid is characterized by delayed reciprocity among the members, depending on need and affordability. The recipient of aid is not expected to repay exactly what is received, but rather to help others in return, when fortunes change. The amount or degree of aid rendered depends on the recipient's own circumstances and on those of the others in need.

An individual's income level is assessed through various mechanisms, to determine both a person's need and affordability. That is, contributions need to be fair and free of adverse-selection motives or concealed anticipation to abuse the system. Likewise, benefits need to be adequate and free of moral hazard motives or willingness to abuse the system. These conditions are sufficient for the sustainability of mutual aid with respect to the willingness of the well-off to continue supporting the system. Fafchamps (1992) highlights how a group solidarity institution can reduce efficiency losses, mainly those that follow moral hazard and adverse selection inherent in voluntary arrangements.

The task of social and political leadership is to create a social solidarity network that promises and ensures adequate and desired behavior from group members. This task also depends on group characteristics, notably its cohesiveness: the strength of the group, its members' desire to remain part of it, and the intention of keeping the quid pro quo. Fafchamps (1992) summarizes that solidarity networks are usually based on family, kinship, lineage and clan membership, neighborhood and geographical proximity, religion, and even wealth (box 17.2). These features help keep the necessary quid pro quo.

BOX 17.2   WILLINGNESS TO BOND

"We find that kinship, geographical proximity, clan membership, religious affiliation and wealth strongly determine group formation. Poor households try to create links with rich households. The rich, however, prefer to build links between each other." (De Weerdt 2002)

BOX 17.3   RWANDA: MICROINSURANCE

Of Rwanda's 8 million inhabitants, 6 out of 10 live below the poverty line. In 1996, after two years of free health care, all providers in the country introduced user fees. By 1999, medical service use in these facilities had dropped from 0.3 to 0.25 per capita. To improve accessibility of care, the population developed a form of microinsurance. The government took notice and decided to pilot microinsurance programs for health.

Under Rwandese law, microinsurers are mutual health associations, managed and owned by the members who meet annually in a General Assembly. Each microinsurer is headed by four volunteers (president, vice president, secretary, and treasurer) elected during the General Assembly. Microinsurance membership gives free access to the benefits package in health centers and district hospitals. Members continue to pay a small copayment per episode of illness. User fees (e.g., for drugs, surgery) are still not covered by microinsurance. At the end of the pilot year, 54 microinsurers covered 88,303 people, about 9 percent of the three district populations. By June 2003, coverage had increased to 189,646 people, about 19 percent of the population.

Group Formation and Its Sustainability for SHI

The fundamental initial challenge of SHI is thus to create effective individual demand for mutual aid as well as microinsurance (box 17.3) schemes. Existing and potential members must be motivated to realize a need that cannot be addressed by the individual or household, as well as the pertinent benefits from group membership, and to be convinced that these benefits would be available when needed.

The state can help organize mutual aid groups, edging toward microinsurance and community SHI, especially in developing environments and the informal sector. This effort can be built around time together and smallness, external threats, and privileged membership.

Time Together and Smallness

Time together is the fundamental asset of existing socioeconomic groups and can serve as the foundation for mutual aid and microinsurance. Small size is more likely to correlate with cohesiveness among members.

The addition of health care insurance to an existing group denominator, with the aid of legitimate leadership, is probably the most effective way to initiate group-based mutual aid and microinsurance in an environment based on out-of-pocket payment and mutual aid. The most efficient strategy is, therefore, to start with existing groups (box 17.4). Though inconsistent with effective insurance principles, starting with small cohesive groups may be inevitable.

External Threats

Examples of relevant threats can be the spreading of HIV/AIDS, malaria, and tuberculosis. Threats such as these can induce group formation consistent with an SHI strategy. While possibly cruel in some respects, this group formation confers privileges and preferential treatments to insurance holders, sending a message about the added value of the mutual aid scheme or microinsurance, rudimentary forms of SHI. Following the strategy suggested here, donor agencies are able to deal concurrently with particular medical issues while, simultaneously, helping shape the system by promoting SHI through the programs they advocate and support.

Privileged Membership

Membership must be a privilege that cannot be (ab)used at will. In Mexico, for example, sick people join the social security scheme (known as IMSS) but can leave it as soon as they recover. This adverse selective behavior undermines desirable insurance by negatively affecting the scheme financially as well as reducing any willingness to join when healthy or to subsidize the unhealthy. This undercuts a basic pillar of SHI. Closing this revolving door may involve some risks to willingness to join, but it can help a scheme establish itself. Such restricted access is essential for the initiation and viability of new mutual aid and microinsurance groups, even those built on existing social and economic groups. Finally, membership benefits from collective activity must be apparent. This can

---

BOX 17.4   TANZANIA: COMMUNITY HEALTH FUNDS

Community Health Funds (CHF) is a voluntary program that covers copayments for members' primary care. CHF membership also helps supplement a household's basic health care services by increasing access to regular supplies of health services, drugs, and medical supplies. Members prepay for this national program when they can afford to—not when they experience illness or injury. The community establishes the membership fee. Households either opt to join CHF or to pay a fee for service. The CHF program covers most of those outside the formal sector. The rural population and the informal sector are the intended members (Chee, Smith, and Kapinga 2002).

be achieved through pooling and managing resources, pooling and sharing risks, and centralized purchasing.

Take-Off (A): Escaping the Out-of-Pocket and Mutual Aid Traps

For the sake of simplifying discussion and maintaining consistency with the literature, the terms mutual aid and microinsurance have been used almost synonymously thus far in this chapter. However, the leap from mutual aid to insurance or to a microinsurance arrangement, especially in a cohesive group setting, is not trivial, even when the insurance premium is fair and affordable.

The transition from out-of-pocket payment and mutual aid toward insurance and pertinent mandatory pay arrangements means shifting from retrospective pay (conditional upon receiving goods and services) to prospective pay (for promised goods and services, depending on eligibility rules). Prospective insurance undercuts, in some fundamental economic and probably cultural ways, the virtues of OOP and, more important from the perspective of this discussion, mutual aid.

The contractual advantages of retrospective pay are compelling, especially in an environment in which services are meager and insecure. Moreover, unaccountable civil workers and unchecked corruption contribute to the advantage of "cash on delivery." This can help explain why, in spite of the advantages of grouping for medical care insurance, the demand for insurance may be lacking in poor communities. The lack of financial markets and insurance infrastructure compounds the problem but may not be its primary source.

There are also social and cultural issues. Mutual aid is based on demonstrated need and use of medical services overseen and supervised by the group. Prospective pay of an insurance premium, especially by the poor and needy, can amount to a declaration of no need for (mutual) aid. Still worse, it may imply that the insured individual left the cohesive group in favor of an alternative arrangement that is external to the group.

These issues are reflected in the development of SHI in Europe where mutual aid was a feature of the group, guild, and eventually the insured group. This transformation from mutual aid to insurance reduces the transaction costs of mutual aid, making the arrangements more structured and transparent, but requires groups to become more coercive in terms of both contributions and membership. Moreover, groups in Europe at that time, as in mainly Latin America today, developed vertically integrated staffed models whereby the group acquired its own medical services by hiring medical staff and acquiring medical facilities. This may have been a way of ensuring service availability as some compensation for prospective payment.

Mandated membership, coupled with a vertical organizational combination between "insurance" and "provision," also compensated for loss of cohesiveness that resulted from the growth of group size and diversity. However, this kind of group, though possibly large and wide, is still not nationwide or public. The group has a common social, and possibly economic, denominator, mostly labor-market or union related.

Take-Off (B): Escaping the Trap of Subsidized and State-Run Services

Many developing and transitional economies support their populations by direct provision of free or heavily subsidized care, provided mostly in state facilities by civil servants. From the perspective of developing SHI, this situation poses several challenges.

First, it may preclude state subsidies for leveraging and promoting insurance, including basic microinsurance, for wider segments of the population and better care. Second, the price subsidies to the state-provided service can be detrimental to SHI in that they may reduce the incentive to acquire insurance by extra private contributions, especially when the service is free altogether. Third, state employees in public facilities may become major stakeholders with an incentive to block change, as they may benefit from the secure civil service status that often enables them to moonlight in the private sector.

Changing the Role of Government

With respect to the state's support to the system, the proposed shift in government responsibility from supporting the supply of care or service-oriented subsidies to supporting the demand for it or insurance-oriented subsidies can be (made) a zero-sum game. The institutional and political flip this transition requires is not, however, effortless, given the number of involved parties with heavily vested interests.

As outlined above, in the process of initiating SHI, the group must become an effective and credible receiving mechanism for resources from the state as well as from NGOs, development agencies, and so on. To this end, groups lacking financial and managerial infrastructure need state aid.

State support can involve assistance with managerial infrastructure, reinsurance, and safety net mechanisms, not least securing preferential availability of services for the insured. Specifically, the state needs to facilitate

- Group-based insurance schemes

- By-laws for self-governing SHI groups

- Affordable community-rated premiums deemed "fair" in an informal environment (van de Ven, chapter 3, this volume). Such premiums may actually subsidize the better-off who are heavier users of services, but are the "lesser evil" compared with out-of-pocket payment.

- Credible and accountable provider institutions identified with the group and whose income may depend on it.

BOX 17.5   GUATEMALA: WHEN THE LONG TERM IS NOT CONSIDERED, AND THE STATE IS NOT INVOLVED

The Asociación por Salud de Barillas (ASSABA) is a community health insurance scheme created by local initiatives in Guatemala. The mayor, local business leaders, midwives, local churches, and others participated in the initiative in 1993. ASSABA was designed to increase access and improve the health care system. It is a prepayment scheme providing primary health care, defined as prescribed drugs, hospital outpatient and inpatient care, and other services provided in the health center, at health posts, and through health promoters. Primary health care is provided at centers of the Department of Ministry of Public Health and Social Affairs (MSPAS). Hospital-based care is available through capitation contracts with a private nonprofit hospital in Barillas. The proposed contribution level was designed to be affordable for most of the families and not designed to cover all the costs of the optimal package. The contributions were initially set according to family size but later changed to pricing per individual. The World Health Organization (WHO) obtained donor funding for preparation and start-up costs. ASSABA collected and disbursed the funds while directly transferring payments to the local MSPAS or hospital. However, there is little interest in the program, due to local political conflicts and little support from regional government. Although this particular scheme did not work, ASSABA became an NGO serving as an intermediary to pay health providers on behalf of MSPAS in a national primary health care program, the System of Integrated Health Care (Ron 1999).

Pertinent state managerial and financial infrastructure gives rise to questions of capacity and governance. These issues need to be squarely addressed in a successful SHI strategy.

Donors

Some potential ethical and political issues pose a particular challenge to the use of donor funds for SHI purposes. Donor funding plays a central role in the funding of care in many poor nations, for example, Tanzania. It is suggested in box 17.5 that donors can be instrumental in shaping SHI by combining the medical benefits they fund with insurance privileges. Securing preferential access to care when the supply of services is meager is the ultimate test of any insurance scheme, including SHI.

SHI TRANSITIONAL CHALLENGES: TRANSFORMING GROUPS AND STAKEHOLDERS

The obstacles inherent in the transition from OOP payment arrangements to mutual aid arrangements, and from these to microinsurance and other forms of financing, show the fundamental challenges involved in SHI development. The reason is that each milestone eventually creates stakeholders that can block progress to milestones further along. Closed groups and even market corporations—critical for the initiation of SHI—can become obstacles to its expansion through the second and third phases of SHI, when subsidies become intergroup, without group brokerage (figure 17.2).

Group and corporate development have been fairly spontaneous, as seen in Europe, Latin America, and the United States. However, the amalgamation of groups and the formation of integrated national systems that secure universal entitlement—through interpersonal and intergroup risk sharing and subsidies—have not been natural and have required strong leadership.

The state-led transition must be based on full understanding of the political economy of the required transitions, with due consideration given to the motives and views of stakeholders, notably existing groups as well as the key elements comprising them (Fox and Reich, chapter 15, this volume). That is, once self-governing groups and corporations are established and exist, the government must expand the circles of SHI to include the community at large—mostly the informal sector—and, eventually, the entire state signifying a universal arrangement. Thus, government needs to help transform nonmarket nonuniversal models (INN, FNN, and FNM) into universal group and pool (UG, UP) models and eventually, when feasible, into a general revenues model (UR). The amalgamation of groups, even those the state has helped establish and sustain, notably civil servant groups, is a key challenge in the advancement of the SHI strategy.

The Group and Market Corporation Revisited

Once formed, the group and the corporation are often statutory entities. They are political as well, balancing various intragroup interests and power sharing, especially those associated with control of the contributions for funding care (D. Chernichovsky, Mizrahi, and Frenkel 2009).

The common stakeholders in the closed group, part of the nonmarket models, are the unions representing labor, employers, and the professions. Internally, one of the three may dominate, and any two can form coalitions. The three can collude against the state or any other external entity that threatens the group's interests.

The same stakeholders may have considerable voice in the market corporation—the insurer, and the plan-HMO—in addition to the influence of shareholders, in the for-profit corporation. In many such situations the insurer or plan, though free-standing, may be an executive arm of a union, a large employer, or the two combined.

Often the state itself can form a "group" akin to the other stakeholders. This follows from several common realities. First and foremost, the state itself can control particular services it may not wish to share with others, as in Mexico (Martinez, Aguilera, and D. Chernichovsky 2011). Second, and related to the first, such services are controlled by unions that often have their own health "plans." Third, these plans benefit from state subsidies in the form of contributions as well as privileges associated with access to state facilities, as in Tanzania, for example.

All key stakeholders, including shareholders, can stand to lose as a collective from advancing SHI to the "next step," and thus oppose change.

Collective Costs and Stakeholder Costs of SHI Expansion

The progress of SHI from one model or phase to the next, and the promise of an eventual universal integrated system, entails costs to the self-governing group and corporation. These costs are associated with the integration of diverse groups, mainly by divesting them from fundraising and fund-allocation responsibilities. The costs to the group or corporation, and by implication, the means required to overcome them are discussed with the aid of figure 17.4.

From Group Homogeneity to Communal Diversity

The erosion of homogeneity and cohesion in favor of increased universality and system integration runs emotionally deeper in an ethnically and religiously

FIGURE 17.4   Social Health Insurance Development: Benefits and Costs

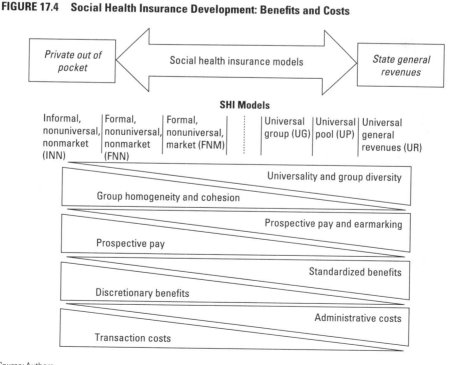

Source: Authors.

diverse environment where suspicion among groups may be substantial, and a new group identity is hard to forge. Economic growth, coupled with widening income disparity, may foster heterogeneity and diversity even in originally homogenous groups. Specifically, the well-to-do and privileged may always wish to keep to themselves (box 17.2). This desire may be reinforced by new and costly medical technology that is harder to share.

The increase in group size and diversity reduces the potential for interaction among members and undermines the psychological advantages of keeping the group small for the sake of willingness to contribute for mutual aid. As the group grows and becomes less cohesive, transparency fades, and transaction costs increase. Accountability of individual members and leaders to the collective may decrease as well.

From Discretionary to Universally Shared Benefits

As universality evolves and widens, the benefits package needs to become more standardized. While standard benefits increase transparency and help earmarking of contributions and, hence, collection of funding, their uniformity can impede free choice, of individuals and groups. This is of particular consequence for the wealthy and well-to-do groups that contribute more and wish to retain their exclusive, often subsidized, benefits.

From Transaction to Administrative Costs

Wide risk-pooling circles of cross-subsidies, grounded in an optimally functioning public finance system, can substantially reduce pertinent transaction costs, mainly those involved in collecting and managing funds and purchasing care. In Israel, for example, the establishment of a national pool reduced collection costs from between 8 and 10 percent to about 2 percent. At the same time, public involvement increases administrative costs, aggravating transparency issues and giving rise to issues of accountability and governance, highlighted above. Thus, as SHI develops, there is a basic need to find ways to introduce and maintain transparency, accountability, and choice, especially for the relatively heavy contributors to the system.

Stakeholders

The privileged group or corporation is clearly the key obstacle to advancing SHI. However, opposition may also exist within other identifiable institutions.

The Privileged Group and the Corporation

To move toward the EP Model (figure 17.3, right) privileged groups need to be persuaded in one way or another to share existing and new state subsidies with the disenfranchised, the uninsured, and the politically unorganized, and to open (for a fee) the closed group to potentially bad risks excluded under existing arrangements. The required change is not purely economic and financial; psychological issues associated with group identity are also involved.

The challenge of well-established market corporations, mainly insurers and HMOs, may not present a lesser challenge than do self-governing groups in the nonmarket situation. Like the self-governing groups, the corporations stand to lose their independence in organizing, funding, and managing the insurance, and may become subject to premium and open enrolment regulations (van de Ven, chapter 3, this volume). President Barack Obama's 2010 health care overhaul bill in the United States is a case in point; because it regulates insurance, the industry objected to the bill. Unlike the groups that stand to lose a social identity, the corporations—mainly insurers—stand to lose their corporate identity. In the end, they become fund-holding plans rather than pure insurers.

The Profession

The potential to increase the supply and lower the cost of medical personnel, physicians in particular, is a clear efficiency gain from funding integration and supporting monopsony purchasing in the system via SHI arrangements. Moreover, price and wage setting associated with collective purchasing of care can serve equity as well by protecting consumer surpluses from monopoly providers.

Thus, the medical profession traditionally objects to more universal coverage that usually involves more collective purchasing, although this approach may be shortsighted, considering the clear benefits to the profession. Insurance increases the demand for care, in part because of moral hazard. This may allow providers even more opportunities to induce demand for care. In addition, insurance arrangements can serve more orderly payment arrangements. For providers, there can be an added measure of secure and stable income.

Medical infrastructure can be an added advantage for the profession from advanced SHI. As the system develops and the cost of technology increases, there can be clear economic and professional gains for medical personnel from centralized fund-holding or purchasing institutions such as insurers that become plans and even from the state. These invest in infrastructure and centralized facilities such as labs, diagnostic facilities, and excellence centers that save individual providers resources and, at the same time, improve the quality of care.

Employers

SHI is usually associated with mandated employer contributions. However, this view may be less significant than commonly thought. It might even be outright wrong. At the outset, employers withhold earnings-related taxes. In this regard a "health tax" (e.g., Israel) is not any different from any other tax withheld by employers. The employer is a collection arm of the state, even when the funds are eventually to be used by the employer-based self-governing group, as has happened in Germany for decades.

The health care contributions withheld by employers signify, first and foremost, their earmarked nature rather than their impact on wages. Even more important, the withholding does not necessarily suggest that employers rather than employees bear the burden of the contributions. This burden is determined by labor supply and demand conditions. Therefore, studies about the impact of the mandated contributions are inconclusive.[10]

An impact of SHI contributions on wages and employment may follow, nonetheless. Even under labor supply and demand conditions favorable to employers (in that the burden of the larger share of mandated contributions would eventually fall on employees), it might take time for employers to shift the burden to employees. In this dynamic situation, employers might finance the contributions even when they will not bear the burden eventually.

Regardless, employers have to bear the administrative as well as the labor relations costs of managing health care coverage. This is a deadweight burden on employers. Hence, regardless of how much they contribute in the short and long runs, employers and the economy overall can do without these costs.

MEETING TRANSITIONAL CHALLENGES

Control over the use of mandated contributions and the pertinent supply of care has been identified as critical for advancing SHI. Individuals, groups, and corporations may agree to surrender this control for the promise of a more equitable and efficient system following the EP principles, provided that the system is accountable and legitimate and provides choice.

Accountability and related legitimacy are served by transparency and good governance. The two are assisted in turn by earmarking contributions and by articulating the benefits they fund. These are key elements of the social SHI contract between individuals and the state (figure 17.2, phase 3), substituting contracts between individuals and groups or corporations, and between the latter and the state (phases 1 and 2).

Choice is potentially best served by competition in internal markets where citizens can enroll freely with competing plans, where feasible, and with providers. These plans, replacing groups and corporations, can be self-governing and accountable—also through competition—both to their membership and the public at large, even when privately owned (D. Chernichovsky, Mizrahi, and Frenkel 2009). As suggested above, all must be supported by stewardship and leadership.

Earmarking

Earmarked mandated contributions are the key identifier of SHI. Earmarking state-mandated contributions is a constitutional-type tool that preserves the control of the contributor community over use of contributions. Contributions can be used only for politically set medical benefits and eligible beneficiaries, and not for other potential state budget uses.[11] Earmarking binds the state's budgetary processes; the state essentially becomes a trustee and a manager of the funds. Moreover, the task is often executed by a public authority that is separate from the state treasury. This institutional arrangement furthers the separation between mandated earmarked contributions and general taxation.

Earmarking is financially the basic separator between the group and the Universal Pool (UP) Model, known as the Continental Funding Model, and the Universal General Revenues (UR) Model, known as the Commonwealth Funding Model. The former is the ultimate SHI model (D. Chernichovsky et al. 2012).

As implied earlier, when compared with other taxes based on the same principles and schedules (such as income taxes), earmarked taxes are inconsequential for the paying individual or enterprise, and even more so for the receiving plan and provider. Israel has moved toward abolishing earmarked funding and yet has maintained other aspects of the system intact; by and large, general revenues fund competing sickness funds responsible for fund holding and provision of entitlement.

As implied, earmarking signifies some distrust in the state and the political process on the part of the contributors. Consequently, earmarking serves the political process: groups surrender their right over fundraising and allocation, in favor of a national covenant, on the condition that the funds are used for socially determined care benefits. Earmarking and its institutional separation from the treasury is thus a way to help preserve transparency and accountability. For that reason, earmarking is probably an indispensable option for widening universal coverage through mandated contributions, especially where the trust of the state is low, and good governance mechanisms are weak. Earmarking can also be an effective tool for the informal sector, which might wish to avoid general taxation because of its deadweight, but would agree to pay an SHI tax, provided that its proceeds are indeed segregated from the "not trusted state."

Trust in the state's good governance and political processes can render earmarking redundant, leading up to the UR Model. By the same token, distrust of the state can reverse this progression from the UG and UP Models to the ultimate UR Model. Former socialist countries backed off the strict UR Model because of distrust of the state and its budgetary process, at least for funding medical care (D. Chernichovsky, Barnum, and Potapchik 1996; Wagstaff and Moreno-Serra, chapter 14, this volume).

Earmarking funds raised through public regulation and principles is, however, a contentious issue that concerns fiscal policy and budget management questions involving macroeconomic issues beyond the health care system. Because earmarking binds the state's budgetary process, treasuries (justifiably, from their perspective) dislike it. When the taxes have not previously existed in the form of group- or corporate-mandated contributions, treasuries can become a major power blocking taxes earmarked for health.

In addition, earmarking is not costless to the health care system. A general tax is more equitable and efficient than an earmarked tax because it provides broader opportunities to use public funds: one of its goals is to serve the public's health through nonmedical spending. In other words, earmarked contributions, though serving medical care, may not serve health optimally. Moreover, since all systems benefit in one way or another from general revenues, the state can always use the earmarked amounts to justify a decrease in its own contribution. And, earmarked funding often requires extra collection mechanisms that raise the cost of running the system.

In addition, general revenues can potentially eliminate the business cycle effect, but an earmarked tax in itself cannot. The latter may expand with an economic upswing and contract with a downswing. General revenues can always include deficit finance to cope with business cycles.

Hence, an earmarked tax can be a double-edged sword. This state of affairs, combined with the reality that earmarked contributions can share identical public finance principles with general taxation, make the debate on this issue normative and political because it deals with the social contract that earmarked taxes represent.[12] For all these reasons, earmarking should be carefully tailored to interact with the general budget to give the health care system financial stability and a safety net against cyclical fluctuations. Earmarked taxes can be phased out in the modern economy where they may still be a debated political issue.

Individual and Plan Choice and Empowerment

In addition to the consequences of loss of control over funding by individuals and groups, the progress of SHI (toward the right in figure 17.4) signifies standardized and uniform entitlement. Grouped and incorporated individuals lose some control over the content and form of care they fund.

The pertinent challenge of advancing developed SHI is dual. It must satisfy diverse and often politically powerful groups that surrender rights. Simultaneously, it must appeal to individuals who might be "liberated" of choices made by unresponsive bureaucrats and stakeholders. Educated and well-to-do clients have different aspirations, demands, and options from those of less-informed and poor clients. Moreover, the demands of the stronger groups continue to pose a risk to the public system, especially where supply of medical personnel and services is limited. Private pay—both over and under the table—can continue, luring civil servants and others paid by the public from serving everyone under public entitlement.

Diversity, and hence political support of the powerful groups, in the UG, UP, and even the UR Models (figure 17.3) can be served by statutory power-sharing between the central state and, where feasible, competing and self-governing health care plans or noncompeting local jurisdictions, about the determination of content and form of entitlement, and nature of voluntary medical insurance.

Contents and Form of Entitlement

Choice concerns content and form of benefits.[13] There is relatively little debate or argument about the form in which entitled care is offered. Competing plans (if any) and providers in the same internal market, operating under mandated contributions, can offer and experiment with variable forms of supplying identical benefits as the offering complies with the entitlement regulations and "common practice." Content of care is more debated than form. The challenge is dual: to allow pluralism in entitlement and to strike a balance between the supplies of publicly funded and privately funded care.

A potential solution entails defining three levels of entitlement: core benefits (CB) under public entitlement, supplemental benefits (SB) regulated by groups or even the central state, and wholly privately funded benefits. The first, basic level is common to all, involving types of care deemed not subject to individual discretion. Notable among these would be prevention and treatment of communicable diseases and treatment of diseases that are potentially "catastrophic" for the household's financial well-being.

The second level is a discretionary package, available on a voluntary basis to groups self-formed around some common denominator, including the extra benefits package itself. Though voluntary, this package may be subject to community rating and open enrolment regulation. The third benefits package is a fully privately funded package of benefits paid by OOP and individually rated insurance. This solution exists in Israel where sickness funds, which provide CB, are regulated to offer "supplemental insurance" for community rating and with open enrolment. In Belgium, enrolment in insurance of this nature is mandatory.

The proposed arrangement might be implemented by a state administration (e.g., the National Health Service), but competition among several plans might be easier. Each plan could offer several combinations of CB + SB, affording a wider choice than would be possible under a single administration.

The proposed arrangements leave some choice about even content of care even under publicly supported or regulated care. The supply of these benefits must be organized to forestall interference with the publicly supported system. If inadequately regulated and organized, the supply of benefits under OOP and voluntary health insurance can interfere with the objectives of the publicly supported system, notably equity and cost containment (Schut and Roos 2008; D. Chernichovsky 2012). Moreover, regulation, notably around open enrolment, should prevent making SB a means for selecting bad risk for the basic package.

Open Enrolment in Competing Plans

Open enrolment with plans, where feasible, and with providers, is critical for exercising choice and minimizing risk selection under universal entitlement.[14] Fund-holding plans can thus be considered "groups," formed by citizens' (or residents') choice and open enrolment, regardless of innate or acquired traits (D. Chernichovsky 2002). As such, competing and open plans can be effective and politically

appealing substitutes to the privileged group, especially if the latter is dominated by an unresponsive interest group and bureaucracy.

Still, some groups may wish to maintain their identity. In that case, they can
become fund holders or plans that have relinquished their fundraising and allocation responsibilities for entitled services, but retained their fund-holding and
provision responsibilities in agreement with the plan's membership. Offering
optional voluntary medical insurance within the plan can even strengthen the
group's political willingness to relinquish control over contributions to fund
entitlement. Hence, while such groups may in the end lose control over spending levels and the full scope of the benefits package, they can express group
preferences by determining the nature of contracting entitlement, and possibly
influence the benefits package.

Governance

Good governance is about rules and regulations that serve transparency and
legal and political accountability, and thereby support a well-functioning system. Good governance is thus also about political legitimacy to widening SHI.
It can be a formidable challenge in "developing" situations where corrupt and
unresponsive group bureaucratic "elites" may be the norm. At times, small,
well-governed groups may provide a better, if second-best, solution than a corrupt, ill-functioning, and legitimacy-lacking government. This implies delicate
balancing acts in the development of an SHI system and suggests trading responsibilities between the state and groups, with transparency and accountability the
fundamental issue.

SHI organized in plans can present an institutional opportunity to introduce pluralism and market-based diversity into the publicly financed health
system. The authority delegated to plans as consumer groups, through their ability to participate actively within the system, means that they can substantially
determine the nature of public entitlement—both its elements and the form of
its delivery (D. Chernichovsky 2002). This arrangement can preserve the powers
of both groups, especially during transition, and of the citizenry at large.

CONCLUSION: THE ROLES OF THE STATE REVISITED

The state's stewardship in devising and implementing SHI is indispensable
because SHI involves integrating—at times through coercion—individuals into
groups, and groups and corporations into larger entities. In view of the prospective nature of commercial insurance and its potential for exploitation, especially
as the risk-sharing and cross-subsidy circles grow, there is a need to promote
systemic legitimacy and trust through transparency and accountability. This
involves setting and enforcing rules and regulations so that institutions and
internal markets function well. To sustain their fiduciary role, plan institutions

must be carefully regulated, while care to preserve their independent nature is exercised.

As for funding, the state needs to see that public funds are protected and used prudently and that the health budget is insulated from fortuitous events, including swings in the business cycle. A critical element in securing an equitable and efficient system is developing and upholding a universal, risk-adjusted capitation allocation mechanism so that groups get their fair share of public-based funding and people are not discriminated against.

The state must ensure citizens' access to plans of their choice through open enrolment. It must also guarantee their access to efficient and equitable services by securing service availability, controlling monopolies and monopsonies, and supporting research, training, and centers of excellence. These support the smooth functioning of internal markets.

Nonetheless, to the extent possible, the government should avoid issuing directives aimed at protecting the paying public's interest. Instead, it should achieve that objective through a fair (risk-adjusted, need-based) allocation system, public information, flexible guidelines, and the support of contractual arrangements between consumers and fund-holding institutions, and between those institutions and providers. Key to all the above is an unbiased government that can serve as an honest and credible broker for all, judging merit on efficiency and equity grounds. These require, first and foremost, that the state itself does not assume and assert vested interests in the systems as a fund holder and provider.

NOTES

1. The *group* is a social entity that comprises two or more individuals who bond to resolve common problems and provide mutual aid. Enrolment is based on innate or acquired social or economic characteristics. Opting out for privileges rendered by the group is forbidden.

2. The *corporation* is an economic entity, for-profit or not-for-profit, which individuals join by paying for the privileges rendered by the corporation. Entry and exit are based on willingness and ability to pay.

3. Nominally there *is* universal coverage in most developing countries.

4. For brevity of discussion, it is assumed here that an insurer's right to refuse to admit a bad-risk individual into an insurance-based group is consistent with an individual's market right. The sick individual always has the right to pay the highest fair premium: the fee for service. The fee amount may be prohibitive in terms of the individual's ability to pay, a situation applicable to many other goods and services in the market.

5. Here *mutual aid* and *microinsurance* are used almost synonymously. Subsequently, this approach is changed.

6. The authors are indebted to D. Dror for this articulation of microinsurance (Dror and Jacquier 1999).

7. At times the contributions for health care might be incorporated in general social security contributions involving notably pensions.

8. Some arrangements with the state, for special groups and in lieu of state subsidies, are possible and common. State support of such groups in general invariably involves subsidies. Those, however, are not necessarily equalizing.

9. About 95 percent of Israeli residents had health insurance coverage through the end of 1994, prior to the enactment of the National Health Insurance Bill, which secured every resident's entitlement to set medical benefits. This example signifies the importance of the integrated national health system, beyond universal coverage.

10. To some extent, these studies may deal with the counterfactual. They cannot establish what the impact would be of an added income tax to fund health care.

11. Earmarked funds may not be entirely immune from general government spending. Earmarked funds can be regulated, and probably should be, to be invested in state bonds that help set the government's spending envelope.

12. For a more formal and detailed presentation of the arguments and the issues, see D. Chernichovsky and M. Chernichovsky (2006).

13. For elaboration, see Chernichovsky (2002).

14. Internal markets supporting plans are not always feasible, especially in nonurban areas where the supply of both providers and managerial and financial infrastructure is limited. Still, ways of empowering local populations need to be sought (D. Chernichovsky and M. Chernichovsky 2006).

REFERENCES

Carrin, G., and C. James. 2003. "Social Health Insurance as a Pathway to Universal Coverage: Key Design Features in the Transition Period." Health Financing Technical Paper, WHO, Geneva.

Chee, G., K. Smith, and A. Kapinga. 2002. *Assessment of the Community Health Fund in Hanang District, Tanzania*. Bethesda, MD: Abt Associates Inc., Partners for Health Reform*plus* Project.

Chernichovsky, D. 1995. "Health System Reforms in Industrialized Democracies: An Emerging Paradigm." *Milbank Quarterly* 73 (3): 339–72.

———. 2002. "Pluralism, Public Choice and the State in the Emerging Paradigm in Health Systems." *Milbank Quarterly* 80 (1): 5–39.

———. 2009. "Not 'Socialized Medicine': An Israeli View of Health Care Reform." *New England Journal of Medicine* 361 (21): 41.

———. 2012. "Semi Public Health Care Finance—Potential and Risks: The Case of Israel." Ben-Gurion University of the Negev, Beer Sheba, Israel.

Chernichovsky, D., H. Barnum, and E. Potapchik. 1996. "Health System Reform in Russia: The Finance and Organization Perspectives." *Economics of Transition* 4 (1): 113–34.

Chernichovsky, D., and M. Chernichovsky. 2006. "Decentralization in the Health Care System: A Framework for Design and Application." World Bank, Washington, DC.

Chernichovsky, D., and D. Chinitz. 1995. "The Political Economy of Health System Reform in Israel." *Health Economics* 4: 127–41.

Chernichovsky, D., R. Donato, A. Leibowitz, A. Maynard, M. Peterson, V. Rodwin, W. van de Ven, and J. Wasem. 2012. "What Can the U.S. Learn from Its Allies?" Ben-Gurion University of the Negev, Beer Sheba, Israel.

Chernichovsky, D., and A. Leibowitz. 2010. "Integrating Public Health and Personal Care in a Reformed U.S. Health Care System." *American Journal of Public Health* 100 (2): 205–11.

Chernichovsky, D., G. Martinez, and N. Aguilera. 2009. "Reforming Underdeveloped Health Care Systems of Mexico, Tanzania and the U.S.A." In *Innovations in Health System Finance in Developing and Transitional Economies*, ed. D. Chernichovsky and K. Hanson. Vol. 21, *Advances in Health Economics and Health Services Research*. Bingley, UK: Emerald Group Publishing.

Chernichovsky, D., S. Mizrahi, and T. Frenkel. 2009. "The Governance of Israeli Sickness Funds." [English version forthcoming.] Jerusalem, Taub Center for Social Policy Studies in Israel.

Davis, K., C. Schoen, S.C. Schoenbaum, M.M. Doty, A.L. Holmgren, J.L. Kriss, and K. Shea. 2007. "Mirror Mirror on the Wall: An International Update on the Comparative Performance of American Health Care." New York: Commonwealth Fund.

De Weerdt, J. 2002. "Risk-Sharing and Endogenous Network Formation." Research Paper, World Institute for Development Economic Research (UNU-WIDER), Helsinki.

Dror, D.M., and C. Jacquier. 1999. "Micro-Insurance: Extending Health Insurance to the Excluded." *International Social Security Review* 52 (1): 71–97.

Ellis, R.P., M. Alam, and I. Gupta. 2000. "Health Insurance in India: Prognosis and Prospectus." *Economic and Political Weekly* 35 (4): 207–17.

Fafchamps, M. 1992. "Solidarity Networks in Preindustrial Societies: Rational Peasants with a Moral Economy." *Economic Development and Cultural Change* 41 (1): 147–76.

Gottret, P., and G. Schieber. 2006. *Health Financing Revisited: A Practitioner's Guide*. Washington, DC: World Bank.

GTZ (German Development Cooperation). 2004. "Social Health Insurance—Systems of Solidarity: Experiences from German Development Cooperation." Federal Ministry for Economic Cooperation and Development, Frankfurt, Germany.

Heller, P.S. 2005. *Understanding Fiscal Space*. Discussion Paper 05/4, International Monetary Fund, Washington, DC.

———. 2006. *The Prospects of Creating "Fiscal Space" for the Health Sector*. Oxford: Oxford University Press in association with the London School of Tropical Medicine.

Hsiao, W.C. 2007. *Social Health Insurance for Developing Nations*. Washington, DC: World Bank.

Londono, J.L. 2000. "Managing Competition in the Tropics." In *Comparative Health Reforms: Asia and Latin America*. Washington, DC: Inter-American Development Bank, Inter-American Institute for the Social Development, INDES.

Mariam, D.H. 2003. "Indigenous Social Insurance as an Alternative Financing Mechanism for Health Care in Ethiopia (The Case of *Eders*)." *Social Science and Medicine* 56: 1719–26.

Martinez, G., N. Aguilera, and D. Chernichovsky. 2011. "The Mexican Health Sector and the Emerging Paradigm in Modern Systems." Inter-American Center for Social Security Studies, Mexico City.

Normand, C., and A. Weber. 1994. *Social Health Insurance: A Guidebook for Planning.* Geneva: WHO.

Ron, A. 1999. "NGOs in Community Health Insurance Schemes: Examples from Guatemala and the Philippines." *Social Science and Medicine* 48: 939–50.

Saltman, R., R. Busse, and J. Figueras, eds. 2004. *Social Health Insurance Systems in Western Europe.* European Observatory on Health Care Systems Series. London: Open University Press, McGraw-Hill Education.

Schoen, C., K. Davis, S.K. How, and S.C. Schoenbaum. 2006. "U.S. Health System Performance: A National Scorecard." *Health Affairs* (Project Hope) 25 (6): 457–75.

Schut, E., and A.F. Roos. 2008. "The Impact of Tied Selling of Mandatory Basic and Voluntary Supplementary Health Insurance: Evidence from the Netherlands." Erasmus University, Rotterdam.

Schwartz, T., ed. 1980. *Socialization as Cultural Communication: Development of a Theme in the Work of Margaret Mead.* Berkeley: University of California Press. Also available online, http://ark.cdlib.org/ark:/13030/ft1p300479/.

van de Ven, W.P.M.M., and D. Chernichovsky. 2003. "Risk Adjustment in Europe." *Health Policy* 65 (1): 1–100.

Wagstaff, A., and R. Moreno-Serra. 2008. "Social Health Insurance and Labor Market Outcomes: Evidence from Central and Eastern Europe, and Central Asia." In *Innovations in Health System Finance in Developing and Transitional Economies,* ed. D. Chernichovsky and K. Hanson. London: Emerald-JAI.

WHO (World Health Organization). 2005. *Social Health Insurance: Selected Case Studies from Asia and the Pacific.* Geneva: WHO.

World Bank. 2004. *World Development Report 2004: Making Services Work for Poor People.* Washington, DC: World Bank.

CHAPTER 18

REGULATORY AND SUPERVISORY CHALLENGES

*Hernán L. Fuenzalida-Puelma, Pablo Gottret, Somil Nagpal,
and Nicole Tapay*

In most countries, health care financing and delivery are fast becoming the "health care business" with the convergence of a public and private mix of interests. "Public" and "private" are no longer opposites. This configuration calls for new approaches in supervision and regulation. This chapter deals with selected issues in the supervision and regulation of social health insurance (SHI) and private voluntary health insurance (PVHI) in developing countries.

REGULATION, SUPERVISION, AND THE PUBLIC-PRIVATE MIX

Social and voluntary health insurance have various meanings in different countries. The OECD taxonomy of health insurance (OECD 2004) distinguishes between public schemes, financed mainly through (a) the tax system, including general taxation and mandatory payroll levies, and (b) income-related contributions to social security schemes. All other insurance schemes financed through private premiums are defined as private, classified into (a) mandatory (by law) and (b) voluntary, distinguishing then two subcategories: (b.1) specific market subgroups (individual and group markets); (b.2) risk rating (community and experience rating).

Social and voluntary health insurance deal with health care financing. In some countries (Albania, the former Yugoslav Republic of Macedonia) the social health insurance funds are considered health institutions and not financial institutions, and there is resistance to having them supervised by an authority different from the Ministry of Health. As financial institutions, they have to meet certain basic institutional and financial standards to ensure their solvency and to honor their financial obligations. Both need to be regulated and supervised to protect the integrity of financial operations and beneficiaries' rights and entitlements and to ensure the delivery of quality care. Both deal with the financing of health care goods and services provided by public and private health care professionals and technicians and by manufacturers and distributors of medical supplies, equipment, and devices. Both offer basic packages of goods and services in the form of health care entitlements. They differ in that one is public and social and the other is private. Social insurance is usually mandatory, and private insurance is usually voluntary (except in Switzerland, where private insurance is mandatory). A mix of taxes, payroll contributions, and state subsidies finances social health insurance. Voluntary health insurance is financed by premiums (for indemnity) and contributions (for prepaid).

Lack of proper distinction between indemnity and prepaid health insurance creates confusion in many countries.[1] For the purposes of this chapter, risk-rated voluntary health insurance can be (a) *indemnity* or *traditional health insurance* (also called fee-for-service health insurance) where patients may choose any physician or hospital, and the insurance company reimburses a percentage of costs, usually after payment of an annual deductible,[2] and (b) *prepaid insurance,* referring to any payment to a provider for anticipated services. Payments are made to organizations/insurers that, unlike an insurance company, take responsibility for arranging for, and providing, needed services as well as for paying for them. This is the case in the various types of health maintenance organizations (HMOs), prepaid group practices, and medical foundations. This chapter deals with social security social health insurance and with private voluntary prepaid health insurance.

The seminal *Investing in Health* (World Bank 1993) did not have a section on regulation. Under "Government Policies in Achieving Health for All," it states, "strong government regulation is also crucial, including regulation of privately delivered health service to ensure safety and quality and of private insurance to encourage universal access to coverage and to discourage practices—such as fee-for-service payments by 'third-party' insurers—that lead to overuse of services and escalation of costs" (World Bank 1993: 6, 133). Regulation appeared as a subsidiary condition for reform and success. Recent studies focus on regulation as a key element for effectiveness in health care financing reforms, among them, Harding and Preker (2003); Afifi, Busse, and Harding (2003); Feeley (2006); and Jost (2009). *The Business of Health in Africa* dedicates a full chapter to regulation because regulation and oversight are at the "heart of effective, high-quality private sector involvement in health care" and a condition for improving health care as a whole in the region (IFC 2008: 17).

There is no one solution for health care financing and its regulation and supervision. The modes of health care financing—costs and prices, access to health care, quality of goods and services, changing roles of public and private sectors, and proper regulation and supervision—are political and operational matters of perennial concern, debate, and experimentation.

But regulating financing is not sufficient. Health care depends on providers and suppliers of goods and services. Chile and the Slovak Republic have integrated the regulation and supervision of financing and provision, while suppliers remain regulated by Ministries of Health. Public-private partnerships (PPPs) in health should be encouraged for infrastructure, delivery of clinical and nonclinical services, and management, provided that appropriate and effective regulation, supervision, and contract monitoring are in place.

How to properly and better regulate health insurance is an issue of global concern. In the United States, health care remains a prime issue in spite of recent reforms as costs escalate and insurance coverage diminishes. In Latin America, health care financing reforms initiated in Chile (1979–80) were followed in

Colombia, Mexico, and Peru with innovative regulatory schemes. In Southeast Asia, voluntary health insurance is making inroads in Thailand and Vietnam. In South Africa, medical schemes follow interesting regulatory modalities. Transition countries in Central Asia and in Central and Eastern Europe (Albania, Bulgaria, FYR Macedonia) struggle with underfunded social health insurance models, while the private sector's expanding role in financing and delivery is not always well integrated and regulated (save in Slovenia). In Sub-Saharan Africa, inadequate public financing, provider shortages, and a diverse and fragmented private sector call for a renewed effort to integrate and regulate the health care sector.

REGULATORY AND SUPERVISORY ACTIVITY

Successful unification of supervision and regulation[3] in countries such as Chile, the Netherlands, and the Slovak Republic shows that the social and voluntary health insurance differences and commonalities can be managed under analogous policies, concepts, and supervisory and regulatory instruments toward an effective public and private mix in health care financing and delivery. As Savedoff states, "unifying supervision for all health insurers—whether public or private, integrated with providers or not—is apparently the best way to ensure fairness and efficiency in terms of financial solvency, consumer protection and equity" (2008: 8).

Deciding *which activities to regulate*[4] involves economic and social considerations. Deciding *who should regulate and how* involves legal and institutional concerns. In the regulatory domain, economics and the law converge. Regulating health care is complex. Political, social, economic, and legal/institutional considerations deal with a matter critical for individuals and society. At the same time, it is an area in which vested and conflicting interests abound. From an economic point of view, controlling market failures such as asymmetric information, adverse selection, and moral hazard justifies regulatory interventions. From a political and legal/institutional perspective, social and equity grounds and interpretations of the constitutional role of the state in protecting the common good or public interest have an impact in justifying regulation.

Regulation requires (a) an institutional/legal framework that would translate policies into norms and procedures; (b) a clear notion of which topics would be subject to regulation; (c) the type of entity or authority that would be entrusted with regulation; and (d) the regulatory instruments that would be necessary for implementation. The environment in which health financing and insurance regulation take place is multifaceted, and it varies depending on a number of national structural and organizational factors (table 18.1).

The point of departure in regulating health insurance lies in health care policy objectives and in the roles assigned to the public and the private sectors in financing and delivery. The definitions determine how to answer questions such as: Would voluntary health insurance be allowed to supplement social health

TABLE 18.1   Factors Influencing the Regulatory and Supervisory Environment

Structure of the state	The state regulatory framework and procedures are critical for determining the type of governmental regulatory organization. Countries vary in whether the state is federal or unitary; the form of government—constitutional monarchy, presidential, parliamentary; and the structure of executive, legislative, and judicial separation of powers.
Prevailing economic model	The prevailing economic model will influence the regulatory environment, depending on the model as central, market-oriented, or mixed economy.
Accepted social values	The consideration of social values by a given society has a profound influence on how health care is perceived and whether or not, or to what extent, social solidarity is an accepted and practiced social value.
Role of local governments	In some countries, municipalities and autonomous regions have their own regulatory frameworks, from simple licensing of pharmacies and clinical establishments to more complex health regulations.
Health policies and priorities	National health policies and priorities have an impact on health insurance regulation. They influence the design and operation of health care financing models, either national health service, social health insurance fund(s); scope of private health insurance; status of public and private health care delivery; and emphasis on hospitals or on primary health care.
Standards, norms, and guidelines	The existence (or not) and the quality of Standards, Norms, and Guidelines have a direct relation to the health care goods and services that are financed and the possible outcomes. Mediocre health care establishment and lax licensing and accreditation standards, outdated clinical protocols, and relaxed guidelines on conduct and responsibilities of physicians and other health professionals determine to a great extent the effectiveness and efficiency of health care financing.
Role for the private sector	Countries vary in what is the accepted role for the private sector in health care financing and delivery. In some countries there is an effective mix and cross-working, while in others the private sector is clearly separated from social health insurance and public health care delivery. Increasingly, countries are converging in the mix of public and private financing and delivery.
Status of consumer and patient rights	The role of consumers is directly related to accountability and quality of care. Law and procedures on informed consent, organ donation, and malpractice serve a purpose of consumer control of the health care goods and services that are financed.
Regulatory instruments	There are many regulatory instruments to consider: laws or acts of parliament; decrees and other instruments issued by the executive branch; ordinances by municipalities; judgments by the judiciary; instructions, standards, circulars, public information by health insurance supervisors/regulators; professional and ethical standards, licensing, and other delegated matters to private self-regulatory organizations.

Source: Authors.

insurance only, or can it also be comprehensive—including benefits under social health insurance but without allowing opt-out?[5] Would private insurance target those who can afford it, or would it be promoted for the less affluent, including the poor and rural populations, with state- or donor-subsidized contributions? Would voluntary health insurance remain totally separated from social health insurance, or could it eventually be allowed to partially manage benefits and service delivery financed by social health insurance?

To answer these questions, policies should take into account realistic assessments of the limitations of social health insurance and the actual potential of voluntary health insurance. It is important to take into account that social health insurance will most likely remain the main financial source of health care and that voluntary insurance will be secondary in global terms. The experience of Chile (a well-structured middle-income country) with a dual health care financing system shows that private health insurance covered 25 percent of the population at the height of the economic boom. Today private coverage is around 15 percent of the population.

Deciding on the autonomy of the social health insurance fund is sometimes a contentious issue. Social health insurance funds should have autonomy, and this means financial, managerial, contractual, and administrative autonomy. Some central governments (mainly the Ministries of Finance and of Health) view the notion of autonomy with some trepidation over a possible loss of power. This should not be so because there is no such thing as absolute autonomy. Social health insurance funds should have a well-regulated autonomy, which is not that different from the regulated "freedom" that private voluntary health insurance companies have. Social health insurance funds are subject to audits (internal, external, and also from the state audit office or state comptroller) and to instructions from Ministries of Finance on the management of public funds; from the Ministry of Health on basic packages and other related health issues, including health care professionals; and in some cases from parliament, alongside various reporting requirements. The degree of autonomy allowed should not be different from the regulated autonomy of voluntary insurers, which are subject to licensing, capital, and solvency requirements, and auditing, reporting, inspections, and customer service obligations under strictly enforced regulations and close supervision and monitoring.

SUPERVISION AND REGULATION: MINIMUM REQUIREMENTS

Legislation defines who the insurance supervisor will be, as well as the roles of Ministries of Finance and Health and self-regulatory organizations (association of voluntary health insurers and professional and trade associations) in matters related to health insurance. There are many options in defining the health insurance supervisor (box 18.1): the Ministry of Health, a separate supervisory authority, a unified supervisory authority for both social and private health insurance, and a special department under the general insurance supervisor or unified financial supervisor.[6]

Private health insurance supervision should target critical issues, such as: solvency; competition to avoid cartel-type practices; transparency in coverage and prices; market stability for expansion and better complementarities with social health insurance; price controls and prohibition of age-rating; open enrolments into minimum products and, up to a certain age, guaranteed renewal and portability; integration with social health insurance without allowing opt-outs, for supplemental and even comprehensive coverage; quality of care by allowing selective contracting[7] of competent providers and respecting their clinical judgment; and advertising and marketing. Regarding health insurance contracts, typical

---

BOX 18.1   OPTIONS FOR REGULATING AND SUPERVISING HEALTH INSURANCE

Who should regulate and supervise social health insurance? (1) The Ministry of Health (the Arab Republic of Egypt), (2) a separate regulator and supervisor (Argentina, the Slovak Republic), or (3) a unified public-private regulator and supervisor (Chile).

Who should regulate and supervise private indemnity health insurance? (1) The insurance supervisor (the United States) or (2) the financial supervisory authorities (Bulgaria, Estonia).

Who should regulate and supervise private prepaid indemnity health insurance? (1) The insurance regulator under a special division and separate from regulation of indemnity health insurance (the United States), (2) a separate regulator and supervisor (Colombia), or (3) a unified public-private regulator and supervisor (Chile).

Who should regulate and supervise health care providers and suppliers? (1) The Ministry of Health is usually the regulator; (2) the new trend is for unified financing and provision supervisor (Chile and the Slovak Republic). Complementarily, professional associations also regulate health care providers (more of ethical and professional behavioral issues).

Source: Authors.

---

regulations refer, for example, to standards of full and fair disclosure related to health policies and health plans, terms of renewal, initial and subsequent conditions of eligibility, coverage of dependents, preexisting conditions, termination of insurance, probationary periods, limitations, exceptions, and marketing of entitlements and prices. In some countries (Chile and the Slovak Republic) the special health supervisor also supervises health care providers, public and private.

Provisions on capital adequacy and solvency need to take into account that voluntary health insurers' liabilities are of short duration and that the revolving nature of clinical and suppliers' expenses also has a short cycle. Catastrophic risk is less frequent, and requiring reinsurance usually covers it. Provisions should also be made in case of malpractice claims and for subscriber compensations.

On price regulation, indirect measures such as restrictions in applying rating procedures selectively between different applicants seem to be effective. On benefits, every insurance plan product must be required to have a minimum set of benefits; and all insurers must be required to offer a minimum product with a standard minimum set of benefits.

MINIMUM REGULATORY REQUIREMENTS

To facilitate the convergence of public and private interests in health care financing, a revision of current regulatory requirements would be helpful. This is because the strict separation of public and voluntary health financing in most legislation does not provide space for the mix in financing and delivery. The issue is how to enable public and private financing of public and private delivery of health care goods and services while retaining their separate public and private identities.

Prepaid Voluntary Health Insurance

Regarding voluntary prepaid health insurance, a first consideration is the need for legislation that distinguishes and separates prepaid from indemnity insurance. Second, there is a need for a regulatory approach based on considerations such as the following:

- Type of prepaid insurance companies (usually joint stock company)

- Minimum capital and solvency (lower than for traditional insurance)

- Governance (boards)

- Fit-and-proper requirements for management (competence)

- Internal auditing and reporting (accountability)

- Approval of new insurance products or health plans, including file and use procedures and risk-compensation schemes

- Innovative payment techniques

- Networking of providers under voluntary insurers' credentialing methods

- Selective contracting

- Norms restricting or impeding preexisting exclusions

- Norms on community rating

- Access to voluntary health insurance provisions (open enrolment) for people for whom coverage would otherwise be unfeasible or too expensive

- Norms on claim processing including internal corporate procedures on appeals to revise claims

- Controlling anticompetitive practices, marketing, and advertising.

Social Health Insurance

Social health insurance benefits from a well-drafted legal foundation in the form of a framework, (not detailed) law, establishing and defining the social health insurance, defining universal coverage, and clearly separating health care financing and public health financing that needs to be financed with state budget and not from health care contributions.

Some minimum requirements could be the following:

- Specific definitions for social health insurance, such as beneficiaries, entitlements, family members, basic package, and contributions

- Legal status for the social health insurance fund, including autonomy, functions and powers, governance (boards), management and design (that is, whether there will be multiple social health insurance funds or one national health insurance fund with local branches as in Albania, Chile, Costa Rica, Estonia)

- Definition of the relations between the social health insurance fund, the Ministries of Finance and Health, and with the legislature

- Criteria for the definition of health care entitlements

- Definitions and basic procedures for the design of basic benefits packages, minimum entitlements, and additional entitlements in the packages

- Operational regulatory capacity (via instructions and mainly through terms and conditions in contracts with providers and suppliers) in coordination with the supervisory authority

- Role of, and relationships with, the private sector in financing and delivery of goods and services

- Relationships between social and voluntary insurance, and areas of partnership and collaboration, including financing, delivery mix, and eventual management of social health insurance activities

- No restrictions for comprehensive voluntary insurance and prohibition of no opting out of social health insurance in the event of purchasing comprehensive voluntary insurance

- Enunciation of basic operational issues to be developed in regulations by the supervisory authority such as pooling financial resources from various sources, risk pooling, purchasing strategies and selective contracting, public-private networking, innovative payment mechanisms, public-private mix, conflict resolution mechanisms (including health insurance ombudsman), and consumer relations

- Accountability through internal and external auditing and reporting on financial, administrative, and health care data

- Supervision and regulation conducted by a special health supervisory authority. Options include a unified health authority regulating and supervising both social and voluntary health insurance.

A fundamental political and policy issue in social health insurance is deciding "what to finance" and "what not to finance" with the available resources. The answer is supposedly found in the specification of the goods and services in the basic benefits package.[8] A legal instrument[9] should translate a defined policy on the scope and content of the basic packages. The details should be regulations, based on proposals by social health insurance funds to finance certain goods and services with the expected available financial resources and limit the services to those resources. These regulations are usually revised annually and approved by Ministries of Health, subject to final sanction by Ministries of Finance and legislatures when approving the annual budget law. Public health services, sick leave, maternity leave payments, and payment for illnesses or accidents should be financed separately from social insurance under workers' compensation insurance programs.[10]

Generous basic packages are still common, despite chronic resource limitations (Albania, Bulgaria, FYR Macedonia). Determining what not to finance or what to finance partially is addressed more on political grounds than on the logic of health care needs and the availability of financial and institutional resources. Usually only timid efforts are made to publicize which goods and services are rationed or excluded and which ones are available with additional formal payments. Unrealistic basic packages, financed with limited contributions, encourage informal financing of health care services, making the content of the packages and the planning of public financing a futile exercise. Public information in plain language about the covered goods and services and the payments expected from the population is a fundamental regulatory area.

Regulations are also needed to solve the problem of what happens when treatment of a medical condition goes beyond the services included in the basic packages. Who pays for the extra costs? How to account for the additional expenditures? On what criteria to decide whether and how to bill the patient? How to obtain reimbursement from the social insurance fund for the added expenses?

Another limitation relates to policies that compel (officially) public health care establishments to provide only services covered in the basic package. Charging, receiving, and accounting for extra-budgetary income is not allowed. Nonetheless, management and staff tend to collude to obtain resources to supplement institutional and personal income by offering additional services for which the patient pays "informally" out of pocket (Mongolia, Nigeria).

Financing should focus on quality health care goods and services, and provider and supplier licensing and accreditation should be obligatory for financing. Clinical protocols and rules for inpatient lengths of stay, use of new technologies and equipment, day surgeries, and strict application of essential drug listings all must be updated, modernized, and incorporated into financing requirements.

A key feature as well as a major limitation of social health insurance is that it is employment based. In developing countries, formal employment in the active labor force making health care contributions is small. Due to low contribution levels, pooling of employment-based financial resources is insignificant and insufficient. Health care contributions may be set at low percentages of income for political—not actuarial—reasons (Albania, Bulgaria, FYR Macedonia). Income is sometimes poorly defined, allowing employers and employees to make even lower contributions in real terms. Employers may collude with workers to keep the payroll base low, complementing income with non-cash benefits. Keeping payrolls at minimum salaries to lower health insurance (and pension) contributions means low income taxes and low fiscal revenues. The percentage of health care contributions may not be explicit but left for annual determinations in budget laws (FYR Macedonia), adding uncertainty to labor cost planning and deterring the creation of formal employment. Lack of information systems precludes detection of compliant and delinquent contributors. Arrears from state budget transfers to pay for government contributions (payment of contributions for civil servants or payment of contributions subsidies for the poor) are not uncommon.

Many self-employed individuals do not pay social contributions (a major issue in Chile). Laws call for the self-employed to pay contributions equivalent to the combined percentages set for employers and for employees. Payments, when made, are usually based on income declarations at the legal minimum for fear that this income information could be shared with tax authorities.

Employers tend to favor labor flexibility that encourages part-time and temporary employment, usually under services contracts. In these cases, employers do not have the legal obligation to pay social health insurance contributions (the United States, Costa Rica, Chile). The contracted employee is left to finance his/her own health insurance. This practice results in lower health insurance contributions, if the employees pay any contributions at all. This means less overall financial resources and less coverage for flexible workers, usually women.

HEALTH CARE PROVIDERS AND SUPPLIERS

Health care providers are the ones that make health care happen. Their competence in terms of education, skills, and updated knowledge is fundamental and is therefore strictly regulated by all countries. Health care facilities need accreditation, certification, and licenses. Health care providers require licensing and relicensing based on continuous education. Public or private financing of inadequate providers leads to bad health care, endangers patients, and consolidates a faulty health care system. The same thing applies to suppliers of goods and nonclinical services. Therefore, regulating health care providers and suppliers is as important as regulating health care financing. The two are inextricably intertwined.

Quality of Care Regulation

Strategies to regulate health care providers and quality of care are essential to protect consumers. This is primarily the responsibility of Ministries of Health and, once objective and transparent rules are in place, self-regulatory organizations can play an increasing role. A major problem is licensing and accreditation procedures. Relicensing and reaccreditation of public health care establishments that produce "success rates" close to 100 percent (Mongolia) cast doubt on the legitimacy of the review processes. Also questionable is the upgrading of public hospitals "by decree" from one level to another (Kenya). As for clinical protocols and pathways, in most developing countries they remain outdated. The absence of regulations on day surgeries and how to finance them by social health insurance creates situations in which patients are kept at hospitals for a determined number of days to qualify for social insurance payments for episodes that could be treated in one day (Mongolia). As long as these issues are unresolved, health care financing pays for an excessive number of providers who deliver suboptimal care and for procedures that are not justified under current technological standards. Regulating and enforcing licensing of health care professionals, accreditation of health care establishments, standardization and application of medical protocols, patients' rights, new payment and claim procedures all help ensure quality of care and disqualify from the pool providers who cannot or will not meet new, higher standards.[11]

Another regulatory issue related to quality of care is supervision and control of pharmacies and suppliers of health care goods. Privatization of pharmacies in transition countries, or proliferation of pharmacies in developing countries, has led to a plethora of small, undersupplied pharmacies in cities. Buyers have no way of knowing whether the products sold are legitimate and within their validly labeled shelf life. Many new private diagnostic laboratories are also springing up, and their licensing, accreditation, regulation, inspection, and control are not well developed.

Of increasing concern is the uncontrolled expansion of health care capacity (clinics, hospitals, laboratories, diagnostic centers). In the public sector, capacity-restructuring efforts—often financed by donor and international lending organizations—do not follow rational assessments of need, but succumb to extraneous considerations such as traditions, ethnic issues, regional competition, and vested political and economic interests. Hospitals and clinics with excess capacity are refurbished without any capacity reduction. In the private sector, new hospitals are built without any assessment of need (the Ministries of Health either lack the competence to assess or cannot go against powerful business interests). In some cases, donor countries (Japan) favor financing hospitals (in Bulgaria, Albania, and FYR Macedonia), or upgrading hospitals with operating theaters (Italy) in places where the district has no staff and ancillary materials (Kenya). Thus, many developing countries face a surge in health care capacity in the capital and other cities where physicians and more affluent consumers prefer to live and shortages in the places where the people most in need of care reside.

A subject that receives less attention despite its critical importance for quality of care is the supply of medical devices, equipment, and pharmaceuticals. Dealing with suppliers of health care goods and technology is an area of urgent concern that requires regulation and supervision. The institutional arrangements and regulatory mechanisms differ for medical devices and pharmaceuticals and involve a distinct group of stakeholders, but their critical relevance for the health care sector (public and private) is undisputed. The potential for harm justifies stricter regulatory requirements than those for average consumer goods (Altenstetter 2005).

Self-Regulation

Professional and industry associations develop their own professional and ethi-cal standards. Self-regulatory organizations can provide a public service when objectivity, transparency, and accountability prevail over self-interest. In devel-oping and transition countries, professional associations are closer to "clubs" than to true professional or trade associations.

Self-regulation includes professional standards and protocols, continuing education as a condition for state relicensing requirements, and the ethical sur-veillance of members' professional behavior. Objectivity, integrity, and account-ability must be established before the law entrusts professional and industry associations with self-regulatory powers. Joint state-professional associations for licensing, relicensing, accreditation, medical protocols, and malpractice complaints facilitate professional quality and performance monitoring. Leg-islation and tax incentives can encourage the development of self-regulatory organizations as part of the process of institutional development of a modern public-private health care sector.

To ensure quality and integrity and to protect the public from fraud and abuse, bylaws of professional associations should provide procedures for claims against members for malpractice. Sanctions usually include monetary penalties, suspension, and revocation of licenses.

Cooperation and coordination among public and private health care financing entities and with public regulatory agencies benefit the planning and implemen-tation of health care financing reforms. When encouraged and given a place in health care financing discussions, nongovernmental organizations representing patient concerns (e.g., cancer, diabetes) can make valuable contributions and mobi-lize additional resources for specific targets.

Finally, private specialized regulatory entities for quality assessment, medical equipment, and clinical protocols should be encouraged. Eventually, authority could be delegated to independent technical assessment agencies to issue recom-mendations to complement state entities in dealing with similar issues. The state could adopt these recommendations in formal regulations.

PUBLIC-PRIVATE PARTNERSHIPS

A new regulatory and supervisory issue is the increased presence of public-private partnerships in health care that could include financing and delivery of health care services, building and renovation of health care infrastructure (health centers, clinics, hospitals, laboratories, diagnostic centers), as well as private management of public health programs and establishments. Europe has many examples of various PPP experiences (Austria, Germany, Portugal, and Romania) (Nikolic and Maikisch 2006).

Although private firms have been involved in public service delivery for a long time, the introduction of PPPs in the early 1990s established a mode of public service delivery that redefined the roles of the public and private sectors. Throughout the 1990s and early 2000s, PPP has expanded in terms of the number of countries where it is used and in terms of the number of sectors and projects funded through this partnership as well.

Governments have introduced PPP for various reasons: to improve the value for money in public service delivery projects, or because PPP had the potential of bringing private finance to public service delivery. Although governments increasingly admit that PPP is an instrument to improve value for money, they do not necessarily consider them an additional source of finance. Nevertheless, there is still a lack of clarity about the definition of PPP as well as the relationships between affordability, budgetary limits, and access to private finance.

In many developing countries, consumers rely on a variety of private sector entities, from individual or group for-profit practitioners, clinics and hospitals, and faith-based and nonprofit nongovernmental organizations, as sources of health care goods and services. Until recently, public health care planners at Ministries of Health have not had the private sector as a substantial component in the health care system. A trend toward public-private partnerships has changed this attitude, and Ministries of Health are seeking the private sector participation in public health initiatives, both health care and public health in attaining national health goals.

Working toward PPP in health is a complex endeavor. Public-private partnerships have the potential of being rewarding in terms of innovation, technology, management, and in multiplying the availability and use of resources and expertise. PPP needs adequate policies and regulations, financing, capacity building, behavioral changes, communication, and social marketing. PPP involves strategies among national and local governments, local businesses, local and international NGOs, multinational companies and international donors. Ideally, PPP should lead to long-term sustainability of partnerships and initiatives that strengthen government and private local organizations and transfer knowledge and skills.

In developing countries PPP in health care generates heated debate. Nevertheless, PPP experience with roads and other public infrastructure projects with concessions for private interests to operate, recuperate investments, and make profits are accepted. PPP may become inevitable to maximize the use of scarce public health care resources and to incorporate the private sector in health care projects for the "public good" that can also be good business opportunities.

PPP in health is a policy for improving the quality and cost-effectiveness of public health care infrastructure and services. It includes the financing of capital investments, access to private sector management, and commercial and creative skills and the use of the expertise of the private sector in providing services. PPPs seek long-term and mutually beneficial relationships between public and private sector partners.

For PPP to be successful, however, it has to be based on a convergence of mutually beneficial interests. Clear advantages include reduced spending, improved efficiency from private sector management of both infrastructure and services, technology transfer, gains in performance-based monitoring and incentives,

TABLE 18.2   Opportunities for Public-Private Partnerships in Health Care

Area	Activity
Infrastructure	Engineering and architectural designs, building construction, medical equipment, capital financing
Nonclinical services	Information technology and services, medical equipment maintenance, general maintenance, dietary (food and cafeterias), laundry, cleaning, security, billing and claims management, banking
Primary care	Expanded primary health care services, including clinical and public health interventions (immunization and prevention), pediatrics, adolescent health, maternal and child care, geriatric care
Clinical support services	Laboratory analysis, imaging services (X-rays, MRIs, and CTs), diagnostic tests, dietary-nutrition therapy, rehabilitation
Specialized clinical services	Dialysis, radio therapy, day surgery, cancer screening, orthopedics and ergonomic service, other specialist services
Hospital management	Management of entire hospital or network of hospitals or clinics or components, (administration, financial accounting, public relations, admissions, public and private insurance management)

Source: Adapted from IFC 2007.

and overall quality improvement. The private sector can use its vast financial, human, technological, and managerial resources to enter new avenues of business, serve the public good, and make a profit.

Because of the risks involved, planning should encompass careful review of the allocation of financial risks and rewards, decision-making mechanisms and responsibilities, and the applicable regulatory and contractual frameworks (Nikolic and Maikisch 2006). Ethical and governance issues, as well as conflicts of interests also need to be properly resolved. Badly managed PPPs can invite corruption, misuse of public funds, fraud, and abuse. Thus, workable regulatory and supervisory mechanisms are needed to deal with these difficult issues by balancing the strengths and weaknesses of public and private partners.

Recently, the International Finance Corporation (IFC 2007) specifically addressed the issue of health care services under PPP. The options envisioned are many and cover a variety of potential projects and services (table 18.2).

CONCLUSIONS

As the convergence of public and private interests in health care business increases, new regulatory and supervisory challenges needing attention emerge. The most obvious areas of intervention are related to health care financing and the role of social and voluntary health insurance, mainly prepaid schemes. Another area of equal importance is the effective regulation of health care providers *and* suppliers of health-related goods and services. Finally, the growing interest and the number of projects on public-private partnerships call for innovative regulatory and supervisory frameworks.

ANNEX 18A   ADAPTING ACCEPTED INSURANCE PRINCIPLES TO PRIVATE VOLUNTARY HEALTH INSURANCE

This annex is a summary (with some deviations) of an innovative draft work for a study on supervision of voluntary health insurance by the Insurance and Contractual Savings Unit, Financial Operations and Policy Department, of the World Bank, prepared by Hernán L. Fuenzalida-Puelma and Mónica Cáceres under the supervision of Vijaysekar Kalavakonda. The authors applied the core insurance principles of the International Association of Insurance Supervisors (IAIS) to indemnity and prepaid private health insurance.

The International Association of Insurance Supervisors has developed core insurance principles that are the standard for the insurance industry worldwide (IAIS 2003). The following is an adaptation of those core principles that are of great interest in regulating and supervising voluntary health insurance.

PRINCIPLE 1: *ALL* FORMS OF PRIVATE HEALTH INSURANCE ARE SUPERVISED AND REGULATED INSURANCE FINANCIAL ACTIVITIES. *Private voluntary health insurance, including all prepaid health care financing schemes, is a financial insurance business requiring public (state) supervision and regulation.*

Private health insurance is either indemnity or prepaid. *Indemnity health insurance* is under the general insurance legislation and subject to supervision and regulation by the insurance supervisor. It can be provided (a) by insurance companies involved in the exclusive business of health insurance as a separate line of insurance (Mexico, Turkey); (b) as a rider to life insurance policies (in almost all countries); and (c) as part of general insurance (India). *Prepaid health insurance* is a special form of health insurance that is different from indemnity insurance. It can be (a) provided as a formal form of insurance by specialized insurers (health maintenance organizations in the United States or in Chile prepaid health insurance schemes [ISAPRES in Spanish]) under special laws on prepaid health care financing (the United States and Latin America), and it is subject to supervision and regulation usually by a special supervisor; (b) conducted on a small scale by physicians and physician group practices and primary health care clinics and ambulatories (Mongolia); (c) carried out on a larger scale by major hospitals and their networks of health care providers (India); and (d) supplied by third-party administrators that are de facto financiers and intermediaries of health care (India). These last three forms of prepaid insurance are usually unlegislated, unsupervised, and unregulated. The principle calls for all forms of health insurance, indemnity and prepaid, to be considered financial insurance activities and to be properly legislated, regulated, and supervised.

PRINCIPLE 2: CONDITIONS FOR EFFECTIVE SUPERVISION. *Supervision of voluntary health insurance relies upon explicit policies, an adequate institutional and legal framework, and an efficient financial market.*

Some jurisdictions have integrated into the health care financing system various forms of prepaid health insurance with the corresponding legislation, and legal and institutional framework for supervision. In the same jurisdictions, however, some prepaid and insurance schemes coexist unlicensed, unsupervised, and unregulated (Argentina, Bolivia, Chile). In most countries a systematic effort is needed to define the role, extent, and supervision of indemnity and prepaid health insurance. In most cases, indemnity health insurance will remain under the mandate of the insurance supervisor. The question is who should be the prepaid insurance supervisor. The trend is to have a separate supervisor (Chile, the Slovak Republic). The principle states that effective supervision of all types of health insurance is a necessary condition to ensure compliance with standards on solvency, capital and reserves investments, payments, and prudential norms.

PRINCIPLE 3: SUPERVISION OBJECTIVES. *The objectives of voluntary health insurance supervision are formally and clearly defined.*

Supervision promotes efficient, fair, transparent, and financially sound markets for voluntary health insurance to the advantage and protection of insurers and beneficiaries. The legal framework should unambiguously stipulate the mandate, scope, competence, and responsibilities of the supervisory authority. Publicly and clearly defined supervisory objectives foster transparency, accountability, and competition and raise the prominence of the supervisory authority. The principle calls for legislation to clearly define the objectives, scope, competence, functions, powers, or attributions of health insurance supervision.

PRINCIPLE 4: SUPERVISORY COOPERATION AND INFORMATION SHARING. *The supervisory authority cooperates and shares information with other relevant supervisors and public entities subject to confidentiality and other legal requirements.*

Information sharing among supervisory agencies helps to avoid contradictions, ambiguities, and unnecessary duplication. Formal agreements among supervisors (financial, health, labor, and among the insurance supervisors if the prepaid insurance has a different supervisor) facilitate prompt and appropriate supervisory action. Cooperation among financial supervisors, or intracooperation in unified financial supervisors (Estonian Financial Supervisory Authority, the Slovak Republic's Financial Surveillance Authority, the United Kingdom's Financial Services Authority), make it possible to harmonize fit and proper standards for managers, capital, and solvency; compliance with prudential and contractual regulations; prevention of fraud, money laundering, and the financing of terrorism. Coordination with Ministries of Health is of utmost importance because the ministries usually regulate the qualifications of health care providers and nonclinical suppliers (materials, drugs, equipment) through licensing, certification, and accreditation. These ministries also define clinical protocols and standards and thus influence the type of health care goods and services that may be included in health insurance policies and prepaid plans.

PRINCIPLE 5: LICENSING. *Voluntary health insurers must be licensed before they can operate within a jurisdiction. The requirements for licensing are clear, objective, and public.*

A *license* is the formal authorization given to indemnity and prepaid health insurance companies to engage in the business of the corresponding health insurance. In many jurisdictions, prepaid insurance is unlicensed, unregulated, and unsupervised. The reason may be that prepaid health insurance is not acknowledged in the legislation (Egypt, Lithuania); only indemnity insurance is recognized. Sometimes, to avoid stringent insurance requirements (minimum capital, reserves, solvency margins), prepaid schemes are designed and marketed without license or regulation (India). Argentina and Bolivia do not have legal licensing requirements for prepaid insurance. Previous registration with the Ministry of Health or another health authority may be required. Colombia and Chile require previous authorization from the National Health Superintendence and the Health Superintendence, respectively. All domestic and foreign entities should be subject to licensing and supervision (both financial and health supervision as appropriate).

PRINCIPLE 6: REPORTING TO SUPERVISORS AND OFF-SITE MONITORING. *The supervisory authority receives necessary information to conduct effective off-site monitoring and to evaluate the condition of each voluntary health insurer as well as the state of the corresponding market.*

The supervisory authority decides on the content, form, obligation, and frequency of the information required, such as quarterly financial reports to assess solvency, risk-control measures, asset and liability management, actuarial reports, and annual audit opinion. The authority also decides whether reinsurance is necessary. Requirements should balance the need for information against the administrative costs of supplying it. All licensed entities must file periodic reports, which provide the basis for off-site analysis. Periodic review of reporting requirements can eliminate unnecessary information or information for which the supervisory authority lacks the capacity to analyze.

PRINCIPLE 7: ENFORCEMENT AND SANCTIONS. *The supervisory authority enforces corrective action and imposes sanctions for infringements of clear, objective, publicly disclosed criteria.*

The supervisory authority must have the powers, range of actions, and enforcement tools to impose timely and effective remedies. Legislative and regulatory powers may include restricting business activities; stopping or withholding approval; requiring the writing of new indemnity contracts or prepaid plans; stopping practices that are unsafe, unsound, or improper; putting assets in trust or restricting disposal of those assets; suspending or revoking licenses; removing directors and managers; and barring individuals from the voluntary health insurance business. Punitive sanctions against insurers or individuals may be appropriate in some cases. Decisions by the supervisory authority may be appealed through internal resolution procedures or by resort to the courts.

PRINCIPLE 8: TERMINATION AND EXIT FROM THE MARKET. *Legal and regulatory frameworks define options for insurers' orderly exit from the marketplace. These instruments define and establish the criteria and procedure for dealing with insolvency. The legal framework gives priority to the protection of policyholders and beneficiaries in case of dissolution.*

The supervisor must determine objectively, technically, and fairly whether a licensed insurer is no longer financially viable, and it may require a takeover or merger of the entity. When all other measures fail, the supervisory authority should be empowered to close or assist in the closure of the entity in difficulty. The legislation should establish the priority of claims by individuals as policy-holders and as beneficiaries of prepaid schemes relative to those of other stake-holders such as employees or the fiscal authorities.

PRINCIPLE 9: RISK ASSESSMENT AND MANAGEMENT. *The supervisory authority must continuously evaluate the range of risks facing voluntary health insurers and their ability to assess and manage them.*

Private health insurers have to identify, understand, and manage market risks relative to the complexity, size, nature, and type of the health insurance business. Risk assessment–risk management is an ongoing process that ranges from routine preventive measures to institutional and financial treatment and rehabilitation. Prepaid insurance faces (a) financial risk and (b) services risk. Unlike other types of insurance, it does not necessarily depend on external, sudden, and fortuitous events although accidents do happen and sudden strokes are not uncommon. Private health insurance, however, faces risks common to any insurer: investment risks (credit, financial market, liquidity), technical risks (premiums, prepayments, reserves), and operational, legal, organizational, and conglomerate issues, includ-ing contagion, correlation, and counterparty risks. Supervisors should require risk-monitoring and control mechanisms and develop prudential regulations and requirements to contain these risks and to ensure that practices are appropriate and enhanced. Corporate boards of directors or governing bodies bear the ulti-mate responsibility for best practices and risk management.

PRINCIPLE 10: HEALTH CARE FINANCIAL ACTIVITY. *Voluntary health insur-ance is a type of financial risk-taking activity. The supervisory authority requires insurers to evaluate and manage the risks they underwrite, including commensurable reinsur-ance if indicated and to set an adequate level for premiums or prepaid contributions.*

Insurers take on risks and manage them with techniques (including pooling and diversification) following underwriting policy approved and monitored by the board of directors or governing body of the insurance company. This allows knowl-edge of the risks and calculation of premiums and prepaid subscriptions to finance coverage while making a profit. Insurers use actuarial, statistical, or financial meth-ods to estimate liabilities and to determine premiums and prepaid subscriptions. Undercalculating liabilities can be adverse if not fatal. To mitigate and diversify risks, insurers use reinsurance as a tool for transferring risk. Insurers should have an appropriate, board-approved reinsurance strategy for the overall risk profile and capitalization as part of the overall underwriting strategy. Prepaid schemes do not necessarily need reinsurance, but the supervisor may consider it prudent to require catastrophic reinsurance in some cases. This may require amending existing gen-eral insurance laws to allow prepaid health insurance companies to reinsure, if the law of prepaid insurance does not include provisions on reinsurance.

PRINCIPLE 11: LIABILITIES. *The supervisory authority requires voluntary health insurers to comply with standards for establishing adequate technical provisions and other liabilities and to make allowance for any necessary reinsurance. The supervisory authority has both the power and the ability to assess the adequacy of the technical provisions and to require provisions to be increased.*

Sufficient technical provisions or amounts set aside on the balance sheet to meet voluntary insurance obligations is an essential insurance feature for a sound capital adequacy and solvency regime. Legal provisions should require sound accounting based on accepted actuarial principles and allow the supervisory authority to define and issue standards for technical provisions, including provisions for claims, claims incurred but not reported; unearned premiums, unexpired risks and other liabilities; and other technical provisions as may be determined. The supervisory authority must have the power and the ability to verify compliance and the power to require reinsurance. In some jurisdictions this may necessitate changes in the insurance legislation allowing prepaid insurers to seek reinsurance. Jurisdictions could also require: (a) technical reserves or financial guarantees (Chile) equivalent to outstanding obligations regarding claims and payments to health care providers; and (b) technical reserves for unearned premiums, outstanding claims, unreported claims, and other reserves (Mexico). The supervisory authority should issue standards on general limits for valuation of the amounts recoverable under reinsurance arrangements for solvency purposes, based on what is ultimately collected and the real transfer of risk; sound accounting principles for booking amounts recoverable under reinsurance arrangements; and credit for technical provisions for recoverable amounts.

PRINCIPLE 12: INVESTMENTS. *The supervisory authority requires voluntary health insurers to comply with standards on investment activities, including investment policy, asset mix, valuation, diversification, asset-liability matching, and risk management, as appropriate to the type of health insurance. These standards address restrictions in their use and disclosure requirements, as well as internal controls and monitoring.*

Investments must be managed in a sound and prudent manner. Investment portfolios carry a range of investment-related risks that might affect the coverage of technical provisions and the solvency margin. Voluntary insurers need to identify, measure, report, and control the main risks. In doing so, they are to address at least the mix and diversification by investment type; limits or restrictions on the amount that may be held in particular types of financial instruments, property, and receivables; safekeeping and custody of assets; appropriate matching of assets and liabilities; liquidity level; and other determinants of risk. In many developing countries risk is concentrated due to the limited number of suitable domestic investment options in the capital markets. The supervisory authority needs to set standards for investment requirements and have the ability to assess risks and their potential impact on technical provisions and solvency. The detailed formulation of investment management policy and internal risk-control methodology is, in the end, the responsibility of the board of directors or governing body.

PRINCIPLE 13: CAPITAL ADEQUACY AND SOLVENCY. *The supervisory authority requires voluntary health insurers to comply with the prescribed solvency regime. This regime includes capital adequacy requirements and suitable forms of capital that enable the absorption of significant unforeseen losses.*

Capital adequacy requirements are part of a solvency regime. The solvency regime addresses consistently the valuation of liabilities: technical provisions and the margins contained therein; quality, liquidity, and valuation of assets; matching of assets and liabilities; suitable forms of capital; and capital adequacy requirements. It also considers the sufficiency of technical provisions to cover all expected and some unexpected claims and expenses and the sufficiency of capital to absorb significant unexpected losses not covered by the technical provisions on the risks for which capital is explicitly required, as well as additional capital to absorb losses from risks not explicitly identified. To protect policyholders and beneficiaries from undue loss, a solvency regime establishes minimum capital adequacy requirements, as well as solvency control levels, as indicators for early supervisory action. Reinsurance, when required for capital adequacy and solvency, should consider the effectiveness of the risk transfer and make allowance for the likely security of the reinsurance counterparty. Experience with prepayments shows that the same principles apply concerning requirements of capital adequacy and solvency. Mexico requires minimum paid capital, minimum guarantee capital that has to be invested at all times, and a solvency margin. Colombia requires minimum corporate capital and solvency margin. Chile requires a minimum capital to total liabilities ratio equal to or exceeding 0.3 and a liquidity ratio of liquid assets to current liabilities equal to or greater than 0.8. The legislation allows a period of regularization when minimum capital and solvency levels diminish.

PRINCIPLE 14: CONSUMER PROTECTION. *The supervisory authority sets minimum requirements for voluntary health and intermediaries in dealing with policyholders and beneficiaries, including foreign insurers selling products across national borders. This includes provision of timely, complete, and relevant information to consumers before a contract is entered into and up to the time all contractual obligations have been satisfied.*

Supervision of insurers and intermediaries (mainly marketing intermediaries) ensures actual and potential policyholders and beneficiaries fair and accurate treatment with reliable and prompt information and responses to queries. This includes contracts, value of premiums (indemnity insurance) and subscriptions (prepaid), and the terms and conditions for their application. Standardized policies and prepayment plans, minimum benefits, and disclosure requirements allow consumers to compare products and make informed decisions. Legislation should allow the supervisory authority to issue general instructions on the drafting of contracts to ensure clarity, facilitate understanding, avoid ambiguous interpretation, and facilitate supervision. Clear, explicit, and expeditious claim-resolution processes ensure fair treatment of consumers and foster consumer confidence. Experience with ombudsman offices as a bridge in resolving complaints quickly and effectively has been positive in

Australia, Germany, India, Poland, the Netherlands, Spain, Switzerland, the United Kingdom, and the United States.

PRINCIPLE 15: INFORMATION DISCLOSURE AND MARKET TRANSPARENCY. *The supervisory authority requires voluntary health insurers to make timely disclosures of relevant information to give stakeholders a clear view of their business activities and financial position and to facilitate the understanding of the risks to which they are exposed.*

Public disclosure of reliable, comprehensive, and timely information facilitates stakeholders' understanding of the financial position and the risks to which insurers are subject, regardless of whether or not they are publicly traded (stock market). Disclosure instruments include financial statements with quantitative and qualitative information on financial position and performance and a description of the basis, methods, and assumptions upon which information is prepared, together with comments on the impact of any changes, on risk exposures and how they are managed, and on management and corporate governance. Insurers should be required to produce audited financial statements, at least annually, and make them available to stakeholders and the public.

NOTES

1. Insurance companies are licensed under insurance legislation by the insurance supervisory authority to conduct indemnity health insurance, which can be offered under life or general insurance. Health insurance contracts are called *health insurance policies,* and payments are called *premiums.* Prepaid health insurance is provided by companies formed under special legislation, and the companies are licensed by a special supervisory authority. Health insurance contracts are called *health plans,* and payments are called *contributions.* This is the case in Argentina, Chile, Colombia, Mexico, and Peru and in the case of health maintenance organizations (HMOs) in the United States. In many other countries (the Arab Republic of Egypt, Mongolia), the absence of social prepaid health insurance legislation and supervision leads to unregulated and unsupervised voluntary health insurance business.

2. Today indemnity insurance is not a significant source of health care financing.

3. *Regulation* entails the issuing and enforcement of norms and procedures to expand the meaning of laws. *Supervision* is the act of overseeing, inspecting, and ensuring that norms and procedures are followed. Regulation and supervision are two sides of the same coin. In this chapter, regulation and supervision are used interchangeably.

4. *Regulation* is the act of controlling through delegated normative authority to issue, interpret, and enforce rules and norms (decrees, orders, instructions, decisions, directives, and regulations proper) issued by a regulatory/supervisory authority to subject certain actions to governing principles and procedures that allow, limit, prohibit, direct, or command. It includes administrative and judicial interpretation. Regulations need to respond to economic and social needs, and to the market dynamics related to the regulated activity. Regulations are subject to administrative and judicial review.

5. In many countries, more for ideological reasons, voluntary private health insurance is defined as supplemental or additional to the goods and services included under

mandatory health insurance. Comprehensive private health insurance is understood to mean implicitly allowing opting out from the mandatory system. A good principle is not to allow opting out from the mandatory health care system. The experience in Chile shows how detrimental for the mandatory health insurance systems this counter-solidarity policy is (Fuenzalida-Puelma 2002).

6. Ministries of Health should not be the supervisors of health insurance, not even of social health insurance. They lack financial expertise, and their tendency to influence management and resource-allocation decisions is too evident (Georgia). In Costa Rica, officially the Ministry of Health supervises the Caja Costarricense del Seguro Social, but in practice, the agency enjoys substantial autonomy, controls its own finances, and has independent political support (Cercone and Pacheco 2008). In Chile, the National Health Fund (FONASA) is supervised and regulated by the Health Superintendence, although the Ministry of Health and the Ministry of Finance have considerable influence and control. FONASA is effectively subordinated to the Ministry of Health and lacks a board of directors (Bitrán, Escobar, and Farah 2008).

7. Selective contracting with a limited number of providers to supply certain agreed-upon goods and services seeks competent and quality health providers and suppliers of goods and other services to potentially lower costs, monitor quality, and increase access to services in underserved areas, and secure an appropriate number of providers in areas in which there are too many providers. Selective contracting either by social or voluntary insurance requires competence, qualified staff, and quality control measures.

8. Capital investments in public facilities should be financed separately.

9. This legal instrument could be a basic health law, a health care law, or a social health insurance law. What is relevant is to have a legal definition specific to the realm of health care for both the public and the private sectors.

10. Sick leave abuses and fraud are frequent in developing and transition countries and impose a substantial financial burden on efforts to rationalize health care financing.

11. An excellent document to consult is Norwegian Board of Health Supervision (2002).

REFERENCES

Afifi, N.H., R. Busse, and A. Harding. 2003. "Regulation of Health Services." In *Private Participation in Health Services*, ed. April Harding and Alexander S. Preker, 219–334. Washington, DC: World Bank.

Altenstetter, Christa. 2005. "International Collaboration on Medical Device Regulation: Issues, Problems and Stakeholders." In *Commercialization of Health Care: Global and Local Dynamics and Policy Responses*, ed. M. Mackintosh and M. Koivusalo, 170–86. London: Palgrave.

Banoob, Samir N. 1994. "Private Financing—Health Care Reform in Central and Eastern Europe." *World Health Forum* 15: 329–34. http://whqlibdoc.who.int/whf/1994/vol15-no4/WHF_1994_15(4)_p329-334.pdf.

Bitrán, Ricardo, Liliana Escobar, and Claudio Farah. 2008. "Governing a Hybrid Mandatory Health Insurance: The Case of Chile." In *Governing Mandatory Health Insurance*, ed. William Savedoff and Pablo Gottret, 161–202. Washington, DC: World Bank.

Cercone, James, and José Pacheco. 2008. "Costly Success: An Integrated Health Insurer in Costa Rica." In *Governing Mandatory Health Insurance,* ed. William Savedoff and Pablo Gottret, 69–99. Washington, DC: World Bank.

Colombo, Francesca, and Nicole Tapay. 2004. *Private Insurance in OECD Countries: The Benefits and Costs for Individuals in Health Systems.* Paris: Organisation for Economic Co-operation and Development. www.oecd.org/.../0,3343,en_2649_34629_2088432_1_1_1_1,00.html.

Feeley, Frank G. 2002. "Regulatory Environment for Microinsurance and Reinsurance." *Social Reinsurance: A New Approach to Community Health Financing,* ed. David M. Dror and Alexander S. Preker, 267–76. Washington, DC: World Bank; Geneva, Switzerland: International Labour Office.

———. 2006. "Law and Regulation." In *Spending Wisely: Buying Health Services for the Poor,* ed. Alexander S. Preker and John C. Langenbrunner, 359–373. Washington, DC: World Bank.

Fuenzalida-Puelma, Hernán L. 2002. "Health Care Reform in Central and Eastern Europe and the former Soviet Union." Budapest, Local Government and Public Service Reform Initiative, Open Society Institute.

Fuenzalida-Puelma, Hernán L., Vijay Kalavakonda, and Mónica Cáceres. 2007. "Financial and Other Regulatory Challenges in Low-Income Countries." In *Private Voluntary Health Insurance in Developing Countries,* ed. Alexander S. Preker, Richard M. Scheffler, and Mark C. Bassett, 325–34. Washington, DC: World Bank.

Harding, April, and Alexander Preker, eds. 2003. *Private Participation in Health Services.* Washington, DC: World Bank.

IAIS (International Association of Insurance Supervisors). 2003. *Insurance Core Principles and Methodology.* http://www.iaisweb.org/__temp/Insurance_core_principles_and_methodology.pdf.

IFC (International Finance Corporation). 2007. "Issues in PPPs in Health Care." IFC Advisory Services, Background paper prepared for Public-Private Partnerships in Infrastructure Days Conference, June 7–8, Washington, DC. http://info.worldbank.org/etools/PPPI-Portal/2007PPPI/sessions.htm.

———. 2008. "The Business of Health in Africa: Partnering with the Private Sector to Improve People's Lives." Washington, DC.

ILO (International Labour Office). 2008. "Social Health Protection: An ILO Strategy towards Universal Access to Health Care." Social Security Policy Briefings, Paper 1, Geneva, Switzerland.

Jesse, Maris. 2008. "Governance of the Health System, Health Insurance Fund and Hospitals in Estonia—Opportunities to Improve Performance." World Health Organization, Europe, Copenhagen. http://www.who.it/document/e91376.pdf.

Jost, Timothy Stoltzfus. 2009. "The Regulation of Private Health Insurance." National Academy of Social Insurance, National Academy of Public Administration, Robert Wood Johnson Foundation. http://ssrn.com/abstract=1340092.

Lagenbrunner, John C., and Xingzhu Liu. 2005. "How to Pay? Understanding and Using Payment Incentives." In *Spending Wisely: Buying Health Services for the Poor,* ed. Alexander S. Preker and John C. Langenbrunner, 89–106. Washington, DC: World Bank.

National Public Health Partnership. 2002. *The Role of Local Government in Public Health Regulation.* Melbourne, Australia. www.dhs.vic.gov.au/nphp/publications/a_z.htm.

Nikolic, Irina, and Harald Maikisch. 2006. "Public-Private Partnerships and Collaboration in the Health Sector: An Overview with Case Studies of Recent European Experiences." HNP Discussion Paper, World Bank, Washington, DC.

North, D.C. 1990. *Institutions, Institutional Change and Economic Performance.* Cambridge, UK: Cambridge University Press.

Norwegian Board of Health Supervision. 2002. "Quality in Health Care—The Role of Government in Supervision and Monitoring in Norway." Norwegian Board of Health Report Series, Report 8/2002, Oslo.

OECD (Organisation for Economic Co-operation and Development). 2004. "Proposal for a Taxonomy of Health Insurance: OECD Study on Private Health Insurance," Paris.

Ogus, A.I. 1994. *Regulation, Legal Form and Economic Theory.* New York: Oxford University Press.

Preker, Alexander S. 2003. "The Evolution of Health Insurance in Developing Countries." In *Private Voluntary Health Insurance in Development: Friend or Foe?* ed. Alexander S. Preker, Richard M. Scheffler, and Mark C. Bassett, 1–22. Washington, DC: World Bank.

———. 2004. "Strategic Purchasing of Priority Health Services under the New National Health Insurance Scheme in Ghana." World Bank, Washington, DC.

Savedoff, William D. 2008. "Governing Mandatory Health Insurance: Concepts, Framework, and Cases." In *Governing Mandatory Health Insurance,* ed. William D. Savedoff and Pablo Gottret, 13–48. Washington, DC: World Bank.

Sekhri, Neelam, and William D. Savedoff. 2006. "Regulating Private Health Insurance to Serve the Public Interest: Policy Issues for Developing Countries." *International Journal of Health Planning and Management* 21: 357–92.

WHO (World Health Organization). 2000. *The World Health Report 2000—Health Systems: Improving Performance.* Geneva, Switzerland: WHO.

World Bank. 1993. *World Development Report 1993: Investing in Health.* Washington, DC: World Bank; New York: Oxford University Press.

Zweifel, P., and Mark V. Pauly. 2007. "Market Outcomes, Regulation, and Policy Recommendations." In *Private Voluntary Health Insurance in Development: Friend or Foe?* ed. Alexander S. Preker, Richard M. Scheffler, and Mark C. Bassett, 115–45. Washington, DC: World Bank.

CHAPTER 19

Implementing Change

*Hong Wang, Kimberly Switlick-Prose, Christine Ortiz,
Catherine Connor, Beatriz Zurita, Chris Atim, and François Diop*

This chapter leads policy makers and health insurance designers through a series of management steps to be taken when introducing and scaling up health insurance.[1] These steps are intended to deepen planners' understanding of health insurance concepts, identify challenges, help them design and implement solutions, and define realistic steps for the development and scale-up of equitable, efficient, and sustainable health insurance schemes.

INTRODUCTION

The World Health Assembly of 2005 called for all health systems to move toward universal coverage, defined as "access to adequate health care for all at an affordable price." A crucial aspect in achieving this goal is to develop a financial risk-pooling system that can provide income and cross-subsidies against risk in health systems in which ability to pay determines financing contributions and use of services is according to need for care. For this, user fees and other out-of-pocket payments must be reduced; and the prepayment level should be increased. To achieve these goals, health insurance has been promoted as the major financing mechanism.

Many high-income countries, as well as some middle-income countries, have achieved universal coverage by introducing various health care financing mechanisms, such as tax-based financing or social health insurance schemes or both. However, little progress has been made in low-income countries. In Africa, several countries have already spent precious time, money, and effort on health insurance initiatives—Ethiopia, Ghana, Kenya, Nigeria, Rwanda, and Tanzania, to name but a few. Similarly to other low-income countries, however, many of those schemes, both public and private, cover only a small proportion of the population, with the poor less likely to be covered than the better off. Although both tax-based financing and social health insurance schemes do exist in low-income countries, the beneficiaries (breadth) or service coverage (depth) or both are rather limited. Most people still have to pay for their health care out of pocket, and illness pushes many of them into poverty. Recognizing the feasibility issue in the introduction of tax-based or social health schemes, community-based health insurance (CBHI) has been introduced or reintroduced in low-income countries as an alternative financing mechanism for the poor in the past two decades. Many low-income countries still face tremendous challenges in developing CBHI in their countries.

Despite the many benefits that health insurance offers, the journey to implement insurance and achieve those benefits is challenging, long, and risky (table 19.1). Policy makers and technicians that support development and scale-up of health insurance must figure out how to increase their country's financing capacity, extend health insurance coverage to the hard-to-reach populations, expand benefits packages, and improve the performance of existing schemes.

TABLE 19.1   Potential Benefits and Risks in Health Insurance Development

Potential benefits	Potential risks
1. Protect households from impoverishment due to high out-of-pocket health spending	• Health system could emphasize expensive curative care over primary and preventive services if insurance schemes do not view primary and preventive services as a way to minimize health insurance costs over the long term
2. Increase access to and use of services where payment is normally required at the time of need	• Institutions and systems that are not ready to handle the burden of insurance implementation could find the process unworkable or highly inefficient and costly
3. Influence provider and consumer behavior to improve quality, efficiency, and effectiveness	• Some provider payment methods do not have positive effects on quality, efficiency, and effectiveness, and their limitations may outweigh the cost of implementing them
4. Harness private providers to address national health goals and objectives	• Low payment levels might not attract quality providers • Insurance agency could lack capacity to ensure quality of private providers • Lack of cost controls could bankrupt the insurance fund • Failure to pay private providers on time could lead to frustration
5. Generate additional and more stable resources for health	• Resources flowing through health insurance schemes could make governments feel free to reallocate general budget resources away from health, leaving the health sector with unchanged or fewer resources • Insurance funds without adequate oversight and accountability can become easy targets for corruption • General public investment could crowd out individual investment and reduce individual responsibility in health care financing
6. Expand resources for and access to priority health services for disadvantaged populations	• Benefits could favor the better off because they are easier to reach with insurance • Benefits to the poor could become false promises if insurance is not purposefully designed to target the poor and if financing is inadequate
7. Assist in redistribution of resources for health to address socioeconomic and geographic inequities	• Countries may launch a broad, but expensive, benefits package that is financially unsustainable and later be forced to limit coverage and thus dash expectations • Redistributive schemes may alienate higher-income groups who subsidize the redistribution of resources

Source: Authors.

DESIGN ELEMENTS FOR A HEALTH INSURANCE SCHEME

The eight design elements (DEs) for a health insurance scheme, and the relationships among them, are depicted in figure 19.1. Each design element is then summarized to give policy makers a concise checklist for design and eventual evaluation of their own insurance programs.

Overarching all is feasibility in terms of the country's political, economic, and sociocultural environment. Monitoring and evaluation should form the foundation. Financing, population coverage, benefits package, provider engagement, organizational structure, and operation are six other components. Although these design elements sequentially help policy makers and other stakeholders work on each element step-by-step, all the elements are intertwined. Stakeholders involved in the design process must be mindful of this interconnectedness, because every decision affects multiple elements simultaneously.

Design Element 1: Feasibility of Health Insurance

DE 1 focuses policy makers' attention on building capacities to identify major political, financial, and sociocultural prerequisites to set up or scale up health insurance in their countries; assess gaps in and obstacles to health insurance development within the political, financial, and sociocultural context of their countries; and plan for laying the groundwork to address these gaps and obstacles.

FIGURE 19.1   Design Elements for a Health Insurance Scheme

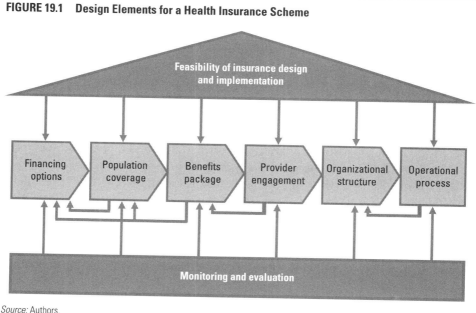

Source: Authors.

It also begins to prepare them for health insurance development or scale-up, including the political process, financing strategies, and sociocultural issues.

Designing and implementing national health insurance is as much a political process as a technical one. Stakeholder views and support determine how a country addresses all seven of the next design elements and overall feasibility. The introduction of insurance in developing countries involves multiple government ministries, health care providers, consumers, employers, and donors. Policy makers and technical experts must work together to manage expectations, ensure decision making based on facts and technical analysis, and find common ground among competing interest groups.

Political mapping is one of the techniques to be used in the political feasibility analysis. This analysis can help discover how much political support there is for different aspects of health insurance design and implementation. It can also help identify where support is lacking and what strategies may be necessary to build consensus.

A country's financial capacity for funding health insurance depends on its current and expected economic status (GDP per capita), the size of the formal sector economy that can be taxed or contribute to employer-based health insurance, the opportunity to find efficiencies in the current health system, and the current level of household health expenditures, some of which might be tapped to finance health insurance. Ministries of Finance and Health must work together to determine the government's capacity and commitment to finance health insurance. Economists, actuaries, and accountants can inform this process by analyzing the country's financial capacity and insurance design under different scenarios. Health insurance financing is discussed in detail in DE 2. In addition, financial capacity is also a function of the country's organizational and operational capacity to collect, pool, and spend funds[2] efficiently and effectively (discussed under DEs 6 and 7).

The feasibility of a particular health insurance design is also affected by ethical, behavioral, and sociocultural dimensions. For example, community-based health insurance is more likely to be feasible in a country where ethnic or geographic groups demonstrate high social cohesion. A social health insurance scheme may be more appropriate for a country with larger numbers of formal sector employees or with a strong sense of national solidarity among the population.

Cultural norms can strongly affect the ultimate success of an insurance program. In some societies, people believe that planning for a bad situation, such as ill health, may bring bad luck. Popular beliefs vary greatly as to whether social or economic equity is an important national objective and the extent to which caring for the poor and the sick should be the responsibility of the population at large. These strongly held social beliefs set the boundaries of what is culturally feasible for a national health insurance program.

Service availability and provider capacity affect feasibility at the following two levels:

- The physical presence of health workers and facilities near enough to target populations and their capacity to deliver quality services covered by insurance (do they have the skills, equipment, and supplies?). If policy makers fail to address gaps in service availability and quality, they risk making existing inequities worse if insurance funds flow to the providers already set up in wealthier, urban areas.

- Providers' willingness to participate in the insurance program. Providers may not be willing to participate if, for example, the insurance payments are perceived as too low, patient volume increases significantly while health worker salaries stay the same, or insurance reduces user-fee income (formal or informal). In Vietnam, providers began refusing to provide services to enrollees in the insurance scheme because the reimbursement rates were much lower than their actual costs, and providers were losing money servicing the insured. In Ghana, the combination of high patient volume and flat income led health workers to strike in 2005. DEs 5 (provider engagement), 6 (organizational structure), and 7 (operations) all offer ways to address these issues.

Typically, the legislative and executive branches of the government must work together to set broad policies for the insurance scheme(s) regarding financing, population coverage, and identification of a body to manage the insurance scheme (a line ministry or a semiautonomous body such as an insurance fund). The insurance scheme authority can then define details such as the benefits package, quality standards for providers, beneficiary eligibility, standards for beneficiary communications, and so forth; or delegate these details to be promulgated by the insurance scheme.

Feasibility of health insurance depends significantly upon a country's existing operational capacity to execute a variety of different technical functions, including actuarial analysis, marketing and communications, enrolment, membership management, collection of funds, claims administration, quality assurance, and financial management. Health insurance often falters because of operational challenges: claims are not paid on time and providers drop out; beneficiaries do not fully understand their benefits and do not access services; or information systems are slow and weak, so nobody knows the insurance fund's balance or its real liabilities. While it is not a prerequisite that a country have all operational functions in place (no country in the world has them completely figured out), administration and management processes need to be taken into consideration while designing and implementing an insurance scheme. These issues are addressed further in DEs 6 and 7.

Design Element 2: Choice of Financing Mechanisms

DE 2 is intended to help policy makers understand the different mechanisms for financing health insurance and the many ways countries combine them; appreciate that health insurance does not automatically improve financial protection and access for the poor; and understand the strengths and challenges of each financing mechanism, particularly as related to the country's health system and health financing goals. Four major health insurance alternatives are discussed: national health insurance, social health insurance, private voluntary health insurance, and community-based health insurance.

- National health insurance (NHI) is government-managed insurance financed through general taxation, usually with mandatory coverage for all citizens. Often, the government directly provides health services as well. The best-known example is the British National Health Service (NHS). This approach is also known as the Beveridge model originating from the Beveridge report in 1942.

- Social health insurance[3] (SHI) generally has four features: independent or quasi-independent management of insurance funds (such as by social security institutes or sickness funds); compulsory earmarked payroll contributions; a direct link between the contributions and defined medical benefits for the insured population; and concept of social solidarity. Social health insurance is sometimes referred to as the Bismarck model reflecting its origin in Germany. Countries such as Germany, Colombia, and the Republic of Korea have extended SHI from employer-based schemes to include other populations, such as, with government financing, low-income groups.

- Private voluntary health insurance (PVHI) is distributed by private for-profit or not-for-profit companies, and premiums are usually based on the purchaser's risk rather than on his or her ability to pay. This insurance is voluntary and can be purchased by either an individual or a group. It can provide primary coverage or it may be purchased to supplement another health insurance policy ("secondary health insurance"). Unregulated PVHI can lead to escalating costs, competition for healthy, wealthy populations (cream skimming), and avoidance of sick, poor populations. However, well-regulated PVHI can induce competition among health care providers, leading to improved efficiency and quality and better customer service.

- Community-based health insurance (CBHI) is not-for-profit private health insurance that is based on an ethic of mutual aid among people in the informal sector and rural areas. CBHI pools members' premium payments into a collective fund that is managed by the members. Several governments have embraced CBHI with national policies and administrative support (e.g., Ghana and Rwanda). Evidence indicates that CBHI schemes can effectively reach marginalized populations and increase access to health care for low-income rural and informal sector workers (Wang and Pielemeier 2012).

Because the population is the source of all of a country's funds, except for external assistance and natural resources, low-income countries face real constraints to raising revenues to finance health care in general and health insurance specifically. Low-income countries are more likely to have high fertility rates and thus a majority of the population under 15 years of age. This is referred to as a high "dependency ratio" when there are many dependents (children and elderly who cost more than they contribute) compared with the working-age people who typically contribute more than they cost.

Government tax revenues on average are about 15 percent of GDP in low-income countries, compared with more than 20 percent among higher-income countries. If all countries in Sub-Saharan Africa were able to meet the Abuja target and allocate 15 percent of government financing to health, 23 countries still would not reach US$34 per capita health spending—the cost of a basic package of essential health interventions, as estimated by the Commission on Macroeconomics and Health (CMH) in 2001. A projection analysis shows that even under optimistic assumptions about economic growth, population growth, and tax revenue collection, most countries in Sub-Saharan Africa will not reach US$34 per capita even by 2020 (Atim et al. 2008).

Financing feasibility is also limited by the size of the formal sector economy from which taxes and payroll contributions can be collected. Generating health financing is usually easier in countries that are more urbanized, where higher population density facilitates registration and revenue collection.

Given low levels of government health spending, it is not surprising to see high out-of-pocket health spending in low-income countries. Heavy dependence on out-of-pocket payments is strongly correlated with households' experiencing catastrophic health expenditures and a lack of financial protection. Equity is a policy priority in many countries because of the strong link between disease burden and poverty. Health insurance can contribute to equity in health.

Design Element 3: Population Coverage

DE 3 is intended to help policy makers identify different types of populations to be covered by health insurance (the beneficiaries); determine how to cover hard-to-reach populations such as low-income, rural, informal sector workers; and understand the trade-off between expanding population coverage and the benefits package (discussed in DE 4).

In May 2005, the World Health Assembly endorsed Resolution WHA58.33 urging member states to work toward universal coverage and ensure that their total populations have access to needed health interventions without risking financial catastrophe (Carrin, Evans, and Ke Xu 2007). Under this resolution, universal coverage incorporates two complementary dimensions in addition to financial risk protection: the extent of population coverage (i.e., who is covered) and the extent of health service coverage (i.e., the benefits covered, addressed in DE 4).

Ideally, a country should develop a health insurance system with universal coverage to provide the entire population with the same health service coverage at the same time. However, this goal may not be achieved at the beginning; it may involve an incremental approach to gradually expand both the covered population and the covered health services with different health insurance schemes. For example, government-financed health insurance typically begins with civil service employees and military personnel. In the private sector, large companies may take the initiative to cover their employees, and possibly their dependents. Wealthy individuals, especially professionals such as lawyers, accountants, and doctors, may elect to purchase private commercial insurance. Subsidized health insurances may need to be developed to cover rural dwellers, the self-employed or informal sector workers, formal employees in small businesses, and the vulnerable population. With limited resources, insurers face a trade-off between extending coverage to low-income and high-risk populations, or covering additional services.

A population-service matrix can help countries visualize the linkages between different target population groups, financing mechanisms, and benefits package options. One risk of segmenting the population is that it could produce a tiered system with inequitable benefits packages for different groups. Another risk is that each segment tends to be homogeneous, limiting cross-subsidization among diverse groups. However, higher-level redistribution of resources among financing pools may be possible.

Design Element 4: Benefits Packages and Cost Containment

DE 4 helps policy makers determine what services should ideally be covered by the benefits package and understand cost-containment methods and the trade-offs between cost containment, benefits, and population coverage.

The benefits package is usually a list or table of general categories of care (e.g., outpatient care and hospital care) with details regarding the level of coverage in each category. The details can include the type of provider, specific services or conditions covered or excluded, limits on services (e.g., number of days in the hospital), and any copayments or deductibles (see cost containment, facing page).

The Commission on Macroeconomics and Health has recommended four criteria for choosing essential health interventions to be included in benefits packages: "(1) they should be technically efficacious and can be delivered successfully; (2) the targeted diseases should impose a heavy burden on society, taking into account individual illness as well as social spillovers (such as epidemics and adverse economic effects); (3) social benefits should exceed costs of the interventions (with benefits including life-years saved and spillovers such as fewer orphans or faster economic growth); and (4) the needs of the poor should be stressed." (CMH 2001: 10). In addition to the CMH criteria, policy makers must also consider the priorities of the population groups that provide most of the financing, who may withdraw their political support for an insurance scheme that does not cover services they value.

Unfortunately, given limited available resources, most developing countries must make difficult choices between covering services most likely to improve population health outcomes and services that protect households from catastrophic health expenditures.

To improve health outcomes, policy makers should consider the population's burden of disease, demographics (age, gender, location, and income), mortality and morbidity rates, epidemiological trends, historical data on service use, and evidence regarding the most cost-effective interventions. Many are public or merit goods with large social benefits (such as immunization), and insurance coverage can help compensate for low willingness to pay for such services. However, these types of services are not considered "insurable risks" because they are not catastrophic and unpredictable. To reduce out-of-pocket expenditures and achieve financial protection, the benefits package will likely need to cover curative outpatient services, drugs, and inpatient care. However, great care must be taken lest incentives be inadvertently created for unnecessary hospitalization and overprescribing.

Selecting an appropriate benefits package requires financial analysis. As noted above, household surveys and health facility data can be used to analyze the target population's current pattern of out-of-pocket health expenditures. Policy makers can then draft a benefits package that balances coverage for the most financially burdensome services and the services with the greatest health impact.

Health actuaries can help estimate the cost of the proposed benefits package to determine if sufficient resources exist to pay for it. They can estimate the costs of services using historical utilization data (e.g., medical claims, household surveys, or facility data), as well as determine the potential rate of increase in utilization of services once health insurance is implemented, which will affect the overall benefits cost. The cost estimate must be compared with revenue projections. If revenues are inadequate, then medical costs must be reduced by removing services, adding cost-containment methods, or reducing the covered population (without reducing revenues). These calculations ensure that premium rates for those participating in the scheme (for voluntary and social insurance systems) or tax revenues (for national health insurance systems) are affordable, politically acceptable, and sufficient for long-term viability.

The goal of cost containment is to make the insurance scheme solvent and financially self-sustaining. As part of the benefits package, cost-containment methods can discourage unnecessary, wasteful spending so there are more funds for needed health care services. Some methods can promote quality, while others may erode quality and must be closely monitored. There are costs incurred when implementing cost containment. Most methods are annoying to beneficiaries and providers, and require administrative systems and labor to implement. Policy makers must confirm that the cost-containment method saves more money than implementing and monitoring compliance with the method costs.

The benefits package design process itself can contribute to cost containment. Many health insurance plans control costs through deductibles and copayments, as these mechanisms control the tendency to overuse health services (moral hazard). These deductibles and copayments may, however, be unaffordable to the poorest groups. Some schemes set a ceiling on the benefits an individual may be paid within a given time frame, such as a year, although such maximums may leave beneficiaries at risk of catastrophic expenditures. Many insurers exclude expensive services such as organ transplants and dialysis. Insurers may cover only generic drugs, or use an essential drugs list. Clear and rational processes, based on evidence of cost-effectiveness, should always be followed for modifying the benefits package and reviewing new interventions, products, and technologies for possible inclusion.

Design Element 5: Engagement, Selection, and Payment of Health Care Providers

DE 5 helps policy makers understand how to lay the groundwork for identifying, selecting, and engaging health care providers; understand how all payment systems create incentives that help (or hinder) quality improvement, efficiency, and reaching the poor; and understand the operational and cost implications of different provider payment systems (further discussed in DE 7).

Provider selection is an important design issue for health insurance because provider behavior is a major determinant of the success of any health insurance scheme. A country should begin by reviewing the current market structure among health service providers, especially in relation to the target population and the benefits package. Issues to be considered include: Where do people go for services—public or private facilities? What are the cost and quality differences for services delivered in the public and the private sectors? What is the geographic distribution of providers (public and private)? What is the population's perception of public and private providers?

Policy makers should review the necessary and available information on providers to determine whether the benefits package is feasible; to decide how to select providers to maximize access by targeting beneficiaries, how to pay the providers, and how to link providers at different levels (referral system); and to identify possible efficiencies that can be realized through better provider payment (e.g., downsizing empty hospitals).

In areas with a mix of providers, how much freedom to give beneficiaries to choose their provider is a key insurance scheme design decision. Can they go to a private provider? Can they go directly to a hospital or specialist, or do they need a referral by a primary care physician? This issue affects beneficiary satisfaction (people prefer to choose their doctor) and medical costs (people tend to choose more expensive levels of care if they do not pay for it directly). Greater provider choice may be possible if the insurer can contract private providers and contain costs. To encourage beneficiaries to use primary health care, many insurers require primary care providers to serve as "gatekeepers" who determine the medical necessity for referral to hospitals and specialists.

Within many countries, shortages of health workers and facilities present a difficult challenge. Health care providers may not be available in all geographic areas or may be disproportionately located in urban areas with few if any in rural areas. If no providers are available, health insurance is irrelevant. In other situations, the quality of providers may be so poor that people choose not to use their services, so again, health insurance could become irrelevant. However, health insurance can offer a powerful means toward improving service quality by linking provider payments to quality standards and outputs.

Payment methods are one of the most sensitive issues for health workers and facilities because payments directly affect their economic interests (Mills 2007). Many different payment methods can be used in combination. All methods create incentives for providers that affect their behavior. The first step in deciding how to select and pay service providers is to review the policy goals of a health insurance scheme—access, quality, revenue, efficiency, administrative simplicity—and select the payment method(s) that create incentives that are consistent with scheme goals. Some payment rates can be for a single service or a package of services.

Performance-based payments, also known as pay for performance (P4P) and results-based financing, can be combined with all the other payment methods. Performance-based payments explicitly link an incentive payment to the achievement of a predetermined result or output. Providers are financially rewarded for achieving measurable health results. In many developing settings, this method has been interpreted as additional payments to providers (on top of salaries and input-based financing) to deliver priority services. Also seen are rewards for achieving performance targets or quality improvements. P4P is currently being implemented around the world, though not always as part of a health insurance system.

In addition, an insurer may choose to contract-out service provision for many reasons: to focus on its role as a purchaser and outsource service delivery (also known as "payer-provider split"), to allow beneficiaries to choose private providers, or to engage desired providers in specific locations or for specific services. Contracts are the written terms and conditions of the agreement between the insurer and the provider to clearly define the services covered, the price/rate to be paid, the payment method, minimum quality, performance incentives for efficiency and quality, and administrative procedures (forms, billing cycles). The contracting process works best when it reflects a partnership instead of an adversarial relationship that requires legal protection. Insurers should state their policy goals for health insurance clearly and specifically and ask providers how they can supply services to meet these goals. Contracting is further discussed in DE 6.

Design Element 6: Organizational Structure

DE 6 helps policy makers understand the functions necessary for health insurance administration and the range of possible organizational structures; critically review their existing institutions to determine how to build on strengths and address gaps; and identify critical organizational characteristics that will help health insurance flourish and ensure accountability.

Although there are many different types of health insurance, several functions or tasks remain more or less constant across every type, from small community-based insurance schemes to national programs (Normand and Weber 1994).

Some ways to execute these functions may be more "sophisticated," faster, and more precise, but also more expensive; there may also be simple and less costly ways. These functions include policy and regulatory functions (Design Elements 1 and 2); provider selection and payment functions (Design Element 5); financial management functions (Design Element 7); beneficiary communication/marketing, enrolment, and revenue collection (Design Element 7); and monitoring and evaluation functions (Design Element 8).

Organizational structures vary across countries and schemes. A wide variety of factors can influence how health insurance should be organized and managed in a country. Although there is no single, optimal organizational structure, there are two universal guiding principles. First, build accountability into the organizational structure. Hold entities accountable for honest and effective execution of their roles through control mechanisms such as regulation, checks and balances, clearly defined management functions, and clear and enforceable contracts (Savedoff and Gottret 2008). Accountability also requires institutional capacity in terms of trained personnel and information systems. Second, build on existing organizations instead of creating entirely new ones for insurance administration. Look for existing capacity and competencies. Not only is establishing new organizations expensive, but it can also generate competition for funds and political influence and confusion about roles and responsibilities.

One national agency may sometimes assume the lead role in the health insurance program, having the mandate to oversee its main functions. In this example, the government is the main overseer of the health insurance company and is responsible for monitoring and evaluating the overall scheme and regulation, while the insurance company interacts directly with providers and consumers. Alternatively, a private provider assumes the lead role in many countries. For instance, a private hospital or association of doctors might form a health maintenance organization (HMO) that combines the roles of insurer and provider. The financial performance of a health insurance scheme will be influenced by the quality and motivation of its managerial and administrative staff, in addition to the behavior of clinical providers.

Without good governance, efforts to expand health insurance could waste resources, destroy public trust, and fail to achieve policy objectives. An earmark of good governance in health insurance is accountable and transparent relationships between health insurance stakeholders, such as the government, the beneficiaries, payers, health care providers, and other insurers.

Good governance within an insurance scheme can be achieved in the following ways (Savedoff and Gottret 2008):

- *Coherent decision-making structure.* Decision makers are empowered with the authority, tools, and resources to fulfill their responsibilities; and face the consequences of their decisions.

- *Stakeholder participation.* Stakeholder input can be incorporated into decision-making and oversight.

- *Transparency and information.* Information should be accessible to decision makers and to the stakeholders to whom they are accountable.

- *Supervision and regulation.* Actors must be accountable for their actions and performance. This type of accountability involves consequences for poor performance.

- *Consistency and stability.* An insurance scheme that is a stable institution behaving consistently helps avoid uncertainty around rulemaking and processes over time and the potential disruptions of political change. This encourages longer-term investments by providers and greater uptake by consumers.

Design Element 7: Operationalizing Health Insurance

DE 7 helps policy makers understand key operational functions necessary for running a health insurance scheme; understand options for performing the functions, and key considerations to be made when determining how functions will be performed; and identify specific operational strengths and weaknesses in the health insurance scheme and specific ways to strengthen the operational system.

Previous design elements took the policy makers through the design issues related to health insurance, as well as the organizational structure. This one focuses on the operational systems that will help ensure smooth running of the health insurance scheme and achievement of health insurance objectives.

In this context, operational systems refer to the administrative and management systems, functions, and processes that support the execution of health insurance, such as enrolment of beneficiaries, premium collection, claims administration, and so on. Once readers determine the critical functions to help the insurance scheme operate (addressed in DE 6), they have to identify what capacity building is needed so that the actors involved in the health insurance scheme are ready to carry out their new responsibilities. Readers may also have to plan to educate other stakeholders in the health system about the overarching management structure and operational issues.

Financial management is critical to ensure adequacy of financial resources to cover operating costs, keep the health insurance funds in financial equilibrium, and ensure transparency for sound monitoring, management, and viability. This includes maintaining an adequate operating reserve to cover known costs and risks and to cover unforeseeable short-term risks. When several stakeholders are involved in the implementation of health insurance and multiple sources of scheme income may be involved (individuals, employers, and government), it is vital that the management and integrity of these funds be maintained to optimize efficiency and effectiveness.

The financial management system should have the following three main elements: a budgeting system to plan for all costs related to the health insurance scheme; an expenditure tracking system to ensure the proper internal controls to manage the flow of funds; and a cost-management system to ensure that payments and costs are in line with what is budgeted for financial viability.

Once a health insurance scheme is established, health care utilization rates will likely increase because of moral hazard and the effectively lower cost to consumers of seeking health care. Moral hazard is inevitable when a traditionally costly service for which there is unmet need becomes financially accessible. The amount of moral hazard a new health insurance scheme will experience is difficult to forecast. That is why it is critical to manage expenses after start-up and maintain flexibility to revise program benefits and payment arrangements; adjustments will probably have to be made along the way to stay within budget. For example, a scheme may need to institute copayments or coinsurance to help generate revenue and limit utilization, or alter the mode in which providers are paid to discourage overprovision of services.

Often, contracting different actors may be necessary if whichever entity (the main managing entity of the scheme) manages the overall health insurance program does not have the skills or capacity needed to accommodate all health insurance functions and therefore, to fulfill specific functions. Possible contractual relationships will depend on the scheme's organizational structure. Functions that might be contracted out include: actuarial analysis; claims management and processing, delivery of health care; grievance redress; risk bearing (sometimes the government is not in a position to bear the risk for health care, so it contracts an insurance company with the necessary capital to bear the risk) or reinsurance; beneficiary enrolment and premium collection; and customer service and marketing/education to beneficiaries.

Continuous monitoring of insurance scheme performance against planned tasks is a key responsibility of the managing entity. Monitoring is critical to every design element discussed above.[4] It must be undertaken routinely throughout the life of the scheme. Key areas for monitoring are both outcomes (i.e., number of individuals enrolled, utilization rates, claims ratios, etc.) and operational processes to ensure the program is running smoothly (Design Element 8).

A functioning management information system (MIS) is necessary for monitoring and evaluating an insurance program. The MIS consists of a series of tools, procedures, and information flows and can be manual or electronic depending on the technology available at different levels of the scheme. Some schemes use existing software programs to manage data at both local and central levels. In other schemes, data are collected on paper at the local level and entered into a software program at the central level. Ideally, one centralized, electronic information system collects and monitors data from all levels, but this may not be feasible in all settings.

The basic MIS administrative and technical monitoring tools and procedures are enrolment and financial contribution data, coordination of benefits and claims, and financial monitoring.

Design Element 8: Monitoring and Evaluation of Health Insurance Schemes

DE 8 helps policy makers become familiar with indicators that scheme operators, managers, and evaluators can use to assess an insurance scheme's performance in achieving desired objectives; understand sources of data for monitoring and evaluating (M&E) insurance schemes; and learn how to use information to make evidence-based decisions to improve the performance of a health insurance scheme.

M&E are complementary but separate functions that often serve distinct purposes. Monitoring shows how the health insurance scheme is doing on an ongoing basis, tracking inputs and outputs to assess whether the scheme is performing according to plan. A functional management information system is essential to do effective monitoring (DE 7). Its day-to-day use facilitates regular follow-up of activities and finances during implementation. MIS data can also be used to evaluate the performance of the health insurance scheme by the management team as well as through internal and external audits (Design Element 7).

Evaluation shows what the scheme achieves by assessing its outcomes and impacts. Evaluation is important for ensuring that the scheme has its intended effects. Is it increasing access to health care? Has coverage of health services increased? Are the benefits going to the targeted individuals? Have out-of-pocket expenditures been reduced? Positive evaluation results can increase political buy-in for a scheme as it scales up and can increase consumer demand for enrolment. Negative evaluation results can help policy makers revise scheme design or operations to achieve desired results. Evaluation results are also important for determining whether the most cost-effective approaches are being used.

Policy makers should consider from the outset how to evaluate the impact and cost-effectiveness of any proposed insurance scheme. Introducing the scheme in a way that facilitates evaluation will ensure more rapidly available, robust, compelling, and policy-relevant results. This can be done, for instance, by piloting the scheme in a randomly selected set of districts matched to control districts. Once an insurance scheme is introduced universally, a robust evaluation system is much more difficult to design retroactively. The results from an evaluation in pilot areas can also be used to modify a scheme's design before national scale-up, as well as to work out solutions to any operational challenges that arise.

Key M&E indicators can be classified into three categories: management performance, financial performance, and impact. Evaluating impacts of a health insurance scheme in terms of equity, efficiency, and effectiveness requires the use of analytical methodology that cannot be fully summarized in this brief space. Nor can a comprehensive evaluation of an insurance scheme be conducted in a short time frame because some impacts, such as changes in health status, are observable only in the long term.

SUMMARY

Health insurance has been considered and promoted as the major financing mechanism to achieve the goal of universal coverage. In Africa, several countries have already spent scarce time, money, and effort on health insurance initiatives.

Despite the many benefits that health insurance may offer, the journey to implement insurance and achieve the benefits is challenging, long, and risky. Policy makers and technicians that support development and scale-up of health insurance must figure out how to increase their country's financing capacity, extend health insurance coverage to the hard-to-reach populations, expand benefits packages, and improve the performance of existing schemes.

This chapter provides policy makers and health insurance designers with practical, action-oriented supports that improve their understanding of health insurance concepts, challenges, and realistic steps for the development and scaling up of equitable, efficient, and sustainable health insurance schemes. In a nutshell the eight basic design elements are:

- DE 1. Assess feasibility of health insurance.

- DE 2. Choose financing mechanisms carefully.

- DE 3. Delineate the population to be covered.

- DE 4. Choose the services to be included in the benefits package and balance them against costs.

- DE 5. Identify, select, and engage health care providers with an eye on the ramifications of payment and incentives packages for quality of care.

- DE 6. Make good governance, founded on strict accountability, the organization's prime objective, no matter what organizational format is chosen.

- DE 7. Understand the requirements for effective administration of health care and choose the organizational format that best corresponds to scheme objectives.

- DE 8. Monitor and evaluate, based on pertinent data gathered daily. These functions are indispensable in a smoothly functioning, flexible system that is capable of policy corrections.

NOTES

1. The chapter is based on Hong Wang and others (2010).

2. These are the three classic health financing functions: revenue collection, pooling, and purchasing (WHO 2010).

3. Definition adapted from Gottret and Schieber (2006).

4. Insurance scheme monitoring is discussed here, separately from evaluation of the scheme and as an aspect of scheme information systems, because it is a critical operational function that must be managed throughout the design and implementation process. Evaluation is addressed in Design Element 8.

REFERENCES

Atim, C.L., L. Fleisher, L. Hatt, S. Musau, and A. Arur. 2008. "Health Financing in Africa 2009: Challenges and Opportunities." Washington, DC, Health Systems 20/20 Project.

Carrin, Guy, David Evans, and Ke Xu. 2007. "Designing Health Financing Policy toward Universal Coverage." *Bulletin of the World Health Organization* 85 (9): 649–732.

CMH (Commission on Macroeconomics and Health). 2001. *Macroeconomics and Health: Investing in Health for Economic Development.* Geneva: WHO.

Gottret, P., and G. Schieber. 2006. *A Practitioner's Guide: Health Financing Revisited.* Washington, DC: World Bank.

Mills, Anne. 2007. "Strategies to Achieve Universal Coverage: Are There Lessons from Middle-Income Countries?" A literature review commissioned by the Health Systems Knowledge Network, WHO Commission on the Social Determinants of Health, London School of Hygiene and Tropical Medicine, London, March 30.

Normand, Charles, and Axel Weber. 1994. "Social Health Insurance: A Guidebook for Planning." Unpublished. World Health Organization, Geneva; http://whqlibdoc.who .init/publications/50786.pdf.

Savedoff, W., and P. Gottret. 2008. "Governing Mandatory Health Insurance: Learning from Experience." World Bank, Washington, DC.

Wang, Hong, and N. Pielemeier. 2012. "Community-Based Health Insurance: An Evolutionary Approach to Achieving Universal Coverage in Low-Income Countries." *Journal of Life* 6: 320–29.

Wang, Hong, Kimberly Switlick, Christine Ortiz, Catherine Connor, and Beatriz Zurita. 2010. "Africa Health Insurance Handbook: How to Make It Work." Health Systems 20/20 Project, Abt Associates, Inc., Bethesda, MD.

WHO. 2010. *World Health Report: Health Systems Financing: The Path to Universal Coverage.* Geneva, Switzerland: WHO.

CHAPTER 20

New Development Paradigm

Onno P. Schellekens, Jacques van der Gaag, Marianne E. Lindner,
and Judith de Groot

Reforming and scaling up health insurance in low-income countries has had a checkered history. The authors review three "laws" of economics that hinder this achievement. Underfunding plays an important role: health systems are severely underfunded in countries where GDP per capita is low. There is a tight relation between GDP per capita and health care expenditures (the first law of health economics), which means that an influx of donor money into the public health sector in a low-income country will not raise the total amount of money in that sector. Instead, it will crowd out private funds or substitute for existing local public expenditures (the third law of health economics). In such countries, out-of-pocket payments will be high (the second law of health economics), easily pushing people into poverty.

Scaling up health insurance through the public sector often fails, as it has in many developing countries, due to weak public sector capabilities and ends up benefiting mainly the interests of groups that have access to state power, which they use for their own benefit. As a result, the public sector often fails to deliver public goods and redistribute income and risk. The institutional framework (legal, financial, and so on) is weak or absent, which leads to high uncertainty and risk. This profoundly influences the behavior of patients, providers, and communities. Health care gets stuck in a vicious circle of inadequate funding arrangements, weak governance, and dysfunctional health systems.

A different approach is needed to lower the overall risk—by working through local communities and nongovernmental organizations providing affordable loans and affordable insurance and, at the same time, raising the quality of supply. By taking the risk out of the market, the willingness to invest and to prepay will grow, generating a virtuous effect and turning the vicious circle into a virtuous one. This will be called the fourth law of health economics.

INTRODUCTION

Despite decades of development policy and billions of dollars spent on health, sustainable health systems have not yet been brought to developing countries. Although improvements have been made on some indicators, many of the Millennium Development Goals will most likely not be reached by 2015. This is enough reason to revisit the approach to development aid in health. It is all the more urgent, given the global economic crisis and increasing pressures on aid budgets. Other chapters in this book shed light on the different and difficult aspects of scaling up health insurance. In this chapter, a possible approach with new potential for scaling up health insurance is presented. An earlier version of our new approach was presented in an essay that won a second prize in the annual IFC/Financial Times essay competition of 2007.

Why has the dominant approach to improving health up until now had such limited results? Why do countries in Sub-Saharan Africa still bear 44 percent of the burden of communicable diseases and account for hardly 1 percent of total health expenditure? Why are more than 50 percent of health expenses still paid out of pocket, and why do most people not have access to affordable and qualitatively good health care? And why is there so little investment in health care in Africa? In the years between 1997 and 2007 the IFC invested a mere US$12 million in Africa, out of total spending of US$12.8 billion by the World Bank on health (World Bank 2009).

In this chapter, the theories from New Institutional Economics are used because these theories open up important insights (box 20.1). According to these theories, the essential characteristics of underdevelopment are low levels

---

BOX 20.1   NEW INSTITUTIONAL ECONOMICS

The school of New Institutional Economics (NIE) looks at economic growth from a different angle. Exchange and transactions play a central role in NIE theories. A crucial concept is that transactions have costs; costs to find and study the product or service, to come to an agreement, and to make sure the agreement is fulfilled. Transaction costs reflect uncertainty by including a risk premium, whose level depends on the chances of defection by the other party and the associated cost (North 1990). Ultimately, all transaction costs are reflected in the price of a product or service. When transaction costs get higher, there will be fewer transactions, and when transaction costs become too high there might be no transactions at all.

The New Institutional Economists argue that institutions play an important role in economic exchange and can help to explain the disparities in economic performance of different countries. *Institutions*, as defined by Douglass North, are the "rules of the game in a society" or "the humanly devised constraints that shape human interaction" (North 1994: 360). Institutions can be informal or formal and determine the way business is done. Informal institutions are, for example, norms of behavior, conventions, and self-imposed codes of conduct. Formal institutions include official rules, laws, and constitutions. North deliberately separates institutions, the rules of the game, from organizations, the players in the game. Institutions are defined by people to create order and reduce uncertainty. They are deeply rooted in history and culture, and their development is "path-dependent" and usually takes decades (North 1990; Williamson 2000).

Transactions among peers or members of a social group are often based on informal institutions. These can be enforced by social pressure, religious pressure, even honor-related violence or the threat of being expelled from the group. As people in the group know each other, there is little effort involved to come to an agreement and make sure the agreement is fulfilled. When social capital and trust are high, the risk associated with the transaction is low, and transaction costs are minimal. For exchange outside a social group, with someone unknown, and for larger and more complex transactions, informal institutions do not suffice. It becomes too lucrative and easy to cheat. In these cases, more effort must be put into specifying the nature of the product, the terms of the agreement, and the measures in case of a breach of the agreement. Risks and transaction costs rise.

Enforcement is the mechanism by which institutions are forced into compliance. Rules work only if one can make sure they are followed. Although some agreements might be self-enforcing (when all parties gain from living up to the agreement), in most cases third-party enforcement mechanisms with some kind of coercion are needed for institutions to be effective (North 1990).

The less personal (in time and place) and the more complex transactions become, the greater is the need for formal institutions and independent enforcement mechanisms to protect the parties' interests and reduce uncertainty (Williamson 2000; North 1994). Extensive formal institutional frameworks exist in developed economies today. These frameworks have not sprung up overnight, but have gradually matured over centuries as organizations have continuously made marginal adjustments to improve their performance, a process called *adaptive efficiency* (North 1990). Although the role of the state has been ambiguous at times, in developed economies today it plays an important role in reducing uncertainty and protecting property rights.

Less-developed countries often reflect what North calls "limited access orders." In such cases, the state has characteristics of a façade state, and does not operate as a neutral third-party enforcer of rules. The countries are de facto ruled by a small elite that use their power for rent seeking. They control violence and protect their interests, which are not necessarily aligned with societal goals. The lack of institutions and their imperfect enforcement create a barrier to market entry for new players, strengthening the monopolies of the "well connected." Keeping inefficient institutions in place often serves the elite well, even though it leads to stagnation and socially inefficient outcomes (North 1990; North et al. 2007).

Without efficient institutions, the scale of economic transactions is limited to the size and level of trust within social groups. Impersonal exchange is too risky, and businesses cannot specialize and increase in size. This inhibits efficiency and economic growth. Especially important in this respect are the definition and enforcement of property rights and contract law (Williamson 2000). The level of trust plays a proven role in decreasing transaction costs in economic exchange. Trust is again related to the existence of efficient formal institutions (Zak and Knack 2001).

The importance of property rights for economic development was brought to the fore by development economist Hernando de Soto, who found that

(continued)

> **BOX 20.1   NEW INSTITUTIONAL ECONOMICS (*continued*)**
>
> people cannot capitalize on their possessions when property rights are not registered and enforced. As a consequence, capital cannot be invested productively and remains "dead" (de Soto 2000). But, as de Soto also admits, property rights are not all that matter (Williamson 2000).
>
> An important measure of a country's institutional efficiency is the average cost of capital, as it reflects the perceived investment risk. Studies have shown that there is a strong (inverse) relation between the strength of institutions and interest rates. In the medieval period, interest rates decreased in the Netherlands and the United Kingdom as a result of the emergence of institutions and development of financial markets. Access to financial instruments such as insurance, savings, loans, or an interest in a ship was broad. These deep and well-integrated markets fueled investment and growth (van Zanden 2009; North 1990). Today in developing countries, the financial sector is still weakly developed, and interest rates are high.

of transactions, high transaction costs, high levels of risk, low levels of trust, high interest rates, and high discount rates. Important determinants are a weak state, unable to provide public goods on a large scale, and a flawed institutional framework.

The main goal of this chapter is to present a new approach that might provide a valuable alternative to the current public sector–based model. A dynamic model to health system development builds on local private sector expertise and on social capital. Its aim is to raise investments. In this way, health systems can be scaled up, using donor funds to catalyze this development of a more sustainable health system, one that is embedded in local social systems and builds on local resources and expertise.

THE OLD PARADIGM

The dominant approach in trying to make health care work with the use of donor money has been either to work through the state—based on the assumption that the state provides health care for all as a public good—or through the direct financing of aid programs. But many public health systems in Sub-Saharan Africa have been unable to meet their people's needs. They suffer from a chronic lack of resources, shortages in qualified staff, and inefficiencies, and often deliver low-quality services (World Bank 2011).

Underfunding: The First and Second Laws of Health Economics

The amount of resources available for health care in a country is directly related to a country's level of economic development. Government per capita funding available for health is low in Sub-Saharan Africa, as GDP per capita is often below

FIGURE 20.1   The First Law of Health Economics

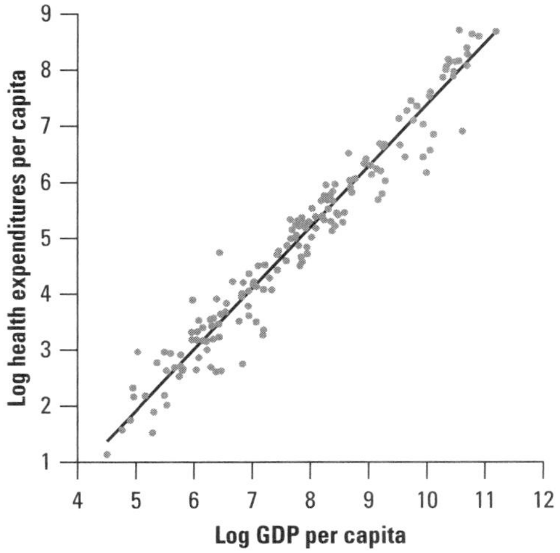

Source: Adapted from Van der Gaag and Stimac 2008: 9.

US$500, and the informal sector in the economy is large.[1] Low-income countries spend on average only US$30 per capita on health care, compared with around US$4,500 on average in OECD countries. This includes donor spending, which amounts to more than 50 percent of national health budgets in some African countries (WHO 2012a).

There is a tight relationship between health expenditure and GDP, as Van der Gaag and Stimac (2008) have demonstrated. This relationship has been stable over time and also holds for developing countries. The authors therefore called it "the first law of health economics" (figure 20.1).

A second observation is that, in low-income countries, private uninsured out-of-pocket expenditures for health care make up a larger share of total financial resources than in richer countries. In other words, when countries grow richer, health insurance coverage increases, and the share of out-of-pocket payments decreases. This can be called "the second law of health economics" (Van der Gaag and Stimac 2008) (figure 20.2). This is important because about 150 million people annually suffer catastrophic financial shocks due to uninsured health care expenditures, while 100 million are pushed below the poverty line (WHO 2010).

Donor Interventions in Health: The Third Law of Health Economics

In the quest to improve health in developing countries, the leading theme on the international policy agenda has been equity or "Health for All." This has prompted donors to align with local governments in their role as the dominant

FIGURE 20.2   The Second Law of Health Economics

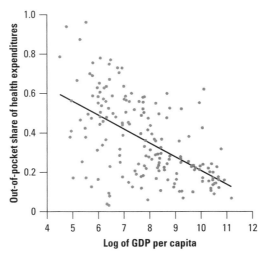

Sources: Adapted from Van der Gaag and Stimac 2008: 21; WHO 2012b.

provider of health care services. This approach was formalized in the 2005 Paris Declaration on Aid Effectiveness (harmonization and alignment around the public sector). Most donor support has thus been channeled as input financing through governments and public health care systems. The underlying assumption is that public health systems are best placed to provide efficient and equitable health care to a population.

Over the last decade, foreign aid spent on health increased from US$10.86 billion in 2000 to an estimated US$27.73 billion in 2011 (IHME 2011: 15, fig. 2). Although remarkable progress has been made in some countries (e.g., Rwanda), in many other developing countries these efforts have not led to universal access to health services or improved health outcomes (World Bank 2011).

How effective, then, are these expenditures? As shown in figure 20.1, there is a tight relationship between per capita GDP and health expenditures. A plausible explanation for the difficulty of raising health expenditure above the level predicted by a country's GDP is the phenomenon of "crowding out": the influx of donor money does not raise the total amount of money in the system, but crowds out private resources for health. This phenomenon has been demonstrated in the context of developed nations by, among others, Cutler and Gruber (1996) and Gruber and Simon (2008). In the context of developing countries, it has also been documented (Van der Gaag and Stimac 2008, 2012).

Besides crowding out private resources, foreign aid spending substitutes for home government spending: money is diverted from the local health budget and replaced by donor money. Lu and others (2010) demonstrated that in Africa development assistance to governments for health had a substantial and significant negative effect on domestic government spending: for every US$1.00 of aid to government for health, government health expenditure from domestic resources went down by between US$0.43 and US$1.14. This means that increased donor or government spending does not increase total resources for health in the same magnitude. We call this the "third law of health economics."

Another aspect of channeling donor money into public programs is that the funds do not reach the right groups of people. Measures intended to benefit the poor (strengthening public health services) are likely to result in an increased use of public services by the better-off, who previously had looked to the private sector. In fact, public health services have been shown to benefit the rich more than the poor (Preker and Langenbrunner 2005; Castro-Leal et al. 2000). Davoodi and others (2010) found that 17 percent of the benefits of public health spending globally accrue to the poorest quintile, compared with 23 percent to the richest. In Sub-Saharan Africa, this difference is even more pronounced (Davoodi et al. 2010).

HOW DID UNIVERSAL HEALTH SYSTEMS GROW?

The three laws of health economics hamper the growth of scalable health systems in Sub-Saharan Africa through the "traditional" approach. A main goal of this traditional approach, one long favored by donors, is the establishment in developing countries of a full-scale, universal health system in which health care is a public good, provided for by the state.

Health Systems in Developed Countries

The traditional approach is based on the example of the comprehensive, universal, and complex health (and social security) systems that exist in many OECD countries today. These systems build not only on the sharing of health risks, but also on income solidarity and age solidarity. OECD countries spend between 25 percent and 35 percent of their GDP on their social systems (Lindert 2004), including, but not restricted to, health.

Since such systems have been regarded as a desirable goal for developing countries, a look at the emerging process of these public systems seems useful (box 20.2). It has taken centuries of incremental, not always deliberate, changes to build today's systems.

These systems are sustainable and have had an enormous impact on generating welfare, equality, and good quality of public health. This proves that there are good reasons to regard health care as a public good[2] and good reason for

BOX 20.2   THE GROWTH OF UNIVERSAL SOCIAL SYSTEMS

The development of universal social systems—related to a growth of GDP per capita and the executive power of the state—can be roughly divided into three phases, as illustrated in figure B20.2.1.

FIGURE B20.2.1   The Three Phases of Universal Social Systems Growth

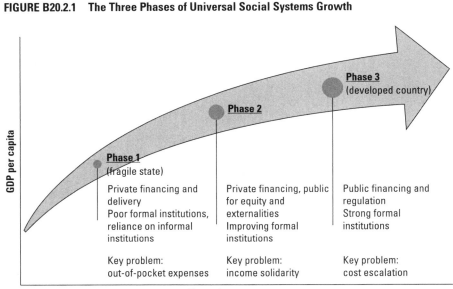

Source: PharmAccess Foundation 2012.

- Until the 19th century, social security systems were mainly a matter of religious charity and were partly provided for within the guilds. Income per head was low, and the executive power of the state was limited. A large segment of the economy was agricultural and informal. In this phase the state played only a minor role in the health system. Most health expenditure was out of pocket, and the associated inequity was de facto accepted. In other words, health care financing and delivery were private or faith-based.

- In the course of the 19th century, when the industrial revolution took its full form, economic production grew rapidly, as did GDP per capita. Health financing and delivery were still predominantly private or faith-based (the guilds had largely disappeared after approximately 1820), but a tendency toward formation of voluntary risk pools such as "mutual funds" was emerging mainly among "small working people." To maintain their sustainability, these private schemes had to live within their means, forcing them to make tough choices on eligibility, benefits packages, and costs (Bärnighausen and Sauerborn 2002; Ogawa et al. 2003; Widdershoven 2005; Companje et al. 2009).

- Later in the century, when large production plants emerged, employers started funds for their workers. In the same period, governments began to assume a role in providing social security and health insurance. The German regime of Bismarck succeeded in 1883 in introducing compulsory health insurance for a large group of workers—this was an important landmark. After that, governments increasingly tried to establish social insurances, but many clashes of interest over the structure and content of these schemes ensued between beneficiaries, providers, and employers on one side and government on the other (De Swaan 2004).

- In the third phase, with further growth and formalization of the economy, state capacity grew. This happened especially after World War II, when the economy boomed and the population grew. Governments took over and consolidated voluntary risk pools, and national systems were created. Solidarity expanded from being purely risk-based to income-based and systems reached (near) national coverage. Depending on the country, this has evolved into either a national health system or a social insurance–based system with a mix of public and private providers. This is where most systems in OECD countries are today, with a low share of out-of-pocket expenses, high-quality care, and a high degree of solidarity. In the 1980s, it became clear that costs had grown out of hand, so cost reduction became a prevalent policy goal. Some privatization took place, but this did not change the universality of social security.

the state to intervene. These reasons include the market failures inherent in the sector, such as the public benefits of, for example, vaccination in reducing the spread of disease,[3] principal-agent issues and information asymmetries in, for example, the doctor-patient relationship. In combination with concerns over equity and efficiency, these market imperfections provide ample justification for governments to intervene in the health sector (Preker 2000). This does not necessarily mean that governments have to be the main provider of health services; they can also take a role as regulator or financer.

The social security systems currently in place in OECD countries have evolved through a bottom-up process from pioneering schemes initiated by professional guilds and communities. These were initially built on the social capital within well-defined groups, based on risk solidarity and were limited in scale. Over time a shift took place toward systems involving income solidarity and age solidarity. The main drivers of the development of health and other social systems have been the growth in income, broadened democratic representation, and the increasing capacity and ability of the state to collect taxes and enforce income redistribution. This is why the growth process of large-scale collective systems cannot simply be transplanted to present-day developing countries.

WHY DOES THE PROCESS WORK DIFFERENTLY IN DEVELOPMENT SETTINGS?

Why is it not so simple to "transplant" the scaling-up process that took place in the richer OECD countries to development settings? And how can more insight be gained into the factors that play a role in developing countries?

The Vicious Circle of Underdevelopment

Theories from New Institutional Economics (refer back to box 20.1) can shed light on these questions. The work of Douglass North and others has done much to clarify the crucial role of transaction costs, institutions, and enforcement in economic growth, in relation to the role of the state. The essence of underdevelopment can be found in high transaction costs and high discount rates due to low levels of trust and high levels of risk, leading to a low level of transactions, and a low level of investments (figure 20.3). Many developing countries suffer from this complex of interlocking factors, given the basic fact that there is no functioning state in the way there is in the OECD countries.

The State: Limited Access Orders

In the richer OECD countries the roles of policy maker, regulator, and central authority are assumed by the state. But in developing countries the state is usually unable to adequately fulfill these roles. In many developing countries,

FIGURE 20.3   The Vicious Circle of Underdevelopment

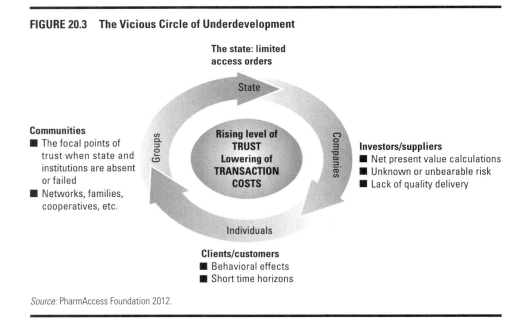

Source: PharmAccess Foundation 2012.

governments have the character of what Douglass North called a "limited access order"—meaning that an elite has a firm hold on the state institutions and uses them for rent seeking, while barring others from access to state power. Consequently, the state does not serve the public interest, but serves the interest of certain groups of people (North et al. 2007).

This has profound consequences. It means that the state cannot take the role of impartial regulator and guarantor of property rights. Neither can it impartially raise taxes and use that money to efficiently provide public goods like security, infrastructure, education, health care, and so on. The state will not be able to establish the large redistribution of income, based on the principles of solidarity, that is characteristic of the welfare states of the OECD countries. This means that insecurity runs high in many aspects of life for the people who live in such a setting.

CLIENTS

Insecurity has a profound impact on individual lives. The effects have been studied by a number of scholars, most prominently Duflo and Banerjee (2011). They find that people refrain from saving when they live in an insecure environment and have little trust that investing today will yield a higher income tomorrow. People at the bottom of the pyramid have scant access to reliable information and therefore make seemingly irrational decisions. For example, in one of the studies in Kenya, only 40 percent of farmers offered a fertilizer associated with a 69.5 percent return on investment actually bought the fertilizer. The authors also describe that in India grocery sellers pay a hefty 4.69 percent interest per day to their suppliers, every day. This translates into an astronomical annual interest rate. Average interest rates for small businesses range from 40 to 200 percent per annum, as compared with perhaps 10 to 20 percent in developed economies. Another interesting observation is that people tend to take on several occupations and save their possessions in different places in an attempt to reduce their risk by diversification.

All in all, the uncertainty and the lack of prospect inhibit people to invest in their future and escape poverty. As Duflo and Banerjee (2011) point out, this is all hard to imagine for anyone who lives in Europe or the United States, where clean water comes from the tap, immunization of children is more or less obligatory, people automatically save for retirement benefits and are entitled to social security, and health care bills are paid in case of illness.

Besides, many people in poor countries have no access to banking services. They keep their money in cash in several places in the house. In such a situation, when people have high discount rates and low trust, they are not automatically willing to prepay for services when quality and delivery are not certain.

Communities

When there is no state that is capable of providing public goods and redistributing income impartially, and when the framework of financial and juridical institutions is weak, families and communities will be the most important institutions for people. The "radius of trust" will be limited to the family, clan, tribe, or religious group. Within the group or network, the level of trust is high, making for low transaction costs because transactions take place within the group or network (Fukuyama 1995, 2000; Rothstein 2005). This means that groups and networks will be the most important unit for transactions to take place.

Investors/Suppliers

Lack of reliable and effective institutions also has an impact on investors and suppliers. People who want to invest in production and delivery of goods and services estimate whether they will get a return on their investment. This is captured in the net present value calculation (box 20.3).

The net present value calculation illustrates the consequences of institutional inefficiencies on investment behavior. For a high-risk investment to be worthwhile, the returns need to be high and quickly realized. Long-term investments can hardly be profitable. As a consequence, companies in developing countries usually have shorter time horizons and little fixed capital (North 1990). This leaves companies unable to invest in productive efficiency, knowledge, or human capital.

When contract enforcement is uncertain, financial transactions become difficult. Companies cannot make sure customers pay their bills, hindering expansion beyond cash-based transactions or outside the social group. But uncertain contract enforcement also has important implications for the financial sector. Lenders and investors enter into financial contracts only when reasonable certainty exists about the relative legal rights of borrowers, creditors, and investors and about fair, speedy, and impartial enforcement of those rights. This again is

---

BOX 20.3   NET PRESENT VALUE CALCULATION

$$NPV = -I_0 + \frac{B-C}{(1+r)^1} + \frac{B-C}{(1+r)^2} \ldots\ldots\ldots \frac{B-C}{(1+r)^n}$$

The *net present value* (NPV) is the value today of the future benefits and costs of a project. To determine the present value of the future cash streams, the latter are discounted against the discount rate (which is equivalent to the perceived risk). The higher the risk, the higher is the discount rate, and the lower the present value.

I_0 = investment, B = benefits, C = costs, r = discount rate, n = number of years.

reflected in the cost of capital. As was noted previously, lending rates in developing countries are considerably higher than in developed economies. However, data on interest rates capture only instances in which a financial transaction actually occurred. It does not take into account that many companies have no access to financing at all and have to rely on their earnings and family members' wealth to invest.

This vicious circle is also manifest in health. Many health systems in developing countries are caught in a vicious circle with low demand, limited risk pooling, and poor quality supply fueling low demand. A major determinant of this circle is the lack of trust among consumers as well as among providers and financiers.

In the next section, how this circle can be broken to increase investments and the availability of quality health care services is explored.

AN ALTERNATIVE MODEL FOR HEALTH SYSTEMS: BEYOND THE THREE LAWS OF HEALTH ECONOMICS

The proposed dynamic model for health system development seeks to break the vicious circle described above and make health care systems viable and scalable, improving access to health care for the poor. This approach seeks to make the unknown risk of transactions known and is based on the leverage of locally existing institutions, social capital, and private sector expertise. It seeks to balance demand and supply, both needed for a sustainable system using risk-pooling mechanisms and stimulating investments. In this way, donor funds can be used to catalyze the development of a more sustainable health system by stimulating investments on both the supply and the demand sides. This might be a way to beat the three laws of health economics and increase the total resources available for health.

The main pillars of the model are: building on existing local institutions and social capital, leveraging the capacity of the private sector, empowering clients and local communities, and balancing demand and supply.

Building on Existing Local Institutions and Social Capital

Donors that have money available to enhance development should aim their interventions at improving health systems that build on existing institutions and local circumstances. This can be achieved by using existing informal institutions (e.g., leveraging social capital of communities and their existing ties with private providers) and contributing to the setting up of formal institutions (e.g., quality standards/accreditation, investment funds for social infrastructure).

Health care delivery should be acknowledged as a service industry. All elements needed to deliver health services need to be present and functioning. These elements are financing (risk pools and prepayment); administrative systems; health care providers such as clinics and hospitals, medication and laboratories; and the client/patient. The demand (financing) side and the supply (delivery) side should be aligned and managed to deliver care to the patient, who will therefore be willing to prepay to ensure the availability of quality services when needed. In this way, both the demand and supply of health care are strengthened.

Leveraging the Capacity of the Risk Capital

In many developing countries, the private sector is an important provider of health care, including for its poor who pay for these private services largely out-of-pocket. Increasingly, many of the facilitating functions for health care—information, quality certification, technology support, human resources—are provided by the private sector. This makes the private sector a potentially important partner to reach the primary beneficiaries, namely, low-income groups, and facilitate systemic change in a bottom-up approach.

Empowering Clients and Local Communities

Ownership by and empowerment of clients and the communities they belong to are of crucial importance for the approach to succeed. A client-oriented approach requires knowledge about what clients want and need and what they can afford and are willing to (pre)pay. It implies the importance of delivering good-quality care to the clients/patients, which requires building a strong health care supply chain: without good-quality supply the willingness to prepay is likely to be low (Carrin 2003; Preker, Harding, and Travis 2000; Litvack and Bodart 1993).

This can be pictured in "the diamond of health care" (figure 20.4).

Interventions

Other elements of the new approach include interventions that are undertaken on both supply and demand sides.

On the *demand side*, the existing private resources for health care (the 50 percent out-of-pocket payments) are used more efficiently through bottom-up voluntary private health insurance schemes to realize solidarity (based on health risk) and protect scheme members from unexpected financial shocks due to ill health. At the same time, the health insurance schemes generate financial resources to build up an efficient supply chain and empower members to insist on high-quality care systems, creating a snowball effect. People who can pay are induced to pay into risk pools, thereby creating stable health care demand. Improved efficiency in the supply chain lowers costs and raises quality, increasing peoples' willingness to pay. As more people buy health insurance, schemes grow, resulting in larger cross-subsidization, which enhances equity. Through volume effects, the costs and premiums can be further reduced. These schemes do not compete with government programs but complement them. Beneficiaries

FIGURE 20.4   The Diamond of Health Care

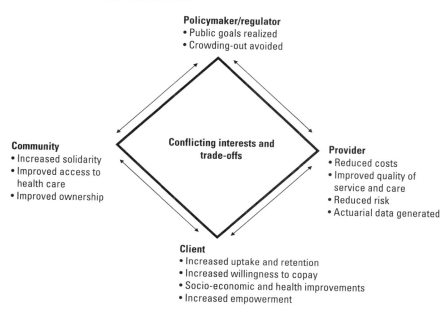

Source: PharmAccess Foundation 2009.

are involved in determining who has access to the schemes, the design of the benefits package, the level of premiums, and the costs to be covered. Mobile telecom companies such as Celtel and MTM have demonstrated that the willingness to prepay for services does exist in Africa, and by first targeting those who can pay and focusing on efficiency in the supply chain, more broad-based coverage can be realized.

The *supply side* is strengthened through facilitating private investments, both debt and equity capital. In addition, supply-chain upgrading is undertaken through quality-improvement programs with rigorous quality monitoring and control, preferably in cooperation with international accreditation organizations. To ensure adequate delivery of care, where regulatory capacity of the government is weak, enforcement of quality standards must be undertaken in another way. Output-based contractual agreements provide a good opportunity to do this (Loevinsohn and Harding 2005).

Donor funds are used to finance the demand-based voluntary health insurance schemes by subsidizing the premiums. Disease-specific donor programs (such as for HIV/AIDS, malaria, tuberculosis) support the insurance schemes through a risk-equalization arrangement built into the program. These long-term donor commitments are made with the solvency of the insurance funds serving as collateral, which lowers the investment risk and makes investments in the health care supply chain feasible. Limited donor funding is also used to upgrade the supply chain. Finally, donor funding is used to mobilize additional resources to scale up the interventions.

For a long time, donors and governments have opposed private sector involvement fueled by concerns over profit motives, issues with regulation, and fears of inequity. But increasingly it is recognized in developing countries that, given the challenges, health systems cannot do without the private sector. This shift is partly motivated by the expectation of decreasing aid budgets due to the global economic turmoil, but also by recognition of the dual realities of the weakness of public systems and the potentially significant contribution of private resources to health care delivery. Asked in a 2011 interview on *Nature News* what was the biggest challenge he had encountered in the global health field, the former president of global health of the Bill & Melinda Gates Foundation said:

> Most people in the developing world, particularly in South Asia, but also in Sub-Saharan Africa, access care through the private sector and pay out of pocket. It's a challenge to know how to impact that sector because most of our programs in global health are meant to be run through the public sector and the government. But, in reality, if you're a mother in Sub-Saharan Africa with a child suffering from malaria, you don't go to the hospital first—you go to, say, a traveling druggist. Figuring how to reach that interface between the front-line private-health system and the patient needing care is going to be a great challenge for all of us.
>
> —Dr. Tachi Yamada[4]

The World Bank and IFC have been instrumental in this paradigm shift with their "Health in Africa" initiative, focusing on the private health sector. A recent report by the World Bank provides recommendations for governments in Africa to engage with the private sector (World Bank 2011).

CONCLUSIONS

In many developing countries in Sub-Saharan Africa, establishing viable and scalable health care systems has proven difficult. Underfunding plays an important role in this. The first, second, and third laws of health economics implicate that donor funding applied through the state and the public system mainly crowds out local private expenses and substitutes for local government spending, limiting the net result. Due to dysfunctional states and weak institutions (legal institutions, financial institutions, property rights) clients are reluctant to prepay for services that may no longer be there when needed, and investors are not eager to invest. As a result, the overall transaction level stays low. The health system is caught in a vicious circle of low trust, low demand, low investment, and low quality supply. Private sector supply suffers from a lack of impartial regulation and enforcement, scarcity of funds, high risks, agency problems, and delivery problems. The private sector has limited access to affordable capital.

The history of the evolution of large welfare states in richer OECD countries shows that such large collective systems grew incrementally over a long period of time and cannot simply be transplanted to low-income countries. Development is path-dependent.

This all pleads for a different approach. The new dynamic model we propose focuses on using donor funds to decrease the risk in the system and to create ownership—on both demand and supply sides at the same time. In this way, the vicious circle is turned into a virtuous circle. New investments are generated, and peoples' willingness to prepay grows. The new money brought into the system creates a multiplier effect.

This approach has modest and high pretensions at the same time. It does not attempt to establish low-cost, universal health care, accessible to all in one step, but it does try to create "islands of efficiency" where the results are sustainable. On that solid foundation, more ambitious plans can be built: health insurance can be scaled up.

NOTES

1. The share of informal employment in nonagricultural employment in Africa, excluding South Africa, is 78 percent.

2. A *public good* is a good that is nonrivaled and nonexcludable, meaning that each individual's consumption of such a good leads to no subtractions from any other individual's consumption of that good (Samuelson 1954).

3. This effect is commonly referred to as an externality. Externalities are indirect effects of consumption or production activity, that is, effects on agents other than the originator of such activity which do not work through the price system (Laffont 2008).

4. Interview, *Nature News,* http://www.nature.com/news/2011/110621/full/news.2011.373 .html; accessed June 22, 2012.

REFERENCES

Bärnighausen T., and R. Sauerborn. 2002. "One Hundred and Eighteen Years of the German Health Insurance System: Are There Any Lessons for Middle- and Low-Income Countries?" *Social Science and Medicine* 5: 1559–87.

Carrin, G. 2003. *Community-Based Health Insurance Schemes in Developing Countries: Facts, Problems and Perspectives.* Discussion Paper No.1, World Health Organization, Geneva.

Castro-Leal, F., J. Dayton, L. Demery, and K. Mehra. 2000. "Public Spending on Health Care in Africa: Do the Poor Benefit?" *Bulletin of the World Health Organization* 78 (1): 66–74.

Companje, K.P., R.H.M. Hendriks, K.F.E. Veraghtert, and B.E.M. Widdershoven. 2009. *Two Centuries of Solidarity: German, Belgian, and Dutch Social Health Insurance, 1777–2008.* Amsterdam: Askant.

Cutler, D., and J. Gruber. 1996. "Does Public Insurance Crowd Out Private Insurance?" NBER Working Papers 5082, National Bureau of Economic Research, Cambridge, MA.

Davoodi, R.H., E.R. Tiongson, and S.S. Asawanuchit. 2010. "Benefit Incidence of Public Education and Health Spending Worldwide: Evidence from a New Database." *Poverty & Public Policy* 2 (2): Article 2; accessed at http://www.psocommons.org/ppp/vol2/iss2/art2.

De Soto, H. 2000. *The Mystery of Capital: Why Capitalism Triumphs in the West and Fails Everywhere Else.* New York: Basic Books.

De Swaan, A. 2004. *In the Care of the State: Health Care, Education and Welfare in Europe and the USA in the Modern Era.* Amsterdam: Amsterdam University Press.

Duflo, E., and A. Banerjee. 2011. *Poor Economics: A Radical Rethinking of the Way to Fight Global Poverty.* New York: Public Affairs.

Fukuyama, F. 1995. *TRUST: Social Virtues and the Creation of Prosperity.* New York: Free Press.

———. 2000. *Social Capital and Civil Society.* IMF Working Paper, Washington, DC.

Gruber, J., and K. Simon. 2008. "Crowd-Out Ten Years Later: Have Recent Public Insurance Expansions Crowded Out Private Health Insurance?" *Journal of Health Economics* 27 (2): 201–17.

Gupta, S., and S. Tareq. 2000. "Mobilizing Revenue." *Finance and Development* 45 (3): 44–47.

IHME (Institute for Health Metrics and Evaluation). 2011. *Financing Global Health 2011: Continued Growth as MDG Deadline Approaches.* Seattle, WA: IHME.

Keynes, J.M. 1936. *The General Theory of Employment, Interest and Money.* London: MacMillan.

Laffont, J.J. 2008. "Externalities." In *The New Palgrave Dictionary of Economics Online.* 2nd ed., ed. S.N. Durlauf and L.E. Blume. Palgrave Macmillan. http://www.dictionaryofeconomics.com/article?id=pde2008_E000200. doi:10.1057/9780230226203.0537.

Lindert, P. 2004. *Growing Public: Social Spending and Economic Growth since the Eighteenth Century.* New York: Cambridge University Press.

Litvack, J., and C. Bodart. 1993. "User Fees Plus Quality Equals Improved Access to Health Care: Results of a Field Experiment in Cameroon." *Social Science and Medicine* 37 (3): 369–83.

Loevinsohn, B., and A. Harding. 2005. "Buying Results? Contracting for Health Service Delivery in Developing Countries." *Lancet* 366 (9486): 676–81.

Lu, C., M. Schneider, P. Gubbins, K. Leach-Kemon, D. Jamison, and C. Murray. 2010. "Public Financing of Health in Developing Countries: A Cross-National Systematic Analysis." *Lancet* 375: 1375–87.

North, D.C. 1990. *Institutions, Institutional Change and Economic Performance.* Cambridge, UK: Cambridge University Press.

———. 1994. "Economic Performance through Time." Nobel Prize lecture, December 19, 1993. Published in *American Economic Review* 84 (3): 359–68.

North, D.C, B. Weingast, S. Webb, and J. Wallis. 2007. "Limited Access Orders in the Developing World: A New Approach to the Problems of Development." Policy Research

Working Paper 4359, World Bank Independent Evaluation Group, Country Relations Division, Washington, DC.

Ogawa, S., T. Hasegawa, G. Carrin, and K. Kawabata. 2003. "Scaling Up Community Health Insurance: Japan's Experience with the 19th Century Jyorei Scheme." *Health Policy and Planning* 18 (3): 270–78.

Preker, A.S., A. Harding, and P. Travis. 2000. "Make or Buy" Decisions in the Production of Health Care Goods and Services: New Insights from Institutional Economics and Organizational Theory." *Bulletin of the World Health Organization* 78 (6): 791–802.

Preker, A.S., and J.C. Langenbrunner, eds. 2005. *Spending Wisely: Buying Health Services for the Poor.* Washington, DC: World Bank.

Rothstein, B. 2005. *Social Traps and the Problem of Trust.* Cambridge, UK: Cambridge University Press.

Samuelson, P. 1954. "The Pure Theory of Public Expenditure." *Review of Economics and Statistics* 36 (4): 387–89.

Van der Gaag, J., and V. Stimac. 2008. *Toward a New Paradigm for Health Sector Development.* Technical Partner Paper 3, Results for Development Institute, Washington, DC.

———. 2012. "How Can We Increase Resources for Health Care in the Developing World? Is (Subsidized) Voluntary Health Insurance the Answer?" *Health Economics* 21: 55–61.

Van Zanden, J.L. 2009. *The Long Road to the Industrial Revolution: The European Economy in a Global Perspective, 1000–1800.* Global Economic History Series 1. Leiden/Boston, MA: Brill.

Widdershoven, B. 2005. *Het dilemma van solidariteit: de Nederlandse onderlinge ziekenfondsen, 1890–1941.* Amsterdam: Askant.

Williamson, O.E. 2000. "The New Institutional Economics: Taking Stock, Looking Ahead." *Journal of Economic Literature* 38: 595–613.

WHO (World Health Organization). 2010. *World Health Report 2010.* Geneva: WHO.

———. 2012a. National Health Accounts (NHA). Country Information, WHO; accessed at http://www.who.int/nha/en/.

———. 2012b. *World Health Statistics 2012.* Geneva: WHO.

World Bank. 2009. "Improving Effectiveness and Outcomes for the Poor in Health, Nutrition, and Population." World Bank, Washington, DC.

———. 2011. *Healthy Partnerships: How Governments Can Engage the Private Sector to Improve Health in Africa.* Washington, DC: World Bank.

Zak, P.J., and S. Knack. 2001. "Trust and Growth." *Economic Journal* 111: 295–321.

Appendixes

APPENDIX A

Theory of Social Health Insurance

Peter Zweifel

1. INTRODUCTION AND OVERVIEW

This appendix develops the theory of social health insurance (SHI). "Public health insurance," the expression used especially in the United States, is viewed here as one variant of SHI. While a good deal is known about the demand and supply of private insurance, the theoretical basis of SHI is much more fragile. Specifically, on the demand side, what are the reasons for social (or public) health insurance to exist, even to dominate private health insurance in most developed countries? With regard to supply, what is known about the objectives and constraints of SHI managers? Finally, economists can predict properties of the equilibrium characterizing private health insurance (PHI). However, what is the likely outcome ("performance") of SHI? At the normative level, one may ask, should the balance be shifted from SHI to PHI?

Accordingly, the plan of this appendix is as follows. Section 2 starts by reviewing the conventional theory of demand for insurance in general and health insurance in particular. However, it also seeks to offer explanations of the demand for SHI, citing efficiency, public choice, and equity reasons. That may explain the existence (but not necessarily the prominence) of SHI. Section 3 is devoted to the supply of health insurance in general and SHI in particular, which comprises more dimensions than just price and quantity. Section 4 reviews the properties of the optimal health insurance contract for providing a benchmark, especially with regard to combating moral hazard. In section 5, the question is asked whether there are factors limiting the apparently inexorable growth of SHI. Section 6 offers a summary and concluding remarks.

2. THE DEMAND FOR SOCIAL HEALTH INSURANCE

This section starts out with the conventional theory of insurance demand. Next, the fact that the subject matter is health insurance rather than property-liability insurance is taken into account. Finally, three types of reasons are given for the existence and prevalence of social rather than private health insurance.

2.1 Theory of Insurance Demand

The standard way to present the theory of insurance demand uses a two-goods model, with wealth in the no-loss state and wealth in the loss state constituting the two goods. Here, a simpler alternative is presented, based on the Von Neumann-Morgenstern function (VNM, henceforth: risk-utility). In figure A.1, there are two levels of wealth, W_l in the loss state and W_n in the no-loss state. The associated utilities are $U[W_l]$ and $U[W_n]$, where $U[W_l] < U[W_n]$, the bracket to be interpreted to mean that the utility function $U(\cdot)$ is to be evaluated at the respective values of the argument. Expected utility is given by[1]

$$EU = \pi \cdot U[W_l] + (1 - \pi)U[W_n] \qquad (1)$$

$$W_l := W_0 - L - P(I) + I$$

$$W_n := W_0 - P(I),$$

with π denoting the probability of loss ($0 < \pi < 1$), P the premium, and I the amount paid by insurance in the event of loss. In figure A.1, the case $\pi = \frac{1}{2}$ is shown. Clearly, the expected utility EU is associated with the expected value of wealth, EW. It is a linear combination of utilities $U[W_l]$ and $U[W_n]$. It is well known that linear combinations of these values lie on the connecting straight line.

FIGURE A.1   The Demand for Insurance

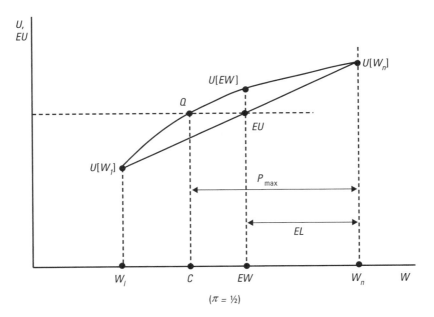

Source: Author.

Now consider an individual who has the possibility of escaping this risky prospect, in which a high value and a low value of wealth may be realized with a certain probability. Given that the alternative providing certainty would be financially equivalent $(W = EW)$, a risk-averse decision maker would opt for it. This means that the risk-utility function must pass above the point EU, for example, through $U[EW] > EU(W)$. The remainder of the risk-utility function can be constructed as follows. The loss-state with probability $\pi = 1$ is no different from the certain unfavorable outcome, and likewise loss-state with probability $\pi = 0$ is equivalent to the certain favorable outcome. Therefore, the risk-utility function at $\pi = 1$ and $\pi = 0$ cannot differ from the extreme points of the linear combination that defines $EU(W)$. On the whole, the risk-utility function must run concave from below, that is, $U''(W) < 0$.

An interesting implication follows from indifference between risky and certain alternatives, depicted as a horizontal line through the point EU, intersecting the risk-utility function at point Q. The associated value of wealth (point C) is called the certainty-equivalent of the risky prospect. It shows that risk-averse individuals accept a reduction in their wealth if this permits them to escape the risky situation. The more marked the curvature of the risk-utility function, the more risk-averse is the individual considered, and the greater is the difference between the expected value of wealth EW and the certainty-equivalent C. This difference can also be interpreted as a willingness to pay for certainty.

Turning to insurance, a policy with full coverage offers certainty in terms of wealth. Therefore, risk-averse individuals also have a willingness to pay for insurance if their assets are exposed to variability. In figure A.1, P_{max} is the maximum total premium that such an individual is willing to pay. It consists of two components. First, EL shows the expected value of the loss. This is also called the actuarially fair premium. The excess of P_{max} over EL is equivalent to the maximum loading for administrative expense and profit that an insurer offering the full coverage contract can charge the consumer depicted in figure A.1. Clearly, this loading also depends on the degree of risk aversion of the individual; without risk aversion, the risk-utility function would run linear, causing P_{max} and EL to coincide. Therefore, there would be no willingness to pay for insurance beyond the actuarially fair amount.

2.2 The Demand for Health Insurance in Particular

The model in the preceding section is not satisfactory for health insurance because it is couched exclusively in terms of wealth. One approach would be to enter health status H in the risk-utility function. A far easier alternative is to continue to work with a risk-utility function in terms of wealth only, but to make its shape depend on health status. First, the risk-utility function conditional on good health has a higher value than that conditional on bad health, that is, $U(W_h) > U(W_s)$, for all levels of wealth W. Second, however, it is not so much the difference in levels but in slopes that is crucial for the optimal amount of coverage. The argument will be developed only for the case where the premium is actuarially fair,

$$P(I) = \pi I. \tag{2}$$

Substituting equation (2) into equation (1), modified to comprise $U_h(W)$ for the healthy state and $U_s(W)$ for the sick state, and taking the first order derivative with regard to insurance coverage I, one obtains

$$\frac{dEU}{dI} = \pi U_s'[W_l](-\pi + 1) + (1 - \pi)U_h'[W_n](-\pi) = 0. \tag{3}$$

Dividing this by $\pi \cdot (1 - \pi)$, one has

$$U_s'[W_l] = U_h'[W_n]. \tag{4}$$

Therefore, given actuarially fair premiums, the optimum for the potential buyer of health insurance is equality of the two marginal utilities of wealth. This makes sense, because as long as additional wealth is worth more in one state than the other, the consumer should reallocate wealth between the two states.

Turning to figure A.2 (panel a), the upper risk-utility function runs steeper throughout than the lower one, indicating that the marginal utility of wealth is higher in the healthy state than in the sick state for all values of W. The two parallel dashed lines show a possible solution that satisfies the equality of marginal utilities as given by equation (4). The optima are given by points Q and R on the state-dependent risk-utility functions. They imply that optimally wealth should be higher in the healthy state than in the sick state. Therefore, insurance coverage

FIGURE A.2   Optimal Degree of Coverage in Health Insurance

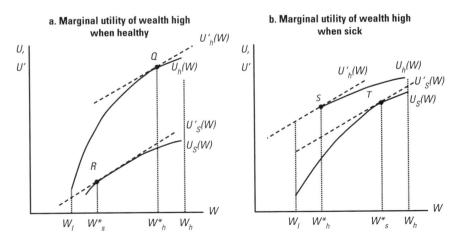

should not be complete but contain a degree of cost sharing (which can also be justified on other grounds, particularly, moral hazard).

In panel b, the situation is exactly reverse. Here, the lower-valued risk-utility function runs steeper than the higher-valued one throughout. Applying the marginal utility criterion of equation (4) once more, one obtains optimal points S and T. This time, these points indicate that wealth optimally should be higher in the sick state than in the healthy state. The interpretation is that possibly, when an individual is ill, good accommodations, healthy food, and comfortable clothing are more important than in the healthy state. For such an individual, health insurance, at least in the absence of moral hazard, should provide compensation for suffering. Of course, a contract that pays more than the medical expenditure needed to reestablish health would strongly invite moral hazard. Therefore, there are considerations that still would call for wealth to be optimally lower in the sick state in order to combat moral hazard.

CONCLUSION 1: The theory of insurance demand predicts that risk-averse individuals derive benefit from health insurance, at least on expectation, provided that the premium does not contain an excessive loading for administrative expense and profit. To the extent that wealth is particularly important when a person is ill, optimal coverage may contain a compensation for suffering; however, this result might not hold under the influence of moral hazard.

2.3 Why Social Health Insurance?

Most developed countries have some kind of collective financing for health services, either through tax (e.g., the National Health Service of the United Kingdom) or through their contributions to "social" health insurance (SHI). This type of insurance is usually characterized by mandatory membership for at least the vast majority of the population, open enrolment, and community rating, that is, a prohibition against charging premiums related to individual risk. From a normative point of view, the institution of SHI can be defended on both efficiency and equity grounds, whereas positive economics seeks to explain its existence in democracies on the basis of public choice models.

2.3.1 Efficiency Reasons: Characteristics of Private Health Insurance Markets

SHI may be efficiency-enhancing if it mitigates or eliminates possible market failures, namely asymmetry in the distribution of information, altruism and free-riding, and optimal taxation.

Asymmetric information. Ever since the seminal contribution by Rothschild and Stiglitz (1976), private competitive insurance markets are suspected of exhibiting adverse selection due to asymmetric information. If the insured has more precise information on his individual risk distribution than the insurer, the only possible Rothschild-Stiglitz equilibrium is a separating one in which the most unfavorable risks are offered complete coverage at actuarially fair premiums.

Lower risks obtain more favorable terms but are rationed in terms of coverage. They would prefer to have more coverage, but this would make their contract attractive to unfavorable risks. Compared with such an equilibrium, SHI, which forces all individuals into a pooling contract with partial coverage, can achieve a Pareto improvement: high risks are made better off because they pay lower premiums for the mandated part of their coverage, whereas low risks benefit from improved total (social plus private) coverage (Newhouse 1996). However, it is unclear to what extent asymmetric information on health risks is really a problem these days since medical exams are used to determine the risk of an insured.

Altruism and free-riding. Altruistic rich members of a society may be willing to subsidize the provision of health care to the poor, especially if they are more interested in the health than in the subjective well-being of the poor (Pauly 1970). Private charity fails to reach an efficient allocation since donations to the poor, whether in cash or in kind, have a public-good characteristic, increasing the utility not only of the donor but also of other altruistic members of society. Either a tax-financed national health service (NHS) or SHI with compulsory membership and contributions according to ability to pay solve this free-rider problem.

Optimal taxation when health and income are correlated. A related justification of SHI is derived from the theory of optimal taxation (Cremer and Pestieau 1996). If abilities cannot be observed by tax authorities, the extent to which income taxation can be used for redistribution from the high-skilled to the low-skilled is limited because the high-skilled can always pretend to be low-skilled by reducing their labor supply. However, if there is a negative correlation between ability and the risk of illness, a mandatory SHI with uniform contributions implicitly redistributes between the ability groups in the desired fashion and thus improves social welfare. It must be emphasized, however, that this justification departs from Paretian welfare economics by postulating a specific redistributive goal.

2.3.2 Equity Reasons

A further justification, also known as the "principle of solidarity," relates to the achievement of equality of opportunity. People differ in their health risk already at birth, and some indicators of risk are readily observable. Moreover, with the rapid progress of genetic diagnostics and the spread of tests during pregnancy, the ability to measure individual health risks of newborns will become more and more pronounced. In private health insurance (PHI), these differences in risk immediately translate into differences in premiums so that persons endowed by nature with a lower stock of "health capital," and thus already disadvantaged, have to pay a higher price for the same coverage on top of this. Behind the veil of ignorance, one would desire at least an equalization of the monetary costs of illness.

There are in principle two ways to achieve solidarity in health insurance (table A.1). First, PHI premiums can be subsidized for people who would have to

TABLE A.1   ALTERNATIVES FOR ACHIEVING SOLIDARITY IN HEALTH INSURANCE

Alternatives		Advantages	Disadvantages	References
Premium subsidy	Current transfer	Permits full competition in PHI (or SHI) both in premiums and products and full information on risk	Means testing; definition of benchmark contract	Pauly et al. (1992)
	Lump-sum transfer for lifetime		Means testing; longevity risk shifted to beneficiaries	
Regulation: Community rating (uniform contributions)		Relieves public budget	Induces cream skimming and RAS as secondary regulation	Van de Ven et al. (2000)

Source: Author.
Note: RAS = risk-adjustment schemes.

pay excessive contributions. The transfer could be on a current basis or a lump sum, equal to the estimated present value of future excess premiums over the whole expected life span of beneficiaries. Both have the important advantage of permitting full competition in PHI (or SHI), including insurers' acquiring information about true risk. Besides means testing and the need to define a benchmark contract to determine the amount of the subsidy, the second variant has the disadvantage of shifting the risk of longevity to beneficiaries. The second alternative is a monopolistic SHI scheme with open enrolment and community rating that prevents differences in health risk from being translated into differences in contributions but induces cream skimming and risk-adjustment schemes (RAS, see below) as a secondary neutralizing regulation.

2.3.3 Public Choice Reasons

In PHI, redistribution occurs purely by chance, from consumers who did not suffer a loss during the life of the contract to those who do. By way of contrast, social insurance mixes in elements of systematic redistribution. The fact that contributions are not (or not fully) graded according to risk alone (OECD 2004) serves to redistribute wealth systematically from high risks to low risks. In SHI, this redistribution affects not only wealth through its financing side but also its benefit side, namely medical services and health. This makes social health insurance an ideal means for a politician who seeks office (or reelection) by catering to the interests of groups that are sufficiently organized to affect the outcome of an election (Gouveia 1997; Hindriks and De Donder 2003; Tullock 2003). The redistributive effects of SHI can be described as follows.

Redistribution of wealth. Using SHI as a vehicle for systematic redistribution has the important advantage that net payers have considerable difficulty determining the systematic component of redistribution. For example, when the contribution to SHI amounts to a payroll tax (as in Germany), high wage earners pay more for their health insurance. However, they are uncertain about the systematic redistribution component of their contribution because the expected value of their benefits may also be higher than average. This may have two reasons: preventive effort may be affected negatively by a higher wage, resulting in higher health costs, and demand for medical services may increase because short-term disability benefits usually increase with wages, creating a spillover moral hazard effect (Zweifel and Manning 2000). Therefore, their higher contribution appears "justified," masking a tax component which, if collected as a tax, would likely be opposed.

Redistribution of medical care. There are two effects here. First, there is an income effect because some individuals who would have demanded less or no medical care without insurance coverage now demand a positive amount of it (Nyman 2003). Indeed there is (macro) evidence suggesting that medical care is a normal good (Gerdtham, Jönsson, and Søgaard 1992; Miller and Frech 2004; Zweifel, Telser, and Vaterlaus 2006). Insurance coverage for everyone then amounts to an in-kind redistribution from the rich to the poor if the supply of medical services is not infinitely elastic and if the price elasticity of demand for medical care is not lower for the rich than for the poor (which is doubtful—see Newhouse et al. [1993: chap. 11]). However, there is also a price effect because health insurance boosts the "true" willingness to pay (WTP) for medical care depending on the rate of coinsurance (Zweifel, Breyer, and Kifmann 2009: chap. 12.3). For example, if "true" WTP is 100 and the rate of coinsurance is 25 percent, observed WTP is 400. To the extent that rich individuals have higher true WTP to begin with, they benefit more strongly (in absolute terms) from this leverage effect of health insurance. Thus, the total redistributive effect of SHI is ambiguous.

Redistribution of health. When it comes to health, altruism is probably more marked than with regard to income, although comparative evidence seems to be lacking (the methodology for measuring distributive preferences for health is still in its infancy [Olsen 2000]). Therefore, politicians can claim to have a mission when seeking to guarantee "health for all" (the famous slogan of the World Health Organization). Equal access to health insurance then may be seen as an important factor for securing equal access to medical care, and to the extent that medical care is effective at the margin, for which there is some evidence (Miller and Frech 2004; Lichtenberg 2004); and for securing equal health status (Culyer and Wagstaff 1993).

If SHI indeed helps win votes and increases the chance of (re)election of a democratic government, one would expect public expenditure for it to increase around election time. One piece of available evidence relates to two types of public expenditure by the Netherlandic government, expressed as GDP shares, between about 1956 and 1993: health (e.g., subsidies to hospitals) and tax contributions to social insurance in general. Van Dalen and Swank (1996), cited in Zweifel (2000a), find that while public expenditure on health does not vary around election time, transfers in favor of social insurance are systematically higher during the years prior to, concurrent with, and after an election. The estimated effect is 13 percent, for example, an increase from 8 percent to 9 percent of GDP. In addition, the share of pensioners in the population is significantly related to both types of public expenditure. Nowadays pensioners are not poor, but they do go to the polls. The evidence thus is compatible with governments proposing SHI schemes to benefit pivotal voter groups.

CONCLUSION 2: While the efficiency reasons for social (health) insurance have received much attention in the economics literature, they are found not fully convincing. As to the equity reasons, targeted premium subsidies emerge as an alternative to community rating. On the whole, the available empirical evidence suggests the public choice reasons (winning votes) may well be the crucial reason for the existence and even more the growth of social (health) insurance.

3. THE SUPPLY OF HEALTH INSURANCE

According to conclusion 2, governments (and public administrations) can be seen as the suppliers of SHI. In systems of the National Health Service type, the government itself provides the insurance function while also acting as the organizer of medical care. Here this type is called "public health insurer." However, in most industrial countries, health insurers are not incorporated in the government's budget; they are called "(competitive) social health insurers." In both cases, the supply of health insurance has several dimensions. It can be characterized by the comprehensiveness and structure of the benefits package, the amount of effort devoted to risk selection, the price of coverage, the amount of integration of health care providers, and the market structure of health insurance.

3.1 Benefits Package

An unregulated private insurer has the option of specifying its offer along three dimensions (figure A.3) (Zweifel and Breyer 1997: 159). First, it can decide to cover only certain types of services and leave out others, for instance, to include inpatient and exclude outpatient care, which is not uncommon in low-income countries (Musau 1999). Second, it can differentiate its offer by covering or excluding services offered by certain provider categories, for instance including only physicians registered with a public agency and excluding those who are not. Third, it may determine the amount of the benefits paid in case of sickness. The compensation may state a certain quantity of services, the compensation per unit of consumption, or the limit up to which expenditures are refunded.

There are many possible combinations between the three dimensions, creating opportunity for product innovation and the building of profitable market segments. The optimal choice is influenced by several factors listed in table A.2, which are discussed starting with the insurer's point of view and moving toward demand-side considerations and regulatory and institutional factors that affect the insurer's decision making.

FIGURE A.3   Differentiation of Benefits

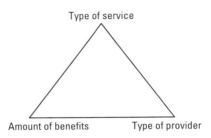

Source: Zweifel, Krey, and Tagli 2007.

3.1.1 Risk Aversion of Insurer

The relevance of risk aversion for the behavior of insurers has been the subject of continued debate (Greenwald and Stiglitz 1990; Chen, Steiner, and White 2001). In industrial countries, owners of insurance companies can be assumed to hold fully diversified portfolios. As such, they are exposed only to nondiversifiable risk, which is reflected in the *beta* of the company.[2] Therefore, diversification is in the interest of shareholders only to the extent it lowers the company's (positive) value of beta. Management, being much less diversified in its assets, has an interest in diversification of its own. Therefore, the extent to which it actually engages in diversification of the underwriting portfolio is a question of corporate governance.

Assuming an interest in risk diversification caused by risk aversion, its impact on the benefits package can still go either way (see table A.2). To the extent that, for example, inpatient and outpatient services constitute complements rather than substitutes, they are positively correlated. Including both in the benefits package then adds to the variance of liabilities, everything else being equal, which runs counter to the interests of a risk-averse insurer. Benefits triggered by communicable diseases have the same effect, motivating their strict limitation. Even if there is negative correlation risk diversification does not necessarily imply more complete benefits packages at the individual level since the insurer can offer different packages to different client groups.

To the extent that domestic investors in low-income countries cannot rely on a sufficiently developed capital market (or are prevented from full international diversification), their risk aversion is more likely to be relevant for management decisions. Management, finding itself in a similar situation, usually reinforces this tendency (assuming corporate governance to be imperfect). In community-based health insurance in particular, which amounts to a mutual insurer, owners are individuals and households, whose degree of asset diversification is far lower. This calls for an even keener interest in diversification.

TABLE A.2   Factors Affecting the Size of the Benefits Package

Factor	*Factor serves to increase (+)/decrease (−) benefits package*				
	Private health insurance	*Community-based health insurance*		*Public health insurance*	
(1) Risk aversion of insurer	+/−	+/−	↓	n.a.	
(2) Synergies among benefits	+	+	↓	n.a.	
(3) Moral hazard	−	−	↓	−	↑
(4) Diversity of preferences	+	+	↓	+	↓
(5) Diversity of risks	+	+	↓	+	↓
(6) Emergence of new health risks	+	+	↓	+	↑
(7) Regulation	+	+		+	↑
(8) Fraud and abuse	−	−	↑	−	↓

Source: Zweifel, Krey, and Tagli 2007.
Note: ↑ = reinforcement of relationship; ↓ = attenuation of relationship; n.a. = not applicable.

A public health insurer is unlikely to be significantly risk averse with respect to its financial results. Its opportunities to shift the financial risk and the responsibility for failure to the government—which can resort to printing money if necessary—are numerous. Therefore, risk aversion cannot have much importance in determining the benefits package.

3.1.2 Synergies among Benefits

Synergies denote economies of scope in production, distribution, and marketing that are unrelated to risk-diversification effects. They cause insurers to benefit from offering a combination of benefits rather than a single benefit. In production, synergies arise when the costs of writing and executing contracts[3] do not rise proportionally with the number of benefits, resulting in decreasing expected unit cost. In distribution, the same channel may be used for selling additional products. In marketing, brand advertising benefits all the products sold by a given insurer.

In a public insurance system, synergies are not a very relevant criteria for a decision maker who aims at providing public and merit goods to the population (see section 3.3). This objective tends to override the economic justification of extending benefits purely because of synergies.

3.1.3 Moral Hazard

The effect of ex post moral hazard[4] on the benefits package can be illustrated as follows. Assume that consumers' willingness to pay out of pocket for a medical service or product is approximately given by the linear demand function $C'C$ of figure A.4. In the case of health insurance with a 50 percent coinsurance

FIGURE A.4   Ex Post Moral Hazard

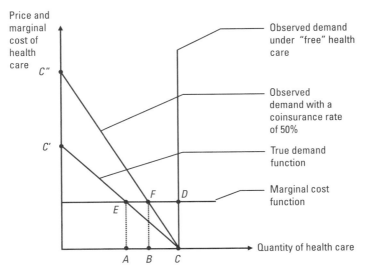

A: Equilibrium quantity without insurance coverage
B: Equilibrium quantity with 50% coinsurance
B-A: Ex post moral hazard effect with a coinsurance rate of 50%
C-A: Ex post moral hazard effect in a scheme without coinsurance

Source: Zweifel, Krey, and Tagli 2007.

rate, maximum willingness to pay is doubled, from C' to C''. More generally, the demand function is rotated outward to become the effective demand function CC''. The lower the rate of coinsurance, the more pronounced is this rotation. With no copayment at all (as is often the case with tax-funded schemes), the curve runs fully vertical from C.

Therefore, the market equilibrium shifts from point E to F, with a higher quantity of the service or product transacted. In terms of equation (5) in section 3.3, the benefits to be paid (I) increase, resulting in an ex post moral hazard effect. As will be argued in section 3.3.6, a decrease in the rate of coinsurance causes both parts of the loading and hence the premium to increase. This creates a negative income effect (shifting the demand curve inward) that is neglected for simplicity.

The moral hazard effect is relevant to the choice of benefits package because it arises with each additional item in the package. The more complete the package, the larger is the loading component in the gross premium and hence the larger is the net cost of insurance. Therefore, moral hazard considerations should lead an insurer to exercise caution in expanding the package. Specifically, an insurer would want to add services characterized by low price elasticity of demand because the moral hazard effect is more limited in this case. In figure A.4, lower price elasticity means that, for a given maximum willingness to pay such as C', the demand function runs steeper, causing point C to shift toward the origin. This serves to reduce the difference between the true and the observed demand curve, and hence the size of the ex post moral hazard effect.

Moral hazard may be less of a problem in community-based schemes (table A.2), which usually consist of small risk-pools. First, asymmetric information is less pronounced in a small community, where each member of the pool can easily monitor the behavior of the others.

In a public insurance system, moral hazard sooner or later becomes an important consideration in the determination of the benefits package. The consumption of health care services usually entails little or no cost sharing for the user, which means that in figure A.4, the vertical observed demand function applies. Therefore, the public insurer must finance the maximum quantity C times the unit price CD for each benefit added. It is subject to the ex post moral hazard effect to a higher degree than a private insurer, who would offer policies with varying degrees of cost sharing. Unless contributions (often levied in the guise of a payroll tax) or tax allocations are increased accordingly, the scheme ends up in deficit.

3.1.4 Diversity of Preferences

The creation of a benefits package depends on its value to consumers. Consumers demand a package that combines benefits to the extent that their marginal rate of substitution is equal on expectation. A unit of benefit will be added to the package until its ratio of expected marginal utility to the premium increase occasioned is equal across all benefits. This expected value importantly depends on the amount of risk aversion and the relevant probabilities of loss. Differences in loss probabilities are addressed below.

Diversity of preferences among the insured causes their optimality conditions to be satisfied at different (sometimes zero) levels of benefits. To attract consumers, insurers customize their products in an attempt to maximize expected profit. The diversity of preferences may relate to, for example, the amount of the deductible, the rate of coinsurance, and the limits on benefits, as well as type of service (e.g., alternative medicine) and type of provider. In this way, permanent innovation and adjustment to changing demand occurs. As a general rule, product differentiation is costly.

Public health insurers, almost by definition, cannot accommodate different preferences because their mission is to administer a uniform product to the entire population (or at least a great majority of it). The more preferences differ, the more likely is a uniform national health insurance scheme to burden the country with a loss of efficiency.[5]

3.1.5 Diversity of Risks

Diversity of risks (in the sense of differences in loss probabilities) promotes a differentiation of degrees of coverage, combined with a differentiation of premiums. If insurers are unable to assess risks, a differentiation of premiums cannot take place, which encourages the purchase of excess coverage by high risks and reduced coverage by low risks. Therefore, the insurer runs the danger of incurring a deficit when expanding the benefits package under these conditions. The same argument holds when the insurer is prevented from differentiating premiums by a mandate to take on every applicant under the same conditions. When combined with asymmetric information, diversity of risks thus hampers the creation of comprehensive benefits packages (table A.2).

For a public health insurer, uniformity of benefits is part of its mission because it acts on behalf of the government, whose likely objective is to provide citizens with a maximum of public and "merit" goods. By assumption, public goods are enjoyed by everyone to the same degree; therefore, if the government views access to health care as a public good, its insurance branch must act accordingly, guaranteeing equal access through equal benefits. Diversity of risks can hardly be reflected in a diversity of (planned) benefits under these circumstances.

3.1.6 Emergence of New Health Risks

New health risks give rise to demand for an extension of the benefits package. However, even under competitive conditions, insurers do not adjust to this demand immediately. First, they need time to assess the probability of loss π. Second, an extension of the benefits package calls for a premium adjustment, which in turn usually requires a cancellation of the policy. It takes new business to provide the insurer with the opportunity to test consumers' willingness to pay a higher premium for the added benefit. Even under competitive conditions, new health risks are thus covered only with some delay (table A.2).

This is even more true of community-based schemes, which still have to deal with communicable diseases causing individual illness probabilities to be positively correlated. Extending the benefits package therefore may increase the risk of ruin, especially since these schemes operate in areas where close personal contact is very common (Nugroho, Macagba, and Dorros 2001).

A public insurer is called upon to cover emerging new risks because public health is at stake. Though hardly concerned about the risk of ruin, the public insurer still has to take into account that the government must cover possibly high deficits.

3.1.7 Regulation

Regulation typically concerns not only premiums but also products because premium regulation can be subverted by product differentiation. Premium regulation typically prevents insurers from differentiating premiums according to true risk. A given uniform premium is associated with a contribution to expected profit in a low-risk case but an expected deficit in a high-risk case. Therefore, it becomes vital for an insurer to attract as many low risks as possible. One way to achieve this is to modify the benefits package, excluding services that attract high risks. More generally, insurers use benefits to compete with differentiated products since price competition is hindered by the regulator. In all, premium regulation in principle serves to increase the variety of benefits packages on the market, unless product regulation neutralizes this tendency.

Overall, regulation of insurance can be efficiency-reducing, especially if it seeks to minimize the social cost of insolvency by avoiding insolvency altogether (annex B and annex table AB.1). Typically, this type of regulation is limited to mitigating the social costs of insolvencies while permitting them in principle. An overview is provided by annex table AB.2.

In many community-based schemes, the members determine the premium. The resulting premium is uniform; however, this triggers but little risk-selection effort through product differentiation (section 3.2) because the risk pool is very homogeneous. Moreover, most schemes are local monopolies and therefore have little incentive to compete for members with differentiated benefits packages.

Since public health insurance can be seen as subject to a maximum degree of regulation (annex table AB.1), it is also most strongly exposed to it in the determination of the benefits package. Expanding benefits is in the logic of a government that seeks to provide a maximum amount of public goods; therefore, a strong tendency in this direction can be expected.

3.1.8 Fraud and Abuse

Fraud and abuse may occur at three levels. First, it constitutes an extreme form of moral hazard on the part of the insured. However, it may be countered by the insurer by inspections, curtailment, or denial of benefits. Second, providers of services may act fraudulently. Here, the countermeasure is to pattern their remuneration in a way that gives them an incentive for honesty.[6] Third, fraud and abuse may occur when health care providers make their purchases. Being one step removed, it cannot easily be neutralized by the insurer unless competition between providers is strong.

Providers of medical supplies may defraud physicians and hospitals, for example, by offering money as an inducement to use their more expensive products for treatment instead of cheaper products from competing suppliers. These products tend to be also of lower quality and quantity because corrupt suppliers have to recover their bribery payments through their sales margins. This results in insurable medical services of a lower quality at a given price. An insurer considering the extension of its benefits package thus has to take into account that such an addition may well be of lower quality, thus failing to induce much willingness to pay higher premiums. This makes more comprehensive benefits packages not very attractive.

Both public and private health insurers are affected by corruption in the same way in that they can offer only fewer services or lower-quality services for the amount of revenue received, be it in the guise of payroll taxes, general taxes, or premiums. This means that the benefits package is less comprehensive than it could be. However, the list of benefits cannot easily be purged of those items whose slots suppliers had bought. This serves to attenuate the negative relationship between benefits and fraud, at least as long as incurring a deficit is an option for the public insurer.

CONCLUSION 3: The comprehensiveness of the benefits package contributes a first dimension of the supply of health insurance. It depends on at least eight factors, with moral hazard exerting an important limiting influence.

3.2 Risk-Selection Effort

Most policy makers and even many economists believe that "cream skimming," namely making an effort to attract the favorable risks, is typical of private health insurers. However, upon closer examination, this belief is not justified. If health insurers were entirely free to grade their premiums according to risk, they would not want to invest in risk selection at all for the following reason. An unfavorable risk would be charged a high premium, whereas a favorable risk would demand and obtain a low premium. Given expected future health care cost, insurers would adjust premiums so that the expected contribution margin is equalized across risk groups. Under the pressure of competition, insurers simply cannot cross-subsidize one risk group to the detriment of another because the discriminated group can generate a more favorable offer from a competing insurer. For this reason, "n.a." is entered in table A.3, where appropriate, to reflect the fully competitive, unregulated benchmark, indicating that the factor considered is not effective. However, in the following discussion it is assumed that premiums are regulated to some extent, imposing more uniformity than warranted by

TABLE A.3   Factors Affecting Risk-Selection Effort

	Factor serving to increase (+)/decrease (−) risk-selection effort		
Factor	Private health insurance	Community-based health insurance	Public health insurance
(1) Risk aversion of insurer	+ (n.a.)	+ ↑	n.a.
(2) Moral hazard	+ (n.a.)	+ ↓	n.a.
(3) Size of the benefits package	+ (n.a.)	+ ↑	n.a.
(4) Diversity of risks	+ (n.a.)	+ ↓	n.a.
(5) Access to risk information	+ (n.a.)	+ ↓	n.a.
(6) Sellers' concentration	− (n.a.)	− ↑	n.a.
(7) Regulation	+ (n.a.)	+	n.a.

Source: Zweifel, Krey, and Tagli 2007.
Note: ↑ = reinforcement of relationship; ↓ = attenuation of relationship; n.a. = not applicable.

actuarial considerations and inducing an interest in risk selection on the part of competitive health insurers. A theoretical model analyzing both risk-selection and product-innovation effort can be found in annex A.

3.2.1 Risk Aversion of Insurer

If premiums have to differ from the expected value of the loss covered plus loading,[7] the underwriting result of the insurer has excessive variance. The predicted response of management to this increased risk exposure depends on the same considerations as expounded in section 3.1.1. If management has leeway to pursue its own interests, inducing risk-averse behavior, it will undertake risk-selection efforts because it can decrease its own risk exposure in this way (table A.3). However, this tendency can be neutralized by implementing a more or less elaborate risk-adjustment scheme (van de Ven and Ellis 2000).

Community-based schemes are subject to risk selection because their member-owners are much less diversified than the typical shareholder of an insurance company, which makes them particularly concerned about excessive exposure to a risk that may ultimately spell insolvency. For a public insurer that wields a monopoly, risk selection is not relevant to begin with, motivating the "n.a." entries in table A.3.

3.2.2 Moral Hazard

A competitive health insurer would want to charge a high premium to consumers who are particularly susceptible to moral hazard.[8] If this is not possible due to premium regulation, risk selection is a substitute measure because it can be used to keep the high–moral hazard types out of the insured population.

3.2.3 Size of Benefits Package

With a limited benefits package, differences in expected contribution margins between high and low risks typically are not large. This means that the incentive to engage in risk selection is not marked either (annex A). Conversely, the more comprehensive the benefits package, the more heavily are health insurers predicted to invest in risk-selection effort. This tendency is likely to be especially strong among community-based schemes because once they begin to offer more benefits, their risk exposure increases, but this increase can be counterbalanced by a more careful selection of risks.

3.2.4 Diversity of Risks

Above all, diversity of risks means that the insured differ widely in terms of their expected value of loss, that is, their illness probability and/or the amount of medical care utilized in the event of illness. The larger such discrepancies are, the more does premium regulation (in the limit: uniformity of premiums) induce excess variance in the underwriting result. A private health insurer is predicted to counter this by stepping up its risk selection effort. However, the same behavior is predicted for a community-based scheme (or in fact any non-profit insurer) as long as running into deficit triggers a sanction of some sort. In community-based schemes, this tendency is weaker because traditionally their insured population has been very homogenous to begin with (table A.3).

3.2.5 Access to Risk Information

Risk selection is an attempt on the part of the health insurer to mitigate or over-come an asymmetry of information resulting from the likelihood that the pro-spective enrollee knows more about his or her future health risks than does the insurer. However, genetic information may change that. Already, the availability of such information permits the insurer to predict an individual's future health care expenditure with much greater precision than in the past. Moreover, refusal to provide genetic information sends a signal that the person has genetic infor-mation indicating he or she constitutes a high risk. This means that the effec-tiveness of risk-selection effort is greatly enhanced by improved access to risk information of this type. Accordingly, risk selection becomes a more attractive alternative for health insurers.

3.2.6 Sellers' Concentration

The importance of sellers' concentration can be seen from the following thought experiment (Wilson 1977). If there were only two companies (A and B) in the market, risk selection would make little sense as soon as the planning horizon of the two competitors extends beyond the current period. True, in period 1 insurer A may be able to filter out the favorable risks. However, it would dump the unfavorable risks on B, who in turn would have to resort to risk selection to stave them off in period 2. Thus, in period 3 these unfavorable risks would again seek coverage with insurer A. In the end, both A and B would lose from investing in risk selection. This consideration makes risk selection in concentrated health insurance markets less likely. This scenario may be less applicable to commu-nity-based health insurance because their members also own the scheme, fully exposing them to the risk of insolvency that may be the consequence of a failure to carefully gauge potential clients. Of course, these arguments do not apply to a public insurer, which wields a monopoly.

3.2.7 Regulation

As stated in the introductory paragraph of section 3.2, a health insurer that has the freedom to grade its premiums by risk usually equalizes expected contribu-tion margins across risks. Unfavorable risks, while expected to cause high health care expenditure, also pay a high premium, whereas favorable risks must be attracted by low premiums that reflect their low future cost. Arguably, it is pre-mium regulation, seeking to relieve the high risks of "excessive" premiums, that induces risk selection by health insurers (Pauly 1984). A means-tested subsidy paid out to potential purchasers of health insurance with low incomes could provide an alternative. In this way, this counterproductive side effect of premium regulation (to be expected regardless of for-profit status) can be avoided (Zweifel and Breyer 2005).

CONCLUSION 4: The amount of risk-selection effort is a second dimension of health insurance supply. Induced by premium regulation, it is of great concern to policy makers. Its extent depends on at least seven factors, the only mitigating one being a high sellers' concentration among insurers.

3.3 Loading: The True Price of Insurance

Since premiums are in part paid back to consumers in the guise of benefits, they do not reflect the price of insurance. Rather, the true price of insurance is the part of the premium that is not used to pay benefits, the "loading for administrative expense" and profit. In more formal terms, insurers pay an indemnity I to cover a loss against a premium. The gross premium can be divided into a net premium ($\pi \cdot I$), with probability of loss π depending negatively on preventive effort on one hand and a loading on the other. The net premium covers the expected amount of benefit to be paid. The loading can be further subdivided into a component that is a per unit amount μ associated with claims processing. The higher the likelihood of a claim's being presented, the more often is an administrative process triggered. The other component is a multiple λ of expected benefits net of copayment (symbolized by a rate of coinsurance c for simplicity), reflecting acquisition cost, a risk premium, and profit. Therefore, a viable insurance contract must be priced to contain the following elements (Zweifel and Breyer 1997: chap. 6.2):

$$P\,(I) = \text{net premium} + \text{loading}$$
$$= \pi(V)\cdot(1-c)\cdot I + \mu\cdot\pi(V) + \lambda\cdot\pi(V)\cdot(1-c)\cdot I \qquad (5)$$

P: Premium
μ: Loading factor for variable administrative expense
π: Loss probability, probability of illness; $0 < \pi < 1$, $\pi'\,(V) < 0$
V: Preventive effort (unobservable)
c: Rate of coinsurance; $c < 1$
λ: Loading factor for acquisition cost, risk premium, and profit
I: Benefit paid in the event of illness

This equation needs to be completed by the following consideration. The more complete coverage, denoted by I, the weaker in general are the insured's incentives for prevention V.[9] Taking into account this ex ante moral hazard effect, the amount of loading can be written

$$\text{Amount of loading} = \mu \cdot \pi(V(I)) + \lambda \cdot (1-c)\cdot\pi(V(I)) \cdot I. \qquad (6)$$

The question arises immediately whether the concept of loading has any relevance to a public health insurer. It does, and for two different reasons. First, a public scheme also has its administrative expense, which rises as the frequency of claims π increases. This frequency depends on preventive effort V precisely as with any private insurer, and V in turn is again negatively related to coverage I (the ex ante moral hazard effect). The term $\mu \cdot \pi(V(I))$ of equation (6) therefore applies to public insurance as well. Second, although a public insurer need not charge for acquisition cost, risk bearing, and profit, it gives rise to a "loading" that is very similar to the second term of equation (6). The larger the expected value of benefits to be paid net of coinsurance $[(1-c) \cdot \pi \cdot I]$, the higher must be the rate of tax levied on labor income or on sales. Now as is well known, taxes cause inefficiencies because they reduce the volume of transactions; some contracts that would have been mutually beneficial are not struck under the influence of tax. These inefficiencies easily amount to 20 percent of transaction value (McMaster 2001) and thus are of a comparable magnitude as λ in equation (6).

In all, the expression for the loading given by equation (6) can be applied to public health insurance as well, at least to a first approximation. The "loading" may differ depending on the type of taxation used to fund the scheme. The amount of loading is influenced by several factors listed in table A.4.

3.3.1 Administrative Expense

Administrative expense must be recovered before the insurer can break even. They are added to the expected loss. The loading factors μ and λ reflect these expenses and thus importantly determine the amount of loading.[10] They depend on possible economies of scale, implying that a critical number of contracts and transactions may be necessary to reach minimum average cost. The loading factors also include capital utilization costs, and surcharges for uncertainty about future cost inflation in the health care sector and about the loss probability π.

TABLE A.4   Factors Affecting the Net Price of Health Insurance (Loading)

Factor	Factor increases (+)/decreases (−) risk-selection effort		
	Private health insurance	Community-based health insurance	Public health insurance
(1) Administrative expenses (including capital charge)	+	+ ↓	+
(2) Reinsurance	+ / −	+ / − ↑	n.a.
(3) Pool size	+ / −	+ / −	−
(4) Benefits package	+	+	+
(5) Copayments and caps	−	−	− ↓
(6) Moral hazard	+	+ ↓	+ ↑
(7) Quality and proximity of health care services	+	+	+
(8) Regulatory framework	+ / −	+ / − ↓	+ / − ↑
(9) Fraud and abuse	+	+ ↓	+ ↑

Source: Zweifel, Krey, and Tagli 2007.
Note: ↑ = reinforcement of relationship; ↓ = attenuation of relationship; n.a. = not applicable.

Community-based schemes are known for their low administrative expenses because they do not employ a large staff, and usually most of the personnel they do have are volunteers. This holds down the loading factors. Members bear part of the costs of organization by spending their time and efforts to decide on the product offering and the premium charged.

Public health insurance constitutes a monopoly, which means that marketing and advertising expenses are reduced but so, too, are pressures to minimize cost. On the whole, the relationship may be comparable to that in private competitive health insurance.

3.3.2 Reinsurance

Generally, reinsurance is an expense that reduces the expected value of profit (if the premium exceeds the actuarial value of losses ceded) (Doherty and Tinic 1981). It is therefore similar to administrative expense, causing the loading to increase, all other things being equal. The benefit of reinsurance is that it improves the solvency of the insurer, permitting a lower value of the loading factor λ. Still, if additional capital is available at lower cost than reinsurance, it is preferable for an insurer to rely on the capital market instead of taking out reinsurance.

Reinsurance can be beneficial to community-based health insurers, whose pool size often is insufficient for the law of large numbers to come to full effect. According to the law of large numbers, insurers are able to estimate π more precisely and hence the expected value of benefits to be paid when the number of risks increases. This facilitates the attainment of a given level of solvency. In addition, the typically undiversified individual (member) owners of such schemes will gain from the lower variance of the surplus (assets minus liabilities) generally afforded by reinsurance. This benefit in terms of variance reduction has to be weighed, however, against the reinsurance premium. Therefore, low-cost reinsurance may become a precondition for the viability of community-based health insurance, which most often does not have access to capital markets.

Reinsurance is hardly an issue for a public health insurer. Its large risk pool allows minimization of per capita reserves (section 3.3.3), to which reinsurance contributes. In addition, these reserves are usually provided by the government as lender of last resort; ultimately, the taxpayers act as the reinsurers of the public health insurer. Compared with a private insurer, these savings on reinsurance entail a cost advantage for the public monopolist (table A.4).

3.3.3 Pool Size

A large number of insured persons of a similar type allows the unknown parameters π and I to be estimated with greater precision. Therefore, the insurer can carry lower reserves per unit risk to attain a given level of solvency (Dror and Preker 2002: 135). The pertinent loading factor λ becomes smaller, resulting in a smaller total loading.

A large pool size shields the individual insurance buyer from social control through other members. This control likely refers to the benefits claimed (I) rather than preventive behavior and hence π. Increased pool size thus strengthens ex post moral hazard and lessens ex ante moral hazard. The second term of equation (6) increases, indicating that the amount of loading increases.

In the case of a community-based health insurer, the trade-off between the two influences can be studied. For instance, the Dana Sehat schemes in Indonesia are organized in several thousand independent groups, with approximately 50 to 100 families in each group. Families are homogenous with regard to household size and income and, due to the community environment, behavior is closely monitored. Although the total number of Dana Sehat participants is large (7 million people in Indonesia), moral hazard can be controlled effectively, resulting in a small loading in spite of small pool size. "Farmer's health insurance" in Taiwan, China, provides a counter example. There, a risk pool typically comprises a few thousand individuals (Bureau of National Health Insurance, Taiwan). This could lead to a lower value of λ; however, greater pool size also calls for more complex management, and social control is undermined. Although information about the total loading is not available, it is likely to be higher than in Indonesia.

Public health insurance schemes start out with risk pool sizes that are too large for moral hazard effects to be mitigated by social control. Therefore, further expansion of the pool causes the loading contained in the contribution to decrease unambiguously.

3.3.4 Benefits Package

An extension of the benefits package increases the likelihood of claims' being submitted. Therefore, the probability of loss π increases even without any behavioral modification on the part of the insured (moral hazard effects are dealt with in section 3.3.6). Likewise, payment may occur under additional titles, resulting in an increased value of payments I. Therefore, the amount of loading must increase according to equation (6).

This argument holds also for community-based and public health insurance (table A.4).

3.3.5 Copayments and Caps

Copayments and caps have three effects on total loading. First, they serve to limit ex post moral hazard. Copayments increase the net price of medical care to consumers, causing them to lower the quantity demanded, while caps increase the net price to its full market value when the threshold quantity is exceeded. Therefore, the value of payments I decreases on average and with it the amount of loading. Caps have the additional feature of excluding very high values of I, thus reducing also the (semi)variance of I and hence the loading factor λ.

Second, copayments relieve the insurer of part of the payment in the advent of illness. As shown in equation (8) in section 3.3.6, an increase in the rate of coinsurance c serves to lower the total amount of loading. Copayments and caps thus unambiguously serve to reduce the amount of loading.

The same arguments hold for community-based schemes. They have even greater force for public health insurance, where the initial rate of copayment is zero, resulting in maximum ex post moral hazard effects. Indeed, according to equation (8) below, the amount of loading reacts most strongly to a variation in the rate of coinsurance c when $(1-c) = 1$, namely when $c = 0$ initially.

3.3.6 Moral Hazard

Moral hazard increases the consumption of health care services by the insured and thus imposes additional costs on the insurer. It is a common phenomenon in the insurance and health care industry. It is convenient to distinguish between ex ante and ex post moral hazard. Ex ante moral hazard refers to the probability of illness π. This probability depends on related preventive effort on the part of the insured, denoted by V.

While preventive effort can hardly be observed in the context of health behavior, it generally decreases when the amount of coverage offered is extended. Ex ante moral hazard thus results in a positive relationship between π and the amount of insurance coverage I.

Indeed, because of ex ante moral hazard an increase in I is associated not only with a higher gross premium, but also with a higher amount of total loading. For convenience, equation (7) is repeated here:

$$\text{Amount of loading} = \Lambda = \mu \cdot \pi(V(I)) + \lambda \cdot (1-c) \cdot \pi(V(I)) \cdot I. \tag{7}$$

The derivative of this expression with respect to I (neglecting possible effects of I on the loading factors μ and λ) is given by

$$\Lambda'(I) = \underset{(-)\quad(-)}{\mu \cdot \pi'(V) \cdot V'(I)} + \underset{(-)\quad(-)}{(1-c) \cdot \lambda \cdot \pi'(V) \cdot V'(I) \cdot I} + \underset{(+)}{\lambda \cdot (1-c) \cdot \pi(V(I))} > 0. \tag{8}$$

With π' and V' negative, the first term is positive. For the same reason, the second term is positive as well, and the third term is positive by definition. In analogy to the development in Zweifel and Breyer (1997: 183), the loading usually increases progressively in I, if $\pi''(V) > 0$ (prevention becoming less effective at the margin) in addition to $V'(I) < 0$.

According to equation (8), some health insurance benefits may be more affected by ex ante moral hazard than others because preventive effort V responds more strongly to an increase in I. Conversely, this effect may be mitigated to some extent if health insurance is provided through the employer, who can at least monitor prevention at the workplace. This difference would be reflected in a more moderate increase of the loading (as well as the gross premium) when coverage becomes more complete or more comprehensive.

Summing up, ex ante moral hazard likely causes an increase in the total loading, which may be even progressive in benefits I. There seem to be no strong reasons to modify this argument for community-based schemes. With regard to public health insurance, the government's objective of maximizing the provision of public and merits goods (see section 3.1.4) frequently militates against imposing a copayment. However, this implies that any increase in benefits must go along with a maximum increase in the loading because of ex ante moral hazard. In equation (7), the amount of loading reacts most strongly to an increase in benefits if $(1-c) = 1$, that is, when $c = 0$.

Turning to ex post moral hazard, this means the tendency of the insured to demand more medical care (or care of higher quality or provided by a more expensive provider) after the onset of an illness. The effect of ex post moral hazard was illustrated in figure A.4; there, the role of coinsurance played a crucial role. It remains to be shown that a decrease in copayment also increases the amount of loading.

For this, a slightly different interpretation of the variable I is needed. Now I becomes the amount of benefits that is actually claimed (rather than promised in the contract), which depends on the rate of coinsurance. Therefore, I has to be replaced by $I(c)$ in equation (6), resulting in the derivative (note that now preventive effort V is predetermined),

$$\Lambda'(c) = -\lambda \cdot \pi \cdot I + \lambda \cdot (1-c) \cdot \pi \cdot I'(c) < 0. \qquad (9)$$
$$\quad (-) \qquad\qquad (-)$$

Therefore, the higher the rate of coinsurance, the lower is the loading, and conversely, the lower the rate of coinsurance, the higher must be the loading. The ex post moral hazard effect is given by $I'(c) < 0$: the more the actual utilization of covered services increases with a decrease in cost sharing, the more marked is the ex post moral hazard effect.

Ex post moral hazard problems in community-based schemes are of minor concern for the same reasons outlined in section 3.1. They benefit from a smaller degree of asymmetry of information, combined with effective sanctioning mechanisms that serve to contain overuse (table A.4).

The "loading" contained in the contributions to public health insurance is affected strongly by ex post moral hazard, again because the rate of coinsurance is usually zero. With $(1-c) = 1$ or $c = 0$, the absolute value of equation (9) is maximum. Put the other way around, this means that moving away from a rate of coinsurance would have a very marked beneficial effect on the loading.

3.3.7 Quality and Proximity of Health Care Services

Health care services of high quality have a direct effect on the total loading because the benefits actually claimed typically are more expensive, as seen in equation (9). High quality of services may also aggravate ex post moral hazard effects (figure A.4). Maximum true willingness to pay for such services must be very high, causing the observed demand function to run steeply. In this case, ample insurance coverage (low c) results in a marked discrepancy between true and observed willingness to pay. Graphically, the distance between quantities

A and B becomes larger. In terms of equation (8), a decrease in the rate of coinsurance c would cause benefits claimed to increase very strongly. With $I'(c)$ large—equivalent to a steep demand function—the loading must increase more strongly with a decrease in c. Therefore, the loading depends positively on the quality of medical services in general.

Increasing proximity of services causes the cost of access and hence total cost of utilizing medical care to fall. Therefore, the amount of services claimed I increases, and with it the amount of loading, as seen in equation (9).

Most members of community-based schemes are located far away from high-quality health care service providers. Any increase in the proximity of a health care provider therefore is likely to have a considerable effect on the cost of access, inducing a particularly marked increase in utilization. However, they benefit from a degree of mutual monitoring of their members that does not prevail in the context of a private insurer. Therefore, the amount of loading may not respond more strongly to an increase in proximity than in industrial countries.

Increased quality and proximity also drive up the loading component in contributions to public health insurance; equation (9) applies once more (table A.4).

3.3.8 Regulatory Framework

The types of relevant regulation in this context are again premium and product regulation. If designed to guarantee solvency, premium regulation typically amounts to an increased safety loading, reflected in λ. Conversely, if regulation is consumer orientated, it may result in increased transparency for consumers, enhancing demand and resulting in a larger risk pool. This means that the reserves held per unit risk can be reduced, causing λ to be smaller. For product regulation, this implies that certain procedures in loss settlement have to be followed, presumably at an increased cost to the insurer. This drives up the value of the other loading factor, μ. Therefore, the overall effect of regulation on the loading is ambiguous, although in the case of U.S. automobile regulation, Frech and Samprone (1980) found that regulation had a demand-decreasing net effect, pointing to a positive relationship between regulation and loading.

In community-based schemes, insurance packages and the premium rate are strictly regulated by the members themselves. This regulation does not aim at creating reserves through a loading surcharge on the risk premium; rather, the insured must come up with additional contributions (often in kind) if the scheme runs a deficit. The downside of reduced loading is an increase in the residual asset variance for members; however, risky insurance is associated with reduced willingness to pay.

Public health insurance is usually governed by an elaborate regulatory framework. (In section 5.2, the view is expounded that public insurance is at the high end of a scale depicting increasing regulatory intensity.) This adds to administrative expense and hence the "loading." Nevertheless, the total amount of loading may still be low due to savings on the cost of acquisition.

3.3.9 Fraud and Abuse

Fraud and abuse are closely related to the institutional framework. In section 3.1.8, emphasis was on the corruption possibly occurring between suppliers of medical inputs and physicians and hospitals. At this juncture, fraud and abuse by the insured are taken up and their impact on the loading discussed.

Fraud and abuse are an extreme form of moral hazard. In the case of ex ante moral hazard, preventive effort V could be said to turn negative, implying that insured's behavior increases the probability of illness to 1. A negative value of V may well be induced by insurance. In terms of equation (8) in section 3.3.6, $V'(I)$ would have to be strongly negative. This means that the amount of loading must increase very rapidly with any increase in I.

Fraud can also occur ex post, for example in the guise of colluding with providers to overstate medical bills. Again, this is an extreme form of ex post moral hazard that is encouraged by a vanishing rate of coinsurance (or more generally, the absence of cost sharing). For as soon as the insured have to pay parts of the medical bill out of pocket, they have an incentive to resist fraudulent overbilling. In general terms, the relationship between the degree of cost sharing c and benefits claimed I is strong in the presence of fraud. For the insurer, the term $I'(c)$ in equation (9) takes on a very large value (in absolute terms), indicating that the total amount of loading must increase strongly with a decrease in cost sharing when fraud is prevalent.

As argued in section 3.1.3, moral hazard in community-based schemes, and as such also any extreme form of it, is mitigated due to the characteristics that prevail in rural communities (close to full information). Therefore, the amount of loading due to fraud and abuse should not increase much in this variant of health insurance.

A public health insurer is under less pressure to control fraud and abuse than private insurers. Unlike private insurers, it does not have to compete for customers through a favorable benefit-cost ratio (to which a low amount of loading contributes).

CONCLUSION 5: The third dimension of supply of health insurance is the loading contained in the premium, which constitutes the net price of health insurance. It depends on at least 10 factors, with copayments and caps an important mitigating one.

3.4 Vertical Restraints/Vertical Integration

Two forms of vertical restraints (in the extreme: full vertical integration) can be distinguished, insurer-driven and provider-driven. A third form of integration, not vertical but lateral, occurs when a firm with main activities outside the sector takes up business in health insurance or health care provision. It will be dealt with only in passing.

3.4.1 Insurer-Driven Vertical Integration

A private insurer can limit its activities to refunding medical expenditures incurred. This amounts to a total absence of vertical restraints, let alone vertical integration. Such a policy is costly to the insurer, however, if the medical care providers have some monopolistic power. In that event, insurance coverage drives up providers' markup over marginal cost. This is illustrated by figure A.5, which builds on figure A.4 in section 3.1.3.

The added feature of figure A.5 is two marginal revenue functions (MR). Without insurance coverage, the health care provider faces the MR function derived from the true demand function (MR_t). The quantity satisfying the optimality condition, "marginal revenue equals marginal cost" (of health care services) is A. Accordingly, the monopoly price is P^*, which already contains a markup over marginal cost. With insurance, the MR function becomes MR_0, associated with the observed demand function. The new optimal quantity of services provided is B, consistent with a higher monopoly price at P^{**}, reflecting an increased markup over marginal cost. In this situation, the moral hazard effect of insurance not only consists of an increased quantity consumed ($B > A$), but also higher prices ($P^{**} > P^*$). Since this boosts payments I, the amount of loading, and hence the price of insurance, increases as well as seen in equation (7), section 3.3.6. One rationale of insurer-driven vertical integration is to avoid this extra moral hazard

FIGURE A.5   Effect of Insurance Coverage on Monopolistic Pricing

Source: Author.

effect, given by ($P^{**} - P^*$). For example, the insurer might employ the health care provider, with the employment contract stipulating fees as low as marginal cost (wage income paid would have to contain a fixed component to make up for the associated loss of revenue on the provider's part).

In more general terms, the provision of health insurance and of health care services may be viewed as two parts of a system. The extra moral hazard effect then amounts to an externality within the system that the insurer may seek to mitigate by imposing vertical constraints on service providers. To be successful, it must itself have a degree of monopoly power (see section 3.4.1.1). Therefore, the objective of the insurer becomes to avoid a double monopoly markup, or double marginalization (Waldman and Jensen 2001: 468f). The solution can be a two-part remuneration scheme. First, the provider agrees to charge a price equal to marginal cost; second the insurer pays a fixed amount sufficient to motivate the provider to sign the contract. In the extreme case, the insurer can opt for fully integrating service providers to avoid this and other externalities. The different possibilities form a continuum between independent provision and full vertical integration (figure A.6).

For example, when full integration would be inefficient, the insurer may limit itself to ownership of hospitals while contracting with ambulatory care providers. It also can mix insurer-managed plans with plans that are governed by contractual relationships devoid of vertical restraints. The imposition of restraints

FIGURE A.6   Forms of Vertical Restraints and Integration Imposed by the Insurer

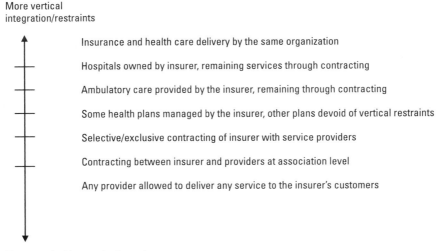

More vertical integration/restraints

Insurance and health care delivery by the same organization

Hospitals owned by insurer, remaining services through contracting

Ambulatory care provided by the insurer, remaining through contracting

Some health plans managed by the insurer, other plans devoid of vertical restraints

Selective/exclusive contracting of insurer with service providers

Contracting between insurer and providers at association level

Any provider allowed to deliver any service to the insurer's customers

Fewer vertical integration/restraints

Source: Zweifel, Krey, and Tagli 2007.

TABLE A.5   Factors Affecting Insurer-Driven Vertical Integration

Factor	Factor serves to facilitate (+)/hamper (–) vertical restraints		
	Private health insurance	Community-based health insurance	Public health insurance
(1) Market power of the insurer	+	+ ↑	+
(2) System efficiency gains to be realized	+	+	+ ↓
(3) Management know-how of insurer	+	+	+
(4) Contestability of health care markets	+	+ ↓	+ ↓
(5) Potential to increase entry barriers to competitors	+	+	n.a.
(6) Contestability of health insurance market	–	– ↓	n.a.
(7) Lack of capital of insurer	–	– ↑	– ↑
(8) Opportunistic behavior and fraud by insurers	–	– ↓	– ↓
(9) Cartelization of service providers	–	– ↓	– ↓
(10) Legislation prohibiting vertical restraints	–	– ↓	–

Source: Zweifel, Krey, and Tagli 2007.
Note: ↑ = reinforcement of relationship; ↓ = attenuation of relationship; n.a. = not applicable.

can finally be delegated, for example, to a medical association, with the likely result that individual provider behavior is not very effectively restrained.

The factors encouraging and hampering vertical integration by the insurer are listed in table A.5.

3.4.1.1 Market Power of the Insurer

This amounts to a necessary condition for the imposition of vertical restraints. If one of many insurers were to impose vertical restraints, a given service provider would always have the opportunity to strike a contract with a competitor that does not seek to impose such constraints. Moreover, as long as these constraints do not amount to exclusive dealings, failure to sign up with a particular insurer has negligible consequences for a service provider. Therefore unless the insurer considered wields a degree of market power, service providers do not need to accept any vertical restraints.

Market power of community-based health insurers typically is high because they, as a rule, wield a monopoly in the rural area they serve. On this score, their degree of market power would certainly enable them to impose vertical restraints.

A public health insurer, being a monopolist, can impose strong vertical restrictions on providers in terms of prices and products delivered if not prevented by legislation. There is, however, a risk of market power abuse. In particular, purchasing prices may be set so low as to drive foreign suppliers of drugs and privately funded hospitals out of the market. This risk is higher in a public insurance scheme than under a competitive private insurance system. K. Grant and R. Grant (2002), citing an unpublished paper, refer to the example of a Sub-Saharan African country where payments by national health insurance are so low that service suppliers have to rely heavily on unofficial charges for finance. The authors also use data from Transparency International (various years), which show that up to 80 percent of recent transactions with health workers in certain countries involve an unofficial fee or bribe.

3.4.1.2 System Efficiency Gains to Be Realized

The double marginalization problem noted above is not the only within-system externality that can be mitigated by vertical restraints. One that is also discussed in the industrial organization literature (Carlton and Perloff 1999: chap. 12) is the risk of the distributor's delivering substandard quality, with adverse reputation effect on the producer. In the present context, this translates into physicians and hospitals skimping on quality in the treatment of patients enrolled with a particular insurer. The solution to this problem can be the creation of a quality assurance scheme by the insurer.

Another problem that is more peculiar to the health care sector is fraud. As emphasized by Ma and McGuire (1997), the insurer has to rely on a report by the physician to be able to establish the appropriateness of treatment. The typical vertical restraint used here is a clause to the effect that service providers are to offer additional information in case of ambiguity.

A third within-system externality, of particular relevance to health care, is the "medical technology race." Given that insurance coverage is complete and density of supply high, service providers cannot compete much by price and location. An important remaining parameter of competition is medical technology. However, for the insurer it suffices to have a few specialized providers offering the most advanced technology for diagnosis and treatment of a given health condition. This implies that a technology race among the providers who are contractual partners amounts to a source of inefficiency. To avoid it, the insurer may assign providers to certain health conditions, at the same time guaranteeing them a minimum number of cases per period. Such a commitment can be supported by a premium-reduction offered to enrollees in return for a restricted choice of provider, as often happens under managed care contracts.

Community-based schemes also face a double marginalization problem. In the rural areas where they operate, an individual physician or hospital may be a local monopolist. The fact that they contract with nonprofit institutions is of limited relevance inasmuch as these providers must recover their cost. Any patients treated free of charge or at a reduced fee quite likely have no insurance coverage at all. The deficit incurred must be neutralized by higher fees from patients that do have insurance protection, namely members of community-based schemes. Provision of substandard quality therefore can be an issue since these providers are also monopsonists in their local labor markets. This induces them to pay a comparatively low wage, which is unlikely to attract the most skilled health care workers. With regard to fraud, community-based health insurers may benefit from the nonprofit status of hospitals; however, public hospitals have a tradition of cheating to ease bureaucratic processes. The technological race between competing providers can be excluded from consideration since community-based insurers are localized primarily in rural areas of low-income countries, where local monopolies prevail.

Another source of efficiency gain is mode of payment. In many rural areas of low-income countries, service providers are still paid in kind. However, most service providers prefer cash. This has led some schemes to use "moneylenders" as intermediaries to transform in-kind contributions into cash, to be paid to providers. In return, hospitals in particular have been willing to accept prospective payment for treating scheme members, which constitutes a vertical restraint.

A public health insurer, protected by a monopoly, is under reduced pressure to reap any system efficiency gains through vertical restraints. Therefore, this particular motivation is seen as less important than for private insurers under competitive pressure (table A.5).

3.4.1.3 Management Know-How of Insurer
Ample management know-how naturally assists in negotiating and monitoring vertical restraints. This is especially true of full vertical integration, which presupposes knowledge on the part of the insurer on how to run provider facilities efficiently.

Management know-how is scarce in community-based schemes, making vertical restraints less likely than conventional, often not fully specified, contracts with service providers. For public health insurance, this type of know-how may be at a level roughly comparable to that of private health insurers operating in the same country.

3.4.1.4 Contestability of Health Care Markets
Contestable markets are characterized by a potential or actual influx of suppliers as soon as incentives to enter become strong enough. As the experience of managed care organizations in the United States suggests, newcomers to the market for medical services are more likely to participate, that is, to accept the corresponding vertical restraints.

With their activity centered in rural areas, community-based schemes cannot count much on the contestability of the health care markets they deal with. Service providers move, if at all, from the countryside to the cities. Therefore, chances for these schemes to find partners that accept vertical constraints are slim.

To a public health insurer, increased contestability of health care markets certainly facilitates vertical restraints. However, public administrators still have to seek out available alternate providers; their incentive to undertake this effort may be undermined by the monopoly status of the scheme.

3.4.1.5 Potential to Increase Entry Barriers to Competitors
One motivation for vertical restraints and integration can also be to keep potential entrants out of the insurance market[11] because, to build a delivery system,

a new health insurer has to establish contractual relationships with insurers. By tying up the supply of scarce health care services, incumbent insurers can indirectly bar the entry of new competitors. Given the complexity of health care services and its high human capital content, controlling a part of health care supply can become a more effective barrier than closing the insurance market itself. Conversely, vertical restraints can be disrupted by an outsider willing to offer high enough compensation to make the health care supplier leave the vertical arrangement. However, such payment is usually above what a newcomer is willing to pay.[12] Community-based schemes benefit from a different type of entry barrier, which obviates the use of vertical integration to protect their market from outside competition. This follows from a likely analogy to credit markets. There, most community schemes are set up along kinship lines, at least in rural areas. In Nigeria, more than 95 percent of borrowing and lending occurs within a given community scheme that usually coincides with a tribe. This suggests that a challenge to an incumbent community-based scheme would have to surmount the high barrier of kinship.

To a public health insurance scheme, the potential of vertical integration to reinforce entry barriers confronting competitors has no relevance because entry by a competitor is prohibited by law (table A.5).

3.4.1.6 Contestability of Health Insurance Markets

As long as insurance markets are contestable, incumbent insurers will be strapped for resources in defending their position, being absorbed mainly with ensuring their survival in the insurance market itself. In addition, when insurers have to compete because entry or exit barriers are low, profitability is driven down to the competitive return; funds and management time will be too scarce to engage in the imposition of vertical restraints or even full vertical integration.

With regard to community-based health insurance, barriers to entry emanate mainly from the characteristics of informal markets. Many health insurers who might consider entry do not accept in-kind payment of the premium. This payment may take the form of not only cattle but also the provision of bonded labor and the cession of land rights. Thus, there are no barriers to entry that hamper the imposition of vertical restraints by community-based health insurance, all other things being equal. In the case of a public health insurer, the contestability of the market for health insurance again has no relevance since the law sees to it that the market is not contestable to begin with.

3.4.1.7 Insurer's Lack of Capital

The insurer's lack of capital is another impediment especially to integration. Often, full vertical integration (but less so vertical restraints) requires a capital investment on the part of the firm acquiring control. If internal finance is available, management enjoys some leeway in deciding about such an investment, monitoring by the owners of the firm being incomplete. Lacking internal finance, the integrating firm has to convince banks and investors that vertical integration will improve profitability and that the debt can be repaid.

Community-based schemes are organized as mutuals and thus do not sell tradable shares of ownership. This precludes external equity finance, except through increasing membership. However, this alternative frequently runs into problems because the scheme may lose its homogeneity and hence an important cost advantage, as argued in section 3.3.3. Finance through, for example, banks is also difficult because the scheme cannot offer marketable collateral. However, in some cases lateral integration may help. Citing the experience of communities in Bangladesh, Desmet, Chowdhury, and Islam (1999) argue that community-based credit schemes in which many individuals are already involved may provide the entry point to finance health insurance. But on the whole, lack of capital constitutes an important impediment to integration for community-based health insurers.

Lack of capital also hampers vertical integration of public health insurance because the scheme is not permitted to accumulate funds or issue debt for such purpose. Initiatives of this type would be interpreted as a sign of for-profit orientation.

3.4.1.8 Opportunistic Behavior and Fraud on the Part of Insurers

Insurers with a reputation for opportunistic and fraudulent behavior have difficulty striking contracts calling for vertical restraints. By engaging in opportunistic behavior, insurers inflict damages on providers, albeit at the expense of their own reputation and credibility. This reduces their chances of successfully arranging vertical restraints with providers. Insurers must therefore first establish their credit and payment reputation among providers to win them over for vertical restraints.

However, fraud seems to be a minor issue in community-based schemes because service providers often wield a local monopoly. If caught cheating, the insurer therefore stands to lose the one available provider in the region. Since this constitutes an effective sanctioning mechanism, it should be easier to agree on vertical restraints (table A.5).

Opportunistic behavior and fraud can also occur with a public insurer, undermining the willingness of service providers to enter into vertical agreements. However, this effect is attenuated by the providers' judgment that they have no choice but to sign up if they want to profit from the demand-enhancing effect of insurance coverage (section 3.3.6).

3.4.1.9 Cartelization of Service Providers

On the provider side, cartelization makes the imposition of vertical constraints more difficult. First, the cartel is a means for providers to jointly increase their incomes. An insurer seeking to negotiate a vertical restraint must beat this benchmark. Second, a cartel must impose discipline on its members to be successful, notably with respect to restricting output. Restrictions on output,

however, conflict with the integrating firm's desire to avoid double marginalization, which may result in the imposition of a minimum volume of sales. In the
present context, a medical association would like to see its members keeping to a
low volume of treatments to support higher fees. However, an insurer may want
to contract for a minimum volume of services at a fixed fee to avoid upward
pressure on fees induced by insurance coverage (figure A.5, section 3.4.1). These
intentions are in conflict.

To community-based schemes, cartelization of health care providers has little
relevance. In rural areas of low-income countries, providers are sufficiently protected from competition through mere distance. They can therefore do without
the protection afforded by a cartel.

For a public health insurance scheme, cartelization of providers constitutes
an obstacle to vertical restraints and integration in much the same way as for a
private insurer. However, since the cartel has no one else to contract with, it may
agree to a uniform set of vertical agreements to secure the viability of the system
(and its demand-enhancing effect) as a whole.

3.4.1.10 Legislation Prohibiting Vertical Restraints

Restraints can be entirely impossible when there is legislation prohibiting vertical restraints and integration in the health care sector altogether. For example,
in several industrial countries, medical practices and/or hospitals may not be
owned by individuals not having a medical degree. At the very least, medical
management must lie in the hands of physicians.

For a community-based insurer, there seem to be few legal impediments to
vertical integration. In fact, they were able to cooperate closely with mission-
ary hospitals in several countries such Kenya, Indonesia, and Uganda. A public
health insurer must presumably respect legislation concerning vertical integration in the same way a private insurer does because the objective of this legislation is to secure the independence of the comparatively small businesses of
health care providers.

CONCLUSION 6: The amount of vertical integration is the fourth dimension
of the supply of health insurance. Its insurer-driven variant depends on at least
10 factors, and the limitation of moral hazard effects is an important motive.

3.4.2 Provider-Driven Vertical Integration

The second type of vertical integration is provider driven. In a typical case, a
hospital chain seeks to avoid double marginalization in its dealings with insurers that wield a degree of market power. The chain may also view an insurer as a
sales channel, where promotional effort is decisive for the market success of its
products. If insurers provide an insufficient amount of advice to future patients,
client matching suffers, with unfavorable effects on hospitals' reputation. A competing insurer could free-ride on these efforts by letting the other company do
the promotion and selling its own policy at a lower premium. Such free-riding
would undermine an insurer's incentive to provide advice. The solution to the

problem can be the assignment of exclusive territories to insurers or even exclusive dealings (Carlton and Perloff 1999: 403–5). In general, the factors encouraging provider-driven vertical restraints and integration (listed in table A.6) are the same ones hampering their insurer-driven counterparts (listed in table A.5, section 3.4.1). With regard to public health insurance, however, provider-driven vertical integration is regarded as not applicable throughout (resulting in the "n.a." entries in the last column of table A.6). The reason is that a hospital or a group of physicians will find it impossible to impose rules on a public agency for example with regard to the amount of contribution to be paid by the insured. For full integration, they would even have to acquire property in the agency, which is not imaginable according to known legal codes.

3.4.2.1 Market Power of Service Provider

As in the case of insurer-driven vertical constraints and integration, market power is a necessary condition for success. This condition usually is not satisfied by a single physician but may be met by a physician network or by a hospital with a large catchment area.

In the rural areas where community-based schemes are typically active, notably hospitals have the market power to impose vertical restraints on insurers or to integrate insurance altogether. An example is provided by the Kisiizi hospitals of Uganda.

3.4.2.2 System Efficiency Gains to Be Realized

The possible efficiency gains are the same as those discussed in section 3.4.1.2. Conceivably, an insurer may have enough market power to increase premiums

TABLE A.6   Factors Affecting Provider-Driven Vertical Integration

Factor	Factor serves to facilitate (+)/hamper (−) vertical restraints		
	Private health insurance	Community-based health insurance	Public health insurance
(1) Market power of service provider	+	+ ↑	n.a.
(2) System efficiency gains to be realized	+	+	n.a.
(3) Management know-how of provider	+	+	n.a.
(4) Contestability of insurance market	+	+ ↓	n.a.
(5) Potential to increase entry barriers to competitors	+	+	n.a.
(6) Contestability of health care markets	−	− ↓	n.a.
(7) Lack of capital of service providers	−	−	n.a.
(8) Market power of insurer	−	− ↑	n.a.
(9) Cartelization of insurers	−	− ↓	n.a.
(10) Legislation prohibiting vertical restraints	−	−	n.a.

Source: Zweifel, Krey, and Tagli 2007.

Note: ↑ = reinforcement of relationship; ↓ = attenuation of relationship; n.a. = not applicable.

independently of the cost incurred from paying service providers. This again results in a double marginalization, hurting the health care provider this time.

Skimping on quality by the insurer is also possible in the guise of delayed reimbursement of patients, but also of having unjustified recourse to small print in its insurance policy. However, whether the consequent loss of reputation falls on the service provider rather than on the insurer is not quite clear. In the latter case, there is no externality affecting the health care provider.

In the same vein, fraud by the insurer (in particular, failure to pay in the event of insolvency) might constitute a source of within-system inefficiency. The ensuing loss of reputation is, however, more likely to fall on the insurer than on the service provider.

Negative external effects because of insurers engaging in a technological race do not seem to be an issue either.

Up to this point, incentives for health care providers to integrate health insurance into their operations seem to be weak. However, provider-driven insurance schemes may have some cost advantages over a nonintegrated competitor since they already have some relevant risk information about the insured. This is an efficiency gain accruing to health care providers.

Health care providers, in particular hospitals dealing with community-based schemes, must take into account double marginalization since a given scheme usually is the monopoly supplier of health insurance in its region. This consideration speaks in favor of vertical restraints or even full integration. However, the possibility of such a scheme's delivering services of substandard quality is rather remote. After all, the insured own the scheme themselves, and it is they who would suffer from a lower quality of service than contracted for (Musau 1999). Also, hospitals are confronted with fraudulent behavior on the part of community-based insurers, as evidenced by Musau's case study of Chogoria Hospital in Kenya. Here, schemes running group policies let nonmembers (who initially were not identifiable as such at the point of service) present themselves for treatment, creating bad debts for the hospital. A technological race is not an issue, most community-based schemes lacking the resources for building up elaborate administrative capacity.

3.4.2.3 Management Know-How of Provider
Management know-how is another factor, facilitating the implementation of vertical restraints and especially vertical integration.

The lack of management know-how is particularly more marked in community-based schemes, leading to even less vertical restraints/integration between health providers and insurers.

3.4.2.4 Contestability of Insurance Market
If the market for health insurance is contestable, a health care provider considering vertical integration has a chance to strike an agreement with newcomers. This serves to increase the likelihood of successfully imposing vertical constraints.

As outlined in section 3.4.1.4, community-based schemes do not face much contestability of their markets. A newcomer would have to incur extremely high investments to match their social control advantages (table A.6).

3.4.2.5 Potential to Increase Entry Barriers to Competitors

Vertical restraints and integration can also serve a strategic purpose by raising the entry barrier, for example, to a new hospital. The same applies to physician networks that set up an insurance scheme to the disadvantage of outside physicians.

Hospitals dealing with community-based insurers, being local monopolies, could in principle attempt to protect their markets through integrating the community-based insurance scheme operating in their catchment area. However, the little evidence available suggests that the main motive for provider-driven vertical integration is the prospect of eliminating within-system inefficiencies (section 3.4.2.2).

3.4.2.6 Contestability of Health Care Markets

Providers find integrating insurers difficult if their market is contestable. In analogy to the arguments proffered in section 3.4.1.6, resources must be spent on defending their position in the market, leaving little room for investing in vertical restraints and integration.

Most health care providers doing business with community-based health insurers are located in poor rural areas. This means that, even if there should be any monopoly rents, their amount must be very limited. Therefore, the incentive for a new competitor to break into such a market is weak, resulting in a small degree of contestability.

3.4.2.7 Lack of Capital of Service Providers

Physician networks may lack capital because their joint liability status impedes their access to capital markets. In a deregulated, competitive market, for-profit hospitals and especially hospital groups may offer an investment with favorable hedging properties. With a measure of independence from the capital market and hence comparatively low beta, they can raise capital at a lower cost than other industries.

Lack of formal capital is a great problem in the case of health care providers dealing with community-based insurers. Located in rural areas, neither physicians nor hospitals have easy access to domestic capital markets. In addition, with intermediation by moneylenders incomplete, health care providers have difficulty raising internal finance.

3.4.2.8 Market Power of Insurer

Insurers with market power require ample compensation to let themselves be constrained or integrated. In community-based schemes, market power of insurers is high since they usually are the only supplier of health insurance coverage. All else being equal, a health care provider considering vertical integration would meet with some difficulties.

3.4.2.9 Cartelization of Insurers

The costs of negotiation are particularly high in the case of cartelization because all members of the cartel must usually be included.

With regard to community-based schemes, cartelization is of little relevance for two reasons. First, the fact that they often operate along kinship lines makes it more difficult to reach horizontal agreements. Second, as stated in section 3.4.1.1, community-based schemes usually constitute a monopoly, causing them to have little interest in the protection from competition afforded by a cartel. In sum, this results in an attenuation of cartelization as a factor influencing vertical restraints.

3.4.2.10 Legislation Prohibiting Vertical Restraints

There may be legislation prohibiting medical providers from owning an insurer. However, no instance is known to this author, relating to either industrial countries or community-based schemes.

3.4.3 Actual Examples of Vertical Integration

As tables A.5 and A.6 and their discussion show, there are factors facilitating and hampering both insurer- and provider-driven vertical integration. This leads to the expectation that, depending on the mix of these influences, imposition of vertical restraints and attainment of full vertical integration does occur.

Table A.7 contains evidence on some of the existing variants of insurer- and provider-driven vertical integration as well as lateral integration. It relates to the

TABLE A.7   Forms of Integration

Form	Variant	Private health insurers	Community-based health insurers
Insurer-driven	• Insurer running clinics and ambulatory care centers • Insurer-owned ambulatory care centers	BUPA (British United Provident Association) offers private health insurance and cooperates closely with domestic health care providers	Atiman Health Insurance Scheme in Tanzania cooperates closely with local health care providers
Provider-driven	• Hospital setting up insurance schemes • Ambulatory care centers/ association of doctors setting up insurance schemes	Community hospitals in rural Pennsylvania, United States, forming a *risk-retention group*, a group of similar entities that pools its resources and insures its own members	• In Uganda the Kisiizi hospital together with the Engozi Society provides a community-based health insurance scheme • The Chogoria Hospital in Kenya offers an insurance scheme
Lateral	Companies/cooperatives active in the credit or insurance sector extending their product line	In Singapore, the product line is extended toward bank assurance activity	Chogoria Hospital Insurance Scheme in Kenya focuses increasingly on the treatment of HIV

Source: Zweifel, Krey, and Tagli 2007.

competitive case and community-based schemes, illustrating that the factors discussed may result in all three types of integration in both settings.

CONCLUSION 7: Vertical integration constitutes the fifth dimension of the supply of health insurance. Its provider-driven variant depends on the same 10 factors, ranging from administrative expense to fraud and abuse. Those facilitating insurer-driven integration usually hamper provider-driven integration and vice versa.

3.5 Market Structure

Market structure has several dimensions, among the more important being the number of buyers and sellers and the amount of product differentiation (Carlton and Perloff 1999: chap. 1). The number of buyers has not been an issue in health insurance markets, even in countries where employers are involved in its provision. With regard to product differentiation, it can be said that its degree increases with the number of sellers unless economies of scope are very marked (see below). Often, the amount of vertical integration is also seen as a dimension of market structure. However, in view of its great importance for the organization of the health care sector as a whole, vertical integration is discussed separately (section 3.4). Thus, the number of sellers (and with it, the degree of their concentration) will be retained as the principal dimension of market structure.

One particular aspect of market structure that will be left out of this exposition is the legal form of the insurance company. Originally, most health insurers were mutuals, presumably because a reasonable degree of homogeneity of risks could be attained in this way. Homogeneity of risks ensures that the variance of total claims to be paid does not increase without bounds when more risks are added (Malinvaud 1972: appendix). A finite variance in turn implies that the expected value of the loss can be estimated with increased precision (a decreased standard error according to the law of large numbers), permitting the insurer to hold less reserves per unit risk while holding its probability of insolvency constant (Cummins 1991). However, mutuals are at a disadvantage when raising capital for expanding their risk pool because they do not issue tradable ownership shares.

For this reason, the preferred legal form of insurers has become the publicly traded stock company in industrial countries. Yet, the mutual form is alive and even thriving in the guise of community-based health insurance in low-income countries. In the wake of development, with increasing demand for capital to finance expansion, these schemes may change their legal form to become stock companies. However, assessing the conditions governing such a transition is not the aim of this chapter. For this reason, it is taken as given that for the foreseeable future private health insurers (which need not be stock companies either) and community-based schemes will continue to coexist in low-income countries.

Focusing on the degree of concentration as the main descriptor of market structure, some important factors influencing it are listed in table A.8. The

TABLE A.8   Factors Affecting the Degree of Concentration of Health Insurance Sellers in Markets for Private Health Insurance

Factor	Private health insurance	Community-based health insurance	Public health insurance
	Factor serves to increase (+)/decrease (−) concentration		
(1) Diversity of preferences	−	−	n.a.
(2) Economies of scale	+/−	+	n.a.
(3) Economies of scope	+	+	n.a.
(4) Barriers to entry	+	+ ↑	n.a.
(5) Barriers to exit	−	− ↑	n.a.
(6) Antitrust policy	−	− ↑	n.a.

Source: Zweifel, Krey, and Tagli 2007.

Note: ↑ = reinforcement of relationship; ↓ = attenuation of relationship; n.a. = not applicable.

discussion starts with factors that relate to the demand side and then shifts to the supply side. Table A.8 has no entries for public health insurance for the simple reason that the scheme is assumed to be a monopoly under all circumstances.

3.5.1 Diversity of Preferences

With greater diversity of preferences, a larger set of differentiated insurance products is necessary for matching supply and demand. This creates potential for niche products written by specialized insurers, and therefore a greater number of companies. However, the theory of consumer demand also says that diversity of preferences becomes effective only if incomes are sufficiently high. With a very small income, the attainable consumption set in attribute space is too restricted to permit choices that lie far apart. Therefore, the number of profitable product varieties (and usually firms) is low when income is low.

In the case of community-based schemes, there is the countervailing effect of lacking access to the capital market, which limits the size of the unit and its geographical expansion. The balance of the two influences is an open issue.

3.5.2 Economies of Scale

In the case of an insurer, the size of its risk pool may be the source of economies of scale, defined as decreasing unit cost as a function of the number of individuals insured. Thanks to the law of large numbers, a larger pool size enables the insurer to reduce its reserves per unit risk without increasing its risk of insolvency (Cummins 1991). This means that the premiums of a large insurer contain a smaller amount of loading (section 3.3.3), which results in a lower premium for a given amount of expected benefits paid. A large insurer could therefore gain even more market share, with the "natural monopoly" as a possible outcome.

However, a growing pool within a given country may require the acceptance of less favorable risks, with a consequent rise in the expected value of the benefit to be paid. Also, a larger pool can be associated with a loss of social control among the insured, encouraging moral hazard. According to equation (6) in section 3.3, both effects cause the amount of loading to increase, thus counteracting economies of scale. There does not seem to be much empirical evidence on this issue in the domain of insurance, let alone health insurance. However, the available evidence points to constant rather than increasing returns to scale.[13] Absent economies of scale, however, there is no reason to expect a particularly high degree of concentration on private insurance markets, at least for this reason.

Fujita, Krugman, and Venables (1999) argue that economies of scale occur due to positive spatial externalities. In the present context, this may explain why health insurers in low-income countries concentrate mainly in urban areas. Strong centripetal forces that draw businesses closer to one another (because firms may want to share a customer base or local services, have access to trained and experienced labor) outweigh weaker centrifugal forces that drive businesses farther apart (because firms compete for labor and land). The first set of influences constitutes spillover effects resulting in economies of scale in the guise of lower administration and advertising costs. As such, they encourage concentration.

Fujita, Krugman, and Venables (1999), though not focusing on community-based schemes, also provide insight into why these are concentrated in rural areas. There, strong centripetal forces (such as the ability to serve certain customers and the acceptance of informal market behavior like barter) outweigh the weaker centrifugal forces (such as small customer base, bad infrastructure, and an underdeveloped capital market). Economies of scale thus may occur due to the first set of influences, serving to lower unit costs, given the market characteristics of community-based health insurance.

3.5.3 Economies of Scope

Economies of scope prevail in insurance if the cost of providing an extra unit of coverage in one line of business decreases as a function of the volume written in some other line. In the context of health insurance, economies of scope may operate at two levels. First, the health insurance line may benefit from other business activities of the same firm. For instance, it may be possible to market health insurance through the existing distribution network for selling, for example, banking services. The tendency toward increased concentration in the health insurance market is indirect and hence not marked in this case. Also, the limited amount of available empirical evidence suggests that economies of scope at this level are not important.[14]

Second, however, health insurers A and B may realize that, while their products are differentiated, the expenses for marketing and administering those of A increase less than proportionately when the quantity of B's products is increased as well. The amount of loading hence would increase less than proportionately with the expected volume of benefits combined, providing a powerful motive for a merger of the two companies. With economies of scope (often also called synergies) of this second type, there is a tendency toward concentration, which does not, however, have to be accompanied by a reduction in the number of product varieties. More generally, the number of product varieties sold in the market does not vary in step with the number of firms in this case. This argument holds for community-based health insurance as well (table A.8).

3.5.4 Barriers to Entry

High barriers to entry exist when a newcomer to the market must make large investments that cannot be recuperated if entry fails (high sunk costs). Barriers to entry thus cause the degree of concentration to be higher than it would be otherwise. These barriers are clearly relevant in the case of health insurance markets, where a newcomer usually needs to launch an extensive advertising campaign to gain even a small share of the market. This investment cannot be recuperated if the newcomer later decides to withdraw.

A small number of sellers make the negotiation and monitoring of collusive agreements less costly. For this reason, concentration poses a threat to price and product competition also in insurance markets. However, collusive agreements can be destabilized by the emergence of an additional competitor. This destabilization is less likely to occur when there are high barriers to entry. Therefore, barriers to entry not only increase the degree of concentration but may also reinforce the anticompetitive effects that usually accompany a high degree of concentration.

Barriers to entry in community-based health insurance are reinforced by the informal nature of the market (e.g., not all insurance companies are willing to accept payment in kind). Furthermore, the relationship between the insurance scheme and its members usually develops over a long period of time (which also helps minimize moral hazard effects). A newcomer to this market thus would have to make a substantial nonrecuperable investment to acquire this experience. This constitutes a barrier to entry, facilitating concentration in the community-based segment of the market for health insurance.

3.5.5 Barriers to Exit

When challenged by a newcomer, one or several of the incumbents may consider exiting from the market rather than defending their position. However, exit is not an attractive alternative if it entails the loss of investments that cannot be recuperated (sunk costs). For instance, a sales force specialized in health insurance is not an asset anymore after the firm leaves the market; even with economies of scope, it has a reduced value, for example, in selling life insurance. Barriers to exit thus keep the degree of concentration lower than it would otherwise be. However, through their stabilizing effect, barriers still help to preserve collusive agreements, reinforcing the anticompetitive effect of concentration. Bailouts of ailing companies also modify the opportunity cost of leaving the market, thus creating a barrier to exit.

Markets in which community-based schemes operate may be characterized by very high barriers to exit. These schemes benefit from advantages due to their favorable reputation and established social control mechanisms (limiting in particular ex post moral hazard, section 3.3.6), which are lost if an exit from the market occurs. Again, this constitutes a factor that contributes to a lower degree of concentration.

3.5.6 Antitrust Policy

In many countries, merger projects must be submitted to antitrust authorities. Mergers that would result in a notable increase in the degree of concentration are subject to scrutiny according to the rules followed both by the U.S. Federal Trade Commission and the Commission of the European Union. Up to this point, few mergers of health insurers have been blocked. This does not mean that antitrust policy does not have an impact on concentration. Indeed, the mere risk of having a merger proposal rejected may well keep concentration lower than it would be otherwise.

Mergers of community-based schemes are rare, but not because of effective antitrust policies. Arguably antitrust policies do not take effect at all in these schemes, which consist of small groups, whose members share common characteristics like close family and long-run community relationships. Mergers thus come at the cost of increased heterogeneity, which seems to greatly outweigh their benefits. The literature on credit markets offers evidence on the importance of market segmentation along geographic and kinship lines. Udry (1993: 95) discovered that loans between individuals in the same village or kinship group accounted for 97 percent of the value of transactions. Hardly any loans were provided to outside communities, as information about repayment possibilities and village sanctions as a mechanism for contract enforcement were lacking. Similar evidence on informal credit markets is reported in a case study of rural China (Feder et al. 1993).

CONCLUSION 8: Market structure as indicated by sellers' concentration constitutes the sixth dimension of the supply of health insurance. It depends on at least six factors, with barriers to entry exerting a positive influence and barriers to exit, a negative influence.

4. THE DESIGN OF AN OPTIMAL HEALTH INSURANCE CONTRACT

The efficiency reasons given above for the existence of SHI with compulsory membership can be convincing only if the design of the SHI contract is in some sense "optimal" from the point of view of the representative consumer (Zweifel and Breyer 1997: chap. 6). In view of the tendency toward full coverage of most SHI schemes, of particular importance are the circumstances justifying copayments, that is, deviations from full coverage of health care expenditures. These issues are: administrative expense, noninsurable loss, ex ante moral hazard, and ex post moral hazard.

Administrative expense. Copayment provisions can be called for to save administrative expense such as costs of handling claims. For this reason, and assuming expected utility maximization on the part of consumers, it is optimal to exclude partially or entirely expenditures on health care items that occur frequently but in limited amounts such as minor medications (Mossin 1968). More specifically, if administrative costs are proportional to the expected volume of health expenditures, a feature of the optimal insurance contract is a fixed deductible (Arrow 1963).

Noninsurable loss. Illness typically involves not only monetary costs but also nonmonetary losses such as pain and suffering. Optimal health insurance equalizes marginal utility of wealth in all states of nature, but this is not equivalent to full coverage if there are complementarities between nonmonetary and monetary losses. In particular, if marginal utility of wealth is lower in case of illness than in good health (e.g., due to reduced ability to enjoy expensive types of consumption), optimal health insurance does not fully reimburse the monetary loss (Cook and Graham 1977).

Ex ante moral hazard. If the insurer cannot observe preventive effort on the part of the insured, a high degree of coverage reduces the incentive for prevention. Hence there is a trade-off between risk spreading through insurance and maintaining incentives to keep the risk of illness low. This trade-off leads to a premium function, which is convex in the degree of coverage, such that full coverage should be particularly expensive (Ehrlich and Becker 1972). In SHI such a premium function is nowhere observed, although it could be easily administered because consumers cannot circumvent the convex schedule by purchasing many insurance contracts, each with limited coverage and low premiums.

Ex post moral hazard. If the insurer could observe the health status of the insured, the optimal type of health insurance would provide indemnity payment; in other words, the insurance payment would not depend on the insured's health care expenditure. With asymmetric information, however, linking reimbursement to expenditure is inevitable. Still, copayment provisions are needed to fend off overconsumption of medical care. The optimal copayment rate is higher, the more price elastic the demand is for the particular type of medical services (Spence and Zeckhauser 1971; Zweifel and Breyer 1997: chap. 6). Empirical evidence, for example, from the RAND Health Insurance Study (Manning et al. 1987) shows that there is a small but significant price elasticity of demand for most medical services.[15]

CONCLUSION 9: The optimal health insurance contract suggests several reasons for stopping short of full coverage. While administrative expense should be recovered by a deductible, the presence of noninsurable losses may, and that of moral hazard definitely does, commend a measure of proportional cost sharing, reflecting the price elasticity of demand for medical care in the last-mentioned instance.

5. THE LIMITS OF SOCIAL HEALTH INSURANCE

There appear to be at least four types of limits to social health insurance. First, the incentive structure of social insurers discussed in section 3 hampers product innovation. Second, the features of the optimal contract as described in section 4 imply that coverage provided by social health insurers needs to be limited in view of moral hazard effects. A third limit of a more institutional character emanates from the fact that health risks, while important, are only one type among several that need to be considered. The fourth and ultimate limit is nothing but the willingness of citizens to pay still higher contributions for higher quality but more expensive health care, about which some evidence will be presented at the end of this section.

5.1 Limits Created by Regulation

Traditionally, social insurance is associated with contributions that are not graded to risk and are uniform across the population. This uniformity would be undermined if competitive social health insurers were to launch new products that fetch a higher premium. The only way to permit innovation is to let competitors with little potential to increase their market share run experiments, which if successful are imposed on the entire market. This is a far shot from the innovation process in actual markets, where most innovations fail, adoption occurs with considerable lags, and some competitors never adopt but already search for a still more promising alternative. In the case of a monopolistic scheme, innovation is possible only through a majority decision in parliament (or a majority decision of the voters in a direct democracy). These impediments cause the current provision of health insurance to lag years, if not decades, behind development of preferences and restrictions prevalent in the population (Zweifel and Breyer 1997: chap 11.1).

5.2 Limits Imposed by the Behavior of Insurers

The analysis in section 3 shows that the capability of innovation—adapting the insurance product to changing demand—is limited in social health insurance as traditionally understood. When risk adjustment is to "marry" uniform premiums in the face of different expected costs with competition, insurers considering innovation fear the financial sanction that goes along with attracting young clients. Finally, in the case of social health insurance not provided by a multitude of suppliers but a monopolistic scheme, the incentive for innovation is stifled even more.

5.3 Limits Imposed by Institutional Design

Undoubtedly, health risks loom large in the lives of citizens. However, other risks also confront people over their life cycles. Adopting the categories of social insurance, one would want to distinguish the risks of accident, disability, old age, unemployment, increase in family size, and death of main breadwinner (Zweifel 2000b). While the relationships between these risks have not yet been fully researched, the available evidence points to positive correlations. This implies that the three assets to be managed over the life cycle—health, wealth, and wisdom (Williams 1998)—are likely positively correlated, an unfavorable situation for risk-averse individuals. Therefore, insurance as a system should at least mitigate those positive correlations, for example, by paying higher-than-expected benefits in one branch if there is a shortfall below expected benefits in another. However, preliminary research at the macroeconomic level suggests that in several important countries, trend deviations of payments are positively rather than negatively correlated across categories. For example, trend deviations in payments of German social unemployment insurance are positively correlated not only with those of old age and pensioners insurance but also of social health and accident insurance (table A.9). Not one out of a total of six correlation coefficients is significantly negative.

TABLE A.9   Correlations of Trend Deviations in the Benefits of U.S. and German Social Insurance

	SOAS (1)	SDI (2)	SMCHI (3)	SMCSM (4)	SMA (5)	SUI (6)	SWC (7)
United States, 1974–92							
SOAS (1)	1						
SDI (2)	−0.41	1					
SMCHI (3)	0.82*	−0.21	1				
SMCSM (4)	−0.29	0.16	−0.31	1			
SMA (5)	−0.55*	0.93*	0.40	0.33	1		
SUI (6)	0.02	0.70*	0.28	0.29	0.63*	1	
SWC (7)	−0.64*	0.77*	−0.65*	0.31	0.84*	0.24	1

	SOAS (1)	SEB (2)	SHI (3)	SAI (4)	SUI (5)
Germany (West[a]), 1975–93					
SOAS (1)	1				
SEB (2)	−0.86*	1			
SHI (3)	0.45	−0.33	1		
SAI (4)	0.91*	−0.81*	0.67*	1	
SUI (5)	0.76*	−0.75*	0.65*	0.83*	1

Source: Zweifel 2000b.
Note: SOAS = old-age and survivors insurance; SDI = disability insurance; SMCHI = Medicare: hospital insurance; SMCSM = Medicare: supplemental medical insurance; SMA = Medicaid; SUI = unemployment insurance; SWC = workers' compensation; SEB = employee benefits; SHI = social health insurance; SAI = social accidents insurance.
a. East under communist rule until 1989.
* Correlation coefficient significant at 5 percent level or better.

Also, social health insurance fails to make up for shortfalls in the benefits of private insurance. While employee benefits for old age, which are counted as social insurance, are negatively correlated with private health insurance (as they should be for portfolio variance reduction), trend deviations of all the other branches of social insurance correlate positively with at least one of the lines of private insurance (table A.10). Conversely, again not one out of 20 coefficients of correlation is significantly negative. On the whole, then, social health insurance in Germany (but in Austria, Switzerland, and the United States as well, see Zweifel and Lehmann 2001) might be largely responsible for present insurance systems keeping the volatility of individuals' assets larger than necessary.

This (admittedly preliminary) evidence suggests that the same amount of resource could produce more security for people or, conversely, that the same amount of security could be afforded for less money. This limits the attractiveness of social health insurance for consumers.

5.4 Limited Willingness to Pay of Citizens

The call for reform of current social security systems frequently is based on the argument that they cannot be financed any longer. However, anything that

TABLE A.10   Correlations of Trend Deviations in the Benefits of U.S. and German Private and Social Insurance

	United States, 1974–92						
	SOAS (5)	SDI (6)	SMCHI (7)	SMCSM (8)	SMA (9)	SUI (10)	SWC (11)
PLDE (1)	0.74*	−0.50*	0.47*	−0.33	−0.64*	−0.37	−0.49*
PLDI (2)	−0.35	0.90*	−0.13	0.13	0.80*	0.58*	0.70*
PAP (3)	0.73*	−0.58	0.58*	−0.45*	−0.74*	−0.38	−0.59*
PHI (4)	0.67*	0.08	0.62*	0.02	−0.10	0.34	−0.19
	Germany (West[a]), 1975–93						
	SOAS (5)	SEB (6)	SHI (7)	SAI (8)	SUI (9)		
PLI (1)	0.27	−0.08	0.26	0.39	0.25		
PHI (2)	0.79*	−0.72*	0.56*	0.92*	0.63*		
PAI (3)	−0.41	0.28	−0.15	−0.41	−0.26		
PGI (4)	0.43	−0.25	0.16	0.54*	0.08		

Source: Zweifel 2000b.

Note: PLDE = life insurance: death payments; PLDI = life insurance: disability payment; PAP = annuity payments; PHI = health insurance; PLI = private life insurance; PAI = private accident insurance; PGI = private general liability insurance; SOAS = old age and survivors insurance; SDI = disability insurance; SMCHI = Medicare: hospital insurance; SMCSM = Medicare: supplemental medical insurance; SMA = Medicaid; SUI = unemployment insurance; SWC = workers' compensation; SEB = employee benefits; SHI = social health insurance; SAI = social accidents insurance.

a. East under communist rule until 1989.

*Correlation coefficient significantly different from zero (5% significance level or better).

does not exceed GDP can be financed in principle. The argument therefore must be watered down to the statement that the willingness to pay (WTP) of consumers is limited, and mandated expenditure on any good or service in excess of that limit causes an efficiency loss. The problem with this argument has been that, until recently, WTP for public goods in the health domain was not known.

In the case of Switzerland, some evidence has become available. In a discrete choice experiment involving 1,000 individuals in 1993, WTP was measured for additional services to be provided (or rather, compensation required for accepting cutbacks) by social health insurance in exchange for an increased premium (Telser et al. 2004; Zweifel, Telser, and Vaterlaus 2006).

Reading table A.11 horizontally, one notes first that the amounts of compensation asked are consistently highest for consenting to a physician list based exclusively on cost criteria (column 1). The sample average is as high as CHF 103 (€67 at 2003 exchange rates), or some 38 percent of Switzerland's average monthly premium of CHF 270 at the time. Still, the fact that it is finite speaks against the claim (often advanced by medical associations) that free choice of physician is virtually priceless. Selecting physicians on quality or quality and cost (i.e., efficiency) criteria already requires a lot less compensation, namely 20 percent and 16 percent of premium, respectively. These premium reductions can be granted by current managed care alternatives available under Swiss social health insurance. A possible delay of access to new therapies and drugs by two years would meet with much more resistance; it would have to be compensated by no less than CHF 6, 24 percent of premium on average. Limiting the drug benefit to generics only would have to be compensated by small amounts only that cannot be distinguished from zero. If the drug benefit were not to reimburse drugs used for the treatment of minor complaints, the Swiss, on average, would even be willing to pay a small amount, which again is not distinguishable from zero and likely reflects "warm glow" (Andreoni 1995). Finally, another cutback would be the concentration of dispersed existing hospital capacity in larger, centralized units. In spite of the alleged superior efficiency of such units, this regulation would have to be compensated by CHF 37, about 14 percent of the average monthly premium.

An argument against SHI in this context is preference heterogeneity. If preferences differ, the uniformity imposed entails an efficiency loss. A first sign of preference heterogeneity is the fact that compensation asked differs importantly between income classes. For example, individuals belonging to the top income class demand a compensation of 220 percent the amount demanded by those of the lowest income class for voluntarily accepting a physician list based on cost considerations only. Wealthy individuals can always opt out by paying extra; however, poor individuals do suffer a loss because the reduction by CHF 67, 25 percent in premiums, could in fact be achieved by at least one health insurer if premium regulation permitted it to pass on its savings from managed care to consumers (Lehmann and Zweifel 2004).

TABLE A.11   Compensation Asked for Cutbacks in Swiss Social Insurance, 2003

Socioeconomic characteristics	Physicians selected on cost criteria (1)	Physicians selected on quality criteria (2)	Physicians selected on cost and quality criteria (3)	Access to new therapies and drugs delayed by 2 years (4)	Reimbursement of generics only (5)	No reimbursement of drugs for minor complaints (6)	No small local hospitals (7)
				Amounts in CHF/month			
Total sample	103 (13.2)	53 (8.8)	42 (7.8)	65 (7.9)	3 (5.5)	–6 (5.3)	37 (5.7)
Region							
German-speaking	88 (11.8)	38 (7.8)	26 (6.8)	56 (7.1)	5 (5.5)	–5 (5.3)	31 (5.2)
French-speaking	191 (76.3)	138 (58.5)	136 (56.9)	117 (45.4)	–14 (19.6)	–13 (19.2)	74 (31.0)
Average monthly income per household member							
< CHF 1,500	67 (17.5)	44 (14.7)	35 (13.4)	52 (12.2)	–5 (10.0)	–2 (9.7)	28 (9.1)
CHF 1,500 to 4,000	108 (17.5)	56 (11.6)	42 (9.9)	66 (10.3)	9 (7.2)	–5 (6.8)	42 (7.8)
CHF 4,000+	148 (55.8)	62 (29.9)	63 (29.7)	81 (29.4)	–14 (17.5)	18 (17.8)	33 (16.8)

Source: Zweifel, Telser, and Vaterlaus 2006.

Notes: 1 CHF equals 0.7 € at 2003 exchange rates. Standard errors in parentheses.

Preference heterogeneity is also reflected in amazingly large regional differences. In the case of accepting a physician list based on cost and quality criteria, the French-speaking minority of Switzerland is so distrustful as to ask for a compensation of no less than CHF 136 per month, more than five times as much as the German-speaking majority. Their WTP to avoid other restrictions is consistently more than twice as high as that of German speakers.

Conclusion 10: There are several limits to social health insurance, ranging from the behavior of social insurers on to moral hazard effects, institutional design preventing correlations between risks to be accounted for, and to a willingness to pay for additional coverage that falls short of its additional cost.

6. SUMMARY AND CONCLUSIONS

This appendix revolves about two related basic issues: (1) What are the reasons for the existence and growth of social health insurance? And (2) Are there limits to social health insurance? As to the reasons, demand for social health insurance may well reflect the demand for an efficiency-enhancing invention that overcomes certain market failures plaguing private insurance markets. In addition, equity considerations may also provide a powerful motive. On balance, however, the (scanty) available evidence points to a preponderance of public choice reasons. Social (health) insurance can be seen as an efficient instrument for gaining votes in the hands of politicians seeking (re)election (Conclusion 2).

Turning to the supply of social health insurance, two settings need to be distinguished. One is provision by competitive health insurers who are regulated with regard to premiums and most products; the other, by a monopolistic public scheme. A simple model generates the prediction that completing regulation by risk adjustment (whereby insurers having an above-average share of low risks must pay into a fund that subsidizes those having an above-average share of high risks) undermines incentives for product innovation. The basic reason is simple. Innovation tends to attract the young, who are deemed to be low risks in all existing risk-adjustment schemes; it therefore induces a financial sanction. The monopolist insurer also pursues product innovation to the extent that it lowers insurance payments (which is of interest to political supervisors); however, its incentives are weaker than the competitive insurer's given reasonable parameter constellations (annex A.1).

The supply of insurance has five dimensions, (1) comprehensiveness of the benefits packages, (2) amount of risk-selection efforts deployed by insurers, (3) amount of loading contained in the premium, (4) amount of vertical integration, and (5) amount of sellers' concentration. Each dimension depends on several factors. Among these factors, the most prominent are moral hazard effects (which can, however, in their turn be influenced by the design of the contract) (Conclusions 3 to 8).

The importance of contract design motivates a review of the theory of the optimal health insurance contract, which also serves as a point of departure for exploring the limits of social health insurance. Indeed, this theory calls for a deductible to recover the administrative cost of providing health insurance. In addition, it may suggest partial coverage only, when the (marginal) utility of wealth is comparatively low in the state of sickness, causing material goods not to be very valuable. It specifically suggests a positive rate of coinsurance to combat moral hazard effects (Conclusion 9). However, there are additional limits to social health insurance. An important one derives from its institutional nature. From the point of view of risk-averse citizens, an "umbrella policy" covering not only the risk of illness but also those of accident, disability, early death of the breadwinner, (unplanned) additions to the family, and insufficient income in old age could be of considerable advantage to the extent that these risks cause their assets health, wealth, and wisdom (skill capital) to be positively correlated. However, consumers may well shy away from creating a public monopoly insurer with the task and authority to cover all these risks jointly. They might be more inclined to entrust this task to a competitive insurer that, if failing to deliver, can be exchanged for another insurer. These considerations put another limit on social health insurance.

Finally, political pressure to constrain social health insurance (and social security more generally) may reflect marginal willingness to pay on the part of citizens below marginal cost. Conversely, compensation asked for accepting restrictions in the domain of social health insurance (in the guise of reduced contributions) could be financed by health insurers through cost savings achieved. Recent evidence from Switzerland relates to this second approach. It suggests that if health insurers were permitted to fully pass on savings accruing, for example, in their managed care options, they could compensate the average consumer sufficiently to make this option attractive. In all, there are clear signs that social health insurance is encountering several limits (Conclusion 10).

These limits will become more important in the future as the cost of health care increasingly occurs toward the end of human life, when they cannot be recouped by increased contributions any more. Moreover, social health insurance, by modifying the incentives of the great majority of a country's health care providers, induces the very change in medical technology that causes the cost of health care to increase so fast (Zweifel 2003). The challenge will be to devise contracts that create incentives for consumers to make do with the second-latest medical technology when they are approaching death. However, competitive private insurers rather than regulated social health insurers are likely better able to meet this type of challenge.

NOTES

1. See, for example, Zweifel, Breyer, and Kifmann (2009: chap. 6).

2. The slope of the regression linking the company's expected rate of return to the expected rate of return prevailing on the capital market at large.

3. Specifically, the processing of claims—cf. the term $\mu \cdot \pi$ in equation (6), section 3.3.

4. For a definition, see section 3.3.6.

5. For some empirical evidence, see section 5.4.

6. This is known as the revelation principle; see, for example, Laffont and Tirole (1993: chap. 1).

7. See equation (5), section 3.3.

8. See equation (7), section 3.3.6.

9. Under certain circumstances, the incentives for prevention are higher when coverage increases. V responds positively to an increase in I when the insured earns a high wage, is risk averse, and/or enjoys generous sick leave. This can be a common situation in developed countries (Zweifel and Manning 2000: 417).

10. See equation (6).

11. For a discussion of the issues in the case of health care, see Preker, Harding, and Travis (2000).

12. "Natural asymmetry," as Carlton and Perloff (1999: 357) put it.

13. See, for example, Fecher, Perelman, and Pestieau (1991).

14. See, for example, Suret (1991).

15. For a survey of the evidence, see Zweifel and Manning (2000).

ANNEX A   FORMAL MODEL OF HEALTH INSURER BEHAVIOR IN TERMS OF INNOVATION AND RISK-SELECTION EFFORT

Among the five dimensions of supply distinguished in section 3 of appendix A, only two are retained here, for simplicity. Moreover, many of the influences listed, particularly in tables A.2 to A.8 of the appendix, are neglected for simplicity. First, the decision situation of an insurer is analyzed under the pressure of competition, then, that of a public monopoly insurer.

1. Competitive Health Insurer

A competitive health insurer can devote effort to innovation (i), resulting in new benefits covered but also—and even more important—in a better control of ex post moral hazard (moral hazard, given that illness has occurred). Developing managed care alternatives or contracts with bonus options for no claims are examples of such costly efforts. Or the insurer can invest in risk-selection effort (s), to "skim the cream," an activity without social value (assuming that the threat of being branded as a "high risk" does not induce preventive effort on the part of consumers). Let $\mu(i,s)$ denote the share of risks in the insurer's population at risk; this share depends not only on s but also on i because innovation typically appeals to younger consumers (which on average are lower risk). The premium (and hence the present value of their flow $\bar{P}$ is regulated to be uniform and constant (despite lowered expected losses thanks to innovative effort to keep things simple). However, high and low risks differ in their probability (π^h, π^l) of claiming benefits during the planning period of the insurer. As noted above, innovation effort also has the effect of lowering the present value of losses L, which are assumed not to depend on the type of insured, again for simplicity. Finally, both innovation and selection efforts have a price of one.

Although social health insurers may not per se pursue the maximization of expected discounted profit $E\Pi$, they still want to ensure their economic survival in the face of competition. To this end, accumulating reserves is of some importance. However, this ultimately implies behavior no different from maximizing expected discounted profit (under regulatory constraint, which also may result in a planning horizon that differs from a for-profit insurer). Therefore, the objective function of such a social health insurer[1] may read as,

$$\max_{i,s} E\Pi = \mu(i,s)\{\bar{P} - \pi^h L(i)\} + \{1 - \mu(i,s)\}\{\bar{P} - \pi^l L(i)\} - i - s \qquad \text{(A.1)}$$

$$\text{with} \quad \frac{\partial \mu}{\partial i} < 0, \quad \frac{\partial \mu}{\partial s} < 0, \quad \frac{\partial L}{\partial i} < 0.$$

Neglecting boundary solutions, the first-order conditions for an optimum are given by

$$\frac{\partial E\Pi}{\partial i} = \frac{\partial \mu}{\partial i}\{\bar{P} - \pi^h L\} + \mu\left(-\pi^h \frac{\partial L}{\partial i}\right) - \frac{\partial \mu}{\partial i}\{\bar{P} - \pi^l L\} + \{1 - \mu\}\left\{-\pi^l \frac{\partial L}{\partial i}\right\} - 1 = 0 \quad \text{(A.2)}$$

$$\frac{\partial E\Pi}{\partial s} = \frac{\partial \mu}{\partial s}\{P - \pi^h L\} - \frac{\partial \mu}{\partial s}\{\bar{P} - \pi^l L\} - 1 = 0. \tag{A.3}$$

Focusing on equation (A.2) first, and multiplying it by (i/μ), one obtains

$$\frac{\partial \mu}{\partial i}\frac{i}{\mu}\{(\bar{P} - \pi^h L) - (\bar{P} - \pi^l L)\} - \left(\frac{\partial L}{\partial i}\frac{i}{L}\right)\{\mu\pi^h L + (1-\mu^*)\pi^l L\}/\mu^* = \frac{i^*}{\mu^*}. \tag{A.4}$$

$\quad$ (−) $\qquad\qquad$ (−) $\qquad\qquad\qquad$ (−) $\qquad\qquad$ (+)

The first term on the left-hand side (LHS) is an elasticity $[e(\mu,i)]$, indicating how much a 1 percent increase in innovative effort serves to decrease (in percent) the share of high risks in the insured population. It is treated as a constant in the following, although its value in general will depend on the levels of both i and s. The term in brackets is also negative. With a common present value of premiums $\bar{P}$, the high risks cause a negative contribution to expected profit and the low risks a positive one. Together, these two terms define a first component of the marginal benefits of innovative effort. The second component again contains an elasticity, which indicates the effectiveness of innovation in terms of lowering the amount of future losses L. The term in brackets multiplied by L is nothing but the overall expected value of discounted future losses. This makes sense: Efforts at controlling ex post moral hazard have a particularly high marginal benefit if the initial amount of expected losses is high; accordingly, the optimal value of innovation $i*$ is higher, all other things being equal—see the right-hand side (RHS) of equation (A.4). However, the last factor $(1/\mu)$ shows that this benefit is dissipated across the high risks; the higher their share, the smaller is this second component of benefits of innovation. The RHS of equation (A.4) is nothing but the marginal cost of innovation, again distributed over the high risks.

Turning now to equation (A.3) and multiplying it through by (s/μ), one obtains

$$\left(\frac{\partial \mu}{\partial s}\frac{s}{\mu}\right)\{(\bar{P} - \pi^h L) - (\bar{P} - \pi^l L)\} = \frac{s^*}{\mu^*}. \tag{A.5}$$

$\qquad$ (−) $\qquad\qquad\qquad$ (−)

The first term on the LHS is again an elasticity $[e(\mu,s)]$, indicating the effectiveness of selection effort. Not surprisingly, the term in brackets shows the negative overall contribution to expected discounted profits. Therefore, the greater the difference between the two types of risk in the face of the uniform premium, the higher is the optimal amount of selection effort $s*$, all other things being equal—see the RHS of equation (A.5). However, its marginal cost can again be distributed over the number of high-risk insured μ.

For comparative-static analysis, the points of departure are equation (A.4) and (A.5), slightly rewritten,

$$e(\mu,i)\{(\bar{P} - \pi^h L) - (\bar{P} - \pi^l L)\} - e(L,i)\{\mu\pi^h L + (1-\mu)\pi^l L\}/\mu = \frac{i}{\mu(i,s)} \tag{A.6}$$

$$e(\mu,s)\{(\bar{P} - \pi^h L) - (\bar{P} - \pi^l L)\} = \frac{s}{\mu(i,s)}. \tag{A.7}$$

The effect of an increase in regulation (possibly from a state of no risk-adjustment scheme) is to decrease the difference in expected margins of high and low risks, that is

$$\frac{\partial}{\partial R}\left[(\bar{P}-\pi^{h}L)-(\bar{P}-\pi^{l}L)\right]:=\frac{\partial A}{\partial R}>0. \tag{A.8}$$

For future reference, one also has

$$\frac{\partial}{\partial i}\left(\frac{i}{\mu(i,s)}\right)=\frac{\mu-i\cdot\partial\mu/\partial i}{\mu^{2}}=\frac{1-e(\mu,i)}{\mu}. \tag{A.9}$$

Now, let the first-order conditions (A.6) and (A.7) be subjected to a shock $dR>0$. Written in matrix form, the comparative statics read, using (A.6) to (A.9),

$$\begin{bmatrix}[e(\mu,i)-1]/\mu & 0\\ 0 & [e(\mu,s)-1]/\mu\end{bmatrix}\begin{bmatrix}di\\ ds\end{bmatrix}=\begin{bmatrix}-e(\mu,i)\cdot\partial A/\partial R\\ -e(\mu,s)\cdot\partial A/\partial R\end{bmatrix}dR. \tag{A.10}$$

Applying Cramer's rule and assuming $|e(\mu,s)|<1$ (which may be deemed realistic), one obtains

$$\frac{di}{dR}=\frac{1}{\underset{(+)}{H}}\begin{vmatrix}\underset{(-)}{-e(\mu,i)\cdot\partial A/\partial R} & \underset{(+)}{0}\\ \underset{(-)}{-e(\mu,s)\cdot\partial A/\partial R} & \underset{(-)}{\left[e(\mu,s)-1\right]}/\mu\end{vmatrix}<0, \tag{A.11}$$

with $H>0$ symbolizing the determinant of the Hessian matrix. Applying Cramer's rule once more yields

$$\frac{ds}{dR}=\frac{1}{\underset{(+)}{H}}\begin{vmatrix}\underset{(-)}{\left[e(\mu,i)-1\right]}/\mu & \underset{(-)}{e(\mu,i)\cdot\partial A/\partial R}\\ 0 & \underset{(-)}{-e(\mu,s)\cdot\partial A/\partial R}\end{vmatrix}<0. \tag{A.12}$$

Thus, both innovative and risk-selection effort are predicted to decrease provided that $e(\mu,i)<1$, which looks like a reasonable assumption.

2. Public Monopoly Health Insurer

Since the manager of a public insurance scheme is a public official, the full set of interactions between a politician, a bureaucrat, and a voter should be specified in principle[2] as here, a much simpler alternative is presented that has the advantage of facilitating comparisons with section A.1.

From the outset, at least two institutional differences need to be noted. First, a public insurance scheme typically is not allowed to build major reserves. Reserves are also unnecessary because economic survival of the scheme is assured by the government. This means that a public official pursuing his or her mission prefers to have a balanced budget. However, if there is a deviation D from a balanced budget, the likelihood $\rho(D)$ that the envisaged utility can be in fact attained decreases. The public official faces a certain probability of losing his or her position (the utility associated with the possible alternative employment is normalized to zero for simplicity). The official's objective function can then be written

$$EU = \rho(D)^*U(D), \text{ with } \frac{\partial U}{\partial D} D < 0. \tag{A.13}$$

If there is a deficit ($D < 0$), then the official has an increase in utility if D increases toward zero ($\partial U/\partial D$); if the scheme has a surplus ($D > 0$), however, a further increase in D causes a decrease in utility.[3] The respective marginal utilities are normalized below to $\partial U/\partial D = \pm 1$.

The second difference concerns the decision variables. Since the public scheme is a monopoly enrolling the entire population, it has no reason to exert any risk-selection effort. Moreover, since the share of high risks μ, is exogenous, this share does not respond to innovative effort i. The only decision variable remaining therefore is i, innovative effort.

In view of these considerations, and focusing on the case of a deficit ($D < 0$, $\partial U/\partial D = 1$), one can write the public health insurer's objective function as

$$\max_i EU = \max \rho(D)D. \tag{A.14}$$

Noting that D depends on i, the first-order condition for an interior solution reads

$$\frac{\partial EU}{\partial i} = \frac{\partial \rho}{\partial D} \cdot \frac{\partial D}{\partial i} D + \rho \cdot \frac{\partial D}{\partial i} = 0. \tag{A.15}$$

This yields

$$\frac{\partial \rho}{\partial D} \cdot \frac{D}{\rho} = -1, \text{ or } e(\rho, D) = -1. \tag{A.16}$$

Note that $e(\rho,D)$ is a constant by assumption. Therefore, the choice of i^{**} by the public health insurer is completely arbitrary. However, since i impinges on its budget, $i^{**} = 0$ is the dominant solution. By way of contrast, $i^{**} > 0$ generally pertains in the case of the competitive health insurer.

NOTES

1. See Zweifel and Eisen (2003: chap. 5.5.2) for a similar model.

2. See, for example, Alesina and Tabellini (2004), Boldrin and Rustichini (2000), and Hammond and Knott (1996). For a comparative description of regulation of social health insurers, see Maarse, Paulus, and Kuiper (2005).

3. For a similar formulation in the case of a public hospital, see Zweifel and Breyer (1997), chap. 9.3.2.

ANNEX B   TYPES AND EFFICIENCY EFFECTS OF REGULATION

The main motive to regulate private health insurance is to (1) eliminate the social costs caused by insolvency by preventing insolvency, or (2) mitigate the social costs caused by insolvency while accepting the possibility of insolvency (Zweifel and Eisen 2003: chap. 8.1). Indeed, individuals losing their health insurance protection may face hardship and poverty that affect society as a whole.

(1) Regulations designed to eliminate insolvencies also seek to avoid instability in insurance markets that may occur due to adverse selection processes. Typically, they are very comprehensive and detailed because current operations of insurers must be monitored to attain the objective. However, this type of regulation generates inefficiency because it prevents insurers from adopting least-cost solutions. Thus, regulation aimed at avoiding insolvency under all circumstances may not maximize social welfare. Once private insurance schemes are fully regulated—such that, for example, prices, quantity, and quality of private insurance products are determined outside the market mechanism—resource allocation is likely to deteriorate. In other words, wrong insurance product pricing, wrong insurance packages, and reduced competitive behavior may lead to an inefficient and inequitable allocation of private health insurance products. Table AB.1 provides an overview of regulations that tend to lower efficiency, along with a short explanation. For example, budget approval (item 6) stifles product innovation because, apart from possible delays, the insurer runs the risk of having the cost of innovation disapproved.

TABLE AB.1   Regulations That Can Lower Efficiency

Imposed premiums	Lack incentive signals
	Undermine price competition
	Fail to reflect expected costs
	Disturb balance of underwriting and investing activities
Obligation to provide specific products, approval of product	Restricts product competition
	Does not reflect individual benefit-cost estimates
Rules on active/passive ownership (vertical integration)	Prevent insurers from finding the optimal degree of vertical integration
Obligation to provide certain benefits and/or to insure certain risks	Can make insurance not viable
	Does not reflect individual benefit-cost estimate
Separation of lines of business	Loss of synergy effects both for insured and insurer (allocation of reserves is not optimal)
Budget approval	Hampers product innovation
Rules on investments	May prevent insurers from obtaining maximum expected return for a given volatility
Subsidies and tax exemptions in favor of insurers	Justified if insurers provide a public good (e.g., cohesion of society)
	Induce overconsumption of insurance
Obligation to contract with providers	Lowers pressure on providers to reach efficiency

Source: Zweifel, Krey, and Tagli 2007.

618   Peter Zweifel

TABLE AB.2 Regulations That Can Enhance Efficiency

Licenses for insurers	Serves to lower probability of insolvency
Minimum capital	Serves to lower probability of fraud
Minimum liquidity requirements	Serves to lower probability of insolvency
Reinsurance schemes	Serves to lower probability of insolvency
Provision of a guarantee fund	Serves to lower probability of insolvency
Industry-wide insolvency fund	Serves to lower probability of insolvency
Provision of information to regulators and consumers	Serves to increase transparency
Agreed-on accounting procedures, internal and external auditing	Serves to increase transparency
Mandatory risk-adjustment scheme among insurers in the presence of adverse selection	Avoids cream skimming by insurers. Often a complement of premium regulation

Source: Zweifel, Krey, and Tagli 2007.

(2) However, regulations can also be designed to reduce social cost once insolvency occurs by making insurers bear them. One way to internalize these costs is to require the deposit of reserves, another, the establishment of a guaranty fund financed jointly by the insurers. These measures go a long way toward eliminating hardship of insured in the advent of insolvency. Even these regulations are not without their cost, however, because, for example, the reserves deposited could usually be invested at a higher rate of return. In addition, there is the direct cost of administering these regulations. On the whole, however, regulations motivated by the objective of internalizing the social cost of insolvency seem to have a better chance of being efficiency-enhancing.

Finally, insurance regulation may have the objective of creating demand for private coverage, which is seen as a precondition for an expanded provision of private health care and the reaping of efficiency gains associated with it (table AB.2) (Griffin 1989: 23).

REFERENCES

Alesina, A., and G. Tabellini. 2004. "Bureaucrats or Politicians?" National Bureau of Economic Research, NBER Working Paper No. 10241, Cambridge, MA.

Andreoni, J. 1995. "Warm-Glow vs. Cold-Prickle: The Effects of Positive and Negative Framing on Cooperation in Experiments." *Quarterly Journal of Economics* 110 (1): 1–21.

Arrow, K.J. 1963. "Uncertainty and the Welfare Economics of Medical Care." *American Economic Review* 53: 941–73.

Boldrin, M., and A. Rustichini. 2000. "Political Equilibria with Social Security." *Review of Economic Dynamics* 3 (1): 41–78.

Carlton, D.W., and J.M. Perloff. 1999. *Modern Industrial Organization*. Reading, MA: Addison-Wesley.

Chen, C., T. Steiner, and A. White. 2001. "Risk-Taking Behavior and Managerial Ownership in the United States Life Insurance Industry." *Applied Financial Economics* (April): 165–71.

Cook, P.J., and D.A. Graham. 1977. "The Demand for Insurance and Protection: The Case of Irreplaceable Commodities." *Quarterly Journal of Economics* 91: 143–56.

Cremer, H., and P. Pestieau. 1996. "Redistributive Taxation and Social Insurance." *International Tax and Public Finance* 3: 281–95.

Culyer, A.J., and A. Wagstaff. 1993. "Equity and Equality in Health and Health Care." *Journal of Health Economics* 12: 431–57.

Cummins, J.D. 1991. "Statistical and Financial Models of Insurance Pricing and the Insurance Firm." *Journal of Risk and Insurance* 58 (2): 261–302.

Desmet, M., A.Q. Chowdhury, and K. Islam. 1999. "The Potential for Social Mobilisation in Bangladesh: The Organisation and Functioning of Two Health Insurance Schemes." *Social Science and Medicine* 48 (7): 925–38.

Doherty, N.A., and S.M. Tinic. 1981. "Reinsurance under Conditions of Capital Market Equilibrium: A Note." *Journal of Finance* 36 (4): 949–53.

Dror, M.D., and A.S. Preker, eds. 2002. *Social Reinsurance: A New Approach to Sustainable Community Health Financing.* Washington, DC: World Bank; Geneva: International Labour Office.

Ehrlich, I., and G.S. Becker. 1972. "Market Insurance, Self-Insurance and Self-Protection." *Journal of Political Economy* 80: 623–48.

Fecher, E., S.D. Perelman, and P. Pestieau. 1991. "Scale Economies and Performance in the French Insurance Industry." *Geneva Papers on Risk and Insurance, Issues and Practice* 60: 315–26.

Feder, G., L.J. Lau, J.Y. Liu, and X. Luo. 1993. "The Nascent Rural Credit Market in China." In *The Economics of Rural Organization*, ed., G. Feder, L.J. Lau, J.Y. Liu, and X. Luo, 109–30. Oxford and New York: Oxford University Press.

Frech, H.E., III, and J.C. Samprone, Jr. 1980. "The Welfare Loss of Excessive Nonprice Competition: The Case of Property-Liability Insurance Regulation." *Journal of Law and Economics* 21: 429–40.

Fujita, M., P. Krugman, and A.J. Venables. 1999. *The Spatial Economy.* Cambridge, MA: MIT Press.

Gerdtham, U.G., B. Jönsson, and J. Søgaard. 1992. "An Econometric Analysis of Health Care Expenditure: A Cross-Section Study of OECD Countries." *Journal of Health Economics* 11: 63–84.

Gouveia, M. 1997. "Majority Rule and the Public Provision of a Private Good." *Public Choice* 93: 221–44.

Grant, K., and R. Grant. 2002. "Health Insurance and the Poor in Low-Income Countries." Institute of Health Sector Development, http://www.ihsd.org.

Greenwald, B., and J. Stiglitz. 1990. "Asymmetric Information and the New Theory of the Firm: Financial Constraints and Risk Behavior." *American Economic Review* 80: 160–65.

Griffin, C. 1989. "Strengthening Health Services in Developing Countries through the Private Sector." Discussion Paper 4, IFD-4, International Finance Corp., Washington, DC.

Hammond, T.H., and J.H. Knott. 1996. "Who Controls the Bureaucracy? Presidential Power, Congressional Dominance, Legal Constraints, and Bureaucratic Autonomy in a Model of Multi-Institutional Policy-Making." *Journal of Law, Economics, and Organization* 12: 119–66.

Hindriks, J., and P. de Donder. 2003. "The Politics of Redistributive Social Insurance." *Journal of Public Economics* 87: 2639–60.

Laffont, J.J., and J. Tirole. 1993. *A Theory of Incentives in Procurement and Regulation.* Cambridge, MA: MIT Press.

Lehmann, H., and P. Zweifel. 2004. "Innovation and Risk Selection in Deregulated Social Health Insurance." *Journal of Health Economics* 23: 997–1012.

Lichtenberg, F.R. 2004. "Sources of U.S. Longevity Increase, 1960–2001." *Quarterly Review of Economics and Finance* 44: 369–89.

Ma, Ching-to A., and T.G. McGuire. 1997. "Optimal Health Insurance and Provider Payment." *American Economic Review* 87: 685–704.

Maarse, H., A. Paulus, and G. Kuiper. 2005. "Supervision in Social Health Insurance: A Four-Country Study." *Health Policy* 71 (3): 333–46.

Malinvaud, E. 1972. "The Allocation of Individual Risks in Large Markets." *Journal of Economic Theory* 14: 312–28.

Manning, W.G., J.P. Newhouse, N. Duan, E.B. Keeler, and A. Leibowitz. 1987. "Health Insurance and the Demand for Medical Care: Evidence from a Randomized Experiment." *American Economic Review* 77: 251–77.

McMaster, R. 2001. "The National Health Service, the 'Internal Market' and Trust." In *The Social Economics of Health Care,* ed. John B. Davis, 113–40. London: Routledge.

Miller, R.D., Jr., and H.E. Frech III. 2004. *Health Care Matters: Pharmaceuticals, Obesity, and the Quality of Life.* Washington, DC: AEI Press.

Mossin, J. 1968. "Aspects of Rational Insurance Purchasing." *Journal of Political Economy* 76: 553–68.

Musau, S. 1999. "Community-Based Health Insurance: Experiences and Lessons Learned from East Africa." Technical Report No. 34. Bethesda, MD: Partnership for Health Reform, Abt Associates Inc.

Newhouse, J.P. 1996. "Reimbursing Health Plans and Health Providers: Efficiency in Production versus Selection." *Journal of Economic Literature* 34: 1236–63.

Newhouse, J.P., and The Insurance Experiment Group. 1993. *Free for All? Lessons from the RAND Health Insurance Experiment.* Cambridge, MA, and London: Harvard University Press.

Nugroho, G., R. Macagba, and G. Dorros. 2001. *Building Community Health: A Practical Handbook for Practitioners.* Claremont, CA: Health Development International.

Nyman, J.A. 2003. *The Theory of Demand for Health Insurance.* Stanford, CA: Stanford University Press.

OECD (Organisation for Economic Co-operation and Development). 2004. *The OECD Health Project—Towards High-Performing Health Systems.* Paris: OECD.

Olsen, J.A. 2000. "A Note on Eliciting Distributive Preferences for Health." *Journal of Health Economics* 19: 541–50.

Pauly, M.V. 1970. "The Efficiency in the Provision of Consumption Subsidies." *Kyklos* 23: 33–57.

———. 1984. "Is Cream Skimming a Problem for the Competitive Medical Market?" *Journal of Health Economics* 3: 87–95.

Pauly, M.V., P. Danzon, P. Feldstein, and J. Hoff. 1992. *Responsible National Health Insurance*. Washington, DC: AEI Press.

Preker, A., A. Harding, and P. Travis. 2000. "Make or Buy Decisions in the Production of Health Care Goods and Services: New Insights from Institutional Economics and Organizational Theory." *Bulletin of the World Health Organization* 78 (6): 779–90.

Rothschild, M., and J. Stiglitz. 1976. "Equilibrium in Competitive Insurance Markets: An Essay in the Economics of Incomplete Information." *Quarterly Journal of Economics* 90: 723–46.

Spence, A.M., and R.J. Zeckhauser. 1971. "Insurance, Information, and Individual Action." *American Economic Review, Papers and Proceedings* 61: 380–87.

Suret, M. 1991. "Scale and Scope Economies in the Canadian Property and Casualty Insurance Industry." *Geneva Papers on Risk and Insurance, Issues and Practice* 59 (April): 236–56.

Telser, H., S. Vaterlaus, P. Zweifel, and P. Eugster. 2004. *Was leistet unser Gesundheitswesen?* [What Are the Benefits of Our Health Care System?] Zurich: Rüegger.

Tullock, G. 2003. "The Origin of the Rent-Seeking Concept." *International Journal of Business and Economics* 2: 1–8.

Udry, C. 1993. "Credit Markets in Northern Nigeria: Credit as Insurance in Rural Economy." In *The Economics of Rural Organization*, ed. K. Hoff, A. Braverman, and J. Stiglitz, 87–108. New York and Oxford: Oxford University Press.

Van Dalen, H.P., and O.A. Swank. 1996. "Government Spending Cycles: Ideological or Opportunistic?" *Public Choice* 89: 183–200.

Van de Ven, W.P.M.M., and R.P. Ellis. 2000. "Risk Adjustment in Competitive Health Plan Markets." In *Handbook of Health Economics*, vol. 1A, ed. J.P. Newhouse and A.J. Culyer, 757–890. Amsterdam: North Holland.

Van de Ven, W.P.M.M., R.C.J.A. van Vliet, F.T. Schut, and E.M. van Barneveld. 2000. "Access to Coverage for High Risks in a Competitive Individual Health Insurance Market: Via Premium Rate Restrictions or Risk-Adjusted Premium Subsidies." *Journal of Health Economics* 19: 311–39.

Waldman, D., and E. Jensen. 2001. *Industrial Organization*. Boston, MA: Addison-Wesley.

Williams, A. 1998. "Makes a Man Healthy, Wealthy, and Wise! Or from Folklore to Systems Science." In *Systems Science in Health Care*, ed. G. Duru et al., vol. 23, 57–60. Paris: Masson.

Wilson, C.A. 1977. "A Model of Insurance Markets with Incomplete Information." *Journal of Economic Theory* 16: 167–207.

Zweifel, P. 2000a. "The Division of Labor between Private and Social Insurance." In *Handbook of Insurance*, ed. G. Dionne, 933–66. Boston, MA: Kluwer.

———. 2000b. "The Future Division of Labour between Private and Social Health Insurance." *Journal of Health Care Finance* 26 (3): 38–55.

————. 2003. "Medical Innovation: A Challenge to Society and Insurance." *Geneva Papers on Risk and Insurance* 28 (2): 194–202.

————. 2005. "The Purpose and Limits of Social Health Insurance." Keynote paper prepared for the 2005 annual meeting of the Verein für Socialpolitik in Bonn, Germany, University of Zurich.

Zweifel, P., and F. Breyer. 1997. *Health Economics*. New York and Oxford: Oxford University Press.

————. 2005. "The Case for Risk-Based Premiums in Public Health Insurance." *Health Economics, Policy and Law* 1 (2): 171–88.

Zweifel, P., F. Breyer, and M. Kifmann. 2009. *Health Economics*. 2nd ed. Heidelberg and New York: Springer.

Zweifel, P., and R. Eisen. 2003. *Versicherungsökonomie* [Insurance Economics]. 2nd ed. Heidelberg: Springer.

Zweifel, P., B.B. Krey, and M. Tagli. 2007. "Supply of Private Voluntary Health Insurance in Low-Income Countries." In *Private Voluntary Health Insurance in Development: Friend or Foe?* ed. A.S. Preker, R.M. Scheffler, and M.C. Bassett, 55–113. Washington, DC: World Bank.

Zweifel, P., and H.J. Lehmann. 2001. "Soziale Absicherung im Portfolio persönlicher Aktiva: Wie kann die soziale Sicherung Teufelskreise verhindern?" [Social Insurance of Personal Assets: How Can Social Security Prevent Vicious Cycles?], ed. E. Theurl, 53–76. Der Sozialstaat an der Jahrtausendwende, Heidelberg: Physica.

Zweifel, P., and W.G. Manning. 2000. "Moral Hazard and Consumer Incentives in Health Care." In *Handbook of Health Economics*, vol. 1A, ed. A.J. Culyer and J.P. Newhouse, 409–59. Boston, MA: North Holland.

Zweifel, P., H. Telser, and S. Vaterlaus. 2006. "Consumer Resistance against Regulation: The Case of Health Care." *Journal of Regulatory Economics* 29 (3): 319–32.

APPENDIX B

Empirical Evidence on Trends in Health Insurance

Yohana Dukhan

This technical appendix extends the analysis of chapters 7 and 8 (on Francophone and Anglophone Africa, respectively) on the factors limiting the development of health insurance in Africa. The main objective is to test the existence of relationships between the development of health insurance—public and private—and a set of structural general factors and factors more specific to the health sector. This appendix is organized as follows. Section 1 recalls the conceptual framework presented in chapter 7 and the main determinants of health insurance development identified. Section 2 discusses the variables used in the empirical analysis as well as the method and the econometric specifications. Section 3 presents the main results of the study.

CONCEPTUAL FRAMEWORK

The literature tends to highlight major economic, social, political, institutional, and cultural constraints that account for the low level of implantation and the relatively slow development of health insurance systems in developing countries (Letourmy 2003, 2005; Carrin 2002; Ensor 1999; Griffin and Shaw 1996). Figure B.1 summarizes the main determinants of health insurance development. These factors can be grouped into two broad categories:

(1) General structural factors related to

- The quality of the political and institutional environment (governance, political stability, domestic resources mobilization capacity, and involvement of the state in the health sector)
- The economic and social context (revenue per capita, revenue growth and stability of revenue growth, labor market structure, and population distribution).

(2) Factors specific to the health sector related to

- The health care supply (existence of medical infrastructure and availability of health care supply, quality of care)
- Direct health care/health insurance demand (capacity and willingness to pay) and indirect (cultural practices and peoples' understanding of health insurance principles).

FIGURE B.1   Determinants of Health Insurance Development

General structural factors	*Political and institutional determinants*	Development of health insurance
	- Governance - Capacity to mobilize domestic resources - Involvement of the state in the health sector - Involvement of donors in the health sector	
	Economic and social determinants	
	- Income per capita - Growth and stability of income growth - Income inequalities - Structure of the labor market - Age structure of the population - Distribution of the population in the territory	
Factors specific to the health sector	*Health care supply*	
	- Existence of infrastructure and availability of health care supply - Quality of health care - Health care payment mechanisms	
	Health care and insurance demand	
	- Capacity and willingness to pay for health care - Existence of health care and insurance subsidies (i.e., subsidized health insurance premiums for the poorest)	- Cultural factors and social practices - Individuals' understanding of health insurance principles	

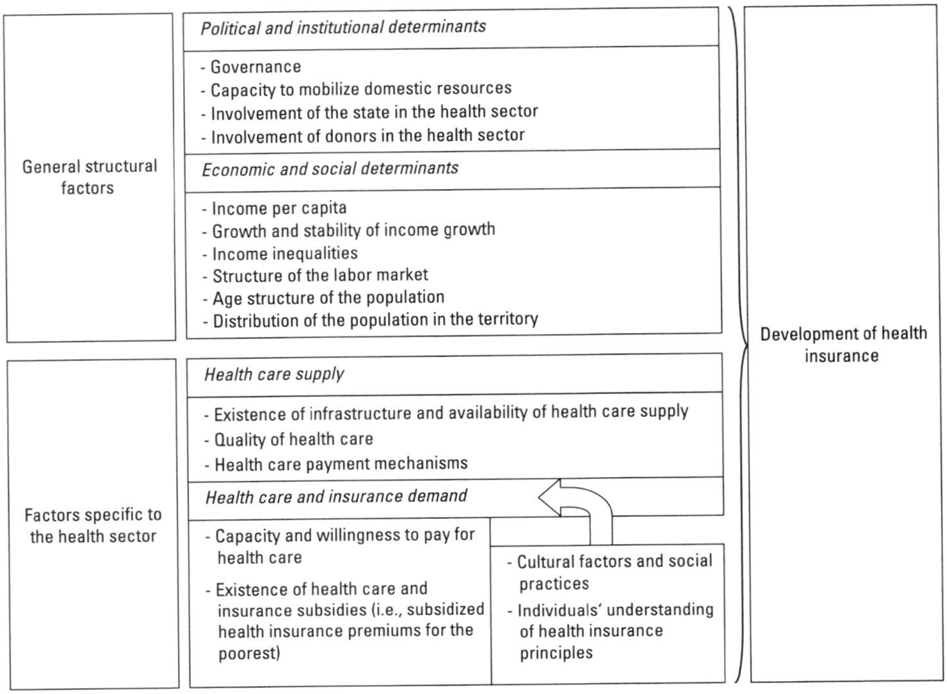

Source: Author.

These factors are frequently discussed in the literature, but they have not been studied in an empirical analysis. This technical appendix tests the role of these factors on the development of health insurance in a sample of 99 developing countries between 1995 and 2010.

EMPIRICAL ANALYSIS OF HEALTH INSURANCE DEVELOPMENT AT THE INTERNATIONAL LEVEL

This section explores whether there are statistically significant relationships between the determinants of the development of health insurance and the degree of development of health insurance at the international level. Estimates are made for a sample of 99 low- and middle-income countries[1] between 1995 and 2010, using data from the World Health Organization (WHO) and the World Bank. First, the choice and measurement of variables are discussed, in particular those measuring the degree of development of health insurance. Second, issues related to the econometric specification and estimation methods are also discussed.

Variables and Descriptive Statistics

Table B.1 provides a list of the variables used, the source, and the expected signs of the coefficients in the regressions. Table B.2 presents descriptive statistics for the variables.

Health Insurance Development

Dependent Variables
Usually, the extent of health insurance development is measured by the rate of population coverage by the health insurance system. For lack of information on health coverage at the international level, data on health insurance expenditure are used in this study.

The share of out-of-pocket (OOP) payments in total health expenditure is sometimes used to approach the degree of financial protection of the population (Gottret, Schieber, and Water 2008). This variable is not relevant in the present

TABLE B.1   Variables and Sources

Variable	Sign[a]	Indicator	Source
		Dependent variables	
Contribution of health insurance to health financing		Total health insurance expenditure as percentage of total health expenditure (HIE/THE)	Author, calculated from NHA (WHO 2012a)
Contribution of social security to health financing		Social security expenditure as percentage of total health expenditure (SSE/THE)	NHA (WHO 2012a)
Contribution of private health insurance to health financing		Private prepaid and risk-pooling expenditure as percentage of total health expenditure (PHIE/THE)	NHA (WHO 2012a)
		Structural factors	
(1) Political and institutional			
Governance	+/+/+	Government effectiveness (Gov.Effec)	WGI (World Bank 2012b)
	+/+/+	Political stability and absence of violence (Pol.Stab)	WGI (World Bank 2012b)
	+/+/+	Voice and accountability (Voice.Acc)	WGI (World Bank 2012b)
Share of health budget devoted to health	?/+/?	Public health expenditure percent Total public expenditure (PHE/TPE)	NHA (WHO 2012a)
External assistance for health	?/?/?	External resources for health percent Total health expenditure (EHE/THE)	NHA (WHO 2012a)
(2) Economic, social, and demographic			
Income per capita	+/+/+	GDP/Cap, constant US$ (2000) (GDP/Cap)	WDI (World Bank 2012a)
Instability of income growth rate	−/−/−	Standard deviation of GDP/Cap growth rate over a 5-year period (S-d.GDP. Growth)	Author, from WDI (World Bank 2012a)
Income inequality	−/−/−	Gini index (Gini)	WIID (UNU-WIDER 2008)

(continued)

TABLE B.1   Variables and Sources *(continued)*

Variable	Sign[a]	Indicator	Source
Dependency ratio	–/–/–	Number of dependents - percent of working-age population (Dep.Ratio)	WDI (World Bank 2012a)
Labor market structure	–/–/–	Population employed in agriculture - percent of total employment (Agri)	WDI (World Bank 2012a)
Urban population	+/+/+	Urban population - percent of total population (Urban.Pop)	WDI (World Bank 2012a)
Specific factors of the health sector			
(1) Health care supply			
Health care supply availability	+/+/+	Number of doctors per 1,000 inhabitants (Doctors)	WDI (World Bank 2012a)
(2) Cultural factors and health care/insurance demand			
Population literacy	+/+/+	Literacy rate of adults - percent of population 15 and above (Literacy)	WDI (World Bank 2012a)
Ethnic diversity	?/–/+	Ethnic fragmentation Index (Ethnic)	Alesina et al. (2003)
Religious diversity	?/–/+	Religious fragmentation Index (Religion)	Alesina et al. (2003)
Africa dummy variable	?/?/?	Dummy variable equal to 1 if country is in Sub-Saharan Africa (0 otherwise, Africa)	Author

Source: Author.

a. Expected signs of coefficients are relative to the three dependent variables considered in the regressions.

TABLE B.2   Descriptive Statistics

Variable	Average	Standard deviation	Minimum	Maximum
HIE/THE	13.36	15.75	0.00	71.11
SSE/THE	10.12	16.20	0.00	71.09
PPRPE/THE	3.65	6.34	0.00	46.82
Gov.Effec	−0.50	0.63	−2.45	1.28
Pol.Stab	−0.42	0.92	−2.50	1.52
Voice.Acc	−0.38	0.83	−2.22	1.43
PHE/TPE	10.16	4.53	0.10	42.38
Ext.HE/THE	11.00	14.96	0.00	93.72
GDP/Cap (constant)	1,808.49	1,938.86	62.24	11,765.60
S-d.GDP.Growth	3.91	4.27	0.12	46.01
Gini	43.04	8.60	16.83	64.34
Dep.Ratio	0.71	0.17	0.39	1.09
Agri	32.30	20.33	0.60	85.40
Urb.Pop	46.07	20.22	7.20	93.66
Med	1.06	1.25	0.01	6.40
Literacy	77.07	21.17	12.85	99.99
Ethnic	0.50	0.25	0.00	0.93
Religion	0.43	0.24	0.00	0.86
Africa	0.33	0.47	0.00	1.00

Sources: National Health Accounts (WHO 2012a); WHOSIS (WHO 2012b); World Development Indicators (World Bank 2012a); Worldwide Governance Indicators (World Bank 2012b).

context as it is to measure the degree of financial protection related to health insurance. A significant share of OOP compared with total health spending may mean that a country's insurance-mechanisms are relatively puny. A low share of OOP in a country may also be associated with weak development of insurance if health care is provided through a National Health System (NHS), free health care programs, or vertical programs.

One could try to estimate the importance of insurance using health insurance spending per capita but, although this indicator is intuitively easy to interpret, it is not satisfactory. Indeed, the political objective sought through the development of health insurance is not to increase health insurance spending per capita but rather to increase the contribution of insurance-based mechanisms to health financing in order to reduce OOP.[2]

The proposed indicator to gauge the degree of development of health insurance is the contribution of insurance to health financing in each country. It is measured by a country's total health insurance expenditure divided by its total health expenditure.[3]

Total health insurance expenditure is divided into two subsets (WHO 2006):

- *Social security expenditure* includes purchases of health goods and services by mandatory schemes that are controlled by government. Also included here are mandatory government-controlled social security schemes that apply only to a selected group of the population, such as public sector employees.

- *Private health insurance expenditure* includes the outlays of private insurance schemes and private social insurance schemes (with no government control over payment rates and participating providers but with broad guidelines from government), commercial and nonprofit (mutual) insurance schemes, health maintenance organizations, and other agents managing prepaid medical and paramedical benefits (including the operating scheme).

The estimates are made at the aggregate level (total health insurance expenditure) but also for each subset (social security expenditure and prepayment and risk pooling) to test the existence of specific relationships to the types of insurance systems. Thus, three dependent variables are used:

- The share of total health insurance expenditure in total health expenditure (HIE/THE)

- The share of social security expenditure in total health expenditure (SSE/THE)

- The share of private health insurance expenditure in total health expenditure (PHIE/THE).

The share of health insurance expenditure in total health expenditure represents on average 13.4 percent in the sample of countries, with a median of only 6.9 percent. This share varies considerably from country to country—from 0 to 71.1 percent (Costa Rica in 1998[4]). The contribution of health insurance to health financing is relatively important in Europe and Central Asia (ECA) and in Latin America and Caribbean (LAC) countries[5] (table B.3). The five countries for which

TABLE B.3   Health Insurance Expenditure, by Level and Region

Health insurance expenditure as percentage of total health expenditure	Number of observations	EAP	ECA	LAC	MENA	SA	SSA
Less than 5 percent	707	160	61	78	16	105	287
From 5 to 30 percent	703	133	53	220	110	16	171
From 30 to 60 percent	193	11	41	99	18	0	24
More than 60 percent	34	0	15	19	0	0	0

Source: Author.
Note: EAP = East Asia and Pacific; ECA = Europe and Central Asia; LAC = Latin America and the Caribbean; MENA = Middle East and North Africa; SA = South Asia; SSA = Sub-Saharan Africa.

health insurance expenditure represents more than 60 percent of total health expenditure are located in Central Europe (Romania, Lithuania, Serbia) and Latin America (Costa Rica and Uruguay). Moreover, in a large number of countries, the share of health insurance expenditure in total health expenditure is zero or very low: 11 percent of the observations in the sample are equal to zero, and almost half of them (43 percent) are less than 5 percent. Most of the countries showing these low values are in Central Asia and Sub-Saharan Africa.

Social security expenditure accounts on average for 10.1 percent of total health expenditure, with a median of 1.5 percent. The contribution of social insurance to health financing is particularly important in Montenegro (69 percent on average over the period), Costa Rica (63.8 percent), Lithuania (60.4 percent), and Romania (66.5 percent between 2003 and 2010). The strong growth of total insurance recorded in these countries really comes from social insurance and not from private insurance.

Finally, *the share of private health insurance expenditure* is very low (an average of 3.6 percent and a median of 1.4 percent). South Africa, Namibia, and Uruguay stand out from other countries in the sample; the contribution of private health insurance to health financing represents on average 41.9 percent, 28.7 percent, and 22.9 percent, respectively, in these three countries over the period of study. This share falls thereafter to 21.5 percent in Chile and 20.4 percent in Brazil.

Determinants of Health Insurance Trends

The main determinants of health insurance development are grouped into two broad categories: general structural factors and factors specific to the health sector.

Structural Factors

(1) Political and institutional

Five variables are used in the analysis. The first three measure the quality of the political and institutional environment; government effectiveness, political stability, voice, and accountability. The last two variables reflect the commitment of the state and donors in health financing. The three governance indicators come from the Worldwide Governance Indicators dataset (WGI, World Bank 2012b) and take values between –2.5 when the results are weak and +2.5 when they improve. A positive relationship is expected between these three variables and those measuring the development of health insurance. The study of simple correlations confirms it, at least for total insurance (figure B.2) and social security, but to a lesser extent for private insurance. The variables measuring the share of the state budget devoted to health and the share of external assistance in

FIGURE B.2   Simple Correlations between Health Insurance Expenditure and Political and Institutional Factors

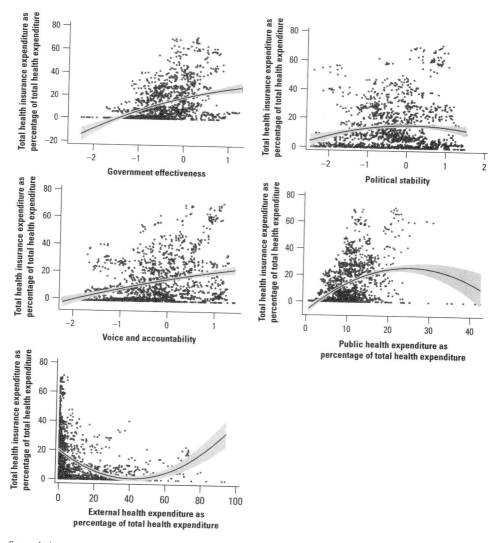

Source: Author.

total health expenditure come from the National Health Accounts (NHA, WHO 2012a). The sign of relations, unknown for these variables, is discussed below.

Government effectiveness measures the quality of public service delivery and the competence of the bureaucracy. The average value of the indicator between 1995 and 2010 in the sample is –0.50 with values ranging from –2.24 in 2010 (Somalia) and 1.18 in 2010 (Chile). Annex figure BA.1 shows a positive correlation between this governance variable and the share of health insurance expenditure in total health expenditure (correlation of 0.17). The coefficients are more important for private health insurance expenditure than social security expenditure (0.43 and 0.21 respectively).

Political stability and absence of violence measures the perception of the likelihood that the government will be destabilized or overthrown by unconstitutional or violent means, including domestic violence and terrorism. The average value of the indicator over the period of study in the sample is –0.42, with a minimum of –2.5 in 2010 (Somalia) and a maximum of 1.52 in 2010 (Palau). Annex figure BA.1 highlights at this stage low correlations between political stability and insurance variables.[6]

Voice and accountability captures perceptions of the extent to which a country's citizens are able to participate in selecting their government, as well as freedom of expression, freedom of association, and a free media. The average value of the indicator over the 1995–2010 period in the sample is –0.38, with a minimum of –2.17 in 2010 (Eritrea) and a maximum of 1.24 in 2010 (St. Lucia).

The share of the state budget devoted to health.[7] The average value of the indicator over the period of study in the sample is 10.2 percent. The countries for which the indicator values are the lowest in 2010 are the Republic of the Union of Myanmar (0.9 percent), Afghanistan (1.6 percent), Guinea (1.8 percent), and Chad (3.3 percent). In contrast, the share of budget spent on health was particularly high in Costa Rica (29 percent) and the Solomon Islands (23.1 percent). This indicator, which aims to reflect the degree of government involvement in financing the health sector,[8] is flawed in that it incorporates external resources for health. The available data do not break down the public health expenditure from internal resources, reflecting a greater effort of the government, and those from external resources. The results should be interpreted with caution because, although the budget spent on health may be relatively high in some countries, external resources can represent a considerable share of health spending. This is the case of Rwanda, for example, for which the state budget spent on health was 20.1 percent in 2010 while at the same time external resources accounted for 49 percent of total health expenditures. The same observation can be made for the Federated States of Micronesia, the Marshall Islands, and Zambia.

The share of external resources in total health expenditure.[9] This variable is used to measure whether the increased weight of foreign aid is also associated with a stronger contribution of health insurance to health financing. The sign of this variable is unknown. A positive relationship can be expected if donors tend to encourage governments to develop insurance mechanisms when the weight of aid is important. The relationship can also be negative if a large part of such aid is used to fund programs such as free health care or vertical programs, as it is in many countries, including African countries. Furthermore, it will be necessary to ascertain whether the level of foreign aid is in part determined by the health insurance level. In other words, this will ensure (using appropriate tests) that this variable is not endogenous. The level of external assistance for a country is in part determined by the degree of development of health insurance. Despite strong unpredictability, the share of foreign aid can represent a significant share of the resources of the health sector for some countries: 83.3 percent for Eritrea in 2006, 80 percent for Malawi in 2010, 72.8 percent for the Federated States of Micronesia in 2005.

(2) Economic, social, and demographic

The success of the establishment or expansion of a health insurance system, whether mandatory or voluntary, also depends on a number of general factors. Among these factors are: the income of the population and its distribution, the rate of economic growth, the population structure, the labor market structure, the distribution of the population within the territory, and the ability of different groups to pay.

Income per capita and instability of income growth rate. The experience of developed countries and countries in transition shows that the income level of the population and stable economic growth would promote the success of health financing reforms and measures to expand insurance mechanisms (Gottret and Schieber 2006). They include the ability to respond to the first function of health financing systems, which is the mobilization of resources (public and private) in a sustainable manner. The identical income growth rate affects insurance differently, depending on whether it is stable or unstable. This variable is used to verify the extent to which average income volatility influences the evolution of insurance for given average revenue. The instability of a variable is always measured relative to a reference value. In empirical work, it is often measured by the standard deviation of the growth rate of the variable, that is, compared with the average rate of growth (Ramey and Ramey 1995).[10] In this analysis, the standard deviation of the growth rate of per capita income over a five-year period is used as a measure of income growth instability. The growth of per capita income is unstable in many countries, especially Liberia, Rwanda, Georgia, Timor-Leste, Albania, and Lebanon (figure B.3).

Income inequality. Insurance is more difficult to develop in a society that has large income inequalities. Indeed, the role of health insurance is to ensure similar health benefits to people with similar health care needs, regardless of the amount each contributes. This principle is often a hard sell to the population, all the

FIGURE B.3   Instability of Income Growth per Capita

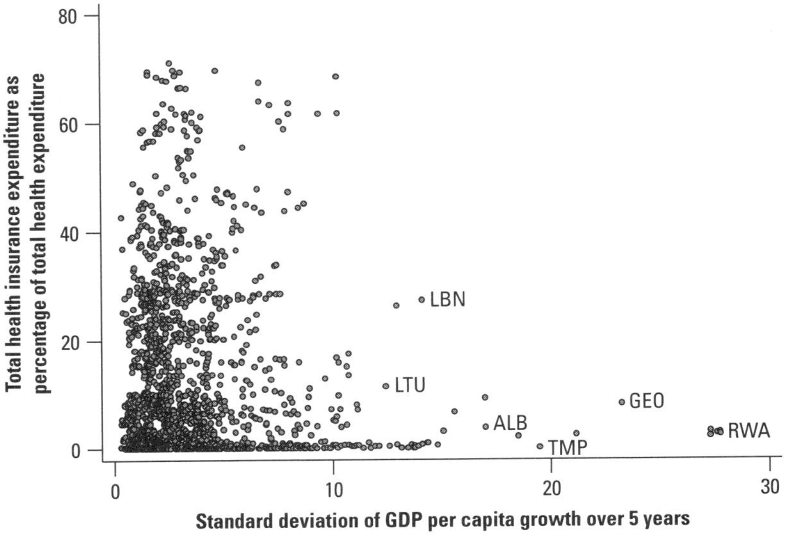

Source: Author.
Note: ALB = Albania; GEO = Georgia; LBN = Lebanon; LTU = Lithuania; RWA = Rwanda; TMP = Timor-Leste.

more so in a country with stark income inequalities. Pooling resources is harder when a society is highly unequal initially (Carrin 2002). The Gini index of UNU-WIDER (2008) is used to test the effect of income inequality on the degree of development of health insurance. The indicator, which has many missing observations, varies between 17 percent and 64 percent. Countries with the highest income inequalities are the Comoros, Lesotho, Ecuador, Swaziland, and Bolivia. These inequalities are relatively low in Azerbaijan, Belarus, Bulgaria, and Ukraine.

Dependency ratio. The sign of this variable is unknown. On one hand, a significant number of dependents relative to the active population may hinder the development of insurance because the number of people who can contribute to the financing of insurance is relatively low. On the other hand, the higher the dependency ratio is, the higher the need for insurance is likely to be. This is because the elderly and children are the most vulnerable to disease. The dependency ratio is relatively high in the sample (0.7 on average). The lowest value is 0.4 (the Russian Federation in 2009) and the highest at 1.1 (Niger in 2009). The highest dependency ratios are registered in Sub-Saharan Africa (average 0.9) and Latin America and the Caribbean (average 0.7).

Labor market structure. Insurance is more difficult to implement or develop in countries that have a high proportion of workers in the informal sector.[11] It is harder for the state to collect resources from informal workers—through taxation, employer contributions, and membership fees—and for private and community insurers through contributions or premiums. Because it is so difficult to find data characterizing the importance of the informal sector at the international level, such variable could not be introduced in this analysis. Moreover, the potential for the development of health insurance in a country may depend on the types of employment most prevalent in an economy. Jobs in the agricultural sector are often characterized by an irregular income during the year, which may compel membership in an insurance system. This assumption is tested by introducing a variable measuring the share of population employed in agriculture.

Urban population. The distribution of the population within the territory may also affect the ease of implementation of insurance. Successful expansion of health insurance, including compulsory, is often linked to high urbanization and high population density, which facilitate the registration of members and the collection of contributions and can benefit from economies of scale.[12] The urban population is on average 49 percent of the total population. The observations range from 10.7 percent in 2009 (Burundi) to 93.7 percent in 2009 (Venezuela). There are also variations of the indicator within countries, with declines in some countries like Tajikistan, Zambia, and Sri Lanka and increases in others such as in Albania, Togo, China, and Bhutan.

Factors Specific to the Health Sector

(1) Health care supply

Many factors related to the provision of health services are essential for the development of health insurance; these include the existence of infrastructure and the availability of health care provision (staff, equipment, and consumables), the quality of health care or existing mechanisms for the payment of health care. Due to a lack of data on these factors, only the availability of health care provision has been approached in this analysis.

The number of doctors (for 1,000 inhabitants). This variable aims to characterize the availability of health care provision in each country. The existence of a network of providers is indeed a crucial component in the development of insurance. This is a purely quantitative variable that can in no way assess the quality of care delivered. The medical density (average of 1.06) is particularly important in Europe and Central Asian countries such as Belarus (4.9 doctors per 1,000 inhabitants), Georgia (4.5), Ukraine (4.4), or Russia (4.3). The ratio is the lowest in Sub-Saharan Africa in countries such as Malawi and Liberia (0.01), Sierra Leone, Rwanda, Niger, Ethiopia, and Liberia (0.02). The average number of doctors per 1,000 population within African countries in the sample is 0.18. These figures are generally well below the standard calculated by the World Health Organization. WHO has indeed estimated that the minimum number of medical workers (doctors, nurses, and midwives) necessary to ensure a sufficient supply of health care in developing countries should be equal to 2.28 per 1,000 inhabitants (WHO 2006).

(2) Health care demand

Data on demand factors could not be obtained for this study. The variables used are rather factors that may affect the development of insurance via their effect on demand for health care or insurance.

Ethnic fragmentation and religious fragmentation. These are proxy indicators of social fragmentation. They each measure the probability that two randomly selected individuals in a population belong to different ethnic/religious groups. In the study sample, ethnic and religious fragmentation values range, respectively, from 0 (the Comoros) to 0.93 (Uganda[13]) and from 0 (Morocco) to 0.86 (South Africa[14]). The signs for these two variables are unknown. In general, theoretical and empirical studies show that societies characterized by high ethnic diversity are more likely to choose suboptimal policies. Ethnically fragmented economies may indeed have more difficulty reaching agreement on policies to implement because the polarization of interest groups leads to the development of rent-seeking behavior and reduces the consensus for public goods (Alesina et al. 2003; Easterly and Levine 1997). Such an assumption might apply in this context since ethnic diversity may complicate the emergence of consensus, particularly in the case of mandatory health insurance projects. Individuals may be reluctant to work with members of another group (Alesina and Ferrara 2000). Different ethnic or religious groups may also not agree on mechanisms for sharing benefits because of potential risks of free-riding behavior. In this case, individuals can then be encouraged to refuse insurance or buy individual, private insurance. Similarly, while religion and belonging to an ethnic group tend to convey solidarity among group members, ethnic or religious fragmentation can dissolve these values and increase the need for individual insurance.

Literacy. This variable aims to measure the influence of cultural variables on the development of insurance. The average of this indicator (79.2 percent) masks significant disparities within the sample, with a minimum of 9.4 percent (Niger in 1997) and a maximum of 99.9 percent (the Republic of Korea in 2010). A positive relationship between this variable and the degree of development of insurance is expected because literacy promotes an understanding of insurance principles.

Africa dummy variable. This variable was created to take into account possible regional specificities of the effect of the determinants of the development of insurance within the sample. The variable includes 25 countries in Sub-Saharan Africa (including 8 Francophone countries[15]).

Econometric Specifications

Three estimation methods are used to reflect the specificity of the dependent variable and to ensure the robustness of the results.

OLS Model

The estimates are initially done with the ordinary least squares (OLS). A Hausman (1978) test is applied to select between panel estimation with fixed effects or random effects. The $x2$ statistics rejects the fixed effects specification and panel estimation with random effects is then used.

The estimated equations are formulated as follows:

$$H.Insu.Exp_{it} = \beta_0 + \beta_1 I_{it1} + \beta_2 X_{it2} + v_{it} \tag{1}$$

$$SS.Exp_{it} = \beta_0 + \beta_1 I_{it1} + \beta_2 X_{it2} + v_{it} \tag{2}$$

$$PPRP.Exp_{it} = \beta_0 + \beta_1 I_{it1} + \beta_2 X_{it2} + v_{it} \tag{3}$$

Where,

$i = 1,..., N$

$i = 1,..., T$

With,

$H.Insu.Exp_{it}$: share of total insurance expenditure in total health expenditure;
$SS.Exp_{it}$: share of social security expenditure in total health expenditure;

$PPRP.Exp_{it}$: share of prepaid plans and risk-pooling arrangements expenditure in total health expenditure;

I_{it}: variables measuring factors related to the political and institutional environment (government effectiveness, political stability, voice and accountability, share of the State budget devoted to health, share of external resources in total health expenditure) and to the economic and social environment (income per capita, standard deviation of income per capita growth, Gini index, dependency ratio, share of population employed in agriculture, and urbanization rate);

X_{it}: variables measuring specific factors to the health sector (number of doctors, ethnic fragmentation, religious fragmentation, and literacy rate);

v_{it}: error term.

OLS might be an imperfect estimation method in the context of this study. Studies considering a dependent variable expressed in percentage often use OLS by applying a logarithmic transformation. In this case, such a transformation is not an option: it would lead to an excessive loss of observations due to the large number of values of the dependent variable equal to 0.[16] Moreover, with this high concentration of observations around 0, OLS may predict values of the dependent variable below 0 as shown in figure B.2.

Tobit Model

The estimates are then carried out as part of a Tobit model with random effects since the dependent variable is a percentage, therefore bounded between 0 and 100. The estimations from the panel Tobit model are defined as follows:

$$Insu.Exp_{it} = f(I_{it}, X_{it}, cons) \tag{4}$$

$$SS.Exp_{it} = f(I_{it}, X_{it}, cons) \tag{5}$$

$$PPRP_{it} = f(I_{it}, X_{it}, cons). \tag{6}$$

Probit Model

Finally, a Probit model is used to treat the problem of distribution of the dependent variable and test the robustness of the results. For this, the dependent variable is converted into a binary variable using the mean of the sample as threshold to characterize the importance of insurance development. The estimated models are:

$$H.Insu.Exp_{it} = \alpha_{it} + \beta_{1it}I_{it} + \beta_{2it}X_{it} + \varepsilon_{it} \tag{7}$$

With $H.Insu.Exp_{it} = 1$ if $H.Insu.Exp > 15.36\%$ and $H.Insu.Exp_{it} = 0$ otherwise (7.1)

$$SS.Exp_{it} = \alpha_{it} + \beta_{1it}I_{it} + \beta_{2it}X_{it} + \varepsilon_{it} \tag{8}$$

With $SS.Exp_{it} = 1$ if $SS.Exp > 10.94\%$ and $SS.Exp_{it} = 0$ otherwise (8.1)

$$PPRP.Exp_{it} = \alpha_{it} + \beta_{1it}I_{it} + \beta_{2it}X_{it} + \varepsilon_{it} \tag{9}$$

With $PPRP.Exp_{it} = 1$ if $PPRP.Exp > 4.03\%$ and $PPRP.Exp_{it} = 0$ otherwise. (9.1)

RESULTS

Results related to total health insurance are presented in table B.4. The first column provides results from the OLS model, the second those from the Tobit model. The last column presents the results of the Probit model using the mean of the sample as threshold to construct the independent variable.

The results are overall unchanged according to the method of estimation used. Variables measuring the political and institutional environment appear among the most significant determinants of the contribution of health insurance to the funding of the health sector. Of these, government effectiveness and state involvement in financing the sector and the variable measuring voice and accountability have a positive effect on the development of insurance in accordance with assumptions. However, political stability appears to have a negative effect on the dependent variable. This suggests that the most stable countries politically are not necessarily those in which insurance is the most developed. This result, contrary to the a priori assumption, however, is not counterintuitive. It emphasizes that more countries are encouraged to develop health insurance when the political context is unstable and the risk of violence is high. In such a context of uncertainty, people may also be more encouraged to participate in insurance programs to protect against health risk.

To overcome multicolinearity issues between the governance variables, regressions were run by adding the variables one by one in the model. The results—signs of the coefficients and significance level—remain unchanged. The same approach applied to per capita income strongly correlated with the government effectiveness variable, for example. The results with and without income per capita, and then again by introducing the governance variables one by one, are identical.

TABLE B.4   Determinants of Total Health Insurance Development

Dependent variable	Total health insurance expenditure as percentage of total health expenditure (HIE/THE)		
	OLS	Tobit	Probit[a]
Goveffec	1.839** (0.879)	2.213** (1.007)	0.720 (0.783)
Pol.Stab	−1.538*** (0.483)	−1.780*** (0.539)	−1.062** (0.540)
Voice.Acc	1.407* (0.721)	1.191 (0.797)	1.442** (0.722)
Pub.Health.Exp/Total.Pub.Exp	0.152** (0.0710)	0.168** (0.0782)	0.189*** (0.0670)
Ext.Ress/THE	−0.0218 (0.0194)	−0.0341 (0.0214)	−0.0522* (0.0313)
Ln GDP/Cap (constant)	7.990*** (1.080)	8.600*** (1.201)	2.513* (1.434)
S-d.GDP.Growth	−0.253*** (0.0694)	−0.284*** (0.0735)	−0.342*** (0.0952)
Dep.Ratio	0.0904** (0.0366)	0.100** (0.0415)	−0.0431 (0.0350)
Urb.Pop	0.0498 (0.0621)	0.0513 (0.0721)	0.183*** (0.0482)
Phys	1.457** (0.709)	1.658** (0.812)	−0.907* (0.474)
Literacy	−0.0119 (0.0568)	−0.0413 (0.0656)	0.0552 (0.0509)
Ethnic	0.122 (5.069)	1.337 (6.666)	−2.712 (3.062)
Religion	−9.678** (4.746)	−8.578 (6.153)	−2.800 (2.713)
Africa	3.117 (2.938)	2.284 (3.864)	2.399 (1.674)
Constant	−46.36*** (9.744)	−51.04*** (11.43)	−27.15*** (10.38)
Observations	1,165	1,165	1,165
Number of countries	88	88	88

Source: Author.
Note: z-statistics in parentheses; * significant at 10 percent; ** significant at 5 percent; *** significant at 1 percent.
The sample mean is used as the threshold for construction of the dependent variable (15.4 percent).

The results for foreign aid do not point to an obvious conclusion. They show an insignificant negative relationship between external resources and the degree of development of health insurance (except at the 10 percent level in column 3). The Nakamura-Nakamura test also shows that this variable is exogenous in the model, suggesting that external resources for health are generally not intended to finance insurance programs.

Among the variables characterizing the economic and social environment, income has a positive effect on the development of health insurance. The results confirm a negative relationship between the instability of income growth rate and the development of health insurance. The results are unchanged when outliers are excluded from the sample.[17] The results for the urban population and the dependency ratio are consistent with hypotheses, but the degree of significance varies depending on the estimation method, especially in the case of urbanization. Finally, the Gini index and the share of population employed in agriculture are insignificant in all regressions. Due to the lack of observations for a significant number of countries, these two variables were excluded.

For variables more specific to the health sector, the sign of the coefficient of the variable measuring the number of doctors is positive and significant. The variables reflecting the cultural environment—literacy, religion, and ethnic fragmentation—are not significant in explaining the level of health insurance development.

Finally, to ensure the robustness of all these results, all the regressions were also performed by removing all values of the dependent variables equal to 0. The results are unchanged from those already shown.

The results for social insurance and private insurance are presented in table B.5. They are relatively equivalent for both types of insurance systems, but with some important differences. Governance variables are still important determinants, especially government effectiveness and political stability, but so, too, is the commitment of the state in the health sector. The variable measuring voice and accountability, however, appears almost always nonsignificant. A significant difference on the variable measuring the degree of state involvement in financing the health sector is important to emphasize. Indeed, although it has a positive effect on the development of social insurance, it appears to negatively influence the development of private insurance. This result shows a substitution effect between the two insurance systems. A relatively large financial commitment of the state in the health sector tends to reduce the size of the available market for insurance, or even to evict some private insurers, if it is intended to fund such development of the social insurance or free care programs.

Among other variables, the results are essentially the same as before. The degree of urbanization seems to contribute to the development of both types of insurance systems, particularly private insurance. The results for ethnic fragmentation do not provide evidence on the sign of the relations. However, religious fragmentation appears negatively related to the development of social insurance and conversely positively related to the development of private insurance. These results are consistent with the assumptions made above. Similarly, the results do not show clear evidence of regional specificity in Africa for the development of health insurance.

The overall results are summarized in table B.6.

TABLE B.5 Determinants of the Development of Social Insurance and Private Insurance

Dependent variable	Social security expenditure as percentage of total health expenditure (SSE/THE)			Private health insurance expenditure as percentage of total health expenditure (PHIE/THE)		
	OLS	Tobit	Probit [a]	OLS	Tobit	Probit [b]
Gov.Effec	0.985	1.562	3.044***	0.494*	0.608*	1.973***
	(0.807)	(1.160)	(0.954)	(0.298)	(0.362)	(0.535)
Pol.Stab	−1.417***	−2.214***	−0.892	−0.267	−0.325	0.0371
	(0.451)	(0.657)	(0.558)	(0.165)	(0.206)	(0.304)
Voice.Acc	1.240*	2.274**	1.064	0.0463	−0.108	−0.276
	(0.660)	(0.969)	(0.661)	(0.255)	(0.309)	(0.411)
Pub.Health.Exp/Tot.Pub.Exp	0.297***	0.424***	0.229***	−0.102***	−0.116***	−0.0943**
	(0.0668)	(0.0948)	(0.0740)	(0.0235)	(0.0286)	(0.0442)
Ext.HE/THE	−0.0212	−0.01000	−0.0494	0.00404	0.00174	−0.00232
	(0.0178)	(0.0288)	(0.0331)	(0.00654)	(0.00799)	(0.0147)
Ln GDP/Cap (constant)	6.531***	12.87***	0.905	1.331***	1.694***	1.503**
	(0.957)	(1.530)	(1.066)	(0.392)	(0.468)	(0.740)
S–d.GDP.Growth	−0.136***	−0.170**	−0.140	−0.0363	−0.0516*	−0.0186
	(0.0484)	(0.0681)	(0.0898)	(0.0235)	(0.0277)	(0.0540)
Dep.Ratio	0.00553	0.0446	−0.154***	−0.00430	−0.0191	−0.0803**
	(0.0346)	(0.0481)	(0.0501)	(0.0133)	(0.0171)	(0.0361)
Urb.Pop	−0.0939	−0.215**	0.185***	0.0942***	0.110***	0.0596*
	(0.0600)	(0.0895)	(0.0438)	(0.0258)	(0.0302)	(0.0320)
Physician	0.860	1.176	−0.712	−0.0537	−0.350	−1.016**
	(0.666)	(0.900)	(0.462)	(0.279)	(0.368)	(0.461)
Literacy	−0.0126	−0.0499	−0.0962**	−0.0540**	−0.0655**	−0.0674***
	(0.0564)	(0.0747)	(0.0390)	(0.0220)	(0.0263)	(0.0224)
Ethnic	7.213	25.25***	1.457	−4.108	−3.455	−2.840
	(5.538)	(7.925)	(2.490)	(2.704)	(3.645)	(1.847)
Religion	−11.83**	−22.17***	−3.009	7.051***	9.015***	3.909**
	(5.264)	(7.996)	(2.066)	(2.537)	(3.167)	(1.704)
Africa	−4.573	−9.277**	−6.408***	2.518*	2.503	2.066*
	(3.142)	(4.460)	(1.710)	(1.514)	(1.864)	(1.107)
Constant	−28.46***	−77.20***	2.088	−5.709	−8.647*	−4.090
	(9.355)	(14.10)	(9.604)	(3.890)	(4.843)	(6.490)
Observations	1,325	1,325	1,325	1,323	1,323	1,323
Number of countries	99	99	99	98	98	98

Source: Author.
Note: z-statistics in parentheses; * significant at 10 percent; ** significant at 5 percent; *** significant at 1 percent.
a. The sample mean is used as the threshold for construction of the dependent variable (10.9 percent).
b. The sample mean is used as the threshold for construction of the dependent variable (4 percent).

TABLE B.6   Summary of Main Results on the Determinants of the Development of Health Insurance in Developing Countries

	HIE/THE	SSE/THE	PHIE/THE
	Structural factors		
Political and institutional			
GovEffec	+++	++	+++
Pol.Stab	− − −	− − −	−
Voice.Acc	+++	++	+
Pub.Health.Exp/Tot.Pub.Exp	+++	+++	− −
Ext.HE/THE	−	−	− −
Economic and social			
GDP/Cap	++	n.d.	n.d.
S–d.GDP.Growth	− − −	− − −	− −
Dep.Ratio	− − −	− − −	− −
Urb.Pop	+	+	+++
	Factors specific to the health sector		
Health care supply			
Doctors	−	n.s.	− −
Cultural factors and health care demand			
Literacy	n.s.	n.s.	+
Ethnic	−	n.d.	−
Religion	n.s.	− − −	++
Africa	+++	n.s.	+++

Source: Author.

Note: n.d. = not determined; n.s. = not significant.

ANNEX A   ADDITIONAL DATA

TABLE BA.1   Countries in the Sample

1	Albania	12	Bosnia and Herzegovina
2	Algeria	13	Brazil
3	Angola	14	Bulgaria
4	Argentina	15	Burkina Faso
5	Armenia	16	Burundi
6	Azerbaijan	17	Cameroon
7	Bangladesh	18	Cape Verde
8	Belarus	19	Chile
9	Benin	20	China
10	Bhutan	21	Colombia
11	Bolivia	22	Comoros

(continued)

TABLE BA.1   Countries in the Sample *(continued)*

23	Congo, Dem. Rep.	62	Mozambique
24	Costa Rica	63	Namibia
25	Cuba	64	Nepal
26	Dominican Republic	65	Nicaragua
27	Ecuador	66	Niger
28	Egypt, Arab Rep.	67	Nigeria
29	El Salvador	68	Pakistan
30	Eritrea	69	Panama
31	Ethiopia	70	Papua New Guinea
32	Gabon	71	Paraguay
33	Gambia, The	72	Peru
34	Georgia	73	Philippines
35	Ghana	74	Romania
36	Guatemala	75	Russian Federation
37	Guinea	76	Rwanda
38	Guinea-Bissau	77	Senegal
39	Honduras	78	Sierra Leone
40	India	79	Solomon Islands
41	Indonesia	80	South Africa
42	Iran, Islamic Rep.	81	Sri Lanka
43	Iraq	82	Sudan
44	Jamaica	83	Suriname
45	Jordan	84	Swaziland
46	Kazakhstan	85	Tanzania
47	Kenya	86	Thailand
48	Kyrgyz Republic	87	Togo
49	Lao PDR	88	Tonga
50	Lebanon	89	Tunisia
51	Lesotho	90	Turkey
52	Liberia	91	Turkmenistan
53	Lithuania	92	Uganda
54	Macedonia, FYR	93	Ukraine
55	Malawi	94	Uruguay
56	Malaysia	95	Vanuatu
57	Mauritania	96	Venezuela, RB
58	Mexico	97	Vietnam
59	Moldova	98	Zambia
60	Mongolia	99	Zimbabwe
61	Morocco		

Source: Author.

TABLE BA.2 Correlations between the Variables

Variable	HIE/THE	SSE/THE	PHIE/THE	Gov.Effec	Pol.Stab	Voice.Acc	PHE/TPE	EHE/THE	lnGDP/Cap	S–d.GDP.Growth	Dep.Ratio	Urban.Pop	Doctors	Literacy	Ethnic	Religion	Africa
HIE/THE	1																
SSE/THE	0.2470*	1															
PHIE/THE	0.1727*	0.0079	1														
Gov.Effec	0.1704*	0.2114*	0.4262*	1													
Pol.Stab	-0.041	0.0184	0.1433*	0.5804*	1												
Voice.Acc	-0.0325	0.2035*	0.2979*	0.6422*	0.6174*	1											
PHE/TPE	0.0568	0.3738*	0.0977*	0.2231*	0.3160*	0.3677*	1										
EHE/THE	-0.1596*	-0.2564*	-0.1925*	-0.2778*	0.0397	0.0277	0.1885*	1									
lnGDP/Cap	0.2227*	0.3317*	0.3785*	0.6289*	0.4728*	0.5037*	0.1828*	-0.4030*	1								
S–d.GDP. Growth	-0.0488	0.0287	-0.0834*	-0.2333*	-0.1879*	-0.1078*	-0.0281	0.0538	-0.1311*	1							
Dep.Ratio	-0.2857*	-0.4686*	-0.1816*	-0.4380*	-0.2478*	-0.2426*	-0.0638*	0.4586*	-0.6409*	0.0407	1						
Urban.Pop	0.2092*	0.3946*	0.3241*	0.2946*	0.1844*	0.2130*	0.1187*	-0.3446*	0.6405*	0.0298	-0.5404*	1					
Doctors	0.1450*	0.3488*	0.0571	0.2409*	0.1620*	0.0803*	0.0914*	-0.3649*	0.4072*	0.1152*	-0.6437*	0.5063*	1				
Literacy	0.1697*	0.3995*	0.2279*	0.3437*	0.2552*	0.2224*	0.1824*	-0.3794*	0.6450*	0.0106	-0.6804*	0.5162*	0.6236*	1			
Ethnic	-0.1006*	-0.1258*	-0.0526	-0.2506*	-0.3038*	-0.2654*	-0.1983*	0.1430*	-0.3740*	0.053	0.3812*	-0.1090*	-0.2836*	-0.4416*	1		
Religion	0.0144	-0.2422*	0.1616*	0.0102	0.0796*	0.1341*	0.0122	0.1537*	-0.1217*	0.0936*	0.1146*	-0.1845*	-0.0750*	-0.021	0.1670*	1	
Africa	-0.1165*	-0.3284*	0.0076	-0.2719*	-0.1352*	-0.2136*	-0.1369*	0.2854*	-0.5234*	0.0193	0.6262*	-0.3548*	-0.4974*	-0.6014*	0.4763*	0.2684*	1

Source: Author.

Note: * significant at 5 percent level.

FIGURE BA.1   Correlations between Political and Institutional Factors and the Development of Health Insurance

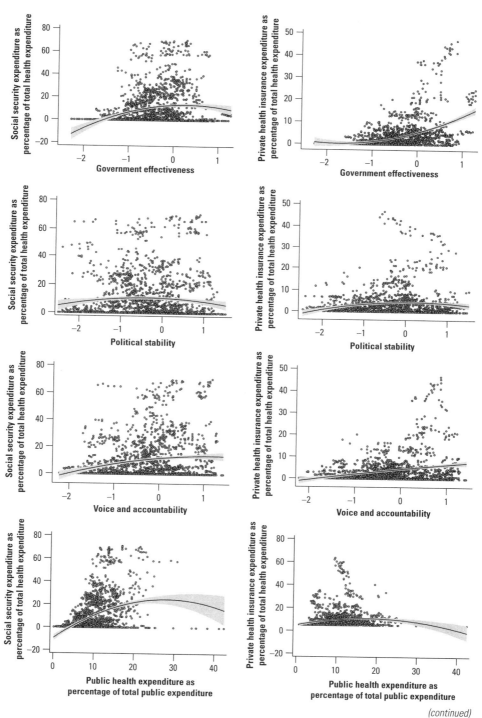

(continued)

FIGURE BA.1   Correlations between Political and Institutional Factors and the Development of Health Insurance *(continued)*

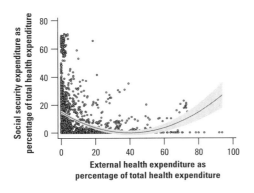
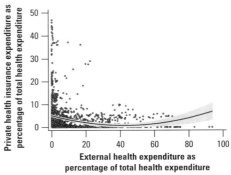

Source: Author.

NOTES

1. The sample comprises 12 countries from East Asia and Pacific, 17 countries from Europe and Central Asia, 21 countries from Latin America and the Caribbean, 8 countries from the Middle East and North Africa, 6 countries from South Asia, and 35 countries from Sub-Saharan Africa (annex table BA.1).

2. This indicator would have been more interesting than the average health insurance expenditure had data on health insurance expenditure by wealth quintiles been available. Indeed, health insurance expenditure data gathered in developing countries often pertains to the richest quintile, which tends to buy private insurance.

3. The data come from WHO National Health Accounts (NHA), gathered and analyzed within a precise methodological framework. The NHAs represent a summary of funding streams and expenditures recorded during the operation of a health system. Further, the NHAs are related to the methodology of macroeconomic and macrosocial accounts.

4. Romania registered the highest value in 2010, with health insurance accounting for 63.1 percent of total health expenditure.

5. According to the classification of regions by the World Bank.

6. The coefficients of correlation are –0.04 for total health insurance, 0.02 for social insurance, and 0.14 for private insurance. But the coefficient is not significant for this last variable.

7. This is the ratio of general government expenditure on health and general government expenditure (GGE) in the WHO terminology. GGHE includes both recurrent and investment expenditures (including capital transfers) made during the year. The classification of the functions of government (COFOG) promoted by the United Nations, the International Monetary Fund (IMF), OECD, and other institutions sets

the boundaries for public outlays. In many instances, the data contained in the publications accessed are limited to those supplied by ministries of health. Expenditure on health, however, should include all expenditure when the primary intent is to improve health, regardless of the implementing entity. An effort has been made to obtain data on health expenditure by other ministries, the armed forces, prisons, schools, universities, and others, to ensure that all resources accounting for health expenditures are included. Furthermore, all expenditures on health include final consumption, subsidies to producers, and transfers to households (chiefly reimbursements for medical and pharmaceutical bills) (WHO 2006).

8. It would have been interesting to use a broader measure of the degree of state involvement in the health sector in order to reflect such political will within the government for sectoral or health insurance reforms. However, available data allowed measurement only of the share of the government budget devoted to health.

9. The external resources are those entering the system as a financing source: all external resources (grants and loans) are included, whether passing through governments or private entities. Information on external resources is taken from the Development Assistance Committee of the OECD (DAC/OECD). Where some member states explicitly monitor the external resources entering their health system, that information has been used to validate or amend the order of magnitude derived from the DAC entries. DAC entries used by WHO relate to disbursements (which reports only bilateral flows from certain countries), wherever available; otherwise commitments are presented.

10. Other studies use the average of deviations from trend, which requires estimating a trend by country (Guillaumont, Korachais, and Subervie 2009).

11. According to the International Labor Office (BIT 1993), the informal sector can be described generally as a set of units producing goods or services primarily to create jobs and income for those involved. These units have a low level of organization; operate on a small scale, with little or no division between labor and capital as factors of production. Labor relations—when they exist—are based mostly on casual employment, kinship, or personal and social relations rather than on contractual arrangements with proper guarantees.

12. This observation must nevertheless be qualified with respect to the development of voluntary insurance because urbanization is often accompanied by a breakdown of social ties between individuals.

13. Uganda comprises eight main ethnic groups: Ganda (17.8 percent), Teso (8.9 percent), Nkole (8.2 percent), Soga (8.2 percent), Gisu (7.2 percent), Chiga (6.8 percent), Lango (6 percent), and Rwanda (5.8 percent).

14. South Africa comprises more than 30 different religions.

15. Burkina Faso, Cape Verde, the Comoros, Guinea, Mauritania, Rwanda, Senegal, and Togo.

16. Recall that 11 percent of the observations in the sample are equal to zero and almost half of them (43 percent) are less than 5 percent.

17. An outlier test was performed on each of the model variables. The test is called Grubbs test (maximum normed residual test). The Grubbs test detects an outlier at each iteration. This latter is discarded from the data and the test is iterated until there is no outlier. Four countries are seen as potential outliers regarding the instability of their rate of income growth: Angola, Moldova, Liberia, and Equatorial Guinea.

REFERENCES

Alesina, A., A. Devleeschauwer, W. Easterly, S. Kurlat, and R. Wacziarg. 2003. "Fractionalization." *Journal of Economic Growth* 8 (2): 155–94.

Alesina, A., and E.L. Ferrara. 2000. "Participation in Heterogeneous Communities." *Quarterly Journal of Economics* 115 (2): 847–904.

BIT (Bureau International du Travail). 1993. *Rapport de la Conférence*. Rapport pour la XVème Conférence Internationale des Statisticiens du Travail, January 19–28, Geneva.

Carrin, G. 2002. "Social Health Insurance in Developing Countries: A Continuing Challenge." *International Social Security Review* 55 (2): 57–69.

Easterly, W., and R. Levine. 1997. "Africa's Growth Tragedy: Policies and Ethnic Divisions." *Quarterly Journal of Economics* 112 (3): 1203–50.

Ensor, T. 1999. "Developing Health Insurance in Transitional Asia." *Social Science and Medicine* 48 (7): 71–79.

Gottret, P., and G.J. Schieber. 2006. *Health Financing Revisited: A Practitioner's Guide*. Washington, DC: World Bank.

Gottret, P., G.J. Schieber, and H.R. Water. 2008. *Good Practices in Health Financing: Lessons from Reforms in Low- and Middle-Income Countries*. Washington, DC: World Bank.

Griffin, C., and P.R. Shaw. 1996. "Health Insurance in Sub-Saharan Africa: Aims, Findings, and Policy Implications." In *Financing Health Services through User Fees and Insurance: Case Studies from Sub-Saharan Africa*, ed. P.R. Shaw and M. Ainsworth. Washington, DC: World Bank.

Guillaumont, P., C. Korachais, and J. Subervie. 2009. "Comment l'instabilité macroéconomique diminue la survie des enfants." *Revue d'économie du développement* 23 (1): 9–32.

Hausman, J.A. 1978. "Specification Tests in Econometrics." *Econometrica* 46 (6): 1251–71.

Letourmy, A. 2003. "L'Etat et la couverture maladie dans les pays à faible revenu." Article préparé pour les XXVIèmes Journées des Economistes Français de la Santé. Santé et Développement, Centre d'Etudes et de Recherches sur le Développement International (CERDI), January 9–10, Clermont-Ferrand, France.

———. 2005. "Assurance maladie: Un cadre général d'analyse en vue de son implantation dans les pays d'Afrique francophone." In *L'assurance maladie en Afrique francophone: Améliorer l'accès aux soins et lutter contre la pauvreté*, ed. G. Dussault, P. Fournier, and A. Letourmy. Washington, DC: World Bank.

Ramey, G., and V.A. Ramey. 1995. "Cross-Country Evidence on the Link between Volatility and Growth." *American Economic Review* 85 (5): 1138–51.

UNU-WIDER (United Nations University World Institute for Development Economics Research). 2008. World Income Inequality Database, Version 2.0c, May. http://www.wider.unu.edu/research/Database/en_GB/database/.

WHO (World Health Organization). 2006. *The World Health Report: Working Together for Health*. Geneva: WHO.

———. 2012a. National Health Accounts (NHA). Country Information, World Health Organization, Geneva. http://www.who.int/nha/en/.

———. 2012b. WHO Statistical Information System (WHOSIS). http://www.who.int /whosis/en/index.html.

World Bank. 2012a. *World Development Indicators 2012*. Washington, DC: World Bank.

World Bank. 2012b. *Worldwide Governance Indicators 2012*. http://info.worldbank.org /governance/wgi/index.asp.

APPENDIX C

Compendium of Health Insurance Terms

Alexander S. Preker and Mark V. Pauly

Ability to pay (ATP). A subjective social judgment usually based on a comparison of a proposed payment amount and a household's income or wealth. ATP for health insurance must be considered in the context of copayments and transaction costs. Reflects a value judgment about whether the household can obtain socially acceptable levels of other goods after paying for care or insurance. This concept of fairness may be an important consideration in designing a micro-insurance scheme and setting premiums.

Accountability. Result of the process that ensures that decision makers at all levels actually carry out their designated responsibilities and that they are held accountable for their actions.

Actual premium. The premium arrived at by estimating the average benefit pay-out, insurer administrative expenses, a safety margin for contingencies, and profits. If profits are at the competitive level the actual premium will be the lowest premium sustainable in the long run.

Actuarially fair premium. A premium equal to average or expected benefit payouts.

Actuary. A professional trained in evaluating the financial implications of contingency events. Actuaries require an understanding of the stochastic nature of insurance and other financial services, the risks inherent in assets, and the use of statistical models. In the context of insurance, these skills are often used, for example, in establishing premiums, technical provisions, and capital levels.

Adverse selection. Also called *antiselection*. Occurs when insurers are unable or are not permitted to charge premiums based on risk levels known to buyers of insurance; can arise either from asymmetric information (buyer knows risk and insurer does not) or regulation (buyer is not allowed to use information it knows in setting premiums). Adverse selection disturbs the operation of the insurance market. The lower-risk insured, knowing the likelihood of events but facing a price higher than that which reflects that risk, chooses not to insure; high risks facing a premium lower than one which reflects risk choose to overinsure. The insurer, having less information, accepts a contract that does not include premiums for low-risk events. Insured temporarily gain from the insurer's inability to distinguish "good" and "bad" risks. In the longer run, adverse selection results in low risks' exiting the insurance market. Providing asymmetric information incentivizes only people who expect to use above-average amounts of care to seek health insurance coverage. Constitutes a key concern for insurers that can lead to higher losses or premiums, which is countered by medical underwriting, which minimizes insuring high-risk individuals.

Affordability. See *Ability to pay.*

Agent, general. Another term for insurer.

Agent, insurer. Someone who assists in the sale of insurance in return for a commission or salary.

Ambulatory care. Outpatient medical care provided in any health care setting except as a stay overnight in a hospital.

Arbitrage. The simultaneous buying and selling of securities, currency, or commodities in different markets or in derivative forms in order to take advantage of differing prices for the same asset.

Asymmetrical information. Parties to a transaction have uneven access to relevant information that governs an informed choice. Such asymmetry can result in an inequitable transaction in favor of the party with the most information, or it can result in the abandonment of the exchange.

Balance sheet. Statement showing the financial position at a particular point in time (for example, at the end of the financial year), listing all assets and liabilities at that time.

Bayesian method. A method (originally enunciated in 1763) for revising the probability of an event's occurrence by taking into account data as they come to hand. The usefulness of this approach depends on the relevance and power of the additional data.

Beneficiary. The person designated to receive payouts from the scheme. This is typically the policyholder or a family member, but it may be an employer.

Benefit exclusion. Refusal of insurer payment for a specific service for an insured. Because this exclusion could be subject to abuse if it is based on arbitrary decisions made at the time of claim rather than as set out in the contract, it tends to be regulated. Reasons for exclusion that are typically allowed include a qualifying period and preexisting illness.

Benefits package. A list of specific benefits agreed upon in the health insurance contract. While private insurance typically offers modules of benefits from which to choose, microinsurers may offer a standard package for simplicity and fairness.

Beta distribution. Beta is a distribution (first used by Gini, 1911) for a real random variable whose density function is null outside the interval [0, 1] and depends on two strictly real parameters. The shape of this distribution depends on the values of the parameters: it can be U-shaped, or J-shaped, or hat-shaped. For this reason, this distribution is very often used for modeling proportions or probabilities.

Bifurcated oversight responsibility. A specialized regulation system in which the supervisory and regulatory functions are broken into a financial component and a health component.

Binomial distribution. A statistical method for understanding the probability of events that have only two possible outcomes—"success" or "failure." These probabilities are constant. In insurance, the binomial distribution is applied to estimate the number of persons in a community who will seek (ambulatory) care in a given period.

Bottom-up. See *Top-down global strategy.*

Broker. An intermediary who sells on behalf of a number of different insurance companies or plans.

Capacity. Has two meanings:

* Insurers' ability to underwrite and pay claims on a large amount of risk on a single loss exposure or many contracts on one line of event. Reinsurance enables a greater capacity among primary insurers.

* Organizational and individual skills. Organizational capacity implies appropriate systems for information and management and adequate resources for handling operations.

Capacity building. Increasing organizational and individual skills and establishing frameworks for that increase to continue.

Capitation payment. Under a capitation payment, the provider receives a fixed fee per individual per month regardless of how many services are provided to any of the individuals covered.

Central limit theorem. States that, as the sample size increases, the characteristics of a sample (e.g., average loss) will more closely approximate those of the population from which that sample was drawn. This theorem is valuable in health insurance as it enables estimates of risk in a population to be based on sample data.

Claim load. The amount of benefits paid to the insured in a period. Fluctuations in claim load in the short term are covered by contingency reserves and in the long run by contribution or premium increases.

Coefficient of variation. The ratio of the sample *standard deviation* to the *sample mean.* It measures the spread of a set of data as a proportion of its mean. It is often expressed as a percentage. This coefficient enables, for example, estimation and comparison of ranges of likely expenses for various risk portfolios or communities.

Coinsurance. An insurance policy provision under which the insurer and the insured share costs incurred after the deductible is met, according to a specific percentage formula. Used to share risk and control moral hazard.

Collection rate or compliance rate. The proportion of possible subscriptions from members that the microinsurer collects. Lack of complete compliance can result from cultural as well as economic factors. It may be used as a measure of a micro-insurer's efficiency/commercial orientation. Members are more likely to pay contributions if their perceived risk is higher.

Community. A group of people with a common characteristic. Often implies locality, but can be occupation-, leisure-, or religion-based.

Community-based health insurance (CBHI) scheme. A voluntary community pre-payment health insurance scheme for pooling and averaging risks. The community's policyholders ideally share social values, are involved in the management of health plans, and elect a group of their members to act as managers. CBHIs are common in many low-income countries, where options are unavailable.

Community financing scheme. See *Community-based health insurance scheme.*

Community participation. Sharing by citizens in any kind of community in communal decision-making processes and definitions of problems.

Community rating. A method for determining insurance rates on the basis of the average cost across all insured regardless of risk level for providing health services in a specific geographic area. This method ignores the individual's medical history or the likelihood of the individual's using the services. All members of a community pay the same premium without considering individual health status or other determinants of expected demand. *Modified* or *adjusted community rating* allows premiums to vary with some characteristics relevant to risk (like age, gender, price levels in the locality, or family size) but not with health indicators or any other characteristics that affect demand.

Compensation. Benefit payout.

Complementary private insurance. Insurance that provides coverage for all or part of the costs not covered under a public program.

Compliance. Payment of contribution owed by members.

Compliance gap. Difference between contributions due and contributions collected.

Compliance rate. The ratio of actual contributions over potential contributions. See *Collection rate.*

Compulsory insurance. Any form of insurance the purchase of which is required by law and subject to a penalty for nonpurchase. Governments typically require the purchase of liability insurance with respect to events associated with losses to others than the insured, such as damage due to negligence. Health insurance against noncontagious diseases is often compulsory because of the desire to provide financial protection to the individual and avoid the need for charity care paid by others.

Confidence interval. A range of values estimated to contain the population parameter. To be 95 percent confident that a range contains the parameter requires a larger range than to be 90 percent confident. For example, analysis of data from a community might suggest a 90 percent chance that the number of people seeking hospitalization in a year will be between 1,100 and 1,500, but the confidence interval for 95 percent confidence is 978 and 1,747.

Conglomerate risk. Insurance companies that are participants in financial groups can be exposed to some additional sources of risk, such as (but not limited to) intragroup exposures, contagion, and risk concentration.

Contingency reserves or equalization reserves. Funds held by the insurer in excess of expected benefit payouts in order to cover unexpected events (contingencies) that cause fluctuations in benefit payouts. They are typically regulated to ensure the insurer's continued solvency and ability to pay claims.

Contribution. Payment of an agreed sum of money by a member to a social insurance system in return for specified benefits. The implied assumption is that any other sources of income complement members' payments. See also *Premium.*

Contribution base. The amount that would be available to the insurer if all members contributed fully. When contributions are set as a percentage of income, this base relies on full disclosure of income (disclosure rate).

Contribution rate. The percentage of contribution base actually, or expected to be, collected.

Cooperative. A group of people who have united voluntarily to realize a common goal by establishing predetermined shares of the necessary capital. Any surpluses above some target amount of reserve capital are distributed to members, and any shortfalls because of large losses are assessed on members. Management is selected by the members of the organization based of prespecified voting rules. Members often also take an active part in its operation, but participation is not always required as a condition of continued membership.

Copayment. An insurance policy provision requiring the insured to pay a fixed monetary amount per unit of service of the type of care insured (e.g., $20 per doctor office visit).

Corporate governance. Set of relationships between an organization's management, its board, its shareholders (if organized as a joint-stock company), and other stakeholders. Corporate governance also provides the structure through which the objectives of the company are set, and the means of attaining those objectives and monitoring performance are determined. It also includes compliance with legal and regulatory requirements.

Cost sharing. See *Copayment* and *Coinsurance.*

Covariance. A measure of the relationship between two variables. Covariance does not specifically imply a cause-and-effect relationship ("causation"), although it may intuitively be inferred to exist, as can its direction. For example, if health problems vary with housing density, it may be possible to infer that density affects health, but the observed covariance of the frequency of schizophrenia with social status may not have a simple unidirectional explanation.

Covariant risk. When events are not independent, the occurrence of one may affect the occurrence of another. For example, the risk of one family member's catching influenza is covariant with that of another family member. Disasters and shocks are classic cases in which proximity influences covariation. When insuring against risk of events, the actuary must consider the covariation between those risks.

Cream skimming (preferred risk selection). An exercise whereby an insurer charging identical premiums to different risks which it can identify selects only a part of a larger heterogeneous risk group ("preferred risks"). When the insurer reduces its loss ratio but continues to charge the same premium as when higher risks were covered, the insurer can retain a profit from cream skimming. This profit depends on the insurer's ability to distinguish several subgroups with different expected costs within the larger group and to predict the (lower) future health care expenditure of individuals in the preferred group. Basing insurance premiums on risk prevents cream skimming.

Creditable coverage. Credit for any prior insurance coverage that provides for a reduction of the length of the waiting or preexisting condition exclusion period by the amount of time an individual already had continuous coverage before enrolment.

Credit risk. Most commonly, the risk of financial loss incurred by an insurer when a vendor or service provider ultimately does not provide the services they have agreed upon and have been paid to provide under a binding contract between the two parties. Credit risk may also result from default or movements in the credit rating assignment of issuers of securities (in the company's investment portfolio), debtors (e.g., mortgagors), or counterparties (e.g., on reinsurance contracts, derivative contracts, or deposits) and intermediaries to whom the company has an exposure. Sources of credit risk include investment counterparties, policyholders (through outstanding premiums), reinsurers, and derivative counterparties.

Cross-subsidies. Amounts effectively paid when some insurance buyers pay more than others relative to expected benefits. The wealthy members may pay higher premiums than the poor, but not use higher benefits, or the healthy may pay the same as the sick for lower expected benefits. The poor and the sick are said to receive cross-subsidies from the wealthy and the healthy.

Crude birth rate. A summary measurement of the total number of live births in a specified population at the end of a specific time period (generally one year), divided by the midyear total population count. Expressed as the number of births per 1,000 people within that population.

Crude death rate. A summary measurement of the total number of deaths in a specified population at the end of a specific time period (generally one year), divided by the midyear total population count. Expressed as the number of deaths per 1,000 people within that population.

Declaration rate. See *Contribution base.*

Deductible. A provision requiring the insured to pay part of the loss before the insurer makes any payment under the terms of the policy. Deductibles typically are found in property, health, and automobile insurance contracts. The purpose of establishing deductibles is to eliminate small claims and reduce the average pure premium and administrative costs associated with claims handling. Deductibles can also reduce moral hazard by encouraging persons to be more careful with respect to the protection of their property and prevention of loss. Annual deductibles and waiting periods are the most common forms of deductibles in health insurance contracts.

Defined benefit pension. The amount, usually formula-based, guaranteed to each person who meets defined entitlement conditions. The formula usually takes into account the individual number of contribution or insurance years and the individual amount of earnings during the same period.

Delphi method or nominal group technique. A method of business forecasting that consists of panels of experts expressing their opinions on the future and then revising them in light of their colleagues' views so that bias and extreme opinions can be eliminated.

Demand. The amounts of a good or service that consumers seek to buy at different prices. *Solvent demand* implies the ability to pay (socially determined sufficient resources left over after payment for the good in question) as well as the willingness to pay. *Elasticity of demand* is a measure of the responsiveness of quantity demanded of a particular good or service to a change in its price. *Elastic demand* implies that as the price goes up the total expenditure falls. *Inelastic demand* implies that as the price goes up total expenditure also goes up. Necessities typically have inelastic demand (given an adequate income base). For example, the imperative to have an aching tooth removed means that the dentist is in a position of power to charge a high price; such dental services have inelastic demand, and it is unlikely that a lower price would attract people not suffering from toothache to have a tooth removed. The concept of "necessity" and therefore of what has an inelastic demand is cultural. In some cultures prenatal care may not be considered a necessity. Demand for some procedures may be truncated in poor communities. *Truncated demand* means that, although the demand for surgery (for example) is inelastic and does not change with price, above a certain price it becomes zero. As half an operation is not an option, the demand is truncated because of poverty.

Derivative. A derivative is a financial asset or liability whose value depends on (or is derived from) other assets, liabilities, or indexes (the "underlying asset"). Derivatives are financial contracts and include a wide assortment of instruments, such as forwards, futures, options, warrants, swaps, and composites.

Derivative contract. A contract whose value derives from an underlying financial instrument like a stock, commodity, or index.

Dual theory of risk. The theory that describes the attitudes of individuals toward insuring themselves, by weighing on the one hand their wealth and on the other hand their aversion to risk. Three possible modifications could swing the balance in favor of insurance: decreasing the premium, increasing the loss probability, or increasing aversion to risk. Even with identical feelings toward monetary loss, individuals would likely adopt different attitudes toward insurance because their feeling is different toward the probability of monetary loss; the higher that assessment, the more attractive insurance is. Two individuals sharing the same utility index for certain wealth cannot have a different degree of aversion to risk (and the converse), but they can have different demands for insurance if they face different premia or risk levels.

Dumping. Termination or transfer of membership (though rules, incentives or marketing) of the higher-risk people by an insurer. Will only happen if the insurer cannot risk-adjust premiums precisely.

Duplicate private insurance. A policy that offers coverage for health services that are already included under a public program. The individual remains covered by the public program but opts to buy and use private health insurance instead in order to obtain broader access or better quality. Individuals are not exempted from making their required contribution towards the public program.

Endemic disease. A sickness habitually present in an area or population.

Epidemic. The occurrence of any disease, infectious or chronic, at a frequency greater than expected, based on prior patterns of disease incidence and prevalence.

Epidemiological transition. The changing pattern of health and disease within a specified population from a predominantly infectious disease pattern of low life expectancy and high mortality, to a predominantly chronic disease pattern of high life expectancy with high morbidity. In the intermediate stage of transition, high survival rates from endemic infectious disease combined with high rates of chronic illness in survivors results in a "double burden of disease." The latter is typical of many developing countries.

Epidemiology. The study of any and all health-related issues in specified populations at specified times, including but not limited to the occurrence and frequency of medical conditions, diseases, or other health-related events; identification of the determinants of medical conditions, diseases, health-related events, and health status; the evaluation of medical procedures and diagnostic tests; the evaluation of a health care system; the evaluation of a population's demand and use of health care services; evaluation of the safety and efficacy of a pharmaceutical product; post-market surveillance of pharmaceuticals to determine product effectiveness and occurrence of side effects or adverse events; and the evaluation of quality of life, access to care, and health status in general.

Equalization reserves. See *Contingency reserves.*

Escrow account management. Implies the use of a special account for managing payments of various obligations. For example, an escrow account may be set up as a savings account to set aside funds for paying insurance premiums and loan repayments.

Estimation. The process by which sample data are used to indicate the value of an unknown quantity in a population. Results of estimation can be expressed as a single value, known as a point estimate, or a range of values, known as a confidence interval. The outcome of estimation is the *estimator.*

Excluded population or excluded communities. Typically agricultural, self-employed, or poor people who have neither formal employers nor steady wages as the basis for access to government-run or commercial health insurance. They may also be excluded from housing, education, disaster relief, and other social services. They may also be unable to access financial services or to secure formal recognition of property they control or own, including property obtained under traditional (tribal) law.

Experience rating. A system in which the insurance company evaluates the risk of individuals or groups by examining their health history and past claims experience when setting premium rates. *Modified experience rating* places limits on the extent to which rates may vary based on claims experience or health status.

Externalities. Benefits or costs with an impact beyond the parties to a transaction. That impact is not considered in the buy/sell decision and so is not reflected in the price. Pollution is an example of an external cost; safe waste disposal has external benefits.

Fairness. See *Ability to pay.*

Fertility rate. A measure of the total number of live births in a specified population during a specific time period (generally one year) in relation to the midyear total number of women in the specified population. Expressed as the number of live births per 1,000 women within that population.

Fiduciary. A person who holds something in trust for another.

First-line insurer. See *Insurer.*

Fit-and-proper requirements. Rules that reduce the risk of failure of regulated institutions due to incompetent, reckless, or improper risk management by responsible persons and ensure that beneficiaries are protected under legislation and regulations. Such necessary qualities must be exhibited by a person performing the duties and carrying out the responsibilities of his/her position with an insurer. Depending on the position or legal form, these qualities could relate to a proper degree of integrity in attitude, personal behavior and business conduct, soundness of judgment, degree of knowledge, experience, and professional qualifications and financial soundness.

Formal sector. The part of the economy/society that is registered with authorities and that is subject to taxation, regulations, and standards.

Free-riding. Exists in health care when persons can benefit from a health care system without contributing to the system.

Gatekeeper. A primary care physician responsible for overseeing and coordinating all of a patient's medical needs. The gatekeeper must authorize any referral of the patient to a specialist or hospital. Except in cases of emergency, the authorization must be given prior to care.

Government failure. Occurs where government does not provide goods and services or an adequate regulatory or support framework for the private sector to provide them.

Gross domestic product (GDP). The annual total value of goods and services produced in a country for use in that country.

Guaranteed access provisions. Rules that can help ensure that any eligible person can purchase health insurance and cannot be refused coverage by a private voluntary health insurance (PVHI) entity on the grounds of bad health status and/or high likelihood for health services utilization. Legal remedies are provided in many developed countries against improper discrimination for a new member, which address discrimination based upon age, frequency of health service use, existence of chronic disease, illness or medical conditions, or health insurance benefits claiming history.

Guaranteed renewability. Insurers subject to guaranteed renewability standards must renew the policy when it expires for all insured regardless of changes in risk.

Health maintenance organization (HMO). See *Managed care plan.*

Imperfect competition. Occurs in markets or industries with free entry that do not match the criteria for perfect competition. The key characteristics of perfect competition are a large number of small firms; identical products sold by all firms; freedom of entry into and exit out of the industry; and perfect knowledge of prices and technology. These four criteria are essentially impossible to reach in the real world. Product differentiation (e.g., automobile service stations in different locations) often result in imperfect competition but not pure monopoly.

Income effect. The effect on demand for a product arising from changes in real income. A price reduction that gives buyers more real income, or greater purchasing power for their income, even though money or nominal income remains the same, can cause income effects.

Incurred but not reported (IBNR) provision. Provision for claims incurred but not reported by the balance-sheet date. That is, it is anticipated that there would be a number of policies that have, but for the advice of the claim to the insurer, occurred and therefore are likely to result in a liability on the insurer. The magnitude of this provision can be expected to reduce as the time since the insurance risk on the contract expired extends. The magnitude is also likely to vary depending on the type of insurance risk covered by any particular class of insurance contract.

Independence. Two events are independent if the occurrence of one of the events gives no information about whether or not the other event will occur; that is, the events have no influence on each other. For example, having a stroke may be independent of being injured in a cyclone.

Induced demand. Demand created by physicians who are able and willing to change information provided to patients for economic reasons. This allows them to affect both the price and the level of care. This ability to determine their own income is difficult to control when it is present and may have impacts on efforts to control medical spending.

Informal risk-protection mechanism. See *Informal sector.*

Informal sector. The part of the society/economy that is not registered with authorities and, whether with legal exclusion or without it (de jure or de facto), is not subject to public regulation and does not benefit from public services or goods. For example, support given by family, friends, and members of a community in times of loss or illness effectively forms an informal risk-protection mechanism. Despite the presumption that such care is voluntarily given, in some cases (for example, providing care to foster children), payment may in fact be given.

Initial capital requirement. Minimum initial capital that is required to obtain a license and must be provided before an insurer commences business, and cannot be used to finance start-up costs.

Inpatient. Individual admitted to a hospital for health care and allocated a bed for the duration of that admission.

Insolvency. Inability to meet current expenses and contractual obligations from current income plus reserves, leading, in the long run, to bankruptcy.

Institution. Social constructs that contain "rules of the games" and thereby both constrain behavior and enable behavior within those rules. By enabling the individual and organization to understand and predict behavior, the social constructs facilitate economic and social interaction. Institutions include regulations and policies of organizations and governments. They also include community-based traditional patterns of behavior and those that have developed in the face of modernization.

Insurability. A risk is insurable if it is independent and outside the control of the insured. If there is a party willing to accept the risk for an agreed premium and another party is prepared to pay that premium, insurance will be furnished by a profit-seeking firm. This situation implies that the probability is known, it is not subject to very serious moral hazard and adverse selection problems, that it is a legal proposition, and that the premium is affordable. Practical problems associated with information availability may render otherwise insurable risks uninsurable.

Insurance. Insurance is any activity in which a set of agents (members of a mutual plan, stockholders of a company) assumes risk by taking payments (premiums) from individuals or companies and contractually agreeing to pay a stipulated benefit or compensation if certain contingencies specified by contract (death, accident, illness) occur during a defined period.

Insurance threshold. Insurers typically request that the insured pay the first part of any claim. This cost-sharing is a form of deductible, used to simplify administration and reduce administrative costs by reducing the number of small claims.

Insured. Also called *principal*; the end user contracting with an insurer for insurance coverage.

Insured unit. See *Subscription unit.*

Insurer (first-line, primary, or ultimate). The company that contracts with the end user for insurance. The first-line insurer may be the ceding insurer if it chooses to reinsure.

Internal rate of return. The discount rate that makes the net present value of an investment project equal to zero. This is a widely used method of investment appraisal as it takes into account the timing of cash flows.

Late-joiner penalties. Payments, often in the form of higher premiums, imposed on consumers who purchase private voluntary health insurance (PVHI) after they reach an older age, become sick, or do not enroll in a scheme once their coverage by another policy ceases. Protects insurers from adverse selection and encourages consumers to purchase PVHI early.

Law of large numbers. The concept that the greater the number of exposures, the more closely will actual results approach the probable results expected from an infinite number of exposures.

Load. The cost of insurance (administration, finance, and so on) as distinct from payouts (benefits). The difference between premiums and benefits. Efficient competitive companies have a low load relative to benefits. Often expressed as a percentage of premiums or claims.

Local government unit (LGU). The term used in the Philippines to describe public authorities at a lower-than-national level (region, province, municipality, barangay).

Macroeconomic. Refers to factors that operate at the national and global levels, for example, exchange rates, inflation rates, and interest rates. The origins of any factors operating at the local level are large scale. Macroeconomic shocks are changes in the large-scale factors that affect the economy and society.

Managed care plan. A scheme that pools risks and directly provides or arranges for health care services. Use is controlled by mechanisms other than patient cost sharing.

Mandated benefits. Minimum coverage standards imposed by government in order to ensure that certain benefits are covered, especially when coverage serves a primary or more extensive role. They provide a protection against insurer's risk selection that is discriminatory toward high-risk individuals.

Mandatory private insurance. A system in which individuals or employers are required by law to purchase some minimum amount of private or public health insurance.

Market failure. A condition in which a market does not efficiently allocate resources to achieve the greatest possible consumer and producer welfare. The four main market failures are public good, market control, externality, and imperfect information. In each case, a market acting without any government-imposed direction does not direct an efficient amount of resources into the pro-duction, distribution, or consumption of the good.

Maximum likelihood estimate (MLE). Provides the best estimate of a population value that makes the sample data most likely. For example, given that a survey of 50 households in a community indicates that 5 percent of individuals have tuberculosis, what is the proportion of tuberculosis sufferers in the community that is most likely to have given rise to this statistic? The MLE techniques enable such calculation.

Mean. Average. It is equal to the sum of the observed values divided by the total number of observations.

Medical underwriting. A process of detailed medical scrutiny of health status, med-ical history, and other information used by insurers to counter adverse selection and accomplish four specific goals: ascertain the level of risk associated with the person or group applying for insurance, decide if a policy should be sold, decide the terms of the policy, and decide the premium level for the policy.

Members. See *Subscription unit.*

Microfinance institution (MFI). Provides financial services to the poor on a sus-tained basis. The services include saving and credit societies, agricultural insur-ance, property insurance schemes, and, more recently, health insurance schemes.

Microinsurance. A mechanism for pooling a whole community's risks and resources to protect all its participating members against the financial conse-quences of mutually determined health risks.

Microinsurance unit (MIU). A very small finance institution specifically designed to offer health insurance to the poor by pooling risks across a community.

Monte Carlo simulation. A statistical technique in which an uncertain value is calculated repeatedly using randomly selected "what-if" scenarios for each calculation. The simulation calculates hundreds and often thousands of scenarios of a model. Uncertain quantities in the model are replaced with fuzzy numbers to see how that uncertainty affects results. Ideally, the simulation aids in choosing the most attractive course of action, providing information about the range of outcomes such as best- and worst-case, and the probability of reaching specific targets.

Moral hazard. An insurance-prompted change in behavior that affects the probability of a loss-producing event or the amount of benefits conditional on occurrence of an event. For example, an insured's demanding tests that would not be demanded in the absence of insurance (demand-side moral hazard). Provider-induced moral hazards include overservicing (supply-side moral hazard).

Morbidity. Refers to illness from a specified disease or cause or from all diseases. It is a change in health status (short of death) from a state of well-being to disease occurrence and thereby a state of illness.

Mortality. Refers to death from a specified disease or cause or from all diseases.

Multilateral utility. See *Utility.*

Nominal group technique. See *Delphi method or nominal group technique.*

Nongovernmental organization (NGO). Generally refers to a not-for-profit or community organization.

Normal distribution. Statistically speaking, values of events fall in a pattern around the average value with known frequencies. For instance, if the average stay in a hospital after childbirth is three days, the values of each stay would be distributed around three, some more, some less, approximately symmetrically, with greater concentration around three than around any other number. The normal distribution is a particular distribution of this kind that is rigorously defined mathematically and gives the typical bell-shaped curve when graphed. This distribution is very powerful in enabling insurers to calculate costs and utilization.

Off-site monitoring. Review not involving physical visits to the regulated entities that evaluates the financial condition and performance of these entities, including checking assets and liabilities valuation, off-balance sheet exposures, and outsourcing.

Ombudsperson. An official appointed to investigate individuals' complaints against maladministration, especially that of public authorities.

On-site inspection. A physical examination of a regulated entity to examine if it meets the required contractual standards of all involved parties. This procedure supplements information needed for analysis of the reports submitted to the supervisory authorities. Inspectors can be staff of the supervisory authority, or the task can be outsourced to specialists certified and supervised by the authority. On-site inspections can be conducted on a full-scale basis or be focused on investigating areas of specific concern.

Outlier. Denotes events that fall outside the norm. For example, in a "review of utilization" a provider who uses far fewer or far more services than the average is called an "outlier."

Outpatient. Person receiving health care in a hospital without admission to the hospital or accommodation in it. The length of stay is less than 24 hours. The care may be a consultation or a technical act (diagnosis or therapeutic procedure).

Pandemic. A disease that is prevalent throughout a locality or population.

Parameter. A number that describes a characteristic of a population. For example, the life expectancy of men in a community might be 56 years. Health insurance uses statistical techniques to estimate the parameter, and the estimation of the parameter is called the statistic. One sample of 50 men taken from the community might estimate the average age statistic to be 54 years while another sample might estimate it to be 57.5 years.

Pay-as-you-go. Refers to a system of insurance financing under which total expenditure (benefit expenditure plus administrative expenditure) in a given period is met by income (contributions and other sources) from the same period. Pay-as-you-go financed insurance schemes do not accumulate reserves, except contingency reserves; surpluses and deficits translate into increases or decreases in the premium.

Per capita premium. The practice of applying a single premium per head across the population. A form of community rating.

Point estimation. An estimate of a parameter of a population that is given by one number.

Poisson distribution. Typically, a Poisson random variable is a count of the number of events that occur in a certain time interval or spatial area. For example, the number of people seeking critical care for malaria in a wet season month in a particular village. The Poisson distribution can sometimes be used to approximate the binomial distribution when the number of observations is large and the probability of success is small (that is, a fairly rare event). This is useful since the computations involved in calculating binomial probabilities are greatly reduced.

Population density. A measure of the size of the population in comparison to the size of a specified geographic area (region, country, province, city). Typically, it is a count of the number of residents per square kilometer.

Preexisting condition exclusion period. A mechanism that protects the insurer against adverse selection by delaying coverage for health expenses incurred by an individual that are related to a condition the individual had prior to applying for health insurance. The rules governing exclusion period vary, but often can limit coverage to conditions which received medical attention, or conditions for which the person arguably should have been aware of, sought treatment for, or for which there were clear signs or symptoms. Premiums are still due during this exclusion period and pay for coverage of care for conditions other than those excluded.

Preferred risk selection. See *Cream skimming.*

Premium. Fee paid by an insured to an insurance company in return for specified benefits. Under social insurance the premium is called *contribution.* See also *Contribution.*

Premium deficiency reserve. Amount set aside on the balance sheet in addition to unearned premiums with respect to risks to be borne by the insurer after the end of the reporting period, in order to provide for all claims and expenses in connection with insurance contracts in force in excess of the related unearned premiums and any premiums receivable on those contracts. Also called *provision for unexpired risks.*

Prevalence. The total number of cases or people who have a specified disease, health condition, attribute, or risk factor within a specified population at a specific point in time.

Preventive health care. Medical care directed primarily toward early detection and treatment or prevention of disease or ill health (for example, immunizations, prenatal care).

Primary health care. The first level of contact by individuals, families, and communities with the health system, bringing health care as close as possible to where people work and live. The organization of primary health care depends upon the socioeconomic and political characteristics of the country, but should address prevention, curative, and rehabilitation services and include education of the population about major health problems and their prevention and control. Such care may be provided by a variety of health workers, acting together as a team, in partnership with the local community.

Primary insurer. See *Insurer.*

Primary private health insurance. Term is used when private health insurance is the only form of health insurance available to an individual because there is no public option available or one is ineligible for it.

Principal. Denotes the client, in the relationship between an insurer (agent) and the insured (principal). See *Insured.*

Probability. The expected relative frequency of occurrence of a particular event with a large number of tries or exposures. Probability is conventionally expressed on a scale from 0 to 1; a rare event has a probability close to 0, a very common event has a probability close to 1. The probability of occurrence of heads in multiple flips of a fair coin is 0.5.

Probability distribution. The probability distribution of a discrete random variable is a list of probabilities associated with each of its possible values. It is also sometimes called the probability function or the probability mass function. For example, the probability of a woman's delivering a single live baby might be 98 percent, twins 1.78 percent, triplets 0.218 percent, more than triplets 0.002 percent.

Providers. Doctors, nurses, hospitals, clinics, laboratories, imaging facilities, pharmacies, and other deliverers of medical services. The insurer or regulating body typically requires that a provider be qualified and/or registered in order to be included in a health insurance scheme.

Prudential regulation system. Standards that facilitate proper functioning of insurers through licensing, reporting, financial standards, capital adequacy, and product regulation, which limit risk-taking of insurance institutions, ensure the safety of depositors' funds, and keep the stability of the financial system.

Public goods. There are two aspects to public goods: it is difficult to prevent nonpayers from consuming them (nonexcludable), and their consumption by one party does not affect their consumption by others (nonrival). Vaccination is an example—those who do not pay and are not vaccinated cannot be excluded from enjoying the lower prevalence of disease; and the fact that they are healthy as a result does not affect another's ability to be healthier as a result of the program. Government usually provides public goods, because private businesses do so profitably.

Pure premium. The pure premium can be defined as the average loss per exposure unit for a specific coverage or, more specifically, the product of the average severity and the average frequency of loss. The result is the amount, which the insurance company should collect to cover all the losses to be met under the predefined types of coverage in a setting with a very large number of exposures. See *Law of large numbers.*

Qualifying conditions. Requirements for acceptance into an insurance plan; also describes the provisions that must be met before a benefit is payable.

Random variable. A function that provides a single numerical value to a particular event or outcome. The value of the random variable will vary from trial to trial as the experiment is repeated. For example, if 10 people visit a hospital as outpatients in a morning, and 7 of them have injuries rather than disease, the random variable for that event is 0.7. Another example: if the life span of a particular baby born 10 weeks premature in a community is 2 days, 4 hours, and 7 minutes, the random variable of that event is that duration.

Rating. See *Risk rating.*

Reciprocating arrangements. Agreements existing between primary insurers to coinsure, the objective being to stabilize funds. These arrangements are sometimes considered an alternative to reinsurance in that they enlarge the pool and reduce risk variance.

Recovery gap. An excess of benefit payouts over income, when the *compliance gap* is assumed to be zero. The recovery gap is not random and so cannot be solved by reinsurance.

Reinsurance. The transfer of liability from the primary insurer, the company that issued the contract, to another insurer, the reinsurance company. This mechanism allows a diversification of the risk and enlarges the risk-pooling base, thereby reducing the risk of insolvency for the reinsuring firm. However, reinsurance extends only to risk defined in the cession contract (called *treaty*). For example, a treaty to cede fluctuations in payouts will not cover the primary insurer against the financial risk of insolvency, for example, because of poorly run or unviable insurance.

Reinsurance premium. The amount charged by the reinsurer to accept an agreed amount of risk.

Reinsurance threshold. Reinsurers typically require that the insurer retains the first proportion of risk for any event. That proportion is the threshold as it is equivalent to the deductible or excess borne by the insured when making a claim against property insurance.

Reinsurer. An insurance company for insurers. A reinsurer offers protection through the sale of a reinsurance contract to a risk-transferring policyholder who is an insurer. If the risk-transferring policyholder is a (re)insurer itself, the risk-assuming insurer is called the reinsurer, and the risk transfer is known as (retro)cession. Usually used to deal with low probability risks that are large relative to the initial insurer's capital or revenues, such as total claims exceeding expected claims by a large amount.

Renewability. See *Guaranteed renewability*.

Reserves. Funds set aside to meet unforeseeable liabilities (i.e., obligations that have not yet materialized) or statutory requirements, and stemming either from shareholders' capital or, in the case of mutuals, members' contributions and from accumulated surplus. Reserves are part of the own funds (in contrast to provisions that support liabilities to parties other than shareholders or other owners). A major financial management goal is to minimize reserves and thus maximize funds available for current use.

Risk. The probability or likelihood that a specified health event (for example, the occurrence of a disease or death) will occur to an individual or population group within a specific period of time.

Risk-based capital model. Applying ongoing solvency standards based on the level of risk assumed by an insurer (including investment, credit, insurance, and operational risks), and weighing out uncorrelated factors to calculate the minimum capital level.

Risk equalization. Provisions under which insurers with higher risk profiles receive a transfer of funds from insurers with lower risk profiles. Used in many countries with community rating schemes.

Risk factor. An attribute (for example, a lifestyle factor or a personal characteristic) or an exposure to an environmental factor associated with an increase in the probability that a specified health event (for example, onset of disease) will occur.

Risk pooling. A health system function in which collected health revenues are transferred to purchasing organizations, and the pooled risk of bearing the financial burden of future unexpected health services is shared and dispersed over large numbers of heterogeneous contributors. Insurers pool risk through reinsurance.

Risk rating. Calculation of health insurance premiums based on the risk of each client. When the premium is calculated based on the risk not of a single individual but of a group, this is called *community rating* or *group rating*. When the premium is set in relation to the client's income, this is called *income rating*.

Risk segregation. Each individual or member of an individual risk class faces a premium based only on that risk class and is not averaged with other distinctive risk classes.

Risk selection. A practice of excluding those who may present a higher risk for the insurer by making more, or more costly, claims.

Risk sharing. Individuals agree to split the cost of future risky events. Insurers share risk through reciprocal relationships and reinsurance. Loan guarantees and insurance are among the many ways of sharing risks.

Safety coefficient. A measure of the difference between the expected annual result of an insurance scheme and the worst possible loss that can be borne. Information on the safety coefficient enables management to make decisions about reserve levels.

Self insurance. A group pays all claims out of its own resources without sharing risk with an outside insurer. For example, a large employer providing coverage to workers under an arrangement in which it pays total claims regardless of their magnitude is self-insuring.

Self-protection. Refers to all the arrangements made by an individual or group to protect themselves from risk. It includes not only saving and establishing contingency reserves but also changing behavior to diminish or avoid risk.

Simulation. The technique of imitating behavior and events during an experimental process. Typically involves a computer.

Small-country [financial system] rationale. Establishing one centralized, integrated supervisory body due to scarce human resources necessary to administer regulation. Common in many transition and developing economies based on a desire to achieve economies of scale in regulation.

Social capital. Refers to the multidimensional "glue" that binds community members together. While concepts of social capital vary from culture to culture, in "Social Capital and Institutional Success" Robert Putnam (1993) defined it as including trust, community involvement, tolerance of diversity, value of life, and extent of connectivity (social and professional).

Social exclusion. Inadequate or unequal participation in social life, or exclusion from a place in the consumer society, often linked to the social role of employment or work.

Social insurance. A compulsory insurance program that is shaped by broader collectively chosen objectives than just interest of each individual principal or agent, while retaining insurance principles that persons are insured against a definite risk.

Social protection. Policies and programs designed to reduce poverty and financial vulnerability. Social protection policies typically focus on labor market policies, social insurance, social assistance, community-based schemes, and child protection.

Social reinsurance. Reinsurance undertaken in pursuit of social goals rather than profit.

Social utility. The alleged gain to society from, in this case, insurance, as distinct from the sum of the gains to the individual members of the society. Where insurance has zero or negative social utility it may be banned; where it has high social utility but low private utility it may be mandated. The choice of rendering a public utility mandatory or not depends on political will or the power of authorities, including community leaders.

Soft budget. A budget with a flexible limit.

Solidarity principle. Applying rules that spread risks and resources across members of a group in a way that provides both insurance coverage and egalitarian distribution. *Risk solidarity* would imply that high-risk individuals receive a subsidy from low-risk individuals, allowing all risk levels to pay the same price for health care coverage. Solidarity between high- and low-income individuals, or *income solidarity,* implies income redistribution through organized transfers. In insurance, the solidarity principle is juxtaposed to the *equivalence principle,* which implies that the insurer seeks to break even on each insurance contract, by applying *risk rating.*

Solvable. An insurance transaction is said to be solvable if the risk is observable, there is no antiselection (adverse selection), and the premium is acceptable to both parties.

Solvency margin. Surplus of assets over liabilities.

Solvency requirements. The whole set of statutory requirements or rules as regards the required solvency margin and eligible capital elements to cover the margin; includes the performance of the solvency test to prove compliance with these requirements.

Solvent demand. See *Demand.*

Spot market transactions. The "spot market" implies transactions for immediate delivery of services as distinct from the insurance requirement of prepayment against (possible) future delivery of services. Populations that are excluded from health insurance rely on spot payments to access health care.

Standard deviation. A statistical term for a measure of the variability in a population or sample.

Subscription unit. Refers to the people covered by a single membership. This may be the individual (usually in developed economies) or the household (usually in developing economies).

Supervisor. An administrator of insurance laws responsible for supervision of the management of an insurer or intermediary. Also supervisory agency/regulator.

Supplementary private health insurance. Provides coverage for health services that are not fully covered by a public program, such as luxury care, elective care, long-term care, dental care, pharmaceuticals, rehabilitation, alternative or complementary medicine, or superior amenity services in the hospital (differs per country).

Swaps. See *Derivative.*

Target group. Refers to both current and future beneficiaries of the insurance system. The target group can comprise several subgroups of people with similar characteristics (for example, income, economic sector).

Technical provisions. Funds for outstanding claims or unearned premiums, required by supervisors. Also called *reserves.*

Top-down global strategy. Implies that a public policy, for instance the approach to improving access to health care or health insurance, was directed by a powerful global body to national governments and down through the rank and file to the community. This contrasts with the "bottom-up" approach based on the empowerment of communities.

Transaction costs. The costs additional to the price of a good or service, arising, for example, from search costs, travel costs, marketing and distribution, or transfer of ownership costs.

Ultimate insurer. See *Insurer.*

Underwriter. A company that receives the premiums and accepts responsibility for the fulfillment of the policy contract; also the company employee who decides whether or not the company should assume a particular risk at a particular premium; also the agent who sells the policy.

Underwriting. The process by which the insurer decides what risks to cover and what premiums to charge. The profit objectives may conflict with what some regard as social obligation. For the reinsurer, underwriting considerations determine the risks of the primary insurer that can be accepted for reinsurance, and which the insurer will retain.

Underwriting assistance. Reinsurance companies gather extensive data on the insured and events. They can share this information with insurers to improve the performance of insurers.

Unearned premiums. A type of technical provision for premiums received but not yet earned. Amount figure on the balance sheet representing that part of premiums written which is to be allocated to the following financial year or to subsequent financial years.

Unilateral utility. See *Utility*.

Uninsurable. See *Insurability*.

Unit cost. The average cost of particular health care treatments. These costs are negotiated between a microinsurance unit and providers. Insurance enables a move away from fee-for-service toward averaging out of unit costs.

Universal coverage. Implies that all members of a country (or a community) have health insurance that covers all or almost all of the cost of all services.

User fees. Charges payable by users, usually at the point of service. See *Spot market transactions*.

Utility. The satisfaction gained from having the desire for goods and services met. *Multilateral utility* means that several parties benefit from outcomes. These parties can be a group of insured or the insurer and the insured. *Unilateral utility* means that only one party gains. The balance between group and individual utility is a delicate component of relations within a community, between insurer/insured, or between insurer/reinsurer.

Utilization. Refers to utilization patterns of medical services in a location over a period. Data on recent utilization, collected at the national and community levels, are valuable in predicting future patterns.

Variation coefficient. See *Coefficient of variation*.

Vector-borne infectious disease. Infections caused by human contact with an infectious agent; transmitted from an infected individual by an insect or other live carrier. For example, malaria is biologically transmitted from an infected individual to a noninfected person by the same mosquito (the vector) biting both people.

Waiting period. A mechanism that protects the insurer against adverse selection by delaying the period before an individual will be covered for any services he or she receives after the effective date of coverage. Access is restricted during the period of delay but not afterward. Policy premiums are still paid during this time.

Willingness to pay (WTP). Willingness to pay for health care or health insurance is affected by a household's income, tastes, and culture and measures the perceived benefit from the good or service. It differs from "ability to pay." There are commonly two ways to estimate WTP:

- Using data on past health care utilization and prices (demand). The price a person pays for the last unit of care purchased equals that person's subjective benefit from that unit. The total amount a consumer would be willing to pay for an amount of a product rather than go without (usually much more than what is actually charged) is a measure of the benefit from that amount of the product compared to none at all.

- Using contingent valuation methods based on surveys.

Working capital. Current assets minus current liabilities. It is the capital available for an organization's short-term financing.

NOTE

This glossary was adapted from "Glossary of Terms," appendix C in *Social Reinsurance: A New Approach to Sustainable Community Health Financing,* David M. Dror and Alexander S. Preker, eds., 465–485, World Bank, Washington, DC, and International Labour Office, Geneva, Switzerland, 2002. Other sources consulted were WebFinance Inc., http://webfinanceinc.com, 2007; and International Association of Insurance Supervisors, *Glossary of Terms,* Basel, 2007.

About the Coeditors and Contributors

COEDITORS

Alexander S. Preker is head of Health Industry and Investment Policy Analysis for the Investment Climate Department of the World Bank Group and a Distinguished Visiting Executive at the Columbia University Business School in New York. He leads a team of advisers and analysts that work with investors, health businesses, and policy makers in improving the investment climate and business operating environment in the health sector in developing countries. Preker has had a distinguished career, working at different times for International Bank for Reconstruction and Development (IBRD), International Development Association (IDA), International Finance Corporation (IFC), and World Health Organization (WHO). Previously, as chief economist for the World Bank's health sector, he coordinated the technical team that prepared the *Health, Nutrition, and Population Sector Strategy* in 1997. For the next 10 years, this strategy provided a vision for the World Bank's engagement in the health sector in low- and middle-income countries, leading to an annual lending pipeline of between US$1 billion and US$2 billion and total portfolio value in the range of US$15 billion. He has recently been involved in the US$1 billion Health in Africa Initiative, which includes a US$500 million debt facility, US$300 million Equity Vehicle for Health in Africa, and US$200 million for analysis and advisory services. He is currently involved in setting up a similar facility for India and other low-income countries.

Preker has published extensively, having written many scientific articles, and is the author of more than 15 books. He is a member of the editorial board for the World Bank's External Operations Publication Department and editor-in-chief of World Bank Business of Health Publications.

In addition to his academic activities at the Columbia University Business School, Preker is an adjunct professor of public administration and health at the Wagner Graduate School of Public Service at New York University. He is a member of the teaching faculty for the Berkeley/Cambridge Health Leadership Forum and teaches periodically at International Masters for Health Leadership, McGill University in Montreal. His training includes a PhD in economics from the London School of Economics and Political Science, a fellowship in medicine from University College London, a diploma in medical law and ethics from King's College London, and an MD from the University of British Columbia/McGill.

Marianne E. Lindner is an economist who worked as senior policy adviser at PharmAccess Foundation, a Dutch nonprofit organization focusing on health systems development in Africa. Previously Lindner held positions in public health consultancy, the UN Children's Fund, the UN Development Program, Oxfam/Novib, and the financial sector. Her working experience is concentrated in the areas of economic and social policy, health systems development, program development, monitoring and evaluation, and related (field) research. Lindner has published in various scientific journals and was involved with the World Bank in the publication of *Global Marketplace for Private Health Insurance: Strength in Numbers*. She received master's degrees in economics (Drs, University of Amsterdam) and health policy, planning, and financing (MSc, London School of Economics and London School of Hygiene and Tropical Medicine, with distinction). She is currently teaching economics in the Netherlands.

Dov Chernichovsky (PhD economics) is a professor of health economics and policy at Ben-Gurion University of the Negev, Israel. He is a research associate with the National Bureau of Economic Research in the United States and a consultant to the World Bank, where he was formerly a staff member. Chernichovsky heads the health program at the Taub Center for the Study of Social Policy in Israel and manages the Negev Health Forum for health promotion in the southern region in Israel. He also serves on the board of the Israeli Cancer Society, the Baxter Prize advisory board, and on the editorial boards of several journals.

Among his numerous commission memberships, Chernichovsky was a member of the Israeli State (Blue Ribbon/Royal) Commission that outlined the reform proposal that led to the national health insurance legislation enacted in Israel in 1995. He was the health system adviser to the Israeli parliament (Knesset), 2005–7. On behalf of the World Bank, he played key roles in health system reform formulations in Romania, the Russian Federation, and more recently in Mexico and Tanzania.

In his research, initially Chernichovsky studied household behavior in various countries around the world. His research in Botswana, Brazil, India, Indonesia, and the United States yielded pioneering economic studies in household investment in human resources, notably education and nutrition. Chernichovsky has become known for articulating "the favored son hypothesis" for investment in children's schooling. Subsequently, Chernichovsky moved to study health care systems. These studies led to the formulation of the Emerging Paradigm in health systems, a framework for studying and reforming these systems. He is also known for his innovative work in the application of Hedonic Prices to estimate hospital costs as well as for the application of Fuzzy Logic to the study of financing in health systems, and formulating a nonconventional view of the effect of aging on health system costs.

Onno P. Schellekens is managing director of PharmAccess Group, an organization dedicated to improving health care services in Africa. The group is active in organizing subsidized health insurance for low-income people (Health Insurance Fund), affordable credit for health care providers (Medical Credit Fund), and private equity for health care in Africa (Investment Fund for Health in Africa); setting clinical standards and quality improvement of care (SafeCare); and conducting impact assessments of health care programs (Amsterdam Institute for Global Health and Development). Schellekens is the author of several publications on health insurance, medical treatment, and HIV/AIDS in Africa. He was one of the winners of the

2008 IFC/*Financial Times* Essay Competition for Private Sector Development with a provocative essay entitled "A New Paradigm for Increased Access to Health Care in Africa." Schellekens graduated from the University of Groningen in the Netherlands with a master's degree from its School of Management and Organization.

OTHER CONTRIBUTING AUTHORS

Chris Atim is a senior health economist on the World Bank's Health Systems Strengthening program, based in Dakar, Senegal. He received his PhD from the University of Sussex in the United Kingdom in 1993 and specializes in health care financing in Africa. He has taught for many years in a health economics masters course on health insurance at the regional Institute for Higher Management Studies (CESAG), based in Senegal. Between 1999 and 2004, he worked as a senior health economist for Abt Associates Inc. and served as the West and Central Africa Regional Adviser for their Partnerships for Health Reform (PHR) project. In that role, he led and supervised technical assistance for the PHR project's program on community-based health insurance schemes in West and Central Africa. Between 2004 and 2009, he worked for a number of international organizations in the areas of health financing as well as cost-effectiveness and evidence-based decision making in introducing new technologies in GAVI-eligible countries. He is currently serving also as the executive director of the African Health Economics and Policy Association (AfHEA).

Mark C. Bassett is a self-employed public policy consultant, specializing in health policy. Over the last 25 years his principal employers have been the National Health Service (1986–97) and Bupa Group (1998–2010), but he has also had long-term secondments to the Department of Health, England (1994–97), and the World Bank (2003–5). Bassett has worked in the Russian Federation, the United States, Australia, China, India, Saudi Arabia, Ghana, the Islamic Republic of Iran, and numerous European countries. He has an MA in health services management from Manchester University and is a Fellow of the Royal Societies of Medicine and Arts in London.

Ricardo Bitrán is a senior health economist from Chile with 30 years of experience as a policy adviser, researcher, and professor in Chile, the United States, and more than 40 developing countries, including nearly all countries in Latin America and the Caribbean. He holds an MS in industrial engineering from the University of Chile and an MBA in finance and a PhD in economics from Boston University. He specializes in the development and evaluation of health sector financing reforms and public and private health investment projects. He is founding partner of Bitrán & Asociados (B&A) since 1995. Previously he worked for 10 years at Abt Associates Inc. in Cambridge, Massachusetts, first as health economist and then as senior scientist. He was on the USAID-financed Health Financing and Sustainability Project. He teaches health economics at the University of Chile and is a member of the core faculty of the Flagship Program in Health System Strengthening. He is the author of academic articles, book chapters, and research papers.

Guy Carrin (1947–2011) was a professor of health economics at the University of Antwerp, Belgium. Between June 1990 and November 2009, he served as a senior health economist in the World Health Organization (WHO) in Geneva, Switzerland. He was also coordinator of health financing policy in the WHO Department of Health Systems Financing. He published extensively in the areas of social security, macroeconomic modeling, and health economics. He held an MA and a PhD in economics from, respectively, the University of New Hampshire, United States, and the University of Leuven, Belgium. He was Takemi Fellow in International Health at the Harvard School of Public Health and adjunct professor of public health at Boston University.

Michal Chernichovsky has an MA degree with distinction in organizational sociology and anthropology from the Hebrew University of Jerusalem. She initiated and ran the "meet the author" programs in the two Israeli leading bookselling chains Zomet Sefarim and Steimatzky. At OzDov Ltd., a consulting group, she has been dealing with issues of industrial organization and relations.

Catherine Connor has 29 years of experience in health, both domestic and international, interacting with governments, nongovernmental organizations, the private sector, and bilateral and multilateral agencies in 30 countries in Africa, Latin America, and Asia. Since 1999, she has managed and delivered technical assistance in health sector reform and system strengthening. As deputy director of the USAID global Health Systems 20/20 project, she oversees health financing activities including health insurance, resource tracking, and pay-for-performance. She works with project teams and counterparts to develop technical approaches and work plans and monitor implementation. She leads selected assignments including the introduction of performance-based incentives in Mozambique, a health system assessment in Angola, a regional health insurance workshop for eight countries in Sub-Saharan Africa, and a technical session on health insurance for the East Central Southern African Health Community. She worked in Brazil for six years in management consulting, including the launch of a private health insurance administrator serving self-insured large employers. Connor has an MBA from Boston University and is fluent in Portuguese.

Judith de Groot obtained an Msc in social and economic history from the University of Amsterdam (cum laude) in 1992. Recently she took courses in economics at the London School of Economics and at the University of Amsterdam. She worked for the Dutch government from 1995 until 2011, in several ministries including the Ministries of Finance, Social Affairs and Employment, and Interior, always on the intersecting point of finance and policy. Outside work, she was active in local politics in Amsterdam. Since 2010 she has been with the PharmAccess Foundation, doing research and policy work.

François Diop, MD, is a senior health economist with extensive experience in health sector reform and health care financing in Africa. Under the Health Finance and Sustainability (HFS) project, he served as the resident adviser to the Ministry of Health in Niger and played a major role in the development of a national policy of cost recovery for primary health care. Under the Partnerships for Health Reform (PHR) project, Dr. Diop provided support to health financing policy debates in Zambia and to the development of national strategies for scaling up community-based health insurance nationwide in Rwanda. Under the Partners for Health Reform*plus* (PHR*plus*) and the AWARE-RH, Dr. Diop provided assistance to Senegal, Benin, and Niger in the development of strategic plans for the development of community-based health insurance. While employed at the World Bank, Dr. Diop provided technical assistance to the elaboration of poverty reduction strategy papers, midterm expenditure frameworks for the health sector, and the health component of country policy matrix. Dr. Diop provided technical leadership in the Health Financing and Policy project in Senegal and the elaboration of the health insurance strategy under the Health Sector Financing Reform project in Ethiopia. Dr. Diop conducted population and health research and provided technical assistance in many African countries for international organizations. Dr. Diop holds a PhD degree from the Johns Hopkins University, Maryland.

Yohana Dukhan is a health economist working in the Human Development Department of the African Development Bank. She previously worked in the Investment Climate Department of the International Finance Corporation. She holds a PhD in economics from CERDI (University of Auvergne, France). Her doctoral research focused on health financing issues in developing countries, particularly health systems efficiency and health insurance. Her main activities cover private sector participation in health, health industry scoping and forecasting, health insurance reforms analysis, and costing analysis. She has also worked at the World Bank, the World Health Organization, and the International Hospital Federation on health financing issues such as health insurance and health systems/hospitals efficiency.

Bjorn O. Ekman is a senior health economist with the World Bank's Middle East and North Africa (MENA) Region. He has a PhD in economics from Lund University in Southern Sweden. Prior to joining the World Bank, he was a researcher at Lund University, focusing on health financing and systems reform in low- and middle-income countries and on the economics of maternal and child health. He has published on these topics in international academic journals. He is currently working on health financing and insurance reform in a number of countries in the MENA Region.

Heba A. Elgazzar is a health economist at the World Bank's Middle East and North Africa (MENA) Region. Her professional experience and publications have been mainly in the areas of comparative health policy, disparities in access to health care, and economic evaluation. She completed her graduate studies at the London School of Economics and Political Science and her undergraduate studies at Columbia University. She is currently leading the Bank's technical and analytical support to several countries in the MENA Region in the areas of health financing and systems reform.

David B. Evans is director of the Department of Health Systems Financing in the Cluster on Health Systems and Services at the World Health Organization (WHO). He has a PhD in economics and worked as an academic in Australia and Singapore before joining WHO in 1990. His work has covered a variety of areas including social and economic aspects of tropical disease control, the assessment of health system performance, and the generation, analysis, and application of evidence for health policy. His current work focuses on the development of effective, efficient, and equitable health financing systems and includes technical support to countries, partnership with other development agencies and initiatives, generation and use of evidence, and capacity building. He has published widely in these areas.

Frank G. Feeley is an associate professor in the Department of International Health at Boston University School of Public Health where he teaches courses on health policy and finance. He holds a JD from Yale University Law School, and began his career with public health insurance and health regulatory agencies in the U.S. state of Massachusetts. In the 1990s, he helped document the shifts in health financing and the extent of out-of-pocket payment for health care in the Russian Federation. His recent international work has focused on the regulation and financing of private health care in developing countries and, more recently, on the impact of HIV/AIDS on employer costs as well as the development of public/private partnerships to address the AIDS epidemic.

Ashley M. Fox is a Fellow of the Agency for Health Care Research and Quality (AHRQ) in the Division of Health Policy and Administration at Yale University. She was previously a postdoctoral fellow in the political economy of health policy with the Department of Global Health and Population at the Harvard School of Public Health. She received her PhD in public health and political science from the Department of Sociomedical Sciences at Columbia University and holds an MA and BA in political science and public policy from the University of Connecticut. Her research focuses on politics of health policy, health inequalities in developing countries, public attitudes toward health reform, and the impacts of policy on health outcomes.

Hernán L. Fuenzalida-Puelma is a senior consultant and adviser on social policy and social security reform. He has worked extensively in 52 countries in projects and activities with private consulting firms and projects financed by international donor organizations including the World Bank, the Asian Development Bank, the U.K. Department for International Development, and the United

States Agency for International Development. His work concerns development of public and private regulatory agencies and insurance industry development, public/private partnerships, as well as policy, legal/regulatory, and institutional issues in financial sector development, social protection financing, and management (social security, pensions, health care, and labor). He has analyzed the health insurance sector in India; assessed the health portfolio in Albania; examined health care reform in Bosnia and Herzegovina, Georgia, and the Slovak Republic; and participated in World Bank missions on health, pension, and labor issues in Albania, Croatia, Lithuania, the former Yugoslav Republic of Macedonia, Mongolia, and Ukraine. Most recently he has been working on social health insurance options for Kenya. A member of the bar associations of Santiago, Chile, and Costa Rica, he holds an LL.M from Yale University.

Sherry Glied is professor of health policy and management at Columbia University's Mailman School of Public Health. A faculty member since 1989, Glied, PhD, is a leading scholar on U.S. health policy reform and mental health care policy. She served as Assistant Secretary for Planning and Evaluation at the U.S. Department of Health and Human Services under President Barack Obama from July 2010 through August 2012. Glied led Columbia University's Department of Health Policy and Management from 1998 to 2009. She was a senior economist for health care and labor market policy on the President's Council of Economic Advisers under Presidents George W. Bush and Bill Clinton, and participated in the Clinton Health Care Task Force. She has been elected to the Institute of Medicine of the National Academy of Sciences and to the Board of Academy Health and has been a member of the Congressional Budget Office's Panel of Health Advisers. Glied's book on health care reform, *Chronic Condition*, was published by Harvard University Press in January 1998. Her book with Richard Frank, *Better But Not Well: Mental Health Policy in the United States since 1950*, was published by the Johns Hopkins University Press in 2006. She is coeditor, with Peter C. Smith, of *The Oxford Handbook of Health Economics*, which was published by Oxford University Press in 2011.

Pablo Gottret is the Social Protection and Labor Sector Manager for the South Asia Region of the World Bank. Previously, he was Lead Human Development Economist in the same region, where he was responsible for overseeing the economic work in Health, Education, and Social Protection. Over the past few years, he has provided extensive cross-support in health insurance, health financing, and Public Expenditure Reviews in several countries in the Latin America and Caribbean, Europe and Central Asia, and Africa Regions.

Before joining the World Bank in 2002, between 1987 and 1990 Gottret was vice minister of budgeting in the Ministry of Finance of his native Bolivia where he managed Bolivia's first Enhanced Structural Adjustment Program for economic stabilization after the hyperinflation period. He was chief executive of the Regulatory Body for Private Pensions, Private Insurance, and Securities between

1998 and June 2002. Gottret led the technical teams that developed Bolivia's Capital Markets Law, Insurance Law, and reforms to the Pension's System Law approved by the Bolivian Congress between 1997 and 1998. Between 1990 and 1998, Gottret worked extensively in health financing, social health insurance, and pension reform programs in different countries of Latin America including Argentina, Mexico, Peru, El Salvador, and Colombia.

Gottret has published several books as well as professional journal articles and acted as speaker in several international conferences. He has a PhD in economics from Texas A&M University with specializations in econometrics, natural resource economics, and finance.

April Harding is an economist and health systems specialist with the World Bank Institute, where she leads the delivery of policy seminars and training courses covering the policy challenges associated with expanding collaboration with the private health sector. She is a sought-after speaker, author, and policy adviser on the private health sector, public-private partnerships, as well as hospital reform and governance. Harding has provided policy advice and analytical support to more than 20 governments on these topics. She recently returned to the World Bank from the Center for Global Development, where she conducted research examining five global health programs, child health, TB, malaria, family planning, and HIV/AIDS, looking at how these programs interact with the private sector in their implementation, and how this contributes to their success or failure. Her findings are presented in her book *Private Patients: Why Health Aid Fails to Reach So Many, and What We Can Do about It* (forthcoming 2013, Brookings/Center for Global Development). She served as a contributing editor at *Health Affairs*, where she helped the journal develop its global health coverage. Prior to joining the World Bank, Harding was a research fellow at the Brookings Institution. She received her doctorate in economics from the University of Pennsylvania.

Peter S. Heller is the former deputy director of the Fiscal Affairs Department of the International Monetary Fund. He has worked on fiscal policy issues in countries as diverse as Japan, China, India, Somalia, Thailand, the Republic of Korea, Indonesia, Bosnia and Herzegovina, Slovenia, and the Russian Federation. He participated in the Commission on Macroeconomics and Health, World Health Organization, and the Millennium Task Force of the United Nations. He has published extensively in a number of areas, relating principally to fiscal policy, economic development, poverty reduction, aging populations, public expenditure policy, and globalization. He is the author of *Who Will Pay? Aging Societies, Climate Change, and Other Long-Term Fiscal Challenges* (International Monetary Fund 2003).

Jürgen Hohmann is an economist, specializing in health and social security, and also holds a PhD in medical sciences and a master's degree in European law. He has been working on health systems and health policies in the European

Union, Asia, and Africa, where he has performed many high-level advisory missions on macroeconomics, health financing, and the development of social security organizations. Since 2007, Hohmann has predominately supported the General Inspectorate of Social Security in Luxembourg, where he manages projects in the field of health and long-term care system development and on cross-border collaboration in health.

William C. Hsiao is the K.T. Li Professor of Economics and leads a new program in health systems studies at Harvard University. Hsiao received his PhD in economics from Harvard University. He is also a fully qualified actuary with extensive experience in private and social insurance. Hsiao has conducted health financing studies for more than three decades. He was actively engaged in designing health system reforms and universal health insurance programs for the United States, China, Colombia, Poland, Vietnam, Sweden, Cyprus, Uganda, South Africa, Hong Kong SAR, China, and Taiwan, China. His current research focuses on developing an analytical model for diagnosing the causes of the successes or failures of national health systems. His analytical framework has shaped how health systems are conceptualized and has been used extensively by various nations around the world in health system reforms. Hsiao is testing his model by conducting large-scale social experiments in several developing nations, including China. Hsiao was elected to membership in the Institute of Medicine and the U.S. National Academy of Sciences. He was also elected to the Board of the National Academy of Social Insurance. Hsiao was named the Man of the Year in Medicine in 1989 for his development of a new payment method (the resource-based relative values) for physician services.

Hsiao has published more than 170 papers and several books and has served on the editorial boards of several professional journals. He has served as an adviser to three U.S. presidents, the U.S. Congress, the World Bank, the International Monetary Fund, World Health Organization, and International Labour Organization. He is a recipient of honorary professorships from several leading Chinese universities and several awards from his profession.

Melitta Jakab is a health economist with 15 years of experience in health system strengthening, policy analysis, and training and education in global health. She joined the World Health Organization (WHO) in 2004 as a policy adviser for the Kyrgyz Republic. Since 2009, she has been working in the Barcelona Office for Health System Strengthening of WHO Europe, Division of Health Systems and Public Health. Her work focuses on health financing and broader health system reform in transition countries, in particular Moldova, Kazakhstan, the Kyrgyz Republic, and Tajikistan. She is coeditor of *Implementing Health Financing Reform: Lessons from Countries in Transition*, with Joseph Kutzin and Cheryl Cashin, published in 2010. She has been codirector of the joint WHO-World Bank Institute Regional Flagship Course for the Europe and Central Asia region as well as of the WHO Barcelona Course in Health Financing. She has a master of science degree in health policy from the Harvard School of Public Health and a PhD in health economics from Harvard University.

Caroline Ly is a doctoral candidate at the University of Pennsylvania's Department of Health Care Management. Ly has consulted for the World Bank on health care financing issues such as social health insurance, performance-based financing, and expanding capital investments in Africa. She holds an MA from the Johns Hopkins School of Advanced International Studies and a BA from the University of Chicago.

Hans Maarse has held a chair in health care policy analysis in the Faculty of Health Sciences of the University of Maastricht in the Netherlands since 1986. His main fields of interest are health care finance, the institutional structure of health care policy making, the international comparative analysis of health care systems, and the impact of the European Union on national health care policies. Recently, he directed a study on the possibilities and effects of market competition in Dutch health care.

Inke Mathauer is a health systems development specialist, holding an MSc and a PhD from the London School of Economics. She works in the Department of Health Systems Financing of the World Health Organization (WHO) in Geneva in the field of health financing policy. Her work involves policy advice to Ministries of Health, conceptual work on health financing performance and the role of organizations and institutions, as well as social health insurance financial/technical feasibility assessments. Prior to WHO, she worked for German Technical Cooperation (GTZ) both at headquarters and in Kenya in health systems development and health financing. Mathauer has also undertaken several institutional analysis consultancies for the World Bank in the field of health and social protection. Earlier, she worked in Benin and Uganda at local and district level.

Alexis Medina studied economics and Chinese as an undergraduate at Williams College and received a master's in East Asian Studies from Yale University. Her recent projects include research for a comparison of China's and India's health systems, econometric analysis for Professor Winnie Yip's well-being study in Shandong, China, and health systems research for Professor William Hsiao.

Rodrigo Moreno-Serra is a health economist currently working as a research fellow at Imperial College London (Business School and Centre for Health Policy). He obtained a PhD in economics from the University of York and an MSc in economics of institutions and development from the University of São Paulo, Brazil. His previous professional appointments include spells at the World Bank, University of São Paulo (Department of Economics), and Federal University of São Paulo (Paulista Center for Health Economics). Moreno's interests include a variety of topics in the health economics field. He has published academic papers and reports dealing with the impact evaluation of health policies and programs in developing and transition countries. He has also done research on economic evaluation in health care. Currently, he is working on the topic of international comparisons of health systems performance, with a particular interest in health systems financing and financial protection issues.

Somil Nagpal is a senior health specialist with the World Bank (South Asia Region), based in New Delhi. His major areas of interest and research are health financing, health insurance, and information technology in health care. Prior to joining the Bank in 2009, he worked for the Insurance Regulatory and Development Authority, India, and was instrumental in setting up and heading the specialized health insurance unit in the country's federal insurance regulator. In prior roles, he also served the Indian Ministry of Health, the National Commission on Macroeconomics and Health, India, and the World Health Organization. Dr. Nagpal is the author and coauthor of several publications on health insurance and health financing, including recent World Bank publications focused on private health insurance regulation, government-sponsored health insurance in India and on creating evidence for better health financing decisions. He is a medical doctor with postgraduate qualifications in health management and financial management and has a fellowship in insurance.

Christine Ortiz is an international health expert with over 20 years' development experience in the United States and abroad. She specializes in health economics and financing. She has international project management experience in health, water and sanitation, and education, with UN agencies, multilateral and bilateral donor agencies, as well as nongovernmental organizations (NGOs). In these activities, she has worked with Abt Associates, Médecins du Monde, UNICEF, the French Cooperation, and the European Commission, among others. She is currently the deputy chief of party on USAID's Health Policy Initiative in Vietnam. Other recent work includes capacity building for universal coverage, institutional strengthening for ministries, Global Fund CCMs and local NGOs, including work force development and governance, supporting community-based health financing in West Africa, costing studies in West and Central Africa, as well as research on maternal mortality. She speaks, reads, and writes fluent English, Spanish, and French. Her undergraduate degree is from the Georgetown School of Foreign Service, and she also earned a joint master's degree in health planning and financing from the London School of Hygiene and Tropical Medicine and the London School of Economics.

Mark V. Pauly is Bendheim Professor in the Department of Health Care Management, Professor of Health Care Management, and Business and Public Policy at the Wharton School, codirector of the Roy and Diana Vagelos Life Sciences and Management Program, and professor of economics in the School of Arts and Sciences at the University of Pennsylvania. A former commissioner on the

Physician Payment Review Commission, Dr. Pauly has been a consultant to the Congressional Budget Office, the Office of the Secretary of the U.S. Department of Health and Human Services, and has served on the Medicare Technical Advisory Panel. He is coeditor-in-chief of the *International Journal of Health Care Finance and Economics* and coeditor of the recently published *Handbook of Health Economics*, volume 2. Dr. Pauly is the 2012 winner of the William B. Graham Prize for Health Services Research from the Baxter International Foundation and the Association of University Programs in Health Administration. He is also the 2011–12 recipient of the University of Pennsylvania Provost's Award for Distinguished PhD Teaching and Mentoring and the 2012 recipient of the Victor R. Fuchs Lifetime Achievement Award from ASHEcon.

Michael R. Reich is Taro Takemi Professor of International Health Policy at the Harvard School of Public Health. He has been a member of the Harvard faculty since 1983, and also serves as director of the Takemi Program in International Health at Harvard. He received his PhD in political science from Yale University in 1981. His current research addresses the political dimensions of public health policy, health system reform, and pharmaceutical policy. He has provided policy advice for national governments, international agencies, nongovernmental organizations, private foundations, and private corporations. During 2008, he worked with the Japanese government and the Takemi Working Group on Global Health Challenges in preparing Japan's global health proposal on health system strengthening for the G8 Summit (in Tokyo, Japan). His recent books include *Access: How Do Good Health Technologies Get to Poor People in Poor Countries?* (with Laura J. Frost, 2008) and *Getting Health Reform Right: A Guide to Improving Performance and Equity* (with Marc J. Roberts, William Hsiao, and Peter Berman, 2004).

Xenia Scheil-Adlung is the Health Policy Coordinator of the Social Security Department of the International Labour Organization (ILO). She holds an MA and a PhD in economics and political science and worked as an academic prior to joining the Federal Government of Germany and the ILO. Her work focuses on social protection in health through social, national, and micro health insurances, national health systems, and other tax-funded approaches such as vouchers and conditional cash transfers. Her main areas of work include policy development and scheme design for effective access to health care and poverty alleviation. Her recent work concentrates on technical cooperation, international partnerships in health at global and regional levels, capacity building, and advocacy. She has published on a number of topics in social health protection and related areas such as HIV/AIDS, privatization of social security, ageing, and long-term care.

Bernd Schramm has a doctorate in social sciences. He studied public administration and sociology in Germany and in the United Kingdom. He specialized in social protection, health insurance, and health system development in developing countries. He wrote his PhD thesis on social policy in Thailand, and published several articles and papers on social health protection in Africa and Asia. In 2002, he started to work for German Technical Cooperation (GTZ) in the field of social health insurance. Soon he became coordinator of an international project on "Social Protection Systems in Developing Countries" at GTZ headquarters. After a few years, he moved to Vietnam to work as technical adviser in the project "Health Care Support to the Poor in the Northern Uplands," funded by the European Commission. In 2008, Dr. Schramm conducted several consultancy missions for WHO in Geneva (in support of the G8 initiative "Providing for Health") and for GTZ, before he was assigned as Interim Programme Coordinator and Social Health Protection Adviser for the GTZ "Support to the Health Sector Reform Programme" in Cambodia. Since July 2009 he has been the coordinator of a new "Social Health Protection Programme," jointly implemented by German Technical Cooperation (now GIZ) and German Financial Cooperation (KfW). In addition to this, he was nominated by German Development Cooperation as Sector Coordinator for the Priority Area of Health in Cambodia.

Mark Stabile is director of the School of Public Policy and Governance at the University of Toronto and associate professor of economics at the Rotman School of Management. He is also a research associate at the National Bureau of Economic Research, Cambridge, Massachusetts, and a fellow at the Rimini Centre for Economic Analysis, Italy. From 2003 to 2005, he was the senior policy adviser to the Ontario Minister of Finance where he worked on health, education, and tax policy. He has been a visiting faculty member at Princeton University, the University of Chicago, and Columbia University. His recent work focuses on the economics of child health and development, the public/private mix in the financing of health care, and tax policy and health insurance. His recent publications include "Child Mental Health and Human Capital Accumulation: The Case of ADHD" in the *Journal of Health Economics*, "Socio-Economic Status and Child Health: Why Is the Gradient Stronger for Older Children?" in the *American Economic Review*, and "The Integration of Child Tax Credits and Welfare: Evidence from the Canadian National Child Benefit Program" in the *Journal of Public Economics*. He has advised the Senate of Canada, Health Canada, and the Ontario Ministry of Health, among others, on health care reform. He is coeditor of *Exploring Social Insurance: Can a Dose of Europe Cure Canadian Health Care Finance?* published in 2008 by the McGill-Queen's University Press. Professor Stabile received his PhD from Columbia University and his BA from the University of Toronto.

Kimberly Switlick-Prose is an international health policy and program manager recognized for helping clients in Africa and Asia increase the scalability and sustainability of health insurance. She was instrumental in redesigning the operational plan and processes for RSBY in Delhi, India, which enhanced enrolment and utilization of insurance benefits and promoted continuity of care to help achieve universal health coverage (UHC). She also has worked with the government of Kenya to expand National Hospital Insurance Fund (NHIF) coverage, benchmarking the NHIF against performance targets and detailing a strategic trajectory for achieving UHC. In addition, she works with countries to help integrate key priority services into insurance mechanisms such as maternal and child health services, family planning, and HIV/AIDS and is developing a business case and road map for mainstreaming HIV/AIDS into health insurance mechanisms. Switlick-Prose codesigned a health insurance workshop in Ghana, "Extending Health Insurance: How to Make It Work," which brought together eight African countries to examine current health insurance activities and develop a blueprint for strengthening and expanding health insurance. She holds an MPH from George Washington University.

Nicole Tapay, JD, is a health care policy expert with over 20 years' experience advising senior government officials, as well as corporate officials, in the United States and internationally in the areas of health care insurance regulation, health care financing, and health care system reform. She currently is a director, Global Public Policy, for Eli Lilly and Company.* Previously, she served as the senior health policy advisor for U.S. Senator Ron Wyden, with responsibility for assisting the senator on health care–related legislation and policy, including U.S. national health care reform. As principal administrator, Private Health Insurance for the Organisation for Economic Co-operation and Development (OECD), she co-authored the OECD book, *Private Health Insurance in OECD Countries*, among other publications on private health insurance in OECD countries. She has also been a senior health specialist with the World Bank, on the research faculty of the Georgetown University Health Policy Institute, and held senior roles for the U.S. Centers for Medicare and Medicaid Services (CMS/HHS) and the National Association for Insurance Commissioners (NAIC), Medco Health Services, Inc. and Novartis AG. She has written or coauthored numerous articles and books on the regulation of private health insurance and health care financing and reform in the United States. She received a JD from Georgetown University Law Center and a Bachelor of Arts from Princeton University, magna cum laude.

The opinions and work contained in chapter 18 are those of the authors and are not in any manner affiliated with Eli Lilly and Company.

Wynand P.M.M. van de Ven is professor of health insurance at the Erasmus University, Rotterdam. His teaching and research focus on managed competition in health care, competitive health insurance markets, risk equalization, risk selection, and managed care. He has experience as a governor and adviser of insurance companies, political parties, government, hospitals, and other health care organizations. He serves (served) as a member of many advisory committees and the editorial board of scientific journals. He is a founder of the European Risk Adjustment Network. Previous positions are: program director of the Master of Health Economics, Policy and Law at Erasmus University and chair of the iHEA Jury-Committee for the annual Arrow Award for the best paper in health economics.

Jacques van der Gaag is a senior fellow at Brookings Institution, Center for Universal Education, where he studies international health care financing as well as the economic consequences of AIDS. He is a professor of development economics at the Faculty of Economics and Business of the University of Amsterdam. He served as dean of the faculty from 1998 until 2006, during which period he founded the University of Amsterdam Business School. Prior to that, he held various positions at the World Bank in Washington, D.C., including chief economist of the Human Development Network.

Van der Gaag studied econometrics at the Erasmus University and received his PhD from Leiden University. He was a visiting professor at the Department of Economics, and a research fellow at the Institute for Research on Poverty, both at the University of Wisconsin, Madison. His research interests include the economics of health, education economics, poverty, and social policies. He has published widely in refereed journals and books and served on the editorial board of the *Journal of Human Resources*, the *Journal of Health Economics,* and the *World Bank Economic Review.*

He is cofounder and codirector of the Amsterdam Institute for International Development and senior economic adviser of the Health Insurance Fund. He currently holds the position of senior fellow at the Brookings Institution in Washington, D.C.

Edit V. Velenyi is a health economist with a focus on health systems development at the Health Nutrition Population (HNP) Anchor Team of the World Bank. Between 2007 and 2011 she acted as the coordinator of the Malaria Impact Evaluation Program (MIEP). In that capacity, she managed an evaluation portfolio that carries out evaluations in a multicountry comparative design, including India and five countries in Africa. In addition to the work on malaria evaluation, in 2011, under the umbrella of a South-South Experience Exchange, she leveraged an exchange between the National Health Insurance Schemes of the governments of Nigeria and India on health insurance for the informal sector. During her work with MIEP, she was responsible for developing the programs of the malaria and health insurance clusters at the Impact Evaluation Workshop for Health Sector Reform (Cape Town, South Africa, 2009).

In 2007, Velenyi was posted to Lagos, Nigeria, by the Amsterdam Institute of International Development (AIID) to serve as Co-PI and field manager for operational research of the Dutch Health Insurance Fund (HIF). Prior to the field work, she was a consultant on health care financing for the World Bank's Africa Region Human Development Technical Unit (2004–5) and the HNP Sector Hub (2002–3) of the World Bank. Before joining the Bank, Velenyi worked for the Hungarian and U.S. governments (1995–2001) at the Ministry of Defense, the Ministry of Foreign Affairs, and the Voice of America.

Velenyi pursued a PhD at the Department of Economics of the University of York (2011). She conducted research at the Centre for Health Economics at the University of York between 2005 and 2007. She has an MA from the School of

Advanced International Relations of the Johns Hopkins University (2001), an MA from the Budapest Business School (1996), and a BA from the University of Szeged, Hungary.

Adam Wagstaff is Research Manager of the Human Development and Public Services team in the World Bank Development Research Group. He holds a DPhil in economics from the University of York, and, before joining the Bank, was a professor of economics at the University of Sussex. He was an associate editor of the *Journal of Health Economics* for 20 years, and has published extensively on a variety of aspects of the field, including health financing and health systems reform; health, equity, and poverty; the valuation of health; the demand for and production of health; efficiency measurement; and illicit drugs and drug enforcement. Much of his recent work has been on health insurance, health financing, vulnerability and health shocks, and provider-payment reform. He has extensive experience with China and Vietnam, but has worked on countries in Africa, Latin America, South Asia, in Europe and Central Asia, as well as other countries in East Asia. Outside health economics, he has published on efficiency measurement in the public sector, the measurement of trade union power, the redistributive effect and sources of progressivity of the personal income tax, and the redistributive effect of economic growth.

Hong Wang, MD, has more than 26 years of experience in health policy globally, with a focus on health economics and financing in developing countries. He received his MD from Beijing Medical University and PhD in health economics from the University of Wisconsin at Madison. Dr. Wang currently serves as a senior program officer for country developing financing in global policy and advocacy at the Bill & Melinda Gates Foundation (BMGF). He works primarily in the areas of country financing, resource tracking, financial access and financial risk protection, and strategic service purchase and provider-payment incentive at both country and global levels. Dr. Wang also holds an adjunct clinical associate professorship at the Yale University School of Public Health. Before joining BMGF, Dr. Wang was a principal associate/senior health economist at Abt Associates Inc. He worked as the technical lead on health financing–related projects, including the PATHS2/DFID project in Nigeria, Vistaar project in India/USAID, Health Sector Financing Reform project in Ethiopia/USAID, Health System 20/20 project/USAID, and CapacityPlus/USAID multicountry project. Dr. Wang's earlier career included positions as associate professor and deputy director for health economics department at Beijing Medical University, adjunct professor and deputy director at the National Health Economics Institute of the Ministry of Health, China, and assistant professor in the Department of Epidemiology and Public Health at Yale University. He taught health economics, comparative health care systems, public policy analysis in global health, and social determinants of health in Beijing Medical University and Yale University.

Ke Xu, MD, also holds a PhD in health economics from the School of Public Health, Fudan University, Shanghai, China. She is a senior health economist in the Department of Health Systems Financing at World Health Organization (WHO) headquarters in Geneva, Switzerland. Her work focuses on health financial protection, catastrophic health expenditure, and the poverty impact of out-of-pocket health payments. Before joining WHO in 1999, she served as a lecturer in the Department of Health Economics, Fudan University, Shanghai.

Beatriz Zurita, MD, has 20 years of experience in health care systems, in Mexico as a public sector senior manager and a program manager for a nongovernmental organization. She has provided technical and policy advice to governments and institutions in several countries in Latin America, Africa, the Middle East, Asia, and the Pacific. Dr. Zurita has been a health lead specialist, Division of Social Protection and Health, at the Inter-American Development Bank since 2010. Previously, she was coordinator of planning and development of the Medical Directorate at the Mexican Institute of Social Security (IMSS), executive coordinator of health economics at the Mexican Foundation for Health (FUNSALUD), and a principal associate at Abt Associates Inc. In addition to an MD from Universidad Anahuac, Dr. Zurita has a master in arts applied economics and a PhD from the University of Michigan, Ann Arbor. She has published and coauthored 10 books, 20 book chapters, and 9 articles in academic journals.

Peter Zweifel, a native of Switzerland, is Professor Emeritus of Economics at the University of Zurich, where he taught until his retirement in 2011. After a visit to the University of Wisconsin at Madison (United States) as an honorary fellow, he became eligible as a professor in 1982 based on a thesis "An Economic Model of Physician Behavior" (in German). Having served as a visiting professor to the University of the Armed Forces in Munich (Germany) and having turned down an offer from the University of Munich, he was given tenure at the University of Zurich in 1984 and promoted to full professor in 1990. Besides health economics (textbook *Health Economics* with Friedrich Breyer and Matthias Kifmann, 1997, 2nd ed. 2009), Zweifel's research and teaching also cover insurance economics (textbook *Insurance Economics* with Roland Eisen, 2012), law and economics, energy economics (textbook with Georg Erdmann, Technical University of Berlin, in German), and international economics (textbook with Walter Heller, formerly International Monetary Fund, in German). In all these fields, he has published in international refereed journals (some 100 articles). Together with Mark Pauly (Wharton School), he was the founding editor of the *International Journal of Health Care Finance and Economics*. From 1996 to 2005, he served on the Swiss Competition Authority and on the Federal Committee for Energy Research. He has been a visiting professor of the Australian National University (Canberra), University of California at Santa Barbara, Duke University, Fudan University (Shanghai), John Curtin University (Perth, WA), University of Western Australia, the Wharton School, and Whitwatersrand University (Johannesburg). He is an honorary professor of Syddansk University (Odense, Denmark).

Index

Boxes, figures, notes, and tables are indicated by b, f, n, and t, respectively.

A

ability to pay (ATP)
  affordability of services and, 15
  catastrophic health care costs and, 46n5
  defined, 649
  financing mechanisms and, 39b, 354
  informal sector and, 237b
  as precondition of purchase of health
    insurance, 51
  revenue collection and, 448
absorptive capacity, 95–96, 97
accepted authority of health
    insurance, 314
access to health services
  in Chile, 246
  out-of-pocket payments and, 102
  social health insurance and, 30–34,
    31–32f, 33t, 34f
  universal coverage and, 14
accountability, 467–96
  administrative costs, 486
  collective costs, 485–86
  cost containment and, 88
  defined, 649
  donors, role of, 483
  earmarking of contributions, 488–90
  employers, role of, 487–88
  governance and, 336, 476–83, 488, 492
  group formation and sustainability,
    479–81
  indirect taxes and, 440
  institutional environment for, 476–83,
    477b, 479b, 480b, 483b
  medical professionals, role of, 487
  mutual aid, 478–79, 481–82
  open enrolment and, 491–92
  organizational structure and, 532
  out-of-pocket payments, 481–82
  for plan choice, 490–92
  of providers, 482
  regulatory and supervisory framework
    for, 503, 504
  solidarity and, 478–79
  stakeholders, role of, 486–88

  state role, 482–83, 483b
  transaction costs, 486
actual premium, defined, 649
actuarially fair premium, defined, 649
actuaries, 529, 649
adaptive efficiency, 541b
addiction care, 64
administrative capacity
  in East Asia and Pacific, 287–89
  economic environment and, 275
  for financing mechanisms, 353
  in Francophone Sub-Saharan Africa, 131
  as government capacity factor, 286
  for multiple-payer systems, 203
  political economy and, 421
  for universal coverage, 42–44
administrative costs, 237b, 363, 486
adverse selection
  asymmetrical information and, 345
  community-based health insurance
    and, 35
  defined, 649–50
  in East Asia and Pacific, 289–90
  informal sector and, 236–37b
  in Latin America and Caribbean,
    235–37, 235f, 236–37b
  mandatory health insurance and, 65, 79
  revenue pooling and, 453
  risk equalization and, 67
  social health insurance and, 72–73, 90n2
  in South Asia, 289–90
  state role in, 443
Affordable Care Act of 2010 (U.S.), 355, 487
Affordable Health Care Act of 2009
    (draft, U.S.), 347
Afifi, N. H., 498
Africa. *See also* Anglophone Africa;
    Francophone Sub-Saharan Africa;
    specific countries
  access to health care in, 30, 31f
  employer-facilitated insurance in, 35
  political will in, 104
  social health insurance development
    in, 71

chronic disease, 170, 191, 209. *See also* noncommunicable diseases

CIDR (Centre International de Développement et de Recherche), 142*n*7

Civil Servant Medical Benefit Scheme (CSMBS, Thailand), 295

civil service employees
  in Anglophone Africa, 160–61
  coverage for, 156
  in East Asia and Pacific, 284
  in Indonesia, 304–5
  in Latin America and Caribbean, 266
  social health insurance for, 80
  in South Asia, 284
  in Tanzania, 182
  in Thailand, 293

Clark, M., 250

classical social health insurance, 17–18, 18*t*

Clinton, Bill, 407

CNAM (Caisse Nationale d'Assurance Maladie, Côte d'Ivoire), 128

CNAM (Caisse Nationale d'Assurance Maladie, Senegal), 128

CNAMTS (Caisse Nationale de l'Assurance Maladie de Travailleurs Salariés, France), 326

CNP (Caja Nacional de Provisión, Colombia), 256

CNSS (Caisse Nationale de Sécurité Sociale, Guinea), 121, 129

CNSS (Caisse Nationale de Sécurité Sociale, Senegal), 128

Code of Hammurabi, 442, 461*n*1

coinsurance/copayments
  cost sharing via, 410, 449
  defined, 651
  in Europe, 325
  in Indonesia, 305
  in Latin America and Caribbean, 239
  revenue collection and, 449
  risk pooling and, 352
  social health insurance and, 87–88
  solidarity and, 410

collection of revenue. *See* revenue collection

collective costs, 485–86

Colombia
  access to health care in, 32
  budget constraints in, 408
  civil service employees in, 266
  coverage rates in, 259, 259*t*, 269

economic environment in, 402
  evasion of social health insurance contributions in, 238, 388*n*16
  health insurance strategies in, 256–61, 257*b*, 258*f*, 259*t*, 261*f*, 267–68*f*
  informal sector in, 237*b*
  interest groups in, 411, 412
  political economy in, 396
  regulatory and supervisory framework in, 499, 502*b*, 517*n*1
  risk-adjusted subsidies in, 58
  social health insurance in, 234, 237, 265, 267, 268, 476, 526
  technocrats in, 407
  unintended consequences of policy choices in, 422–23
  value added tax (VAT) in, 408

Commission on Macroeconomics and Health (CMH), 116, 133, 148, 527, 528

Commonwealth Funding Model, 489

communicable diseases. *See* infectious diseases

Community-Based Fund (Tanzania), 156

community-based health insurance (CBHI)
  in Anglophone Africa, 147–48, 164–65, 175
  defined, 652
  in Ghana, 177
  implementation of, 522
  informal sector and, 30
  in Nigeria, 178
  as policy design option, 526
  premiums collected by, 17
  as social health insurance, 18, 18*t*, 35
  in Tanzania, 181
  in Uganda, 182

Community Health Funds (CHF, Tanzania), 172, 480*b*

community rating, 50, 67, 482, 503, 652

Compagnie de Bauxite de Guinée, 143*n*14

complementary services, 83

compulsory participation, 350, 470–71, 652. *See also* mandatory health insurance (MHI)

Concertation, 122, 142*nn*5–6

Confédération des Syndicats Medicaux Français (CSMF), 322

conflict-affected countries
  governance in, 132
  in Middle East and North Africa, 191, 204, 214, 226*t*

Congo. *See* Democratic Republic of
	Congo; Republic of Congo
Connor, Catherine, 521
Continental Funding Model, 489
contract enforcement, 550
Convention 102 on Social Security (ILO),
	13, 42
Cooperative Medical System (CMS,
	China), 282, 297, 310
cooperatives, 17, 653
copayments. *See* coinsurance/copayments
core benefits (CB), 491
core health care financing functions, 5–6
corporatism, 328, 653
corruption, 93, 143*n*17, 337, 417–18
Costa Rica
	civil service employees in, 266
	coverage rates in, 269
	dependency ratio in, 238
	formal sector in, 252, 255
	health insurance strategies in, 250–56,
		251*f*, 251*t*, 253–54*t*, 255*f*,
		267–68*f*
	quality of care in, 253
	reform timeline in, 105
	regulatory and supervisory framework
		in, 518*n*6
	social health insurance in, 234, 265,
		267, 268
	universal health system in, 387*n*8
cost containment
	design elements for health insurance
		scheme, 528–30
	OECD countries, 354
	in South Africa, 183*b*
cost recovery, 115, 142*n*8
cost sharing. *See* coinsurance/copayments
Côte d'Ivoire
	governance in, 131, 132
	health expenditures in, 116, 119
	institutional environment in, 133
	mandatory health insurance in, 116,
		121, 122, 125, 128, 134
	public health expenditures in, 119, 133
Council for Cooperative Health Insurance
	(CCHI, Saudi Arabia), 205
Country Policy and Institutional
	Assessment (CPIA), 131, 143*n*16
coverage. *See also* breadth of coverage;
		depth of coverage
	constraints for, 5
	defined, 14

as design element for health insurance
		scheme, 527–28
coverage map, 38
cream skimming, 345, 526, 654
Criel, B., 122
Croatia
	out-of-pocket payments in, 198
	social health insurance transition in, 360
cross-subsidies
	defined, 654
	Latin America and Caribbean, 237–38
	mandatory, 55
	social health insurance and, 15, 71,
		88–89, 474–75
	taxes as, 439
	transaction costs for, 65, 486
	universal coverage and, 107
crowding-out effects, 97, 544
CSA (Caisse Sociale Agricole, Côte
	d'Ivoire), 128
cultural influences, 136, 524
Czech Republic
	health expenditures in, 368
	provider payment methods in, 389*n*29
	public health expenditures in, 368
	universal coverage in, 342

D
Dana Sehat (Indonesia), 305–6, 310
Davoodi, R. H., 545
deadweight losses, 75, 80, 86, 488
debt-cancellation initiatives, 94, 98, 99*n*3
debt financing, 94, 98, 99*nn*2–3
decentralization
	efficiency and, 43
	in India, 308
	in Latin America and Caribbean, 231
	in Mexico, 241–42
	in Nigeria, 178
	public health care providers and, 171
	on subnational level, 414
Decent Work Strategy (ILO), 13
deficit financing, 355
de Groot, Judith, 539
delegation, 418–20
demand
	defined, 655
	health insurance development and, 634
	induced, 659
	in new development paradigm,
		552–53, 553*f*
	supply-induced, 52

Maghreb region, 202–4
majoritarian voting systems, 413–14,
    416, 417
Malawi
    debt financing in, 94, 98
    donor dependence in, 98
    inflation in, 95
    spending ratio in, 92
    tax burden in, 92
Malaysia, UK establishment of health
    service in, 285
Mali
    debt financing in, 99n3
    governance in, 131
    health expenditures in, 116, 119
    institutional environment in, 133
    mandatory health insurance in, 116,
        122, 129, 134
    mutual health organizations in,
        116, 134
    subsidization of the poor in, 135
    voluntary health insurance in, 122,
        129, 138, 139
managed competition model, 411
management capacity
    institutional environment and,
        459–61, 460f
    as reform constraint, 6–9, 8b
    universal health systems and, 346
management information system (MIS),
    209–10, 534
mandated contributions, 79, 470–71.
        See also mandatory health
        insurance (MHI)
mandatory community rating
    defined, 50
    drawbacks of, 61–62
    popularity of, 62–63, 67
mandatory health insurance (MHI)
    adverse selection, prevention of, 65
    cross-subsidies, transaction costs of, 65
    defined, 185n1, 661
    in Francophone Africa, 116, 121–22,
        125–31, 126–27t, 137–38
    free-riding problem and, 64
    motives for, 63–65
    paternalistic motives for, 64
    transaction costs, 65
Mandatory Health Plan
    (POS, Colombia), 257
Mandatory Workers' Insurance
    (Chile), 245

market structure, 599–603, 600t
Martin, S., 388n11
Mashreq region, 201
Mastruzzi, M., 131, 132, 314, 336
maternal health care services, 31, 64,
    138–39, 143n15, 253
Mathauer, Inke, 101, 110
Mauritania
    economic environment in, 136
    voluntary health insurance in, 122
Mauritius, employer-facilitated insurance
    in, 35
McIntyre, Di, 183b
McKnight, R., 390n35
means-tested contributions, 472
medical associations, 411, 413, 427
Medical Care Act of 1967 (Canada),
    349, 350
Medical Care Recommendation (ILO),
    45n1
medical coverage. See coverage; health
    insurance
medical education, 344
medical professionals. See also providers
    as design element for health insurance
        scheme, 530–31
    in Europe and European Union,
        320–22
    national health insurance and,
        320–22, 329
    regulatory and supervisory framework
        for, 506–8
    social health insurance and, 487
medical savings accounts, 232, 300
Medical Schemes Act of 1998 (South
    Africa), 184
Medical Welfare Scheme (Thailand),
    294, 296
Medicare (Philippines), 287, 301
Medicare (U.S.), 83, 401
Medigap policies (U.S.), 83
Medina, Alexis, 273
MedX, 181b
Mexican Institute for Social Security
    (IMSS), 241–42
Mexico
    budget constraints in, 408
    change teams in, 406–7
    civil service employees in, 266
    coverage rates in, 269
    democratization in, 399
    electoral cycle in, 419, 420